# LIST OF ABBREVIATIONS

| | |
|---|---|
| ABM | Antiballistic missile |
| ACDA | United States Arms Control and Disarmament Agency |
| ACLU | American Civil Liberties Union |
| AEC | United States Atomic Energy Commission |
| AMA | American Medical Association |
| APCD | Air Pollution Control District |
| BHC | b |
| bwu | b |
| CBW | c |
| CEQ | C |
| CIAT | In |
| CIMMYT | In |
| CSM | co |
| DDD | di |
| DDE | di |
| DDT | d ... de |
| EDF | E |
| EPA | E |
| FAO | U |
| FDA | U |
| FOE | F |
| FPC | U |
| FPC | fis |
| GNP | g |
| 2,4-D | a |
| 2,4,5-T | a |
| HEW | U |
| IITA | In |
| INCAP | In |
| IPPF | In |
| IR-8 | a |
| IRRI | In |
| IUD | In |
| IWC | In |
| MIRV | M |
| NAWAPA | N |
| NPG | N |
| NRR | N |
| OAS | O |
| PCBs | p ... s |
| ppb | p |
| ppm | p |
| SCP | si |
| TEPP | a |
| UAR | U |
| UN | U |
| UNCTAD | U |
| UNESCO | United Nations Educational, Scientific and Cultural Organization |
| UNFPA | United Nations Fund for Population Activities |
| USAID | United States Agency for International Development |
| USDA | United States Department of Agriculture |
| WHO | World Health Organization |
| ZPG | Zero Population Growth, the name of an organization and the state of a population which is neither growing nor shrinking |

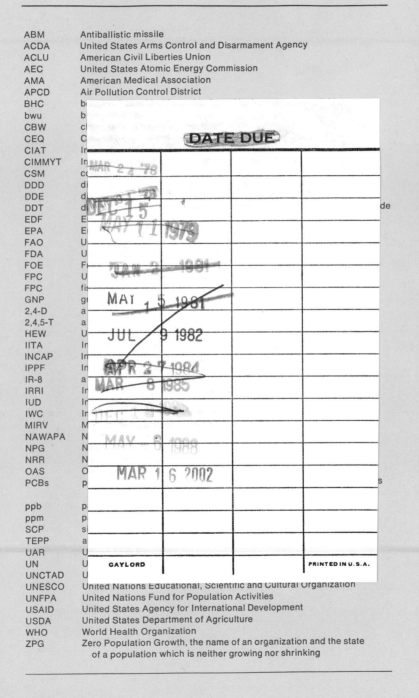

Population

Resources

Environment

## A SERIES OF BOOKS IN BIOLOGY

EDITORS:
Donald Kennedy
Roderic B. Park

*SECOND EDITION*

*Paul R. Ehrlich*
*Anne H. Ehrlich*
STANFORD UNIVERSITY

# Population

# Resources

# Environment

ISSUES IN HUMAN ECOLOGY

W. H. Freeman and Company
San Francisco

Printed in the United States of America

Library of Congress Catalog Card Number: 70–179799

International Standard Book Number: 0–7167–0695–4

6   7   8   9

To Dorothy Decker
with love and thanks

# Preface

With many of the crucial variables that affect human ecology changing almost daily, any text dealing with the subject can rapidly become out of date. For this reason we have decided to revise *Population, Resources, Environment* in two years, rather than on a more conventional four or five year revision basis.

The statistics have been updated throughout and substantial additions and revisions have been made in most sections. Entirely new sections have been added on many topics, including forest resources, net reproductive rates and zero population growth, the impact of population growth upon the environment, heavy metals pollution, ecocide in Indochina, and Thomas Malthus. The material dealing with energy, weather, pesticides, integrated control, the Green Revolution, novel foods, radiation hazards, air pollution, crowding, birth control, population policies, abortion, and other major topics have been considerably reworked or expanded. In response to requests for more thorough documentation, the annotated bibliographies have been greatly enlarged. The index for this edition has been done by Jeanne D. Kennedy, and reflects, we think, the touch of one of the top professionals in the field.

In short, this edition is really a new book, based on the old. We hope that we have retained the flavor of the original while making the work more comprehensive and useful. We have tried to adhere to our philosophy as expressed in "About this Book" (p. 445) by clearly stating where we stand on various matters of controversy. Our apprehension about the course on which humanity is embarked has not lessened in the past two years; we hope the next two will bring changes that will permit a more cheerful prognosis.

*Stanford, California*  
*January, 1972*

*Paul R. Ehrlich*  
*Anne H. Ehrlich*

# Contents

## 12 The international scene  403

## 13 Conclusions  441

Population

Resources

Environment

# CHAPTER 1

# The Crisis

*"The Generations pouring
From times of endless date,
In their going, in their flowing,
Ever form the steadfast State;
And Humanity is growing
Toward the fullness of her fate."*

Herman Melville
(1819–1891)

The explosive growth of the human population is the most significant terrestrial event of the past million millenia. Three and one-half billion people now inhabit the Earth, and every year this number increases by 70 million. Armed with weapons as diverse as thermonuclear bombs and DDT, this mass of humanity now threatens to destroy most of the life on the planet. Mankind itself may stand on the brink of extinction; in its death throes it could take with it most of the other passengers of Spaceship Earth. No geological event in a billion years—not the emergence of mighty mountain ranges, nor the submergence of entire subcontinents, nor the occurrence of periodic glacial ages—has posed a threat to terrestrial life comparable to that of human overpopulation.

Most of the members of modern societies have now seen pictures of the Earth as seen from the vicinity of the moon, and they must have a new awareness of the finite size of our planet. In comparison with many celestial bodies, it is a rather small ball of rock. It is also possibly a unique ball of rock, for its surface is populated by a vast variety of living organisms that depend for their existence on a thin film of atmosphere, which is itself, in part, a product of those living things.

If *Homo sapiens* is to continue as the dominant species of life on Earth, modern man must come soon to a better understanding of the Earth and of what he has been doing to it. Yet many people—as a result of the excitement over the successful landings of men on the moon—are better informed (and perhaps more curious) about conditions on the surface of that dead satellite than they are about the damage being done by overpopulation and over-development to the only life-supporting planet we know.

Only recently have Americans been astounded to learn that many millions of their own fellow citizens go to bed hungry every night. Most of us, of course, have vague ideas about starvation in India or about Brazilians living in squalid *favelas,* but all too many of us have no real appreciation of the dimensions of the world food problem. Why should we? The concept of one or two *billion* people living on this planet without adequate diets truly staggers the imagination. How can it be that 10 or 20 million people, mostly children, are starving to death each year while we pay some of our farmers *not* to grow food? How many presumably well-educated Americans realize that their pets receive a better diet than hundreds of millions of their fellow human beings? How many are aware that many poor Americans resort to eating pet food as a cheap source of high-quality protein?

Look for a moment at the situation in those nations that most of us prefer to label with the euphemism "underdeveloped," but which might just as accurately be described as "hungry." In general, underdeveloped countries (UDCs) differ from developed countries (DCs) in a number of ways. UDCs are not industrialized. They tend to have inefficient, usually subsistence food production systems, extremely low gross national products and per capita incomes, high illiteracy rates, and incredibly high rates of population growth. For reasons that are made clear in this book, most of these countries will never, under any conceivable circumstances, be "developed" in the sense in which the United States is today. They could quite accurately be called "never-to-be-developed countries."

The people of the UDCs will be unable to escape from poverty and misery unless their populations are controlled. Today these countries have larger populations than they can properly support, given their physical and biological resources and their social systems. Furthermore, their population growth rates make it clear that conditions are going to get steadily and rapidly worse. The populations of most UDCs are doubling every 20–30 years. Consider what it would mean for a country like the Philippines or Honduras to double its population in some 20 years. There would be nearly twice as many families in 20 years; today's children would be adults and have their own children. In order to maintain present living standards, such a country must, in two decades, duplicate every amenity for the support of human beings. Where there is one home today there must be two (or their equivalent). Where there is one schoolroom there must be two. Where there is one hospital, garage, judge, doctor, or mechanic, there must be two. Agricultural production must be doubled. Imports and exports must be doubled. The capacity of roads, water systems, electric generating plants, and so on, must be doubled (although economies of scale would reduce needs to something less than a physical doubling in some cases). It is problematical whether the United States could accomplish a doubling of its facilities in 20 years, and yet the United States has abundant capital, the world's finest industrial base, rich natural resources, excellent communications, and a population virtually 100 percent literate. The Philippines, Honduras, and other UDCs have none of these things. They are not even going to be able to maintain their present low standards of living.

Even if some UDCs should manage to maintain their living standards, this will not be acceptable to the people in those countries. The "have-nots" of the world are in an unprecedented position today: they are aware of what the "haves" enjoy. Magazines, movies, transistor radios, and even television have brought them news and pictures of our way of life—our fine homes, highly varied diet, and so forth. They have also seen in their own countries our automobiles, airplanes, tractors, refrigerators, and other appliances. Naturally they want to share our affluence. They have "rising expectations," but a few simple calculations show that they also have plummeting prospects. It takes no political genius to guess the results of not just a continual frustration of these expectations, but an actual deterioration of living standards as well. Population pressure has been described as numbers of people pressing against values. For many people in the UDCs there are relatively few values left to press against, and even these are doomed if mankind continues on its present course.

Many people in the UDCs—the Colombian mothers forced by hunger to practice infanticide, the refugees of Bangla Desh ravaged by cholera, the Indian women who, during the Bihar famine in the mid-1960s, spent days sitting in the sun picking up grains of wheat one by one from railroad beds, and the several hundred thousand residents of Calcutta who live in the streets—have virtually nothing left to lose but their lives. The inhabitants of the DCs have much to lose. Overpopulation right now is lowering the quality of life dramatically in these countries as their struggle to maintain affluence and grow more food leads to environmental deterioration. In most DCs the air grows more foul and the water more undrinkable each year. Rates of drug usage, crime, and civil disorder rise and individual liberties are progressively curtailed as governments attempt to maintain order and public health.

The global polluting and exploiting activities of the DCs are even more serious than their internal problems. Spaceship Earth is now filled to capacity or beyond and is in danger of running out of food. And yet the people traveling first class are, without thinking, demolishing the ship's already overstrained life-support systems. The food-producing mechanism is being sabotaged. The devices that maintain the atmosphere are being turned off. The temperature-control system is being altered at random. Thermonuclear bombs, poison gases, and super-germs have been manufactured and stock-piled by people in the few first-class compartments for possible future use against other first-class passengers in their competitive struggles for dwindling resources—or perhaps even against the expectant but weaker masses of humanity in steerage. In the past few years some people have begun to face the immensity of the spaceship's peril and have begun to grope for ways of avoiding catastrophe. But, unaware that there is no one at the controls of their ship, most of the passengers ignore the chaos or view it with cheerful optimism, convinced that everything will turn out all right.

# CHAPTER 2

# Numbers of People

*"Prudent men should judge of future events
by what has taken place in the past,
and what is taking place in the present."*

Miguel de Cervantes (1547–1616)
*Persiles and Sigismunda*

Assuming that the first "man" appeared between one and two million years ago, we can estimate that between 60 and 100 billion representatives of *Homo sapiens* have lived on the planet Earth. Today some 3.7 billion people inhabit the Earth, roughly 4–5 percent of all those who have ever lived.

We do not have substantial historical data on which to base estimates of population before 1650; such estimates must be based on circumstantial evidence. For instance, we believe that agriculture was unknown before about 8000 B.C.; prior to that date all human groups made their living by hunting and gathering. No more than 20 million square miles of the Earth's total land area of some 58 million square miles could have been successfully utilized in this way by our early ancestors. From the population densities of the hunting and gathering tribes of today, we can estimate that the total human population of 8000 B.C. was about 5 million people.

Population sizes at various times, from the onset of the agricultural revolution until census data first were kept in the seventeenth century, have also

TABLE 2-1

*Doubling Times*

| Date | Estimated world population | Time for population to double |
|------|----------------------------|-------------------------------|
| 8000 B.C. | 5 million | |
| | | 1,500 years |
| 1650 A.D. | 500 million | |
| | | 200 years |
| 1850 A.D. | 1,000 million (1 billion) | |
| | | 80 years |
| 1930 A.D. | 2,000 million (2 billion) | |
| | | 45 years |
| 1975 A.D. | 4,000 million (4 billion) Computed doubling time around 1972 | |
| | | 35 years |

been estimated. This was done by projection from census figures that exist for agricultural societies, and by examination of archaeological remains. Such data as number of rooms in excavated ancient villages prove especially useful for calculating village populations. It is thought that the total human population at the time of Christ was around 200 to 300 million people, and that it had increased to about 500 million (½ billion) by 1650. It then doubled to 1,000 million (1 billion) around 1850, and doubled again to 2 billion by 1930. The course of human population growth can be seen in Figure 2-1. Note that the size of the population has, with minor irregularities, increased continuously, and that *the rate of increase has also increased*.

Perhaps the best way to describe the growth rate is in terms of "doubling time"—the time required for the population to double in size. To go from 5 million in 8000 B.C. to 500 million in 1650 meant that the population increased 100-fold. This required between 6 and 7 doublings:

$$5 \text{ million} \rightarrow 10 \rightarrow 20 \rightarrow 40 \rightarrow 80 \rightarrow 160 \rightarrow 320 \rightarrow 640 \text{ million}$$

in a period of 9,000 to 10,000 years. Thus, on the average, the population doubled about once every 1,500 years during that period. The next doubling, from 500 million to a billion, took 200 years, and the doubling from a billion to 2 billion took only 80 years. Barring a catastrophic increase in the death rate, the population will reach 4 billion around 1975, having doubled in 45 years. The rate of growth around 1972 would, if continued, double the population in about 35 years. Table 2-1 summarizes our population history in these terms. To take a slightly different perspective, it took 1 or 2 million years to achieve a population size of 1 billion around 1850. The next billion was added in 80 years (1850–1930). The third billion came along in only 30 years (1931–1960), and the next will have taken only about 15 years (1960–1975), when the population size reaches 4 billion. If this trend continues, the United Nations forecasts that the fifth billion will be added in just slightly more than a decade.

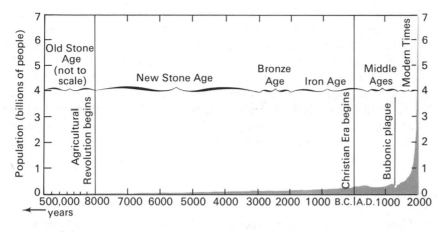

FIGURE 2-1

Growth of human numbers for the past one-half million years. If Old Stone Age were in scale, its base line would extend about 18 feet to the left. (After *Population Bulletin,* vol. 18, no. 1.)

The sort of graph shown in Figure 2-1 does not reveal details of trends in the long, slow growth of the human population before the current millennium. But if population size and time are plotted against one another on logarithmic scales (a log-log graph), as in Figure 2-2, a greater range of time can be shown, and more detail in the lower range of population sizes is revealed. Notice that the log-log graph shows three surges of population growth, one about 600,000 years ago, one about 8,000 years ago, and one about 200 years ago.

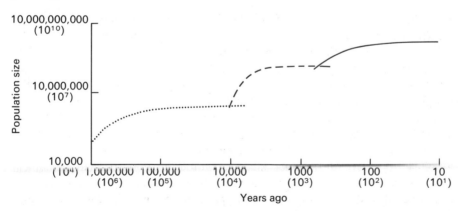

FIGURE 2-2

Human population growth plotted on a log-log scale. Plotted in this way population growth is seen as occurring in three surges, as a result of the cultural, agricultural, and industrial-medical revolutions, which are discussed later in this chapter. (After Deevey, "The Human Population." Copyright © 1960 by Scientific American, Inc. All rights reserved.)

The reasons for the patterns shown on both graphs are reasonably clear, but before these reasons are examined, some details of population dynamics —the ways in which populations change size—must be considered. The size of a population is essentially the result of additions and subtractions. Additions to local human populations consist of births and immigrations; subtractions consist of deaths and emigrations. Demographers (scientists concerned with the statistical study of human populations) who are interested in the total population of the planet work primarily with birth and death rates, since there has been no migration to or from the Earth.

## Birth and Death Rates

The birth rate is usually expressed as the number of babies born per thousand people per year. The total number of births during the year is divided by the estimated population at the midpoint of the period. For example, in the United States there were 3,729,000 live births during the 12 months ending April 30, 1971. The population on October 31, 1970 (the midpoint of that period) was estimated to be 205,200,000. The birth rate for that period was therefore $3,729,000/205,200,000 = 0.0182$. There were 0.0182 births per person or $0.0182 \times 1,000 = 18.2$ births per thousand people. Similarly, there were 1,919,000 deaths during the period, giving a death rate of $1,919,000/205,200,000 = 0.0094 \times 1,000 = 9.4$ deaths per thousand people in the year from May 1, 1970 to April 30, 1971.

## Growth Rate

Since birth rate represents additions and death rate represents subtractions, we can calculate the rate of growth (or shrinkage) of the population by subtracting the death rate from the birth rate. During the year ending April 30, 1971, the growth rate was 18.2 minus 9.4, or 8.8 per thousand. That is, in the period from May 1, 1970, to April 30, 1971, 8.8 people were added to each 1,000 people in the American population. Technically this is the "rate of natural increase," since migration is not considered. Demographers express this growth rate as a percent annual increase —that is, not as a rate per thousand but as a rate per hundred. In the example cited above the annual increase would be 0.88 percent, a typical rate for an industrialized nation. In 1971 the estimated world birth rate was 34, and the death rate 14. The population growth rate was thus $34 - 14 = 20$, or 2 percent.

If the world rate of increase is 2 percent and remains constant, then the population will double in 35 years. A 2 percent rate of increase means that 20 persons per thousand are added to the population each year. Note that if you simply *add* 20 persons per year to a population of 1,000 people, it will take 50 years to double that population ($20 \times 50 = 1,000$). But the doubling time is actually much less, because populations grow in the way that money grows when interest is compounded. Just as the interest dollars themselves earn interest, so people added to populations produce more people. It is growth at compound interest rates that makes populations double so much more rapidly than seems possible (see Box 2-1). The relationship between the annual percent increase (interest rate) and the doubling time is shown in Table 2-2.

TABLE 2-2

| Annual percent increase | Doubling time (years) |
| --- | --- |
| 0.5 | 139 |
| 0.8 | 87 |
| 1.0 | 70 |
| 2.0 | 35 |
| 3.0 | 23 |
| 4.0 | 17 |

## History of Population Growth

The story of human population growth is not primarily a story of changes in birth rate, but of changes in death rate. The populations of our ancestors a few million years ago (*Australopithecus* and relatives) were confined to Africa and numbered perhaps 125,000 individuals. By that time, these ancestors of ours had already "invented" culture, the body of nongenetic information passed from generation to generation. The volume of culture is, of course, vastly greater today than in the days of *Australopithecus*. In those days human culture was transmitted orally and by demonstration from the older to the younger members of the group. It doubtless consisted of information about methods of hunting and gathering, rules of social conduct, dangerous enemies, and the like. Today, of course, human culture includes information transmitted and stored in such diverse places as books, phonograph records, photographs, videotapes, and computer tapes.

The possession of a substantial body of culture is what differentiates man from the other animals. During man's evolutionary history the possession of culture has been responsible for a great increase in human brain size (the australopithecines had small brains, with an average volume of only about 500 cubic centimeters). Early men added to the store of cultural information, developing and learning techniques of social organization and group and individual survival. This gave a selective advantage to individuals with the large brain capacity necessary to take full advantage of the culture. Larger brains in turn increased the potential store of cultural information, and a self-reinforcing coupling of the growth of culture and brain size resulted. This trend continued until perhaps 200,000 years ago, when growth of brain size

BOX 2-1    INTEREST AND GROWTH RATES

If $N_0$ dollars are placed in a bank at a 2 percent rate of interest compounded semiannually, the principal plus the interest at the end of $t$ years will be

$$N_t = N_0(1.01)^{2t}.\tag{1}$$

More generally, if the interest rate is expressed as a decimal $r$ (where $100r =$ interest rate as a percent) and interest is compounded $x$ times per year, then

$$N_t = N_0\left(1 + \frac{r}{x}\right)^{xt}.\tag{2}$$

If interest is compounded continuously, then $x \to \infty$. Expression (2) may be rewritten, substituting $y = r/x$

$$N_t = N_0(1 + y)^{rt/y} = N_0[(1 + y)^{1/y}]^{rt}.\tag{3}$$

Those who have had calculus will understand that as $x \to \infty$, $y \to 0$, and in the limit

$$\lim_{y \to 0} (1 + y)^{1/y} = e.$$

The base of natural logarithms, $e$, is approximately equal to 2.718. Therefore, when interest is compounded continuously (3) becomes

$$N_t = N_0e^{rt}.\tag{4}$$

If

$N_0 =$ population at time 0,

$N_t =$ population at time $t$,

$r =$ growth rate per year (assumed to be calculated from instantaneous birth and death rates),

$t =$ time in years,

then expression (4) will apply to population growth instead of to the accumulated sum of principal and interest. For instance, given the growth rate, the doubling time may be computed by setting $N_t/N_0 = 2$.

Then

$$2 = e^{rt}$$

Taking the natural logarithm of each side (and remembering that $\ln e = 1$) gives

$$\ln 2 = rt \quad \text{or} \quad \frac{\ln 2}{r} = t \quad \text{or} \quad \frac{0.6931}{r} = t.$$

For example, if the annual growth rate is 2 percent, then $1.02 = e^r$ and $r = .0198$, and

$$t = \frac{0.6931}{.0198} = 35 \text{ years.}$$

In general, therefore, the doubling time is 69.31 years divided by the instantaneous growth rate (in percent). It can be closely approximated by dividing by the annual growth rate.

leveled off at an average of some 1,350 cubic centimeters (Box 2-2), and man considered to belong to the same species as modern man, *Homo sapiens,* appeared.

The evolution of culture had an important side effect. Although the human birth rate remained around 40 to 50 per thousand, cultural advances caused a slight decline in the average death rate. But, up until the agricultural revolution the average death rate could not have been much less than .02 per

---

BOX 2-2   NATURAL SELECTION

Natural selection is the prime mover of evolution. It is essentially the differential reproduction of genetic types. In all human populations, individuals differ from one another because each individual has a different hereditary endowment. For instance, people differ from one another in such traits as eye color, height, and blood type, which are at least partially hereditary. If people with one hereditary trait (that is, one kind of genetic information) tend to have more children than those with another, then natural selection is occurring with respect to that trait. Natural selection can cause one kind of genetic information—for example, that producing people with blue eyes—to become more and more common in the gene pool of a population. These changes in the gene pool are what is called *evolution.* Thus the statement that an evolutionary premium was placed on brain size is a convenient shorthand for a statement that might go like this: in early human populations there was variation in brain size. This variation was in part caused by differences among individuals in their genetic endowment. Individuals with slightly larger brains were better able to utilize the cultural information of the society. This permitted them more ready access to mates, a better chance of surviving, or perhaps a better chance of successfully rearing their offspring; and they reproduced more than did individuals with smaller brains. The result was a gradual increase in the genetic information producing larger brain size in the gene pools of human populations. In turn this increased the capacity for storing cultural information and produced a selective advantage for further increase in brain size. This reciprocal evolutionary trend continued until other factors, such as the difficulty of getting the enlarged brain case of a baby through the female's pelvis (which was not enlarged commensurately) at birth removed the selective premium on further increase in brain size.

Understanding natural selection will help to illuminate a number of other points in this book. Further on we will discuss the development of pesticide resistance in insect populations, a process that occurs through natural selection. The insect individuals vary in their natural resistance to a pesticide, and this variation has a genetic basis. Those that are naturally more resistant have a better chance of surviving, and thus of reproducing, than their less fortunate fellows. In this way the entire population becomes more and more resistant, as in each generation the most resistant individuals do most of the breeding.

The key thing to remember is that natural selection is *differential reproduction* of genetic types. It may involve survival, but differentials in reproduction may occur while the life expectancies of all genetic types remain identical—all may live the same length of time, but some may be relatively sterile while others are highly fertile.

thousand below the birth rate. In prehistoric times there unquestionably were sizable fluctuations in birth and, in particular, death rates, especially during the difficult times associated with glacial advance. The end result, however, was a population of about 5 million around 8000 B.C. Mankind had by that time spread from Africa to occupy the entire planet. It is thought that man first entered the Western Hemisphere around 30,000 B.C. As he became ubiquitous, man's increased hunting and gathering efficiency may have led, among other things, to the extinction of many large mammals, such as the great ground sloths, sabre-toothed tigers, and woolly mammoths.

The consequences of cultural evolution for human population size and for man's environment were minor compared with those that were to follow in the agricultural revolution. It is not certain when the first group of *Homo sapiens* started to supplement their hunting and food gathering with primitive farming. On the basis of studies of archaeological sites in the Middle East, there is firm evidence that established village-farming communities functioned between 7000 and 5500 B.C., and archaeologists estimate that agriculture began around 9000–7000 B.C. Around that time, certain groups of people in the hills flanking the Fertile Crescent, in what is now the border area of Iraq and Iran, gradually began to add a new dimension of security to their lives. Like modern Eskimos, these people practiced intensive food collection, and were presumably intimately familiar with the local flora and fauna. It was a natural step from gathering food to producing it. This step, accompanied by settlement in one place with the consequent possibilities for storage of vegetable foods in granaries and bins, and meat on the hoof, freed men from the constant search for food. As a result some members of early agricultural communities were able to turn entirely to other activities, all of which helped to raise the general standard of life. Wheeled vehicles appeared; copper, tin, and then iron were utilized; and dramatic sociopolitical changes occurred along with urbanization. Existence began to lose some of its hazards, and man's life expectancy began to creep upward from its primitive level of perhaps 25–30 years.

The growth of human populations was not continuous after the agricultural revolution. Civilizations grew, flourished, and disintegrated; periods of good and bad weather occurred; and those apocalyptic horsemen, pestilence, famine, and war, took their toll. Of course, there has been no accurate record of human population sizes until quite recently, and even today demographic statistics for many areas are unreliable. A general picture, quite adequate for the purposes of our discussion, can, however, be reconstructed. Although the global trend, indicated in Figure 2-1, was one of accelerating increase, a great many local population "explosions" and "crashes" are concealed in that trend. For example, bubonic plague (Black Death) killed an estimated 25 percent of the inhabitants of Europe between 1348 and 1350. From 1348 to 1379 England's total population was reduced by almost 50 percent from an estimated 3.8 million to 2.1 million. Many cities lost half or more of their inhabitants in the second half of the fourteenth century. The demographic effect of repeated visitations of plague on the population

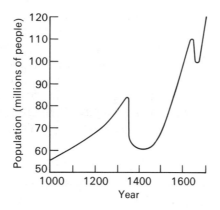

FIGURE 2-3

Effects of bubonic plague epidemics on
European population size in the
fourteenth and seventeenth centuries.
Curve is an estimate based on historical
accounts; actual data are scarce. (After
Langer, "The Black Death." Copy-
right © 1964 by Scientific American,
Inc. All rights reserved.)

is shown in Figure 2-3. The plague also triggered a great deal of social unrest, a typical concomitant of both dramatic increases and reductions in
population size.

Famine has also been an important periodic contributor to high death rates
even after the agricultural revolution. Floods, droughts, insect plagues, warfare, and other causes often have pushed populations over the thin line
between hunger and famine. One study, by Cornelius Walford, lists more than
200 famines in Great Britain alone between 10 and 1846 A.D. (Box 2-3).
Many of these, of course, were local affairs, which could nevertheless be
very serious in the absence of efficient transport systems for relocating surplus
food from other areas. Another study counts 1,828 Chinese famines in the
2,019 years preceding 1911, a rate of almost one per year. Some of these
famines, and similar ones in India, have been known to result in many
millions of deaths. Even in this century famine has killed millions. For
example, perhaps 5–10 million deaths have been attributed to starvation in
Russia (1918–1922, 1932–1934), perhaps as many as 4 million deaths in
China (1920–1921), and 2–4 million deaths in West Bengal, India
(1943).

Warfare has often created conditions in which both pestilence and famine
thrived, but it is difficult to estimate what the direct effects of war on population size have been. In many areas of the world, wars must have made a
major contribution to the death rate, even when the conflict was between
"primitive" groups. Indeed, the effect of warfare on population size and
distribution in New Guinea was rather dramatic until quite recently. For

security, villages in many areas were placed exclusively on hilltops, some of them thousands of feet above the nearest available water. A likely demise for a New Guinean man, woman, or child was death at the hands of a hostile group. Throughout the history of Western Civilization, war has been essentially continual, which doubtless helped to maintain high death rates, particularly by creating food shortages and the preconditions of plagues. Barbarian invasions of the Roman Empire (375–568 A.D.), the Hundred Years' War (1337–1453), and especially the Thirty Years' War (1618–1648)

---

BOX 2-3    FAMINES

A small sampling of quotes from Cornelius Walford's 1878 chronology of 350 famines will give some feel for the ubiquity in time and space of this kind of catastrophe. (Quotation marks indicate where Walford was quoting directly from his sources.) Those who have seen films of recent famines in India and Africa are unlikely to consider scenes like those described below as things of the past.

| | | |
|---|---|---|
| B.C. | 436 | *Rome.* Famine. Thousands threw themselves into the Tiber. |
| A.D. | 160 | *England.* Multitudes starved. |
| | 192 | *Ireland.* General scarcity; bad harvest; mortality and emigration, "so the lands and houses, territories and tribes, were emptied." |
| | 331 | *Antioch.* This city was afflicted by so terrible a famine that a bushel of wheat was sold for 400 pieces of silver. During this grievous disaster Constantine sent to the Bishop 30,000 bushels of corn, besides an immense quantity of all kinds of provisions, to be distributed among the ecclesiastics, widows, orphans, etc. |
| | 695–700 | *England and Ireland.* Famine and pestilence during three years "so that men ate each other." |
| | 1193–1196 | *England, France.* "Famine occasioned by incessant rains. The common people perished everywhere for lack of food." |
| | 1299 | *Russia.* Ravaged by famine and pestilence. |
| | 1412–1413 | *India.* Great drought, followed by famine, occurred in the Ganges-Jumna delta. |
| | 1600 | *Russia.* Famine and plague of which 500,000 die. |
| | 1769–1770 | *India.* (Hindustan) First great Indian famine of which we have a record. It was estimated that 3,000,000 people perished. The air was so infected by the noxious effluvia of dead bodies that it was scarcely possible to stir abroad without perceiving it; and without hearing also the frantic cries of victims of famine who were seen at every stage of suffering and death. |

caused substantial increases in the death rate in Europe. To give a single instance from the last of these conflicts, the storming and pillaging of Magdeburg by Catholic forces in 1631 caused an estimated 20,000 deaths. Indeed, some historians feel that as many as a third of the inhabitants of Germany and Bohemia died as a direct result of the Thirty Years' War.

The Peace of Westphalia ended the Thirty Years' War in 1648, and a period of relative tranquility and stability began. At that time the commercial revolution was in full swing. Power was concentrated in monarchies,

| 1770 | *Bohemia.* Famine and pestilence said to carry off 168,000 persons. |
|---|---|
| 1789 | *France.* Grievous famine; province of Rouen. |
| 1790 | *India.* Famine in district of Barda . . . so great was the distress that many people fled to other districts in search of food; while others destroyed themselves, and some killed their children and lived on their flesh. |
| 1877–1878 | *North China.* "Appalling famine raging throughout four provinces (of) North China. Nine million people reported destitute, children daily sold in markets for (raising means to procure) food. . . . Total population of districts affected, 70 millions. . . ." The people's faces are black with hunger; they are dying by thousands upon thousands. Women and girls and boys are openly offered for sale to any chance wayfarer. When I left the country, a respectable married woman could be easily bought for six dollars, and a little girl for two. In cases, however, where it was found impossible to dispose of their children, parents have been known to kill them sooner than witness their prolonged suffering, in many instances throwing themselves afterwards down wells, or committing suicide by arsenic. |
| 1878 | *Morocco.* ". . . If you could see the terrible scenes of misery—poor starving mothers breaking and pounding up bones they find in the streets, and giving them to their famished children—it would make your heart ache." |

after having been decentralized in the loose feudal structure, and mercantilism was the economic order of the day. Perhaps the most basic idea of mercantilism was that of government invervention to increase the power of the state and (most important from our point of view) the prosperity of the nation. Planning by government was extended to provide economic necessities for the population.

In the mid-seventeenth century, then, a period of relative peace started in a post-feudal economic environment. Simultaneously, a revolution in European agriculture—a revolution that was largely a result of the commercial revolution—began to gather momentum, and it accelerated rapidly in the eighteenth century. Rising prices and increasing demand from the growing cities added to the commercial attractiveness of farming. The breakdown of the feudal system gradually destroyed the manorial estates. On these estates each serf had assigned to him several scattered strips of land and these strips were farmed communally. The peasants grew increasingly unhappy with the communal farming, and strips were rearranged into single compacted holdings leased by individual peasants from the landholder.

As landowners wished to put more land to the plow there was an increasing trend toward the enclosing of old communal woodland and grazing lands with hedges and walls barring the peasants from resources essential to their subsistence. This movement was especially pronounced in Great Britain, where it was promoted by a series of special Acts of Parliament. Furthermore, much of the peasantry was dispossessed, or forced out of agriculture by competition from the more efficient large farming operations. Agriculture was transformed into big business.

Accompanying these changes were fundamental improvements in crops and farming techniques. For instance, the role of clover in renewing soil (by replacing lost nitrogen) was discovered in England by Lord Charles Townshend. This made the practice of letting fields lie fallow every third year unnecessary. Other improvements were made in methods of cultivation and in animal breeding. Agricultural output increased and, consequently, so did the margin over famine. It seems plausible that a combination of commercial and agricultural revolutions, a period of relative peace, and the disappearance of the Black Death* all combined to reduce the death rate and produce the European population surge which started in the mid-seventeenth century. Between 1650 and 1750 it is estimated that the populations of Europe and Russia increased from 103 million to 144 million. An additional factor that may have contributed to this burst of growth was the opening of the Western Hemisphere to European exploitation. In 1500 the ratio of people to available land in Europe was about 27 per square mile. The addition of the vast, virtually unpopulated frontiers of the New World reduced the ratio for

---

* The disappearance was possibly due to the displacement of the black rat, which lived in houses, by the sewer-loving brown rat. This lessened rat-man contact, and thus reduced the chances of plague-carrying fleas reaching human beings. In London the great fire of 1666 destroyed much of the city, which consisted largely of rundown wooden buildings that provided excellent rat harborage. By orders of the king, the city was rebuilt with brick and stone, thus making it much more secure from plague.

Europe plus the Western Hemisphere to less than five per square mile. As historian Walter Prescott Webb wrote, this frontier was, in essence, "a vast body of wealth without proprietors." Thus not only was land shortage in Europe in part alleviated, but several major European nations were enriched, both factors encouraging population growth.

Although we can speculate with ease about the causes of Europe's population boom between 1650 and 1750, it is somewhat more difficult to explain a similar boom in Asia. The population there increased by some 50–75 percent in this period. In China, after the collapse of the Ming Dynasty in 1644, political stability and the new agricultural policies of the Manchu emperors doubtless led to a depression of death rates. Much of the Asiatic population growth during this period probably took place in China, since India was in a period of economic and political instability caused by the disintegration of the Mogul Empire. When the last of the Mogul emperors, Aurangzeb, died in 1707, India was racked by war and famine. Robert Clive and the East India Company established British hegemony in India during the period 1751–1761. At a time when China may have had the world's most advanced agricultural system under the efficient Manchu government, India was a battleground for the British and French. And the rapid increase in power of the British East India Company following the Peace of Paris in 1763 did not bring rapid relief. Indeed, in the famous famine of 1770 about one-third of the population of Bengal is reputed to have perished—a circumstance that did not prevent industrious agents from increasing the East India Company's revenue from Bengal by more than 50 percent during that year!

World population seems to have grown at a rate of about 0.3 percent per year between 1650 and 1750. The growth rate increased to approximately 0.5 percent between 1750 and 1850. During this period the population of Europe doubled in response to a number of favorable changes: agricultural techniques advanced fairly rapidly, sanitation improved and, at the end of the period, the introduction of smallpox vaccination signalled improvements in public health. Furthermore, this growth was achieved in the face of substantial emigration to the New World, where the population jumped from some 12 million to about 60 million in the same period. Growth in Asia between 1750 and 1850 was slower than in Europe, amounting to an increase of about 50 percent. Most of the developments that favored rapid increase in Europe's population were to appear in Asia only much later, if at all.

Little is known about the past population size of Africa, a continent which remained virtually unknown until well past the middle of the nineteenth century. It is generally accepted that the population remained more or less constant at around 100 million, plus or minus 5–10 million, between 1650 and 1850. Then European technology and medicine began to take effect in Africa, death rates started to drop, and the population increased some 20–40 percent between 1850 and 1900, doubling to 200 million by 1950.

The average growth rate of the world population between 1850 and 1950 was about 0.8 percent per year. Population increased in that time from

TABLE 2-3
*Populations in Millions*

| | *World* | *Africa* | *North America* | *Latin America* | *Asia (except USSR)* | *Europe and Asiatic USSR* | *Oceania* |
|---|---|---|---|---|---|---|---|
| *1850* | 1,131 | 97 | 26 | 33 | 700 | 274 | 2 |
| *1950* | 2,495 | 200 | 167 | 163 | 1,376 | 576 | 13 |

SOURCE: United Nations (1963) and estimates (somewhat modified) by Willcox, *Studies in American Demography* (1940) and Carr-Saunders, *World Population* (1936).

slightly more than 1 billion to almost 2.5 billion. The estimated populations shown in Table 2-3 indicate that between 1850 and 1950 the population of Asia did not quite double, but population more than doubled in Europe and Africa, multiplied about fivefold in Latin America, and increased more than sixfold in North America.

The death rate continued to decline during the period 1850–1900 as a result of the industrial revolution and the accompanying advances in agriculture and medicine. Although the horrible conditions that prevailed in the mines and factories during the early stages of the rise of industry are well known to all who have read the literature of the period, the overall conditions in areas undergoing industrialization actually improved. Life in the rat-infested cities and rural slums of pre-industrial Europe had been grim almost beyond description. Advances in agriculture, industry, and transportation had, by 1850, substantially bettered the lot of Western man. Improved agriculture reduced the chances of crop failures and famine. Mechanized land and sea transport made local famines less disastrous when they occurred, and provided access to more distant resources. Great improvements in sanitation around the beginning of this century helped to reduce death rates further, as did knowledge of the role of bacteria in infection, which transformed medical practice and saved many lives. European death rates, which had been in the vicinity of 22–24 per thousand in 1850, decreased to around 18–20 per thousand and went as low as about 16 per thousand in some countries. For instance, combined rates for Denmark, Norway, and Sweden dropped from about 20 per thousand in 1850 to 16 in 1900.

In Western Europe in the latter half of the nineteenth century low death rates (and the resultant high rate of population increase) contributed to a massive emigration. And, as the industrial revolution progressed, another significant trend appeared. Birth rates in Western countries began to decline. In Denmark, Norway, and Sweden the combined birth rate was around 32 per thousand in 1850; by 1900 it had decreased to 28. Similar declines occurred elsewhere. This was the start of the so-called "demographic transition"—a falling of birth rates which has characteristically followed industrialization.

The demographic transition carried on into the first half of the twentieth

century. By the 1930s decreases in the birth rate had, in some countries, outpaced decreases in the death rate. By then the combined death rate of Denmark, Norway, and Sweden had decreased to 12 per thousand, but the birth rate had dropped precipitously to about 16. Populations in the industrial countries of Europe in the 1930s were in a demographic situation that, if continued, would have led to population declines. True, birth rates were still above death rates, but they would not have stayed that way for long. Death rates rise to meet declining birth rates. If the fertility rates for women of each age class in these European populations (that is, the number of births per thousand women of a given age) had remained at the low levels reached during the 1930s, the growth rate of the population would have continued to decrease. This is because as the average age of the population increased, the proportion of women in their reproductive years—especially the years of highest fertility, from 20 to 29—would decrease, further lowering the overall birth rate of the population. At the same time, proportionately more and more people would enter the older age classes of the population and become subject to higher age-specific death rates, which would raise the death rate for the population as a whole. However, stimulated by improving economic conditions and World War II, birth rates rose again during the 1940s and 1950s. European growth rates have generally averaged between 0.5 and 1.0 percent since the war.

What is the cause of the lowered birth rates in industrialized countries? No one knows for certain, but some rather good guesses can be made. In agrarian societies, children are often viewed as economic bonuses. They serve as extra hands on the farm and as old-age insurance for the parents. This pronatalist point of view was beautifully expressed by Thomas Cooper in his book, *Some Information Respecting America,* published in 1794. He says (p. 55), "In America, particularly out of the large towns, no man of moderate desires feels anxious about a family. In the country, where dwells the mass of the people, every man feels the increase of his family to be the increase of his riches: and no farmer doubts about the facility of providing for his children as comfortably as they have lived. . . ."

In an industrial society these things are changed. Children are not potential producers; they are consumers. They require expensive feeding and education. Large families, which became more likely with lowered death rates, tended to reduce mobility and to make the accumulation of capital more difficult. The result of this in Europe was a trend toward later marriage (which reduces birth rates by reducing each woman's years of reproductive activity) and toward control of the number of births within marriage (Fig. 2-4).

The demographic transition was not, however, limited to the urban areas in Europe. Population increase created a squeeze in rural areas as well, a squeeze that was compounded by the modernization of farms. A finite amount of land had to supply a livelihood for more people. At the same time, mechanization, which reduced the need for farm labor, made it more and more difficult for a young couple to establish themselves on a farm of

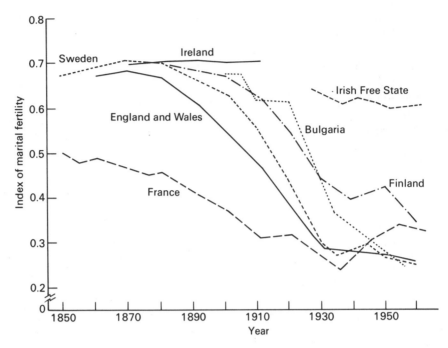

FIGURE 2-4

Demographic transition in selected European countries as indicated by changes in the index of fertility of married women. Scale on the ordinate indicates the number of births by married women divided by the number of births that a population of the same age structure would have if it were reproducing at the highest age-specific rates ever recorded for a population of substantial size. Highest value for the index would be 1. (After Coale, "Decline of Fertility in Europe." *In* Behrman et al., *Fertility and Family Planning,* Univ. of Michigan Press, 1969.)

their own. As a result, rural birth rates dropped and many people moved to the cities.

There was, of course, no demographic transition outside the industrialized countries. For instance, the Indian birth rate in 1891 was estimated to be 49 per thousand per year, but in 1931 it was still 46 per thousand. In the decade 1930–1940 the rate of population growth in North America and Europe was 0.7 percent, whereas that of Asia was 1.1 percent, Africa 1.5 percent, and Latin America 2.0 percent; even though the death rates were relatively higher in the last three areas. The world growth rate for the decade was 1.1 percent.

Thus far two principal demographic trends in the modern world have been discussed. The first was a decline in the death rate in countries undergoing industrialization, and the second was a decline in the birth rate following industrialization. The first of these trends resulted in a relatively rapid growth rate in Western countries, a growth rate above the world average. The second trend moved the growth rate of these countries below the world

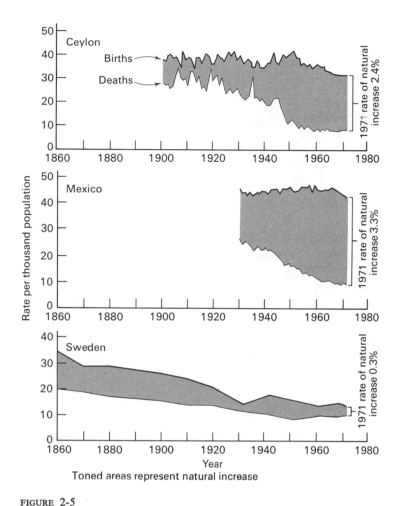

Toned areas represent natural increase

FIGURE 2-5

Different patterns of change in birth and death rates and rate of natural increase. Death rates dropped gradually in western industrial countries such as Sweden and precipitously in UDCs such as Ceylon and Mexico. (Courtesy of the Population Reference Bureau.)

average, Europe making the demographic transition around the turn of the twentieth century, and the United States and Canada more recently.

A third major demographic trend began around the time of World War II. A dramatic decline in death rates occurred in the underdeveloped countries. In some areas, such as Mexico, the decline started before the war. In others, such as Ceylon, it did not start until the end of the war. Compare, for instance, the trend for Sweden since 1860 with that in Mexico since 1930 (Fig. 2-5). This decline was caused primarily by the rapid export of modern drugs and public health measures from the developed countries to the underdeveloped countries. The consequent "death control" produced the most rapid, widespread change known in the history of human population dynamics.

The power of exported death control can be seen by examining the classic case of Ceylon's assault on malaria after World War II. Between 1933 and 1942 the death rate due directly to malaria was reported as about 2 per thousand. This rate, however, represented only a fraction of the malaria deaths, as many were reported as being due to "pyrexia," a fancy name for fever. Actually, in 1934–1935 a malaria epidemic may have been directly responsible for fully half of the deaths on the island, about 17 per thousand. The death rate at that time rose to 34 per thousand. In addition, malaria, which infected a large portion of the population, made many people susceptible to other diseases and thus contributed to the death rate indirectly as well as directly.

The death rate in Ceylon in 1945 was 22 per thousand. The introduction of DDT in 1946 brought rapid control over the mosquitoes that carry malaria. As a result, the death rate on the island was reduced by about 50 percent in less than a decade. It dropped 34 percent between 1946 and 1947 and moved down to 10 per thousand in 1954; it has continued to decline since then, and in 1971 stood at 8 per thousand. Although part of the drop is due to the killing of insects that carry nonmalarial diseases and to other public health measures, most of it can be accounted for by the control of malaria.

Victory over malaria, yellow fever, smallpox, cholera, and other infectious diseases has been responsible for similar decreases in death rates throughout most of the UDCs. The decline in death rate has been most pronounced among children and young adults. These are the people with proportionately the highest death rates from infectious diseases—the diseases most efficiently dealt with by modern medical and public health procedures. Congenital problems in infants and degenerative diseases of older people reduce the proportionate effects of infectious disease in those age brackets. This differential reduction of mortality can be clearly seen in data from Jamaica and Ceylon (Table 2-4).

In the decade 1940–1950 the death rate declined 46 percent in Puerto Rico, 43 percent in Formosa, and 23 percent in Jamaica. In a sample of 18 underdeveloped areas the average decline in death rate between 1945 and 1950 was 24 percent. Figure 2-6 shows the dramatic change in death rates from the 1945–1949 average to 1960–1961 in selected Asian nations.

A critical point to remember is that this decline in death rate is different in kind from the long-term slow decline that occurred throughout most of the world following the agricultural revolution. It is also different in kind from the comparatively more rapid decline in death rates in the Western World over the past century. The difference is that it is a response to a spectacular environmental change in the UDCs, largely through control of infectious diseases, not a fundamental change in their institutions or general way of life. Furthermore, the change did not originate within these countries, but was brought about from the outside. The factors that led to a demographic transition (to low birth rates) in the DCs were not and are not present in

TABLE 2-4
*Change in Age-specific Death Rates of Males in Two UDCs*

| | 1950–1952 rate as a percentage of 1920–1922 rate | |
| Age class | Jamaica | Ceylon |
| --- | --- | --- |
| 0–1 | 45.1 | 39.8 |
| 1–5 | 38.3 | 34.7 |
| 5–10 | 34.6 | 21.7 |
| 10–15 | 28.7 | 15.6 |
| 15–20 | 25.9 | 16.1 |
| 20–40 | 31.7 | 21.4 |
| 40–60 | 59.2 | 32.4 |
| 60–70 | 73.1 | 48.2 |

SOURCE: Kingsley Davis, *Population Review* (1965).

the UDCs. Instead, a large proportion of the world's population has moved rapidly from a situation of high birth and death rates to one of high birth and low death rates. As a result, the annual rates of increase have risen sharply. Egypt, for instance, moved from a growth rate of slightly more than 1.5 percent before 1945 (birth rate 40–45, death rate about 28) to 2.5–3.0 percent after 1945 (1971 birth rate 44, death rate 15, growth rate 2.8 percent).

Because of the death rate reduction in the UDCs, the world growth rate moved from 0.9 percent (doubling time 77 years) in the decade 1940–1950

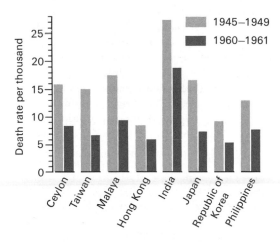

FIGURE 2-6

Change in death rates in selected Asian nations. The average rates of 1945–1949 are compared with those of 1960–1961. (After *Population Bulletin,* vol. 20, no. 2.)

to a rate of 1.8 percent (doubling time 39 years) in the decade 1950–1960. The world's population grew from a total of about 2.3 billion in 1940 to 2.5 billion in 1950, 3.0 billion in 1960, and 3.6 billion in 1970. According to the Population Reference Bureau's *1971 World Population Data Sheet* (reproduced here in Appendix 1), the world's population size in mid-1971 was estimated to be 3.71 billion, the growth rate 2.0 percent, and the doubling time 35 years. During the 1960s the world growth rate fluctuated between 1.8 and 2.0 percent. These figures are only approximations (because census data from many countries are inadequate—see introduction to Appendix 1), but they are more than sufficient for the purposes of discussion in this book. If there were actually only 3.5 billion people or as many as 3.9 billion people in the world as of mid-1971, or if the world growth rate were actually 1.7 or 2.2 percent, our conclusions would not change one iota.

# Bibliography

Adams, Robert M., 1960. The origin of cities. *Scientific American,* vol. 203, no. 2 (Sept.). Scientific American Offprint No. 606, W. H. Freeman and Company, San Francisco.

Agarwala, S. N., 1967. *Population.* National Book Trust, India.

Behrman, S. J., L. Corsa, Jr., and R. Freedman (eds.), 1969. *Fertility and family planning: A world view.* Univ. of Michigan Press, Ann Arbor. Useful source for recent demographic history.

Braidwood, Robert J., 1960. The agricultural revolution. *Scientific American,* vol. 203, no. 3 (Sept.). Reprinted in Ehrlich et al. (see below).

Carr-Saunders, A. M., 1936. *World Population.* Oxford Univ. Press, Fairlawn, N.J.

Curwen, E. C., and G. Hatt, 1953. *Plough and Pasture,* Henry Schuman, New York. Deals with the early history of farming.

Dalrymple, Dana G., 1964. The Soviet Famine of 1932–34. *Soviet Studies,* vol. 14, pp. 250–284. An excellent and detailed account.

Davis, Kingsley, 1956. The amazing decline of mortality in underdeveloped areas. *Am. Econ. Rev.,* vol. 46, pp. 305–318.

Davis, Kingsley, 1963. Population. *Scientific American,* vol. 209, no. 3 (Sept.). Scientific American Offprint No. 645, W. H. Freeman and Company, San Francisco.

Davis, Kingsley, 1965. The population impact on children in the world's agrarian countries. *Population Review,* vol. 9, pp. 17–31.

Deevey, Edward S., 1960. The human population. *Scientific American,* vol. 203, no. 3 (Sept.). Scientific American Offprint No. 608, W. H. Freeman and Company, San Francisco. Reprinted in Ehrlich et al. (see below).

Ehrlich, P. R., and R. W. Holm, 1963. *The Process of Evolution.* McGraw-Hill, New York. See especially Chapter 12.

Ehrlich, P. R., J. P. Holdren, and R. W. Holm (eds.), 1971. *Man and the Ecosphere.* W. H. Freeman and Company, San Francisco. Important papers from *Scientific American* with critical commentaries.

Keyfitz, Nathan, 1966. How many people have ever lived on Earth? *Demography,* vol. 3, pp. 581–582.

Keyfitz, Nathan, 1966. Population density and the style of social life. *BioScience,* vol. 16, no. 12, pp. 868–873 (Dec.).

Langer, William L., 1958. The next assignment. *American Historical Review,* vol. 63, pp. 283–305. Includes an excellent discussion of the long-term effects of the Black Death on society.

Langer, William L., 1964. The Black Death. *Scientific American,* vol. 210, no. 2 (Feb.). Scientific American Offprint No. 619, W. H. Freeman and Company, San Francisco. Reprinted in Ehrlich et al. (see above).

Martin, Paul S., 1967. Pleistocene overkill. *Natural History,* pp. 32–38 (Dec.). Describes early man's effects on other large animals.

Martin, Paul S., 1970. Pleistocene niches for alien animals. *BioScience,* vol. 20, no. 4, pp. 218–221 (Feb. 15). Discusses the ecological impact of Pleistocene extinctions.

Population Reference Bureau, 1962. How many people have ever lived on Earth? *Population Bulletin,* vol. 18, no. 1. Contains a good brief summary of population growth. An arithmetic error in the calculation of the total number of people who have lived is corrected by Keyfitz (see *Demography* reference above). *Population Bulletin* is a major source of information for the educated layman on all aspects of demography. The Bureau also produces an invaluable annual "Population Data Sheet." For more information write Population Reference Bureau, 1755 Massachusetts Avenue, N.W., Washington, D.C. 20036.

Reed, Charles A., 1970. Extinction of mammalian megafauna in the Old World late Quaternary. *BioScience,* vol. 20, no. 5, pp. 284–288 (March 1). More on early man's effects on large animals.

Thompson, W. S., and D. J. Lewis, 1965. *Population Problems,* 5th ed. McGraw-Hill, New York. An excellent, comprehensive source.

United Nations, Statistical Office. *Demographic Yearbook.* This annual compilation is *the* source for world data on population.

Walford, Cornelius, 1878. The famines of the world: past and present. *Royal Stat. Soc. Jour.* vol. 41, pp. 433–526.

Waterbolk, H. T., 1968. Food production in prehistoric Europe. *Science,* vol. 162, pp. 1093–1102.

Willcox, Walter F., 1940. *Studies in American Demography.* Cornell Univ. Press, Ithaca, N.Y.

Wrigley, E. A., 1969. *Population and History.* McGraw-Hill, New York.

# CHAPTER 3

# Population Structure and Projection

*"We shall see finally appear the miracle of an animal society, a complete and definitive ant-heap"*

Paul Valéry
(1871–1945)

The discussion of population so far has dealt mainly with population sizes and growth rates, but there is more to demography than just sizes and growth rates. Populations have structure: age composition, sex ratio, and distribution and dispersion (the geographic position and relative spacing of individuals). Both distribution and age composition will be considered in the first part of this chapter. The second part is a discussion of projections of future population sizes—projections that usually depend on various assumptions about population structure.

## Age Composition

During the Depression in the 1930s, some European countries were in an interesting demographic situation. If age-specific birth and death rates had held constant, the populations in these countries eventually would have stopped growing and begun to decline. But in fact these populations continued to increase, although slowly. This increase was due to the *age composition* of the population—the percentage of people in different age classes.

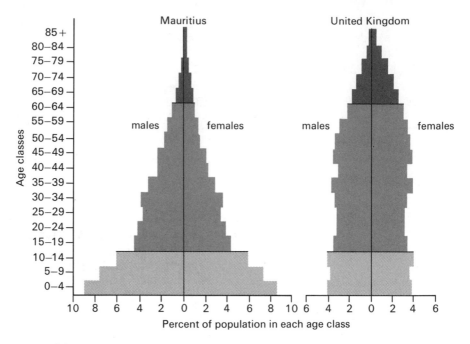

FIGURE 3-1

Age composition of population of Mauritius and United Kingdom in 1959. These age profiles contrast the age distribution in a rapidly growing UDC with a very slowly growing DC. In Mauritius young people predominate; in the United Kingdom the population is more evenly distributed over the age spectrum. Note that in each profile the percentage of males of each age class in the population is shown to the left of the center line and that of females to the right. In Figures 3-1 to 3-5 the working ages (15–64) are shown in medium gray, the young dependents (0–14) in pale gray, and the elderly dependents (65 or over) in dark gray. (After *Population Bulletin,* vol. 18, no. 5.)

Contrast, for instance, the age compositions of the populations of Mauritius (an island in the Indian Ocean) and the United Kingdom in 1959 as shown by their population profiles (Fig. 3-1). These profiles are a graphic means of showing the age compositions of the populations. Because the profiles are based on proportions, they both have the same area in spite of the great difference in the absolute sizes of the populations. This permits one to focus easily on their comparative shapes, which, of course, are an indication of their comparative age compositions. Mauritius' profile exemplifies rapidly growing countries with high birth rates and declining death rates. Most of its people are young; 44 percent are under age 15. The U.K., however, has had low birth and death rates for many decades. It has a much narrower population profile than Mauritius. Only 23 percent of the population of the United Kingdom in 1959 was under age 15.

In Mauritius (Box 3-1) and many other UDCs, high birth rates and increasing control over infant and child mortality have greatly inflated the younger age groups in the population. There has not yet been sufficient time for individuals born in the period of "death control" to reach the older age classes, whose death rates are higher than those of the younger age classes. In most of these countries the greatest decreases in death rates among infants and children occurred in the late 1940s, and the large numbers of children born in that period will be in their peak reproductive years in the early 1970s. Their children will in turn further inflate the lower tiers of the popu-

---

BOX 3-1    MAURITIUS, CHILDREN, AND THE DEPENDENCY LOAD

Mauritius, one of the Mascarene Islands in the Indian Ocean, has one particular claim to fame—it was once the home of the now-extinct dodo, a flightless bird larger than a turkey. By 1969 more than 800,000 people were jammed onto the island, more than 1,100 per square mile, and the island's population had a growth rate of 2 percent a year. The story of Mauritius' postwar population growth is similar to that of other UDCs, and the result has been a dependency load of 47 percent; that is, 47 percent of the population is either under 15 (44 percent) or over 65 (3 percent). The society is faced with a tremendous burden in the form of vast numbers of children who are non-productive or relatively unproductive.

The huge proportion of young people in the population has put a tremendous strain on Mauritius' school system. Many primary schools had to go on double shifts, and an extreme shortage of teachers developed. In order to staff the schools, teachers had to be put in charge of classes before their training could be completed. Most of the country's educational effort went into primary schools; as of 1962 only one out of seven elementary school students went on to high school.

The education problem in Mauritius is a good example of what demographer Kingsley Davis meant when he said that children "are the principal victims of improvident reproduction." Many UDCs simply cannot afford to educate their children adequately. The governments of DCs are able to spend almost twice as much proportionately on education as opposed to health as are governments of the UDCs. The government of Mauritius spent more on both health and public assistance in 1958–1959 than it did on education, yet, after the first five years of life, children in the UDCs enter the portion of the population that has the lowest mortality rates. These children desperately need education, for their own good and for the future of their society, but the sorry fact is that in the absence of population control, solving the problems of health in the UDCs makes solving the problem of education extremely difficult.

High fertility and low income also tend to force children out of school and into the labor pool as early as possible. Even the chances for education in the home are reduced when families are large and mothers overburdened. Child labor is used at a very high level in underdeveloped countries, although the productivity of that labor may be quite low. United Nations statistics, which may understate the case, show that 31 percent of males between 10 and 14 years of age are economically active in UDCs, in contrast to only 5 percent in DCs.

It is a brutal irony that children must bear the brunt of the suffering caused by the population explosion. As Davis says, "the old philosophy that their coming is a just and divine punishment for their parents' sexual indulgence, and therefore not to be mitigated by deliberate control is one of the cruelest doctrines ever devised by a species noted for its cruel and crazy notions."

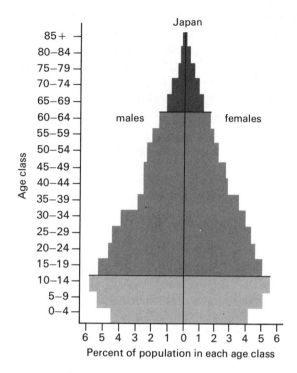

FIGURE 3-2

Age composition of population of Japan in 1960.
Note narrow base of profile, caused by a sharp
decrease in the birth rate. (After Thompson and
Lewis, *Population Problems,* 5th ed. McGraw-Hill,
1965.)

lation pyramid. Eventually, either population control will lower birth rates in
these countries, or famine or other natural checks on population will once
again increase mortality in the youngest age classes—or possibly in all age
classes. If birth rates are lowered, there will also be a rise in the death rate
as the population ages. In the absence of both birth control and natural
checks, however, death rates in the extraordinarily young populations of
these UDCs may temporarily fall below those of the DCs. For instance, in
1971 the death rate in the United Kingdom was 11.9 per thousand, in
Belgium 12.4, and in the United States 9.3. In contrast, the death rate in
Costa Rica was 8.0, Trinidad 7.0, Ceylon 8.0, Singapore 5.0, and Hong
Kong 5.0.

Rapid and substantial decreases in birth rate, which can be produced by
the onset of a successful population control program, may temporarily
produce a population profile that is sharply constricted at the base. Such
is the shape of Japan's 1960 profile (Fig. 3-2), which shows the effects of
an extremely rapid postwar decline in the birth rate. Japan is a DC today,
but the profile resembles that of a typical UDC from the 10–14 age class
upward. However, the 0–4 and 5–9 classes are considerably smaller than in

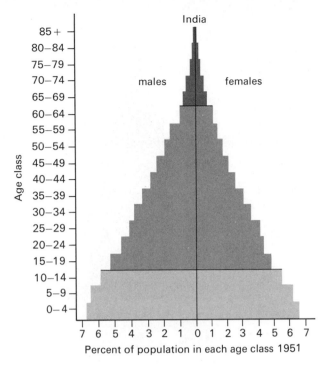

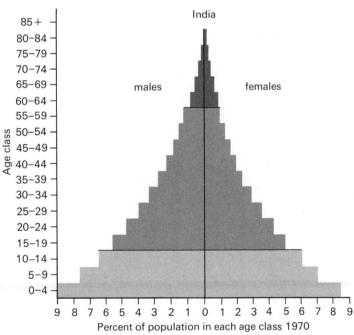

FIGURE 3-3

Age composition of population of India in 1951. Declining death rates have not
yet produced the "pinched" profile characteristic of rapidly growing UDCs such as
Mauritius. (After Thompson and Lewis, *Population Problems,* 5th ed. McGraw-Hill,
1965.) Age composition of population of India in 1970; profile now resembles
typical UDC. (After *Population Bulletin,* vol. XXVI, no. 5, Nov. 1970. Population
Reference Bureau, Inc.)

32

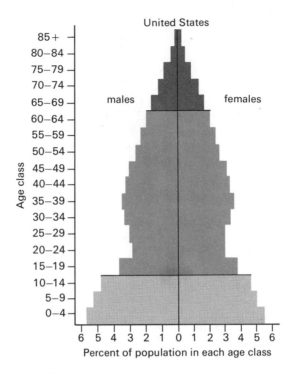

FIGURE 3-4

Age composition of population of United States in
1960. Large "bulge" in 0–14 age class represents the
age group that will be reproducing in the 1970s and
1980s. (After Thompson and Lewis, *Population
Problems,* 5th ed. McGraw-Hill, 1965.)

most UDCs, so only 30 percent of the population is under 15.

Two additional profile shapes are commonly found. One is the more or
less equilateral triangle characteristic of countries that have both high birth
rates and high death rates. Such profiles must have typified most human
populations until fairly recently. They lack the extremely broad base
of profiles like that of Mauritius (Fig. 3-1) and most other UDCs today.
India's profile was essentially triangular in 1951 (Fig. 3-3). Since then,
however, India's death rate has dropped by about 10 per thousand, and the
base of her profile has broadened to give her the sort of "pinched triangle"
shape of the other UDCs. The second additional profile is exemplified by that
of the United States in 1960 (Fig. 3-4); such bell-shaped profiles result when
a population that once had low birth and death rates undergoes a subsequent
rise in birth rate and starts growing relatively rapidly again.

One of the most significant features of the age composition of a population is
the proportion of people who are economically productive in relation to
those who are dependent on them. For purposes of convenience, the segment
of the population in the age class 15–64 is chosen as an index of the pro-

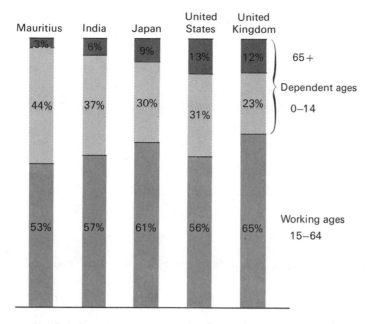

FIGURE 3-5

Dependency loads in Mauritius (1959), India (1951), Japan (1960), United States (1960), and United Kingdom (1959). Note contrast in proportions of economically active people in a typical UDC, Mauritius, and a typical DC, the United Kingdom. (After *Population Bulletin,* vol. 18, no. 5; and Thompson and Lewis, *Population Problems,* 5th ed., McGraw-Hill, 1965.)

ductive portion of the population (Fig. 3-5). In the population profiles (Figs. 3-1 to 3-4) and in Figure 3-5, the working ages are shown in medium gray, the young dependents in pale gray; and "senior citizens" in dark gray. Figures 3-1 to 3-5 provide a comparison of the proportion of dependents in these same populations. The proportion of dependents in UDCs is generally much higher than in the DCs, primarily because a large fraction of the population is under 15 years of age. Thus the ratio of dependents to the total population size is higher in the poor countries, and lower in the rich countries, although the ratio is somewhat misleading because of the heavier utilization of child labor in UDCs (Box 3-1). This unfortunate dependency ratio is an additional heavy burden to the UDCs as they struggle for economic development.

The high percentage of people under 15 years of age is also indicative of the explosive growth potential of their populations. In most UDCs this percentage is 40–45; in a few as high as 50. By contrast, the percentage under age 15 in DCs is usually 20–30. Thus UDCs have a much greater proportion of people in their prereproductive years. As these young people grow up and move into their reproductive years, the size of the childbearing

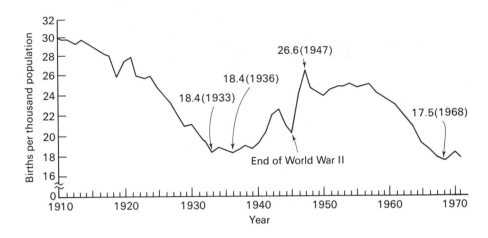

FIGURE 3-6

Birth rate in United States, 1910–1971. (After *Population Profile,* Population Reference Bureau, March 1967.)

fraction in the population will increase astronomically. In turn their children will further inflate the size of the youngest age groups. These masses of young people in the UDCs are the gunpowder of the population explosion.

The birth and death rates used thus far, which are expressed in births and deaths per thousand population, are known technically as *crude birth rates* and *crude death rates.* They are called "crude" simply because they do not allow for differences in the structure of populations. They are the most readily available (and thus most widely quoted) figures, and although they are often quite useful, comparison of crude rates may be misleading.

An outstanding example was the recent highly publicized drop in the birth rate in the United States, which some people and publications misinterpreted as heralding the end of the U.S. population explosion. The birth rate in 1968 was 17.4, a record low for the country, going below the previous low of the depression year 1936. Note the trend in birth rates between 1959 and 1968 shown in Figure 3-6. In this period the crude birth rate declined about 25 percent. This could, of course, have been caused by a decrease in the number of women in the childbearing years rather than by a change in the desired family size of individual women. One check on this may be made by looking at another demographic statistic, the *fertility rate.* The fertility rate—the number of births per 1,000 women 15–44 years of age—is a more refined indicator of birth trends, because it compensates for differences in sex ratio (such as are sometimes the result of wars) and for gross differences in age composition. Differences in age composition might be revealed if two populations had identical crude birth rates but widely differing fertility rates. This might mean, for instance, that one had a relatively low proportion of its people in the 15–44 age group and a high fertility rate, while the other had a relatively high proportion in the 15–44 age group and a lower fertility rate.

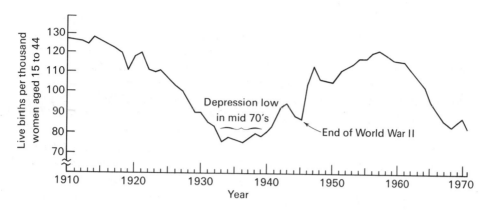

FIGURE 3-7

Fertility rate in United States, 1910–1971. (After *Population Profile,* Population Reference Bureau, March 1967.)

As is shown in Figure 3-7, the fertility rate in the U.S. *was also declining* during the period 1959–1968, and at just about the same rate as the crude birth rate. So not only were fewer babies being born in proportion to the entire population, but fewer babies were being born in relation to the population of females in their childbearing years. But does this mean that the population explosion in the United States was coming to an end in the late 1960s?

The fertility rate *has* been on a downward trend, but the 1968 fertility rate of about 85 was still higher than the lows reached during the Depression (when it was well below 80). In 1970, the fertility rate had risen again to about 87. The crude birth rate reached a record low in 1968 because a smaller proportion of the total population were women in the 15–44 age group in the late 1960s than in 1936. In 1936, 24 percent of the population consisted of women in those childbearing years; in 1967, only 20 percent. In 1967 there were an estimated 40.2 million women in the 15–44 age class. By 1970 the U.S. Census Bureau estimated that there were about 42.3 million women in this class. In 1975 the number of women of childbearing age is projected to be about 46.9 million, an increase of 17 percent over 1967.

Of the women in the 15–44 age group, those in the 20–29 subgroup bear most of the children. This subgroup, which accounted for some 60 percent of the children born in 1967, increased from 14.3 million in 1968 to 15.5 million in 1970, and is projected to increase to 18.3 million in 1975, and to 20 million by 1980. After that the size of the subgroup will begin to decline as the babies of the low-birth-rate 1960s enter their reproductive years. From these data it is apparent that, barring a tremendous drop in the fertility rate, a considerable rise in the American *crude birth rate* can be expected during the 1970s. Unless the death rate also rises this will result in an increase in the growth rate of the population.

Many other factors influence birth rates in addition to the number of women in their childbearing years. Severe economic conditions, epidemics, and wars may cause declines. For instance, the shipment of young men overseas during World War I and the great influenza epidemic of 1918 led to a drop in the American birth rate from 28.2 in 1918 to 26.1 in 1919. Similarly, improvements in economic conditions and the return of World War II servicemen led to a birth rate jump from 20.4 in 1945 to 26.6 in 1947.

The optimists who greeted the decline in birth rates in the 1960s with pronouncements about the end of the population explosion would probably interpret a December thaw as a sign of spring. It is too early at this writing to predict the magnitude of the baby boom of the 1970s, which will result from the increased number of women in their prime reproductive years. But surveys during the late 1960s indicated a rising preference among Americans for large families, which was not an encouraging sign. Gallup polls periodically ask the question, "What do you think is the ideal number of children for a family to have?" In 1936, 34 percent of Americans answered "four or more." In 1945 the percentage was up to 49, from which point it descended to 35 percent in 1966. In 1968 it was back up to 41 percent. That figure is itself 70 percent higher than the highest equivalent figure in eleven European countries where similar surveys have been conducted. Results there, for those wanting four or more children, ranged from 7 percent in Austria to 24 percent in the Netherlands during the 1960s.

By 1971, however, the percentage of Americans who thought four or more children was the ideal number had dropped abruptly to 23 percent. Not only was this an extraordinary change in only three years' time, it represented a new all-time low for the United States, far below the previous level reached in 1936. The reasons for this change of attitude toward family size are unclear. Publicity about the population explosion apparently influenced some people. Other factors were the economic recession and social unrest, which make U.S. society today appear less desirable as a place to raise children than in the past.

There is often, of course, a substantial difference between opinions or plans expressed about family size and actual reproductive performance. Moreover, both ideals and plans are subject to change during a period of time, as the fluctuations in stated ideals since 1936 demonstrate. A wide variety of factors could lead either to larger or smaller family sizes in the 1970s than those now voiced as "ideal."

## Age-specific Vital Rates and the Potential for Population Growth

Fertility and death rates (vital rates) may be separately calculated for any age class in the population. For instance, the number of babies born to each thousand women of age 25 is the age-specific fertility rate for 25-year olds. The number of 25-year olds who die per thousand people of that age in the population is the age-specific death rate for 25-year olds. At any given time a population has a schedule of age-specific fertility and death rates. Most human populations show rather high age-specific death rates in the age 0–1 and considerably lower rates in the next nine years. Infants are more likely to die than young children. After the age of 10, there is generally a slow rise in death rates until around 45 to 50, and then a rapid rise. There is, of course, considerable variation from country to country. UDCs, for instance, tend to have proportionately much higher infant and child mortality rates than do DCs.

The reason for the enormous growth potential inherent in the age composition of most UDCs can be seen by considering their schedules of age-specific vital rates. In rapidly growing UDCs, roughly 40 to 45 percent of the population are less than 15 years of age. That population of young people will soon be moving into age classes with high age-specific fertility rates, *but it will be some 50 years before they are subject to the high age-specific death rates associated with old age.* Fifty years is about two generations, which means that those youngsters will have children and grandchildren before they swell the upper part of the age pyramid and begin to make heavy contributions to the crude death rate. Therefore, even if the fertility in the population dropped precipitously to a level which would eventually result in an end to population growth, that end would not be reached for 50 years or more. That is, *assuming there is no rise in the age-specific death rates,* there will be a long "braking-time" before even very successful birth control programs can halt growth in these nations. The momentum inherent in the age composition means that population size will go far beyond the level at which the "brakes" are successfully applied.

Demographer Nathan Keyfitz has calculated the magnitude of that momentum. He showed what would happen if a birth control miracle were to occur and the average number of children born to each woman in a typical UDC were to drop immediately to the replacement level (so that each couple would on the average have just the number of children which would lead to their replacement in the next generation). In such an event, a typical UDC would continue to grow until it was about 1.6 times its present size. Should the fertility rates drop to the replacement level gradually over the next 30 years, the final population size would be some 2.5 times the present size. Even a drop to replacement level in 30 years is, of course, extremely unlikely to occur. Not even the most optimistic U.N. demographic projections foresee such a pattern of fertility decline.

## NRR, ZPG, and NPG

If age-specific vital rates remain constant the age composition of a population eventually becomes *stable,* a situation in which the proportion of people in each age class does not change through time. A population with a stable age composition can be growing, shrinking, or constant in size. When a population is constant in size (crude birth rate equals crude death rate), demographers refer to it as stationary; colloquially we say that zero population growth

(ZPG) has been achieved. In the work described above, Keyfitz was interested in how rapidly a stationary population would result if fertility rates dropped to replacement level. Replacement level is normally defined by demographers in terms of a statistic known as the net reproductive rate (NRR). The net reproductive rate of a population is the projected ratio of the number of women in one generation to that of the next. It is calculated by applying the age-specific birth and death rates of the population to a hypothetical group of 1,000 newborn female babies, seeing how many live female babies they would eventually produce, and dividing that number by 1,000.

If the average completed family size of a population with typical DC death rates is three children, the NRR will be about 1.3. An NRR of 1.3 means that, barring changes in birth and death rates and assuming a stable age composition, the population will grow 30 percent per generation (a generation is usually 25 to 30 years). As long as the NRR remains above 1, such a population will continue to grow. An NRR of 1 (fertility at replacement level) indicates either a stationary population or one that will become stationary after time has permitted the age composition to stabilize. Similarly, if the NRR drops below 1 and stays there, the population will shrink sooner or later (how soon will depend on the initial age composition). Note that the NRR describes what will happen *between generations,* if the age-specific vital rates remain constant at the same values that they had when the NRR was calculated. Even if these rates (and thus the NRR) are unchanging, the age composition of the population must be known in order for population projections to be made, since several generations normally live side-by-side. Suppose in a young population, such as that of one of the UDCs studied by Keyfitz, there were a rapid drop in age-specific fertility rates leading to a constant NRR smaller than 1. In that case the next generation would be slightly smaller than the one preceding it, but the population will continue to grow for a while because it has a very large population of reproductive age and hence a higher crude birth rate than it will have later.

Demographer Tomas Frejka, using 1965 as a base year, has shown what would happen to the United States population under a variety of assumptions. For instance, instant ZPG (zero population growth—a stationary population) could be achieved only by reducing the NRR to slightly below .6, with an average family size of about 1.2 children, for the years between 1965 and 1985. Thus, to bring the crude birth and death rates immediately into balance (so that the growth rate is zero), the average completed family size would have to drop far below that which would *eventually* lead to such a balance. After that, in order to hold the population size constant, the crude birth rate and NRR would have to oscillate wildly above and below the eventual equilibrium values for several centuries. The age composition would correspondingly change violently, undoubtedly causing a variety of severe social problems. These problems could be ameliorated by reducing the fertility rate less abruptly and then accepting the desirability of temporary negative population growth (NPG), rather than attempting to hold the population precisely at ZPG. As will be discussed later, there are powerful

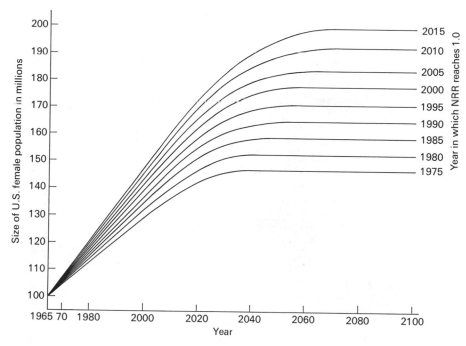

FIGURE 3-8

Projections of the course of population growth in the U.S. if NRR reaches 1.0 in various years. Total population size would be slightly less than twice the size of the female population, since there are slightly fewer men than women (after Frejka *Population Studies,* Nov. 1968).

arguments for reducing the size of the American population well below its present level.

Frejka also describes what would happen if the NRR declined from its 1965 level of about 1.3 to 1.0. From the time that the NRR reaches 1.0 until population growth actually stops would take about 65 to 75 years. Figure 3-8 shows projected population growth if NRR reached 1.0 and stayed there in a series of years starting with 1975, assuming no immigration. The projections clearly show that substantial population growth will occur after a pattern of replacement reproduction is established, no matter when that may be. For instance, if an NRR of 1.0 were reached in 1985, the population would not stop growing until 2055, and there would be an ultimate population of around 300 million (slightly less than twice the female population).

## Distribution

Mankind is not uniformly distributed over the face of the Earth. Figure 3-9 shows the rough pattern of population density in 1965. Population density

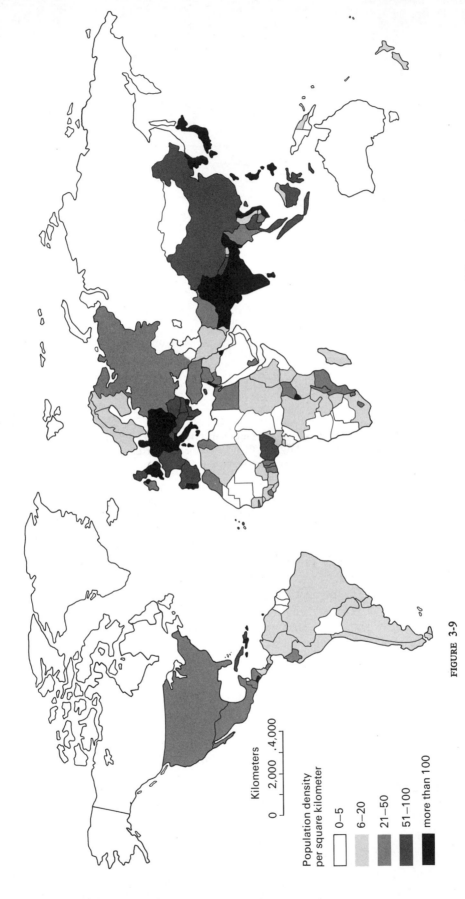

FIGURE 3-9

Patterns of population density, 1969. Figures are given in persons per square kilometer. A square kilometer is 0.3861 square miles. (Data from UN Demographic Yearbook, 1969.)

Population density
per square kilometer

0–5

6–20

21–50

51–100

more than 100

Kilometers

0    2,000  .4,000

is the number of individuals per unit area. For human populations this figure is normally expressed as people per square mile or per square kilometer. Some rough estimates (people per square mile) of population densities in the 1960s are:

| | |
|---|---:|
| Earth (land area) | 65 |
| United States | 55 |
| Japan | 700 |
| Tokyo | 20,000 |
| New York City | 25,000 |
| Manhattan | 75,000 |

In contrast, before the arrival of Europeans in the continental United States, its population density was about 0.33 people per square mile; the density rose to 5 people per square mile by about 1800. Of course, one must be cautious in picturing densities in terms of people per square mile because of man's tendency to gather in clusters. Although the U.S. in 1971 had about 57 people per square mile *on the average* (67 per square mile in the coterminous 48 states), there are, of course, many square miles that have no people. Furthermore, within any given square mile people will not ordinarily be uniformly distributed.

The densities and distributions of populations, especially in relation to resources, have played critical roles in many important events in human history. Densities that are perceived by the members of populations themselves as "high" generate what is generally referred to as "population pressure." Overpopulation is usually thought of in relation not to the absolute size of a population but to its density. There must have been many thousands of occasions in prehistory when one tribe or another decided that it had pretty much exhausted the berries and game in its home territory, and moved in on its neighbors. Many of the famous migrations of history, such as the barbarian invasions of Europe in the early Christian era, may have been due to population pressures. In 1095 when Pope Urban II preached the First Crusade, he referred to the advantages of gaining new lands. The crusaders were mainly second sons who were dispossessed because of the growing European trend toward primogeniture (inheritance by the first-born son only).

Considerable evidence indicates that population pressures were building up in fifteenth-century Europe. There is, for instance, evidence of attempts at land reclamation. The addition of the New World frontier to Europe at the end of the fifteenth century reduced the overall population density of Europe plus the Western Hemisphere from about 27 people per square mile to less than 5 people per square mile. European exploitation of the spatial, mineral, and other material wealth of the New World led to the creation of a basic set of institutions attuned to frontier attitudes. The economic boom that ensued lasted for 400 years. As far as land is concerned, the boom is now plainly over. The population density of the European metropolis (Western Europe and the Western Hemisphere) increased until it exceeded 27 per square mile before 1930. Since all of the material things on which the boom depended came ultimately from the land, the entire boom is clearly limited. In fact, the institutions and attitudes that evolved in the frontier setting now constitute a major threat to the survival of mankind.

Many wars were fought by European nations as they scrambled to occupy the Western Hemisphere. They warred among themselves and against the small native populations in the New World. More recently, population pressure contributed to Nazi Germany's famous drive for "lebensraum" (literally, room for living), especially in the East, where it reached its climax in "Operation Barbarossa"—the ill-fated invasion of the Soviet Union. Historian D. L. Bilderback comments that in the early years of Hitler's power, "large numbers of intelligent and humane persons believed that the Eastern adventure was a matter of necessity for their own survival." Whether Germany in 1941 was overpopulated in some absolute sense is not the point. The nation perceived itself as overpopulated. Germany is probably more pressed for space today than she was then. The Bonn Government, however, in contrast to Hitler, is not calling attention to overpopulation as a problem; indeed, it almost certainly does not realize that by many standards Germany today *is* overpopulated. On the contrary, Germany today is importing workers from southern Europe and North Africa.

Japan's expansionist moves in the 1930s and early 1940s can be traced in part to the high population density on her small islands. The population growth of Japan in the last third of the nineteenth century and the first third of the twentieth century was unprecedented among industrialized nations. It doubled in size (from 35 to 70 million) and therefore in density during the 63 years between 1874 and 1937. When the attempt to conquer additional territory failed, and population growth continued to accelerate, Japan moved to take drastic steps to limit her population (see Chapter 10). Japan is now again feeling the pinch, and is looking toward the continent of Asia for at least economic lebensraum.

Population pressures are certainly contributing to international tensions in the world today. Russia, India, and other neighbors of grossly overpopulated China guard their frontiers nervously. Chinese forces have already occupied Tibet. Population growth in China may leave her little long-range choice but to expand or starve, unless her population control policies are successful. Australians are clearly apprehensive about the Asian multitudes. This attitude is reflected in their nation's immigration laws and foreign policy. They have reason to be fearful, since the generally unfavorable and unreliable climate over much of Australia, together with its history of disastrous agricultural practices, mean that the entire continent lacks the resources for absorbing even a single year's increment to the Asian population. Such an increment would more than *quadruple* Australia's population from 12.8 million to 61 million. The number of people added *annually* to India's population alone is more than the entire population of Australia today.

# Urbanization

One of the oldest of all demographic trends is the one toward urbanization. Preagricultural man, by necessity, had to be dispersed over the landscape. Hunting and gathering required perhaps a minimum of 2 square miles of territory to produce the food for one person. Under such conditions, and without even the most primitive of transportation systems, it was impossible for people to exist in large concentrations. But the agricultural revolution began to change all that. Because more food could be produced in less area, people began to form primitive communities. The ability of a farmer to feed more than his own family was obviously a prerequisite of urbanization. A fraction of the population first had to be freed from cultivation of the land in order to form cities. But the division of labor and specialization of a nonfarming population does not in itself seem to have led immediately to urbanization. For example, some scholars feel that Egyptian agriculture and society was such that considerable numbers of people were freed from the land by the time their culture reached the condition we call civilized (ca. 3000 B.C.). It was, however, another 2,000 years before they developed the complex interrelated variety of urban population form that we would call a city. Similarly it is doubted whether the Mayan civilization produced cities. It is thought that, in ancient Mesopotamia at least, and perhaps in Cambodia, the development of large and complex irrigation systems helped lead to the formation of cities. Then, as today, shortage of water formed the basis of political disputes, and people may have gathered together for defensive purposes. Mesopotamian cities also would have served as storage and redistribution centers for food. As anthropologist Robert M. Adams has written, ". . . the complexity of subsistence pursuits on the flood plains may have indirectly aided the movement toward cities. Institutions were needed to mediate between herdsman and cultivator; between fisherman and sailor; between plowmaker and plowman." Whatever the actual impetus for urbanization was, the first cities arose along the Tigris and Euphrates rivers between 4000 and 3000 B.C.

The trend toward urbanization continues today, as it generally has since those first cities were formed. The move to the cities has at times been accelerated by agricultural advances that have made possible the establishment of larger, more efficient farms. It seems also to have been accelerated by growth in rural areas, which necessitated either the subdivision of farms among several sons, or the migration of "surplus" offspring to the cities. In the past, advances in agriculture were generally accompanied by advances in other kinds of technology, which provided new opportunities for employment in cities. Beyond providing places for those displaced from the land, cities have always been attractive in themselves to people who hoped to improve their economic condition. The movement into large urban concentrations has been especially accelerated in the last century. For instance, in the United States about 6 percent of the population lived in urban areas in 1800,

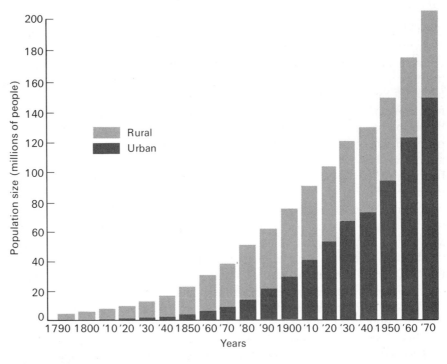

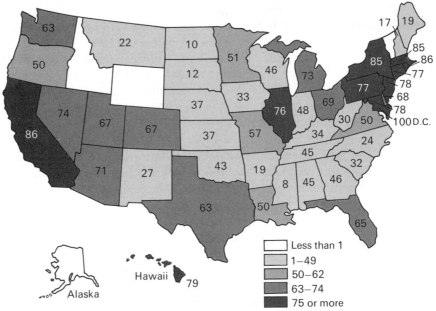

Percentage of population living in metropolitan areas, 1960

FIGURE 3-10

Urbanization of the United States. In 1960, 70 percent of Americans were living in towns or cities, and 63 percent were living in large cities and their surroundings (metropolitan areas). The 1970 census indicated that the percentage had increased to 73.5. (After *Population Bulletin,* vol. 19, no. 2.)

15 percent in 1850, 40 percent in 1900; today, nearly 75 percent live in cities or their suburbs (Fig. 3-10).

Rapid urbanization has not been confined to industrialized countries, however. Between 1950 and 1960, the populations of cities in the DCs increased 25 percent, while those of cities in the UDCs increased 55 percent. In Latin America, especially since the end of World War II, there has been an increasing flood of impoverished peasants into urban areas. Yet employment opportunities there have not materialized. The result has been the development of characteristic huge shanty-towns, given different names in each country: *favelas* in Brazil, *tugurios* in Colombia, *ranchos* in Venezuela, and *barriadas* in Peru. In Peru some three-quarters of a million squatters live in such settlements—a substantial fraction of Peru's population of 14 million.

The trend in Africa has been similar, with hundreds of thousands migrating to the cities annually in search of a better life. Nairobi, the capital of Kenya, had a 1968 population of 460,000 and was growing at a rate of 7 percent per year. That is more than double the growth rate of Los Angeles in the decade 1950–1960. Accra, the capital of Ghana, is growing at almost 8 percent per year; Abidjan, capital of the Ivory Coast, at almost 10 percent; Lusaka, capital of Zambia, and Lagos, capital of Nigeria, both at 14 percent. In both Latin America and Africa the trend to the cities seems to be caused in large part by the kind of hope for a better life that has drawn many people from rural areas of the southern United States and Puerto Rico to a slum life in New York, Chicago, and other Northern metropolises. And in the cities of underdeveloped countries where there is little industry, the opportunities are much more limited than in the United States. Yet, miserable as their condition is, nearly all evidently prefer to remain in the cities rather than return to what they left. Of course, many may also have burned their bridges behind them and have no way of successfully returning to their former homes.

The rate of urbanization in Asia has also been rapid in this century, but in many areas the increases have been from a rather low base. For instance, at the turn of the century about 11 percent of India's population was urban. Today more than 20 percent of India's people live in cities. Most of this increase has occurred since 1931, with the largest percent increase occurring in the decade 1941–1951 and the largest absolute increase in the decade 1951–1961. Data for the period since the 1961 census are not available, but the figure of 20 percent is based on the 1961 figures corrected for comparability with previous censuses and projected. Even under the new, more restricted definition of "urban," the figure would be close to 20 percent today.

One problem that is inevitably encountered when discussing urbanization is the definition of "urban area." This varies from country to country, and from time to time. And, of course, urban areas in different countries or different areas of the same country often are quite dissimilar. Los Angeles, New York, and Chicago have certain features (and problems) in common— good art museums, major universities, slums, disadvantaged minorities, numerous TV stations, dangerously congested airports, diverse specialty shops, and air pollution, to name a few. But their differences are as apparent as their similarities. The air-pollution problems of Los Angeles and New York are fundamentally different because the "smogs" over each city have different compositions and the cities are in different physical settings. Water supply problems are unique in each of the three cities. Los Angeles has a hopeless surface transportation problem and smoggy "sunshine slums." Mexican-Americans are one of its largest minority groups. Chicago has substantial problems with a "hillbilly" minority. New York has been unable to absorb satisfactorily the masses of immigrants from Puerto Rico and has been overwhelmed with welfare recipients migrating from the rural South. The problems of government in all three cities have their own peculiar twists.

Urbanization seems to have one almost universal effect, the breaking down of the traditional cultures of those who migrate to the cities—a loss of roots, or alienation. In rural or tribal societies each individual has a well-defined role in the organization of the society, a role that he or she has matured into and that is recognized by all other members of the society. In contrast, anonymity is a major feature of the city. City-dwellers typically are on close terms with no more people than are village-dwellers, and they tend to go to great lengths not to "get involved" with the vast majority of the human beings with whom they come into daily contact.

Urbanization in the United States differs dramatically from urbanization in most UDCs. For instance, the difference between city-dwellers and country-dwellers in the United States has become increasingly blurred, especially in recent years, with urban culture becoming dominant. Rapid transportation and mass media have exposed the country folk to the ways of the city. The image of the hick has less and less validity today, especially when some "hicks" fly their wives several hundred miles to the city in their private aircraft for shopping sprees and a night at the theater. Furthermore, in the United States especially, the phenomenon of suburbanization has developed. Suburbanites, who take advantage of high-speed transport and general affluence, attempt to enjoy the advantages of city and countryside simultaneously, working in the former and living close to the latter.

In the UDCs, communications and transportation are much less efficient, and the peasant culture is less influenced by the urban. According to demographer Nathan Keyfitz, the overwhelming majority of urban dwellers in the UDCs are migrants from the countryside who have brought their peasant culture with them. Unlike most DC urbanites, whose specialized education, training, and skills assure them of a place in the city's complex social web, the UDC immigrant has no such talents to offer. Cities in developed countries are a source of wealth and power, generated through technology and manufacturing. The goods they produce are exchanged for food from the countryside. In contrast, many UDC cities subsist in times of shortage primarily on food imported from other countries. Attracted by the opportunity to obtain a share of the imported food, inhabitants of the countryside move into these cities when the countryside can no longer support them. Inevitably, they find that their limited skills render them incapable of contributing to the economy, and as a consequence they are not much better off than they were where they came from. In many UDC cities these unproductive squatters now make up a majority of their populations, and their number in most places is growing very rapidly.

Many migrants to the UDC city maintain contact with their home villages or form modified village societies within the city, and thus tend to transfer the village culture to the city. This may explain why the reproductive rates and attitudes of the inhabitants of these cities closely resemble those of their rural relatives.

## Demographic Projections

Once there was a young man who proposed a novel pay scheme to a prospective employer. For one month's work he was to receive one cent on the first day, two cents on the second, four on the third, and so on. Each day his pay was to double until the end of the month. The employer, a rather dull-witted merchant, agreed. The merchant was chagrined, to say the least, when he found that the young man's pay for the 15th day was more than $160. The merchant went bankrupt long before he had to pay the young man $167,733 for the 25th day. Had he remained in business he would have had to pay his new employee wages of more than $10 million for the month.

This is just one of many stories that illustrate the astronomical figures that are quickly reached by repeated doubling, from even a minute base. Another is about a reward that consists of a single grain of rice on the first square of a chessboard, 2 on the second, 4 on the third, and so forth, until the board is filled. It turns out that completing the reward takes several thousand times the world's annual rice crop.

Similar horrendous figures may be generated by projecting the human population of the world into the future. After all, the doubling time for that population is now only about 35 years. If growth continued at that rate the world population would exceed a billion billion people about 1,000 years from now. That would be some 1,700 persons *per square yard* of the Earth's surface, land and sea! Even more preposterous figures can be generated. In a few thousand more years everything in the visible universe would be converted into people, and the diameter of the ball of people would be expanding with the speed of light! Such projections should convince all but the most obtuse that growth of the human population must stop eventually.

Of primary interest and significance to us are predictions of population sizes in the next few decades. The most complete of these are the low, medium, and high population projections for the period 1965–2000 made by the United Nations in 1963. These are not simple extrapolations of past trends or present rates into the future. Instead, these population projections are computed on a component basis. That is, specific forecasts are made of trends in age-specific fertility, death rates, migration, and so forth. These are based on the best available demographic data for the nations or regions of the world, and the scope of future variation in these rates is estimated on

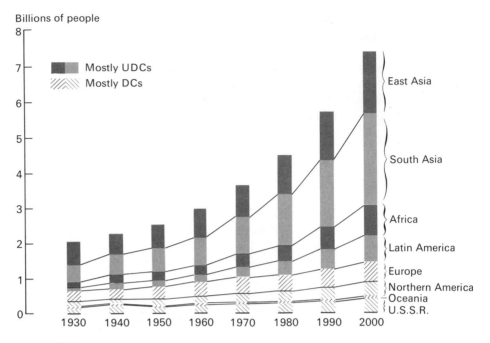

Billions of people

FIGURE 3-11

Projected growth of world population, based on the United Nations "constant fertility" projection. (After *Population Bulletin,* vol. 21, no. 4.)

the basis of past trends in developed and undeveloped areas. Possible major disasters, such as thermonuclear war, are not considered. All of these data are integrated to provide medium, low, and high projections, the last two of which the demographers hope will bracket the actual figures. The accuracy of the projections depends, of course, on the degree to which the various realized rates differ from the predicted rates. Another projection, called the "constant fertility, no migration" projection, is made on the simpler assumption that current fertility and the current trend in mortality will continue and that there will be no migration between areas. A revision of the 1963 projections was made in 1968, but only the medium variant was prepared for areas within the developed regions. In the following discussion the 1968 figures are used whenever they are available (Fig. 3-11).

The low 1963 U.N. forecast projects a world population of about 5,449 million in the year 2000, the medium forecast 6,130 million, and the high 6,994 million. Data for the regions denoted in Figure 3-12 are given in Table 3-1. The map also indicates level of development of the areas. If, however, present high birth rates should continue and be accompanied by a continuing decline in death rates, the constant-fertility projection would be for 7,522 million people at the turn of the century. The U.N.'s low, medium, and high projections all rest on an assumption that fertility rates will be lowered in those areas where they are now dangerously high. For convenience

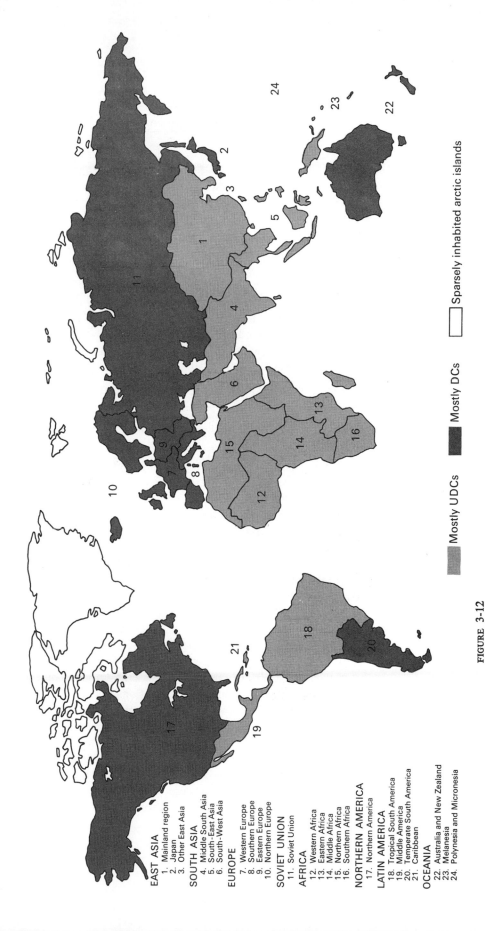

EAST ASIA
  1. Mainland region
  2. Japan
  3. Other East Asia

SOUTH ASIA
  4. Middle South Asia
  5. South-East Asia
  6. South-West Asia

EUROPE
  7. Western Europe
  8. Southern Europe
  9. Eastern Europe
 10. Northern Europe

SOVIET UNION
 11. Soviet Union

AFRICA
 12. Western Africa
 13. Eastern Africa
 14. Middle Africa
 15. Northern Africa
 16. Southern Africa

NORTHERN AMERICA
 17. Northern America

LATIN AMERICA
 18. Tropical South America
 19. Middle America
 20. Temperate South America
 21. Caribbean

OCEANIA
 22. Australia and New Zealand
 23. Melanesia
 24. Polynesia and Micronesia

Mostly UDCs    Mostly DCs    Sparsely inhabited arctic islands

FIGURE 3-12

Regions of world for which United Nations demographic projections are made.

TABLE 3-1

*Estimate of Population in the Year 2000* (in millions)

| Region | 1971 population | Low | | Medium | | High | | Constant Fertility, No Migration | |
|---|---|---|---|---|---|---|---|---|---|
| | | *1963* | *1968* | *1963* | *1968* | *1963* | *1968* | *1963* | *1968* |
| World Total | 3,706 | 5,449 | | 6,130 | 6,494 | 6,994 | | 7,522 | |
| East Asia | 946 | 1,118 | | 1,287 | 1,424 | 1,623 | | 1,811 | |
| South Asia | 1,157 | 1,984 | 2,119 | 2,171 | 2,354 | 2,444 | 2,617 | 2,702 | 2,989 |
| Europe | 466 | 491 | | 527 | 568 | 563 | | 570 | |
| Soviet Union | 245 | 316 | | 353 | 330 | 403 | | 402 | |
| Africa | 354 | 684 | 734 | 768 | 818 | 864 | 906 | 860 | 873 |
| Northern America | 229 | 294 | | 354 | 333 | 376 | | 388 | |
| Latin America | 291 | 532 | | 638 | 652 | 686 | | 756 | |
| Oceania | 20 | 28 | | 32 | 35 | 35 | | 33 | |
| Developed Regions | 1,105 | 1,293 | | 1,441 | 1,454 | 1,574 | | 1,580 | |
| Underdeveloped Regions | 2,601 | 4,155 | 4,523 | 4,688 | 5,040 | 5,420 | 5,650 | 5,942 | 6,369 |

SOURCE: United Nations, *World Population Prospects as Assessed in 1963 and 1968*. 1971 data from World Population Data Sheet, Population Reference Bureau.

in comparing future trends against the projected figures, detailed tables for each of these areas appear in Appendix 2. Both 1963 and 1968 projections are given. Note in the appendix that the 1970 world population size fell between the U.N.'s 1963 medium and high projections.

The history of population projections and forecasts in the past few decades has been that they have erred fairly consistently on the low side. For instance, in its November 8, 1948, issue, *Time* magazine quoted the opinions of un-named "experts" who felt then that a prediction (by the U.N. Food and Agriculture Organization of the United Nations) of a world population of 2,250 million in 1960 was probably too high. The actual population in 1960 was about 3,000 million. In 1949 economist Colin Clark predicted a world population in 1990 of 3.5 billion, and in 1950 demographer Frank Notestein predicted that by the year 2000 there would be 3.3 billion people alive. Both figures were exceeded well before 1970. In 1957 the demographers of the United Nations offered the following population projections for 1970: low, 3,350 million; medium, 3,480 million; and high, 3,500 million. The actual population size passed the high projection for 1970 sometime near the end of 1968. In the depression years it was common for demographers to show great concern over the possibility of population declines. Their appre-hensions were based on projections of trends in both the birth rate and the death rate. Depression declines in birth rates were more than compensated for by the baby boom of the 1940s and 1950s. And the unprecedented effect of death control exported from DCs to UDCs was not foreseen.

The changes between the 1963 and 1968 projections are based on the findings that during the 1960s birthrates dropped only slightly, mainly in DCs, while death rates declined considerably in UDCs and remained low in DCs. The new figures are higher for most regions, but particularly for those UDC areas where death rates have declined from previous high levels in Asia and Africa (Table 3-1). Table 3-2 summarizes the history of United Nations projections of the population size in 1980 and indicates what a tricky business the making of such forecasts can be.

TABLE 3-2

*Projections of World Population in 1980 as made by the United Nations at several points of time from 1951 to 1968*

| Made in | Low | Medium Variant | High |
|---------|-----|----------------|------|
| 1951 | 2,976 | | 3,636 |
| 1954 | 3,295 | | 3,990 |
| 1957 | 3,850 | 4,220 | 4,280 |
| 1963 | 4,147 | 4,339 | 4,550 |
| 1968 | | 4,457 | |

Courtesy of Nathan Keyfitz

Since prediction is a favorite sport of almost everyone concerned with the population problem, we might as well stick our necks out. We feel that U.N. projections for the year 2000, with the possible exception of the low forecast, are too high. This is not, however, because we share their optimism about the future impact of family planning programs on birth rates. Instead, for reasons explained in subsequent chapters, we predict that a drastic rise in the death rate will either slow or terminate the population explosion, unless efforts to avoid such a tragic eventuality are immediately mounted.

Regardless of whether today's trends continue, it is instructive to assess the effects of their continuation on various regions of the world. All current figures used here are from the Population Reference Bureau's mid-1971 estimates (see Appendix 1), and the projections are those of the United Nations.

## NORTH AMERICA

Canada and the United States have a population of 229 million. A growth rate of 1.2 percent per year gives a doubling time for the area of 58 years, which is fast for DCs. If catastrophe is avoided, North America could have as many as 375 million people in the year 2000 or as few as 300 million.

52

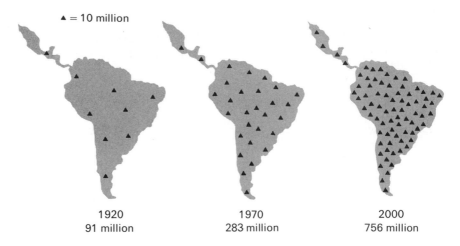

▲ = 10 million

|   1920    |    1970    |    2000     |
| 91 million | 283 million | 756 million |

FIGURE 3-13

Population growth in Latin America, 1920–2000. If fertility rates do not drop, the population of the area will undergo a more than 8-fold increase in 80 years. (After *Population Bulletin,* vol. 23, no. 3.)

LATIN AMERICA

This area (the Western Hemisphere south of the United States) has a population of 291 million and a growth rate of 2.9 percent, the highest rate for any major region. As a whole the population of the area is doubling every 24 years. Some Latin American countries have incredibly high growth rates and rapid doubling times. Costa Rica shows a growth rate of 3.8 percent and a doubling time of 19 years. Other representative doubling times are for Mexico, 21 years; Peru, 23 years; Brazil, 25 years; Jamaica, 33 years; Bolivia, 29 years; and Cuba, 37 years. A few countries in temperate Latin America are growing more slowly; that is, Argentina and Uruguay (doubling in 47 years and 58 years, respectively). According to various projections, the population of this area in the year 2000 will be 550–750 million (see Fig. 3-13); but our prediction is that it won't even get close to 650 million because of rising death rates.

EUROPE

Europe is the demographic antithesis of Latin America. Today's European population (excluding European U.S.S.R. and Turkey) is 466 million, more than half again that of Latin America. The growth rate for the continent is 0.8 percent, which gives a doubling time of 88 years. The more rapidly growing countries, such as Poland, Switzerland, and the Netherlands, have doubling times of about 60–80 years. But most European countries are doubling much more slowly than that: Italy every 88 years; Czechoslovakia and the United Kingdom, 140 years; Ireland, 100 years; West Germany, Austria and Hungary, 175 years; and East Germany, 700 years. In the year 2000 Europe's population is projected to be about 570 million.

The Soviet Union has a present population of 245 million, a growth rate of 1.0 percent, and a doubling time of 70 years. For several years its growth rate has been similar to that of the U.S., but it is now lower. Its population is projected to reach some 330 million by the year 2000.

### AFRICA

The present population of Africa is 354 million people. Its current rate of population growth is 2.7 percent, and its doubling time 26 years. The pattern of doubling times is not unlike that of Latin America, except that generally higher death rates result in a somewhat lower growth rate. Sample doubling times are for Morocco, 21 years; Kenya, 23 years; Zambia, 24 years; the United Arab Republic, 25 years; Nigeria, 27 years; South Africa, 29 years; Madagascar, 26 years; the Congo, 31 years; and Angola, 33 years. Projections for the year 2000, based on the assumption that the death rate will not increase, give Africa a population of 730–900 million, second only to the projected high for Asia. Some experts on Africa cite evidence that the high death rates there will drop rapidly in coming years, while the birth rates will remain high. If this occurs, growth rates of 3.5 or even 4.0 percent per year could become commonplace in Africa, and the population estimates given here would be too low.

### ASIA

Today's population giant, Asia, has a population of 2,104 million—over 2 billion people. That figure, which amounts to more than half of the world's population, does not include the population of Asiatic U.S.S.R. Asia's current growth rate is 2.3 percent, and her doubling time is 31 years. Among the Asian nations, only Japan shows a pattern similar to that of Europe and North America. Japan's growth rate is 1.1 percent, and the doubling time is close to that of North America, 63 years. For the rest of Asia the doubling times tell the same old story of the UDCs: Philippines and Pakistan, 21 years; Malaysia, 25 years; India, 27 years; and Afghanistan, 28 years. Mainland China presents a special problem. The size and growth rate of its population are uncertain. Estimates of size range from 700 to 950 million people, the 1971 U.N. figure being 773 million. The Population Reference Bureau's growth rate estimate is 1.8 percent (39-year-doubling time), and this is basically an informed guess. Projections for the year 2000 put Asia's population between 3,000 and 4,800 million, and uniformly predict that she will continue to be the home of more than one-half of all *Homo sapiens.*

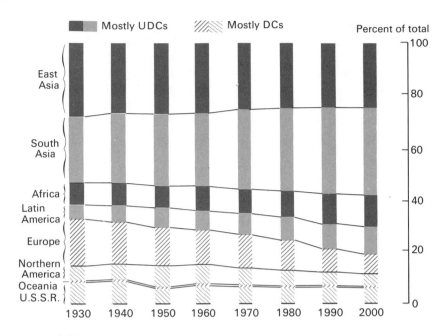

FIGURE 3-14

Percentage distribution of world population, 1930–2000. Future figures are those of the United Nations "constant fertility" projection. In 1930, DCs had 32.7 percent of the people. In 1965 they had 27.5 percent, and if the United Nations constant fertility projection is the one that holds, that percentage will shrink to 18.8 by the year 2000. (After *Population Bulletin,* vol. 21, no. 4.)

## Projected Changes in Density and Distribution

Aside from changes in population size one may also examine trends in population distribution (Figs. 3-14, 3-15). Obviously changes in density, calculated by nation or by region, are directly proportional to projected size changes, assuming that borders remain constant. More interesting are projections of trends in urbanization. For instance, one projection leads to a population estimate for Calcutta in the year 2000 of 66 million people, more than eight times today's population. Needless to say, this will not be reached. But there is a realistic expectation that the population of this festering city, which has several hundred thousand people living homeless in its streets today, will increase from 7.5 million to 12 million in the next two decades. Calcutta is already a disaster area, and the consequences of further growth at such a rate are heart-rending to contemplate, especially in view of the recent pressure of refugees from East Pakistan. The population of relatively prosperous Tokyo is projected to reach 40 million in the year 2000 (as opposed to perhaps 16 million in 1970). Tokyo is using 7,000 tons of garbage a day to fill Tokyo Bay, in a desperate attempt to create land for expansion. Flat, empty land is at a premium in mountainous, overpopulated

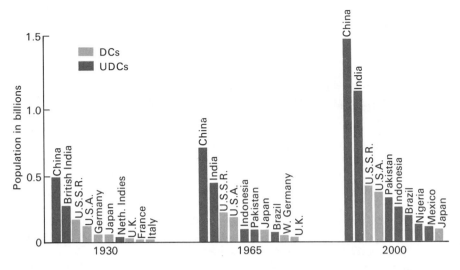

FIGURE 3-15

"Top Ten" nations in population size: 1930, 1965, 2000. China and India are each projected to have populations of more than a billion by the year 2000. Japan will have dropped to tenth place by then, and Nigeria and Mexico will have joined the "Top Ten," replacing the U.K. and West Germany. (After *Population Bulletin,* vol. 21, no. 4.)

Japan. Middle-class apartments are already so scarce that there is a 2-year waiting list. Tokyo's incredible crowding seems destined only to get worse.

Demographer Kingsley Davis has made some extrapolations of urbanization trends, and has produced some startling statistics. If the urban growth rate that has prevailed since 1950 should continue, half of the people in the world would be living in the cities by 1984. If the trend should continue to 2023 (it cannot!), everyone in the world would live in an urban area. Most striking of all, in 2020 most people would not just be in urban areas; half of the world's human beings would be in cities of over one million population, and in 2044 *everyone* would be existing in "cities" of that size. At that time the largest "city" would have a projected population of 1.4 billion people (out of a projected world population of 15 billion). The word "city" is in quotes because, should such a stage be reached, world living conditions would make the term meaningless in its usual sense.

# Bibliography

Adams, Robert M., 1960. The origin of cities. *Scientific American,* vol. 203, no. 2 (Sept.). Scientific American Offprint No. 606, W. H. Freeman and Company, San Francisco.

Bogue, D. J., 1969. *Principles of Demography.* Wiley, New York.

Davis, Kingsley, 1965. The population impact on children in the world's agrarian countries. *Population Review,* vol. 9, pp. 17–31. Contains details of the argument that children get a disproportionately bad deal in the UDCs.

Davis, Kingsley, 1965. The urbanization of the human population. *Scientific American,* vol. 213, no. 3, pp. 41–53 (Sept.). Scientific American Offprint No. 659, W. H. Freeman and Company, San Francisco. Reprinted in Ehrlich et al. (see below).

Demko, G. J., H. M. Rose, and G. A. Schnell (eds.), 1970. *Population Geography: A Reader.* McGraw-Hill Book Co., New York. Background information on population structure and distribution, urbanization, etc.

Ehrlich, P. R., J. P. Holdren, and R. W. Holm (eds.), 1971. *Man and the Ecosphere.* W. H. Freeman and Company, San Francisco. Important papers from *Scientific American* with critical commentaries.

Enke, Stephen, 1970. Zero population growth, when, how and why. *Tempo,* General Electric Co., Santa Barbara, Jan. A relatively non-technical discussion of population momentum.

Frejka, Tomas, 1968. Reflections on the demographic conditions needed to establish a U.S. stationary population growth. *Population Studies,* vol. XXII, pp. 379–397 (Nov.).

Hance, William A., 1970. *Population, Migration and Urbanization in Africa.* Columbia University Press, New York.

Keyfitz, Nathan, 1966. Population density and the style of social life. *BioScience,* vol. 16, no. 12, pp. 868–873 (Dec.). Information on the origin of cities and differences between DC and UDC cities.

Keyfitz, Nathan, 1971. On the momentum of population growth. *Demography,* vol. 8, no. 1, pp. 71–80 (Feb.).

Keyfitz, N., and W. Flieger, 1971. *Population: Facts and methods of demography.* W. H. Freeman and Company, San Francisco. Gives life tables and other calculations for most countries where birth and death statistics exist, and explains methods used in these calculations. Age distributions, sex ratios, and population increase are among its themes. Highly recommended.

Mangin, William, 1967. Squatter settlements. *Scientific American,* vol. 217, no. 4 (Oct.). Provides some insight into recent migrants into UDC cities. Scientific American Offprint No. 635, W. H. Freeman and Company, San Francisco.

Marshall, A. J. (ed.), 1966. *The Great Extermination.* Heinemann, London. This book details much of the destruction of the Australian environment.

Mumford, Lewis, 1961. *The City in History: Its Origins, Its Transformation and Its Prospects.* Harcourt, Brace and World, Inc., New York.

Population Reference Bureau, Washington, D.C. *Population Data Sheet.* Published annually.

Population Reference Bureau, 1962. The story of Mauritius from the dodo to the stork. *Population Bulletin,* vol. 18, no. 5. This issue details a UDC "population explosion" in a microcosm and is the basis of Box 3–1. Many issues of the *Population Bulletin* are pertinent to this chapter.

Population Reference Bureau, 1971. The future population of the United States. *Population Bulletin,* vol. 27, no. 1. Discusses the latest U. S. Census Bureau projections.

Reissman, Leonard, 1964. *The Urban Process: Cities in Industrial Societies.* The Free Press, New York. Sociological study of cities and urbanization.

Stockwell, Edward G., 1968. *Population and People.* Quadrangle Books, Chicago. A demographic study of the U.S.

United Nations, 1966. World population prospects as assessed in 1963. *Population Studies,* no. 41. This is the major source for detailed population projections.

United Nations, 1969. *World Population Situation.* Economic and Social Council, Population Commission report (E/CN.9/231), 23 Sept. Source of revised population projections.

United Nations, *Population Newsletter.* Population Division of the Department of Economic and Social Affairs. Source of information on U.N. activity in demography and population affairs.

United States Public Health Service, National Center for Health Statistics. *Monthly Vital Statistics Report.* These provide current statistics, both "provisional" and "final," on live births, marriages, deaths, and infant deaths. They are available from Health Services and Mental Health Administration, Washington, D.C. 20201.

# CHAPTER 4

# The Limits of the Earth

*"The power of population is infinitely greater than the power in the earth to produce subsistence for man."*

Thomas Malthus (1766–1834)

*"The image of the frontier is probably one of the oldest images of mankind, and it is not surprising that we find it hard to get rid of."*

Kenneth E. Boulding, *The Economics of the Coming Spaceship Earth*, 1966.

Photographs of the Earth taken from the vicinity of the moon make the finite nature of our planet apparent to us in a way that no writing can. What is the capacity of the Earth to support people? Unfortunately, there is no simple answer to this question, although certain theoretical limits may be calculated. More than 100 years ago Justus von Liebig established a principle that has become known as the "law of the minimum." It says, in essence, that the size of a population or the life of an individual will be limited by whatever requisite of life is in the shortest supply. It is not yet clear what that requisite will be for the human population, which, as we have seen, is growing at an increasingly faster rate. In this chapter and the next the following potential limiting factors are considered: space, heat, available energy, nonrenewable resources, water, and food.

## Outer Space

Many Americans, who see science fiction dramas on television and movie screens, in addition to being tax-paying participants in the real-life performances of our astronauts, think it entirely reasonable to regard space as the next frontier. Actually, the obstacles to interstellar or even interplanetary migration are stupendous and far beyond present or foreseeable technological capabilities. Even if the technology should become available, in the end we would be defeated by the very source of our present difficulties: numbers. Since this chapter deals with the limits of the Earth, it is necessary to demonstrate clearly that we are, in fact, confined to our own small planet. To make this clear, let us examine for a moment the possibilities for shipping surplus people to other planets. For the sake of this discussion, let us ignore the virtual certainty that the other planets of the solar system are uninhabitable. Consider some interesting calculations that have been made on how much time we could gain if we insisted on postponing direct action against the population explosion by occupying the planets of our solar system. For instance, at any given time, and at current population growth rates, it would take only about 50 years before Venus, Mercury, Mars, our moon, and the moons of Jupiter and Saturn all had the same population density as Earth.

What if the fantastic problems of reaching and colonizing the larger and more distant planets of the solar system, such as Jupiter, Uranus, and Pluto, could be solved? It would take only about 200 years of time to fill them "Earth-full." So we could perhaps gain 250 years for population growth in the solar system after reaching an absolute limit on Earth. Then, of course, we would still have the problem, but in greater dimensions.

A fundamental aspect of such a migration scheme would be the cost of the venture. Let us make some optimistic assumptions. Suppose that a small modern spaceship like Apollo, instead of carrying three men to the moon, could transport 100 people to one of the planets for the same cost. In order to hold the present population of the Earth constant, we would have to export about 70 million people per year (assuming no change in the growth rate). To do so would require the launching of very nearly 2,000 spaceships each day, year in and year out. The cost, not counting the expense of recruiting and training migrants, would exceed $300 billion daily. Three days' launches would equal the present annual gross national product of the U.S.

On the optimistic grounds that anything is possible, though, let us suppose that the immense problems of reaching and colonizing the planets of our own solar system are somehow solved. What then? The optimists would have us next expand to occupy the planets of *other* stars. Interstellar transport for surplus people presents an amusing prospect. Since the ships would take generations to reach most stars, the only people who *could* be transported would be those willing to exercise strict birth control. Population explosions on spaceships could not be tolerated.

We could continue to outline other speculations and fantasies, but hopefully you are now convinced that the extremely remote possibility of expanding into outer space offers no escape from the laws of population growth. The population will have to stop growing sooner or later.

## Heat

A British physicist, J. H. Fremlin, has calculated an ultimate terrestrial population density of some 100 persons per square yard of the Earth's surface. At that point a "heat limit" would be reached. People themselves, as well as their activities, convert other forms of energy into heat, which must be dissipated. Indeed, whenever energy is put to work, heat is produced. This is a basic law of the universe, one of the Laws of Thermodynamics (Box 4-1). According to Fremlin, at about the density described, the outer surface of the planet (by that time an artificial "world roof" covering the entire planet) would have to be kept around the melting point of iron to radiate away the excess heat.

Fremlin, however, made a series of extremely unlikely assumptions to permit the population to build to his limit of 60,000,000,000,000,000 (60 quadrillion) people. He assumed, for instance, that all social, political, and technological problems of crowding people into a 2,000-story building covering the entire surface of the Earth would be solved. It is more likely that a different sort of heat limit would prevail long before any such astronomical population size is reached. Meteorologists caution that world climates could be drastically altered if the additional heat that man dissipates in his global environment reaches about one percent of the solar energy striking the Earth's surface. At the present rate of increase of about 5 percent per year in world energy consumption, this situation will be reached in about a century. The consequences of altering the heat balance, locally and globally, are discussed in detail in Chapter 7.

In many aspects of population, resources, and environment, the restrictions imposed by the laws of thermodynamics can be critical. Many futuristic proposals for expanding energy supplies, utilizing new resources, and increasing food production lose their luster in the cold perspective of the efficiencies to which these laws restrict us.

## Energy

Will the availability of energy impose a limit on human population growth? The energy situation is uncertain and complex, but it can be summarized as follows: we are not yet running out of energy, but heavy environmental costs attend both its production and consumption; moreover, people in the DCs are using the richest and most accessible energy resources at a rate not justified by legitimate needs. Our supplies of high-grade fossil fuels—coal, petroleum, and natural gas—are finite and will probably be consumed within a few hundred years, possibly much sooner. (This does not mean that *all* the coal, oil, and gas will be gone, of course. We will simply reach the point

BOX 4-1   THE LAWS OF THERMODYNAMICS

Essential to an understanding of a number of important environmental problems is a grasp of the two fundamental Laws of Thermodynamics. It should be noted at the outset that these laws apply to all known phenomena—no exception to either has ever been observed. The First Law is the formal statement of "conservation of energy": energy can neither be created nor destroyed. The law makes sense only when it is realized that energy takes on a myriad of forms, and it is only the *total* of the energy in all its guises which is required to be constant. Examples of the various forms are energy of motion (kinetic energy), potential energy (gravitational, elastic), chemical energy, heat, nuclear energy, and the energy associated with mass itself (given explicitly by Einstein's famous formula, $E = mc^2$). Although physicists concern themselves with the details of relations among the kinds of energy (actually some of the "different" forms listed above are identical), the reader need remember only that physical processes change just the *distribution* of energy among its various categories, never the sum in all of the categories. Apparent violations of the First Law invariably stem from overlooking a category.

The Second Law of thermodynamics is subtler and more difficult to grasp, but fully as important in its implications. It specifies the *direction* in which physical processes proceed. General statements of the Second Law tend to be inscrutable; it is more fruitful to begin with specifics. In spontaneous processes, for example, the Second Law declares that heat flowing between two objects moves from the hotter to the colder, that concentrations (of anything) tend to disperse, that structure tends to disappear, that order becomes disorder. Thus, if a partitioned container is filled with hot water on one side and cold water on the other and is left to itself, the hot water cools and the cold water warms—heat flows from hotter

to colder. Note that the opposite process (the hot water getting hotter and the cold getting colder) does not violate the First Law, conservation of energy. That it does not occur illustrates the *Second* Law. Indeed, many processes can be imagined that satisfy the First Law but which violate the Second, and therefore are not expected to occur. As another example, consider adding a drop of dye to a glass of water. Intuition and the Second Law (both based on experience) dictate that the dye will spread, eventually coloring all the water—concentrations disperse, order (the dye-no-dye arrangement) disappears. The opposite process, the spontaneous concentration of dispersed dye, is consistent with conservation of energy, but *not* with the Second Law.

Unfortunately, the Second Law is this simple only for spontaneous processes with isolated and obvious effects. It applies as well to the most complicated biological and technological phenomena, but for each application must usually be restated in a different form: one is, "the disorder of the universe is always increasing"; another is, "no process is possible whose *sole* result is the flow of heat from a cold body to a hot one." The first formulation also applies to localized phenomena, as long as no effects are left out. For instance, both biological organisms and the technology of man are capable of filtering and concentrating dispersed substances from their environment. But when all the consequences of this activity are considered, including the expenditure of energy and the disposition of the heat produced, the "disorder" in the system as a whole (pond, planet, universe, depending on how far-reaching the activity) invariably increases. As an example of the other formulation of the Second Law, consider a refrigerator, which certainly causes heat to flow from cold bodies (contents of the refrigerator) to a hot one (the room). The "catch" is that this heat flow is not the *sole* result of the operation of the refrigerator: energy must be supplied to the refrigeration cycle from an external source, and this energy is converted to heat and discharged to the room, along with the heat removed from the interior of the refrigerator. As with the First Law, apparent violations of the Second Law can always be traced to leaving something out of the accounting.

Another, and for our purposes more pertinent, perspective on the Second Law of thermodynamics comes from relating disorder to the degradation of energy. Order, it seems, is related to the ability of energy to do work, and while the First Law insists that the total *amount* of energy in the universe remains constant, the Second Law requires that the fraction of *energy available to be used* is continually being diminished. For this reason it is often said that the Second Law tells us that the universe is "running down." This idea can be understood from the fact that energy is most usable where it is most concentrated—for example, in highly structured chemical bonds (gasoline, sugar) or at high temperature (steam, incoming sunlight). Note that the "temperature" of radiant energy, for the purposes of thermodynamic discussions, is the temperature of the radiating body—in this case, the sun. Since the Second Law says that the *overall* tendency in all processes is *away* from concentration, *away* from high temperature, it is saying that, overall, more and more energy is becoming less and less usable. Typically, the manifestation of this degradation of energy is the production of heat at relatively low, hence relatively useless, temperatures—for example, the heat of a car's exhaust, the heat of tire friction against the road, the heat radiated by your body, the heat of a decomposing animal carcass.

The Laws of Thermodynamics often can be used quantitatively to determine the minimum loss of useful energy (ideal efficiency) associated with a given process. But the reader need note only that, on thermodynamic grounds alone, such losses *always* occur, even in the complete absence of friction. In the real world, of course, some sort of friction or its equivalent is always present, so the losses are even larger. For instance, in the basic process by which cells extract energy from the chemical bonds of food molecules, almost half the useful energy is lost: more than one food-molecule bond must be broken for each equivalent bond synthesized in the organism eating the food. Thus the Laws of Thermodynamics tell us why we need a continual input of energy to maintain ourselves, why we must eat much more than a pound of food in order to gain a pound of weight, and why the total weight of plants on the face of the Earth will always be much greater than the weight of the plant-eaters, which will in turn always be much greater than the weight of flesh-eaters. They also make it clear that all the energy used on the face of the Earth, whether of solar or nuclear origin, will ultimately be degraded to heat. Here the laws catch us both coming and going, for they put limits on the efficiency with which we can manipulate this heat. Hence they pose the threat (discussed elsewhere) that man may make this planet uncomfortably warm with degraded energy well before he runs out of high-grade energy to consume.

It has been asked whether a revolutionary development in physics, like Einstein's theory of relativity, might not open the way to circumvention of the Laws of Thermodynamics. The answer is no: knowledge will expand and theories will change, but the practical consequences of the Laws of Thermodynamics will persist—just as Newton's Laws of classical physics remain valid for describing the vast majority of human activities and observations today, in the age of relativity.

where the quality of the remaining supplies is so low, or the effort required to get at it so high, that extraction is not worth the cost.) Coal will probably be the last of the conventional fossil fuels to be depleted in this way, perhaps 300–400 years from now—or sooner in the unlikely event that the present growth rate in world coal consumption persists for as much as a century.

Petroleum and natural gas will go much sooner. The most recent and thorough estimate, by geologist M. King Hubbert, gives us about a century before world petroleum reserves (including recent Alaskan discoveries) are substantially depleted, and the prognosis for natural gas is no better. The rise in costs as scarcity increases will be a continuous process, possibly accelerated by energy demands associated with limited development in the UDCs. All indications point to increasing energy costs for Americans even in the next few years, as higher extraction costs and the expense of even nominal pollution control efforts make themselves felt. Of course, increases in the cost of energy should encourage us to waste less in overpowered cars, heating and air conditioning of poorly insulated homes, and other frivolous uses.

Threatening future shortages of liquid and gaseous fossil fuels can and presumably will be postponed by converting coal to oil and gas. The liquefaction and gasification processes are fast approaching economic competitiveness with conventional sources of liquid and gaseous fuels, and both processes seem destined to see large-scale commercial use within the 1970s. Reliance on coal for all fossil fuel needs would of course shorten the life expectancy of our coal reserves considerably. One possible alternative is the oil shales, which constitute a potential energy resource much larger even than coal. However, there is vigorous disagreement about how much of the vast oil shales will even be economically exploitable. Also, the shale must be crushed and heated to extract the oil, and the huge volume of solid residue could constitute an unprecedented blight on the landscape. Possibly the oil shales will serve as the eventual source of hydrocarbons for lower volume, recyclable uses such as lubrication and the production of plastics, after the cheaper and more accessible sources have all been burned.

Hydroelectric energy and the energy of the wind and tides are inexhaustible in the sense that they will always be available, but their role is limited in scale by the number of suitable sites at which these sources can be exploited. The world's potential production of hydroelectric power is roughly half of the amount of power now being produced by fossil fuels. There are, however, serious problems in utilizing it to the utmost. Much of the potential lies in UDCs, where the power could not be used unless those countries become industrialized; and global ecological factors and inability to mobilize capital and high-grade resources will prevent industrialization in most of them. Furthermore, reliable hydroelectric power depends on dams, which under present conditions of technology are temporary structures. In a few hundred years—sometimes more, sometimes less, depending on the river— their reservoirs fill with silt and become useless. Thereafter, power production from the waterfall occupying the dam site hinges on the daily and seasonal vagaries of river flow. Some additional environmental problems associated with dams and their reservoirs are treated in Chapter 6. Finally, there is an aesthetic question: do we really wish to impound and control all of the wild rivers of the Earth? Unfortunately, tidal power does not have more than a minute fraction of the potential of water power, and will presumably never be of more than local importance. Wind energy has the disadvantages of low concentration and, in most locations, unpredictable intermittency.

There is some dispute about the exploitable power potential of the heat of the Earth's interior (geothermal energy). Some experts say that geothermal energy will never supply more than a very small fraction of the power used by man; others connected with companies attempting to harness this energy are much more optimistic. Perhaps the major uncertainty is the *lifetime* of the underground reservoirs of superheated water or steam which constitute the exploitable form of geothermal energy. One expert has estimated that the world's exploitable geothermal resources could sustain one-third the present electrical consumption of the U.S. alone for only about 50 years.

For many years men have speculated about the sun as a source of non-depletable power. Large-scale utilization of solar energy presents serious technological problems arising mainly from the irregularity of the energy flow in space and time and the low concentration of the energy. The collecting device for an electric generation plant with a capacity of 1,000 megawatts (enough power to supply electricity to a city of perhaps 750,000) would have to cover an area of about 16 square miles, if the solar to electric conversion efficiency were 10 percent. In a recent proposal for a large-scale, solar-electric power facility in the southwestern U.S., two Arizona astronomers, Aden and Marjorie Mienel, argued persuasively that the efficiency can be raised to about 25 percent, reducing needed collecting area. They also claimed that the other obstacles can be overcome. However, the greatest potential of solar power may be in dispersed uses—such as air conditioning and space heating—that take advantage of the sun's having done the distribution of power for us. Because of its obvious environmental advantages and inexhaustible nature, solar power certainly deserves more research support than it has been receiving.

Many people who are concerned about the rapid consumption of our fossil fuel resources (and the attendant environmental problems) assume that nuclear power (Box 4-2) from the fission of uranium will replace the fossil fuels quickly, cheaply, and with particular benefits for the UDCs. Unfortunately, there are several flaws in this view. Today's fission reactors use uranium very inefficiently, managing to extract only 1 to 2 percent of the potential energy of this fuel. Breeder reactors will do much better in this respect, but they will probably not see large-scale use until the late 1980s. The danger of running out of uranium before then has certainly been exaggerated, but the inefficient use of the highest quality deposits is a questionable tactic. Unfortunately, the environmental costs of nuclear power may prove to be considerable, and the breeder reactor could easily be worse in this respect than today's "burner" reactors (Chapter 6). Also, contrary to a persistent misconception, nuclear power is not particularly cheap today, and it is thus no panacea for the UDCs. The largest nuclear generating stations now in operation are, even with their considerably hidden subsidies, just competitive with or marginally superior to modern coal-fired plants of comparable size (in areas where coal is not scarce). At best, both produce electricity for approximately 4 or 5 mills (one mill = one-tenth of a cent) per kilowatt-hour. Smaller nuclear plants are less economical than small plants that operate on fossil fuels. In this connection it is important to note

---

BOX 4-2   FISSION AND FUSION REACTORS

Nuclear fission power plants are identical in many respects to plants fueled with coal or oil or gas. Water is heated to make steam, and the steam is passed through a turbine that turns a generator that produces electricity. The essential difference between nuclear fission and fossil fuel plants is the source of the heat: in the nuclear plant, it is obtained from the splitting—or fissioning—of uranium, which converts some atomic mass into energy.

Natural uranium consists of 99.3 percent uranium-238, which does not fission, and 0.7 percent uranium-235, which does. Fission occurs when a uranium-235 nucleus "captures" a slow moving neutron. Among the fission fragments are an average of 2.5 additional neutrons, which, after being slowed down in colliding with other particles, may initiate the splitting of more uranium-235. This is the famous "chain reaction" that makes fission bombs and reactors work.

Although uranium-235 is the only naturally occurring "fissile" substance, it is possible to produce others by bombarding "fertile" substances with neutrons. For example, if uranium-238 captures a fast neutron (one that has not yet experienced many collisions since being "born" in a fission reaction), it undergoes a series of spontaneous changes that transform it into fissile plutonium-239. Similarly, thorium-232 can capture a slow neutron and be transformed into fissile uranium-233. Since thorium-232 and uranium-238, between them, are hundreds of times as abundant as uranium-235, they represent a vast potential source of energy—needing only neutrons to convert them into usable fuel.

Today's commercial power reactors contain a uranium mixture in which the concentration of uranium-235 has been "enriched" from its natural concentration of 0.7 percent to a few percent. Most of the energy is produced by the fissioning of this uranium-235, but some excess neutrons react with uranium-238, which comprises the bulk of the mixture, to form plutonium. Some of the plutonium fissions in the course of events in the reactor, and some is recovered from the spent fuel in reprocessing plants, to be recycled. Of every hundred atoms of natural uranium that enter the fuel cycle of contemporary nuclear reactors, only one or two are eventually fissioned, either as uranium-235 or as plutonium made from uranium-238. These reactors are called *burners* because of the rapid rate at which they consume the scarce uranium-235.

By means of drastic changes in design, it is possible to devise a reactor that transforms fertile material into fissile fuel—for example, uranium-238 to plutonium-239—faster than it consumes fissile fuel itself. Such a reactor is called a *breeder,* and the time it takes to double its initial inventory of fissile fuel by this means is called the *dou-*

that UDCs rarely can use the outputs of large power plants. There are simply not enough industries, lightbulbs, appliances, neon signs, electric trains, buses, streetcars, and so on, to utilize that much electricity. Large transmission networks to share the output of a single large plant among several UDCs are possible, but the capital cost of such networks is high. It is also impractical for several countries or even one country to depend on only a single plant for all their electrical capacity, since shutdowns then become disastrous. Furthermore, the potential political difficulties of multinational powergrids based on single plants should be obvious.

*bling time.* It is to be emphasized that such a reactor is not giving us something for nothing, nor is it a perpetual motion machine, because it must be continuously supplied with the fertile material it converts to fuel. A reactor that appreciably stretches its fuel supply by converting fertile to fissile material, but which cannot meet the self-refueling criterion of the breeder, is called a *converter.*

The energy of the sun and the hydrogen bomb is derived from the fusing together of light atoms, rather than from the splitting of heavy ones. In fusion as in fission some of the mass of the nuclei is converted into energy. The most suitable fuels for controlled, earthbound fusion are deuterium and tritium, which are heavy isotopes of hydrogen, and helium-3. Tritium is rare and radioactive, but it could be produced from abundant lithium in a fusion reactor much as plutonium is produced in a fission breeder. All other potential fusion fuels and reaction products are nonradioactive, and tritium is considerably less dangerous than many reaction products in fission reactors. Achieving a sustained fusion reaction is far more difficult than in the case of fission: the fuel must be heated to a temperature of tens to hundreds of millions of degrees; the density of the fuel must be high enough to yield an appreciable reaction rate; and the fuel must be confined under these conditions long enough that the energy output more

than repays the energy investment in heating and confinement. The necessary combination of conditions has not yet been achieved in the laboratory, and a commercial reactor can hardly be expected before 1990. The goal is worth striving for because of the abundance of the fuel, the low environmental impact of extracting it from the ocean, the relatively low amount of radioactivity involved, and the inherent safety of the process. The safety can be understood from the following comparison. In a fission reactor, one goes to great lengths to keep the reaction from running too fast; in a fission reactor there is always the possibility of the chain reaction escalating out of control. The end result can be the melting of the reactor core or (especially in the case of the breeder reactor) a substantial explosion, rupturing the containment vessel enclosing the reactor and releasing enormous amounts of dangerous radioactivity into the atmosphere. Although the explosion in such an accident would be much smaller than that of a Hiroshima-size A-bomb, the quantity of radioactive material released could be much larger. On the other hand, in a fusion reactor, one must go to great lengths to get it to run at all—any malfunction would tend to quench the reaction by loss of temperature or loss of confinement or both.

Significantly, the cost of modernization and industrialization required to utilize the electrical power greatly exceeds the cost of the power itself. In the U.S., the cost of energy accounts for only 4 percent of the value added by the process of manufacturing raw materials. The cost of the needed power clearly is not the limiting factor in development today, and the proliferation of nuclear plants (or any other kind) would not bring that development about.

A second common misconception about nuclear power is that it can reduce our dependence upon fossil fuels to zero as soon as that becomes necessary or desirable. In fact, nuclear power plants produce only electrical energy, and electrical energy constituted only 22.5 percent of the total energy consumed in the United States in 1968. Thus the length of time that nuclear fuels can postpone the exhaustion of our coal and oil depends in part on how much the use of electrical energy increases. Even the rather ambitious forecasts of the U.S. Atomic Energy Commission assume that only half of U.S. energy consumption will be electrical in the year 2000 and that only half of that will be generated from nuclear fission.

Nuclear energy, then, is a panacea neither for the DCs nor the UDCs. It may relieve, but not remove, the pressure on fossil fuel supplies, and may provide reasonably priced power in certain parts of the world where these fuels are not abundant. It has substantial, if expensive, potential applications in increasing food production, which are discussed in the next chapter.

Some technologists have argued that the advent of a safe and practical breeder reactor or the as yet theoretical thermonuclear fusion reactor will cause a major drop in the cost of power and make feasible a host of development-related projects. Actually, the real importance of both breeder and fusion reactors is that either would solve civilization's fuel problems for many millenia—a breeder reactor can in theory extract from a pound of granite 50–100 times the energy contained in a pound of coal; the fusion reactor could, again in theory, extract from a gallon of seawater 300 times the energy in a gallon of gasoline. But the time scale for availability and the ultimate cost of energy are uncertain for both possibilities. Experimental breeder reactors exist, but owing to the technological complexity and attendant safety problems of this kind of fission process, they are unlikely to be put in routine operation on the power grid until at least the mid-1980s. When they are in operation, it is not obvious that they will produce power particularly cheaply; the fuel seems certain to be cheap by today's standards, but the construction costs for the plant itself might more than compensate. This seems particularly likely because of the extensive (and expensive) safeguards and waste-handling systems that will be required (including, perhaps, putting the entire plant deep underground).

Fusion reactors, on the other hand, have not yet been conclusively demonstrated to be scientifically feasible. The more optimistic scientists working in this field believe such a demonstration will be achieved within a decade. If it is (and this is by no means certain) fusion reactors would probably need at least an additional decade of development time before being ready for the power grid. Again, the fuel costs would be low, but the construction costs are uncertain (no one can yet say what such a device will look like!). The major benefits of fusion would be the near inexhaustibility of the fuel supply and the inherent safety and relatively low (but not zero) radioactivity burden associated with the process.

It is clear that mankind, if it survives for another century or so, will witness drastic changes in the use of energy sources. It does not appear, however, that availability of energy itself will place a limit on population growth, although difficulties accompanying the transition from one source to another might well do so. The ultimate limits to the use of energy (assuming radioactive pollution and other safety problems associated with nuclear energy can be solved) come not from its shortage, but from the problem of dissipating the heat to which all useful energy is eventually degraded.

## Nonrenewable Mineral Resources

Geologist T. S. Lovering wrote in 1968: "Surprisingly enough, many men unfamiliar with the mineral industry believe that the beneficent gods of technology are about to open the cornucopia of granite and sea, flooding industry with any and all metals desired." Lovering was responding to the outpouring of propaganda from technological optimists who discount the problems posed by the unprecedented consumption of nonrenewable resources and by their sporadic distribution. How well-fixed is mankind for the fossil fuels, the metals, and the other minerals extracted from the Earth? Should we believe the technological optimists, who hold that science and technology can solve resource problems? Or should we listen to those who argue that mineral resources, whether they be extracted from undiscovered rich deposits or from the minute quantities present in such common rocks as granite, are exhaustible and irreplaceable? The answer goes something like this: for the next 30 years, the DCs will probably not fare too badly, since most of the UDCs will be unable to industrialize on any more than a modest scale. For approximately a century after that, mankind in general will do rather poorly, especially if any of several current trends continue. Beyond that time, the costs of energy required to extract whatever resources remain will tax far more than man's ingenuity (those costs, of course, include the environmental ones).

The resources of the Earth's crust are very unevenly distributed—a result of the uneven distribution of the processes that led to their deposition and concentration. The distribution of coal, for instance, presumably represents the pattern of distribution of certain types of swamp plant communities that existed several million years ago. Some minerals have been formed by sedimentation; others have been deposited in fractures in the Earth's crust. The concentration of some minerals varies more or less continuously from very high-grade ores to below the average abundance of the element in the crust of the Earth. Certain types of copper ores exhibit such a pattern of deposition, as do the ores of other important metals, such as iron and aluminum. Many others, including ores of lead, zinc, tin, nickel, tungsten, mercury, manganese, cobalt, precious metals, and molybdenum do not. They show sharp discontinuities in concentration. As a result of this uneven distribution, some areas of the Earth (and thus some nations) are richly endowed with mineral wealth, while others are depauperate.

The frequent discontinuous distribution of ores, as well as other factors, make untenable the views of certain economists who think that only economic considerations determine the availability of mineral resources. They have the idea that as demand increases, mining will simply move to poorer and poorer ores, which are assumed to be progressively more and more abundant. These economists have misinterpreted a principle called the "arithmetic-geometric ratio" (A/G ratio)—a principle that geologists developed for application to certain types of ore deposits within certain limits. It is valid only for those ores (such as porphyry copper deposits) and only within those limits. The idea is that as the grade of ore decreases arithmetically, its abundance will increase geometrically until the average abundance in the Earth's crust is reached. It is further assumed that the additional cost of mining the low-grade ores can easily be absorbed, since the dollar value of mineral resources is at present only a small part of the gross national product. But, as noted above, the geological facts of mineral distribution do not support the simplistic views of the cornucopians, any more than the physical and biological facts of life support their views about the imagined panacea of unlimited power from atomic energy. Although some ores approximate a distribution where the A/G ratio may be applied, most do not.

Our present level of affluence depends on much more than the availability of relatively common substances, such as iron, aluminum, zinc, phosphate rock, coal, and oil. Also necessary are such "mineral vitamins" as vanadium, tantalum, tungsten, molybdenum, and helium. Although these are little known to the layman, they are critically important to industrial processes. Like the familiar vitamins in our diets, these minerals are often required only in small amounts, but they are indispensable, which by analogy gives them the "vitamin" label.

Figure 4-1 gives estimated time spans for depletion of various mineral reserves. Implicit in the chart are certain assumptions: these are that the population would remain constant at 3.3 billion, that consumption would not increase above 1965 rates, that no ore now uneconomical to mine would be exploited, and that there would be no discovery of presently unknown reserves. Moreover, the figures for the U.S. assume that *all* U.S. consumption would have to be derived from domestic reserves; no imports are considered. Thus, the chart shows certain substances, of which the U.S. has very small reserves, being exhausted in this country almost immediately. These assumptions, of course, had to be made to reduce variables; otherwise the chart could not have been made up.

Population and consumption have obviously both grown since 1965. Some

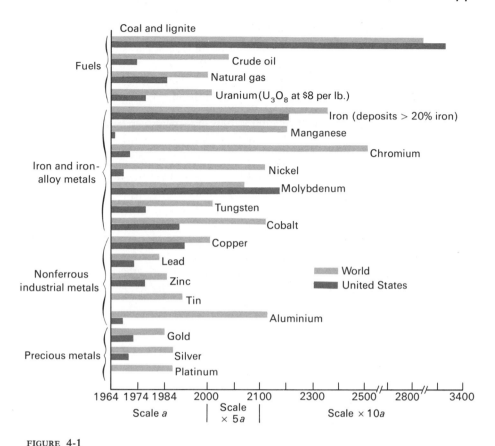

FIGURE 4-1

Lifetimes of estimated recoverable reserves of mineral resources. Reserves are those that are of high enough grade to be mined with today's techniques. Increasing population and consumption rates, unknown deposits, and future use of presently submarginal ores are not considered. (After Cloud, *Realities of Mineral Distribution,* 1968.)

low-grade ores have become economically competitive, and perhaps more will. Nor is there any doubt that new reserves of at least some of the minerals will be found. But how future developments will interact (or counteract) is totally unknown, so the chart is probably as good an estimate of today's reserves as is possible.

Clearly, these estimates hardly give us reason for optimism. A considerable amount of substitution and extraction from low-quality ores will be necessary well before the end of this century. Unless oil exploration is extraordinarily successful we will be well into our reserves of oil shales, and we will almost certainly be converting coal into liquid and gaseous fuels. There has been a rather gradual rise in domestic oil production from 319 million metric tons in 1953 to 450 million metric tons in 1968. In the same period, world oil production more than doubled—from 658 million metric tons to 1,641 million metric tons. At present the United States produces about one-fourth of the world's oil, but consumes about eight times the per capita figure for the non-socialist world—about 900 gallons per year for every man, woman, and child in this nation. Nuclear energy will possibly relieve some of the demand on oil reserves. In 1967 Charles F. Jones of the Humble Oil Company estimated, however, that during the 13 years between 1967 and 1980 the consumption of oil in the United States would be more than twice the amount of our known reserves. We will of course continue trying to supplement these reserves by importing oil. Unfortunately, however, we have already experienced some trouble in making trade agreements for oil and minerals with foreign countries, and these troubles are likely to increase.

In general, the United States is highly dependent on foreign sources for most of its basic industrial raw materials, except bituminous coal. For instance, in 1968 we mined 50,172,000 metric tons of iron ore, but we consumed 137,757,000 metric tons of steel. In 1961 we were importing more than 90 percent of our nickel and 30 percent of our copper. At the same time, our industrial production and affluence have reached unprecedented levels far beyond the highest levels plausible for the UDCs. Our national per capita income is some 33 times that of India, and both our per capita gross national product and our per capita steel production are more than 50 times those of India. (The GNP ratio is higher because it includes such things as depreciation and other kinds of "duplication.") In 1968 our per capita steel *consumption* (production plus imports minus exports) was some 342 times that of Indonesia, 86 times that of Pakistan, 68 times that of Ceylon, 23 times that of Colombia, 9 times that of Mexico, 2 times that of France and Switzerland, 1.4 times that of Japan, 1.5 times that of the United Kingdom and the USSR, and marginally (10 percent) higher than that of our nearest rival, Sweden. The United States in 1968 accounted for more than one-third of the world's energy consumption, well over a third of its tin consumption, about a fourth of its phosphate, potash, and nitrogenous fertilizer consumption, almost half of its newsprint and synthetic rubber (produced from a variety of resources), more than a fourth of its steel, and about an eighth of its cotton. Using the figures for energy resources, steel, tin, and fertilizers as indicators, it seems reasonable to estimate that the U.S. is currently accounting for about 30 percent of the world's consumption of raw materials. Obviously, our consumption is far beyond our "share" on a basis of population. We number less than 6 percent of the world's people!

The DCs account for only about 30 percent of the world's people but consume the vast majority of the world's resources. The U.S., Canada, Europe, U.S.S.R., Japan, and Australia in 1968 consumed about 90 percent of both the energy and the steel produced in the world.

The availability of critical resources has a considerable bearing on the possibilities of industrialization in the UDCs. Even if world population growth stopped in 1972, world iron production would have to be increased about sixfold, copper production almost sixfold and lead production about eightfold to bring global per capita consumption to the present United States level. Such considerations ignore the enormous amounts of these metals already mined, refined, and in use in the railroads, automobiles, girders, electrical wiring, and so on in the United States. If one takes into account this enormous capital stock which, far better than annual consumption alone, measures the true standard of living, the picture appears even gloomier. One then finds that to raise all of the 3.8 billion people of the world of 1972 to the American standard of living would require the extraction of almost 30 billion tons of iron, more than 500 million tons of copper and lead, more than 300 million tons of zinc, about 50 million tons of tin, as well as enormous quantities of other minerals. That means the extraction of some 250 times as much tin, 200 times as much lead, 100 times as much copper, 75 times as much zinc, and 75 times as much iron. The needed iron is theoretically available, and might be extracted by tremendous efforts over a long period of time, but a serious limit could be imposed by a shortage of molybdenum, which is needed to convert iron to steel. Needed quantities of the other materials far exceed *all* known or inferred reserves. Of course, to raise the standard of living of the projected world population of the year 2000 to today's American standard would require nearly doubling all of the above figures. But, far from concentrating on ways to help UDCs while making a maximum effort to husband limited resources, economists in the DCs want to *increase* the rate of domestic consumption of nonrenewable resources far above that of 1970, while population growth continues. Our environment probably cannot stand "world industrialization," mainly because of the simplification and resulting destabilization of life-supporting ecosystems which would accompany it (Chapter 7). But even if it could, the problem of supplying the raw materials alone staggers the imagination.

It is questionable whether the DCs will be able to obtain the steadily increasing amounts of critical resources that are projected as future "needs." In the short term, say until the end of this century, the United States *might* do all right by increasing its imports, assuming that the UDCs will continue to let us exploit their mineral resources, and by developing substitutes. Maintaining imports will be especially important. In common with almost all industrial nations, with the possible exception of the U.S.S.R., we are already net importers of most of the metals and ores we use (Fig. 4-2). Some of these, of course, are imported simply because importing them is cheaper than it would be to mine very poor-grade domestic deposits. Others we just do not have in exploitable form. Consequently, should any unforeseen events limit our access to imports, we would be in trouble immediately. Unfortunately, such "unforeseen events" are likely in our future.

The long-run solution to world shortages of most mineral resources is seen by technological optimists to be in extracting them from such common rock as granite and from sea water, where 63 out of 92 naturally occurring elements have been found (although the important metals dissolved in sea water are present only in extraordinarily low concentrations). They further assume that in an era of cheap energy this will be feasible, but they are apparently unaware of the problems of thermal pollution and other ecological consequences of such a program. Both the geological and the economic facts of

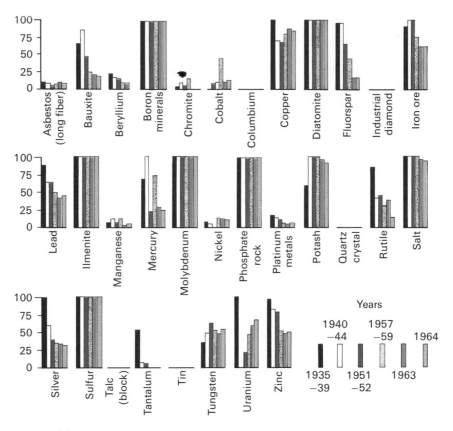

FIGURE 4-2

Self-sufficiency of the United States in selected minerals, calculated as the percentage of primary consumption mined in the country. (Data from the U.S. Department of the Interior, Bureau of Mines, Division of Minerals, 1965.)

life make it probable that, as one knowledgeable geologist put it, "average rock will never be mined."

It is unlikely that cheap nuclear energy, even if it materializes, can greatly reduce the cost of mining, partly because most mining will presumably continue to be subterranean; there are definite limits to the feasible depth of open-pit mining. Most plans call for underground nuclear blasts to fragment rock, followed by hydrometallurgical or chemical mining. These techniques present enormous problems. Rocks must be fractured to the proper particle size, and then brought into contact with special solvents (which must also be derived from natural resources). Ways must be found to contain the solvents and to prevent them from being consumed by dissolving unwanted materials. In attempting to extract low concentrations underground, electrolysis also seems very unpromising, as are biologically catalyzed metallurgical reactions. If extraction below ground is successful, then the reagent and the dissolved material must be pumped to the surface, both possibly hot and extremely radioactive. After the separation both the waste rock and the solvent must be disposed of.

In reality, labor costs would probably remain quite high in any prospective programs to extract desired minerals from low-grade deposits. It seems likely that it will remain much cheaper to search out mineral concentrations well above the average than to mine average rock, even if it means keeping human miners with picks at the mine face. As geologist Preston Cloud has observed: "The reality is that even the achievement of a breeder reactor offers no guarantee of unlimited mineral resources in the face of geologic limitations and expanding populations with increased per-capita demands, even over the middle term. To assume such for the long term would be sheer folly."

## Water

"Water is the best of all things," said the Greek poet Pindar. It is also, in the broad sense, a renewable resource. It circulates on the Earth in a complex series of pathways known collectively as the hydrologic cycle (Fig. 4-3). The oceans serve as the principal reservoir, from which an estimated 875 cubic kilometers ($km^3$) evaporate per day. About 775 $km^3$ return to the ocean through condensation and precipitation, there being a net windborne transfer of some 100 $km^3$ from the seas to the land. About 260 $km^3$, or $686 \times 10^{11}$ gallons, daily fall upon the land, 100 $km^3$ of which are blown in from the sea and 160 $km^3$ have been previously evaporated from the land. The cycle is balanced by about 100 $km^3$ of daily runoff from land to sea via the streams, rivers, and flow of groundwater. But even though it circulates, the finite supply of fresh water still places limits on the numbers of people that can be supported, both in specific locations and on the Earth as a whole.

Some 97 percent of the world's water is sea water. Of the remaining 3 percent, which is fresh water, almost 98 percent is tied up in the ice caps, principally of Antarctica and Greenland. Since freeing all of this water would raise the sea level some 50 meters, inundating many of our cities and much of our crop land, it would seem best to leave most of that water tied up as it is, even if it were feasible to free it.

Water is needed in prodigious quantities just to produce food. Plants are constantly absorbing water from the soil and evaporating it from their leaves, which is the basic reason for the extreme water requirements of vegetable food production and the even greater requirements of meat production. A single corn plant may take from the soil and evaporate as much as 200 quarts of water in a growing season. The water needed for the production of one pound of meat includes that necessary for growing about 10 pounds of forage plants, plus the water required by the animal directly for drinking, and further water for meat processing. To produce a pound of dry wheat re-

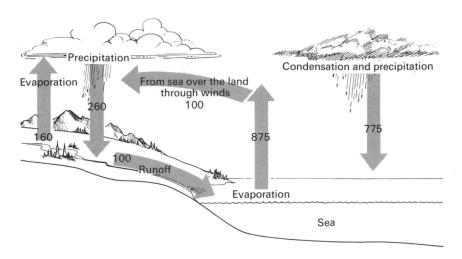

FIGURE 4-3

Hydrologic cycle (in cubic kilometers per day). (Data from Borgstrom, *Too Many,* Macmillan, New York, 1969.)

quires some 60 gallons of water; a pound of rice, 200–250 gallons; a pound of meat, 2,500–6,000 gallons; and a quart of milk, about 1,000 gallons. Industrial processes are even more water-greedy. Directly and indirectly, it takes an estimated 100,000 gallons of water to produce a single automobile. In 1900 each American used about 525 gallons daily. This increased to almost 1,500 gallons per capita in 1960, and is expected to reach almost 2,000 gallons by 1980. These figures do not include the use of rainwater by crops, but roughly 50 percent of the consumption given here is for irrigation.

These prodigious quantities of water are supplied almost entirely by tapping the runoff portion of the hydrological cycle: the rivers and streams that flow over the surface, and the subsurface aquifers that are fed by percolation and underground streams. The only exception is a statistically insignificant amount of water obtained directly from the sea by desalting. Withdrawals from the runoff do not necessarily constitute consumption, because much water is simply used (for washing, cooling, flushing, etc.) and returned to the river or aquifer from which it came. If suitably purified, this water can be used over and over again; in fact, the water in some river systems of developed countries is reused up to 50 times. However, almost all use involves some depletion in the form of evaporation and, in the case of irrigation, transpiration. Indeed, depletion from irrigation ranges from 60 to 90 percent of withdrawals. Water is also effectively depleted if it is discharged so polluted as to make reuse impossible, or if it is discharged directly into the ocean.

The second major aspect of water demand is flow requirement. This term means that after all the consumptive demands have been met, there must still be enough water flowing in the river to carry off wastes, to meet hydropower and navigational needs, and (perhaps) to maintain wildlife habitat and recreational opportunities. On the assumption that waste capacity will be the limiting factor, and using a nominal figure for acceptable concentration of pollutants, it was estimated in the 1963 study, *Resources in America's Future,* that the U.S. flow requirements in 1980 and 2000 would be 332 and 447 billion gallons per day (bgd), respectively. Their "medium" projections for depletions in those years were 178 and 247 bgd.

At first glance, even the numbers for 2000 seem unalarming, because the U.S. runoff averaged over a year comes out 1,100 bgd. In practice, however, much of the runoff occurs in a short wet season, so the *dependable* flow is much smaller than the "average." This problem can be ameliorated to some extent by building reservoirs to catch and store the high flows that would otherwise be wasted. With the storage facilities existing in the U.S. in 1954, however, the flow maintainable 95 percent of the time (a standard measure of "dependable flow") was only 93 bdg, or less than 10 percent of the impressive average runoff. It seems unlikely that the dependable flow can be increased fast enough to meet the projected needs for the year 2000, even setting aside the environmental costs of water projects and the reduction of older storage capacity by silting.

The situation looks even worse when one breaks it down by geographical regions. More than 75 percent of the annual runoff occurs in the eastern half of the U.S. In many parts of the western half of the country, the dependable flow is *already* inadequate. Excluding Washington and Oregon, the total runoff for the western U.S.—assuming it could *all* be exploited—will be inadequate to meet projected needs in this part of the country before the year 2000.

When needs cannot be met from dependable flow, one "solution" is to sacrifice the flow requirement for waste dilution, with serious consequences for water quality. Another is to withdraw water from underground aquifers faster than it is replenished by runoff. Both practices are already occurring in the U.S. and other DCs.

Michigan State's Georg Borgstrom, an authority on food production, estimates that the people of Europe extract three times what the cycle returns to accessible reserves, and that North Americans take out about twice what is returned. The groundwater supply in some areas will soon be below that necessary to meet withdrawal demands, and those branches of the water bank will fail.

Similar squeezes will occur in many other areas of the world, especially in connection with the immense water needs related to agriculture. For instance, India, in her desperate struggle to grow more food, has greatly increased her tapping of groundwater. Between July 1968 and June 1969 the government drove 2,000 new tube wells, and private enterprise drove 76,000. In addition, 246,000 new pumps were installed on old and new wells. Even in areas such as the Ganges Plain, which is underlain by a huge groundwater reservoir, the supplies are not infinite. Sustained pumping will have to be accompanied by careful planning for recharge if three-crop agriculture is to be developed over much of the plain without depleting the groundwater supply.

## Forests

Intimately related to fresh water supplies are another renewable resource: forests. That deforestation results in heavy soil erosion, floods, and local changes in climate has been known for centuries—known but not always heeded. The annual floods that have plagued northern China since ancient times are due to deforestation during the early dynasties. The Chinese are now attempting to restore some of those forests. The once fertile hills of central Italy have been arid and subject to regular, occasionally devastating floods since the Middle Ages when the trees were removed. It is interesting that medieval writers and others since accurately predicted the results of deforestation without replanting. The ancient Greeks and Romans apparently were relatively conscientious in maintaining the forests and understood their value in protecting watersheds. But this understanding seems to have been partially lost during the Middle Ages, when the demands of a growing population for fuel, construction materials, and grazing land destroyed the forests in much of southern Europe.

Today, similar demands are encroaching on forests around the world. Many valuable tracts have disappeared entirely. Most of Europe, northern Asia, the eastern one-third of the U.S., and vast areas of the northwest were once covered with forests. Only a fraction of the forest of the eastern U.S. and of western Europe remains today, largely preserved through conscious conservation and reforestation policies. The Soviet Union has the greatest remaining reserves of temperate and subarctic forest, including nearly half of the world's coniferous forest. About two-thirds is virgin, largely because it is relatively inaccessible. However, the best quality trees for lumbering are in European Russia, and as a result those have been heavily exploited. Large reserves of coniferous forest also remain in North America, from Nova Scotia to Alaska. Forest management practices have been established in most DCs, including the U.S.S.R. and the U.S., to preserve their forests for the future. But reforestation takes from 50–100 years, depending on the tree and the climate. Vast forest reserves also still exist in the tropics, especially in the Amazon Valley, Southeast Asia, and central Africa. Inaccessibility and economic factors have until recently protected these areas from destruction, but the more accessible forests have now vanished or have been selectively depleted of the most valuable species. The rate of clearing tropical rainforests has accelerated in the past decade or so to the point that many fear that they will all but disappear by the end of the century.

What remains of temperate forests is under increasing pressure, especially in the U.S. Lumber interests, in an effort to meet rising demand for construction wood and paper, are increasing their harvest often at considerable expense to the forest environment. Particularly damaging is the practice of "clear-cutting"—the wholesale removal of large tracts of mature forest. Even if this is followed by immediate replanting, which it sometimes is not, a good deal of erosion and flooding can ensue before the young trees are well established. Large stands of young trees are also more susceptible to disease, pests, and fire than are forests containing trees of varied age. Loggers defend the practice of clear-cutting on the grounds that certain valuable species of trees need direct sunlight and space in which to grow; that is, cleared land. Presumably some less destructive procedure can be used, such as clear-cutting of small stands, if selective cutting and replanting of individual trees is unsatisfactory.

Forests in the U.S. and, to varying degrees elsewhere, are threatened by more than a demand for lumber and fuels. Much privately owned forested land (which amounts to about 80 percent of that in the eastern U.S.) disappears each year under highways, subdivisions, airports, and other development projects. Strip-mining destroys thousands of acres, in a process even more destructive of the soil than clear-cutting. Inevitable erosion and flooding follow, often accompanied by severe water pollution; reforestation is often not even attempted (although with care it can be achieved). In publicly owned tracts in National Forests, under the "multiple-use" policy, trees are cleared for recreational facilities (and often damaged by the crowds of visitors), access roads, powerline cuts, mining activities, and sheep and cattle grazing. And in some areas, for example, near Los Angeles, trees are being killed by smog.

The situation is equally bad or worse in many other countries. Half of the trees cut down in the world are used for fuel, regardless of their potential value as lumber. Clearing for agricultural land, especially in the tropics, is another great threat to this resource, often with disastrous results (see Chapters 5 and 7 for more on the special problems of tropical soils and agriculture). Because of poor transportation facilities and various economic factors, many of the felled trees, often valuable hardwoods, are not harvested and used as lumber, but are wasted or used for fuel. Brazil's forests once covered 80 percent of the country; by 1965 they had been reduced to 58 percent. Vast stretches of the Amazon forest are now being cleared for a transcontinental highway. Much of the best quality forest has been cut to clear land and for fuel. What replanting there is has been with fast-growing, inferior trees. This is not to say that tropical forests have not also been exploited for lumber. The mahogany of Haiti, for example, has long since disappeared and that of Honduras is nearly gone. Replanting in tropical forests has seldom been practiced in the past, although a few countries are now becoming aware of their value and introducing forest management practices. If tropical forests are not to vanish as did the European and much of the U.S. forest, conservation and management policies will need to be established soon.

Many values are associated with forests besides the lumber and pulp that can be harvested from them: these include the maintenance of watersheds, oxygen production, their function as reservoirs for a variety of plant species, fish, and wildlife, and the recreational opportunities and aesthetic pleasure they afford to people.

Careful management of forests could assure us of the opportunity to benefit from these values more or less in perpetuity. This management would include preservation of trees of mixed species and ages as much as possible to discourage losses from pests, disease, and fire, logging on a long-term rotation basis for the best quality of lumber, reforestation, and careful protection of the soil. But lumbering companies in the U.S. have not always strictly adhered to these principles, with the result that recently their abuses have been loudly protested by conservation groups. At the same time, the present and predicted housing shortage will create huge demands on our forests in the next 10 to 15 years. In 1970 President Nixon sanctioned an increase of 60 percent in National Forest logging to help meet housing needs. Conservationists find this a questionable expedient at a time when vast quantities of U.S. timber are being exported to Japan, a country that tightly restricts logging on its own soil.

At the present time, forest cutting apparently is proceeding faster than areas are being reforested. The National Forest Service estimated that demand for wood products (including paper) will have doubled between 1969 and 2000. Even if massive recycling of paper can compensate for much of this, the pressures against our forest resources are obviously growing severe. Unless a comprehensive national land use policy, including careful management of forests, is soon established, the U.S. may one day find it has housed one generation rather well, but at the expense of the next.

## Food and Nutrition

The most pressing factor now limiting the capacity of the Earth to support *Homo sapiens* is the supply of food. In the rest of this chapter, man's needs for food and his current nutritional situation are discussed. The next chapter takes up the all-important subject of our attempts to meet these needs today, and our prospects for meeting them in the future.

Despite the emphasis on the need for a "balanced diet," which has been a part of school curricula and general public information in the United States since the 1920s and 1930s, some Americans are still convinced that the typical Asian can live happily and healthily on one bowl of rice per day. The truth is that an Asian's nutritional requirements are essentially the same as those of an American, although the total amount of some nutrients needed may be less owing to smaller size (itself probably the result of poor nutrition during the years of growth). The Asian, however, meets his nutritional needs through a quite different assortment of foods from those an American would choose. The traditional diets of various peoples of the world differ tremendously, from the East African Masai diet of berries, grain, vegetables, milk, and blood from cattle, and sometimes sheep or goat meat, to the Polynesian diet of coconut, fish, breadfruit, taro, and tropical fruits, and occasionally pork or poultry. American and European diets—once based on relatively few foods, such as beef, mutton, poultry, dairy products, eggs, wheat (bread) and other grains, potatoes (more recently), and vegetables and fruits—have grown in the past generation to include a fantastic array of foods from all parts of the world. Nevertheless, the relatively limited traditional diets of most of the people in underdeveloped countries, where under-nutrition and malnutrition are today very widespread, could be basically adequate to meet their needs. The existing nutritional deficiencies result either from insufficient supplies of some or all of these foods, or from poverty or ignorance.

To comprehend fully the nutritional problems of today's hungry millions, one must be conversant with problems of agricultural development and production, agricultural economics, food distribution patterns, cultural food preferences, and even public health situations. But above all, the nutritional needs that are common to all people, regardless of what they recognize as "food," must be understood.

Some 45 compounds and elements found in foods are considered "essential nutrients," necessary for life and health in human beings (see Appendix 3 for details). These nutrients fall into five general categories: carbohydrates, fats, proteins, vitamins, and minerals. Each nutrient can be found in a wide variety of foods, although no one food contains all of them. Each performs some particular function or functions within the body, providing energy, building and repairing tissue, or maintaining the physiological processes of life.

Human nutritional requirements can be met by eating some foods from each of four groups daily. These are:

1. Milk and dairy products for protein, vitamins, calcium, and other minerals. In some countries soybeans are substituted for milk, but they are not as rich in calcium. Using lime in the preparation of foods, and eating whole small fishes or pickled pigs' feet are ways in which some people without dairy products obtain their calcium (the acid in the pickling fluid dissolves the calcium from the pig's bones and makes it available).

2. Meat, fish, poultry, or eggs for protein, fats, and vitamins. These are luxury foods for most of the world. They are more expensive both in terms of the price the purchaser pays and in terms of the agricultural and environmental cost of producing them.

3. Grains and starchy vegetables for carbohydrates, vitamins, and some protein. This category includes the staple foods, such as wheat, rice, potatoes, corn, cassava, and taro. Among poor people these foods make up the bulk of the diet, and provide a large proportion of their protein intake.

4. Fruits and vegetables for carbohydrates, vitamins, minerals, and some protein. These are often absent in the diets of poor people in both DCs and UDCs because of their expense, and sometimes as a result of faulty food distribution. Peas, beans, and other of the legumes are important protein sources for people living in poverty.

## A Hungry World

"Basically there are not many oases left in a vast, almost worldwide network of slums; about 450 million well-fed people living in comparative luxury . . . as against 2,400 million undernourished, malnourished, or in other ways deficiently fed and generally poor . . ." This vivid description of the present world situation appears in Georg Borgstrom's 1969 book, *Too Many*.

In 1967 the President's Science Advisory Committee Panel on the World Food Supply estimated that 20 percent of the people in the underdeveloped countries (which include two-thirds of the world population) were undernourished (that is, were not receiving enough calories per day) and that 60 percent were malnourished (seriously lacking in one or more essential nutrients, most commonly protein). This means that as many as a billion and a half people are either undernourished or malnourished. This is a conservative estimate; others place the number of "hungry" people at more than 2 billion. The President's Panel further estimated that perhaps a half billion people can be described as either chronically hungry or starving. These numbers do not include the hungry and malnourished millions in the lower economic strata of developed countries such as the United States or the numbers of people who can afford to eat well but are malnourished because of their ignorance of elementary nutrition. Figure 4-4 shows the areas of the world where hunger is most widespread.

Even in the face of such staggering numbers, one might be tempted to shrug and say, "Oh well, there have always been famines and hungry people." The truth is that today's situation is totally unprecedented, in part because of the absolute numbers of people involved. Famines, which have existed throughout human history, have generally been cataclysmic, short-term events caused by weather or human intervention and have been limited to relatively small, local populations. Though such famines are undeniably tragic affairs that result in a great deal of human suffering and death, they are an entirely different phenomenon from the unceasing privation now endured by more than one billion people around the globe. Today's hunger is also unprecedented because the multitudinous hungry are increasingly aware of the dietary condition of the affluent few and have high hopes of emulating them, a situation which has important political implications for the future. Nigeria's recent famine represents the traditional type; the relatively adequately nourished Biafran population in Nigeria was suddenly faced with a catastrophic reduction in food supply. Produced by a political revolution that failed, the famine was a temporary affair. Except in the cases of severest deprivation, most adults who survived have probably not suffered permanent harm from hunger, although many very young and vulnerable children unquestionably have, and older children may have suffered some retardation of physical growth. The worst effects on the younger children will be permanent mental deficiency due to a lack of protein during critical stages in brain development (discussed later in this chapter).

Contrast this situation, which is sad enough, with the sort of grinding pov-

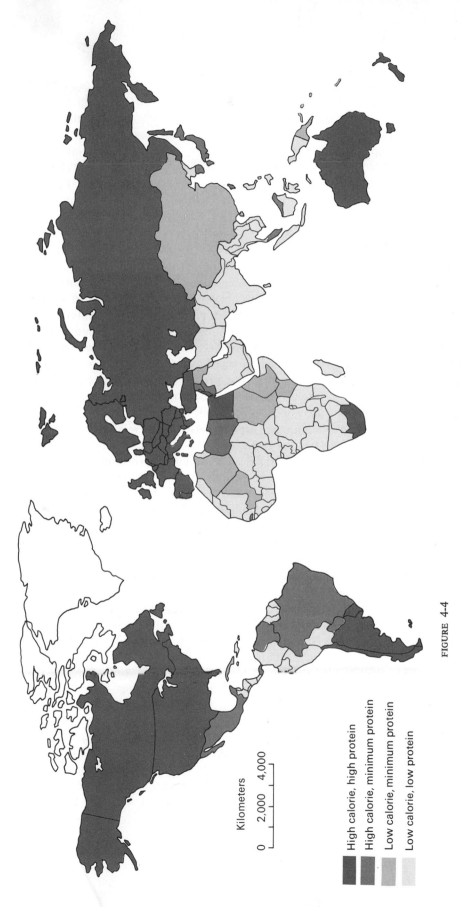

Kilometers

0    2,000    4,000

High calorie, high protein

High calorie, minimum protein

Low calorie, minimum protein

Low calorie, low protein

FIGURE 4-4

The geography of hunger. (Data derived from FAO *Production Yearbook 1968.*)

erty in some other underdeveloped areas, which has been gradually worsening for a number of years. Population growth has outstripped increases in food production in many areas. Before World War II, many countries in Africa, Asia, and Latin America were grain exporters. By the mid-1960s, they were importing grain in far greater quantities than they had ever exported it. The per capita food production in most of Asia, Africa, and Latin America dropped during the early 1960s. While 1968 brought new production records following the disastrous years of 1966 and 1967 in Asia, world food production in 1969 showed no net increase over 1968. Because the population grew 2 percent during the year, there was a per capita decline. The small net gain in agricultural production was offset by a 2 percent drop in fisheries production. For details of recent per capita food trends, see Table 5-1.

Although individual needs for calories vary according to age, sex, body size, and activity, the United Nations Food and Agriculture Organization (FAO) has established standard "reference" body weights and standard daily per capita calorie requirements for estimating a population's caloric food needs. Children's caloric needs, which are higher than those of adults in proportion to their body weights, are standardized according to age groups. For adults, allowances are also made for pregnancies and differences in age and sex. On the basis of these FAO standards, which were considered generous, the President's Science Advisory Committee placed 1965 world average calorie needs at 2,354 calories per capita per day. The FAO estimated that an average of 2,420 calories per capita per day in food was available at the market level in the middle 1960s. These estimates would indicate that there was enough food—just—to feed the entire population adequately with calories. But unhappily there are vast inequities of distribution between and within countries. The rich get more than their share; the poor get less. If an additional loss of at least 10 percent between market and consumption to waste, pests, and spoilage is taken into account, the reality of the gap between needed and available calories becomes clear.

Individual protein requirements also vary with body size and age, although activity makes very little difference. These needs must be calculated according to the quality of the protein sources. Where animal foods are a rare element in the diet, more protein is needed to compensate for the lower quality of the protein in vegetable sources (see Appendix 3). Maldistribution of proteins in UDCs, even within households, is perhaps an even more serious problem than maldistribution of calories (Figs. 4-5, 4-6). Pregnant and nursing women, and children, who have the greatest needs for protein, are often left the smallest portions.

Conflicting accounts of the actual food situation sometimes result from different ways of comparing figures. Food production figures are usually quoted only in calories and take no account of whether adequate protein or other nutrients are available. In addition, there is a vast difference between what is produced and what reaches the marketplace, as well as losses between the market and the family table. Estimates of losses to insect and

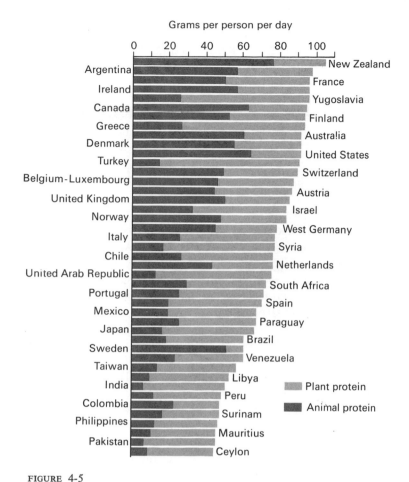

Grams per person per day

0   20   40   60   80   100

Argentina — New Zealand
Ireland — France
Canada — Yugoslavia
Greece — Finland
Denmark — Australia
Turkey — United States
Belgium-Luxembourg — Switzerland
United Kingdom — Austria
Norway — Israel
Italy — West Germany
Chile — Syria
United Arab Republic — Netherlands
Portugal — South Africa
Mexico — Spain
Japan — Paraguay
Sweden — Brazil
Taiwan — Venezuela
India — Libya
Colombia — Peru
Philippines — Surinam
Pakistan — Mauritius
— Ceylon

Plant protein
Animal protein

FIGURE 4-5

Daily per capita total protein supplies in 43 countries. (After *Introduction to Livestock Production,* 2d ed., by H. H. Cole. W. H. Freeman and Company. Copyright © 1966.)

rodent pests and to spoilage before food reaches the market range from 20 percent to as high as 50 percent in some areas.

To feed the projected population of 1985 even at the inadequate 1965 level, the President's Science Advisory Committee Panel estimated that world food production must be increased between 43 and 52 percent over 1965 production. The low estimates assume that effective population control measures will have reduced fertility by 30 percent by 1985 and that food distribution will have been improved. The greatest increase in food needs will occur in the UDCs, which are growing most rapidly. For example, the requirements of India, Pakistan, and Brazil for calories will more than double, unless there is a decline in population growth. The increase in protein requirements will be even higher. In some UDCs the protein increase may

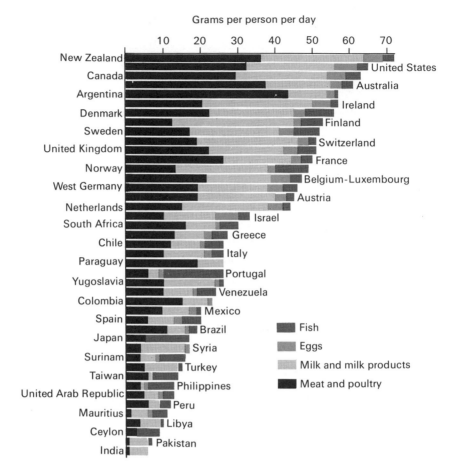

FIGURE 4-6

Daily per capita animal protein supplies in 43 countries. (After *Introduction to Livestock Production,* 2d ed., by H. H. Cole. W. H. Freeman and Company. Copyright © 1966.)

need to be as much as 150 percent. If the world is successful in making these prodigious increases in available food, and if distribution is made more equitable, in 1985 we can look forward to a population of around 5 billion, perhaps 15 percent of which will still be undernourished and 40 percent malnourished.

The present failures of food distribution are the result of a number of interacting factors, including poverty, ignorance, cultural and economic patterns, and lack of transport systems. Although the worldwide supplies of food might theoretically be adequate, the average diet within many countries in Southern Asia and tropical Latin America is significantly below FAO minimum nutritional standards. Within these countries individuals in the poorest quarter of the population may be receiving only three-fourths of the calories and proteins of even this inadequate average diet. These shortages show up in widespread malnutrition and hunger to an obvious degree, especially among such vulnerable groups as infants, preschool children (ages 1–4), and pregnant and nursing women. Correcting this situation alone would require a massive effort to raise total food production, since those who now consume more than their minimal share can hardly be expected to approve of a redistribution plan that would place everyone on a minumum calorie—low protein diet.

Deaths from starvation and malnutrition are commonplace. Of the 60 million deaths that occur each year, between 10 and 20 million are estimated by French agronomists René Dumont and Bernard Rosier to be the result of starvation or malnutrition. In most countries the cause of death is usually officially attributed to some infectious or parasitic disease, which in most cases only dealt the final blow. Diseases that are usually only minor nuisances in well-nourished individuals are devastating to the malnourished. Even if they do not kill, they tend to intensify the malnourishment by draining the individual's reserves. Cases in which normally minor diseases have precipitated a severe deficiency disorder are often seen by public health workers. Extremely poor sanitary conditions further complicate the picture; dysentery and infestations of various kinds of worms are commonplace. Diarrhea, dangerous even in a well-fed, protected baby, is disastrous to an ill-fed one. *For our purposes, any death that would not have occurred if the individual had been properly nourished may be considered as due to starvation, regardless of the ultimate agent.* Dumont's and Rosier's estimates are contested by some agronomists and may be too high. But even if they are five times too high, some 2 to 4 million human beings starve annually; a tragedy of vast proportions.

These interacting factors are a major cause of the high infant and even higher child mortality rates in the UDCs compared with those of the DCs (Tables 4-1 and 4-2). Infants are somewhat protected from both parasites and severe nutritional deficiencies while they are nursing. Mother's milk is extremely nourishing and does not transmit parasites. Nevertheless, the infant mortality rate in some poor countries is 2 to 8 times higher than that in the United States, which is by no means the world's lowest (Table 4-1). The preschool mortality rate has been considered the best indication of the nutritional level of a population, since children of this age are usually no longer protected by nursing and are therefore the most susceptible segment of the population (Table 4-2). In many parts of Latin America, Asia, and Africa these rates are three to forty times higher than in the U.S. Although dependable statistics are hard to come by, India's mortality rate for children under 4 (including infants) has been estimated to be as high as 250 per thousand. There is little question that at least half of these deaths are basically due to malnutrition, usually protein starvation.

TABLE 4-1

*Infant Mortality Rates, Under 1 Year, 1969 or most recent available figure*

| Continent and country | Rate per 1,000 live births | Continent and country | Rate per 1,000 live births |
|---|---|---|---|
| *Africa* | | *Europe* | |
| Kenya | 49.9 | Austria | 25.4 |
| Madagascar | 75.0 (1967) | Belgium | 22.9 (1967) |
| Mauritius | 69.1 (1968) | Bulgaria | 30.5 |
| Réunion | 62.4 | Czechoslovakia | 22.9 |
| United Arab Republic | 118.5 | Denmark | 15.8 (1967) |
| *North and Central America* | | Finland | 13.9 |
| Barbados | 45.7 (1968) | France | 16.4 |
| Canada | 20.8 (1968) | Germany, East | 20.4 (1968) |
| Costa Rica | 62.3 (1967) | Germany, West | 22.8 (1968) |
| Dominican Republic | 72.6 (1968) | Greece | 31.9 |
| Guatemala | 93.8 (1968) | Hungary | 35.6 |
| Mexico | 65.7 | Ireland | 20.6 |
| Puerto Rico | 28.3 (1968) | Italy | 30.3 |
| Trinidad and Tobago | 36.6 (1968) | Netherlands | 13.1 |
| United States | 20.8 | Norway | 13.7 (1968) |
| *South America* | | Poland | 34.3 |
| Argentina | 58.3 (1967) | Portugal | 61.1 (1968) |
| Chile | 91.6 (1967) | Spain | 29.8 |
| Colombia | 78.3 (1967) | Sweden | 12.9 (1967) |
| Ecuador | 87.9 (1968) | Switzerland | 16.1 (1968) |
| Peru | 61.9 (1967) | United Kingdom—England | |
| Venezuela | 41.4 (1967) | and Wales | 18.3 (1968) |
| *Asia* | | Yugoslavia | 56.3 |
| Taiwan | 19.0 (1968) | *Oceania* | |
| Hong Kong | 20.9 | Australia | 17.8 (1968) |
| Indonesia | 87.2 (1965) | Fiji | 24.8 (1968) |
| Israel | 23.0 | New Zealand | 16.9 |
| Japan | 15.3 | | |
| Kuwait | 35.9 (1968) | | |
| Pakistan | 142.0 (1965) | | |
| Philippines | 72.0 (1966) | | |
| Thailand | 27.9 (1967) | | |

SOURCE: United Nations, *Demographic Yearbook 1969.*

TABLE 4-2
*Child Mortality Rates 1-4 Years, 1960–1962 (Average Annual)*

| Continent and country | Rate per 1,000 children (ages 1-4) per Year | Continent and country | Rate per 1,000 children (ages 1-4) per Year |
|---|---|---|---|
| *Africa* | | *Europe* | |
| Mauritius | 8.7 | Austria | 1.3 |
| Réunion | 9.6 | Belgium | 1.0 |
| United Arab Republic | 37.9 | Bulgaria | 2.4 |
| *North and Central America* | | Czechoslovakia | 1.2 |
| Barbados | 3.7 | Denmark | 0.9 |
| Canada | 1.1 | Finland | 1.1 |
| Costa Rica | 7.2 | France | 1.0 |
| Dominican Republic | 10.8 | Germany, East | 1.6 |
| Guatemala | 32.7 | Germany, West | 1.3 |
| Mexico | 13.8 | Greece | 1.9 |
| Puerto Rico | 2.9 | Hungary | 1.6 |
| Trinidad and Tobago | 2.5 | Ireland | 1.2 |
| United States | 1.0 | Italy | 1.9 |
| *South America* | | Netherlands | 1.1 |
| Argentina | 4.2 | Norway | 1.0 |
| Chile | 8.0 | Poland | 1.6 |
| Colombia | 17.4 | Portugal | 8.0 |
| Equador | 22.1 | Spain | 2.0 |
| Peru | 17.4 | Sweden | 0.8 |
| Venezuela | 5.9 | Switzerland | 1.2 |
| *Asia* | | United Kingdom—England, and Wales | 0.9 |
| Ceylon | 8.8 | Yugoslavia | 5.2 |
| China (Taiwan) | 7.2 | *Oceania* | |
| Hong Kong | 4.4 | Australia | 1.1 |
| Israel | 1.8 | Fiji Islands | 3.7 |
| Japan | 2.2 | New Zealand | 1.2 |
| Kuwait | 3.6 | | |
| Philippines | 8.4 | | |
| Syria | 8.3 | | |
| Thailand | 9.1 | | |

SOURCE: United Nations, *Statistical Series,* K/3, 1967.

## Common Deficiency Diseases

The most commonly encountered deficiency diseases in UDCs are marasmus and kwashiorkor (Fig. 4-7). Marasmus is probably indicative of overall undernutrition, but it is often referred to as a "protein-calorie deficiency." It seems to be related to early weaning or to a failure in breast-feeding that results in the provision of inadequate substitutes for mother's milk, and it often appears following a bout of diarrhea or some other disease. Most victims are babies less than a year old. Since poor people in the UDCs (particularly those who migrate to cities and fill up the shanty towns) have begun to adopt from the wealthier urban classes the habit of early weaning, marasmus is on the increase. Unlike their more affluent neighbors, these mothers have

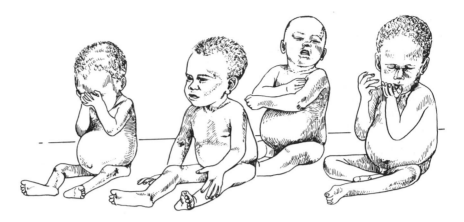

FIGURE 4-7

Symptoms of kwashiorkor (protein deficiency) in African children.
[Drawn from a photograph by Eva D. Wilson.]

no adequate substitute to offer for their milk. Out of ignorance and poverty combined, the babies are likely to receive corn flour, sago, or arrowroot gruels, with a tiny amount of milk added "for color," or, if they are luckier, dried or condensed milk that has been diluted. The child with marasmus is very thin and wasted, and has wrinkled skin and enormous eyes.

Kwashiorkor is a West African word that means "the sickness the child develops when another baby is born." Kwashiorkor is the result of protein starvation, and can occur even if calories are abundantly provided. It most frequently follows weaning, when the child of one or two years is offered mainly starches or sugars for his diet (the Jamaican "sugar baby" is an example). In mild cases the child's physical growth is retarded, the hair and skin are discolored, and he has a pot-belly. He may also lose his appetite. When the disease is more acute, the discoloration is more pronounced, hair is loosely rooted and pulls out in tufts, legs and feet swell with fluids, digestive problems arise, and the child becomes markedly apathetic. After this stage is reached, death will follow unless the best medical care can be provided. The President's Science Advisory Committee reports that the high mortality rates of children 1–4 years old in UDCs "suggest that moderate protein-calorie malnutrition affects at least 50 percent of these children."

Vitamin A deficiency often accompanies protein malnutrition and shows up in a drying of eye membranes (xerophthalmia) or softening of the cornea (kerotomalacia), which soon leads to blindness if not treated. Supplementing protein-deficient diets with high-protein foods without adding vitamin A, as has been done under American food-aid programs in which non-fat dry milk was distributed, will cause a previously unsuspected deficiency to be manifested in an acute form. Since 1965 American non-fat dry milk shipped overseas has been fortified with vitamin A. Vitamin A deficiency is widespread in most of the underdeveloped world and most frequently afflicts preschool children.

Beriberi is a disease caused by a deficiency of thiamine. It often accompanies a high-carbohydrate diet, usually one based on polished rice. The thiamine in rice is in or just under the outer skin of the grain, which is removed in milling. Where rice is hand-pounded, undermilled, or parboiled (soaked and partly cooked) before milling, at least some of the thiamine is preserved. But polished rice is preferred in many countries for its keeping qualities and because the product of milling (the polishings or husks) may be used as feed for stock. Infantile beriberi, an acute form of the disease, strikes suckling infants and soon leads to death unless it is treated promptly. Severe thiamine deficiency in the mother is the cause of infantile beriberi.

Beriberi is widespread in Southeast Asia and the Philippines, and it appears to be increasing. This is partly due to the introduction of modern community rice mills, which eliminate the need for hand-pounding, formerly done at home. Pregnant and nursing women in these areas are often, by tradition, restricted to very limited diets, which further curtails their intake of thiamine as well as that of other vitamins and proteins.

Another prevalent form of malnutrition in UDCs, particularly among women and small children, is anemia, usually iron-deficiency anemia. Lack of protein, vitamin $B_{12}$, or folic acid can also play a part in anemia. During pregnancy, a fetus absorbs from the mother's stored reserves a large supply of iron, which it needs during the months after birth (mother's milk contains very little iron). Successive pregnancies can very quickly lead to exhaustion of a mother's reserve supply; if her diet does not replenish it, the result is anemia for both mother and child. This not only produces a lack of energy and low productiveness in the mother but can increase the likelihood of stillbirth and premature birth. The incidence of death from anemia in UDCs ranges from 6 to 16 times higher than that in the United States. It is common wherever poverty and poor sanitation prevail, where it is often aggravated by such parasitic infections as hookworm. These parasites consume large amounts of blood.

Rickets and osteomalacia (softening of the bones) are due to lack of vitamin D or calcium, or both. Vitamin D is synthesized in the skin when it is exposed to sunlight. Rickets first became a health problem for Europeans in smoky, congested cities during the Industrial Revolution, where children had only dim, narrow alleys for playgrounds, and often were kept indoors to work. Like many other deficiencies, this syndrome also affects both mother and child, for the calcium deprivation may begin in the prenatal period. During pregnancy, the fetus draws from the mother's body minerals and vitamins that may not be replenished by her food. Lactation draws still greater amounts of calcium. Successive cycles of pregnancy and lactation may leave the mother virtually crippled by the drain on her bone structure. She may even be unable to leave her house. Thus she is denied the sunlight that would help replenish her vitamin D and is denied the chance of working to obtain better food.

Rickets, the childhood form of osteomalacia, is not very common in tropical countries, where sunshine is abundant. Nevertheless, it does exist, more commonly in the cities and towns. It is found also in India, Pakistan, China, and parts of the Middle East. Customs of keeping children indoors and of keeping women secluded or heavily veiled undoubtedly contribute to the incidence of both diseases.

Scurvy, pellagra, and ariboflavinosis are deficiency diseases which are less widespread than the others. Scurvy (deficiency of vitamin C), which is prevented by eating fresh fruits and vegetables, occasionally appears in arid countries during drought or famine, or among urban poor, especially the elderly. Pellagra (deficiency of niacin) usually occurs among people whose staple food is corn. In Latin America it somehow seems to be avoided through the practice of soaking the corn in lime-water before grinding it. Ariboflavinosis (lack of riboflavin) usually seems to accompany other forms of malnutrition, especially vitamin A deficiency. (See Appendix 3 for details of these diseases.)

## Implications of Severe Malnutrition and Hunger

The serious malnutrition prevalent in our overpopulated world causes incalculable suffering, wasting of human life, and loss of human productivity. Malnourishment, especially protein deficiency, inhibits the development of protective antibodies and lowers resistance to diseases. Even more alarming is the growing body of evidence which shows that protein malnutrition has permanent effects, especially on small children. It has been known for a long time that malnourishment during the years of growth and development will result in a certain amount of dwarfing and delayed physical maturity, even if the deficiency is temporary and a normal diet is later restored. What is far more ominous is the evidence that protein deficiency in infancy and early childhood may result in permanent impairment of the brain.

A child's body grows to 20 percent of its adult size in the first three years, while the brain grows to 80 percent of its adult size. This rapid brain growth is primarily a result of protein synthesis (more than 50 percent of the dry weight of brain tissue is protein). When protein is not available in the diet to supply the amino acids from which brain proteins are synthesized, the brain stops growing. Apparently it can never regain the lost time. Not only is head size reduced in a malnourished youngster, but the brain does not fill the cranium.

Studies in Central and South America have established a strong correlation between nutritional levels and physical and mental development in preschool and school age children. Among underprivileged youngsters studied in rural Mexico, height and mental achievement were positively correlated; all these children were near the lower end of the height and mental achievement scales for their ages, indicating that their development was affected by their nutrition. Among well-fed, middle-class children in the same society, height and mental development showed no relationship.

In another study in Chile, comparisons were made among Santiago slum children on inadequate diets, other slum children receiving supplemented diets and medical care, and middle-class children. The slum children on supplemented diets more closely resembled the middle-class youngsters in physical and mental development than they did their neighbors with poor diets, although the two groups of slum children came from otherwise very similar environments. Of the malnourished children only 51 percent reached the normal range of development, compared with 95 percent of the supplemented group and 97 percent of the middle-class group. Another group of children who had had marasmus as infants and had subsequently been given medical care and supplemental food were all found to have considerably below normal intelligence 3 to 6 years later.

Similar results have been obtained in studies conducted in the U.S. on severely malnourished children, comparing their later development with siblings and children of similar backgrounds without histories of malnutrition. Although human implications must be inferred with care from research on laboratory animals, studies on rats suggest that malnourished pregnant mothers may also produce children with impaired brain development. At the very least, the stress of the pregnancy represents a threat to the mother's health and her ability to care for the child.

There is some evidence that even adults do not fully recover from episodes of severe deprivation. After apparent recovery, former prisoners of Nazi concentration camps (living in Norway 20 years later) exhibited reduced brain sizes and a variety of emotional and mental problems. How much of this was due to the starvation they endured and how much to other factors such as torture and severe emotional stress is impossible to say.

Governments must be made aware of nutritional levels in their populations and of what these can allow them to expect and demand of people. Undernutrition, together with parasitism and disease, typically produces apathy, listlessness, and low productivity. Well-fed Europeans and North Americans, seeing these symptoms but neither recognizing them as such nor understanding their cause, often conclude that natives of underdeveloped areas are "lazy." By contrast, the improvement of inadequate diets may lead to rebelliousness and aggressiveness—characteristic of the behavior of humans during the recovery period following starvation experiments with volunteers. The implications of the prevalence of malnutrition for the undeveloped countries in the future, when it is more likely than not to be even more widespread and severe, are frightening to say the least. All proposals to increase food production in the UDCs are inevitably attached to elaborate plans for economic development. Can they possibly achieve either with a weakened, malnourished populace and with the prospects of physical and mental impairment in a large portion of the coming generation?

## The Picture in America

Americans were shocked in 1968 when the extent of hunger, malnutrition, and clinical deficiency diseases in the U.S. was made public. Although it was not the first report, a CBS television special program was the first to reach a substantial number of Americans. As in UDCs, this hunger and malnutrition appears to be related to poverty and an accompanying syndrome of unemployment, displacement from the land, and appalling sanitary conditions, often accompanied by a high incidence of parasitism. A U.S. Public Health Service doctor testified before the Senate Select Committee on Nutrition and Human Needs that the nutritional level of the segment of the population examined in a government survey conducted by the Public Health Service in 1969 was as low as those found in many underdeveloped countries. Investigation revealed that between *10 and 15 million* Americans were constantly and chronically hungry. A large proportion of these, as in UDCs, were children. Another 10 to 15 million had incomes too low to provide an adequate diet.

Among a random sample of 12,000 American men, women, and children from low-income areas in Texas, New York, Louisiana, and Kentucky, the survey found seven extremely severe cases of marasmus and kwashiorkor, eighteen of rickets, and evidence of widespread goiter, which is caused by iodine deficiency; 4 percent showed milder symptoms of kwashiorkor and a similar proportion had mild cases of rickets. About 17 percent of these 12,-000 people had serious protein deficiencies, and as many were described as "real risks" nutritionally. Among the children, most were below average size for their ages, and 3.5 percent were definitely stunted. One-third of those less than 6 years of age were anemic, and nearly as many showed signs of being vitamin A deficient, many seriously so. Altogether, from 35 to 55 percent of all the people surveyed exhibited signs of serious nutritional deficiencies of various kinds.

The high incidence of deficiencies of vitamins A and D and iodine found by the Public Health Survey is embarrassing, since they are easily preventable. Nonfat dry milk, which is now fortified with vitamin A for overseas food aid, is still not fortified for domestic programs; nor is vitamin D added, as it clearly should and easily could be by irradiation. The need for the use of iodized salt may be forgotten or unknown among some of the poor, yet the government survey found that it was not even available in the markets in parts of Texas, a goiter area.

The underlying causes of this level of malnutrition and hunger in a country as rich as the U.S. resemble in some respects those in UDCs, including inadequate food distribution, poverty, and ignorance. But there is an essential difference between under- and malnourishment in the United States and the same situations in a UDC: in a UDC they often exist because of a lack of the needed foodstuffs to provide a sufficient diet for a burgeoning population; in the United States they have existed only because of the lack of will on the part of the well-fed to do anything about them. U.S. government food-aid programs have clearly failed to achieve their supposed aims. Free surplus foods have indeed been distributed to the poor by the U.S. Department of Agriculture, whose primary interest, unfortunately, seems to have been in the expeditious elimination of the surpluses rather than in the nutritional needs of the recipients. Food stamps have been used in some places to enable the poor to buy food at lower prices, but for the lowest income groups, families with less than $1,000 per year, even the stamps are too expensive. In addition, participation in the government programs was optional, and city and county governments administered them. Many local governments declined to participate, even when they had large eligible populations. Poor administration probably accounts for some of the failure as well. Free school lunch programs have also had a long history of mismanagement of funds and, at the legislative level, have been hampered by food industry lobbying.

A candid Senator, Ernest F. Hollings of South Carolina, made a major contribution toward forcing the Federal government and the public to recognize and attack the problem of hunger in America. In early 1969 he testified to the Senate Select Committee on Nutrition that when he was Governor of South Carolina from 1959 to 1963, he and other state officials deliberately concealed their state's hunger problem in an attempt to boost its industrial development. They feared that knowledge of South Carolina's difficulties would discourage industry from locating there.

Although President Nixon made a strong speech in May 1969 in support of eliminating hunger in America as soon as possible, this was not followed by prompt action. A congressional request for $1 billion to feed the hungry and provide free food stamps for the destitute had already been turned down by the Administration as inflationary. A subsequent bill was emasculated by conservative committee chairmen in the House, while the Administration returned to the treasury $36 million originally appropriated for food stamps. When the Family Assistance Program for welfare reform was presented to Congress, it was at first announced that the food stamp program was to be eliminated when the program took effect, but this was later reversed.

In December 1969, delegates to a White House Conference on Food, Nutrition, and Health severely criticized the Administration's inaction against hunger and made several strong recommendations. It demanded emergency funds to meet the situation, a minimum income of $5,500 for a family of four under the Family Assistance Program, expansion of existing food programs, and the transfer of food programs from the U.S. Department of Agriculture to the Department of Health, Education, and Welfare.

In early 1970 an expanded food stamp program was put into effect. The cost of food stamps to the poor was reduced considerably and the program was extended into many areas where it had not previously existed. Funding for the program has risen to $1.5 billion for fiscal 1971 and a request for $2 billion for 1972. Free or low-cost school lunch programs for children have also been expanded. The number of children served by this program had grown from 2.5 million in 1968 to 6.4 million by the beginning of 1971. The commodity distribution program has remained about the same, presumably fluctuating according to available supplies of surplus food. Overall, there has unquestionably been progress, although the latest expansion was accompanied by a tightening of regulations. Federal spending has increased from less than $1 billion for all programs in 1968 to a projected $3.3 billion in 1972, when it will reach about 16 million of the poor and hungry. Since some 24 million people live in poverty in the U.S., there is still clearly a gap to fill. Congressional hearing testimony in spring 1971 revealed that severe malnutrition still exists among the children of migrant workers in western states. Nevertheless, if the food programs continue to be expanded, the disgraceful existence of widespread hunger and malnutrition in the world's richest country may be eliminated within a few years.

# Bibliography

Altman, P. L., and D. S. Dittmer (eds.), 1968. *Metabolism.* Federation of American Societies for Experimental Biology. Bethesda, Md. Good source of detailed information on nutrition.

Barnett, J. J., and C. Morse, 1963. *Scarcity and Growth.* Johns Hopkins Press, Baltimore. This book presents the views of the Cornucopian economists.

Borgstrom, Georg, 1967. *The Hungry Planet.* Collier Books, New York (Revised edition).

Borgstrom, Georg, 1969. *Too Many.* Macmillan, New York.

Borgstrom, Georg, 1970. The dual challenge of health and hunger: global crisis. *Bulletin of Atomic Scientists,* Oct. pp. 42–46.

Brown, H., J. Bonner, and J. Weir, 1957. *The Next Hundred Years.* Viking Press, New York. A classic of futurism, this work is updated in *The Next Ninety Years,* published in 1967 by the California Institute of Technology. *The Next Hundred Years* has a discussion of the theoretical possibility of extracting needed minerals from granite, sea, and air.

Carter, Luther J., 1970. Timber management: improvement implies new land-use policies. *Science,* vol. 170, pp. 1387–1390 (25 Dec.).

Chase, H. P., and H. P. Martin, 1970. Undernutrition and child development. *New England Journal of Medicine,* vol. 282, no. 17, pp. 933–939 (April 23). An account of a U.S. study of infant malnutrition.

Cloud, Preston, E., Jr., 1968. Realities of mineral distribution. *Texas Quarterly,* vol. 11, pp. 103–126. A fine brief summary of the nonrenewable resource situation, with commentary on some of the premises of technological optimists.

Cloud, Preston, E., Jr. (ed.), 1969. *Resources and Man.* W. H. Freeman and Company, San Francisco. See especially Chapter 8 by M. King Hubbert on energy resources, Chapter 6 by T. S. Lovering on mineral resources from the land, and Chapter 7 by P. E. Cloud on mineral resources from the sea.

Cravioto, J., E. R. DeLicaride, and H. B. Birch, 1966. Nutrition, growth and neurointegrative development: an experimental and ecological study. *Pediatrics* (supplement), vol. 38, no. 2, part II (Aug.).

Dumont, R., and B. Rosier, 1969. *The Hungry Future.* Praeger, New York. These authors estimate that in 1969, 300–500 million human beings were undernourished and 1,600 million people malnourished. That 10–20 million people die of starvation each year is their estimate.

Ehrlich, P. R., J. P. Holdren, and R. W. Holm (eds.), 1971. *Man and the Ecosphere.* W. H. Freeman and Company, San Francisco. Important papers from *Scientific American* with critical commentaries.

Eichenwald, H. F., and P. C. Fry, 1969. Nutrition and learning, *Science,* vol. 163, pp. 644–648 (14 Feb.).

Farmer, F. R., 1970. Safety assessment of fast sodium-cooled reactors in the United Kingdom. *Nuclear Safety,* vol. 11, p. 283. Candid treatment of safety problems in breeder reactors by an expert.

Food and Agriculture Organization of the United Nations, 1969. *Production Yearbook* 1968. FAO-UN, Rome.

Food and Agriculture Organization of the United Nations, *The State of Food and Agriculture.* An annual volume of information.

Gilluly, James, Aaron C. Waters, and A. O. Woodford. 1968. *Principles of Geology,* 3d ed. W. H. Freeman and Company, San Francisco. See especially Chapter 12 on mineral resources.

Gough, W. C., and B. J. Eastlund, 1971. The prospects of fusion power. *Scientific American,* Feb. Good survey of the status and potential of controlled fusion. Reprinted in Ehrlich et al. (see above).

Hirschleifer, J., J. C. DeHaven, and J. W. Milliman, 1969. *Water Supply Economics, Technology, and Policy.* Univ. of Chicago Press, Chicago. Analysis of ways to meet rising demand for water. Includes discussion of California Water Plan.

Holdren, J. P., and P. R. Ehrlich (eds.), 1971. *Global Ecology.* Harcourt, Brace and Jovanovich, New York. Significant papers on a number of the topics discussed in this chapter.

Holdren, J. P., and P. Herrera, 1972. *Energy.* Sierra Club Books, New York. Thorough, readable, and well-documented treatment of the energy situation: technology, economics, environmental impact, and a history of utility-environmentalist confrontations. By far the best book available on the subject.

Holling, Ernest F., 1970. *The Case Against Hunger.* Cowles Book Co., Inc., New York. A moving account of hunger in the U.S.

Janick, J., R. W. Schery, F. W. Woods, and V. W. Ruttan, 1969. *Plant Science.* W. H. Freeman and Company, San Francisco. Contains some useful information on forests.

Klein, Richard M., 1969. The Florence floods. *Natural History,* Aug.–Sept. pp. 46–55. An historical account of the consequences of deforestation.

Landsberg, H. H., L. L. Fischman, and J. L. Fisher, 1963. *Resources in America's Future.* Johns Hopkins Press, Baltimore. Data pertaining to supply, demand, and technology for renewable and nonrenewable resources; also helps sort out accounting practices that sometimes render more condensed data sources unintelligible.

Lessing, Lawrence, 1969. Power from the earth's own heat. *Fortune* (June). This article paints an optimistic picture of the future of the generation of electricity from geothermal power.

Loomis, W. F., 1970. Rickets. *Scientific American* (Dec.). Scientific American Offprint No. 1207. W. H. Freeman and Company, San Francisco. History of the first appearance of rickets in Europe during the industrial revolution and the discovery of vitamin D.

Lovering, T. S., 1968. Non-fuel mineral resources in the next century. *Texas Quarterly,* vol. 11, pp. 127–147. A critical discussion of the views of the Cornucopian economists, and of the practical problems of extracting minerals from common rock. Reprinted in Holdren and Ehrlich (see above).

Meinel, A. B., and M. P. Meinel, 1971. Is it time for a new look at solar energy? *Science and Public Affairs.* (*Bulletin of the Atomic Scientists*), vol. 27, no. 8 (Oct.). Description of an ambitious proposal for large-scale electricity generation from solar energy.

Mental retardation from malnutrition: irreversible, 1968. *Journal of the American Medical Association,* vol. 206, no. 1, pp. 30–31. A report on the study of malnourished children in Chile.

Odum, Howard T., 1971. *Environment, Power and Society.* John Wiley & Sons, Inc., New York. Interesting treatment of man's involvement in energy flows and the energetics of ecosystems.

Ogburn, Charlton, Jr., 1970. Population and resources: the coming collision. *Population Bulletin,* vol. XXVI, no. 2 (June), Population Reference Bureau, Washington, D.C.

Paddock, William, and Paul Paddock, 1964. *Hungry Nations.* Little, Brown & Company, Boston. Good descriptions of conditions relating to UDC food production.

Park, Charles F., Jr., 1968. *Affluence in Jeopardy.* Freeman, Cooper & Co., San Francisco. An important discussion of mineral resource problems in a world with an exploding population. There are a few rather minor technical errors, but the book generally gives an accurate picture of resource depletion. The discussion of mineral policy is, in contrast, disappointing.

Payne, Philip, and Erica Wheeler, 1971. What protein gap? *New Scientist,* 15 April, pp. 148–150. Discussion of the complex factors affecting nutrition in UDCs.

President's Science Advisory Committee Panel on the World Food Supply, 1967. *The World Food Problem* (3 vols.). Washington, D.C. A very detailed, basic source.

Pyke, Magnus, 1970. *Man and Food.* World University Library, McGraw-Hill, New York. Basic information on nutrition and food technology.

Rasmussen, Clyde L., 1969. Man and his food: 2000 A.D. *Food Technology,* vol. 23, no. 5, pp. 56–74. Good summary of the food gap and economics of food distribution.

Robinson, Gordon, 1971. Sierra Club position on clear-cutting and forest management. *Sierra Club Bulletin,* vol. 56, no. 2 (Feb.), pp. 14–17. The advantages of the best forest management practices written by an experienced forester.

Robinson, H. F., 1969. Dimensions of the world food crisis. *BioScience,* vol. 19, no. 1 (Jan.), pp. 24–29.

*Science and Public Affairs.* (*Bulletin of the Atomic Scientists, 1971.*) The September and October issues are devoted to extensive discussion of the "energy crisis."

Scrimshaw, Nevin S., and John E. Gordon, 1968. *Malnutrition, Learning and Behavior.* MIT Press, Cambridge. A comprehensive source of information on the effects of malnutrition.

Seaborg, G. T., and J. L. Bloom, 1970. Fast breeder reactors. *Scientific American,* Nov. Technical description of breeders that sweeps safety issues under the rug. See Farmer, cited above, for a more responsible discussion.

Sebrell, William H., Jr., and James J. Haggerty, 1967. *Food and Nutrition.* Time, Inc., New York.

Sherrill, Robert, 1970. Why can't we just give them food? *New York Times Magazine,* March 22. Feeding the hungry in the U.S.

Simpson, David, 1968. The dimensions of world poverty. *Scientific American,* vol. 219, no. 5 (Nov.). Includes a somewhat understated discussion of the food problem. Reprinted in Ehrlich et al. (see above).

Singer, S. Fred, 1970. Human energy production as a process in the biosphere. *Scientific American,* vol. 223, no. 3, pp. 174–190 (Sept.).

Sukhatme, P. V., 1966. The world's food supplies. *Royal Statistical Society Journal,* Series A., vol. 129, pp. 222–248. Contains some information from FAO.

Thomas, H. E., 1970. Ganges Plain: irrigation potential. *Science,* vol. 168, p. 1042 (29 May).

*Technology Review,* 1970. Vol. 72, no. 4 (Feb.). Special issue on nutritional problems in UDCs and their significance in development programs. Many interesting articles. The paper by Millikan is reprinted in Holdren and Ehrlich (see above).

U.S. Department of Agriculture, 1964. *The World Food Budget, 1970.* Foreign Agricultural Report no. 19. Washington, D.C.

Watt, K. E. F., 1969. *Ecology and Resource Management.* McGraw-Hill, New York.

Williams, Roger J., 1962. *Nutrition in a Nutshell.* Dolphin Books, Garden City, N.Y. Popular summary of nutrition by a distinguished scientist in the field

# CHAPTER 5

# Food Production

*"The human brain, so frail, so perishable, so full of inexhaustible
dreams and hungers, burns by the power of the leaf."*

Loren Eiseley, *The Unexpected Universe,* 1969

*". . . industrial man no longer eats potatoes made from solar energy;
now he eats potatoes partly made of oil."*

Howard T. Odum, *Environment, Power and Society,* 1971

All flesh is grass. This simple phrase summarizes a basic principle of biology
that is essential to an understanding of the world food problem. The basic
source of food for all animal populations is green plants—"grass." Human
beings and all other animals with which we share this planet obtain the
energy and nutrients for growth, development, and sustenance by eating
plants directly, by eating other animals that have eaten plants, or by eating
animals that have eaten animals that have eaten plants, and so forth.

## Solar Energy and Food

One may think of the plants and animals in an area, together with their
physical surroundings, as comprising a system through which energy passes,
and within which materials move in cycles. Energy enters the system in the
form of radiation from the sun. Through the process of photosynthesis, green
plants are able to "capture" some of the incoming solar energy and use it to
bond together small molecules into the large (organic) molecules that are
characteristic of living organisms. Animals that eat plants are able to break

down these large organic molecules and put to their own use the energy that once bound the molecules together. The animal expends some of this energy in its daily activities and uses some of it to build large molecules of animal substance (for growth or repair of tissue). Animals that eat other animals once again break down the large molecules and put the energy from them—energy that originally arrived in the form of solar energy—to their own uses. According to the First Law of Thermodynamics (see Box 4-1), energy can be neither created nor destroyed, although it may be changed from one form to another (as in the change from light energy to the energy of chemical bonds in photosynthesis). The Second Law of Thermodynamics says, in essence, that in any transfer of energy there will be a loss of usable energy; that is, a certain amount of the energy will be degraded from an available, concentrated form to an unavailable, dispersed form. The practical consequence of this law as it applies to food production is that no transfer of energy in a biological system may be 100 percent efficient; there is always some loss of usable energy at each transfer. In the photosynthetic system, usually one percent or less of the sunlight falling on green plants is actually converted to the kind of chemical bond energy that is available to animals eating the plants. Roughly 10 percent of that store of energy in the plants may turn up as available energy in the chemical bonds of animals that have eaten plants. And roughly 10 percent of that energy may in turn be incorporated into the chemical bonds of other animals that eat the animals that ate the plants.

Thus, one may picture the flow of energy through this system as a stepwise progression along what is known as a food chain. A food chain starts with the green plants, which are known as the producers. They are the first *trophic* (feeding) *level*. Then at the second trophic level come the herbivores (plant-eating animals), the primary consumers. At the third trophic level are the secondary consumers, the carnivores (or meat-eaters), which eat herbivores. Tertiary consumers are the carnivores that eat other carnivores, and so forth. Man plays many roles in food chains, but his most common one is that of a herbivore, since grains and other plant materials make up a very great proportion of the diet of most human beings. Man may also be a secondary consumer, as when he eats beefsteak (or the meat of any other herbivorous animal). When he consumes fishes, he often occupies positions even further along the food chain, because many fishes are tertiary or even quaternary consumers themselves. A food chain including man is shown in Figure 5-1.

At each transfer of energy in a food chain, perhaps 90 percent of the chemical energy stored in organisms of the lower level becomes unavailable to those of the higher level (in certain situations the percentage loss may be much higher or lower than this). Since the total amount of energy entering the food chain is fixed by the photosynthetic activity of the plants, obviously more usable energy is available to organisms occupying lower positions in the food chain than is available to those in higher positions. For instance, as an oversimplification, it might take roughly 10,000 pounds of grain to

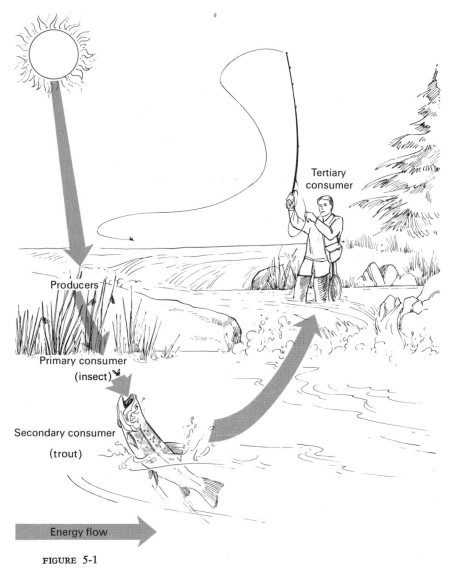

Producers

Primary consumer
(insect)

Secondary consumer
(trout)

Tertiary
consumer

Energy flow

FIGURE 5-1

A food chain including man. A mosquito feeding on the man would be
a quaternary consumer.

produce 1,000 pounds of cattle, which in turn could be used to produce
100 pounds of human being. By moving man one step down the food chain,
ten times as much energy would be directly available—that is, the 10,000
pounds of grain used to produce 1,000 pounds of cattle could be used
instead to produce 1,000 pounds of human beings.

It follows from this application of the Second Law of Thermodynamics that
in most biological systems the biomass (living weight) of producers will be

greater than that of primary consumers; the biomass of primary consumers in turn will be greater than that of secondary consumers; and so forth. The weight of organisms possible at any trophic level is dependent upon the energy supplied by the organisms at the next lowest trophic level; and some energy becomes unavailable at each transfer.

Mankind has always been dependent on the process of photosynthesis for his food. Whether primitive man ate berries, roots, fishes, reindeer, or whatever, the energy he derived from his food had the same ultimate source: the radiant energy of the sun. Not, however, until the agricultural revolution did man begin to exercise some control over plant growth, and attempt to concentrate and increase the yield from desirable food plants. His earliest attempts at agriculture doubtless were based on the astute observation that certain accidental disturbances of the land by human activities increased the growth of some useful plants. Indeed, today in some tropical areas so-called "slash-and-burn" agriculture consists of little more than cutting and burning clearings in which seeds of various desirable plants are then scattered. It would have been a small step from such practices to the reduction of competition for the desired plants by the simple hoeing of weeds and the protection of the crop from animals, and to the utilization of the fertilizing effects of excreta and other organic wastes from human activities.

Modern agriculture, of course, differs completely from primitive slash-and-burn methods. The changes in temperate agriculture over the past few hundred years could quite fairly be considered a second agricultural revolution. The science of plant breeding has produced a vast diversity of crop varieties that are adapted to various growing conditions, high in yield, resistant to diseases, and so forth. Mechanical cultivation and harvesting, improved methods of fertilization and irrigation, the use of chemical and biological controls against plant and insect pests, weather forecasting (and, to a small degree, weather control), and many other technological advances have greatly increased the quantity of food that can be produced on a given area of land. Technology has also increased the quality of some crops, but not of all crops. For instance, high yields in grains are sometimes gained at the expense of lowered protein content.

It is important to note that modern, high-yield agriculture can be reasonably described as a system which turns calories of fossil fuel into calories of food. Fossil fuels are, of course, used extensively in both the manufacture and the operation of farm machinery. They are also used in the construction and operation of the systems that transport materials to the farm and carry farm produce to market. They are used as fuel in the mining and manufacture of fertilizers, and both as energy sources and raw materials in the production of pesticides. Recent statistics indicate that, conservatively, for each calorie of food produced in the United States, about 1.5 calories of fossil fuels are consumed by agriculture and related activities.

Although man is able to modify many of the conditions of plant growth, limits are imposed upon agricultural production by geographic variation in the amount of solar energy reaching the surface of the Earth, temperatures of both soil and air, amount of soil moisture available, and so forth. And, because of the key role played by photosynthesis in agriculture, it is inevitable that farming will remain a highly dispersed human activity. Agriculture must remain spread over the face of the Earth, because the energy of sunlight can only be utilized in photosynthesis at its point of arrival. Furthermore, when populations are large, agricultural production and the transport of agricultural goods will always remain intimately intertwined: food production cannot be considered in isolation from food distribution. It is not possible to concentrate agriculture in regions of need, as it is so often possible to concentrate production of other substances required by human beings. Indeed, the existence of high concentrations of human beings tends to be inimical to agriculture. For instance, as anyone knows who has lived in the country around such cities as Philadelphia, Chicago, or Los Angeles, much farmland is taken out of production each year; prime agricultural land is "developed" into subdivisions and highways. For each additional 1,000 people in California, an average of 238 acres of arable land has been covered by buildings and pavement. By 1960 some 3 million acres of California farmland, most of which was of high quality, had been converted to nonagricultural use. By the year 2020 that figure is projected to increase to 13 million acres—half of the state's arable land. In addition, smog kills crops. If current trends continue, California eventually will not be able to feed herself, let alone export food.

Man has domesticated many species of food plants. In addition he has improved most of them by selective breeding and/or hybridization. In prehistoric times some 80 kinds of food plants of major importance were domesticated, as opposed to only about two dozen kinds of animals. But in spite of this diversity of food plants, a relatively small number of crop plants supplies the vast majority of the world's food. If one had to pick the three most important food plants in the world, the almost inevitable choice would be three species of grasses: rice, wheat, and corn. So important are these cereal grains that slightly more than one-half of the harvested land of the world is used to grow them. Wheat and rice together supply roughly 40 percent of man's food energy (Fig. 5-2).

Rice is the most important of all; it is the staple food for an estimated 2 billion people. The People's Republic of China grows about 32 percent of the world's rice, India and Pakistan 28 percent, Indonesia 6 percent, and Japan 5 percent. The great bulk of the remaining 29 percent is grown in Southeast Asia and Latin America. Total world production in 1970 was an estimated 295 million metric tons (before milling). New strains of rice that produce very high yields per acre when properly cultivated have been developed at the International Rice Research Institute (IRRI) in the Philippines. The IRRI strains have been introduced to farmers in Southeast Asia, where they are beginning to have dramatic effects on rice production.

Close behind rice in importance in the diet of human beings comes wheat, with a slightly smaller total production than rice. In 1970 some 288 million metric tons were produced. Unlike rice, wheat does not grow well in the tropics, in part because one of its major diseases, wheat rust fungus, thrives in warm, humid climates. Wheat is grown mostly where winters are cold and wet, and summers hot and rather dry (although in the U.S. wheat belt most of the precipitation is in the summer). The Soviet Union produces some 28 percent of the world's wheat, the United States 13 percent, the People's Republic of China 8 percent, India 7 percent, Canada and France 4 percent each, Italy, Turkey, and Australia 3 percent each, and all the rest of the world 27 percent.

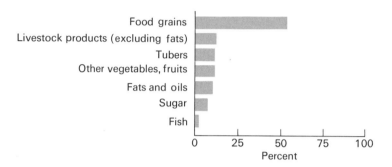

FIGURE 5-2

The sources of mankind's food energy. More than half of the calories people consume come from cereals, with wheat and rice each providing about 20 percent. (After Brown. Copyright © 1970 by Scientific American, Inc. All rights reserved.)

Corn, or maize, is the third great cereal crop, with 1970 production being about 250 million metric tons. The long, warm, moist summers of the eastern half of the United States are ideal for corn production, and more than 40 percent of the world supply is grown there. The People's Republic of China grows about 10 percent. Brazil ranks third in corn production, growing about 5 percent of the world total. About 20 percent is accounted for by the U.S.S.R., Mexico, Argentina, Yugoslavia, Rumania, and South Africa combined, and the other countries of the world grow 25 percent.

Rice, wheat, and corn together account for well over ¾ billion metric tons of grain annually. The rest of the world's crop of about one billion metric tons is made up by other grains: barley, oats, rye, millet, and sorghum. Somewhat more than half of the world's production of these grains comes from the United States, the U.S.S.R., and western Europe.

The protein content of modern high-yield grains tends to be about 5 to 13 percent and is not complete protein (protein with the proper balance of amino acids for human nutrition), being too low in content of some essential amino acids, especially tryptophan and lysine. Grains are all rich in protein, however, in comparison with the only other staple crop that approaches them in global significance: potatoes. Roughly a third of a billion metric tons of potatoes are grown annually, but the water content of the potato is so high (75 percent) and its protein content so low (1–4 percent wet weight) that the food value of the crop is considerably less than that of any of the "big three" grains. The potato is well adapted to cool climates. Of potato production outside of mainland China, fully 30 percent comes from the Soviet Union. Poland comes second with 16 percent, and West Germany third with about 7 percent. The United States and East Germany produce about 4 percent each, and France slightly more than 3 percent. The rest of the world accounts for some 34 percent, mostly produced by European and Latin American countries. China's production is probably about 30 million metric tons.

Although legumes cannot compete with grasses in volume in world food production, they have two to four times the protein content, and are thus critically important in human nutrition. They are not only an important source of protein for man but are also the ultimate source of much of the protein in domestic animals. Bacteria associated with the roots of legumes have the ability to fix gaseous nitrogen from the atmosphere and convert it to a form that may be directly used by plants. As a result legumes also serve man as fertilizer, "green manure," and thus contribute indirectly to the protein he derives from other plants.

Two legumes, soybeans and peanuts, are grown primarily as oil sources. They account for about half of the world's legume production of some 80 million metric tons. Soybean and peanut oil are used for making margarine, salad dressings, and shortenings, and are used in various industrial processes. The material remaining after the oils are pressed out (press cake) is valued as a feed for livestock. Little of the soybean crop is directly consumed by man, whereas a significant portion of the peanut crop is eaten in the nut form or in candy or peanut butter. The remaining legumes—beans and peas —are known collectively as pulses. There is a wide variety of these, including lima beans, string beans, white beans, kidney beans, scotch beans, peas, cowpeas, garbanzos, lentils, and so forth. Legumes are grown all over the world; production of soybeans is concentrated in the United States and mainland China, that of peanuts in India and Africa, and of pulses in the Far East and Latin America.

Grains and legumes are the mainstays of man's vegetable diet on a global basis, but a vast variety of other plants is cultivated and consumed. Cassava, sweet potatoes, and yams (all root crops) supply starch to many people in the world, especially the poor. The roots of the sugar beet plant and the stem of the cane sugar plant (a grass) supply us with our sugar. The roots, stems, and leaves of many plants are eaten as vegetables: cabbage, lettuce, celery, carrots, cauliflower, spinach, and rhubarb to name a few. Fruits and berries are also widely eaten: apples, peaches, pears, citrus fruits, tomatoes, eggplants, peppers, pineapples, bananas, passion fruits, papayas, mangoes, apricots, dates, grapes, strawberries and many dozens more.

Many plants are also used as forages—food for domestic animals. Although domestic animals are often just turned loose to graze and fend for themselves, many crops are grown specifically as feed for animals. For instance, some 60 million acres of the world are planted to the most nutritious of all forage crops, the legume alfalfa (called lucerne in Europe), which is especially rich in protein. Clovers and other legumes are also grown as forage, as are various grasses.

The primary importance of domesticated animals today is as a source of high-quality protein. As noted previously, the selection of animals to domesticate for food has been more limited than the selection of plants. Only nine species—cattle, pigs, sheep, goats, water buffalo, chickens, ducks, geese, and turkeys—account for nearly 100 percent of the world's production of protein from domesticated animals. Beef and pork together, in roughly equal amounts, account for some 90 percent of the nonpoultry meat production. Cows produce more than 90 percent of the milk consumed, water buffalo about 4 percent, and goats and sheep the remainder (ignoring tiny amounts from reindeer and some other minor domestic mammals).

Although certain breeds of domestic animals are adapted to the tropics, one can say that animal husbandry is generally easier and more productive in temperate areas than in the tropics. It is primarily in the Temperate Zones that geneticists have produced animals capable of extraordinary yields of meat, milk, and eggs. The year-round high temperatures and possibly the high humidity of the tropics tend to slow growth and, in milk-producing animals, lower the production of milk and milk solids. High temperature and humidity also often provide ideal conditions for parasites and carriers of disease. For instance, in parts of Africa where rainfall and other conditions are suitable, tsetse flies carry a serious disease, nagana (caused by single-celled animals called trypanosomes), which makes cattle herding impossible. However, herding indigenous species of antelope which are resistant to nagana might overcome this problem. Unfortunately, although forage may grow luxuriantly in many tropical areas, it is commonly low in nutrient value.

Domestic animals, especially cattle, are often more than mere meat or milk producers in the UDCs. In the semiarid zones of East and West Africa, cattle are the basis of entire cultures. They are regularly tapped for blood as well as milk, and are intimately related to the social and economic life of certain groups. Cattle provide their owners with wealth and prestige, are used ceremonially, and have aesthetic value. In India there is a large population of "sacred cattle," so called because of the Hindu taboo against slaughter. Visitors to India rather commonly conclude that the Indian food situation could be ameliorated by slaughtering these "useless" animals. This judgment is based on a fundamental misunderstanding of the situation. Like so many folkways and taboos, the Indian taboo has a vital influence on the local ecology. Most of the cattle feed on forage and waste vegetation that are not human foods: they do not compete with man. The cattle *do* supply milk, and above all they supply power. Bullocks (castrated bulls) are the tractors of India; they are absolutely essential to her agricultural economy. Finally, the cattle also supply dung, which is the main cooking fuel of India, and which is also used as plaster in houses and as fertilizer. Of an estimated 800 million tons of dung produced each year, some 300 million are used as fuel. This fuel produces heat equivalent to that obtained from burning 35 million tons of coal (about half of India's coal production).

## Recent History of Agricultural Production

Following the Second World War there was a steady worldwide upward trend in the amount of food produced for each person on Earth. This trend has generally continued in the DCs, with some exceptions, to the present day. In the UDCs, however, this steady increase was halted between 1956 and 1960, depending on the country, and things have been nip and tuck ever since. Table 5-1 shows the FAO index numbers of per capita food production for the years 1956–1968. In 1968 the average country in Africa and Latin America grew less food per person than it did 12 years before. The average country in the Far East improved its condition from 1956 to 1964, dropped back in 1965–1967, and showed a recovery after that. This situation obtained in spite of substantial increases (roughly 30–35 percent) in absolute food supplies in these areas during that period; population growth offset the gains. One cannot judge directly from per capita food production figures exactly what happened to the average diet of individuals in these areas, since consumption equals production plus or minus trade. The trade position of many of these countries changed markedly between 1956 and 1968. Many of them became heavy grain importers. Furthermore, the averaging process obviously conceals great dietary differences between regions within countries.

Local weather conditions are extremely important to food production. Bad weather (drought) affected the growing seasons of 1965–1966 and 1966–1967 in many parts of the world, especially in South Asia. As a result, per capita index numbers for 1965 and 1966 were very low. Good weather in 1967–1968 brought per capita production in the UDCs almost back to the 1964 level. Weather was less favorable in 1968–1969, and as a result there was a per capita decline in food production in all underdeveloped areas except the Far East. In that region, the accelerating program of agricultural development using new varieties of high-yield grains (the Green Revolution) apparently compensated somewhat for the poor weather.

Figure 5-3 shows the general trends of population growth, total food production, and per capita food production in the underdeveloped areas. Note that per capita food production in 1969 remained roughly what it was in the base period 1952–1956. *This, of course, indicates an enormous increase in human misery.* Something on the order of a *billion* people have been added to those hungry populations in the decades of the 1950s and 1960s. While the average nutritional condition of the poverty-stricken of our planet may have remained about the same, both the absolute numbers of the poor and their proportion of the total world population are increasing rapidly.

India is often considered to be the indicator for the UDCs. Agricultural ex-

TABLE 5-1

Index Numbers of Per Capita Food Production, by Regions (1952-56 = 100)

| Region | 1948–52 | 1954 | 1955 | 1956 | 1957 | 1958 | 1959 | 1960 | 1961 | 1962 | 1963 | 1964 | 1965 | 1966 | 1967 | 1968 | 1969 | 1970 |
|---|---|---|---|---|---|---|---|---|---|---|---|---|---|---|---|---|---|---|
| Western Europe | 86 | 101 | 101 | 101 | 104 | 105 | 107 | 112 | 111 | 117 | 118 | 118 | 117 | 119 | 126 | 128 | 127 | 126 |
| Eastern Europe and U.S.S.R. | 87 | 96 | 103 | 111 | 112 | 121 | 121 | 120 | 122 | 123 | 117 | 126 | 127 | 141 | 141 | 146 | 140 | 142 |
| North America | 100 | 97 | 99 | 100 | 93 | 98 | 98 | 98 | 96 | 98 | 102 | 99 | 99 | 99 | 101 | 101 | 99 | 97 |
| Oceania | 99 | 98 | 101 | 100 | 94 | 107 | 106 | 107 | 107 | 110 | 112 | 113 | 106 | 116 | 108 | 123 | 120 | 116 |
| Other developed countries (Israel, Japan, and South Africa) | 86 | 98 | 109 | 107 | 110 | 111 | 111 | 112 | 115 | 121 | 121 | 122 | 121 | 124 | 142 | 141 | 139 | 137 |
| Developed Regions | 92 | 98 | 101 | 104 | 102 | 107 | 108 | 110 | 109 | 112 | 113 | 114 | 114 | 119 | 121 | 124 | 121 | 121 |
| Latin America | 97 | 100 | 100 | 102 | 102 | 105 | 102 | 101 | 104 | 104 | 103 | 102 | 104 | 100 | 102 | 99 | 100 | 100 |
| Near East (excl. Israel) | 91 | 98 | 98 | 104 | 106 | 106 | 107 | 106 | 103 | 109 | 109 | 109 | 108 | 108 | 109 | 111 | 110 | 107 |
| Far East* (excl. Japan) | 95 | 100 | 101 | 103 | 101 | 102 | 104 | 106 | 107 | 106 | 106 | 106 | 103 | 101 | 103 | 105 | 107 | 108 |
| Africa (excl. South Africa) | 95 | 101 | 99 | 101 | 99 | 100 | 101 | 105 | 97 | 102 | 103 | 103 | 102 | 100 | 100 | 100 | 99 | 99 |
| Developing Regions | 94 | 100 | 100 | 102 | 102 | 103 | 104 | 105 | 105 | 106 | 106 | 106 | 104 | 102 | 104 | 104 | 105 | 105 |
| World* | 93 | 99 | 101 | 103 | 101 | 105 | 106 | 106 | 106 | 108 | 108 | 108 | 107 | 109 | 110 | 112 | 110 | 109 |

SOURCE: Food and Agriculture Organization of the United Nations (FAO), Monthly Bulletin of Agricultural Economics and Statistics, vol. 20, Jan. 1971.
NOTE: The indexes are calculated as a ratio between the index numbers of food production and the corresponding index numbers of population using all data available as of 15 November 1970. For further information consult the FAO Production Yearbook.
* Excluding People's Republic of China (mainland).

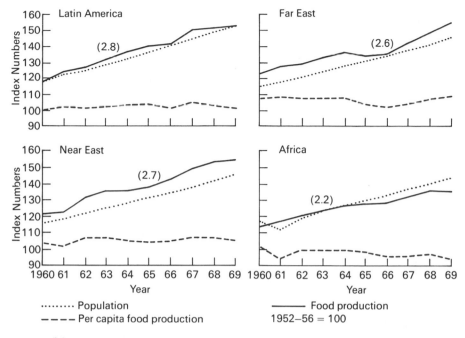

FIGURE 5-3

Food production and population trends in underdeveloped regions. Figures in brackets
show annual rate of growth of food production in the decade 1956–1958 to 1966–1968,
(1) excluding Israel; (2) excluding Japan, Peoples Republic of China (mainland),
and other Asian communist nations; (3) excluding South Africa. (After FAO, *State of
Food and Agriculture,* 1970).

pert Raymond Ewell made an interesting analysis of India's food-grain
production from the 1949–1950 growing season to the 1969–1970 season.
Figure 5-4 presents his data. The trend line is fitted by the statistical method
of least squares, a method of plotting the line through the data points so that
the sum of the squared deviations of the points from the line is minimized.
The trend line shows a growth rate of 2.9 percent per year, an improvement
over Dr. Ewell's previous analysis which indicated a growth rate of 2.3 percent. India's current population growth rate is 2.6 percent per year. There
are optimistic forecasts that India can reach and sustain a grain production
growth of 3 percent a year or better. As long as the current pace can be maintained or accelerated, India should be able to postpone further famine.

Of course, index numbers or total grain production figures are at best crude
indicators of the food situation. Even within a single country conditions
may vary tremendously from area to area. For instance, by mid-1968 most
of northern India was completely out of the famine conditions that had held
sway for several years before. In most parts of the provinces of Bihar, Pun-
jab, Uttar Pradesh, Bengal, and Orissa, wheat and rice were superabundant,
and as a result prices were dropping steadily. But in spite of this surplus of

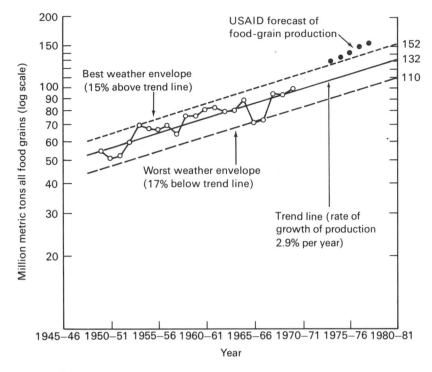

FIGURE 5-4

Trends in Indian food-grain production from 1949–1950 to 1969–1970. Solid circles indicate USAID forecasts of production. If they are achieved India will have made a substantial breakthrough in agricultural production. (Courtesy of Dr. Raymond Ewell.)

food, 7 million people were in danger of starvation in Orissa alone. At that time within northern India as a whole, some 20 million people were described as being in "acute distress," due largely to local droughts in areas adjacent to those producing surpluses. The people are so poor that they cannot create effective demand for food, producing the spectacle of surpluses and dropping prices in close proximity to starvation. This local situation is a microcosm of the story of food distribution throughout the world.

To picture the UDCs simply as net food importers would be an error. Although the DCs annually deliver some 2.5 million tons of gross protein to the UDCs, the latter send to the DCs about 3.5 million tons of higher quality protein in fish meal, presscakes of oilseeds, and soybeans. Peru exports to the DCs large catches of various fishes that could greatly alleviate severe protein deficiencies in Latin America. The DCs, however, use nearly all of it to feed poultry, livestock, and pets. More than sixty countries, including Mexico, Panama, Hong Kong, and India, supply the United States with shrimp, which could otherwise be a life saver for the protein-starved children of those countries. Georg Borgstrom describes the advantage held by the rich countries of the world in the present pattern of protein flow as a "treacherous exchange." That it is based primarily on the present world economic system is an indictment of that system and its values.

The food supply in the UDCs is at best marginal. *Large-scale efforts are required simply to avoid drops in per capita food production.* In order to *improve* the lot of the Earth's 1 to 2 billion hungry people, food production will have to increase at an unprecedented rate. What are the prospects for continuing to increase the food production of the world? Within the framework of any system of technology or any economic system, the environment imposes limits on agricultural production. As noted earlier, for the foreseeable future terrestrial food production will depend on the availability of sunlight, fertile soil, water, and a growing season long enough for crops to mature. Unfortunately, these conditions are unevenly distributed over the Earth. For example, although many tropical forest areas have a year-round growing season and abundant rainfall, their soils are often extremely poor, making large-scale agriculture there virtually impossible at present.

## Amount of Land Under Cultivation

In 1967 the report of the President's Scientific Advisory Committee estimated the amount of potentially arable (farmable) land on the Earth to be 7.86 billion acres. This amounts to only 24 percent of the total ice-free land area, but is more than triple the area actually planted and harvested in any given year. About 4.13 billion acres, more than half of the estimated total, lies in the tropical areas. Warm-temperate and subtropical areas account for another 1.37 billion potentially arable acres, and cool-temperate areas account for most of the rest, 2.24 billion acres. The distribution of cultivated and potentially arable land in relation to population and area of continents in 1965 is shown in Table 5-2. As you can see, the majority of potentially arable land is in Africa and South America, with Asia close behind.

But the term "potentially arable" can be misleading. Actually, almost all the land that can be cultivated under today's economic circumstances is now under cultivation. Most of the "potentially arable" land in Asia could not support one four-month growing season without irrigation; subtracting this land leaves very little additional arable land available in Asia. Irrigation is just one factor among many that will have to be considered if the potential of this land is to be realized. Technical expertise must be available to evaluate the fertility of soils, the feasibility of irrigation, the availability of capital and labor for both farming and support activities, such as constructing farm roads. Such surveys cost money. So do farm roads, which account for 10 to 30 percent of the cost of developing new agricultural land. Clearing land, removing stones, improving drainage, and other necessary improvements also cost money, and these costs are extremely variable from area to area. Other costs that must be considered include the expense of irrigation when irrigation is necessary, the costs of administering new developments, resettling people, supplying them with homes, schools, services, and so on. The per-acre costs

TABLE 5–2
*Present Population and Cultivated Land on Each Continent,*
*Compared with Potentially Arable Land*

| Continent | Population in 1965 (millions of persons) (1) | Area in billions of acres | | | Acres of culti-vated* land per person (5) | Ratio of culti-vated* to potentially arable land (percent) (6) |
| --- | --- | --- | --- | --- | --- | --- |
| | | Total (2) | Poten-tially arable (3) | Culti-vated* (4) | | |
| Africa | 310 | 7.46 | 1.81 | 0.39 | 1.3 | 22 |
| Asia | 1,855 | 6.76 | 1.55 | 1.28 | .7 | 83 |
| Australia and New Zealand | 14 | 2.03 | .38 | .04 | 2.9 | 2 |
| Europe | 445 | 1.18 | .43 | .38 | .9 | 88 |
| North America | 255 | 5.21 | 1.15 | .59 | 2.3 | 51 |
| South America | 197 | 4.33 | 1.68 | .19 | 1.0 | 11 |
| U.S.S.R | 234 | 5.52 | .88 | .56 | 2.4 | 64 |
| Total | 3,310 | 32.49 | 7.88 | 3.43 | 1.0 | 44 |

SOURCE: President's Science Advisory Committee, *The World Food Problem* (1967).
\* Our cultivated area is called by FAO "Arable land and land under permanent crops." It includes land under crops, temporary fallow, temporary meadows, for mowing or pasture, market and kitchen gardens, fruit trees, vines, shrubs, and rubber plantations. Within this definition there are said to be wide variations among reporting countries. The land actually harvested during any particular year is about one-half to two-thirds of the total cultivated land.

of seven sample projects in UDCs ranged from $32 to $973, with a median of $218.

How much time could we buy in the population-food crisis by concentrating on the development of new lands? Under the optimistic assumption that one acre of land will support one person, and the even more optimistic assumption that development costs will be only $400 per acre (the cost of irrigating alone now averages almost $400 per acre), the world would have to invest $28 billion per year simply to open new lands to feed the people now being added to the population annually. And, since there is an inevitable "lag time" in opening up new lands, it would seem reasonable to start immediately with the financing of at least a 10-year program costing at least $280 billion.

The chances are, however, that such a program would be as unsuccessful as previous attempts have been at opening "potentially arable" lands. In 1954 large sections of the dry plains of Kazakhstan in the U.S.S.R. were put into grain production. Premier Khrushchev had great hopes for this highly promoted "virgin lands" program, but unfortunately the virgin turned out to be a harlot in disguise. Rainfall there is marginal, roughly 12 inches per year, and drought has afflicted the area. In the 1950s Turkey also expanded grain plantings into grassland areas that subsequently had to be allowed to revert to grass because of inadequate rainfall.

A classic example of lack of attention to the agricultural limits imposed by local conditions was the ill-fated British groundnut (peanut) project started in Tanganyika (now Tanzania) after World War II. Although agricultural experts predicted that weather conditions would be satisfactory in only 8 years out of 19, millions of dollars were spent on the program. All the expertise of the British was to no avail; the program was a catastrophic failure.

Brazil's attempts to set up an agricultural colony in the Amazon basin have been utterly defeated by poor tropical soils. Unlike temperate soils, which are rich storehouses of nutrients for plants, tropical soils contain relatively little of the nutrients that exist in a tropical forest. Most of these are stored in the forest trees and shrubs themselves (for details, see chapter 7). Small wonder forest clearing so often results in disaster!

A most poignant account of the realities of agricultural development of virgin lands is "The Myth of Fertility Dooms Development Plans," by Darryl G. Cole. In 1955 Cole took his family to Cañas Gordas, Costa Rica, where they attempted to clear a piece of highland rain forest and set up a diversified farm. They failed from the beginning, in spite of their farming experience in the United States, extensive consultation with experts, and considerable experimentation with fertilizers, insecticides, fungicides, various cover crops and methods of tillage. The basic reason for failure was the thin soil, whose fertility quickly vanished in the heavy rain when the forest was removed. The Coles were reduced to dependence on a monoculture of coffee, a bush crop grown in the shade of trees. Cole wrote, "I would like to submit that such hopes [of prosperity for farmers on virgin lands] have not been realized in the Cañas Gordas–San Vita area, that they are not being realized in other areas of Costa Rica, and that, on the basis of our present knowledge of tropical agriculture, they will not be realized in similar new lands in underdeveloped nations. The myth of the fertility of these virgin lands has been too long in dying."

The Coles' experience was by no means unique. Through trial and error they ended up with a version of the sort of agriculture that has proven most successful in other tropical forest areas: "mixed cropping." This technique usually involves the planting of a shade-loving crop (in this case, coffee) under trees. The trees could be valuable hardwood, which would represent a long-term investment, or fruit, rubber, or some other potentially profitable tree.

Successful agricultural development of tropical lands clearly involves a much more sophisticated approach than simply transplanting Temperate Zone agriculture. New techniques will have to be developed for these areas through experimentation with different crops and methods. Quite possibly much can be learned by studying and comparing the practices of indigenous populations in similar climates.

Perhaps the most discussed approach to bringing substantial amounts of new land under cultivation lies in the irrigation of arid (but otherwise arable) lands. This must be done with great care, as the danger of ruining the land is great. In West Pakistan it has been estimated that salinization and water-logging take an acre of irrigated land out of production every 5 minutes. Future attempts to bring large areas under irrigation may be limited to large-scale water projects that would include dams and canals or the removal of salt from ocean and brackish water (desalination). Supplies of usable groundwater are already badly depleted in most areas where they are accessible, and natural recharge is so low in most arid regions that such supplies do not offer a long-term solution in any case.

Some recent statistics will give perspective to the following discussion of water projects and desalting. Withdrawals of water in the U.S. in 1970 totaled about 400 billion gallons of water per day, of which 160 billion gallons per day were consumed by agriculture, and 250 billion gallons per day by municipal and industrial users. The bulk of the agricultural water cost the farmer from 5 to 10 cents per 1,000 gallons; the highest price paid in 1960 for agricultural water was 15 cents per 1,000 gallons. For small industrial and municipal supplies prices as high as 50 to 70 cents per 1,000 gallons were paid in arid regions of the United States. Some communities in the Southwest were paying about $1 per 1,000 gallons for "project" water, the extremely high cost of which was due largely to transportation costs, which have been estimated at 5 to 15 cents per 1,000 gallons per 100 miles.

What are the implications of such numbers with reference to the irrigation of arid lands? The most ambitious water project yet conceived in this country is the North American Water and Power Alliance, which proposes to distribute water from the great rivers of Canada to thirsty locations all over the United States. Formidable political and ecological problems aside, this project would require the expenditure of $100 billion in construction costs over a 20-year completion period. At the end of this time, the yield to the United States would be 69 million acre-feet of water per year, or 63 billion gallons per day. If past experience with massive water projects is any guide, these cost and water figures are overly optimistic. Such projects virtually always have cost more than the estimates of the original promoters. But even if the figures are assumed to be accurate, it is instructive to note that this monumental undertaking would provide for an increase of only 21 percent in the water consumption of the United States, during a period in which the population is expected to increase by between 25 and 43 percent. For the sake of argument, it may be assumed that *all* of the additional water could be devoted to agriculture, although extrapolation of present consumption patterns indicates that only about half would be. Using the rather optimistic figure of 500 gallons per day to grow enough food for one person, it is found that this project could feed 126 million additional people. Since this is somewhat less than the number of people expected to be added to the North American population between 1970 and 2010, it should be clear that even the most massive water projects can make but a token contribution to the long-term solution of the world food problem. And in the crucial short term, the years preceding 1980, *no* additional people will be fed by projects that exist only on the drawing board today.

The costs of such projects are staggering, the scale insufficient, and the lead time too long. And we need not merely speculate about the future of such projects to produce evidence of the failure of such technological "solutions" in the absence of population control. The highly publicized and expensive Aswan Dam project will ultimately supply food (at the present miserable diet level) for much less than Egypt's population increment during the time of its construction. In addition, as is discussed in Chapter 12, it is creating a series of ecological disasters. Moreover, as is true of all water projects of this nature, silting of the reservoir will eventually impair and finally destroy the project's usefulness.

Desalting water for irrigation also has serious economic limitations. The desalting plants operational in the world today produce water at individual rates of 7.5 million gallons per day and less at a cost of 75 cents per 1,000 gallons and up, the cost increasing as the plant size decreases. The most optimistic proposal that anyone seems to have made for desalting with present or soon-to-be-available technology was for a 150-million-gallon-per-day nuclear-powered installation studied by the Bechtel Corporation for the Los Angeles Metropolitan Water District. Bechtel's original figures indicated that water from this proposed complex would be available at the site for 27–28 cents per 1,000 gallons, or $88–90 per acre-foot. Spiralling construction cost estimates caused the project to be shelved after the anticipated water cost had reached 40–50 cents per 1,000 gallons. But even using the earlier low figures does not alter the verdict. At those figures the water that would be supplied by the largest and most economical municipal desalting facility yet proposed in the United States would cost approximately twice the highest price that farmers have hitherto been willing to pay for irrigation water. The transportation costs for farmers a few hundred miles from the sea might easily double the on-site cost. Moreover, studies have shown that at present and short-term future energy costs, no further economies are to be gained by building desalination facilities with a greater capacity than that of the proposed plant, whether conventional or nuclear. On purely economic grounds, then, it is unlikely that desalting will revolutionize food production in the foreseeable future. Technology may improve this outlook with the passage of time, especially if new strains of crop plants that are more tolerant to slightly brackish water can be produced. Indeed, it may eventually be possible to select high-yield strains of salt-tolerant grasses and raise grains with salt-water irrigation. Experiments with this technique are being carried out in Israel. However, there are many difficult problems, and any eventual success can be expected to come, at best, in the distant future. Unfortunately, world population growth will not wait.

Desalting becomes more promising if the high cost of the water can be off-set by increased agricultural yields per gallon and, perhaps, by the use of a single nuclear installation to provide power for both the desalting process and a profitable on-site industrial process. This prospect has been investigated in a thorough and well-documented study headed by nuclear engineer E. A. Mason at Oak Ridge National Laboratory. The result is a set of preliminary figures and recommendations regarding nuclear-powered "agro-industrial complexes" for arid and semiarid regions, in which desalted water and fertilizer would be produced for use on an adjacent, highly efficient farm. In underdeveloped countries incapable of using the full excess power output of the reactor, this energy would be consumed in on-site production of industrial materials for sale on the world market. Technologies for both near-term (10 years hence) and far-term (20 years hence) projects are considered, as are various combinations of farm and industrial products. The representative near-term project for which a detailed cost breakdown is given consists of a seaside facility with a desalting capacity of a billion gallons per day, a farm size of 320,000 acres, and an industrial electric power consumption of 1585 megawatts. The initial investment for this complex is estimated at $1.8 billion, and annual operating costs at $236 million. If both the food and the industrial materials produced were sold (as opposed to giving the food to those who could not pay) the estimated profit for such a complex, before subtracting financing costs, would be 14.6 percent.

Mason and the co-authors of the study are commendably cautious in outlining the assumptions and uncertainties upon which these figures rest. The key assumption is that 200 gallons of water per day will grow the 2,500 calories required to feed one person. Water to calorie ratios of this order or less have been achieved by the top 20 percent of farmers specializing in such crops as wheat, potatoes, and tomatoes, but more water is required for urgently needed protein-rich crops such as peanuts and soybeans. The authors recognize the uncertainty that crops usually raised separately can be grown together in tight rotation on the same piece of land. Also mentioned are problems of water storage between periods of peak irrigation demand, optimal patterns of crop rotation, and seasonal acreage variations. And, of course, a suitable seaside location is required. These important "ifs" and assumptions, and those associated with the other technologies involved, are unfortunately often omitted when the results of such painstaking studies are put forth in oversimplified terms for popular consumption. As a result, the general public tends to assume there are easy solutions where none exist and to foresee panaceas where, in fact, scientists in the field concerned see only potential palliatives which would require much time and huge sums of money.

It is instructive, nevertheless, to examine the impact that the complexes proposed by the Oak Ridge group might have on the world food problem if construction were to begin today, and if all their assumptions about technology 10 years hence were valid *now*. The food produced at an industrial-agricultural establishment of the sort described above would be adequate for just less than 3 million people. This means that 23 such plants per year, at a total cost of $41 billion, would have to be put into operation merely to keep pace with world population growth, without even trying to improve the substandard diets of between one and two billion members of the present population. Fertilizer production beyond that required for the on-site farm might conceivably be used to raise food production elsewhere, but the substantial additional costs of transporting the fertilizer to where it is needed would have to be accounted for. From the start of construction, approximately 5 years would be required to put such a complex into operation, so we should commence work on at least 125 units at once, and plan to begin at least another 25 per year thereafter. If the technology *were* available now, the investment in construction during the five-year construction period would be $315 billion—about 20 times the United States foreign aid expenditure during the past 5 years. By the time the technology is available, the cost will be even greater. This example, too, illustrates how scale, time, and cost can work against technology. Of course, if humanity redefined its priorities in favor of such development, many of the cost obstacles would disappear—but time would still be lacking.


## Improving Yields on Land

A great deal of publicity has been given to the so-called Green Revolution, an agricultural transformation that some claim has the potential for keeping agricultural production in the UDCs well ahead of population growth. Dr. Norman Borlaug was given the Nobel Peace Prize in 1970 for his excellent work in developing "miracle" wheats—one of the mainstays of the revolution. There are two general components in this revolution: increased use of fertilizers and, especially, increased use of the new "high-yield" varieties of grain.

Probably the most widely recommended means of increasing agricultural yields is through more intensive use of chemical fertilizers. Their production is straightforward, and a good deal is known about their effective application. But the environmental consequences of heavy fertilizer use are poorly understood and dangerous (Chapter 7). Even if we could ignore such problems, we find staggering difficulties barring the implementation of fertilizer technology on the scale required. The accomplishments of Japan and the Netherlands are often cited as offering hope to the underdeveloped world. Some perspective on this point is afforded by noting that if India were to apply fertilizer at the per capita level employed by the Netherlands, Indian fertilizer needs alone would amount to nearly half the present world output. Per capita use in the Netherlands is more than 12 times that of India (the Netherlands is nonetheless a net importer of food).

Although the goal for nitrogen fertilizer production in 1971 under India's fourth five-year plan was 2.4 million metric tons, Raymond Ewell (who has served as fertilizer production adviser to the Indian government for the past 12 years) suggests that less than 1.1 million metric tons would be a more realistic figure for that date. The most recent FAO figures show the 1968–1969 production to be 563,000 metric tons of nitrogen in fertilizer. Ewell cites poor maintenance, shortages of raw materials, and power and transportation breakdowns as factors that contribute to continuing low production by Indian factories. Moreover, even when fertilizer is available, increased productivity does not necessarily follow. In parts of the under-

TABLE 5-3

*Estimated Acreages Planted In New High Yielding Grain Varieties (non-Communist Nations)*

| Crop Year | Wheat | Rice | Total |
|-----------|-------|------|-------|
| 1965–66 | 23,000 | 18,000 | 41,000 |
| 1966–67 | 1,542,000 | 2,505,000 | 4,047,000 |
| 1967–68 | 10,173,000 | 6,487,000 | 16,660,000 |
| 1968–69 | 19,699,000 | 11,620,000 | 31,319,000 |
| 1969–70 | 24,664,000 | 19,250,000 | 43,914,000 |

Most of wheat and all reported rice acreages were in South and East Asia; of 1969–1970 total, 59 percent was in India, 20 percent in Pakistan. Limited areas of wheat have been planted in West Asia, North Africa, and Latin America.
SOURCE: Dalrymple, 1971.

developed world, lack of farm credit limits fertilizer distribution; elsewhere, internal transportation systems are inadequate to the task. Nor can the difficulties of educating farmers on the advantages and techniques of fertilizer use be ignored. A recent study of the Intensive Agriculture District Program in the Surat district of Gujarat, India (in which scientific fertilizer use was to have been a major feature) notes that "on the whole the performance of adjoining districts which have similar climate but did not enjoy the relative preference of input supply was as good as, if not better than, the programme district. . . . A particularly disheartening feature is that the farm production plans, as yet, do not carry any educative value and have largely failed to convince farmers to use improved practices in their proper combinations." Obviously, increasing agricultural production requires much more than just supplying more fertilizer.

A main area of hope in conventional agriculture is the development and distribution of new high-yield or high-protein strains of food crops. That such strains can potentially make a major contribution to the food supply of the world is beyond doubt. There are some heartening indications that fundamental changes are occurring in UDC agriculture, especially in Asia. There has been a rapid increase in the estimated acreage planted to new high-yielding grain varieties in Asia (Table 5-3).

In 1968 the Indian wheat harvest was 35 percent above the previous record, and the Pakistani crop was 37 percent higher than any other year. There were also large gains in rice production in the Philippines and Ceylon in 1966–1968. These gains were in large part due to the new grain varieties. These grains have several advantages over traditional varieties. Not only do they tend to mature early, but unlike traditional varieties they are relatively insensitive to day length; these two characteristics make multiple cropping (growing two or three crops a year) more practical. In Mysore State in India, farmers are growing three corn crops every 14 months. When adequate water is available, Indian, Indonesian, and Philippine farmers can grow two and even three rice crops each year. Where there is a dry season with inadequate water available for growing rice, some farmers are growing new high-yielding grain sorghums (which require less water). In some areas of northern India and western Pakistan, farmers are alternately planting rice in the summer and wheat in the winter.

Such advances do indicate that significant increases in yields are *possible* in some UDCs. There are, however, many unanswered questions about the ultimate scale and duration of the Green Revolution. Typically the new grain varieties *must* have high fertilizer inputs in order to realize their potential. This means that the problems mentioned above must be dealt with: fertilizer must be produced within the UDC or purchased from outside, and it must then be transported to the fields. Capital is required for fertilizer plants, fertilizer purchases, road construction, railroad construction, trucks, and so forth. Abundant water is also essential for most of the grains, requiring investment in tubewells, pumps, and irrigation ditches. Similarly pesticides and mechanized planting and harvesting are necessary to get the most out of the new varieties. These too are expensive, and capital is in chronically short supply in most UDCs.

There are other economic problems. For instance, in some areas farmers' yields are increased by the new grains to the point where their marketable surplus is doubled. This can produce a grain glut that the marketing system cannot handle. Transport facilities are inadequate for distribution, and there is not sufficient "demand" for the food. After all, demand is purchasing power, and starving people may create no demand at all. It is common for agricultural economists to speak of helping hungry peoples by increasing the *demand* for food in a country. High grain production all too often means low grain prices. When this happens, the poor can afford to buy more food, but the farmer's incentive is destroyed. The end result is that *less* food is available. Governments in UDCs thus may be forced into grain price support programs that they can ill afford. The Mexican government, for instance, supports local wheat prices at about double the world market price. Finally, in some countries progress is hindered by a lack of farm credit. New grains are first introduced to "progressive" farmers, usually those with the largest, richest farms. They are in the best position to pay for the inputs of fertilizer, pesticides, irrigation water, and so forth. This advantage of the large landholders over small farmers is intensified when the higher yields bring in more money, which can be further invested in more land and more fertilizer. As attempts are made to spread the Green Revolution to smaller farmers, the need for credit becomes acute.

India has provided an example of how these economic problems can lead to serious trouble. Prices of farm land have been greatly increased by competition among landholders eager to take advantage of subsidies, while the landless rural population, already over 50 million people, is being squeezed out. The peasants are in some areas abandoning the land and moving to the already overcrowded cities. Resentment of the big landholders by the landless in India led to massive landgrabs in 1970. Hundreds of thousands of landless farmers seized, at least temporarily, an estimated 32,000 acres in a single week. The amount of land occupied in 1969 and 1970 was probably over 300,000 acres. There is a growing trend toward both rural and urban violence in India, much of it apparently connected with the Naxalite movement, which gets its name from the Naxalbari area near the Himalayas, the site of a tribal revolt in 1967. Naxalites have begun "executing" rich landlords and other "class enemies." By 1971 Naxalites had largely withdrawn from the country-side and were concentrating their activities in the cities, especially Calcutta. But the underlying conditions of revolution still exist in the countryside and seem likely to be exacerbated as the Green Revolution progresses. It seems clear that only long-needed land and tenancy reforms have any chance of preventing major disaster.

Another serious problem in spreading new agricultural technology is a critical shortage of agricultural research workers and technicians in the UDCs. Table 5-4 summarizes the number of such workers in various

TABLE 5-4

*Agricultural Research Workers per 100,000 People Active in Agriculture, 1960*

| India | 1.2 | Iran | 10.0 |
|---|---|---|---|
| Philippines | 1.6 | Argentina | 14.0 |
| Mexico | 3.8 | Japan | 60.0 |
| Pakistan | 4.5 | Taiwan | 79.0 |
| Thailand | 4.7 | Netherlands | 133.0 |
| Colombia | 9.0 | | |

SOURCE: USDA, *Changes in Agriculture in 26 Developing Nations, 1948–1963.*

countries in 1960. Many more research organizations like the International Maize and Wheat Improvement Center (CIMMYT) in Mexico and the International Rice Research Institute (IRRI) in the Philippines are needed. Two units with broader missions in tropical agriculture have recently gone into operation: the International Center for Tropical Agriculture (CIAT) in Colombia, and the International Institute for Tropical Agriculture (IITA) in Nigeria. The IRRI and the CIMMYT were set up and supported by private foundations (Ford and Rockefeller) and are now partly funded by other foundations and USAID; the CIAT and IITA also will be supported by foundations. Many more institutions such as these, supported where necessary by government funds from the DCs, should be established all over the tropical world as trained researchers become available to staff them.

In many ways the problem of revolutionizing UDC agriculture is inextricably tied up with the general problem of UDC "development." Shortages of capital, demand, resources, and trained technicians, lack of effective planning, and the absence of adequate transport and marketing systems all tend to combine with extremely high rates of population growth, malnutrition, and disease to make any kind of development extremely difficult, and thus retard agricultural development. It is a vicious cycle—one that the Green Revolution may not be able to break.

Perhaps even more important than the effects of these economic problems on agricultural development are those of potential biological problems. For instance, the new grain varieties were rushed into production in places like West Pakistan, where the climate is most favorable. How they will fare in less favorable climates remains to be seen. They are also going into production without adequate field testing, which is very time consuming, so that we are unsure of how resistant they will be to the attacks of insects and plant diseases. Continuous breeding efforts are, however, being carried out in order to develop varieties suitable for different conditions. In general, though, when crops are selected for high yield, something is sacrificed, such as protein content or resistance to bacteria or insects. We suspect that in the next few years escalating pest problems will cut heavily into "miracle yields." William Paddock has presented a plant pathologist's view of crash programs designed to shift agriculture in the UDCs to the new varieties. With reference to India's dramatic program of planting improved Mexican wheat, he writes: "Such a rapid switch to a new variety is clearly understandable in a country that tottered on the brink of famine. Yet with such limited testing, one wonders what unknown pathogens await a climatic change which will give the environmental conditions needed for their growth." Introduction of the new varieties creates enlarged monocultures of plants with unknown levels of resistance to diseases and pests. Clearly, one of the prices that is paid for higher yield is a higher risk of widespread catastrophe.

This potential for catastrophe was given meaning for many Americans by an epidemic which attacked their corn crop in 1970. An estimated 710 million bushels, roughly 17 percent of the anticipated crop, was lost to southern corn leaf blight. A new genetic strain of a fungus, *Helminthosporium maydis* proved to be especially damaging to corn with "T cytoplasm," a type used widely in seed production. About 80 percent of the American corn crop was potentially susceptible. It is hoped that measures being taken to replace the susceptible corn will prevent a repetition of the 1970 epidemic. The chance remains, however, that the fungus will evolve the ability to attack other strains. As L. A. Tatum of the Plant Science Research Division of the U.S. Department of Agriculture stated, "The corn blight epidemic is a dramatic demonstration that gains in crop production, especially from high yield varieties, may be short-lived unless supported by constant alertness and an aggressive research program . . . The epidemic illustrates the vulnerability of our food crops to pests."

One of the most serious side-effects of the Green Revolution may be acceleration of the loss of reserves of genetic variability in crop plants, variability badly needed for continuing development of new strains. This process is already well under way as old varieties, reservoirs of variability, are re-

placed by high yielding varieties over large areas. FAO agronomists estimate that seed stock reserves must be collected within the next five years, or
"mankind will have lost them for good and ever."

Since the new varieties may require more input of pesticides, with all of
their deleterious ecological side-effects, part of the price of agricultural development may be increased pollution of the environment and a decrease
in the harvest of food from the sea. (These and similar biological problems
are discussed in detail in Chapter 7). Because biological problems usually
develop over considerable periods of time, it is possible that early successes
in the Green Revolution may have given the world a false impression of what
rates of improvement in yield can be sustained. The new grain varieties were
adopted primarily by progressive farmers in the most suitable areas; it remains questionable whether their success will be duplicated by less progressive farmers who may not do as well with the new strains, or may not
even be willing or able to try them. On the other hand, it can be argued that
the Green Revolution may break the crust of tradition and become self-
accelerating. Only time will tell.

A final problem must be mentioned in connection with these strains of
food crops. In general, the hungriest people in the world are also those with
the most conservative food habits. In South China a local vitamin B deficiency was caused because people refused to eat their rice unmilled. They
objected to the additional cooking time required, they did not like the flavor,
and it gave them upset stomachs. Even rather minor changes, such as from a
rice variety in which the cooked grains stick together to one in which the
grains fall apart, may make food unacceptable. It seems to be an unhappy
problem of human nutrition that people would sometimes rather go hungry
than eat a nutritious substance that they do not recognize or accept as food.

Beyond the economic, ecological, and cultural problems already mentioned in connection with high-yield agriculture, there is the overall problem of time. We need the time to breed the desired characteristics of yield
and hardiness into a vast array of new strains (a tedious process indeed),
time to convince farmers that it is necessary to change their traditional ways
of cultivation, and time to convince even hungry people to change the
staples of their diet. Agricultural experts William and Paul Paddock give
twenty years as the rule-of-thumb for a new technique or plant variety to
progress from conception to substantial impact on farming. They state: "It
is true that a *massive* research attack on the problem could bring some
striking results in less than twenty years. But I [we] do not find such an attack remotely contemplated in the thinking of those officials capable of
initiating it." The International Rice Research Institute did produce and introduce a high-yield strain of rice, IR–8, in just six years, which shows that
under ideal circumstances the lead time can be reduced, as the Paddocks
noted. But the IRRI was able to take advantage of previously completed breeding work. Even so, the report in late 1969 was that the new rice variety was
proving to be of poorer quality than the traditional rice varieties, being less
palatable and having poor milling qualities. In addition, it was very suscepti-

ble to pests. New varieties are now being developed which avoid these problems, and in many areas IR–8 is now obsolete. But it would seem that a decade would be an *optimistic* average under most circumstances for lead time in properly developing plant varieties. As promising as high-yield agriculture may be, the funds, the personnel, the ecological expertise, and the necessary time to develop its full potential are unfortunately not at our disposal. Fulfillment of the promise will come too late for many of the world's hungry, if it comes at all. Even the most enthusiastic boosters of the Green Revolution admit that it cannot possibly keep food production abreast of population growth for more than two decades or so. Since a birth control solution to the population explosion will inevitably take longer than that, the prospects for avoiding massive increases in the death rate from starvation are dim indeed.

## Food from the Sea

Perhaps the most pervasive myth of the population-food crisis is that mankind will be saved by harvesting the "immeasurable riches" of the sea. Unfortunately, the notion that we can extract vastly greater amounts of food from the sea in the near future is an illusion promoted by the uninformed. Biologists have carefully measured the riches of the sea, considered the means of harvesting them, and have found them wanting as a solution to the food problem.

The basis of the food-from-the-sea myth seems to be theoretical estimates that fisheries productivity might be increased to many times current yields. However, an analysis by J. H. Ryther of the Woods Hole Oceanographic Institution in 1969 (Box 5-1) put the maximum sustainable fish yield in the vicinity of 100 million metric tons, considerably less than twice the record 1968 harvest of 64.3 million metric tons (U.N. estimates do not include the People's Republic of China, which is calculated to harvest an additional 6–8 million metric tons). Some other marine biologists think a yield of 150 million metric tons is conceivable.

Since 1950, when the world fisheries production total was about 21 million metric tons, production has risen at an average rate of about 5 to 6 percent per year. This rapid sustained increase was largely due both to more intensive fishing and increasing use of technology, and probably also in part to more accurate and complete reporting. In 1969 the rise in fisheries production came to an abrupt halt; in fact there was a decline of 2 percent. The total catch was 63.1 million metric tons.

To surpass the potential annual fish production of 100–150 million metric tons would require moving down the food chain from the big fish ordinarily found in fish markets to the harvesting of plankton. All signs at the moment indicate that this will not be feasible or profitable in the foreseeable future, if ever. More calories of fuel and human energy would be spent on harvesting the plankton than could be gained, the expenditure of money would be

BOX 5-1 PRODUCTIVITY OF THE SEA

It is common for laymen to consider the oceans of the world a virtually limitless source of food. They would do well to heed the words of marine biologist J. H. Ryther, "The open sea—90 percent of the ocean and nearly three-fourths of the earth's surface—is essentially a biological desert. It produces a negligible fraction of the world's fish catch at present and has little or no potential for yielding more in the future." The upper layer of open sea, where there is enough light for photosynthesis, lacks the nutrients necessary for high productivity. The photosynthetic producer-organisms (phytoplankton) that live in this layer are extremely small in size. As a result very small herbivores and lower order carnivores are able to function in food chains, and roughly five steps in the chains are interposed between the producers and man. Thus not only are the basic mineral resources for the producers in short supply, but the energy losses in repeated transfers up the long food chains result in further reductions in the potential harvest.

Close to shore, in certain offshore areas, and in a few coastal areas where powerful upwelling currents bring nutrients to the surface, productivity is 2–6 times higher; phytoplankton are larger, and food chains thus tend to be shorter. It is these areas that supply man with virtually all of his fishes. These are also the areas where pollution is the most serious. Indeed, in many areas one-quarter to one-half of fishing production is dependent on estuaries, directly or indirectly, and mankind is busily destroying many of the world's estuaries.

The fisheries situation is summarized in the following table.

| Area | Percent of ocean | Area (square kilometers) | Average productivity (grams of carbon per square meter per year) | Average number of trophic levels (approximate) | Annual fish production (metric tons) |
|---|---|---|---|---|---|
| Open ocean | 90 | 326,000,000 | 50 | 5 | 1,600,000 |
| Coastal zone[a] | 9.9 | 36,000,000 | 100 | 3 | 120,000,000 |
| Coastal up-welling areas | 0.1 | 360,000 | 300 | 1.5 | 120,000,000 |
| | | Total annual fish production | | | 241,600,000 |
| | | Amount available for sustained harvesting[b] | | | 100,000,000 |

SOURCE: After Ryther, *Science*, 1969.

[a] Including certain offshore areas where hydrographic features bring nutrients to the suface.

[b] Not all the fishes can be taken; many must be left to reproduce or the fishery will be overexploited. Other predators, such as sea birds, also compete with us for the yield.

colossal in relation to the yield, and the product would require considerable processing to be made palatable as human food. In addition, harvesting plankton would result in the depletion of desirable stocks of larger fish living farther up the food chain. The most careful analysis indicates that the world harvest might be increased to 70 million tons or so by 1980. On a per capita basis, however, an increase of this amount would actually constitute a small *decline*—unless the human population growth rate were to decrease in this decade.

But two things stand between man and the future achievement of even that 70 million or more tons of yield. The first is overexploitation, the second is oceanic pollution (which is discussed in Chapter 7).

The 1969 setback may mean that these two problems have already overtaken us. The story of the whale fisheries* serves as a model of overexploitation. In 1933, a total of 28,907 whales was caught, producing 2,606,201 barrels of whale oil. In 1966, a third of a century later, 57,891 whales were killed; almost exactly twice as many as in 1933. But twice as many whales yielded only 1,546,904 barrels of oil, just about 60 percent of the 1933 yield. The reason can be seen in the charts of Figure 5-5. As the larger kinds of whales were driven toward extinction, the industry shifted to harvesting not only the young individuals of large species but, with time, smaller and smaller species.

After the Second World War, the 17 countries interested in whaling established the International Whaling Commission (IWC). This commission was charged with regulating the annual harvest, setting limits to the catch and protecting whale species from extinction. In theory, commissioners from the various nations were to be responsible for ensuring the compliance of their nation's whalers with IWC decisions, but in fact their powers of inspection and enforcement were nonexistent. Instead of setting quotas on individual whale species, the IWC unfortunately established quotas on the basis of "blue whale units." A blue whale unit (bwu) is one blue whale or the equivalent in terms of other species: two fin whales, two-and-a-half humpback whales, or six sei whales. The nations engaged in whaling in the antarctic fishery were allowed a combined quota of 16,000 blue whale units. Since the blue whales were the largest, they were the most sought after. Up until about 1950, although blues continued to be taken, their numbers declined sharply, which meant that the next largest, the fin whales, were hunted more vigorously.

In 1960 the Commission appointed a committee of biologists to investigate the stocks of antarctic whales. Catches of blues and fins continued to decrease in the interval between establishment of the committee in 1960 and its report in 1963. The report detailed the overexploitation of the fisheries and warned that blues and humpbacks were in serious danger of extinction. It recommended that blues and humpbacks be totally protected, and that the

---

* Although whales are mammals, not fishes, the hunting of them is arbitrarily called a "fishery."

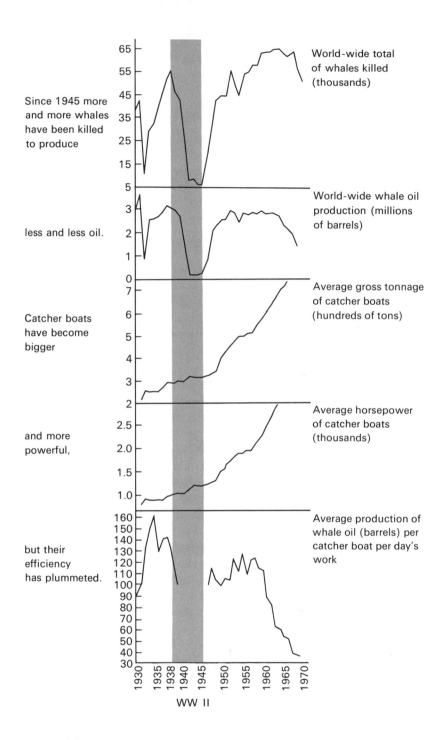

FIGURE 5-5

Overexploitation of whale fisheries. (After *N.Y. Zoological Society Newsletter*, Nov. 1968.)

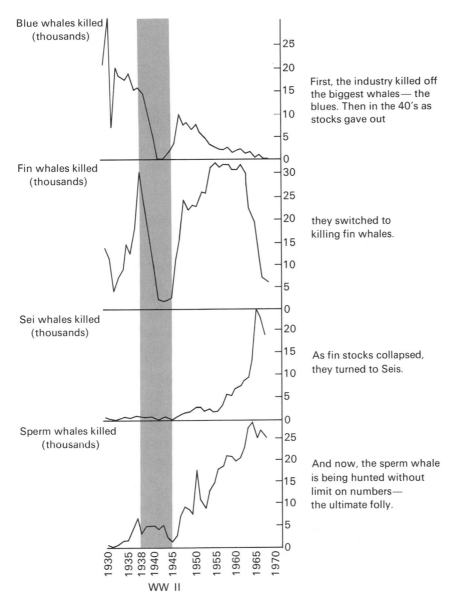

Blue whales killed (thousands)

First, the industry killed off the biggest whales— the blues. Then in the 40's as stocks gave out

Fin whales killed (thousands)

they switched to killing fin whales.

Sei whales killed (thousands)

As fin stocks collapsed, they turned to Seis.

Sperm whales killed (thousands)

And now, the sperm whale is being hunted without limit on numbers— the ultimate folly.

WW II

take of fins be strictly limited. It also urged abandonment of the system of blue whale units in favor of limits on individual species.

The committee also made some predictions. Their report stated that if unrestricted whaling continued in 1963–1964, no more than 8,500 blue whale units would be taken, and that 14,000 fins would be killed. Predictably, the warnings were ignored, and the limits were set at 10,000 bwu. The whalers killed 8,429 bwu that season, and 13,870 fins were taken: the biologists' predictions proved uncannily accurate. An ominous note in these figures is that the catch of fin whales was about 35 percent of the estimated total fin population—probably three times the estimated *sustainable* yield.

When the results for 1963–1964 were in, the biologists recommended a bwu total for 1964–1965 of 4,000, 3,000 bwu in 1965–1966, and 2,000 bwu in 1966–1967, in order to allow for recovery of the whale stocks. Again their advice was ignored. All four countries then engaged in antarctic whaling—Japan, the Netherlands, Norway, and Russia—voted against accepting the recommendation, and instead agreed only to limit the 1964–1965 season's catch to 8,000 bwu, double the recommended number of units.

What happened in 1964–1965? Only 7,052 blue whale units were taken, well short of the 8,000 quota. Furthermore, only 7,308 fins were taken, and the majority of the remaining bwu consisted of almost 20,000 seis, well over a third of the total estimated population of that species. In both 1963–1964 and 1964–1965 the total antarctic catch of whales was less than that from other areas of the world—an unprecedented situation. Meanwhile, the Netherlands had given up whaling and sold her fleet to Japan.

In an emergency session in May of 1965, the IWC decided to limit the 1965–1966 catch to 4,500 bwu, which again exceeded the biologists' recommendation. The IWC also tried unsuccessfully to give the now heavily fished sperm whales some protection. The whaling industry did not catch the 4,500-bwu limit in 1965–1966; the total was only 4,089 units, and sei whales made up the majority. Meanwhile, whaling stations in Peru and Chile (not members of the IWC) killed 449 more blue whales, which were already dangerously near extinction.

Subsequent attempts to reach agreements to limit the take of fin, sei, and sperm whales in antarctic and other waters have failed. In 1966–1967 there were four Japanese, two Norwegian, and three Russian antarctic whaling expeditions; the take was 3,511 bwu (4 blues, 2,893 fins, and 12,893 seis). Outside of the Antarctic, seven factory ships and 24 land stations processed 29,536 whales, many of them sperms. In the calendar year 1967 a grand total of 52,046 whales were slaughtered, 25,911 of them sperm whales. In addition, Japan, desperate for protein, killed 20,000 porpoises. In 1968 Norway was forced out of the whaling industry, leaving the field to Japan and Russia.

Setting aside any consideration of the aesthetics of such unrestricted slaughtering of these magnificent and intelligent animals, what can be said about the whaling industry's performance? For one thing, of course, their drive toward self-destruction tends to contradict the commonly held notion that people would change their behavior if they realized that it was against their own self-interest. The whaling industry has operated against its own long-term self-interest continually since 1963, in full knowledge of what it was doing. Short-term self-interest, the lure of the "quick buck," clearly is too strong to allow the long-range best interest of everyone to prevail. This is just one example of a cost-benefit analysis done over too short a term (see Chapter 12).

Cetologist Roger Payne of Rockefeller University has pointed out the ultimate absurdity of the whaling industry's behavior. It is now in such difficulties that the Soviet Union has moved into the business of harvesting krill, the abundant antarctic shrimp that is the primary source of food for the baleen whales. All of the species mentioned above except the sperm whale belong to a group called baleen whales—those that sieve their food out of vast amounts of sea water by means of a hairlike mesh of whalebone in their mouths (they do not have functional teeth). The best krill-catch rates achieved thus far by large ships in the densest clouds of krill have been about 12 tons per day. Even if this rate could be maintained for 24 hours a day, and if oil and protein could be extracted at 80 percent efficiency (an extremely high efficiency), the catch would still be less than the krill equivalent of the whale catch (krill is 6 percent oil and 20 percent protein). As Payne says, killing whales and harvesting krill "is like wiping out beef cattle in order to have the pleasure of eating grass-protein-concentrate." What the whalers do not seem to recognize is that the most efficient way to utilize the krill is not by harvesting it, but by leaving it unexploited so that the catch of whales could be sustained.

Technological "space-age" advances have greatly aided the whalers in their overexploitation. Ship-based helicopters locate whales and then guide killer boats to the quarry. The killer boats hunt by sonar, killing the quarry with an explosive harpoon head attached to a nylon line with an 18-ton test strength. The dead whale is inflated with compressed air so it will not sink, and a radio beacon is attached to the catch so that the towboat can find it and tow it to the factory ship, where it is rapidly processed.

Similar technological advances are already being applied to other major fisheries around the world. The Soviet Union and other eastern European nations have moved into big-time fishing with a vengeance. A single Rumanian factory ship equipped with modern devices caught in one day in New Zealand waters as many tons of fish as the whole New Zealand fleet of some 1,500 vessels. *Simrad Echo,* a Norwegian periodical published by a manufacturer of sonar fishing equipment, boasted in 1966 that industrialized herring fishing had come to the Shetland Islands, where 300 sonar-equipped Norwegian and Icelandic purse-seiners had landed undreamed-of quantities of herring. An editorial in the magazine queried, "Will the British fishing industry turn . . . to purse-seining as a means of reversing the decline in the herring catch?" Another quotation from the same magazine gives further insight: "What then are the Shetlands going to do in the immediate future? Are they going to join and gather the bonanza while the going is good—or are they going to continue drifting and if seining is found to have an adverse effect on the herring stocks find their catches dwindling?" The answer is now clear. In January 1969, British newspapers announced that the country's east coast herring industry had been wiped out. The purse-seiners took the immature herring that had escaped the British drifter's nets, which are of larger mesh, and the potential breeding stock was destroyed.

The April 1967 issue of *Simrad Echo* contains another example of activities in the modern fishing industry. In an article discussing a newspaper item about a purse-seiner that was being built by a Norwegian shipyard for Peru, which has one of the world's major anchovy fisheries in the rich Humboldt Current, *Simrad Echo* says:

> Fish-rich Peru nurses an ever-growing apprehension. Increasingly it is asked: surely the anchovy stocks off the coast—seemingly limitless at present—cannot sustain catch losses running into millions of tons year after year?
>
> Behind the news item lies what many people consider to be the answer to the Peruvian question—bigger and better equipped boats to augment the hundreds of small 'day trip' purse-seiners engaged in the stupendous coastal fishery.
>
> They theorize that if the present abundant stocks *do* start to get scarce there will be boats on the scene able to go much further afield and be suitably equipped to track fish down.
>
> They theorize further that *now* is the time for action, while things are still relatively good, not at the last moment of truth. In the meantime valuable experience can be gained in operating the latest fish-finding devices, such as echo sounders and sonars.

One wonders whether the author of these words (and the captains of industry who promote these electronic marvels) ever heard of the fable of the goose that laid the golden eggs.

Other examples of overexploited stocks are East Asian and California sardines; Northwest Pacific salmon; cod in many areas; menhaden; tunas in the Atlantic, Pacific, and Indian Oceans; flat-fish in the Bering Sea; plaice in the North Sea; hake and haddock in the North Atlantic; and bottom fish in the West Pacific and East Atlantic oceans. Some fish stocks, such as Pacific hake, South Atlantic herring, Yellow Sea bottom fish, anchovy off California, and clupeids in the Atlantic and Indian oceans, are at present underexploited. It seems unlikely they will remain so for long, at least wherever their numbers are not too dispersed for efficient fishing.

Unfortunately, as biologist Garrett Hardin of the University of California at Santa Barbara has pointed out, the sea is a "commons," analogous to a communal pasture open to all. From the point of view of an individual herder exploiting such a pasture commons, there seems to be every reason to keep adding to his herd. Although the grass is limited he will get a larger share if he has a larger herd. If his animals do not eat the grass, someone else's will. Such reasoning is, of course, followed by each user of the commons. Individuals struggle to increase their herds until, at some point, the carrying capacity of the pasture is exceeded and it is destroyed by overgrazing. Similarly, in the sea each individual, company, or country exploiting a fish stock (equivalent to the grass of the pasture) strives to get a maximum share of the catch because each increment represents further immediate profit. Unless some strict agreement is reached about the degree of utilization of the fishery commons, maximum utilization seems the best short-range strategy from the point of view of each user. After all, the Japanese reason, if we don't get the fish, the Russians will. The Russians take a similar view, as do the Peruvians and all the others. Unhappily, the end result of all these individual optimum strategies for dealing with the commons is disaster for all.

The race to loot the sea of its protein is now in full swing. Fish catches more than doubled between 1953 and 1968. Peru, Japan, and Russia took the lion's share in 1968, jointly landing almost 40 percent of the catch (the catch of the People's Republic of China is not included here). The United States and Norway, who came next, landed some 7 percent between them. The pressures of competition are beginning to show. Soviet fishing ships make headlines by penetrating waters off both coasts of the United States and Canada. In 1971, they were accused of interfering with the activities of American lobstermen and destroying some of their equipment. Between 1961 and 1971 the Peruvian government seized 30 United States tuna fishing boats, and Ecuador had taken 70 others in disputes over the limits of territorial waters. Ecuador and Peru each claim sovereignty over the ocean within 200 miles of their shores. In early 1971, Ecuador seized 24 U.S. tuna boats, and the issue threatened to bring on a serious diplomatic crisis. The activities of far-ranging Japanese fishing fleets have aroused the antagonism of the Mexicans, and Cuban fishing boats have been seized in Florida waters. The list of conflicts grows, and will undoubtedly continue to do so unless competition is regulated.

Since only a few percent of the world's calories come from the sea, one might easily draw the conclusion that a reduction of per capita yield is not particularly important. Unhappily, it is extremely serious. Although food from the sea provides comparatively few calories, it supplies almost one-fifth of the world's animal protein, and two-fifths of it exclusive of milk and eggs (see Fig. 4-6). For some countries the loss of this protein would be catastrophic. Japan's fisheries, for instance, supply her with more than one-and-one-half times as much protein as is provided by her agriculture.

What about "farming" the sea? Unfortunately, the impression that sea farming is here today, or just around the corner, is illusory. For the most part we still hunt the sea today, or in a realtively few cases herd it (for example, we herd oysters). It is certainly true that we can increase our yields from sea-herding. In 1965 some 66 thousand metric tons of yellowtail were produced in Japan's Inland Sea, more than 80 percent from fishes raised in net cages, and yields since then show an upward trend. The potential of both fresh- and salt-water herding (fish culture or aquaculture) is considerable, although it must be emphasized that the potential is small compared to the scale of the world food problem, and increasing pollution now threatens our hope of realizing even this potential.

Farming the sea presents an array of formidable problems, especially of fertilizing and harvesting. About the only planting and harvesting of marine plant crops done today is some seaweed culture in Japan, and this is really best viewed as an extension of land agriculture into shallow water. Perhaps if the sea is finally emptied of its fishes and shellfishes, some kind of phytoplankton farming could be attempted (if the sea is not by then too badly poisoned by pollution). The crop would be extremely costly at best, and it would not be very tasty, but in desperation we might give it a try. For the immediate future, however, sea-farming offers no hope at all.

Plans for increasing the yield of fishes from the sea have disregarded the effects of pollution and are based on the premise that the fish stocks will be harvested rationally. The history of fisheries so far gives little hope that rationality will prevail. One can, for instance, expect continuation of attempts to harvest simultaneously young and old of the same species, and both the big fishes and the little fishes that big fishes must eat to live. And one can expect pollution to help reduce the size of many or all fish populations.

Thus, far from being a food panacea, the sea may not even be able to continue to support the limited yield we now extract from it. The 1969 setback may be the beginning of a long downward trend. Judging from the fishing industry's behavior toward the sea, one might conclude that if they were to go into the chicken-farming business they would plan to eat up all the feed, all the eggs, all the chicks, and all the chickens simultaneously, while burning down the henhouses to keep themselves warm.

## Novel Sources of Food

What about some of the other proposed solutions to the world food problem that we often see in the public press? Certain food novelties do have potential for helping to alleviate the protein shortage. For instance, protein-rich material can be produced by culturing single-celled organisms on petroleum or other substrates. Theoretically, much, if not all, of the world's protein deficit in the last two decades of this century *could* be made up with protein from such sources. Knowledgeable people think it conceivable that single-cell protein (SCP) could be made sufficiently pure for human consumption by 1980, although whether the purification costs would make it uneconomical is another question. After that the problem would be one of building the requisite plants, arranging for distribution, and solving local political and economic problems relative to SCP use. Perhaps most important of all, people will then have to be convinced that SCP is food. As has been mentioned before, people tend to be extremely conservative in their food habits. The hungriest people are precisely those who recognize the fewest items as food. They have always existed on a diet of limited variety. Even though most Americans are used to an extremely varied diet, many would choose to starve to death rather than eat grasshoppers and snakes—which are perfectly nutritious, but are not generally acceptable as food in our culture.

British Petroleum has built an SCP plant in France which opened in 1971 with an annual production capacity of 16,000 tons. Earlier pilot plants produced yeasts grown on paraffins from refining wastes. The yeasts have been successfully used as a livestock feed supplement under the name "Tropina." The new French plant will grow bacteria on another refining waste, gas oil. The protein content of this form of single-cell protein ranges between 40 and 65 percent, but there is usually a lack of one or two essential amino acids. BP hopes to be producing 100,000 tons of SCP per year by 1974. Meanwhile, other companies in a number of countries including the U.S., Japan, Taiwan, India, Nigeria, U.S.S.R. and possibly China have begun pilot projects using hydrocarbons as substrates. Total production by 1975 may range between 300,000 and 500,000 tons, or somewhat less than .5 percent of the protein content of the world food grain harvest. While it will be many years before SCP suitable for human food will be available, it can fairly soon begin making an indirect contribution as animal food. It could, for instance, replace fish protein concentrate and oilseed cakes, which can alternatively be fed to people. SCP from petroleum hydrocarbons obviously will be available only as long as supplies of petroleum last and are not prohibitively expensive. However, since the substrates usually are otherwise waste byproducts, SCP may have an important role to fill, if all the technical, social and economic problems can be worked out.

Other ways of reducing the protein deficit are being actively promoted. Work is going ahead on the production of grains with higher quality proteins, those which contain a better balance of the protein building-blocks (amino acids) that are necessary for human nutrition. This is being done both by breeding new varieties and by fortifying grain grown from traditional varieties. This is critically important work, and, if successful, it could make a substantial contribution to the improvement of the human diet. The plant breeding programs take a good deal of time, but would doubtless be more satisfactory in the long run. Lysine-enrichment of wheat has been shown to be beneficial to rats and human babies under rigidly controlled conditions. Whether its benefits are well enough demonstrated to warrant large-scale introduction is still a matter of debate.

New protein foods have been produced by adding oilseed protein concentrates to foods made from cereals. The best known of these is Incaparina, developed by INCAP (Institute of Nutrition for Central America and Panama). It is a mixture of corn and cottonseed meal enriched with vitamins A and B. Another is CSM formula (corn, soya, milk), a mixture of 70 percent processed corn, 25 percent soy protein concentrate, and 5 percent milk solids. A third is Vita-Soy, a high-protein beverage now being marketed very successfully in Hong Kong. These and all similar products should be viewed more as "future hopes" than as current cures. As valuable protein and vitamin supplements, they hold considerable promise, but the economics of their production and distribution are not well worked out. More important, the question of their general acceptability remains open. Incaparina has been available in Central America for more than a decade, but its impact, to quote the Paddock brothers, "remains insignificant." It remains insignificant in the face of determined efforts by private and commercial organizations to push its acceptance, and in spite of tremendous worldwide publicity. The Paddocks consider the principal problem to be its bland taste and texture. As they say, "The food tastes of a people are truly puzzling and as difficult to alter as their views on family planning." Efforts should nonetheless be continued to promote Incaparina and other protein-rich products made from oilseeds. The presscakes that remain after oil is squeezed out of soybeans, cottonseed, peanuts, and sesame seeds are perhaps the most accessible untapped source of protein for human consumption. Today much of it is wasted; the rest is used as livestock feed or fertilizer.

Other unorthodox ways of providing more food are presently being discussed or are under preliminary development. These include herding such animals as the South American capybara (a rodent) and the African eland (an antelope), which are not now being herded except experimentally; converting water hyacinths and other aquatic weeds to cattle feed, making cattle feed from wood, extracting protein from leaves and little fishes, and culturing algae in the fecal slime of sewage treatment plants. Some of these hold promise, at least to help local situations. But most are subject to serious problems.

For instance, although herding native antelopes instead of cattle might improve meat yields from African plains, this would be practical only where cattle herding is not already practiced. Many African herders base their culture on an extraordinarily intricate relationship with their cattle. The economy, social structure, indeed their entire lives revolve around their animals. These groups would not take kindly to antelope herding. And, although water hyacinths are abundant (and pestiferous—they clog waterways) and contain protein that is high in the essential amino acid lysine, their dry weight is only 5 percent of their wet weight, which presents a tremendous obstacle in processing them even into cattle feed. An attempt to herd manatees (walrus-like animals), which eat the hyacinths, has proven unsuccessful.

Much has been written about fish protein concentrate (FPC) as a valuable protein source. It may help, but it is no panacea. Its chief advantage might be that it would exploit fish stocks that are largely unexploited at present; but the corollary disadvantage is that these often supply food for stocks that we do catch at present. FPC harvesting is subject to all the problems of fishing in general, and the processing is relatively complex and demands an expensive factory. It also seems to be more costly, at least at the present stage of development, than protein concentrates from other sources. The acceptability of FPC involves the same problems as for SCP and Incaparina.

Leaf protein extracts present the same social and economic drawbacks that affect SCP and FPC. A technical difficulty is the extraction of the protein concentrate from the fiber content of the leaves, but this has been done successfully in small-scale projects and presumably could be done on a large scale if a sufficient investment were made in the equipment. The leaves of forage crops such as alfalfa and sorghum produce large proportions of high quality protein. Alfalfa yields 2,400 pounds of protein per acre. It has been estimated that enough alfalfa could be raised in an area equivalent to about 7 percent of the land now under cultivation to provide the minimum protein needs of the world's present population. The fibrous residue can still be used as fodder for ruminant animals such as cattle, and these crops can be grown on soils too poor or hilly to support grains. The advantages of leaf protein would certainly appear to justify a reasonably large effort to develop it. But it would obviously be many years before production could reach the point where it made a significant contribution to the world food problem.

Finally, the reaction of people in the UDCs (or in DCs for that matter) to proposals to feed them protein grown on sewage can well be imagined, although algae grown in other ways may prove to have some value, especially as animal feed.

We must, of course, press ahead to develop novel foods and, especially, to find ways to make them acceptable to diverse peoples. But it is reasonably clear that few of them will be a major factor in the world food picture during the critical decade or two ahead. Hopefully, if mankind can survive, the most ecologically, economically, nutritionally, and aesthetically desirable of these processes will eventually be integrated into normal food supplies.

## Reduction of Food Losses

One area in which technology can greatly help to improve the food supply is in reduction of losses in the field, in transit, and in storage. For instance, the Indian Food and Agriculture Ministry estimated that in 1968 rats consumed almost 10 percent of India's grain production, and others think 12 percent is more nearly accurate. It would take a train almost 3,000 miles long to haul the grain India's rats eat in a single year. And yet in 1968 India spent $265 million on importing fertilizers, about *800 times* as much as was spent on rat control. The rats in two Philippine provinces in 1952–1954 consumed 90 percent of the rice, 20–80 percent of the maize, and more than 50 percent of the sugar cane. Since 1960, birds in Africa have destroyed crops worth more than $7 million annually. Insects in UDCs may destroy as much as 50 percent of a stock of grain in a year's storage period. Spoilage from molds, mildews, and bacteria also takes a heavy toll, even in the DCs. As a guess, the development of good storage and transport facilities alone might increase UDC food supplies by as much as 10 to 20 percent.

The problems of controlling populations of insect pests in fields are discussed in Chapter 7. Reducing these losses requires great care to avoid serious ecological problems. Controlling rats, birds, rusts, and other non-insect pests in fields also presents similar problems. Protection of foods once they are harvested, however, is much more straightforward and ordinarily involves much less ecological risk. Storage facilities may be made rat-proof, be refrigerated, and be fumigated with nonpersistent pesticides which are not released into the environment until they have lost their toxicity. Transport systems may be improved so that more rapid movement, proper handling, refrigeration where necessary, and other measures greatly reduce spoilage en route. Perhaps the safest investment man could make toward improving the quantity and quality of food would be to improve his methods of handling, shipping and storing crops after the harvest.

## Should We Be Pessimistic?

As must be apparent by now, we tend not to share the enthusiasm of many for various proposed "solutions" to the world food problem. The most practical solution, that of increasing yield on land already under cultivation (the Green Revolution), presents great difficulties. This and other programs are usually carried out with little consideration for their ecological consequences, and all too often they neglect the critical importance of high-quality protein in the human diet. Still, if we press on with many of these programs simultaneously, we may buy some badly needed time to start bringing the population explosion to a halt. It is certainly evident that no conceivable increase in food supply can keep up with the current population growth rates over the long term. We emphatically agree with the report of the President's Science Advisory Committee's Panel on the World Food Supply, which in 1967 stated: "The solution to the problem that will exist after about 1985 *demands* that programs of population control be initiated now."

The basic questions for the next decade or so seem to be:

1. Will the weather be favorable?
2. Can apparent breakthroughs in UDC agriculture be sustained and converted into real revolutions in spite of the substantial problems associated with their achievement?
3. Will the ecological price paid for a Green Revolution be too high?
4. Can we rapidly develop international agreements for rational use of the sea?

Only time will bring the answers. Obviously, the most prudent course is to work for the best but prepare for the worst.

# Bibliography

Addison, Herbert, 1961. *Land, Water and Food.* Chapman & Hall, Ltd., London. Describes barrages, tube wells, etc., in a general discussion of irrigation and land reclamation.

Allaby, M., 1970. One jump ahead of Malthus. *The Ecologist,* vol. 1, no. 1, pp. 24–28 (July). Discussion of FAO's Indicative World Plan for agricultural development.

Allaby, M., 1970. Green revolution: social boomerang. *The Ecologist,* vol. 1, no. 3 (Sept.)

Altschul, Aaron M., 1967. Food proteins: new sources from seeds. *Science,* vol. 158, pp. 221–226 (13 Oct.). Describes a potential source for protein supplement.

Altschul, A. M., 1969. Food: Protein for humans. *Chemical and Engineering News,* vol. 47, pp. 68–81 (24 Nov.) On possible sources of protein supplement.

Altschul, A. M., and D. Rosenfield, 1970. Protein supplementation: Satisfying man's food needs. *Unilever Quarterly,* vol. 54, no. 305, pp. 26–84 (March). On protein-fortified foods.

Alverson, D. L., A. R. Longhurst, and J. A. Gulland, 1970. How much food from the sea? *Science,* vol. 168, pp. 503–505 (24 April). Discussion of Ryther's estimates on potential fish production and Ryther's reply.

*Asian Agricultural Survey,* 1969. Asian Development Bank. University of Washington Press, Seattle.

Bardach, John, 1968. *Harvest of the Sea.* Harper & Row, New York. An overview of the oceans—reasonably optimistic.

Berg, Alan. 1970. Role of nutrition in national development. *Technology Review.* Feb.

Boerma, Addeke H., 1970. A world agriculture plan, *Scientific American,* vol. 223, no. 2, pp. 54–69. An optimistic view of the FAO's Indicative World Plan for agricultural development.

Borgstrom, Georg, 1967. *Hungry Planet.* Collier-Macmillan, Toronto. See especially the discussion of fisheries.

Borgstrom, Georg, 1968. *Principles of Food Science.* Collier-Macmillan, New York. Useful for those interested in food technology.

Borgstrom, Georg, 1969. *Too Many.* Collier-Macmillan, Toronto. An excellent discussion of the limits of food production.

Borgstrom, Georg, 1970. Dual challenge of health and hunger: global crisis. *Bulletin of Atomic Scientists.* Oct. pp. 42–46.

Borlaug, Norman, 1971. The green revolution, peace and humanity. *PRB Selection no. 35.* Population Reference Bureau, Washington, D.C. A condensation of Dr. Borlaug's speech on receiving the Nobel Prize in December, 1970, for his work in developing high-yield varieties of wheat.

Boyko, Hugo, 1967. Salt water agriculture. *Scientific American,* pp. 89–96 (March).

Brown, Lester R., 1970. Human food production as a process in the biosphere. *Scientific American,* vol. 233, no. 3, pp. 160–170 (Sept.). Scientific American Offprint No. 1196, W. H. Freeman and Company, San Francisco; reprinted in Ehrlich et al. (see below).

Brown, Lester R., 1970. *Seeds of Change: The Green Revolution and Development in the 1970's.* Frederick A. Praeger, New York. A current analysis of the Green Revolution and its impact on the various aspects of development strategy by an author eminently qualified to discuss the topic.

Brown, L. R., and G. Finsterbusch, 1971. Man, food and environment. *In* W. N. Murdoch (ed.), *Environment: Resources, Pollution and Society.* Sinauer Associates, Stamford, Conn. An excellent summary.

Carefort, G. L., and E. R. Sprott, 1967. *Famine on the Wind*. Rand-McNally, New York. Popular story of the battle against plant diseases.

Champagnat, Alfred, 1965. Protein from petroleum. *Scientific American,* vol. 213, no. 4, pp. 13–17 (Oct.). Scientific American Offprint No. 1020, W. H. Freeman and Company, San Francisco. A paper on a possible form of protein supplement: yeast grown on petroleum.

Chao, Kang. 1970. *Agricultural Production in Communist China, 1949–1965.* Univ. of Wisconsin Press, Madison.

Chedd, Graham, 1969. Famine or sanity? *New Scientist* (Oct. 23). A critical review of plans to increase world food production.

Chedd, Graham, 1970. Hidden peril of the green revolution. *New Scientist,* 22 Oct. pp. 171–173. A discussion of the loss of genetic variability in crops.

Christy, Frances T., Jr., and Anthony Scott, 1965. *The Common Wealth in Ocean Fisheries.* Johns Hopkins Press, Baltimore. See especially the discussion of the productivity of the sea.

Clawson, M., H. H. Landsberg, and L. T. Alexander, 1969. Desalted seawater for agriculture: is it economic? *Science,* vol. 164, pp. 1141–1148. Detailed critique of desalting procedure.

Cloudsley-Thompson, John, and Anne Cloudsley-Thompson, 1970. Prospects for arid lands. *New Scientist,* 5 Nov. pp. 286–288.

Cole, Darryl G., 1968. The myth of fertility dooms development plans. *National Observer* (April 22).

Cole, H. H., ed., 1966. *Introduction to Livestock Production, Including Dairy and Poultry,* 2d ed. W. H. Freeman and Company, San Francisco. A basic source.

Curwen, E. C., and Gudmund Hatt, 1953. *Plough and Pasture.* Henry Schuman, New York. Deals with the early history of farming.

Dalrymple, Dana G. 1971. Imports and plantings of high yielding varieties of wheat and rice in the less developed nations. *Foreign Economic Development Report* No. 8, USDA/USAID.

DeGarine, Igor, 1971. Food is not just something to eat. *Ceres,* vol. 4, no. 1, pp. 46–51 (Jan.–Feb.). A study of food habits in various cultures.

Deneven, William M., 1970. Aboriginal drained-field cultivation in the Americas. *Science,* vol. 169, pp. 647–654 (14 Aug.). Ancient land reclamation techniques which might usefully be restored.

Dumont, René, and Bernard Rosier, 1969. *The Hungry Future.* Frederick A. Praeger, New York. See especially the discussion of agricultural problems in socialist countries.

Dyson-Hudson, Rada, and Neville Dyson-Hudson, 1969. Subsistence herding in Uganda. *Scientific American,* Feb. On an African cattle culture.

Ehrlich, P. R., and J. P. Holdren, 1969. Population and panaceas—A technological perspective. *BioScience,* vol. 19, no. 12 (Dec.) p. 1065. Reprinted in Holdren and Ehrlich, *Global Ecology* (see below). Discussion of limitations imposed by logistics, economics, and lead time on large-scale technological attempts to increase world food supply.

Ehrlich, P. R., J. P. Holdren, and R. W. Holm (eds.), 1971. *Man and the Ecosphere.* W. H. Freeman and Company, San Francisco. Important papers from *Scientific American* with critical commentaries.

Environmental Systems Group, 1969. *A Model of Society.* Institute of Ecology, University of California, Davis.

Food and Agriculture Organization of the United Nations. *Fisheries Year-book*. FAO, Rome. Issued annually.

Food and Agriculture Organization of the United Nations, *Production Yearbook*. FAO-UN. Rome. A basic source for agricultural data.

Food and Agriculture Organization of the United Nations. *Ceres*. A journal on world agriculture.

Food and Agriculture Organization of the United Nations. *State of Food and Agriculture*. Annual volume.

Foreign Agricultural Service. *Foreign Agriculture*. U.S. Department of Agriculture. Washington, D.C. A monthly journal.

Frankel, O. H., W. K. Agble, J. B. Harlan, and Erna Bennett, 1969. Genetic dangers in the green revolution. *Ceres* (FAO) vol. 2, no. 5, pp. 35–37 (Sept.–Oct.). Describes the loss of genetic variation in crops as new varieties replace diversity of older ones.

Frankel, O. H., and E. Bennett, 1970. Genetic Resources in Plants—Their Exploration and Conservation. F. A. Davis Company, Philadelphia. A comprehensive sourcebook.

Galston, A., 1971. Crops without chemicals. *New Scientist,* 3 June, pp. 577–580. How genetic manipulation may someday allow creation of nitrogen-fixing and disease resistant plants.

Goldblith, Samuel A., 1968. World food crisis, *Technology Review,* vol. 70, no. 8 (June) pp. 20–29. Discusses role of technology in agricultural development.

Hardin, Garrett, 1968. The tragedy of the commons. *Science,* vol. 162, pp. 1243–1248. Reprinted in Hardin, *Population, Evolution, and Birth Control,* 2d ed. W. H. Freeman and Company, San Francisco, and in Holdren and Ehrlich (see below).

Harlan, Jack R., and Daniel Zohary, 1966. Distribution of wild wheats and barley, *Science,* vol. 153, pp. 1074–1079 (2 Sept.). About early agriculture.

Heiser, Charles B., Jr., 1969. Some considerations of early plant domestication. *BioScience,* vol. 19, no. 3, pp. 228–231 (March).

Hendricks, Sterling B., 1969. Food from the land. *In* P. E. Cloud, Jr. (ed.), *Resources and Man.* (chapter 4.) W. H. Freeman and Company, San Francisco. A hardheaded look at the food problem; the last section contains a good summary of what might be possible if an all-out effort to feed the world were undertaken.

Holdren, J. P., and P. R. Ehrlich (eds.) 1971. *Global Ecology*. Harcourt Brace and Jovanovich, New York. This collection contains several important papers on world food supplies, as well as many other aspects of the interaction of population with resources and environment.

Howe, E. E., G. R. Jansen, and M. L. Anson, 1967. An approach toward the solution of the world food problem with special emphasis on protein supply. *American Journal of Clinical Nutrition,* vol. 20, no. 10, pp. 1134–1147 (Oct.).

Hunter, J. R., and E. Camacho, 1961. Some observations on permanent mixed cropping in the humid tropics. *Turrialba,* vol. 11, no. 1, pp. 26–33. Jan.–March.

Idyll, C. P., 1970. *The Sea Against Hunger*. Thomas Y. Crowell Co., New York.

Iowa State University Center for Agricultural and Economic Development,

1967. *Alternatives for Balancing World Food Production and Needs.* Iowa State University Press, Ames, Iowa. Somewhat out of date, but contains interesting papers.

Janick, J., R. W. Schery, F. W. Woods, and V. W. Ruttan, 1969. *Plant Science.* W. H. Freeman and Company, San Francisco. A fine survey covering all aspects of man's use of plants.

Janzen, Daniel H., 1970. The unexploited tropics. *Bulletin of the Ecological Society of America,* Sept. pp. 4–7. A distinguished ecologist's view of agriculture in the tropics.

Johnson, Willard, 1968. Current innovation in world food production. *Journal of Law and Economic Development,* vol. II, no. 2. Contains some information on unorthodox foods.

Ladejinksy, Wolf, 1970. Ironies of India's green revolution. *Foreign Affairs,* July, pp. 758–768.

Leeds, Anthony, and Andrew P. Vayda (eds.), 1965. *Man, Culture and Animals.* American Association for the Advancement of Science, Washington, D.C. See especially chapters on cattle herding in Africa and sacred cows of India.

Martin, Paul S., 1970. Pleistocene niches for alien animals. *BioScience,* vol. 20, no. 4, pp. 218–221 (Feb. 15). Discussion of potential animal husbandry of so far unexploited animals.

McKenzie, John, 1968. Nutrition and the soft sell. *New Scientist,* 21 Nov. On the difficulties of introducing unorthodox foods.

McNeil, Mary, 1964. Lateritic soils. *Scientific American,* vol. 211, no. 5 (Nov.). Scientific American Offprint No. 870, W. H. Freeman and Company, San Francisco. Reprinted in Ehrlich et al. (see above).

Meier, Richard L., 1969. The social impact of a nuplex. *Bulletin of the Atomic Scientists,* March, pp. 16–21. Describes the many nontechnical problems of establishing nuclear agro-industrial complexes.

Morris, Ian, 1970. Restraints on the big fish-in. *New Scientist,* 3 Dec., pp. 373–375. Discussion of the limits on food from the sea.

The Nutrition Foundation, Inc., 1968. *Food Science and Society.* The Nutrition Foundation, Inc., Berkeley.

Odum, Howard T. 1971. *Environment, Power, and Society.* Wiley, New York. An interesting treatment of the energetics of ecosystems and man's involvement in energy flows. See especially the material on the energy subsidy of agriculture.

Ogburn, Charlton, 1970. Population and resources: the coming collision. *Population Bulletin,* vol. XXVI, no. 2 (June). Population Reference Bureau. Contains discussion of limitations on food production.

Owen, D. F., 1966. *Animal Ecology in Tropical Africa.* W. H. Freeman and Company, San Francisco.

Paddock, William C., 1967. Phytopathology in a hungry world. *Annual Review of Phytopathology,* vol. 5, pp. 375–390.

Paddock, William C., 1970. How green is the green revolution? *BioScience,* vol. 20, no. 16, pp. 897–902 (Aug. 15).

Paddock, William, and Paul Paddock, 1964. *Hungry Nations.* Little, Brown & Co., Boston. Good descriptions of conditions relating to UDC food production.

Paddock, William, and Paul Paddock, 1967. *Famine 1975!,* Little, Brown & Co., Boston. Discussion of the possibilities for revolutionizing UDC agriculture. Many consider the Paddocks overly pessimistic; "realistic" is a better appraisal, even though the Green Revolution may have slightly changed the timetable.

Patton, S., P. T. Chandler, E. B. Kalan, A. R. Loeblich III, G. Fuller, and A. A. Benson, 1967. Food value of red tide (Gonyaulax polyedra). *Science,* vol. 158, pp. 789–798. An example of a possible protein food developed from algae.

Paulik, G. J., 1971. Anchovies, birds and fishermen in the Peru Current. *In* W. W. Murdoch (ed.) *Environment: Resources, Pollution and Society.* Sinauer Associates, Stamford, Conn. A fine discussion of the oceanographic, economic, and sociological aspects of the Peruvian anchovy fishery by a distinguished figure in the field of mathematical analysis of resource management. Paulik's best conjecture of the potential production of all marine fish is 125 million tons per year.

Payne, Philip, and Erica Wheeler, 1971. What protein gap? *New Scientist,* 15 April, pp. 148–150. Discussion of complex factors affecting nutrition in UDCs.

Payne, Roger, 1968. Among wild whales. *New York Zoological Society Newsletter* (Nov.). A good summary of the whaling situation. Reprinted in Holdren and Ehrlich (see above).

Phillips, John, 1961. *The Development of Agriculture and Forestry in the Tropics.* Faber and Faber, London. Introduction to many of the problems faced by the UDCs.

Pirie, N. W., 1966. Leaf protein as human food. *Science,* vol. 152, pp. 1701–1705, (24 June). One of the most promising of the unorthodox sources of protein.

Pirie, N. W., 1967. Orthodox and unorthodox methods of meeting world food needs. *Scientific American,* vol. 216, no. 2, (Feb.), pp. 27–35. Scientific American Offprint No. 1068, W. H. Freeman and Company, San Francisco.

Pirie, N. W., 1969. *Food Resources, Conventional and Novel.* Penguin Books, Baltimore. See especially the material on novel foods.

The President's Science Advisory Committee Panel on the World Food Supply. 1967. *The World Food Problem* (3 vols.), Washington, D.C. A very detailed and basic source. Summaries and individual papers.

Pyke, Magnus, 1970. A taste of things to come. *New Scientist,* 17 Dec. On synthetic food supplements; today vitamins, in the future amino acids and fatty acids.

Ramsey, James E., 1969. FPC, *Oceans,* vol. 2, no. 2, pp. 76–80 (Aug.). On the potential value of fish protein concentrate.

Rasmussen, Clyde L., 1969. Man and his food: 2000 A.D. *Food Technology,* vol. 23, no. 5, pp. 56–74. Good summary of the food gap and economics of food distribution.

Ravenholt, A., 1971. Can one billion Chinese feed themselves? *Fieldstaff Reports,* East Asia Series, vol. XVIII, no. 2. American Universities Field Staff, P.O. Box 150, Hanover, N.H. 03755. An interesting look at the population food situation in China.

Ricker, William E., 1969. Food from the sea. *In* P. E. Cloud, Jr. (ed.), *Resources and Man* (Ch. 5). W. H. Freeman and Company, San Francisco. Slightly more optimistic than the estimates by Ryther.

Rounsefell, G. A., 1971. Potential food from the sea. *Journal of Marine*

*Science,* Bayou La Batre, Alabama, vol. 1, no. 3. Good summary article.

Ryther, John H., 1969. Photosynthesis and fish production in the sea. *Science,* vol. 166, pp. 72–76. An excellent discussion of the potential maximum sustainable fish yield to man. Reprinted in Holdren and Ehrlich (see above).

Schaeffer, Milner B., 1965. The potential harvest of the sea. *Transactions of the American Fisheries Society,* vol. 94, no. 2 (April), pp. 123–128. One of the more optimistic estimates of potential fish production.

Sewell, W., R. Derrik, Vincent Ostrom, Jones A. Crutchfield, E. Roy Tinney, and William F. Roger, 1967. Nawapa: a continental water system. *Bulletin of the Atomic Scientists,* Sept., pp. 8–27. A series of articles on the North American Water and Power Alliance.

Stanton, W. R., 1964. Some social problems in tropical agriculture. *Tropical Science,* vol. 6, no. 4, pp. 180–186.

Stauls, W. J., and M. G. Blase, 1971. Genetic technology and agricultural development. *Science,* vol. 173, pp. 119–123 (9 July). On some of the problems of the Green Revolution.

Sukhatme, P. V., 1966. The world's food supplies, *Royal Statistical Society Journal,* Ser. A, vol. 129, pp. 222–248.

Thurston, H. David, 1969. Tropical agriculture, a key to the world food crises. *BioScience,* vol. 19, no. 1, pp. 29–34 (Jan.).

Tatum, L. A., 1971. The southern corn leaf blight epidemic. *Science,* vol. 171, pp. 1113–1116 (19 March). On the corn blight that ruined an estimated one-sixth of the 1970 corn crop.

United Nations, *U.N. Statistical Yearbook,* New York. Annual volume full of information.

U.S. Department of Agriculture, 1964. *The World Food Budget, 1970.* Foreign Agriculture Report no. 19. Washington, D.C.

Walthen, Pat, 1969. Plant protein extracts may feed world's hungry. *University-Industry Research Progress.* University of Wisconsin, Feb., p. 17.

Watt, K. E. F., 1968. *Ecology and Resource Management.* McGraw-Hill, New York. See especially Chapters 4 and 5 of this fine book.

Went, Frits W., 1957. Climate and agriculture. *Scientific American,* vol. 196, no. 6 (June ). Scientific American Offprint No. 852, W. H. Freeman and Company, San Francisco.

Wharton, Clifton R., Jr., 1969. The green revolution: cornucopia or Pandora's box? *Foreign Affairs,* vol. 47, pp. 464–476 (April). An excellent summary of economic and social consequences of the Green Revolution.

Williams, G., and W. J. A. Payne, 1959. *An Introduction to Animal Husbandry in the Tropics.* Longmans, Green & Co. Ltd., London.

Yarwood, C. E., 1970. Man-made plant diseases. *Science,* vol. 168, pp. 218–220 (10 April). How efficient agriculture can foster plant diseases.

# CHAPTER 6

# Environmental Threats to Man

*"He will manage the cure best who foresees what is to
happen from the present condition of the patient"*

Hippocrates (ca. 460–377 B.C.)

*"Don't drink the water and don't breathe the air."*

Tom Lehrer, *Pollution,* 1965

In many ways man has made his environment much more hospitable in the past few centuries, as was noted in Chapter 2, but in some ways he has made it more hostile. Overpopulation and industrialization have contributed in various ways to the general deterioration of the environment upon which humanity is completely dependent for life. Only relatively recently has man been made somewhat aware of the harmful effects of the ever-increasing number of biologically active substances that he has produced and exposed himself to—substances with which *Homo sapiens* has had no evolutionary experience and against which human cells have evolved no natural defenses.

Direct threats to human health are the most obvious aspect of environmental deterioration, and of these direct threats the phenomena commonly lumped under the term "pollution" are the most widely discussed. Pollutants reach us through the air we breathe, the water we drink, the food we eat, and the sounds we hear. But these direct threats are not the only ones; they are merely the most obvious. Less obvious are the indirect effects of mankind's activities on the Earth's ecosystems—those complex environmental systems upon which all human existence ultimately depends. Because the problem of environmental deterioration is exceedingly vast and complex, we have chosen to discuss the direct and indirect effects in separate chapters; this chapter considers the direct assaults upon human physical and mental health; Chapter 7 explores the indirect effects upon ecosystems. Actually, many kinds of deterioration have both direct and indirect effects.

Before discussing some specific kinds of pollution in detail, it is helpful to clarify just what a pollutant is. Substances that are naturally present in the environment but that are released by man in significant additional amounts, we call *quantitative pollutants*. Synthetic substances—those produced and released only by man—we call *qualitative pollutants*.

Within the category of quantitative pollutants, there are three distinct criteria by which a man-made contribution may be judged significant. First, man can perturb a natural cycle with a large amount of a substance ordinarily considered innocuous, either by overloading part of the cycle (nitrogen, Chapter 7), by destabilizing a finely tuned balance ($CO_2$, Chapter 7), or by swamping the natural cycle completely (heat, in the very long term, Chapter 7). Second, an amount of material negligible compared to natural flows of the same thing can create a disaster if released in a sensitive spot, over a small area, or suddenly (oil, Chapter 7). Third, *any* addition of a substance that is dangerous even at its natural concentrations is significant (mercury, Chapter 6; sulfur dioxide, Chapter 6; many radioactive substances, Chapters 4 and 6). Such considerations show that it is meaningless to assert, as some have, that man's pollution is negligible compared to "nature's."

In the category of qualitative pollutants, of course, the situation is even more clear cut. There can be no question of the potential for harm from poisonous substances with which organisms have had no prior evolutionary experience (synthetic organic pesticides, PCBs, and herbicides, Chapters 6 and 7).

## Air Pollution

"The air nimbly and sweetly recommends itself unto our gentle senses." So wrote William Shakespeare in *Macbeth*. Would a poet of comparable skill living in a modern city be likely to express a similar sentiment? Probably not; the form of pollution that most of us are aware of is air pollution. Those of us who live in or near cities can see it, and we can feel it when it burns our eyes and irritates our lungs. Virtually every major metropolis of the world has serious air-pollution problems. Travelers know how often their first sight of a city can be spoiled by a pall of smog. Pollution at times cuts down the amount of sunlight that reaches New York by nearly 25 percent, and that reaching Chicago by approximately 40 percent, giving a foretaste of what the world can expect if current trends are allowed to continue. Today, however, it is not only the air over our cities that is polluted. The

*entire atmosphere* of our planet is now afflicted to some degree. Meteorologists talk about a nebulous veil of air pollution encircling the entire Earth.
Smog has been observed over oceans, over the North Pole, and in other unlikely places. Mankind is taxing the capacity of the atmosphere to absorb and
to transport away from areas of high population density the enormous
amounts of waste exhausted into it. Air pollution is now recognized not
only as an agent that rots nylon stockings and windshield wiper blades, that
corrodes paint and steel, blackens skies and the wash on the clothesline, and
damages $500 million worth of crops annually; it is recognized as a killer
of people.

Air pollution comes from many sources. According to the United States
Public Health Service, in the late 1960s our 90 million motor vehicles annually
spewed into the atmosphere 66 million tons of carbon monoxide, 1 million
tons of sulfur oxides, 6 million tons of nitrogen oxides, 12 million tons of
hydrocarbons, 1 million tons of particulate matter, and assorted other
dangerous substances, such as tetraethyl lead. Translated into daily amounts,
the figures mean that each day American cars exhaust into our atmosphere
a variety of pollutants weighing more than a bumper-to-bumper line of cars
stretching from Cleveland to New York.

The principal industrial sources of air pollution, according to the U.S.
Public Health Service, are pulp and paper mills, iron and steel mills, petroleum refineries, smelters, and chemical plants. Their annual contribution to
the atmosphere includes 2 million tons of carbon monoxide, 9 million tons of
sulfur oxides, 3 million tons of nitrogen oxides, nearly 1 million tons of
hydrocarbons, and 3 million tons of particulate matter. The fuel burned for
heating houses, apartments, and offices sends another 2 million tons of
carbon monoxide, 3 million tons of sulfur oxides, 1 million tons of hydrocarbons, and 1 million tons of particulate matter up flues and into the atmosphere each year. And, finally, trash burning adds about 1 million tons of
carbon monoxide, nearly 1 million tons of nitrogen oxides, 1 million tons of
hydrocarbons, 1 million tons of particulate matter, and about 100,000 tons
of sulfur oxides. In total, more than 140 million tons of these pollutants are
added annually to the atmosphere, almost three-quarters of a ton for every
man, woman, and child in the United States.

For many human beings air pollution has already proven lethal. Death
rates are above normal when and where smog occurs. The demise of the
very old, the very young, and those with respiratory ailments is accelerated.
Perhaps the most dramatic case thus far recorded was the London smog
disaster of 1952 (see Box 6-1). But such disasters have still been of less
significance to public health than have the less spectacular but ultimately
more far-reaching effects that day-to-day exposure has on people living in
seriously polluted localities. In 1969, sixty faculty members of the Medical
School of the University of California at Los Angeles made a recommendation
to the residents of southern California's smoggy areas. Their statement read,
in part: "air pollution has now become a major health hazard to most of
this community during much of the year . . . ," and they advised "anyone

who does not have compelling reasons to remain to move out of smoggy portions of Los Angeles, San Bernardino, and Riverside counties to avoid chronic respiratory diseases like bronchitis and emphysema." It is estimated that physicians in private practice around Los Angeles recommend to about 10,000 patients a year that they leave the area as part of their treatment.

What are the general effects of individual air pollutants on health? Carbon monoxide combines with the pigment hemoglobin in our blood, displacing the oxygen that hemoglobin normally transports. In fact, carbon monoxide binds to hemoglobin more efficiently and tightly than oxygen does.

---

BOX 6-1   AIR POLLUTION DISASTERS

Donora, Pennsylvania, is a small town in the steep valley of the Monongahela River; in 1948 it had a population of 12,300. Because of the steepness of the surrounding hills it tends to be even smokier than other mill towns. In the autumn, fog is often added to the smoke, making the mixture smog (smog equals smoke plus fog in the strict sense of the word, but air pollution not involving fog, such as that found in Los Angeles, is now commonly called "smog"). On Tuesday, October 26, 1948, a thermal inversion (a layer of warm air above a layer of cold air; see Fig. 6-2) trapped fog and smoke producing a lethal situation. The red, black, and yellow smoke from Donora's huge wire factory, zinc and sulfuric acid plants, and steel factory lingered for days over the grimy town, and the upper layer of fog absorbed the sun's heat, creating more warm air above the cold and intensifying the inversion. The smog persisted through Sunday, and 6,000 people, nearly half the people in the area, were made ill as a result. Fifteen men and five women died, and the lives of many others may have been shortened.

A similar smog occurred in London in 1952; the combination of fog and thermal inversion was accompanied by severe cold weather. London's homes were heated by coal, and the cold greatly increased fuel consumption and the production of smoke. The atmospheric content of sulfur dioxide rose to double its usual level. The episode started on Friday, December 5, and by Sunday the smog had reduced visibility to only one yard in parts of London, and created multitudes of hard-to-credit situations. For example, so much smog seeped into theaters that only people in the first four rows could see the cinema screen. People inadvertently walked off of quays along the Thames and fell into the river. A pilot trying to taxi to the terminal at London Airport after an instrument landing got lost, as did the party sent to search for him. The consensus is that about 4,000 deaths were directly attributable to the London smog.

There have, of course, been other smog disasters, as well as many close calls. Two often-cited cases occurred in the Meuse Valley of Belgium in 1930 and at Poza Rica near Mexico City in 1950. When the next smog "disaster" will come, no one knows. But in August 1969 citizens of both Los Angeles and St. Louis were warned by doctors not to play golf, jog, or do anything that involved deep breathing because of the air-pollution hazards that prevailed. The activities of school children in the Los Angeles basin are curtailed on doctors' orders with increasing frequency, and attrition of the health of asthmatics and others with respiratory or cardiovascular problems continues.

Carbon monoxide tends to cause suffocation by occupying the high-speed transport system which in the human organism normally guarantees a steady renewal of the supply of oxygen necessary to maintain metabolism in the cells. When oxygen supply to the cells is reduced, the heart must work harder, as must the respiratory mechanism. These effects may produce a critical strain in people with heart and lung diseases. When a person lives for eight hours in an atmosphere containing 80 parts per million (ppm) of carbon monoxide, the oxygen-carrying capacity of the circulatory system is diminished by about 15 percent. This has about the same effect as the loss of more than a pint of blood. When traffic is badly snarled, the carbon monoxide content of the air may approach 400 ppm. Symptoms of acute poisoning, often experienced by people in traffic jams and on freeways, include headache, loss of vision, decreased muscular coordination, nausea, and abdominal pain. In extreme cases, unconsciousness, convulsions, and death follow. Cases of chronic carbon monoxide poisoning have been reported, and an association between high concentrations of atmospheric carbon monoxide with higher mortality in Los Angeles County has been demonstrated for the years 1962–1965.

Oxides of sulfur are contributors to respiratory disease. Sulfur dioxide has caused attacks of severe respiratory illness in older patients with chronic lung disease. Most sulfur compounds are harshly irritating to respiratory passages, causing coughing and choking. Their effects are thought to be a major cause of the abnormal death tolls that have occurred during smog disasters. A 1968 press release put out by the University of Chicago Toxicity Laboratory stated, "sulfur dioxide produced by coal burning adheres to coal dust particles and spreads through urban air. These particles get into our lungs and create sulfuric acids, which can be highly dangerous."

Sulfur dioxide has been implicated in the increased rates of acute and chronic asthma, bronchitis, and emphysema observed in people exposed to severe air pollution. Asthma is an allergic supersensitivity of the bronchial tree, the set of branching tubes that carry air from the trachea to the lungs (Fig. 6-1). An asthmatic attack causes the muscles that encircle the "twigs" of the bronchial tree to contract and narrow the tubes. The victim is able to inhale air, but is unable to exhale with sufficient force to clear the lungs. The result is a distension of the lungs: input exceeds output. Carbon dioxide builds up in the lungs, and the victim also suffers oxygen deprivation. Asthma attacks kill several hundred Americans a year; even those that are not lethal often last for long periods and may lead to more or less permanent changes in the breathing apparatus.

Bronchitis, inflammation of the bronchial tree, leads to difficulty in expelling foreign matter from the lungs by coughing. The muscles surrounding the bronchial tubes weaken, and mucus accumulates. There is a progressive loss of breathing ability. Bronchitis is often accompanied by emphysema, a disease of the air sacs in the lungs. These air sacs tend to fuse, essentially coalescing from clusters of small pouches to form larger ones. This is accompanied by a narrowing of the finer branches of the bronchial tree. The

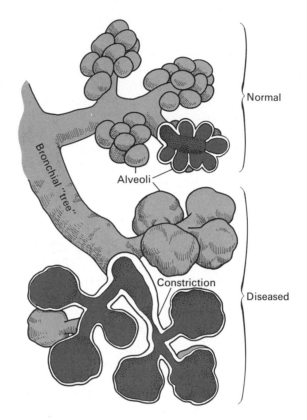

FIGURE 6-1

Bronchitis-emphysema, a disease that is caused or aggravated by air pollution. In the normal lung the bronchial tubes branch into millions of tiny chambers (alveoli), where transfer of oxygen to blood takes place. In the diseased lung the alveoli coalesce, reducing the amount of surface available for oxygen transfer. Furthermore, the "twigs" of the bronchial tree are constricted, reducing the rate at which air is exchanged. (After McDermott, "Air Pollution and Public Health." Copyright © 1961 by Scientific American, Inc. All rights reserved.)

combined results are a reduction of total surface area for the exchange of oxygen between air and blood stream and a reduction of the amount of air flow through the lungs. This process takes place gradually over a period of years, while the lungs become progressively less capable of proxiding oxygen for activity. The victim of emphysema ultimately dies of suffocation.

Nitrogen oxides affect man in much the same way as carbon monoxide, by reducing the oxygen-carrying capacity of the blood. The hydrocarbon pollutants are a diverse lot and, among other things, are almost certainly involved in rising cancer death rates (the best known suspected carcinogen is the complex benzpyrene molecule). Similarly, some components of "particulate" pollution, such as asbestos and certain metals, are strongly suspected of contributing to the cancer load of the human population. An association between particulate air pollution and mortality from cirrhosis of the liver has been shown, but it is not clear which components are the toxic agents or whether the effect is direct or synergistic with other substances. Asbestos exposure is implicated in raising the incidence of lung cancer among cigarette smokers. Unfortunately, it is difficult to make definitive statements about the precise health effects of air pollution, for reasons explained in Box 6-2.

In spite of these problems, the evidence pointing to the seriousness of air pollution as a definite hazard is now massive. Consider just a few sample findings. Cigarette smokers from smoggy St. Louis, Missouri, have roughly

---

BOX 6-2    ASSAYING THE HAZARDS OF AIR POLLUTION

The effects of cigarette smoking on health might be considered a problem in "micro air pollution." We now know that cigarette smoking has many harmful effects. Yet even with the great advantage of being able to measure the amount and length of exposure, and having a relatively uniform pollutant source, it took many years to do the research required to convince doctors, scientists, and eventually the general public of the extreme hazards of smoking.

In contrast, here are some of the problems of assaying the dangers of air pollution:

1. Pollutants are numerous and varied, and many of them are difficult to detect. Their concentrations vary geographically. In many areas techniques for monitoring pollutants are highly inadequate, and long-term records are unavailable. Long periods of study are usually needed to reveal delayed and chronic effects.

2. It is usually impossible to determine with precision the degree of exposure of a given individual to specific pollutants.

3. Degree of air pollution is correlated with other factors, such as degree of exposure to various kinds of stress, other kinds of pollution, and food additives. Such factors must be considered in data analysis.

4. Research is complicated because pollutants that do not cause problems when tested alone may be dangerous in combination with other pollutants. For instance, many of the asbestos particles inhaled by nonsmokers are carried out of the lungs in an ever-moving sheet of mucus propelled by the beating of cilia (tiny active appendages of living cells). Smoking interferes with this natural cleansing function, and increases the chance of coming down with an asbestos-induced mesothelioma, a kind of cancer of the lungs. Sulfur dioxide also tends to interfere with this cleaning function. It is thought that the length of exposure of lung surface to airborne carcinogenic hydrocarbons such as benzpyrene may determine whether a cancerous growth is started. When benzpyrene occurs as a pollutant in combination with sulfur dioxide, the exposure and the hazard are greatly increased. Such interactions are called *synergistic;* the danger from the two combined pollutants is greater than the sum of the individual dangers.

four times the incidence of emphysema as smokers from relatively smog-free Winnipeg, Canada. At certain times, air pollution increases the frequency of head colds. Ten years after the Donora smog disaster of 1948, those residents who had reported severe effects during the smog showed the highest subsequent death rates. (This, of course, does not *prove* that the smog hurried them toward their graves; perhaps only previously weakened people suffered severe effects.) Pneumonia deaths are more frequent in areas of high pollution. Chronic bronchitis is more serious among British postmen who work in areas of high air pollution than in those who serve in relatively smog-free areas. Emphysema death rates have skyrocketed as air pollution has increased. England has higher overall rates of air pollution than the United States, and death from lung cancer is more than twice as common among British men as it is among American men. The lung cancer death rates in England are correlated with the density of atmospheric smoke. The lung cancer rate for men over 45 in the smoggiest part of Staten Island, New York is 55 per 100,000. In a less smoggy area just a few miles away, the rate is 40 per 100,000.

Some of the effects we have just described are still the subject of controversy within the scientific community, undoubtedly owing to the sorts of difficulties described in Box 6-2. However, much of the debate begins to take on the character of the cigarette-smoking-and-cancer arguments of a few years ago—the evidence is "only statistical," but to those knowledgeable in statistics, it is already persuasive and becoming overwhelming. In short, air pollution kills. It usually kills slowly and unobtrusively, and the resulting deaths are not dramatically called to the attention of the public. Published estimates of the annual American financial loss resulting from air pollution's effects on health run as high as $14–29 billion. An article in *Science* put the *lower limit* on the annual savings (in medical care and lost income) that a 50 percent reduction in air pollution in major urban areas would provide at slightly more than $2 billion.

If current trends are allowed to continue, death from air pollution *will* become obtrusive. The Public Health Service has predicted that annual sulfur dioxide emission will increase from the 1960 level of 20 million tons to 35 million by the year 2000. Similarly, nitrogen oxides will increase from 11 to almost 30 million tons, and particulates from about 30 million to more than 45 million tons. Unless the United States alters present trends in transportation, the number of automobiles will quadruple between the years 1960 and 2000, as will the number of gallons of fuel consumed. Although population and environmental limitations make it unlikely that these trends will continue to the end of this century, these projections do give some indication of what we may have to live with as long as they do continue.

## Air Pollution and Population Growth

The clear connection between air pollution and population growth may be seen by examining the history of pollution in Los Angeles. Even four cen-

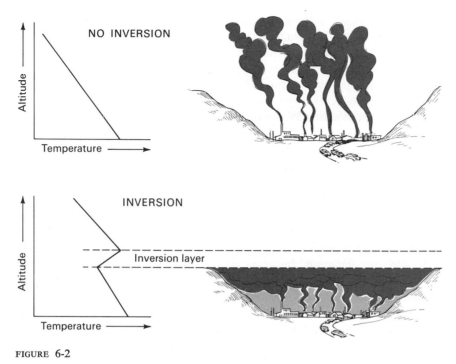

FIGURE 6-2

Temperature inversion, in which a layer of warm air overlies a layer of cooler air, trapping air pollution close to the ground.

turies ago, Juan Rodriquez Cabrillo recorded in his diary that smoke from Indian fires in the basin went up for a few hundred feet and then spread to blanket the valley with haze. Because of this phenomenon, he named what is today called San Pedro Bay "The Bay of Smokes." Cabrillo was observing the effect of a thermal inversion. Normally the temperature of the atmosphere decreases steadily with increased altitude, but during an inversion a layer of warm air overlying cooler air below severely limits vertical mixing of the atmosphere, and pollutants accumulate in the layer of air trapped near the Earth's surface (Fig. 6-2). Because of the wind patterns in the eastern Pacific and the ring of mountains surrounding the Los Angeles Basin, it is an ideal place for the formation of inversions, usually at about 2,000 feet above the floor of the basin. They occur there on about 7 days out of every 16.

Los Angeles has abundant sunshine, another climatic feature that contributes to its air-pollution problems. Sunlight acts on a mixture of oxygen, nitrogen oxides, and hydrocarbons to produce what is known as photochemical smog. Characteristic of photochemical smog are such compounds as peroxyacetyl nitrates. Combustion products from well over 3 million cars are exhausted into the atmosphere of the Los Angeles Basin in addition to the wastes discharged by oil refineries and other industries. As a result, the air that residents of Los Angeles breathe contains far more than the usual mixture of nitrogen, oxygen, and carbon dioxide; it also contains carbon monoxide, ozone, aldehydes, ketones, alcohols, acids, ethers, peroxyacetyl nitrates and nitrites, alkyl nitrates and nitrites, benzpyrene, and many other dangerous chemicals.

Smog first became prominent in Los Angeles during World War II. Since then the Los Angeles County Air Pollution Control District (APCD) has pursued a vigorous policy of smog abatement. A "Devil's Dictionary of Air Pollution" published in a San Francisco newspaper in 1969 defined *Air Pollution Control* as "a phrase used in answering the telephone at many public agencies which are involved in watching the growth of air pollution. It describes a modern myth." This definition might be accurate for most agencies, but not for the Los Angeles APCD. The district has imposed strict controls on industry, setting rigid emission standards for power plants, re-fineries, and other sources of pollution. Some 1.5 million domestic inciner-ators, a dozen large municipal incinerators, 57 open burning dumps, and most incinerators in commercial buildings have been eliminated. Coal burning has been made illegal, and so has (for most of the year) the burning of oil with a high sulfur content. Control is exercised over the escape of vapors from petroleum storage tanks and gasoline loading facilities; also controlled are commercial processes that require organic solvents, the olefin content of gaso-line sold in Los Angeles County, and many other contributors to air pollution. Furthermore, all cars sold in California were required to have smog-control devices designed to reduce crankcase emissions of hydrocarbons before the devices were required nationwide.

The Los Angeles area has partially "controlled" its smog by generating a portion of its electricity in areas of low population in New Mexico, using low quality coal which would not be tolerated under the air quality laws of California or Arizona. This is roughly equivalent to throwing garbage in a neighbor's yard because his yard is larger and he is too ignorant or weak to prevent it.

And what has all this smog control effort accomplished? At best, it has more or less permitted a holding of the line. There has been little or no im-provement in the air quality in the Los Angeles Basin since 1960. Un-expectedly, pollution from nitrogen oxides has soared, partly because manu-facturers have increased the compression ratios of automobile engines, and partly because of the fitting of crankcase antismog devices, which were designed to reduce the emission of hydrocarbons. Since 1970, nitrogen oxide emissions in new cars have been reduced and should be further reduced by 1974. Fortunately, hydrocarbon levels have remained about even, as have those of carbon monoxide. Sulfur oxides have fluctuated, but they are currently decreasing. Since 1962 there has been an increase in the number of smog alerts in which public health warnings are broadcast. Furthermore, although there has been no spectacular rise in the *density* of smog since 1960, the *volume* of heavily polluted air is increasing. The smog is spreading in area and in height as the heat generated by the city forces the base of the inversion cap higher. According to one estimate, the Los Angeles Basin now receives only 94 percent of its heat from the sun; fully 6 percent comes from the burning of fossil fuels. Air pollution is now reported to be causing damage to living plants growing hundreds of miles east of Los Angeles.

Why has Los Angeles been unable to improve its air quality in spite of the strenuous efforts of the APCD? A basic answer is population growth. Even though the per capita amount of pollution has declined, the number of people has increased. Each new worker is faced with the virtual necessity of using an automobile to move around in an immense city that lacks an adequate public transportation system. And, of course, more people means more business and industry, which in turn tend to attract more people. In California the situation is especially critical, but many urban areas of the U.S. face similar problems. More people and more automobiles, plus systematic resistance to smog control from industry and industry-hungry local governments, have combined to work against successful pollution abatement.

By 1970, public concern and growing activism on the part of environmental organizations began to have an effect on government apathy and industrial resistance to pollution control. Nationwide, laws against automobile and smokestack emissions became increasingly stringent, with California's standards generally being stricter than federal ones. Both federal and state governments began to prosecute companies that violated standards, imposing heavy fines or closing down offending plants. Automobile manufacturers and industrialists complained that it was impossible to keep up with constantly changing standards; what was acceptable one year was unacceptable the next. Many 1970 model automobiles failed to meet emission standards for that year. Some of the tests previously used were also found not to be sensitive enough to measure emissions accurately. To add still another complication, cars that were "clean" when new were usually found to deteriorate after a few thousand miles.

In late 1970 Congress passed a new Clean Air Act, setting strict new standards for air pollution both for factories and automobiles. Most of the standards must be met by 1975, although a clause permits a delay until 1976 if the company in question can prove well ahead of time that it cannot possibly meet the requirements sooner. For automobiles, emissions of hydrocarbons and carbon monoxide must be reduced by 90 percent by January 1, 1975, and nitrogen oxides by 90 percent by January 1, 1976. The Administration's new Environmental Protection Agency (EPA) is charged with setting national air quality standards and enforcing the act.

One can hope that continued public awareness of the problem will lead to further change during the 1970s, that perhaps the internal combustion engine will gradually come to play a much smaller role in American life while pollution control becomes more effective. One early practical step might be to reduce the size, horsepower, and compression ratios of internal combustion engines, while making every effort to improve the control of emissions. The amount of pollution from an automobile is not necessarily related to engine size, although this varies depending on how it is measured. But small engines certainly consume less fuel.

Eventually, the presently dominant form of the internal combustion engine may be replaced by one or perhaps a variety of less polluting alternatives: steam engines, electric motors, gas turbines, diesels, or the pistonless, rotary Wankel engines. All of these are being actively developed, and some are in use in certain applications today (for example, diesels in trucks and a few cars). Large-scale use of most of these potential substitutes for today's engines would involve new problems, including a different spectrum of pollutants in some cases and considerable economic adjustment to new forms of fuel or power in others. Electric cars, for instance, merely shift the pollution from the air over highways and cities to the air above power plants because of the increased electricity used to recharge the cars. However, it may prove easier to control the pollution in such a system. Since many of the other problems associated with automobiles, including resource depletion, both for power and materials, solid waste disposal, and urban and highway congestion, will still remain, even the best of the alternatives can provide only a partial solution. They will ultimately have to be supplemented by efficient forms of mass transportation. Perhaps the ideal situation would combine zoning regulation to curtail urban sprawl and a network of mass transport with minimum use of small private vehicles in an efficient, integrated system. Of course, any move to reduce substantially our dependence on large automobiles is likely to meet determined resistance not only from the manufacturers, but also from the American public.

## Water Pollution

In many communities direct threats to human health arrive through the faucet as well as through the air. The drinking water that flows from the tap in some localities has already passed through seven or eight people. Graffiti in public washrooms in numerous towns along the Mississippi River read: "Flush the toilet, they need the water in St. Louis." Yet the water in St. Louis is chlorinated and filtered, and therefore it should be safe to drink. Unfortunately, the water in many cities is often unsafe to drink (Box 6-3). Although proper chlorination may help, there is growing evidence that high contents of organic matter in water can somehow protect viruses from the effects of chlorine. Infectious hepatitis is spreading alarmingly in the United States, and a major suspect for the route of transmission is the "toilet-to-mouth pipeline" of many water systems not made safe by chlorination. Indeed, the safety of purifying water with chlorine has been questioned by Nobel Laureate Joshua Lederberg of Stanford University who wrote in *The Washington Post* in 1969, "Many geneticists have raised cautions about chemicals that may cause mutations, and I will join them by adding chlorine to the lengthy list that cry out for close scrutiny." The principal difficulty with chlorination is that certain chlorine compounds, which are sometimes formed by the chlorination process, cause mutations; but considering the high level of dangerous germs in many of our water supplies, we probably will have to continue to accept any risks involved in chlorination.

As the populations of many municipalities grow, their sewage treatment facilities, though once adequate, are quickly outgrown. Funds for new facilities can be obtained only at the expense of those needed for better schools, police departments, water systems, roads, and other public services. Inevitably, it seems, the available funds are insufficient to meet all of these needs, which are created in part by increases in population. Lax inspections and public health standards permit construction of septic tanks too close together or in unsuitable soils in many of the rural and suburban areas where there are no general sewage facilities. In some rural areas public health measures are so lax that many people have no sanitation facilities at all; people "just go to the woods."

As population in a DC grows, so does industry, which pours into our water supplies a vast array of contaminants: lead, detergents, sulfuric acid, hydrofluoric acid, phenols, ethers, benzenes, ammonia, and so on. As population grows, so does the need for increased agricultural production, which results in a heavier water-borne load of pesticides, herbicides, and nitrates. A result is the spread of pollution not just in streams, rivers, lakes, and along seashores, but also (and most seriously) in groundwater, where purification is almost impossible. With the spread of pollution goes the threat of epidemics of hepatitis and dysentery, and of poisoning by exotic chemicals.

Another hazard is the problem of nitrate pollution. Current agricultural practices result in the flow of a heavy load of nitrates into our water supply; nitrates also accumulate in high concentrations in our crops. Nitrates themselves are not especially dangerous, but when certain bacteria are present in

---

BOX 6-3    IS YOUR WATER SAFE TO DRINK?

Where did you live in the late 1960s? In Wilmington, Delaware; New London, Connecticut; Chattanooga, Tennessee; or Eugene, Oregon, the quality of your water was not completely protected from the source to your tap. Did you live in Grand Junction, Colorado; Fort Myers, Florida; or Bayonne, New Jersey? Your water in those cities did not come from the purest possible source. In Savannah, Georgia, or North Platte, Nebraska? Your water was not checked frequently enough for dangerous bacteria. Fairbanks, Alaska? Your local regulations were not adequate to prevent health hazard. Pueblo, Colorado? Surveys to detect potential health hazards were too infrequent. Wilmington, North Carolina? The bacterial level in your water was too high. Altoona, Pennsylvania? There were too many chemical impurities in your water. Charleston, South Carolina? Your water department used nonapproved tests. Some of the abovementioned cities had more than one of these problems, and many other cities have similar ones. These facts were revealed in a Public Health Service Provisional List, in which water supplies of more than 60 American cities were rated as "unsatisfactory" or "potential health hazard." If you are living in one of the cities mentioned you might wish to check with your public health agency as to the current status of your water supply. Indeed, periodic inquiry would be a good idea no matter where you live.

the digestive tract, they convert the nitrates into highly toxic nitrites. In addition, conversion of nitrates to nitrites can occur in any opened container of food, even if it is subsequently refrigerated. Farm animals and human infants are particularly likely to include in their digestive tracts the proper types of bacteria and the appropriate conditions for the conversion of nitrate to nitrite. When this nitrite is absorbed into a baby's bloodstream, it reacts with the oxygen-carrying pigment of the red blood cells, forming methemoglobin, which does not have hemoglobin's oxygen-transport capability. The resulting disease, methemoglobinemia, is characterized by labored breathing; in some cases, it terminates in suffocation. Nitrate water pollution in lakes, streams, and wells probably is most dangerous in the Central Valley of California, where it is a severe public health hazard and where doctors often recommend that infants be given only pure bottled water. It is also serious, however, in some other states, such as Illinois, Wisconsin, and Missouri. The city of Elgin, Minnesota, has been forced by nitrate pollution to find a new water supply.

A United States Department of Agriculture official estimated that the use of inorganic nitrogen fertilizer would be increased some ten times between 1970 and 2000. Should this occur, it would contribute to a general ecological catastrophe, as well as to the possible poisoning of large numbers of children and farm animals.

The Public Health Service, which monitors municipal water supplies for drinking safety, is empowered only to set standards to prevent the introduction or spread of disease organisms. As of 1970, it had no power against any of the myriad of known dangerous or possibly dangerous chemicals that have been appearing in increasing amounts in U.S. waters, including various kinds of pesticides. The PHS is presumably revising its standards to include such chemicals in its monitoring, and hopefully steps will be taken to remove them as much as possible from our drinking water.

Water pollution with sewage provides one of the classic examples of diseconomies of scale accompanying population growth. If a few people per mile live along a large river, their sewage may be dumped directly into the river and natural purification will occur. But if the population increases, the waste-degrading ability of the river becomes overstrained, and either the sewage or the intake water must be treated if the river water is to be safe for drinking. Should the population along the river increase further, more and more elaborate and expensive treatments will be required to keep the water safe for human use and to maintain desirable fishes and shellfishes in the river. In general, the more people there are living in a watershed, the higher the *per capita* costs of avoiding water pollution will be.

The history of water pollution abatement in the U.S. has largely paralleled that of air pollution: generally too little effort applied too late. By the late 1960s, despite a growth of federal involvement in setting standards and providing financial assistance, the situation was getting out of hand. Since 1969, the emphasis has been on pouring money into municipal waste treatment plants. These are certainly needed, but inadequate to solve all our water pollution problems. The Environment Protection Agency and the Army Corps of Engineers have been given the joint task of regulating industrial water pollution under the 1899 Refuse Act, a strict piece of legislation that has never really been enforced.

National standards for water quality and federal regulation and enforcement of them are sorely needed to replace the present hodgepodge of state, local, and federal standards. Let us hope that a new Clean Water Act, similar to the 1970 Clean Air Act, will soon be passed by Congress.

## Solid Wastes

An extremely serious problem facing the United States and other affluent countries is the accumulation of solid wastes in open dumps or inadequate fills. These dumps are not just aesthetic disasters; if they are burned they contribute to air pollution, water percolating through them pollutes groundwater supplies, and they serve as breeding grounds for such annoying and disease-bearing organisms as rats, cockroaches, and flies. Each year in the United States we must dispose of some 55 billion cans, 26 billion bottles and jars, 65 billion metal and plastic bottle caps, and more than half a billion dollars worth of other packaging materials. Seven million automobiles are junked each year, and the amount of urban solid wastes (trash and garbage) collected annually is approximately 200 million tons. Every man, woman and child in the United States is, on the average, producing nearly a ton of refuse annually. In addition to junked cars, some 10 million tons of iron and steel are scrapped each year, more than 3 billion tons of waste rock and mill tailings are dumped near mine sites, and huge amounts of slag, ash, and other wastes are produced by smelters, power plants, other industries, and agriculture.

It is becoming universally recognized that current methods of dealing with the solid waste problem are utterly inadequate. A report by the Department of Health, Education and Welfare has labeled 94 percent of the 12,000 disposal sites in the United States as "unacceptable." Many cities are facing disposal crises as population growth simultaneously produces more waste and reduces the available land for dumping. Waste disposal is another classic case where per capita costs tend to go up as population grows. San Francisco considered having its refuse hauled to distant dumping sites by train, and cities on the eastern seaboard considered hauling their wastes to the coalfields of Pennsylvania for disposal in abandoned mines. But, curiously enough, people living near the selected sites were not happy with the idea, and costs would have been very high. Sanitary landfill, where space is available, is a more satisfactory (and expensive) solution than dumping, but it also generates many problems. Water pollution continues, dust pollution is created, and nonbiodegradable materials (those not quickly broken down by microorganisms) which do not compact easily, lessen the utility of the fill. Incineration of wastes is another answer which in France and other European countries has been combined with power production in trash-fired power plants. Unless great care is taken, of course, this answer may merely substitute air pollution for land pollution.

Besides the obvious necessity of limiting the size of the human population, a number of other measures would help ameliorate the solid waste problem. Laws might be passed that would place heavy taxes upon any product or wrapping that is designed to be discarded rather than returned or recycled, and the manufacture of nonbiodegradable products could be prohibited. Heavy deposits, perhaps 5 or 10 cents per beer can or "pop" bottle, should be required to encourage the return of such containers, and give a boost to those recycling programs already under way. Then even those that might be discarded would be gleaned from roadsides and beaches by ambitious children. Many of our products, as well as our refuse-collection system, could be so designed that the materials which might be used as soil conditioners could be separated from those to be recycled in other ways. New apartment buildings should be equipped with separate disposal chutes for different kinds of wastes. Automobiles could be designed not only to minimize air pollution, but also for ease of disassembly into recyclable components. Indeed, in view of the obvious need to minimize the wasteful scattering of nonrenewable resources, the design of all of man's manufactured devices, from home appliances to computers, should take into account the possibility of recycling their components.

## Pesticides and Related Compounds

Some substances, such as chlorinated hydrocarbons, lead, mercury, and fluorides, reach us in so many ways that they must be considered as general pollutants. Chlorinated hydrocarbons are among the most ubiquitous manufactured chemicals in the environment. Of these, DDT has been employed the longest, having been put into mass use late in World War II. It is the most commonly used and most thoroughly studied of all synthetic insecticides. It often occurs in concentrations of more than 12 parts per million (ppm) in human fat, and as high as 5 ppm in human milk (though the usual range is some 0.05 to 0.26 ppm). Most mother's milk in the United States contains so much DDT that it would be declared illegal in interstate commerce; the permissible level in cow's milk is set by the FDA at 0.05 ppm. Other chlorinated hydrocarbon insecticides, including aldrin, dieldrin, and benzene hexachloride, have also been found in human milk.

Recently another class of chlorinated hydrocarbon compounds, polychlorinated biphenyls (PCBs), has also been found to be a serious pollutant. These compounds are used in a variety of industrial processes, and are released into our environment in a variety of ways. They vaporize from storage containers, are emitted from factory smokestacks, are dumped into rivers and lakes with industrial wastes, and, along with a variety of other hydrocarbons, are added to the load of particulate atmospheric pollutants as automobile tires are worn down. Like the pesticides, they show up in the milk of nursing mothers. Zoologist Robert W. Risebrough of the University of California recently stated that PCBs "are highly toxic to man when inhaled as vapors, and the more heavily chlorinated components have greater toxicity. No tolerance limits have been set for human food supplies, and their cancer-causing properties remain to be determined."

Chlorinated hydrocarbons are present in very low concentrations in our drinking water, in our fruits and vegetables, and in the air we breathe. Greater amounts are present in meat, fish, and eggs. At times the dosage is direct and high. Farmers sometimes far exceed legal residue levels of insecticides on their crops and get away with it because inspection is inadequate. Some ill-informed grocers spray their produce to kill fruit flies. In the summer of 1968, our research group found leaking cans of chlordane dust (a chlorinated hydrocarbon insecticide) on a narrow shelf above the onion bin in a supermarket. The dust was present on the produce. The manager, on being informed, took prompt corrective action—but not before some of his customers had added to their loads of chlorinated hydrocarbons. By the summer of 1969 the pesticides had reappeared on the shelf over the produce, and complaints had to be renewed. Obviously the sale of all pesticides should be prohibited in food stores.

A colleague of ours has observed massive anti-roach spraying—presumably of chlordane—in a restaurant kitchen, where the spray drifted over exposed food. Some restaurants formerly used lindane vaporizers; fortunately these have now been banned. Regardless of whether such practices and the resultant heavy doses are common or not, continuous "light" exposure is virtually unavoidable. For example, at least a dozen states have reported that residual pesticide levels in fishes may be well above the FDA recommended limits, and in some individual fishes DDT concentrations are ten times higher.

Can this light exposure be dangerous? Doesn't the government specify how much exposure to these chemicals is safe on the basis of long-term experiments? Haven't the medical and biological sciences protected us? Isn't it true that DDT has been proven to have no adverse effects on humans unless taken in massive doses? Unfortunately the answer to the last three questions is a resounding "No!". But there is no reason why the average citizen should know that, even though the dangers of pesticide poisoning have been given increasing and much-needed attention in the news media during the past decade. Because of the variety of problems enumerated in the discussion of air pollution, it has been very difficult to evaluate the long-term and chronic effects of pesticides. Biologists have long been warning that we have no evidence that DDT, even though its effects may not be immediately obvious, might not have subtle or long-term effects. In fact, we have every reason to believe that these biologically active molecules are downright dangerous. Rachel Carson wrote, "For the population as a whole, we must be more concerned with the delayed effects of absorbing small amounts of the pesticides that invisibly contaminate our world." But, as often happens, the possibility of subtle chronic effects has been discounted by industry, ignored by the government, and forgotten by the public. That DDT has very low immediate toxicity to mammals, including humans, has been known since it was first put in use, and this has never been questioned. Promoters of pesticides have even resorted to the dangerous extreme of eating spoonfuls of pure DDT in an effort to prove how harmless it is, but such actions in no way demonstrate that DDT is safe for human consumption over the long run.

People can understand acute poisoning, but they find subtle physiological changes difficult to grasp. Why should it matter if high concentrations of chlorinated hydrocarbons are being stored in our bodies? Haven't scientists carried out experiments in which convicts ate DDT without apparent harm? Hasn't a study of workers in a DDT plant and another done with convicts shown that no ill effects resulted from heavy exposure? The answer is that these two studies attesting to the "safety" of DDT were poorly designed and utterly inadequate to assure us of its long term safety. Both were done with people whose first exposure occurred as *adults,* and the convict study followed individuals over *less than two years.* The study of exposed workers did not investigate what had happened to workers who were no longer employed. The effects on the delicate developmental systems of fetuses and infants were not investigated; nor were there any women or children in the study. No attempt was made to investigate the possible effects of DDT exposure on large populations over several decades, and the causes of death in large numbers of people with high and low exposures were not statistically compared.

Biologists have just started to get an inkling of what our "harmless" chlorinated hydrocarbon load may be doing to us over the long run. Animal studies give us some clues. In high doses DDT has recently been shown to increase the incidence of cancers, especially liver cancers, in mice. This indicates that DDT might also be carcinogenic in human beings. At around 10 ppm DDT has been shown to induce abnormally high levels of certain liver enzymes which break down many prescribed drugs and render them ineffective. As pharmacologist Richard M. Welch of the Burroughs Wellcome Research Laboratory has pointed out, DDT in rats not only induces the production of these enzymes, but also increases the weight of the uterus and the deposition of dextrose in the uterus. Moreover, it stimulates the production of enzymes that break down steroid sex hormones. We know that DDT affects the sex hormones of rats and birds and may produce sterility in rats. We also know that rat reproductive physiology shows many similarities to human reproductive physiology. DDT induces these same liver enzymes in humans, but we do not know whether hormonal changes occur or what their effects will be if they do.

Results of other recent studies are even more ominous. One study, the results of which were obtained by autopsies, showed a correlation between DDT levels in fat tissue and cause of death. Concentrations of DDT and its breakdown products, DDE and DDD, as well as dieldrin (another chlorinated hydrocarbon pesticide), were significantly higher in the fat of patients who died of softening of the brain, cerebral hemorrhage, hypertension, portal cirrhosis of the liver, and various cancers than in groups of patients who died of infectious diseases. The histories of the patients in the study showed that concentrations of DDT and its breakdown products in their fat were strongly correlated with home use of pesticides, heavy users having much higher concentrations than light or moderate users.

More conclusive investigations of these effects are urgently needed, but in the light of what is known about the deleterious effects of chlorinated hydrocarbons on laboratory animals, the results of this study alone leave little room for complacency. Neurophysiologist Alan Steinbach of the University of California at Berkeley claims that DDT is an irreversible nerve poison. There is also some evidence that chlorinated hydrocarbon exposure can cause abnormal changes in electroencephalograph (brain wave) patterns. These observations are not surprising, since experiments with other animals indicate that exposure to chlorinated hydrocarbons causes changes in the central nervous system. For example, in experiments conducted by J. M. Anderson and M. R. Peterson, biologists at Carleton University, Ottawa, Canada, trout exposed to 20 parts per *billion* DDT showed a complete inability to learn to avoid an electric shock, whereas *all* unexposed fishes learned to do so quite easily. Furthermore, previously trained fish lost their ability to avoid electric shock after exposure to DDT.

There is evidence that the amount of DDT stored in human tissue has not increased over the past decade or so in the United States, but has probably reached a mean concentration of some 7–12 ppm. At a given exposure level it apparently takes about one year for an equilibrium to be established between intake and loss through excretion and breakdown, after which continued exposure produces no increase in DDT storage. The mean concentration of DDT in human populations varies widely from one geographic location to another, both within and among countries. It also varies with diet, race, age, and undetermined individual differences. For reasons that are not entirely clear, the black population has a considerably higher average level of DDT concentration in the blood than does the white population. This includes those who live in cities, as well as farm workers who might be expected to have more than average exposure to insecticides. Table 6-1 shows the DDT concentrations that have been found in a series of studies.

Generally, people in the most northern countries, where growing seasons are short and insects not a year-round problem, have substantially smaller DDT burdens than people in the United States. Intensive agriculture in Israel, as well as increased household usage of pesticides, is probably responsible for the high levels found there. Unfortunately, there are no available reports of DDT loads from other countries with intensive agriculture, such as Japan and the Netherlands. High levels in Delhi, India, may be related to the use of DDT to preserve stored food.

In a recent study of individuals from Dade County, Florida, a significantly

164

TABLE 6-1
*Mean Concentration of DDT in Human Body Fat*

| Population | Year | Number in sample | DDT (ppm) |
|---|---|---|---|
| United States | 1942 | 10 | 0 |
| United States | 1950 | 75 | 5.3 |
| United States | 1955 | 49 | 19.9 |
| United States | 1954–1956 | 61 | 11.7 |
| United States | 1961–1962 | 130 | 12.6 |
| United States | 1961–1962 | 30 | 10.71 |
| United States | 1962–1963 | 282 | 10.3 |
| U.S. (all areas) | 1964 | 64 | 7.0 |
| U.S. (New Orleans) | 1964 | 25 | 10.3 |
| U.S. (white, over 6 yrs.) | 1968 | 90 | 8.4 |
| U.S. (nonwhite, over 6 yrs.) | 1968 | 35 | 16.7 |
| Alaskan Eskimo | 1960 | 20 | 3.0 |
| Canada | 1959–1960 | 62 | 4.9 |
| Canada | 1966 | 27 | 3.8 |
| United Kingdom | 1961–1962 | 131 | 2.2* |
| United Kingdom | 1963–1964 | 65 | 3.3 |
| United Kingdom | 1964 | 100 | 3.3* |
| Germany | 1958–1959 | 60 | 2.2 |
| Hungary | 1960 | 50 | 12.4 |
| France | 1961 | 10 | 5.2 |
| Israel | 1963–1964 | 254 | 19.2 |
| India (Delhi) | 1964 | 67 | 26.0 |

SOURCE: Various. DDT is expressed as DDT plus its breakdown product DDE converted to equivalent DDT units. Some figures include minor amounts of other breakdown products.
* Geometric mean.

lower DDT-DDE concentration was found in children under 5 years of age, suggesting that they had not yet reached their equilibrium levels. Six still-births and fetuses were examined, and found to have loads more closely reflecting concentrations in their mother's tissues. Passage of DDT across the placental membrane into the fetus has now been demonstrated to take place as early as the 22nd week of pregnancy, and may occur well in advance of that.

Recent studies in dogs show that DDT storage concentrations will rise dramatically if aldrin, another chlorinated hyrdocarbon insecticide, is also ingested. This is an example of synergism between pollutants, a general phenomenon about which too little is known. Whether aldrin also affects DDT storage concentrations in humans is not known, but it is certainly possible.

Other studies have shown that certain anti-convulsant drugs can act to reduce DDT concentrations in blood and fat tissues of people. Nothing is known about how this occurs or what long-term side effects may follow the use of these drugs for DDT reduction. Since DDT is ubiquitous, the treatment would be only temporary, unless the drugs were taken frequently or continuously.

It is difficult at this juncture to evaluate the magnitude of the direct threat to human health represented by the present level of chlorinated hydrocarbon contamination. Most analyses have dealt with DDT, although human beings are also being exposed to a wide range of related compounds, some of which have considerably higher immediate toxicity. There are indications that dieldrin, perhaps four times as toxic as DDT, may be involved in portal cirrhosis of the liver, and that benzene hexachloride may contribute to liver cancer. The critical question is not immediate toxicity, but long-term effects. The oldest people who have been exposed to high concentrations of DDT since conception are now just in their early twenties. It is possible that their life expectancies may already have been greatly reduced; it is also possible that there will be no significant reduction of life expectancies. We will not know until more time has passed. Breastfed babies in Sweden get 70 percent more than what is considered the maximum acceptable amount of DDT, and British and American breastfed babies consume about 10 times the recommended maximum amount of dieldrin. Some babies in Western Australia are exposed to as much as *30 times* the maximally acceptable amount of dieldrin. What effect these poisons may be having on the sensitive developmental systems of infants is unfortunately unknown. Göran Löfroth of the Institute of Biochemistry, University of Stockholm, wrote in 1968 that "Many parents are faced by a difficult choice. Should they expose their child . . . to an unknown and high amount of organochlorine pesticides, or should they deprive the child of nutritious milk and warm contact with its mother? The danger notwithstanding, it looks as if the positive advantages of breast-feeding outweigh the organochlorine hazard. But the outlook for the future is, to say the least, distinctly disturbing."

At any rate, we shall almost certainly find out what the overall effects of the chlorinated hydrocarbon load will be, since the persistence of these compounds guarantees decades of further exposure, even after their use has been discontinued. The continued release of chlorinated hydrocarbons into our environment is tantamount to a reckless global experiment, and we humans, as well as all other animals that live on this globe, are playing the role of guinea pigs.

## Pollution by Heavy Metals

### LEAD

Although biologists are just beginning to understand the effects of chlorinated hydrocarbons on people, and are beginning to realize that they previously underestimated the danger, there is no lack of understanding with regard to acute lead poisoning. We *know* what lead can do, although we do not know what the results of chronic low-level exposure to lead are, especially atmospheric lead from automobile exhausts. Lead poisoning symptoms include loss of appetite, weakness, awkwardness, apathy, and miscarriage; it causes lesions of the neuromuscular system, circulatory system, brain, and gastrointestinal tract. It is a sobering thought that over-exposure to lead may have been a factor in the decline of both the Greek and Roman civilizations. As S. C. Gilfillan has pointed out, the Romans lined their bronze cooking, eating, and wine-storage vessels with lead. They thus avoided the characteristic unpleasant taste of copper and the obvious symptoms of copper poisoning, trading them for the pleasant flavor of lead and the more subtle symptoms of lead poisoning.

Although lead pipes were commonly used to carry water, it is doubtful whether much of the lead that accumulated in the bones of Roman citizens entered their systems through the water supply. The reason is that most waters are slightly alkaline, and insoluble compounds would have formed on the surfaces of the pipes, thus preventing the metal from entering the water. Most of the lead undoubtedly entered their bodies with food and drink, particularly their wines. The acids in foods and in wines combine with lead to form soluble salts that can be absorbed by the body. Examination of the bones of upper class Romans of the classical period shows high concentrations of lead. The lower classes lived more simply, drank less wine from lead containers, and thus may have picked up less lead.

We too are constantly exposed to lead in our environment, in the form of air contamination from lead smelting and the combustion of gasoline containing tetraethyl lead. We are exposed to lead in various other ways as well—via pesticides, paints, solder used to seal food cans, lead piping, abraded particles of lead-containing ceramics and glassware, and so forth. Clair C. Patterson, a geochemist at the California Institute of Technology, stated in 1965, "There are definite indications that residents of the United States today are undergoing severe chronic lead insult. The average American ingests some 400 millionths of a gram of lead per day in food, air, and water, a process which has been viewed with complacency for decades."

The pattern of increase in the lead contamination of the atmosphere has been revealed by studies of the lead content of the Greenland ice cap. The ice cap "lead load" increased some 400 percent between 1750 and 1940, and it rose another 300 percent between 1940 and 1967! By comparison, studies show that the content of sea salts in the Greenland ice cap have not changed since 1750, indicating that changes in the overall pattern of deposition of materials in the ice is not the cause of the lead increase. That similar patterns of lead contamination are not found in antarctic snows lends strong support to the thesis that atmospheric lead pollution originated first with lead smelting and then more recently with the combustion of gasoline. Both sources of contamination are concentrated in the Northern Hemisphere, and the spread of pollution to Antarctica and the Southern Hemisphere in general is largely blocked by atmospheric circulation patterns.

It is now suspected that airborne lead is becoming a major source of exposure, at least for people in urban areas, although the overall exposure from food and beverages is still higher. But in Los Angeles and a few other cities, it is possible that more lead is now being absorbed through the lungs than through the digestive tract. Since 1924 the American consumption of tetraethyl lead in automobile fuel has risen from less than one million pounds per annum in 1924 to 285 million in 1950 and 700 million in 1968. In 1968 another 50–60 million pounds were used in aviation gasoline. About 75 percent of this ends up in the atmosphere. The average concentration of lead in the blood of Americans in 1968 was about 0.25 ppm, which is a little less than half the level at which removal from exposure is recommended for people who work with lead in industry. Garage mechanics and parking lot attendants tend to have about 0.34–0.38 ppm in their blood. Government samples of atmospheric lead concentrations taken during 1968 and 1969 in Philadelphia, Cincinnati, and Los Angeles, showed sharp increases over samples taken seven years earlier. The increases ranged between 2 percent and 36 percent for Philadelphia and Cincinnati, and in Los Angeles from 32 to 64 percent.

Lead is a cumulative cellular poison. It seems hardly prudent to wait until much of the population begins to show chronic or acute symptoms before we attempt to lower its level in the environment. Chronic lead poisoning is unusually difficult to diagnose, and low-level effects could be quite common already. Moreover, there is always the possibility of synergistic interactions with the other poisons to which we are exposed.

Low-lead and lead-free gasolines were offered for sale in the U.S. by most major oil companies during 1970. By mid-1971, they still accounted for only about 5 percent of sales. Possibly the public was still largely unaware of lead's role in air pollution. But the major reasons for the low sales doubtless were the price difference—from 2 to 6 cents per gallon more than leaded gasoline—and the fact that many cars, especially older ones and high-powered models, could not operate well without lead. Cars produced since 1970 are more tolerant of unleaded gas. Engines designed to meet the 1975 pollution requirements will be unable to use leaded gasolines, so a conversion to non-leaded gas will certainly take place during the next few years. Presumably the cost differential can be eliminated as the new gasolines come into wider use. Even at a penny or two more per gallon, unleaded gasoline is quite a bargain, provided that substitute additives will not cause other problems.

## MERCURY

Man adds mercury to his environment in many ways. It is lost from industrial processes, especially those that produce chlorine (which, in turn, is used in large quantities in the manufacture of plastics) and caustic soda (which has many industrial uses). It is lost by the pulp and paper industry.

It is a prime ingredient of agricultural fungicides, which have been used extensively for treating seeds. Small amounts of mercury are found in fossil fuels and are released when the fuels are burned. Despite the low concentration, the enormous volume of fossil fuels consumed each year may make this the dominant source of mercury in the environment. Medicines flushed down drains and even broken medical thermometers may make significant contributions to the environmental mercury load. It was estimated in 1971 that over 23 million pounds of mercury were being released into the environment annually.

The natural "background" level of mercury in waters is a matter of some dispute. The mercury content of seawater varies with such things as salinity and depth and seems to average close to 1 ppb (part per billion). Calculations indicate that man's activities have not added significantly to the mercury already present in the ocean from natural sources, and mercury levels in oceanic fishes caught almost a century ago seem to be comparable to those caught today. This, of course, does not mean that mercury is harmless just because it may come from natural sources. Indeed modern fishing techniques may be increasing human intake of mercury because large oceanic fishes are more widely marketed. But man himself is probably an important factor in raising oceanic mercury levels only in estuarine and coastal waters.

The picture in fresh water is quite different; there mercury concentrations are correlated with sources of mercury pollution. The Saskatchewan River in Canada had .05 ppb above the city of Edmonton and .12 ppb below. Sediment below a plant using mercury to produce chlorine and caustic soda had 1,800 ppm (parts per million). Measurements taken in many North American streams show a similar picture. Man is making substantial contributions to the mercury load in lakes, rivers, and streams.

Metallic (elemental) mercury is relatively non-toxic to man. Certain microorganisms, however, are able to convert metallic mercury to more toxic organic forms, methylmercury and other alkyl-mercury compounds. This process goes on continuously, so that the metallic mercury deposited in freshwaters serves as a reservoir from which the more poisonous form may continually be added to ecosystems for decades or even centuries *even after release of mercury is halted.*

Methylmercury is concentrated by organisms and amplified by food chains. Fishes, for instance, seem to absorb it both from their food and through their gills, and may show concentrations in their bodies thousands of times higher than that of the water in which they live. Methylmercury is far more easily absorbed than inorganic mercury and excreted far more slowly. Buildup in the food chains also occurs, as indicated by high levels of mercury in tuna, swordfish, and in animals that live near the tops of marine food chains. Concentrations in tuna are often in the 0.13–0.25 ppm range, and swordfish averages even higher. The FDA found that most of its tested samples of swordfish exceeded the maximum allowable concentration, and 8 percent of the samples exceeded it by three times.

The symptoms of methylmercury poisoning are varied. Blindness, deafness, loss of coordination, madness, or death may be the fate of those exposed to high concentrations. Individuals vary both in their sensitivity to methylmercury and in their exposure. Populations which eat large amounts of fish are, for instance, likely to have a much higher exposure than those that do not. Symptoms have been recorded in association with blood concentrations as low as 0.2 ppm, a level thought to result from a regular daily intake of 0.3 milligrams of methylmercury for a 70 kilogram (154 pound) man. The FDA has established 0.5 ppm as the maximum allowable concentration in fishes for human consumption. In order to maintain that 0.2 ppm blood level, a 70 kilogram man would have to consume 4.2 kilograms (over 9 pounds) per week of fish containing 0.5 ppm.

There have been local disasters connected with high levels of mercury pollution. For instance, in 1953 a chemical plant in Minamata City, Japan, greatly increased its production and its release of mercury. The result was the appearance of "Minimata disease" in the population eating seafood from Minamata Bay. More than 100 people died or suffered serious damage to their nervous systems. In the mid-1960s a woman in New York went on a strict diet which involved eating 10 ounces of swordfish daily. She lost 45 pounds, but suffered "dizziness, memory loss, hand tremors, tongue quivers, hypersensitivity to light, difficulty in focusing her vision and physical uncoordination." At first diagnosed as suffering from psychosomatic illness, it was realized in 1971 that she was suffering from mercury poisoning, the first known case attributable to eating marketed food.

In spite of these and similar cases it seems unlikely that we are on the verge of an epidemic of mercury poisoning. But in the light of our lack of knowledge of many aspects of the problem (including the long term effects of exposure to subclinical mercury loads and possible interactions of methylmercury with other chemicals now assaulting our cells), extreme caution is clearly required. The fact that some of our mercury exposure is due to the natural "background" is no reason to discount the problem. Small man-induced increases over the background level may be extremely serious. Some steps are being taken to limit release of mercury into the environment, and some foods (such as swordfish) seem destined to disappear from the market. Hopefully, mankind has recognized the mercury menace in time to avoid disaster.

CADMIUM, ARSENIC, AND OTHER HEAVY METALS

Lead and mercury are the best studied of the heavy metal pollutants, but some others also pose environmental threats. Cadmium is now being detected in suspicious concentrations in oysters and elsewhere, but we are ignorant both of the significance of these levels and of the pathways cadmium follows in the environment. Cadmium poisoning causes a serious disease called *itai-itai* (ouch-ouch) in Japan because it is so painful. Fatal cases have been reported in Japan, whose cadmium pollution of food supplies is now a recognized problem. The U.S. Geological Survey found concentrations of cadmium above U.S. Public Health Service standards in the raw water (before treatment) supplies of 20 cities. The amounts ranged from 10 to 130 ppb. Unacceptably high levels of both cadmium and chromium have been found in ground waters in one part of Long Island. The contamination originated with wastes deposited during World War II, and the polluted zone is slowly expanding. Contamination should not reach the nearest well being used for a public water supply until around 2000 A.D., but the situation plainly calls for careful monitoring. This incident is an excellent example of the degree to which ground water supplies are vulnerable to long-term contamination.

Arsenic is another pollutant found both in food and in water supplies in trace amounts. The main sources of this pollutant are arsenical pesticides and detergents, which contain a possibly less toxic form, arsenate. But there is a real possibility that under conditions of heavy water pollution the arsenate may be broken down to the more toxic arsenite. Moreover, many plants and animals concentrate arsenic in their tissues; some of the organisms are human food.

The toxic metals characterized by the M.I.T. Study of Critical Environmental Problems as being "the most toxic, persistent, and abundant in the environment" are lead, mercury, cadmium, chromium, arsenic, and nickel. We are seriously in need of more information on environmental effects and short and long term human toxicity of all of these. Until such information is available, the intelligent course clearly is to limit as stringently as possible their release into the environment. We suspect that this will also prove to be the wisest course when the information is available.

## Fluoride Pollution

Fluoridation of water supplies is an emotion-charged subject, but it is linked with a potentially serious health hazard, flouride pollution, and it must be discussed. The scientific evidence supporting the efficacy and safety of mass fluoridation is not as good as it ought to be, but neither is there convincing evidence that it is harmful. Although there are certainly some "cranks" in the antifluoridation school, there are also some serious and competent scientists and responsible laymen who have been unmercifully abused because of the position they have taken on this controversial issue. Individual treatment with fluoride is simple and can be supplied cheaply on public funds for those desirous of using it.

Fluoride pollution is a serious problem. Fluorides are discharged into the air from steel, aluminum, phosphate, glass, pottery, and brick works. It can add to the fluoride uptake of individuals who drink fluoridated water. In addition, increased fluoride concentration has been detected in foods and beverages processed in communities supplied with fluoridated water. The difference between "safe" and "unsafe" levels of fluoride uptake is small, and it is clear that some people in fluoridated communities and elsewhere are now taking in more than the official "safe" level (there is evidence that even this level may be unsafe for certain people). Fluoride pollution and water fluoridation should be monitored much more closely, and a way must be found to assay the benefits and dangers of fluoridation in a much calmer atmosphere than has prevailed over the past decade or so.

## Radiation

We live in what has been called a "sea" of ionizing radiation from which we cannot escape. Known as the natural background, this radiation comes from cosmic rays, from radioactive substances in the Earth's crust, and from certain natural radioisotopes (such as potassium-40) that circulate through the living world. It amounts to an average of from 0.08 to 0.15 rad per person per year. (The rad is the customary unit of absorbed ionizing radiation, and amounts to 100 ergs per gram of absorber.) That man has evolved in the presence of this inescapable background does not mean that it is "safe," however, nor does it mean that we should take lightly any man-made additions to the background that happen to be smaller than or comparable to it.

Actually, there is no reason to doubt that a burden of genetic defects, cancers, and stillbirths has always been and will continue to be associated with the natural background, and that any additional radiation exposure that man brings upon himself will increase this burden. We know, for example, that ionizing radiation causes mutations—random changes in the structure of DNA, the long molecule that contains the coded genetic information necessary for the development and functioning of all organisms, including man. Mutations occur at random. Therefore, the vast majority of them are harmful, just as a random change in any complex apparatus, such as a TV set, is much more likely to do harm than good. When a cell in which a mutation has occurred is in the germ line—that is, in any cell that will produce sperm or eggs—the mutation may be passed on to future generations. It is true that repair of genetic material by certain enzymes has been demonstrated to occur. But since many mutations are passed on, we know that such repair processes are imperfect—perhaps too slow, perhaps not versatile enough, perhaps capable of error. Whatever the details that remain to be understood, repair processes do not "solve" the genetic aspect of radiation exposure.

The mechanisms which induce cancer and other consequences of radiation (such as life shortening irrespective of cause of death) borne by the generation exposed are also not well understood. It is clear that the incidence of such effects increases with the dose, although disagreement exists over whether this is in direct proportion to exposure or whether there is some more complicated relationship at the lower doses.

Naturally, all these costs of increased radiation exposure must be balanced against whatever social benefits are perceived as deriving from the activities generating the exposure. We will nevertheless dwell here on the costs, secure in the knowledge that the promoters of the activities in question will focus ample attention on the benefits.

At the moment, by far the bulk of man-made radiation exposure (over 90 percent) is attributable to the medical and dental uses of X-rays for diagnosis and therapy. Karl Z. Morgan, head of health physics at Oak Ridge National Laboratory and member of the International Commission on Radiation Protection, has argued that superfluous medical radiation exposures today may be causing between 3,500 and 36,000 unnecessary deaths annually in the U.S. alone. Morgan has also suggested that medical uses of radiation be included as contributing to the maximum recommended genetically significant dose to the public at large, currently deemed to be 0.17 rad per person per year. This allowance does not include the natural background. If medical uses were brought into the accounting, as Dr. Morgan suggests, the remaining allowable budget for man-induced radiation exposure would be reduced to about 0.10 rad per person per year. Averaged over the population, medical and dental uses today amount to more than 0.06 rad per person per year.

Another source of radiation exposure is fallout from nuclear weapons. This source has not accounted (for Americans) for more than 1 or 2 percent of the natural background. However, the rate of increase at the time the test-ban treaty was signed in 1963, stopping above-ground testing by the U.S., U.K., and U.S.S.R., was such that we should consider ourselves fortunate to have stopped when we did. Unfortunately, both the French and the Chinese have continued with surface tests. We cannot assume that there have been *no* adverse consequences of fallout, particularly since the doses in some cases have been unevenly distributed. (Averaging radiation doses over the entire population is often deceptive—it is a bit reminiscent of the old story of the statistician who drowned in a lake averaging only 2 feet deep.)

A potentially important source of radiation exposure is the use of nuclear reactors as a source of electric power. While nuclear reactors accounted for less than 1 percent of all the energy consumed in the U.S. in 1969, the amount seems to be doubling roughly every 2 years. Such a rate, if it persists, means a ten-fold increase every 6.5 years, which very quickly becomes a great deal of nuclear power.

Nuclear power can result in the release of radioactivity to the environment in a number of ways: mining and processing the fuel, the generation process itself, the transportation and reprocessing of the spent fuel elements, and the storage of the long-lived radioactive wastes. In addition to these "routine" processes, there is the possibility that an accident at a nuclear plant will release much larger quantities of radioactivity—potentially comparable to the fallout from hundreds of Hiroshima-sized fission bombs.

Obviously, no one would like to see such an accident occur, and the Atomic Energy Commission and reactor builders assure us that the probability is near zero. But because the consequences would be so great—

ranging from thousands to perhaps millions of casualties, depending on the location of the reactor, and billions of dollars in property damage—some people have called this situation "the zero-infinity dilemma." After all, "impossible" things have happened before, including the sinking of "unsinkable" ships and the cascading failure of fail-safe power grids. An AEC document on reactor safety published in 1964 records 11 "criticality accidents" in *experimental* reactors, which resulted in unusual radiation exposure to personnel, damage to the reactor, or both. An accident at the Fermi fast breeder reactor near Detroit in 1966 exceeded the "maximum credible accident" specified in the official Hazards Summary for that installation. Partly by good luck, no injuries resulted. This "near miss" for the people of Detroit casts suspicion on the system of checks and balances in the AEC regulatory bureaucracy, which permitted this highly experimental and potentially very dangerous device to be built near a population center in the first place.

The complexities of reactor safety make this a difficult area for judgments by laymen or scientists trained in other fields. It is instructive, though, that the Western Hemisphere's largest insurance companies (which presumably can afford competent advice) have refused, even as a coalition, to underwrite more than about 1 percent of the potential liability for a major nuclear power plant accident. This has led to the curious situation in which, by act of Congress (the Price-Anderson Act), the bulk of the liability is absorbed by the American public, who would shell out up to some $478 million from the U.S. treasury in the event of an accident, and the victims, who would be uncompensated for any damages in excess of that.

The issues are hardly simpler when it comes to the routine storage of radioactive wastes and to the routine emissions occurring during generation and reprocessing. Highly radioactive liquid wastes are presently stored in steel tanks at several locations around the country. This is acknowledged to be a temporary measure, since these wastes must be isolated from the biosphere for centuries. Several thousand gallons (out of some 80 million gallons stored) are known to have leaked from the "tank farm" at Hanford, Washington, already. For the longer term, the AEC seems to have made a plausible case for reducing the high-level wastes to solid form and storing them in abandoned salt mines. However, the Kansans who live near the first candidate salt mine have already expressed doubts about the potential for accidents during transportation and interment.

On the matter of less radioactive but still very dangerous low-level wastes, it would appear that economic considerations have dominated prudence. The Committee on Resources and Man of the National Academy Sciences/National Research Council summarized the situation concerning these low-level wastes as follows: "In fact, for primarily economic reasons, practices are still prevalent at most Atomic Energy Commission installations with respect to these latter categories of waste that on the present scale of operations are barely tolerable, but which would become intolerable with much increase in the use of nuclear power."

The effects of exposure to low levels of radiation and the implications of present standards are the subjects of vigorous controversy among scientists qualified in the field. The current phase of the debate was initiated by nuclear chemist (and M.D.) John Gofman and biophysicist Arthur Tamplin of the Biomedical Division at the Lawrence Radiation Laboratory, who argued in an outspoken 1969 report, and a series of supporting documents, that existing guidelines for radiation exposure should be lowered ten-fold. The validity of the numbers being debated is again difficult to judge. But a number of more fundamental issues have been raised which are relevant to all of the matters discussed in this section and to which the AEC has offered no satisfactory answer: Why should promotion and regulation of *any* technology be vested in a single agency? If it is not the intent to expose the public to a hazard permitted by present regulations, why not tighten the regulations to be *sure* the public is not so exposed? In matters of public health where the data admit the *possibility* of serious harm, should the public be required to prove harm or should the promoter be required to prove safety?

The ultimate folly in our development of nuclear energy is that the AEC is charged with the inherently contradictory responsibilities of developing nuclear power generation as expeditiously and as inexpensively as possible *and* safeguarding the public against the hazards involved in this development. In any industrial process, one buys safety at the expense of time and money.

In the matter of atomic power generation and in all matters relative to the protection of the environment, we are faced with problems so new that we are forced to examine our basic rules for individual and collective protection. Traditionally, our legal system has assumed that a person or group should be allowed to proceed so long as their activities are not harmful to others. When a person claimed that he was in danger of being harmed, the burden of proof lay upon him to demonstrate the nature of the harm. Our society now has a technology which bombards the air we breathe, the water we drink, and the natural processes upon which we depend with a volume and variety of substances the exact consequences of which are unknown. It is clear that when we are dealing with forces of unknown but certainly profound and longlasting effect on all human beings, including the unborn, the burden of proof must in some part be shared by those who are loosing the forces. Not knowing the consequences of one's actions must be a reason for restraint in this vital area.

## Chemical Mutagens

Biologists have recently become seriously concerned about sources of mutations other than radiation, namely chemical mutagens. Increased interest in the causes of congenital defects, combined with the progress being made toward an understanding of the chemical basis of heredity, have led to an awareness that mankind is being exposed to many thousands of synthetic chemicals whose mutagenic potential is unknown. Such chemicals as caffeine and LSD have been alleged to be dangerously mutagenic in man, but the results of tests on experimental animals have been variable and therefore inconclusive. Caffeine has been shown to be mutagenic in fruit-flies, but not in mice. Among the many other chemicals that have been shown to be capable of causing mutations are nitrogen mustards (from which organo-phosphate insecticides are derived), hydrogen peroxide, formaldehyde, cyclohexylamine (a breakdown product of the artificial sweetener, cyclamate), and nitrous acid (this is what the food additive sodium nitrite becomes in the stomach). In 1971, DDT was shown to be mutagenic in mice.

In order to get through the next few decades with civilization intact, we will have to focus our attention primarily on the *quantity* of *Homo sapiens*. But it would be foolish for us to neglect, even in the face of crisis, the question of the future *quality* of the human population. Every reasonable effort should be made to determine the extent of mutational hazards and to reduce them.

## Geological Hazards

Geological hazards, such as landslides—or even earthquakes—are sometimes caused by human activities. These include changing the land for housing or industrial construction or the building of large dams to meet the need of growing populations for additional supplies of fresh water.

When Lake Mead was filled (1939) following the completion of Hoover Dam, thousands of seismic events—the largest of which was an earthquake with a magnitude of 5 on the Richter scale—were recorded in that previously inactive area. Large dams in other usually inactive regions of the world have caused numerous earthquakes with magnitudes greater than 6, large enough to do substantial damage to urban areas. An earthquake that registered 6.4 on the Richter scale was triggered by the filling of the Kogna Dam in India in 1967, causing 200 deaths. Some geologists suspect that the lowering of water tables (underground water), now a worldwide occurrence, could have similar effects.

In 1967 the consequences of four years of pumping fluid chemical wastes into an underground reservoir near Denver became clear. A series of earthquakes occurred, the three largest of which had magnitudes of about 5; slight damage was reported in Denver. The amount of energy released in the series of earthquakes was slightly greater than that released by a 1 kiloton A-bomb, more energy than was expended in pumping the fluid into the reservoir. The remaining energy had been stored in the Earth's crust by geologic processes, and its release was triggered by the injection of fluid into the underground reservoir.

In 1963, the bottom of the Baldwin Hills reservoir in the Los Angeles area ruptured, causing water to burst through the dam, flooding suburbs below. Fortunately there was enough warning that the inhabitants could be evacuated in time. The cause of the reservoir failure was eventually traced to the fact that it had been situated over ancient faults which evidently were reactivated by fluid injection in nearby oil fields for oil recovery and waste disposal.

Underground nuclear explosions also have the potential for releasing such stored energy. Although the widely discussed Amchitka test in 1971 did not induce a major quake, that in no way guarantees that future tests will not serve as triggers to set off earthquakes which may be far more serious than any yet caused by human intervention in the dynamics of the Earth's crust. On the other hand, knowledge gained from underground injections and explosions may permit us to use them to relieve stresses which, if allowed to accumulate, could lead to major earthquakes.

Another man-induced geological hazard is ground subsidence. The problem here is the destruction of homes and other structures when the surface sinks due to the removal of water, oil, or large quantities of ore from beneath.

In addition to man's capability of triggering geological misfortunes, poor planning, partly abetted by rapid population growth, increases the human impact of natural geological phenomena. Thus we find homes and apartment buildings on potentially unstable landfill in the earthquake-prone San Francisco Bay area, schools and homes virtually astride the infamous San Andreas fault in the same vicinity, and residences everywhere covering steep hills subject to downhill creep and mudslides in the wet season. An equally absurd situation is heavy settlement in flood plains. (How, then, can the inevitable flood be called a "natural" disaster?) This problem has often been compounded by clear-cut logging of associated watersheds, which destroys the ability of the land to retain water and thus intensifies flooding.

## Noise Pollution

People everywhere have recently become aware of a new kind of pollution —noise pollution. The problem has been thrown into sharp focus by the discovery that some teen-agers were suffering permanent hearing loss following long exposures to amplified rock music, and by public concern about the effects of sonic booms that would be caused by supersonic transports (SST), if they were put into commercial service. Possible serious effects of the SST, in addition to the booms, are discussed in Chapter 7.

Noise is usually measured in decibels. A 10-fold increase in the strength of a sound adds 10 units on the decibel scale, a 100-fold increase adds 20. Silence, an arbitrary threshold level is represented by zero decibels. The formal definition of the decibel scale is

$$\text{decibels} = 10 \, \log_{10}\left(\frac{\text{measured intensity}}{\text{average human hearing threshold intensity}}\right).$$

Table 6-2 gives the decibel values of some representative sounds.

Even a brief exposure to intense noise can cause temporary loss of hearing acuity. Permanent loss of hearing follows chronic exposure to high

TABLE 6-2
*Noise Levels (in decibels)*

| | |
|---|---|
| Threshold of hearing | 0 |
| Normal breathing | 10 |
| Leaves rustling in breeze | 20 |
| Whispering | 30 |
| Quiet office | 40 |
| Homes | 45 |
| Quiet restaurant | 50 |
| Conversation | 60 |
| Automobile | 70 |
| Food blender | 80 |
| Niagara Falls at base | 90 |
| Heavy automobile traffic, or jet aircraft passing overhead | 100 |
| Jet aircraft taking off, or machine gun at close range | 120 |

noise levels. Noise levels as low as 50–55 decibels may delay or interfere with sleep and result in a feeling of fatigue on awakening. Recently there has been growing evidence that noise in the 90-decibel range may cause irreversible changes in the autonomic nervous system. Noise may be a factor in many stress-related diseases, such as peptic ulcer and hypertension, although present evidence is only circumstantial. In any case, noise pollution is clearly a growing threat to our health and happiness. Even if we are not subjected to the booms of the SST, the problem of noise abatement will continue to be a serious one for our society. Unless action is taken against the proliferation of motor cycles, "tote-goats," power lawnmowers, motor boats, noisy appliances, and the like, they will make aural tranquility, even in the wilderness, a thing of the past. Fortunately, however, this problem is more readily solvable with technology, imagination, and determination than most pollution problems.

## The Environment of Modern Cities

The deterioration of the environment, both physically and aesthetically, is most apparent in our cities. The dehumanizing effects of life in the slums and ghettoes particularly, where there is little hope for improving conditions, have often been cited as causes contributing to urban rioting and disturbances. Crime rates usually reach their zenith in these neighborhoods. Such symptoms of general psychological maladjustment suggest that modern cities provide a less than ideal environment for human beings.

There seems to be abundant evidence that traditional cultural patterns break down in cities, and also that the high numbers of contacts with individuals not part of one's circle of regular social acquaintances may lead to mental disturbance (defined here merely as behavior generally considered "disturbed" by the majority of the society). It is important to note that antisocial behavior and mental illness are found in all cultures, and that indeed the same disorders recognized by Western psychiatrists are found even in primitive peoples. Therefore we can be reasonably certain that lack of an evolutionarily "natural" environment is not the sole cause of such behavior. Nevertheless, that lack may well serve to aggravate the problems of people living in our most crowded, smoggy, and impersonal metropolises.

Stanford psychologist P. G. Zimbardo has concluded that urban pressures are transforming Americans into potential assassins. He based his conclusions on experimental studies of the connection between anonymity and aggression, and on field studies of vandalism. He noted an estimated 230 violent urban outbreaks in the period 1964–1969, and reported that in 1967 vandals in New York City alone wrecked 360,000 pay telephones, broke 202,712 school windows, and did damage to parks and transit systems costing some $850,000. Cars were abandoned on streets of a large city (New York) and a small one (Palo Alto, California), and secretly watched to see if there was a difference in vandalism between the two localities. The New York car was virtually demolished within three days by 23 separate attacks by looters and vandals, nearly all in view of passersby and during the daytime. The Palo Alto car was not molested during more than a week. How much (if any) of such behavior might be reduced if density were lowered is unknown, but at least the anecdotal evidence seems to indicate that factors associated with high density are involved in such problems. Crime rates are some five times as high in urban as in rural areas. Though some of this difference may be due to disparities in reporting, not all of it can be explained on this basis. Such factors as unemployment, poverty, and a poor social environment undoubtedly contribute as well. Rates for violent crimes have been shown to be positively correlated with actual population densities in American cities. This general correlation held for statistics taken in three different years, 1940, 1950, and 1960, in the same cities. The rises in assault and robbery with higher density were particularly striking, although murder and rape both also reflected the trend. Robbery is the only one of the four that does not most commonly occur between acquaintances. Interestingly, crime rates in the suburbs have been rising in the past few years, especially among teenagers from relatively affluent areas, although their crimes are more often acts against property than crimes of violence. It is important to note that none of these data show that crowding in itself causes crime (see chapter 8).

Other symptoms of mental disturbance and emotional stress are also prevalent in cities, although by no means exclusive to them. Incidence of divorce, suicide, child abuse, and various forms of mental breakdown are higher in urban areas. In an intensive study conducted in the late 1960s in Manhattan on the effects of density on people, all but 18.5 percent of the people interviewed were found to be suffering from some degree of neurotic or psychotic disturbance. This survey did not include the poorest neighborhoods, nor did it include people who were hospitalized. A different study of mental problems among children in Manhattan indicated that only 12 percent of these children were entirely free of any mental problems, and that 12 percent were seriously disturbed. Poverty and racial discrimination were found to be associated with mental disturbance, especially after the onset of adolescence. But the evidence is conflicting, and some studies tend to indicate that little or no increase of mental illness accompanies urbanization. Much more work is needed before the effects of urbanization can be clearly separated from other factors.

Diseases associated with stress, particularly ulcers, coronary disease, and high blood pressure, are also prevalent in cities. Lung cancer, associated with air pollution, is much more common in cities, even among nonsmokers, than in the country. But so are several other forms of cancer, the causes of which are unknown. Studies with animals, especially rats, which, like people, also form social systems (but whose social systems differ from those of men), indicate that overcrowding leads to severe stress on individuals. Under extreme conditions of crowding, the social system of rats breaks down and various sorts of aberrant behavior appear, including cannibalism, violent aggression, and gross neglect of offspring. Miscarriage and failures of reproduction become more common and the death rate rises. Autopsies of these animals reveal exhaustion of the adrenal cortex, brought on by stress. Similar symptoms of stress pathology were found in autopsies of many people who died in World War II concentration camps. Although there has been no direct investigation of adreno-cortical stress as a factor in deaths of urban dwellers, the prevalence of stress-related diseases in cities suggests that there might be a relationship. The possibility that our cities could eventually deteriorate to the point of causing complete social breakdown is something to consider.

The environmental deterioration of American cities is most obvious to the poor who live in them, especially to racial minorities. For them, "environmental deterioration" has nothing to do with the disappearance of fish and wildlife in national forests or litter in campgrounds. Their concern is "ghetto ecology," including the wildlife in their homes—rats, mice, and cockroaches. Air pollution reaches its highest levels in city centers; here also are there most likely to be inadequate sewage disposal and solid waste disposal systems. Heat in winter is often insufficient, space is at a premium, crime rates and vandalism high, food often inadequate, medical care poor at best, opportunities for recreation virtually nil, schools at their worst, and public transportation expensive and inconvenient. In short, all the problems and disadvantages of cities are greatly intensified for the poor. This environmental syndrome is reflected by higher mortalities among the poor, especially infant and child mortalities, than for the general population.

Of course, many, if not most, of the present hazards and discomforts of city life could be eliminated or mitigated by more creative design of houses and neighborhoods, by the development of alternative, less-polluting means of transportation, by finding solutions to the problems of the minorities and the poor in general, and by more efficient and equitable forms of administration. If urban areas were planned and developed so that people could live near their places of employment, many transportation-related problems would be alleviated, including congestion and pollution from automobiles. Making the vicinities of factories pleasantly habitable would present some problems, but would result in considerable pollution abatement. Similarly, the social problems created by the separate existence both of suburban bedroom communities and city-center ghettoes might also be relieved. Of course, all of this requires vast infusions of time, talent, imagination, and money. But no amounts of these, however vast, can bring lasting success as long as our cities continue to grow rapidly.

## Aesthetic Considerations

Some destitute mountain folk from the Appalachians, who were moved to New York where jobs were available, promptly fled back to the mountains, preferring poverty amid pleasant surroundings to life in such a horrible place. The aesthetic poverty of our cities and suburbs has reached such a degree that most citizens are aware of it. Newspapers are replete with stories describing slums, ghettos, rats, trash, and garbage. This is one of the reasons why weekends and holidays invariably bring on a mass exodus from the cities. Unfortunately, our frontier habits of thoughtless littering and defacement seem likely to reduce our attractive rural areas and state and national parks to similar levels of ugliness.

Studies with young animals and indirect evidence from young children indicate that the richness of the sensory environment early in life influences the extent of later mental development. Sensory stimulation in young rats resulted in measurably larger brain sizes in adulthood than in their sensorily deprived litter-mates, and it affected their learning and problem-solving abilities as well. Children who have been exposed to a variety of sights, sounds, and experiences when they are very young may learn faster, and later on be more likely to develop attitudes of inquiry and exploration.

Yet our cities, once a rich source of varied sensory experiences, are becoming more monotonous and dismal. Modern urban development programs flatten blocks at a time—blocks that once included a mixture of buildings of different ages and styles—and then replace them with concrete monoliths that lack aesthetic quality. The variety of sounds, at least some of which were pleasing to hear, in smaller towns and on farms, is also coming to be replaced by an incessant din of traffic, construction, and household appliances.

A zoologist with an interest in environmental psychology, A. E. Parr of the American Museum of Natural History, has written that city children of a generation or two ago spent much of their time exploring and participating in the activities of the city, while today children are confined to dreary school rooms, their homes, and the local park. Poorer ones may play in the streets, and in this respect perhaps they are luckier. But many of today's city children are being deprived of firsthand knowledge about the city they live in and how the social organizations within it function, which creates a sort of alienation from their surroundings. At the same time their surroundings are becoming more and more monotonous and less attractive. Children's urges toward inquisitiveness, exploration, and ingenuity (qualities we will desperately need during the next generation) may thus be stifled outside the schools as well as in them.

Suburbs are often better than the cities in aesthetic qualities and sensory stimulation, but not invariably so. Although the environment is usually more natural and includes trees and gardens, many suburbs tend to reduce everything to a common denominator. All the houses in a given area are similar if not identical, and so are the gardens, parks, and shopping centers. Each modern real estate development is generally inhabited by people of about the same age, educational level, type of employment, and economic status. There is not much opportunity for children to meet people whose points of view differ from their own or those of their parents. Although the children may be freer to explore in the suburbs than in the city, there is sometimes even less of interest to find there than in the city. The absence of men most of the time may result in an even greater alienation of youngsters (and wives as well) from the functioning society. Of course, television may compensate somewhat for the lack of sensory and social variety in our lives, but it does not encourage inquisitiveness or offer opportunities for exploration, ingenuity, or direct experience. On the contrary, it seems to foster passiveness and a tendency to regard life as a spectator sport.

## The Epidemiological Environment

Today the population of *Homo sapiens* is the largest in the history of the species, it has the highest average density, and it contains a record number of undernourished and malnourished people. The population, or rather a small but important segment of it, is also unprecedentedly mobile. People are in continual motion around the globe, and they are able to move from continent to continent in hours. The potential for a worldwide epidemic (pandemic) has never been greater, but people's awareness of this threat has probably never been smaller.

We do not completely understand the behavior of viruses but we do know that the spontaneous development of highly lethal strains of human viruses and the invasion of humanity by extremely dangerous animal viruses are possible. We also know that crowding increases the chances for development of a virus epidemic. Should, say, an especially virulent strain of flu appear, it is doubtful that the United States and other developed countries could produce enough vaccine fast enough to save most of their populations. Needless to say, the problem would be even more severe in the UDCs. Certainly little effort could be made to save most of humanity. Consider, for example, the difficulty the United States had in coping with the mild Asian flu epidemic of 1968. It was not possible to manufacture enough vaccine to protect most of the population, and the influenza death rate in 1968 was more than four times as high as that of 1967. Only 613 deaths were attributed to flu, but society paid a high price for the disease in extra medical care and loss of working hours. That the number of deaths was not higher was due primarily to the relatively mild character of the virus, rather than to modern medicine.

In 1967 an outbreak of a previously unknown disease occurred among a shipment of vervet monkeys that had been imported into laboratories in Marburg, Germany, and in Yugoslavia. This severe, hemorrhagic disease infected 25 laboratory workers who came into contact with the monkeys and their tissues. Seven of these people died. Five secondary infections occurred in individuals who came into contact with the blood of the original patients; all of these individuals survived. Mankind was extremely fortunate that the first infections of *Homo sapiens* by Marburgvirus occurred around laboratories where the nature of the threat was quickly recognized, and the disease contained (it was not susceptible to antibiotics). If it had escaped into the human population at large, and if the disease had retained its virulence as it passed from person to person, an epidemic resulting in hundreds of millions or even billions of deaths might have occurred. Among well-fed laboratory workers with expert medical care, 7 out of 30 patients died. Among hungry people with little or no medical care, mortality would be much higher. The infected monkeys passed through London airport in transit to the laboratories. If the virus had infected airport personnel, it could have spread over the entire world before anyone realized what was happening.

Our highly mechanized society is also extremely vulnerable to disruption by such events as power failures, floods, and snowstorms. What would happen if the United States were confronted with an epidemic that kept masses of sick people from work and caused the uninfected to stay home or flee the cities because of their fear of infection? This might slow or even stop the spread of the disease, but hunger, cold (in the winter), and many other problems would soon develop as the services of society ceased to operate. We have substantial knowledge of the almost total breakdown of much less complex societies than ours in the face of the "Black Death"— a breakdown that occurred among people far more accustomed to a short life, hardship, disease, and death than the population of the Western World today. The panic may well be imagined if Americans were to discover that "modern medical science" either had no cure for a disease of epidemic proportions, or had insufficient doses of the cure for everyone. The disease itself would almost certainly impede the application of any ameliorating measures. Distribution of vaccines, for instance, would be difficult if airlines, trains, and trucks were not running.

In many parts of the world, public health conditions are developing that have a high potential for disaster. The rats that live on stored grain in India have renewed the spectre of a major outbreak of bubonic plague. Indeed, a returning Vietnam veteran could bring plague to rat-infested New York City and create an extremely dangerous situation. Nitrate pollution of water is creating conditions in which dangerous soil organisms are brought into contact with man for the first time. The organism that has recently caused cases of a fatal meningitis has been identified as a soil-dwelling amoeba. It may be just the first of many such agents to infect man.

Irrigation projects connected with the Aswan Dam are spreading the conditions that promote the serious parasitic disease bilharzia (schistosomiasis). The broadcast use of chemotherapy and antibiotics has created a serious medical problem through the induction of resistance in bacteria and other parasites. Modification of the climate would also inevitably influence disease patterns; for example, the length of time viruses remain infectious is in part a function of humidity. A trend toward drying would encourage some, whereas others would thrive in increased moisture.

As if the threat of a natural pandemic were not gruesome enough, there is always the threat of biological warfare, or of an accidental escape of lethal agents from a biological warfare laboratory. Although most laymen have long been afraid of thermonuclear war, they are just beginning to grasp the colossal hazard posed by chemical and biological warfare (CBW). Any country with one or two well-trained microbiologists and even a modest budget can build its own biological doomsday weapons. Constructing lethal viruses against which there is little or no resistance in human populations can easily be done in theory; it may have already been done in practice. There have been rumors of the development by the American CBW establishment of a pneumonic rabies, one which, instead of being transmitted by bite, is transmitted in the same way as the common cold: from person to person via exhaled droplets. This is certainly possible, since under special conditions (such as those that sometimes occur in caves full of rabid bats) rabies has already been shown to have been transmitted through the air. Such a disease would be a disastrously effective weapon if it were transmitted by infected individuals before symptoms appear, since once they do appear, rabies is (with one notable recent exception) 100 percent fatal. Other possibilities for lethal agents are many— anthrax, plague, tularemia, and $Q$-fever, to name a few. These might be disseminated in their natural form or in the form of special "hot" strains that are drug resistant or superlethal. Besides direct assaults on man, overt or covert attacks on a nation's food supply might be made by introducing plant diseases. The more crowded a population is, and the smaller its per capita food supplies, the better a target it would be for a biological warfare attack.

Why would nations develop such weapons? For the same reason they develop others. They hope to immunize or otherwise protect their own populations and thus avoid a biological backlash. These weapons have a special appeal for small and poor powers, which see themselves threatened by larger, richer ones, and which lack the funds or the expertise to develop nuclear weapons systems. Presumably CBW would hold a special interest for countries like Taiwan, Cuba, Egypt, Israel, and North Vietnam.

Probably the full arsenal of CBW will never be used but that does not rule out the possibility of an accident. Virus laboratories, especially, are notoriously unsafe. To date, some 2,700 laboratory workers have become accidentally infected with viruses transmitted by insects, and there have been 107 fatalities. These deaths were caused by just one group of viruses. Fatal accidents occur in laboratories where work is done on other kinds of viruses, as well as other microorganisms. The inability of government CBW agencies to avoid accidents has been made clear by the Skull Valley, Utah, CBW disaster of 1968, in which many thousands of sheep were poisoned when a chemical agent "escaped," and by the possible escape of Venezuelan Equine Encephalitis from the Dugway, Utah, Proving Ground in 1967. Congressman Richard D. McCarthy of New York announced in 1969 that CBW agents were being transported around the country in small containers *on commercial airliners!* Biological warfare laboratories are potential sources of a man-made "solution" to the population explosion. It is essential that some way be found to block all further work on biological weapons—the risk for mankind is simply too great.

In November 1969, President Nixon announced the unilateral renunciation by the United States of the use of biological warfare, even in retaliation. He directed that the U.S. stocks of biological agents were to be destroyed and that further work on defenses against biological weapons was to be transferred from the Department of Defense to the Department of Health, Education and Welfare. President Nixon's warning that ". . . mankind already carries in its own hands too many of the seeds of its own destruction" is one that must be heeded by people in all nations. Destruction of U.S. biological warfare materials was systematically carried out in 1970 and 1971. Even though this action might later be reversed by reactionary leadership in this country or nullified by actions elsewhere, it is encouraging that the President of the world's most powerful nation has taken this most constructive step.

# Bibliography

Aaronson, Terri, 1969. Tempest over a teapot. *Environment,* vol. 11, no. 8, pp. 23–27. On steam engines as an alternative to internal combustion.

American Chemical Society, 1969. *Cleaning our Environment: the Chemical Basis for Action.* American Chemical Society, Washington, D.C. On pollution control for air, water, solid wastes, and pesticides.

Anderson, J. M., and M. R. Peterson, 1969. DDT: sublethal effects on brook trout nervous system. *Science,* vol. 164, pp. 440–441.

Angino, E. E., et al., 1969. Arsenic and water pollution hazard. *Science,* vol. 170, pp. 870–872.

Anthrop, Donald F., 1969. Environmental noise pollution: a new threat to sanity. *Bulletin of the Atomic Scientists,* May, pp. 11–16. Contains some material on SST noise and sonic booms.

Bache, C. A., W. H. Gutenmann, and D. J. Lisk, 1971. Residues of total mercury and methylmercuric salts in lake trout as a function of age. *Science,* vol. 172, pp. 951–952 (28 May). Shows buildup of mercury concentrations as fish grow bigger.

Bates, Marston, 1968. Crowded people. *Natural History* (Oct.)

Beranek, Leo L., 1966. Noise. *Scientific American,* vol. 215, no. 6 (Dec.) pp. 66–76. Scientific American Offprint No. 306, W. H. Freeman and Company, San Francisco.

Berelson, B., and G. A. Steiner, 1964. *Human Behavior: An Inventory of Scientific Findings.* Harcourt, Brace & World, Inc. An invaluable source for information on subjects ranging from perception to mental illness and cultural change.

Bragdon, Clifford R., 1968. Noise—a syndrome of modern society. *Scientist and Citizen,* March, pp. 29–37. Extensive bibliography.

Burnham, David, 1969. Psychologist says pressures of big-city life are transforming Americans into potential assassins. *New York Times,* April 20, p. 49. An account of Dr. Phillip G. Zimbardo's studies on aggression and vandalism in large and small cities.

Calhoun, John B., 1962. Population density and social pathology. *Scientific American,* vol. 206, no. 2 (Feb.). Studies of crowding in rats. Scientific American Offprint No. 506, W. H. Freeman and Company, San Francisco.

Carr, Donald E., 1965. *The Breath of Life.* W. W. Norton & Co., Inc., New York. A general discussion of air pollution.

Chesters, G., and J. G. Konrad, 1971. Effects of pesticide usage on water quality. *BioScience,* vol. 21, no. 12, pp. 565–569 (June 15).

Chow, T. J., and J. L. Earl, 1970. Lead aerosols in the atmosphere: increasing concentrations. *Science,* vol. 169, pp. 577–580 (7 Aug.). On lead as a component of air pollution.

Cole, LaMont C., 1966. Man's ecosystem. *BioScience,* vol. 16, no. 4 (April).

Consumer's Union, 1971. Will the new gasolines lick air pollution? *Consumer Reports,* March, pp. 156–159. Discusses non-leaded gasolines and other components of automibile emissions.

Council on Environmental Quality (U.S.), 1971. *Environmental Quality: Second Annual Report* (Aug.). Washington, D.C. This report concentrates on the costs of environmental protection; what is being spent now and what will be needed in the future.

Curley, A., and R. Kembrough, 1969. Chlorinated hydrocarbon insecticides in plasma and milk of pregnant and lactating women. *Arch. Environmental Health,* vol. 18, pp. 156–164.

Curley, A., V. A. Sedlak, E. T. Gerling, R. E. Hawk, W. F. Barthel, P. E. Pierce, and W. H. Lekosky, 1971. Organic mercury identified as the cause of poisoning in humans and hogs. *Science,* vol. 172, pp. 65–67. Documentation of the first episode of mercury poisoning in the U.S., caused by eating meat of animals that had consumed mercury in their food.

Curtis, Anthony, 1971. Is cleanliness three-cornered? *New Scientist,* 25 Feb. pp. 415–417. Describes a low-pollution alternative to the internal combustion engine, the Wankel.

Curtis, Richard, and Elizabeth Hogan, 1969. *Perils of the Peaceful Atom: The Myth of Safe Nuclear Power Plants.* Doubleday & Co., New York. This and Novick's book (below) summarize the dangers in today's headlong rush to use nuclear energy to produce electrical power.

Davies, J. E., W. F. Edmundson, C. H. Carter, and A. Barquet, 1969. Effects of anticonvulsant drugs on dicophane (DDT) residues in man. *Lancet,* July 5, pp. 7–9. Certain drugs have been shown to reduce DDT levels in human tissue. Long-term side effects have not been studied, and therefore their value is unknown.

Deichmann, W. B., W. E. MacDonald, and D. A. Cubit, 1971. DDT tissue retention: sudden rise induced by the addition of Aldrin to a fixed DDT intake. *Science,* vol. 172, pp. 275–6 (16 April). Another example of synergistic effects among pollutants.

Demaree, Allan T., 1970. Cars and cities on a collision course. *Fortune,* Feb. pp. 124–129+. Discussion of the disadvantages of an automobile transport system and some possible alternatives.

Dubos, Rene, 1965. *Man Adapting.* Yale Univ. Press, New Haven. Deals with many of the problems covered in this chapter.

Ehrlich, P. R., J. P. Holdren, and R. W. Holm (eds.), 1971. *Man and the Ecosphere.* W. H. Freeman and Company, San Francisco. Important papers from *Scientific American* with critical commentaries.

Elsaesser, H. W., 1971. Air pollution: Our ecological alarm and blessing in disguise. *Transactions of the American Geophysical Union,* vol. 52, no. 3, pp. 92–100 (March). Argues that air pollution acts as a valuable stimulant for arousing action against more subtle environmental problems.

*Environment,* 1970. The June issue contains three articles on automobile emissions and some possible alternatives to the internal combustion engine.

*Environment,* 1971. The May issue (vol. 13, no. 4) of this journal on environmental problems contains three important articles on mercury, and references to the literature.

Esposito, John C., 1970. *Vanishing Air.* Grossman Publishers, New York. Ralph Nader's Study Group's report on air pollution.

Evans, D. M., and A. Bradford, 1969. Under the rug. *Environment,* vol. 11, no. 8 (Oct.) pp. 3–13+. On industrial wastes in deep injection wells.

Fabricant, N., and R. M. Hallman, 1971. *Toward a Rational Power Policy: Energy, Politics, and Pollution.* Report by the Environmental Protection Agency of New York City. George Braziller, New York.

Falk, H. L., S. J. Thompson, and Paul Koten, 1965. Carcinogenic potential of pesticides. *Arch. Environmental Health,* vol. 10, pp. 848–858.

Fischer, Ames, 1967. Community psychiatry and the population explosion. *California Medicine,* vol. 106, pp. 189–195. Contains information on relation between high population density and incidence of mental illness.

Flawn, P. T., 1970. *Environmental Geology.* Harper and Row, New York. Excellent material on earthquakes, subsidence, man as a geological agent, etc.

Forbes, I. A., D. F. Ford, H. W. Kendall, and J. H. Mackenzie, 1971. Nuclear reactor safety: an evaluation of new evidence. *Nuclear News,* September. The best paper available on accident hazards in existing nuclear power reactors.

Friedman, I., and N. Peterson, 1971. Fossil fuels as a source of mercury pollution. *Science,* vol. 172, pp. 1027–1028 (4 June). Pollution from fossil fuels is shown to be comparable to that from industrial waste.

Gilfillan, S. C., 1965. Lead poisoning and the fall of Rome. *Journal of Occupational Medicine,* vol. 7, no. 2 (Feb.) pp. 53–60.

Gofman, J. W., and A. R. Tamplin, 1971. *Poisoned Power.* Rodale Press, Emmaus, Pa. Scientists from the Lawrence Radiation Laboratory present their case on radiation and the hazards of nuclear power.

Goldsmith, J. R., and A. C. Hexter, 1967. Respiratory exposure to lead: Epidemiological and experimental dose-response relationships. *Science,* vol. 158, pp. 132–134.

Goldsmith, John R., 1970. The new airborne disease. *California Medicine,* vol. 115, no. 5, pp. 13–20 (Nov.). A general discussion of the effects of air pollution on health.

Graham, Frank, Jr., 1966. *Disaster by Default. Politics and Water Pollution.* M. Evans & Co., Inc., New York.

Graham, Frank, 1970. *Since Silent Spring.* Fawcett-Crest, Greenwich, Conn. Details of the pesticide controversies in recent years.

Grinstead, Robert R., 1970. The new resource. *Environment,* vol. 12, no. 10, (Dec.), pp. 2–17. On possible means of using solid waste.

Gross, Edward, 1969. Digging out from under. *Science News,* vol. 96, pp. 278–279. Discusses the problem of disposal of solid wastes.

Groth, N., 1970. *Air Pollution in the San Francisco Bay Area.* Report of the Stanford Workshop on air pollution. Ecology Center Press, San Francisco.

Hall, E. T., 1966. *The Hidden Dimension.* Doubleday, Garden City, New York. Basic source on man's use of personal space.

Hamilton, D. H., and R. L. Meeham, 1971. Ground rupture in the Baldwin Hills. *Science,* vol. 172, no. 3981, pp. 333–344. How fluid injection can trigger surface faulting.

Hanson, R. P., S. E. Sulkin, E. L. Buescher, W. McD. Hammon, R. W. McKinney, and T. H. Work, 1967. Arbovirus infections of laboratory workers. *Science,* vol. 158, pp. 1283–1286. Describes incidence of laboratory accidents with arthropod-borne viruses.

Harris, Robert J. C., 1971. Cancer and the environment. *International Journal of Environmental Studies,* vol. 1, pp. 59–65.

Hayes, W. J., Jr., W. F. Durham, and C. Cueto, 1956. The effect of known repeated oral doses of chlorophenothane (DDT) in man. *Journal of American Medical Association,* vol. 162, pp. 890–897. In this study high oral doses of DDT did not produce detectable symptoms in adult men over a period of 1–2 years. It is often erroneously cited as "proof" that DDT is harmless to human beings.

Herber, Lewis, 1968. *Crisis in our Cities.* Prentice-Hall, Inc., Englewood Cliffs, N.J. Describes the negative aspects of the urban environment.

Hersch, Seymour M., 1969. *Chemical and Biological Warfare.* Doubleday (Anchor Book), Garden City, N.Y.

Hersch, Seymour M., 1969. Dare we develop biological weapons? *N.Y. Times Magazine,* Sept. 28.

Herschaft, Alex, 1969. Solid waste treatment. *Science & Technology,* June, pp. 34–42.

Hexter, A. C., and J. R. Goldsmith, 1971. Carbon monoxide: association of community air pollution with mortality. *Science,* vol. 172, pp. 265–267 (16 April). A study showing the association of deaths in Los Angeles with high levels of carbon monoxide in the atmosphere.

Holdren, J. P., and P. R. Ehrlich (eds.), 1971. *Global Ecology.* Harcourt Brace Jovanovich, New York. Includes basic papers on several classes of environmental hazards.

Holdren, J. P., and P. Herrera, 1971. *Energy.* Sierra Club Books, New York. This book deals extensively with the threat to human life inherent in today's methods of producing energy.

Iltis, H. H., O. L. Loucks, and P. Andrews, 1970. Criteria for an optimum human environment. *Science and Public Affairs,* the *Bulletin of the Atomic Scientists,* vol. 26, no. 1, pp. 2–6. Discusses some of the less obvious requisites of human existence. Reprinted in Holdren and Ehrlich (see above).

Innes, J. R. M., et al., 1969. Bioassay of pesticides and industrial chemicals for tumorigenicity in mice: a preliminary note. *Journal of the National Cancer Institute,* vol. 42, no. 6, pp. 1101–1114 (June). Study of cancer induction in mice by a variety of chemicals, including DDT and several other pesticides.

Jahns, R. H., 1968. Geological jeopardy. *Texas Quarterly,* vol. 11, no. 2, pp. 69–83. Reprinted in Holdren and Ehrlich (see above).

Kazantis, G., 1971. The poison chain for mercury in the environment. *International Journal of Environmental Studies,* vol. 1, pp. 301–306.

Kissling, R. E., R. Q. Robinson, F. A. Murphy, and S. G. Whitfield, 1968. Agent of disease contracted from green monkeys. *Science,* vol. 160, pp. 888–890. Source on Marburgvirus.

Kryter, K. D., 1970. *The Effects of Noise on Man.* Academic Press, New York. Useful for detailed information.

Kyllonen, R. L., 1967. Crime rate vs. population density in United States Cities: A model. *Yearbook of the Society for General Systems Research,* vol. 12, pp. 137–145.

Lave, L. B., and E. P. Seskin, 1970. Air pollution and human health. *Science,* vol. 169, no. 3947, pp. 723–733 (21 Aug.). Concludes that there is a close association between air pollution and ill health and estimates the health cost in dollars. Extensive bibliography.

Law, Steven L., 1971. Methylmercury and inorganic mercury collection by a selective chelating resin. *Science,* vol. 174, pp. 285–287 (15 Oct.). A possible means of collecting methylmercury and inorganic mercury from our waters.

Laws, E. R., Jr., A. Curley, and E. F. Biros, 1967. Men with intensive occupational exposure to DDT. *Archives of Environmental Health,* vol. 15, pp. 766–775. This study, like that of Hayes et al. cited above, tends to indicate little or no toxicity of DDT to adults over periods of a decade or more. It says nothing about the effects of exposure over longer time stretches, especially when exposure begins before birth. Information on the causes of death of men who have worked for chlorinated hydrocarbon manufacturers would be of greater interest on the subject of adult toxicity than this sort of study.

Lerner, I. Michael, 1968. *Heredity, Evolution, and Society.* W. H. Freeman and Company, San Francisco. Excellent background reading for hazards associated with mutagenesis.

Lewis, Howard R., 1965. *With Every Breath You Take.* Crown Publishers, New York. Another general discussion on air pollution.

Lewis, Oscar, 1966. The culture of poverty. *Scientific American,* vol. 215, no. 4 (April). Scientific American Offprint No. 631, W. H. Freeman and Company, San Francisco.

Lindsay, Sally, 1970. How safe is the nation's drinking water? *Saturday Review,* May 2, pp. 54–55.

MacDonald, G. J. F., 1969. The modification of planet earth by man. *Technology Review,* Oct./Nov. See especially the section on man-made earthquakes.

Marine, Gene, 1969. *America the Raped.* Simon & Schuster, New York.

Marwick, Charles, 1968. A revival for the steam car? *New Scientist,* 20 June, pp. 638–639. On the advantages of steam over internal combustion engines.

McCaull, J., 1971. Building a shorter life. *Environment,* vol. 13, no. 7 (Sept.). A documented study of cadmium as a potentially dangerous pollutant.

Morgan, Karl Z., 1969. Tainted radiation. *Science and Technology,* no. 90, pp. 47–50 (June).

Morgan, Karl Z., 1970. *Hearings on environmental effects of producing electric power.* Joint Committee on Atomic Energy, part 2, vol. 1, U.S. Congress. An important statement by a distinguished health physicist.

National Wildlife Federation, 1970. National Environmental Quality Index. *National Wildlife Magazine,* Oct–Nov. Also issued as a separate pamphlet. Shows decline of environmental quality in the U.S. and estimates costs of damage.

Novick, Sheldon, 1969. *The Careless Atom.* Houghton-Mifflin, Boston. General source on radiation hazards.

Novick, Sheldon, 1969. A new pollution problem. *Environment* (May). Discussion of mercury pollution. The same issue of *Environment* contains two other articles on the same subject.

Parr, A. E., 1967. Urbanity and the urban scene. *Landscape,* vol. 16, no. 3. Contrasts the psychological impact of city life today with that of two generations ago, especially on children.

Parr, A. E., 1968. The five ages of urbanity. *Landscape,* vol. 17, no. 3. Describes the impact of modern city life on people of different ages.

Patterson, Clair C., 1965. Contaminated and natural lead environments of man. *Archives of Environmental Health,* vol. 11 (Sept.) pp. 344–360. Documented study of human exposure to lead.

Perlmutter, M., and M. Lieber, 1970. *U.S. Geological Survey, Water Supply Paper 1879 G*. Discusses chromium and cadmium pollution of Long Island ground water.

President's Science Advisory Committee, Environmental Pollution Panel, 1965. Restoring the quality of our environment. Washington, D.C. Somewhat out of date but still a useful reference.

Pryde, P. R., 1970. Victors are not judged. *Environment,* vol. 12, no. 9, pp. 30–39 (Nov.). Water pollution problems in the USSR.

Radomski, J. L., W. B. Deichmann, E. E. Clizer, and A. Rey, 1968. Pesticide concentrations in the liver, brain and adipose tissue of terminal patients. *Food and Cosmetic Toxicology,* vol. 6, pp. 209–220. This study is one of the most frightening yet to appear on the direct threat of the human chlorinated hydrocarbon load.

Rienow, Robert, and Leona T., 1967. *Moment in the Sun*. Dial, New York. Well written introduction to American environmental problems.

Russell, Claire, and W. M. S. Russell, 1970. The sardine syndrome. *The Ecologist,* vol. 1, no. 2 (Aug.) pp. 4–9. Interesting article on aggression, stress, and crowding.

Sachs, David P., 1968. Drink at your own risk. *McCalls* (Nov.), p. 100. Describes the state of water supplies in a series of American cities. Based on data from the Public Health Service.

Salvia, Joseph D., 1968. A little pest in the alfalfa. . . . a little trouble in Montana. *Scientist and Citizen,* Aug. pp. 143–153. On pesticide residues in food.

Sanders, Howard J., 1969. Chemical mutagens. 1. The road to genetic disaster. 2. An expanding roster of suspects. *Chemical and Engineering News,* May and June. An excellent popular summary of what is known about chemical mutagens.

Sax, Karl, and Hally J. Sax, 1968. Possible mutagenic hazards of some food additives, beverages and insecticides. *Japan Journal of Genetics,* vol. 43, no. 2, pp. 89–94.

Schapiro, S., and K. R. Vukovitch, 1970. Early experience effects upon cortical dendrites: a proposed model for development. *Science,* vol. 167, pp. 292–294 (16 Jan.). Experiments on rats indicating that enriched sensory experience in infancy results in increased brain growth.

Schmitt, Robert C., 1957, Density, delinquency, and crime in Honolulu. *Sociology and Social Research,* vol. 41, pp. 274–276. Study linking high population density with criminal behavior.

Schmitt, Robert C., 1966. Density, health and social disorganization. *AIP Journal.* Jan., pp. 38–40. More on the effects of high density.

Schroeder, H. A., and J. J. Balassa, 1966. Abnormal trace metals in man: Arsenic. *Journal of Chronic Diseases,* vol. 19, pp. 85–106. A basic source.

Selikoff, I. J., E. C. Hammond, and J. Churg, 1968. Asbestos exposure, smoking and neoplasia. *Journal of the American Medical Association,* vol. 204, pp. 106–112 (April 8). Demonstrates an apparent synergism between asbestos particles and cigarette smoke in inducing lung cancer.

Smith, C. E. G., D. I. H. Simpson, E. T. W. Bowen, and I. Zlotnik, 1967. Fatal human disease from vervet monkeys. *Lancet,* vol. 2 for 1967, no. 7526, pp. 1119–1121. See also pp. 1129–1130 of the same issue. Source on Marburgvirus.

Sommer, Robert, 1969. *Personal Space.* Prentice-Hall, Inc., Englewood Cliffs, N.J.

Study of Critical Environmental Problems (SCEP), 1970. *Man's Impact on the Global Environment.* MIT Press, Cambridge. An excellent assessment of some of the most important environmental problems.

Tamplin, A. R., and J. W. Gofman, 1970. *Population Control through Nuclear Pollution.* Nelson Hall Co., Chicago. An angry book dealing with AEC irresponsibility.

T.–W.–Siennes, R. N., 1963. Stress in a crowded world. *New Scientist,* no. 357, pp. 595–596 (Sept. 19).

Tarjan, R., and T. Kemeny, 1969. Multigeneration studies on DDT in mice. *Food and Cosmetic Toxicology,* vol. 7, pp. 215–222. On the induction of cancer in mice by DDT.

Tinker, Jon, 1971. Ouchi-ouchi: your cadmium's showing. *New Scientist,* 22 April, pp. 186–187. On cadmium pollution.

United States Congress, Joint Committee on Atomic Energy, 1969–1970. *Hearings on Environmental Effects of Producing Electric Power.* Parts I and II (3 vols.). U.S. Government Printing Office, Washington, D.C. Contains complete testimony of Gofman, Tamplin, K. Z. Morgan, and many others on all sides of radiation and nuclear power controversies.

Viets, F. G. Jr., 1971. Water quality in relation to farm use of fertilizer. *BioScience,* vol. 21, no. 10, pp. 460–467 (May 15).

Waggoner, P. E., 1971. Plants and polluted air. *BioScience,* vol. 21, no. 10, pp. 455–459. Discusses the destructive effects of smog on plants and the ameliorating effects of plants on smog.

Wakefield, Ron, 1970. Are the smog laws really fighting smog? *Road and Track,* May, pp. 88–90. A technical discussion of emission control of automobiles.

Wallace, R. A., W. Fulkham, W. D. Shults, and W. S. Lyons, 1971, *Mercury in the Environment: the Human Element.* A report from the Oak Ridge National Laboratory (available from Operations Division, National Technical Information Service, Springfield, Va. 22151; order by title and identification no. ORNL-NSF-EP-1, $3.00).

Warren, C. E., 1971. *Biology and Water Pollution Control.* W. B. Saunders Co., Philadelphia. A search for solutions to water pollution problems in a biological context.

Winklestein, W., and M. R. Gay, 1971. Suspended particulate air pollution. *Archives of Environmental Health,* vol. 22, pp. 174–177 (Jan.). Indicates that particulate air pollution may act directly or synergistically to cause cirrhosis of the liver.

Wright, Jim, 1966. *The Coming Water Famine*. Coward-McCann, Inc., New York.

Wurster, Charles F., 1971. Persistent insecticides and their regulation by the federal government. Testimony before the U.S. Senate Committee on Agriculture and Forestry, 25 March. Excellent summary of what is known about DDT as a threat to human health.

Zaron, M. R., R. Tyre, and L. Lattore, 1967. Chlorinated hydrocarbon pesticide levels in newborn. *Proc. Conf. Biological Effects Pesticides Mammalian Systems*. N.Y. Academy of Sciences (in press).

Zeidberg, L. D., R. A. Prindle, and E. Landau, 1964. The Nashville air pollution study. III: morbidity in relation to air pollution. *American Journal of Public Health,* vol. 54, no. 1, pp. 85–97.

# CHAPTER 7

# Ecosystems in Jeopardy

*". . . the fouling of the nest which has been typical of man's*
*activity in the past on a local scale now seems to*
*be extending to the whole world society."*

—Kenneth Boulding
*The Economics of the Coming*
*Spaceship Earth* (1966)

The plants, animals, and microorganisms that live in an area and make up a biological community are interconnected by an intricate web of relationships, which includes the physical environment in which these organisms exist. These interdependent biological and physical components make up what biologists call an *ecosystem*. The ecosystem concept emphasizes the functional relationships among organisms and between organisms and their physical environments. These functional relationships are exemplified by the food chains through which energy flows in ecosystems, as well as by the pathways along which the chemical elements essential to life move through the ecosystem. These pathways are generally circular; the elements pass through the system in cycles. The cycling of some elements is so slow, however, that in the time span of interest to us, movement appears to be one-way. An understanding of the flow of energy and the cycling of materials in ecosystems is essential to our perception of what is perhaps the most subtle and dangerous threat to man's existence. This threat is the potential destruction, by man's own activities, of those ecological systems upon which the very existence of the human species depends.

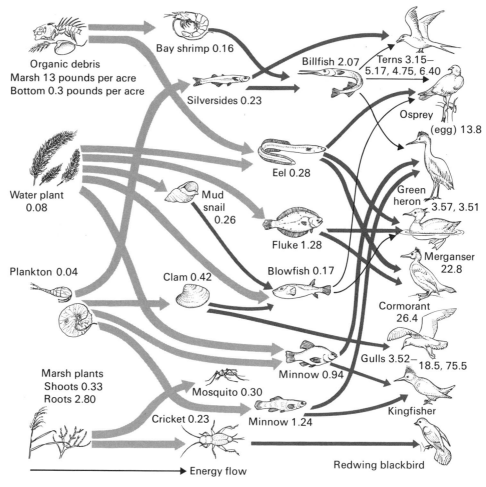

Organic debris
Marsh 13 pounds per acre
Bottom 0.3 pounds per acre

Bay shrimp 0.16

Silversides 0.23

Billfish 2.07

Terns 3.15—
5.17, 4.75, 6.40

Osprey
(egg) 13.8

Eel 0.28

Water plant
0.08

Mud
snail
0.26

Green
heron
3.57, 3.51

Fluke 1.28

Merganser
22.8

Plankton 0.04

Clam 0.42

Blowfish 0.17

Cormorant
26.4

Marsh plants
Shoots 0.33
Roots 2.80

Mosquito 0.30

Minnow 0.94

Gulls 3.52—
18.5, 75.5

Cricket 0.23

Minnow 1.24

Kingfisher

Redwing blackbird

Energy flow

FIGURE 7-1

Portion of a food web in a Long Island estuary. Arrows indicate flow of energy. Numbers are the parts per million of DDT found in each kind of organism. (After Woodwell, "Toxic Substances and Ecological Cycles." Copyright © 1967 by Scientific American, Inc. All rights reserved.)

## Food Webs

The food web of a Long Island estuary has been thoroughly investigated by biologists George M. Woodwell, Charles F. Wurster, and Peter A. Isaacson. The relationships they discovered are illustrated in Figure 7-1; their study illustrates several important characteristics of most food webs. One is complexity. Although only some of the kinds of plants and animals in this ecosystem are shown in this figure, it is evident that most of the consumers feed on several different organisms, and that most prey organisms are attacked by more than one predator. To put it another way, the food chains are interlinked. Ecologists believe that complexity is in part responsible for the stability of most ecosystems. Apparently, the more food chains there are in an ecosystem and the more cross-connecting links there are among them, the more chances there are for the ecosystem to compensate for changes imposed upon it.

For example, suppose that the marsh plant-cricket-redwing blackbird section of Figure 7-1 represented an isolated entire ecosystem. If that were the case, removing the blackbirds—say, by shooting—would lead to a cricket plague. This in turn might lead to the defoliation of the plants, and then to the starvation of the crickets. In short, a change in one link of such a simple chain would have disastrous consequences for the entire ecosystem. Suppose, however, that the cormorants were removed from the larger system. Populations of flukes and eels would probably increase, which in turn might reduce the population of green algae (*Cladophora*). But there would be more food for mergansers and ospreys, and their populations would probably enlarge, leading to a reduction of eels and flukes. In turn, the algae would recover.

Needless to say, things do not normally happen that simply and neatly in nature. But we have both observational and theoretical reasons to believe that the general principle holds: complexity is an important factor in producing stability. Complex communities, such as the deciduous forests that cover much of the eastern United States, persist year after year if man does not interfere with them. An oak-hickory forest is quite stable in comparison with an ultrasimplified community, such as a cornfield, which is a man-made stand of a single kind of grass. A cornfield has little natural stability and is subject to almost instant ruin if it is not constantly managed by man. Similarly, arctic and subarctic ecosystems, which are characterized by simplicity, tend to be less stable than complex tropical forest ecosystems. In arctic regions the instability is manifested in frequent, violent fluctuations in the populations of such northern animals as lemmings, hares, and foxes. In contrast, outbreaks of one species do not occur as often in complex tropical forests. Ecologist Robert MacArthur suggested in 1955 that the stability of an ecosystem is a function of the number of links in the web of food chains. He developed a measure of that stability using information theory. Although the bases of stability now appear somewhat more complicated than those proposed by MacArthur in his pioneering work, the idea that complexity promotes stability still appears to be theoretically sound.

## Concentration of Toxic Substances in Ecosystems

Nowhere is man's ecological naiveté more evident than in his assumptions about the capacity of the atmosphere, soils, rivers, and oceans to absorb pollution. These assumptions all too often take the following form: if one gallon of poison is added to one billion gallons of water, then the highest concentration of poison to which anything will be exposed is about one part per billion. This might be approximately true if complete mixing by diffusion took place rapidly, which it often does not, and *if only physical systems were involved*. But because *biological systems* are involved, the situation is radically different. For example, filter-feeding animals may concentrate poisons to levels far higher than those found in the surrounding medium. Oysters make their living by constantly filtering the water they inhabit, and they live in shallow water near the shore, where pollution is heaviest. Consequently, their bodies often contain much higher concentrations of radioactive substances or lethal chemicals than the water in which they live. For instance, they have been found to accumulate up to 70,000 times the concentration of chlorinated hydrocarbon insecticides found in their environment. Food chains may lead to the concentrations of toxic substances; as plant physiologist Barry Commoner of Washington University once put it, they act as a kind of "biological amplifier." The diagram of the Long Island estuary food web (Fig. 7-1) shows how the concentration of DDT and its derivatives tend to increase in food chains from one trophic level to another. This tendency is especially marked for the chlorinated hydrocarbons because of their high solubility in fatty substances and their low water solubility. Although the clam and the mud snail are at the same trophic level, the filter-feeding clam accumulates more than half again as much DDT as the mud snail because of the difference in their food-capturing habits.

The mechanism of concentration is simple. Because of the Second Law of Thermodynamics, the mass of herbivores normally cannot be as great as the mass of plants they feed on. With each step upward in a food chain the *biomass* is reduced. Energy present in the chemical bonds of organisms at one level does not all end up as bond energy at the next level, because much of the energy is degraded to heat at each step. In contrast, losses of DDT and related compounds along a food chain are small compared to the amount that is transferred upward through the chain. As a result, the concentration of DDT increases at each level. Concentrations in the birds at the end of the food chain are from tens to many hundreds of times as high as they are in the animals farther down in the chain. In predatory birds, the concentration of DDT may be a *million* times as high as that in estuarine waters.

Clear Lake, in California, has long been a favorite of fishermen, and now attracts water-skiers and vacationers of all kinds. Unfortunately, a midge (known locally as the Clear Lake "gnat") reproduces in great numbers in certain years. This insect is considered a pest merely because it is phototropic (attracted to light), and for no other reason. In an attempt to control the gnat, a program was begun in the late summer of 1949 using DDD, a less toxic but equally persistent relative of DDT. The rate of application to the lake water was 14 parts per billion (ppb). The first application of what was then thought to be a relatively harmless pesticide eliminated about 99 percent of the gnats, as did the next application of 20 ppb in 1954. By the time the lake was treated for the third and last time in 1957, the gnat plus many other species of insects and other pests had developed some resistance to the pesticide. (It should be pointed out that within two weeks after each treatment, no DDD could be detected in the lake waters.)

Before 1950 Clear Lake had been a nesting ground for about 1,000 pairs of western grebes (ducklike diving birds that feed primarily on small fishes and other aquatic organisms). Not only did many grebes die soon after the 1954 and 1957 treatments, but fairly large die-offs occurred in subsequent years. Furthermore, the survivors were unable to reproduce. From 1950 to 1961 no young were produced; in 1962 a single grebe hatched. Reproduction remained unsuccessful until 1969, many years after the first introduction of DDD into the lake. Studies designed to determine the concentration of DDD from the lowest trophic levels to the highest revealed that the microscopic plankton of the lake contained about 250 times that of application (the original concentration in the lake water). The concentration in frogs was 2,000 times that of application, in sunfish, about 12,000, and in grebes, as high as 80,000 times. The figures given for frogs and the other animals higher in the food chain are for the visceral fat. The flesh of several species of game fish were also examined. Some white catfish contained almost 10,000 times the original concentration of DDD in the water. These data make it obvious why no DDD could be detected in the lake water only two weeks after application: because of its high solubility in the fatty materials of biological systems, the insecticide had been absorbed almost completely by the *living* components of the lake's ecosystem.

## Biogeochemical Cycles

Energy from the sun is constantly entering and passing through the Earth's ecosystems. But our ecosystems have no similar extraterrestrial source of the carbon, nitrogen, phosphorus, potassium, and sulfur, and many other substances that are required for life. These substances must be continually recycled through the ecosystem if the ecosystem is to persist. Let us now consider the cycling of three of these essential elements: carbon, nitrogen, and phosphorous.

### CARBON CYCLE

Carbon is the basic constituent of all the large molecules characteristic of living beings. In a real sense life on Earth is "carbon-based"; life is possible only because of the properties of this element. The major reservoir of carbon is the gas carbon dioxide ($CO_2$), which occurs in the atmosphere of our planet and in solution in its waters. As shown in Figure 7-2, the process of photosynthesis forms the primary pathway by which carbon (as $CO_2$) is

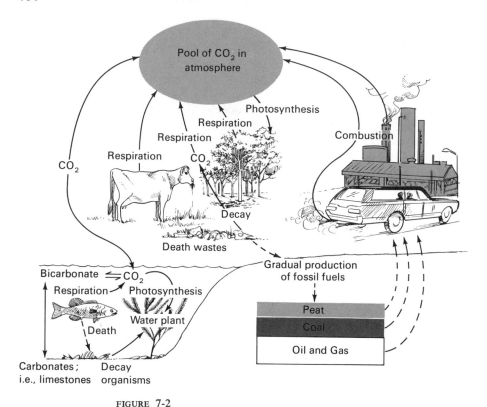

FIGURE 7-2

Carbon cycle. Solid arrows represent flow of CO₂.

withdrawn from the carbon dioxide "pool" and is used by plants to build carbohydrates and other organic compounds. These compounds transfer the carbon to herbivores, which eat the plants. When herbivores are eaten by carnivores, the carbon moves farther along the food chain. Both plants and animals extract energy from these organic compounds by the complex biochemical process called *cellular respiration*. Photosynthesis is the process by which energy from the sun is used to form the bonds of chemical energy that hold organic molecules together. The inorganic raw materials used in photosynthesis are $CO_2$ and water. Oxygen, which is released into the atmosphere, is one of its most important by-products. In respiration, which occurs in both plants and animals, the organic molecules are broken down by oxidation (a slow combustion), and the energy of their chemical bonds is extracted. The end products of respiration are water and carbon dioxide.

Thus an essential part of the carbon cycle is the movement of carbon-containing molecules from the pool of $CO_2$ in air and water to plants and animals farther up the food chain. From plants and animals at various positions along the chain, respiration returns $CO_2$ to this pool. Carbon is also returned to the pool through the agency of the bacteria and fungi that cause decay. These microorganisms serve as the ultimate link in food chains, reducing the complex carbon-containing molecules of dead plant and animal matter, and animal wastes, to their simple components.

The amount of carbon extracted from the $CO_2$ pool by photosynthesis is balanced, on the average, to within one part in 10,000 by the amount added to the pool through respiration and decay. Part of the small imbalance leaves the carbon cycle for millions of years and enters the crust of the Earth. This happens when incompletely decomposed organic matter accumulates and is transformed by geologic processes into fossil fuels—coal, oil, and natural gas. Carbon also is temporarily withdrawn from the cycle by the formation of limestone, often through the life processes of organisms (as in the formation of coral reefs). Such carbon is returned to the $CO_2$ pool by the burning of fossil fuels and by the weathering of limestone rocks.

## NITROGEN CYCLE

Air is almost 80 percent nitrogen, another element required by all living systems (it is an essential ingredient of proteins). Nitrogen moves within ecosystems through a series of complex pathways, some of which are shown in Figure 7-3. Unlike the oxygen and carbon dioxide of the atmosphere, gaseous nitrogen cannot be used directly by most organisms. But some microorganisms, such as certain bacteria and blue-green algae, can convert gaseous nitrogen into more complex compounds that can be utilized by plants and animals. The best known of these nitrogen-fixing organisms are the bacteria associated with the special nodules on roots of legumes, which are plants of the pea family. These and other nitrogen-fixing bacteria that live free in the soil use the atmospheric nitrogen directly in making their own proteins. Nitrogen-containing compounds become available to plants when these bacteria die, and eventually to animals that eat the plants.

Decay of dead plants and animals (by bacteria and fungi) leads to the production of ammonia, as does animal excretion. A special group of bacteria, nitrite bacteria, utilizes the energy in the chemical bonds of the ammonia, degrading it to nitrites (compounds containing nitrogen atoms each combined with two oxygen atoms—in the shorthand of the chemist, $NO_2$). Then another group of bacteria, nitrate bacteria, changes the nitrites to nitrates (compounds with combinations of single nitrogen atoms with three oxygen atoms, $NO_3$). The nitrate bacteria remove more energy in degrading $NO_2$ compounds to $NO_3$. Nitrates are the commonest form in which plants obtain nitrogen from the soil; thus a loop of the nitrogen cycle may be completed without the formation of gaseous nitrogen.

Nitrogen, then, enters the living part of the cycle in two ways: directly from the atmosphere via nitrogen-fixing bacteria, and as nitrates taken up from the soil by plants:

$$NO_3 \rightarrow protein \rightarrow ammonia \rightarrow NO_2 \rightarrow NO_3.$$

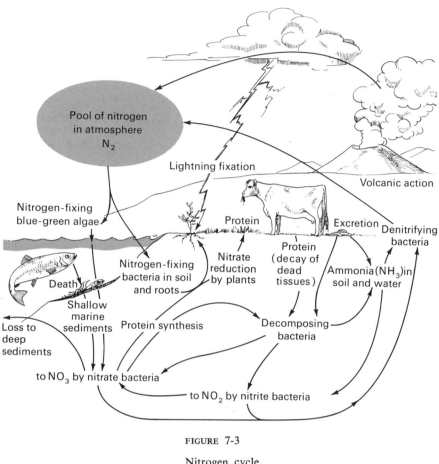

FIGURE 7-3

Nitrogen cycle.

Another kind of bacteria, denitrifying bacteria, returns nitrogen to the atmosphere. These bacteria break down nitrates, nitrites, and ammonia, and liberate gaseous nitrogen.

Some nitrogen is lost to the system. In the form of nitrates, which are highly soluble, it is washed from the soil and eventually becomes deposited as deep-sea sediments.

## PHOSPHORUS CYCLE

A famous German biochemist introduced the epigram: "Ohne Phosphor kein Leben"—without phosphorus there is no life. Phosphorus is an essential element in the DNA and RNA molecules involved in the transmission of genetic information (heredity), and phosphorus compounds are the prime energy-manipulating devices of living cells. Phosphorus does not cycle in ecosystems as readily as nitrogen does. The principal phosphorus reservoirs are phosphate rocks, deposits of guano (sea-bird excrement), and deposits of fossilized animals (Fig. 7-4). Phosphorus is released from these reservoirs through natural erosion and leaching, and through mining and subsequent use as fertilizer by man. Some of this released phosphorus becomes available to plants in the form of phosphates in the soil, and thus enters the living part of the ecosystem. It may pass through several animals and microorganisms before returning to the soil through decay. Much of the phosphate washed or dug from rock deposits eventually finds its way to the sea—man's mining and distributing activities accelerate this process. There it may be utilized by marine ecosystems or deposited in shallow or deep marine sediments. Although some of this may be returned by upwelling currents, much of it is lost semipermanently. It can be returned by geological processes leading to the uplifting of sediments, but it seems unlikely that these in the future will be sufficient to balance the loss. A 1971 report by the Institute of Ecology states: "Known potential supplies of phosphorus, a non-renewable resource essential to life, will be exhausted before the end of the 21st century. Without phosphate fertilizers, the planet can support between one and two billion people." It obviously would behoove humanity to make a

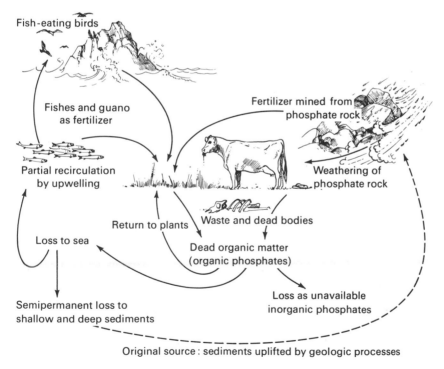

FIGURE 7-4

Phosphorous cycle.

maximum effort to recycle phosphates to extend the life of our reserves, rather than permit them to become pollutants as now commonly occurs.

## Modifying Ecosystems

Let us look now at some of the ways in which mankind modifies ecological systems. Obviously, some ecosystems are destroyed outright by such diverse activities as planting crops, logging forests, starting fires, building dams, applying defoliants to jungles, and constructing buildings and laying pavement. The results of man's activities are as varied as the activities themselves. When prairie is converted to cornfield, an unstable, simple ecosystem replaces a stable, complex one. Man's attempts to stabilize such systems artificially can lead to further destabilization and bring about changes elsewhere as well.

Wholesale logging of forests creates extreme changes that effectively destroy the forest ecosystem. Numerous animals that depend on the trees for food and shelter disappear. Many of the smaller forest plants depend on the trees for shade; they and the animals they support also disappear. With the removal of trees and plants, the soil is directly exposed to the elements, and it tends to erode faster. Loss of topsoil reduces the water-retaining capacity of an area, diminishes the supply of fresh water, causes silting of dams, and has other serious consequences for man. The flooding along many of the world's rivers, from the Yang-tse in China to the Eel River in California, is greatly aggravated by heavy logging in their watersheds. Deforestation changes the water cycle in other ways. It reduces the amount of water transferred from ground to air by the trees in the process known as "transpiration." This modifies the weather downwind of the area, usually making it more arid and subject to greater extremes of temperature. Finally, if reforestation is not carried out, the deforested area is invaded by "pioneer" weedy plants that often have much less desirable characteristics for human use than did the forest that was removed.

Man's activities have already produced a great increase in the amount of desert and wasteland. In 1882 land classified as either desert or wasteland amounted to 9.4 percent of the total land on Earth. In 1952 it had risen to 23.3 percent. (Part of this increase may be the result of better information or changes in the definition of wasteland.) During the same period land classified as carrying inaccessible forest *decreased* from 43.9 percent to 21.1 percent. The vast Sahara Desert itself is in part manmade, the result of overgrazing, faulty irrigation, and deforestation, combined with natural climatic changes. Today the Sahara is advancing southward on a broad front at a rate of several miles per year. The great Thar Desert of western India is also partly the result of man's influence. Some 2,000 years ago, what is now the center of this desert was a jungle. The spread of this desert has been aggravated by poor cultivation practices, lumbering, and overgrazing. Man's activities can lead to repetition of the Sahara and Thar stories in many parts of the globe.

Erosion is an increasingly serious problem. It is estimated that one-half of the farmland in India is not adequately protected from erosion, and on fully one-third of the farmland erosion threatens to remove the topsoil completely. As Georg Borgstrom has pointed out, soil conservation procedures are especially difficult to institute in areas where the population is poorly fed. He cites a study that recommended a one-fifth *reduction* in the amount of cultivated land and a one-third reduction in the size of livestock herds in Turkey. It was hoped that these reductions would help to diminish the danger of catastrophic erosion caused by overgrazing. Unfortunately, the program was not initiated, presumably because the local people were dependent upon the land and the herds for food and other necessities. As so often happens, a short-run need took precedence over long-run wisdom.

In most tropical areas the soils are extremely poor. They cannot maintain large reserves of minerals needed for plant growth, such as phosphorus, potassium, and calcium, primarily because heavy rainfall and the resultant leaching cause a high rate of water flow through the ground to the water table. The soils also have very high contents of iron and aluminum oxides in their upper levels. Most of the nutrients in a tropical jungle are concentrated not in the soil, but in the vegetation. Nutrients that are released to the soil through the decay of dead plant parts are quickly returned to the living vegetation. The extensive shallow root systems of the forest trees absorb the nutrients as soon as they are released. Since most jungle trees are evergreen, the process is continuous. There is no chance for nutrients to build up in the soil as they do in temperate deciduous forests, which are dormant each year following a general leaf fall.

When a tropical forest is defoliated or cleared for agriculture, this continual recycling of nutrients is interrupted. Heavy rains wash away the thin supply of soil nutrients, and the last substances to leach out are iron and aluminum oxides. The soil is exposed to sun and oxygen, and a series of complex chemical changes takes place, often resulting in the formation of a rocklike substance called *laterite* (from *later,* the Latin word for brick). Such laterization has occurred over wide areas of the tropics, starting long ago and continuing in recent years. Those who have been fortunate enough to visit Angkor Wat in Cambodia have seen magnificent cities and temples built by the Khmers some 800 to 1,000 years ago. The construction materials were sandstone and laterite, and laterization may have been a principal reason for the disappearance of the Khmer civilization.

Farming small clearings for a year or two and then letting the jungle reclaim them is the ancient method of agriculture in many areas where soils are subject to laterization. Tropical forests are usually able to reinvade small areas before laterization is complete. Whether large areas that have been kept cleared for substantial periods of time can be reforested is an open question. Reforestation has been successful in some areas where the soil crust has been carefully broken up, fertilizers applied, and the whole system carefully cultivated. But natural reforestation seems unlikely, and even most of the attempts supported by man have failed. Laterization is continuing throughout the tropics and will doubtless proceed more rapidly as mankind grows increasingly desperate for food. According to geologist Mary McNeil, "The ambitious plans to increase food production in the tropics to meet the pressure of the rapid rise of population have given too little consideration to the laterization problem and the measures that will have to be undertaken to overcome it." Along with other data supporting her contention, she provides a description of the fiasco at Iata in the Amazon Basin, where the government of Brazil attempted to found a farming community. Laterization destroyed the project when, "in less than five years the cleared fields became virtually pavements of rock."

## Insecticides and Ecosystems

Besides being direct threats to human health, synthetic insecticides (Box 7-1) are among man's most potent tools for simplifying, and thus destabilizing, ecosystems. The increase in the concentration of the most persistent of these compounds with each upward step in a food chain exposes the populations *least* able to survive poisoning to the highest concentrations.

There are several reasons why the organisms that occupy positions near the upper end of food chains are less able to cope with the poisons than are, for example, herbivores. The first reason traces back again to the Second Law of Thermodynamics. Because of the loss of energy at each transfer, the higher the position that a given population occupies in a food chain, the smaller that population will be. This means that if a poison were applied that would kill most of the predators and herbivores in an area, it would be more likely to exterminate the population of predators than the population of herbivores, simply because there are fewer predators. Purely by chance, members of the larger population would be more likely to survive. It would not be necessary to kill all individuals of any one species of predator to force it to extinction. If survivors were too scattered for the sexes to find one another and produce offspring, extinction would surely follow. Or, if survivors were few, various genetic problems might result from inbreeding and cause the population to dwindle to zero.

Another reason that small populations of animals occupying high positions in food chains are more vulnerable is that larger populations tend to have greater stores of genetic variability. Assume, for instance, that one individual per hundred thousand in each of two insect populations, A and B, carries a mutant gene that makes it naturally resistant to pesticide X. Assume that A is a herbivore and that its population in a field consists of one million individuals. Assume that B is a parasite on A and that its population is one hundred thousand individuals. If the field is thoroughly treated with pesticide X, ten individuals of A will survive, but only one of B will survive, each of these being naturally resistant mutants. In this oversimplified example, the consequences are clear. The small group of resistant A insects can quickly reproduce a large population, free of the attack of B. But because most individuals of the new population of *A* will be resistant, the next treatment with insecticide *X* will have little effect. If dosage of *X* is increased, species *A* will respond by becoming more and more resistant with each new generation. Not only herbivorous pests, but other large populations can easily develop such resistance; for example, resistance to DDT has developed in many mosquito populations and has hampered malaria control programs.

There is an additional reason why our artificial poisons are so much more effective against predators and parasites than they are against herbivores. For many millions of years plants have been evolving defenses against the assaults of herbivores. Many of these defenses are familiar to everyone. They include the spines of the cactus, the thorn of the rose bush, and a wide variety of compounds ranging from the irritants in poison ivy and poison oak to such useful substances as quinine and pepper. These plant substances are natural pesticides; in fact, mankind has utilized some of them, such as nicotine (extracted from tobacco) and pyrethrins (extracted from a small marigoldlike flower), for their original purposes—as insect poisons. Although the use of nicotine as an insecticide has fallen off since the introduction of synthetic pesticides, pyrethrins are still the active ingredient in many insect sprays intended for home use.

Insects, of course, have in turn evolved mechanisms for evading the plants' chemical defenses. Long before man appeared, this reciprocal "coevolutionary war" was being waged between the plants and insects; the plants continually building better defenses, the insects countering with better attacks. Small wonder that herbivorous insects have had little trouble in dealing evolutionarily with man's recent attempts to poison them.

Pesticides may often lead to *higher* concentrations of pests rather than lower, either because they directly poison the natural enemies of the pest, or because they indirectly decrease the efficiency of those enemies as control agents. As Carl B. Huffaker of the Division of Biological Control at the University of California (Berkeley) has pointed out, they may accomplish the latter in several ways. One is through the very success of the pesticide in reducing the target pest population. This may deprive the pest's natural enemies of their prey and thus reduce the predator or parasite population to a level where it is ineffective as a control when the pest population resurges. Similarly, the natural enemies of the pest may be decimated if the pesticide kills off another species preyed on by the same predator or parasite. Such an alternate host may be necessary to keep the predator population going all year round; if it is destroyed, the natural control will be destroyed also.

There are, of course, many actual cases in which differential kill of predators has released some of their prey species from their natural restraints. It is fair to say, for instance, that mites, as pests, are a *creation* of the pesticide industry. Careless overuse of DDT and other pesticides has promoted many of these little insect-like relatives of spiders to pest status by killing the insects that previously preyed on the mites and kept them under control. The emergence of the European red mite as a major pest in apple orchards followed the use of DDT to control the codling moth. This is only one of many examples in which pesticides intended for one pest have led to the flourishing of others. The usual response of the pesticide industry to such situations is to use more of the original pesticide, or to develop more potent poisons which then create another array of pollution problems; for instance, some miticides seem to be powerful carcinogens.

---

BOX 7-1   SYNTHETIC INSECTICIDES

Two groups of compounds contain the majority of synthetic insecticides: chlorinated hydrocarbons and organophosphates.

*Chlorinated Hydrocarbons*

This group includes DDT, benzene hexachloride (BHC), dieldrin, endrin, aldrin, chlordane, lindane, isodrin, toxaphene, and similar compounds designed to kill insects. DDT is the most thoroughly studied of the chlorinated hydrocarbons, and much of the following discussion is based on it. In its behavior it is more or less typical of the group, although other chlorinated hydrocarbons are more soluble in water, more toxic, less persistent, etc. In insects and other animals these compounds act primarily on the central nervous system in ways that are not well understood, but the effects range from hyperexcitability to death following convulsions and paralysis. Chronic effects on vertebrates include fatty infiltration of the heart, and fatty degeneration of the liver which is often fatal. Fishes and other aquatic animals seem to be especially sensitive to chlorinated hydrocarbons. Oxygen uptake is somehow blocked at the gills, causing death from suffocation. That chlorinated hydrocarbons apparently can influence the production of enzymes may account for their wide range of effects.

Chlorinated hydrocarbons tend to be selectively soluble in fats and fatty tissues. In animals this means that they may be stored at sites remote from the primary active site in the nervous system and rendered rela-

tively harmless. Chlorinated hydrocarbons vary a great deal in their toxicity to plants. They are known to slow the rate of photosynthesis, but the exact cause of this effect is unknown. The greater toxicity of chlorinated hydrocarbons in insects as compared to mammals is primarily a function of the greater ease with which these compounds are absorbed through insect cuticle compared with mammalian skin. Four properties make chlorinated hydrocarbons a particular threat to ecosystems:

1. Chlorinated hydrocarbons have a wide range of biological activity; they are broad-spectrum poisons, affecting many different organisms in many different ways. They are toxic to essentially all animals including many vertebrates.

2. They have great stability. It is not clear, for instance, how long DDT persists in ecosystems. Fifty percent of the DDT sprayed in a single treatment may still be found in a field 10 years later. This does not mean, however, that the other 50 percent has been degraded to biologically inactive molecules; it may only have gone somewhere else. Probably DDT (including its biologically active breakdown product DDE) has an average half-life (time required before 50 percent has been degraded) of much more than a decade. Indeed, DDE may be virtually immortal.

3. Chlorinated hydrocarbons are very mobile. For example, the chemical properties of DDT cause it to adhere to dust

In such cases one or more pests were being held in check by natural biological controls, which were upset by the introduction of the chemical. That so many organisms can be "promoted" to pest status by the killing of predators and parasites with pesticides is itself a powerful testimonial for biological controls. These controls are constantly at work suppressing potential pests at no economic cost. One of the most successful biological controls ever used

particles and thus get blown around the world. Four different chlorinated hydrocarbons have been detected in dust filtered from the air over Barbados; frog populations in unsprayed areas high in the Sierra Nevada of California are polluted with DDT. Furthermore, DDT codistills with water; when water evaporates and enters the atmosphere, DDT goes with it. Chlorinated hydrocarbons thus travel in the air and surface waters.

4. Finally, chlorinated hydrocarbons become concentrated in the fats of organisms. If you think of the world as being partitioned into nonliving and living parts, then these pesticides may be thought of as moving continually from the physical environment into living systems. To attempt to monitor DDT levels merely by testing water (as has frequently been done) is ridiculous. Water is saturated with DDT—that is, can dissolve no more—when it has dissolved 1.2 parts per billion. Besides, the chemical does not remain for long in water; it is quickly removed by any organisms that live in the water.

It is these four properties—extreme range of biological activity, stability, mobility, and affinity for living systems—that cause biologists' fears that DDT and its relatives are degrading the life-support systems of our planet. If any one of these properties were lacking, the situation would be much less serious, but in combination they pose a deadly threat.

### Organophosphates

This group includes parathion, malathion, Azodrin, diazinon, TEPP, phosdrin, and several others. These poisons are descendants of the nerve gas Tabun (diisopropylfluorophosphate), developed in Nazi Germany during World War II. All of them are cholinesterase inhibitors; they inactivate the enzyme responsible for breaking down a nerve "transmitter substance," acetylcholine. The result is, in acute cases of poisoning, a hyperactivity of the nervous system; the animal dies twitching and out of control. Unlike chlorinated hydrocarbons, organophosphates are unstable and non-persistent; thus, they tend not to produce chronic effects in ecosystems or to accumulate in food chains.

Organophosphates inhibit other enzymes as well as cholinesterase. Indeed, some of those that show relatively high insect toxicity and low mammalian toxicity do so because they poison an esterase that is more critical to the functioning of insect than of mammalian nervous systems. Malathion, which is violently poisonous to insects, is relatively nontoxic to mammals because the mammalian systems contain an enzyme, carboxy-esterase, that destroys malathion. But toxic effects on mammals can occur when malathion is used in combinations with other organophosphates, which apparently inhibit the carboxy-esterase enzyme.

by man was the introduction of vedalia beetles to attack the cottony cushion scale—a pest that threatened the existence of California's infant citrus industry in the 1880s. Complete control was achieved by the beetles in the 1890s and no further problems arose until DDT was used on or around citrus in the 1940s. The DDT killed the vedalia beetles, and the scale insects became pests again. When DDT use was stopped and the beetles reintroduced, control of the pest was regained.

Biological controls have been tried against 223 out of about 1,000 recognized important insect pests, with some success against 55 percent of them. Clearly, much more attention should be paid to promoting these more ecologically sensible techniques for keeping pest populations at a reasonable level.

### SIDE-EFFECTS OF INSECTICIDES

Of all the synthetic organic pesticides, probably more is known about DDT than any other. It is the oldest and most widely used chlorinated hydrocarbon insecticide. It is found everywhere—not only where it has been applied, but all over the Earth. Virtually every kind of animal on Earth has been exposed to it. As noted earlier (Table 6-1), concentrations in the fat deposits of Americans average about 12 ppm, and the people of India and Israel have much higher concentrations. More startling and significant in some ways has been the discovery of DDT residues in the fat deposits of Eskimos, and in antarctic penguins and seals. Seals from the east coast of Scotland have been found to have concentrations of DDT as high as 23 ppm in their blubber. Pesticide pollution is truly a worldwide problem.

Because DDT breaks down so slowly, it lasts for decades in soils. For instance, in the Long Island estuary studied by Woodwell and his colleagues, the marsh had been sprayed for 20 years for mosquito control. Up to 32 pounds per acre of DDT were found in the upper layer of mud there. Such concentrations in U.S. soils are not unusual. As a result of the concentration of DDT as it moves up food chains, the danger to the life and reproductive capacity of fish-eating birds is extreme. Nesting failures among bald eagles attributable to DDT have now reached proportions that bring the survival of the species into severe jeopardy. In addition, reproductive difficulties in populations of such diverse birds as the peregrine falcon, the brown pelican, and the Bermuda petrel have been traced to residues of DDT and other chlorinated hydrocarbon insecticides. These chemicals interfere with the birds' ability to metabolize calcium, which results in the laying of eggs whose shells are so thin that they are crushed by the weight of the incubating parents. Similar effects have been suggested for the polychlorinated biphenyls (PCBs; chlorinated hydrocarbons used extensively in industry), which are closely related to the insecticides. They may share with the insecticides the blame for high rates of nesting failure in raptorial birds, and they may be five times more potent as killers than DDT.

The evidence against DDT in the case of birds' eggs is now overwhelming. Studies have been done of the thickness of raptorial bird eggshells in museum collections. Among those species investigated that feed high on food chains, there is virtually always a sharp drop in eggshell thickness for the period 1945–1947, when DDT was generally introduced (Fig. 7-5). In Britain a strong correlation has also been shown between the level of chlorinated hydrocarbon contamination in various geographical regions and eggshell thickness in peregrine falcons, sparrowhawks and golden eagles nesting in those regions. The exceptions make the case even more convincing. The shells of one Florida population of bald eagles first thinned in 1943, not in 1945–1947. Investigations disclosed that this population lived in a county where large-scale DDT testing took place in 1943. One pair of peregrine falcons on the coast of California was an exception to the general rule of nesting failure. Examination of their nest revealed that they were feeding inland on mourning doves. Mourning doves are herbivores; thus the peregrines were feeding much lower in the food chain than if they had been feeding on fish-eating sea birds. They picked up less DDT, and were therefore able to reproduce successfully.

Experimental feedings of DDT to mallard ducks, American sparrowhawks, and Japanese quail all produced thin egg shells and reduced hatch rates. DDE, the widely distributed, stable breakdown product of DDT, has also been shown to reduce the thickness of mallard egg shells and to reduce hatchability, and dieldrin produced similar results with mallards. At one time it was thought that the thin eggshell phenomenon was produced by alterations in estrogen levels, which in birds are involved in the storage of calcium. However, biologist D. B. Peakall of Cornell University did a series of experiments in which DDE was injected into ringdoves shortly before they laid eggs. The eggs, when laid, had thin eggshells. The DDE greatly reduced the activity of carbonic anhydrase, an enzyme which plays a critical role in providing calcium for eggshell production.

Dieldrin, when injected shortly before egglaying, did not cause thinning of the eggshell. It and other chlorinated hydrocarbons (especially PCBs) do, however, produce a lowered estrogen level which in turn delays breeding. DDT does not have as large an estrogen effect as dieldrin, nor apparently is it as potent an inducer of liver enzymes. Late breeding is an important component of the observed declines of predatory birds, since breeding is normally timed to coincide with optimal food supplies for the young. Interestingly, some of the most spectacular population declines in these birds occurred years after thin eggshells first began to appear—about the time that dieldrin was introduced.

Birds are not the only organisms suffering from the chlorinated hydrocarbon problem. Coho salmon in Lake Michigan, which also feed at high trophic levels, have been laying eggs that contain DDT residues. In 1968 almost 700,000 young salmon died as they absorbed the last DDT-rich drop of oil from their yolk sacs. Trout have been having similar problems, and rising DDT levels are now found in such commercially important marine fishes as tuna, mackerel, and hake.

One spectacular example of the destruction of nontarget organisms by

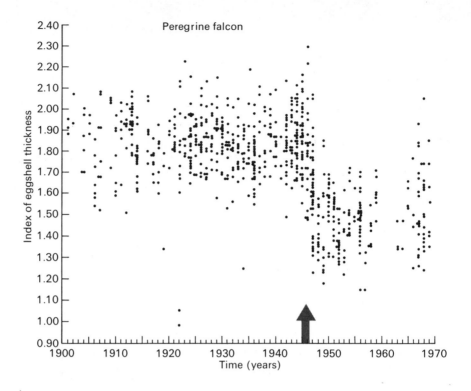

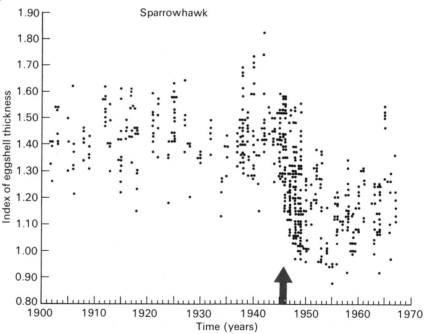

FIGURE 7-5

Changes in thickness of eggshells of peregrine falcon and sparrowhawk in Britain. Arrows indicate first widespread use of DDT. (After Ratcliffe, *J. Appl. Ecol.* 7, 67–115, 1970.)

pesticides is described in detail by reporter Frank Graham, Jr., in his fine book *Disaster by Default*. He recounts the story of the great Mississippi fish kill in the early 1960s. Rough estimates give the total loss in the four years 1960–1963 as between 10 and 15 million fishes in the lower Mississippi and its bypass, the Atchafalaya. The fishes killed included several kinds of catfish, menhaden, mullet, sea trout, drumfish, shad, and buffalo fish. The die-offs were ruinous to the local fishing industry. A thorough investigation by government (Public Health Service) and private laboratories placed the blame primarily on the highly toxic insecticide endrin and one of its derivatives. It was found not only in the blood and tissues of dying fishes and water birds but also in the mud in areas where fishes were dying. In experiments, extracts, made both from the mud and from the tissues of dying fishes, killed healthy fishes. It was found that fish kills were greatest in 1960 and 1963, when endrin was used commonly to treat cotton and cane crops in the lower Mississippi Valley, and that fish kills were smallest in 1961 and 1962 when very little endrin was used.

The Public Health Service found that runoff from agricultural lands following dusting and spraying was one major source of the endrin. The other source was the Memphis plant of the Velsicol Chemical Corporation; waste endrin from the manufacturing process was getting into the river. Graham describes the interesting reaction of the Velsicol Corporation:

"Velsicol, under fire, shot back. Bernard Lorant, the company's vice-president in charge of research, issued strong denials. In a statement to the press, he said that endrin had nothing to do with the Mississippi fish kill, that the symptoms of the dying fish were not those of endrin poisoning, and that Velsicol's tests proved that the fish had died of dropsy."

Unfortunately for the Velsicol defense, dropsy happens to be a disease of fishes that is *never epidemic*. Considering the facts cited above, and the small detail (apparently ignored by the Velsicol researchers) that the fishes had the symptoms of endrin poisoning, one would have to conclude that some 10 million fishes had simultaneously contracted a new form of dropsy that produced the symptoms of endrin poisoning and that, coincidentally—perhaps only to confuse investigators—the fishes had even produced endrin in their tissues and excreted it into the mud of the Mississippi!

At a 1964 conference on the Mississippi fish kill, a theme promoted by the pesticide industry was that only communist sympathizers would criticize the extravagant way pesticides are used. This approach is exemplified by a statement made well before the conference by Parke C. Brinkley, president of the National Agricultural Chemicals Association: "Two of the biggest battles in this war [against communism] are the battle against starvation and the battle against disease. No two things make people more ripe for Communism. The most effective tool in the hands of the farmer and in the hands of the public health official as they fight these battles is pesticides."

In June 1969 a vast fish kill occurred in the Rhine River. Preliminary investigations indicated that containers holding at least 200 pounds of the insecticide Endosulfan, which had dropped off a barge, were responsible.

The encouraging increase in public understanding between 1964 and 1969 of the ecological dangers of pesticides was perhaps indicated by the refreshing absence of any comments from the pesticide industry about either dropsy or communists.

Another example will illustrate how complex, subtle, and far-reaching the effects of pesticide pollution may be. Ecologist L. B. Slobodkin of the State University of New York has described a plan to block the seaward ends of lochs in western Scotland and use them as ponds for raising fishes. One of the problems has been to find ways to raise the young fishes in the laboratory so that they can be "planted" in the ponds. It has been discovered that newly hatched brine shrimp serve as a satisfactory food for the kinds of fishes that will be raised. These may be obtained from brine shrimp eggs that are gathered commercially in the United States and sold to tropical fish fanciers for use in feeding young tropical fishes. The American supplies come from two places: San Francisco Bay in California, and Great Salt Lake in Utah. Sufficient eggs for the project can no longer be obtained from San Francisco Bay because of the demands of local aquarists and because large areas of former brine shrimp habitat are now residential subdivisions. Unfortunately, the Utah supply is of no use to the British, because brine shrimp hatched from Utah eggs kill their young fishes. The Utah shrimp have absorbed the insecticides that drain into Great Salt Lake from surrounding farmlands. Thus, insecticide pollution in Utah hampers fish production in Scotland!

### AGRICULTURE, ECOLOGY AND INSECT CONTROL

World agriculture today is an ecological disaster area. We carefully breed out of plants their natural chemical defenses. The poisons usually taste unpleasant to us, although some of our spices, which we use in small quantities, are produced by plants to serve as insecticides. We plant our crops in tight, simple monocultures, inviting pest outbreaks, to which we then respond with synthetic pesticides, often killing a higher proportion of some nontarget populations than of the target population of pests. Because synthetic pesticides, whether intended for insects or pest plants, have toxic effects on so many nontarget organisms, they are more accurately called "biocides." There are a few hopeful signs that ecologically sound agricultural practices may eventually be adopted, but so far the general trend has been in the opposite direction.

The percentage of crop losses to insects in the U.S. seems to have remained about the same for more than 20 years, despite enormously increased use of pesticides. In 1948, ecologist William Vogt noted in his book, *Road to Survival,* that "one-tenth of all crop plants are destroyed by insects in the U.S. every year." Vogt based his comment on statistics published by the USDA. In 1969, Georg Borgstrom, also using USDA figures, observed that crop losses due to insects amount to the yield from about a fifth of our total acreage, or about a sixth of the cash value of our total crop production.

When the storage-loss component is subtracted, the field losses amount to slightly more than a tenth of total production, about the same as 1948. The President's Science Advisory Committee Panel on the World Food Problem estimated insect losses in the field during the 1950s as between 4 percent and 14 percent, depending on the crop. In 1948, according to zoologist Robert L. Rudd of the University of California, DDT, benzene hexachloride, and lead arsenate were the only insecticides of any significance used. By 1958, production of DDT in the U.S. had increased seven-fold (about half was then exported), production of lead arsenate had dropped about a third, and production of six other chlorinated hydrocarbons amounted to nearly five times the 1948 production of DDT. The production of Benzene hexachloride tripled by 1953, then dropped again in 1958 to about half the 1953 figure. Overall, pesticide usage in the U.S. more than doubled between 1960 and 1970, with about one billion pounds being used in 1970. In *Pesticides and the Living Landscape* (1964), Rudd points out that it is difficult to get accurate estimates of pest losses and that standards of pest damage have changed through time. Nevertheless, the consistency of insect loss estimates over time is rather striking. Despite huge inputs of insecticides, insects still claim a substantial share of the American farmers' greatly increased agricultural production.

What proportion of this increased production is due to the use of synthetic pesticides? Certainly not as much as the pesticide industry would like us to believe, but synthetic pesticides may play a more significant role than is indicated in the relatively constant percentage loss figures. High-yield strains of crops, heavily fertilized, probably require more protection per acre than lower yield strains. That is, one might expect a higher percentage loss in fields today if we were still using the control techniques of 1940.

Could similar or greater yields have been achieved since World War II with control methods which are more ecologically sophisticated than current pesticide practices? It is the opinion of systems ecologist K. E. F. Watt of the University of California that when measured against successful biological and integrated control programs, "most pesticide projects have been failures." We believe that the procedures in use in the 1950s and 1960s will eventually be seen as one of mankind's most tragic blunders, and that when the total accounting is done, it will be found that other methods of control would have provided higher yields at less direct cost and with fewer deleterious consequences for mankind.

Pesticides, especially the persistent ones, simplify the ecosystems to which they are applied, and into which they are transported by wind and water. The results of direct application are all too often the same: the freeing of pests from natural restraints. The pest, at first seemingly controlled, is soon back in even larger numbers than before. This destabilizing effect of pesticides is so common that it is often cited in the scientific literature as evidence that ecosystem simplification leads to instability. Unfortunately, things do not end there in agricultural practice, and higher doses of pesticides are applied thus aggravating the situation still further.

The history of attempts to control cotton pests in the coastal Cañete Valley of Peru has been reported by entomologist Ray F. Smith of the University of California. Against the advice of ecologically sophisticated entomologists, who recommended the use of cultural control methods and inorganic and botanical insecticides, synthetic organic pesticides were widely introduced in the valley in 1949. At first the use of these pesticides, principally the chlorinated hydrocarbons, DDT, BHC, and toxaphene, was very successful. Cotton yields increased from 494 kilograms per hectare (440 lbs/acre) in 1950 to 728 kilograms per hectare (648 lbs/acre) in 1954. The cotton farmers concluded that if more pesticide were applied, more cotton would grow. Insecticides "were applied like a blanket over the entire valley. Trees were cut down to make it easier for the airplanes to treat the fields. The birds that nested in these trees disappeared. Other beneficial animal forms, such as insect parasites and predators, disappeared. As the years went by, the number of treatments was increased; also, each year the treatments were started earlier because of the earlier attacks of the pests."

Trouble started in 1952 when BHC proved no longer to be effective against aphids. In 1954 toxaphene failed against the tobacco leafworm. Boll weevil infestation reached extremely high levels in 1955–1956, and at least *six new pests had appeared,* pests that were not found in similar nearby valleys that had not been sprayed with organic pesticides. In addition, the numbers of an old pest, larvae of the moth *Heliothis virescens,* exploded to new heights, and showed a high level of DDT resistance. Synthetic organic phosphates were substituted for the chlorinated hydrocarbons, and the interval between treatments was shortened from one or two weeks down to three days. In 1955–1956, cotton yields dropped to 332 kilograms per hectare, in spite of the tremendous amounts of insecticide applied. Economic disaster overtook the valley. In 1957 an ecologically rational "integrated control" program was initiated in which biological, cultural, and chemical controls were combined. Conditions improved immensely, and yields rose to new highs.

This example should not be taken to mean that ecologically unsound pesticide programs have been instituted only in other places and in former times. Many examples can be cited of mistakes made here in the United States. For example, in both California and Arizona, profit margins have been dropping for cotton farmers because of insect attacks and the rising costs of chemical pesticide applications. In an attempt to evaluate the control measures used by agriculturalists, biologists uncovered some astounding facts. The programs designed to "control" cotton pests in these states were reviewed in 1968 by Kevin Shea, Scientific Director of the Committee for Environmental Information. Shea reported that "controlled experiments on small plots suggest that cotton growers in California may have spent thousands of dollars to fight an insect, the lygus bug, that has no appreciable effect on the final production per acre." Reduction of the number of lygus bugs per acre *did not lead to increased yields,* apparently because the bugs fed on "surplus" bolls of cotton, which would not ripen in any case. Spraying for lygus bugs early in the season with some pesticides not only did not help yields, but lowered them by killing insect predators of the bollworm, which caused outbreaks of bollworms. What is still more intriguing is that recent research has begun to indicate that the bollworm itself may not be a threat to yields even at population levels considerably higher than what had previously been considered a dangerous infestation.

Most disturbing of all is the Azodrin story. Azodrin is a broad-spectrum organophosphate insecticide manufactured by the Shell Chemical Company (a subsidiary of the Shell Oil Company). Azodrin kills most of the insect populations in a field, but like other organophosphates (and unlike the chlorinated hydrocarbons) it is not persistent. Its effects are devastating to populations of predatory insects. Therefore, when the field is reinvaded by pests, or when pest survivors make a comeback, their natural enemies are often absent, and overwhelming population booms of the pest may occur. Experiments by University of California entomologists clearly indicated that, rather than controlling bollworms, Azodrin applications, through their effect on the bollworms' natural enemies, actually *increased* bollworm populations in treated fields. Figure 7-6 summarizes the experimental results.

Other Azodrin experiments, and the similar results obtained with the use of other broad-spectrum pesticides, make it clear that the control procedure, rather than helping the farmer, often has precisely the opposite effect. One might reasonably expect the pesticide manufacturer to withdraw his product, or at least warn customers and advise them how to avoid these disastrous effects. However, Shea writes: "Shell Chemical Company, manufacturer of Azodrin, was aware of the University's findings through publications and from a seminar given at the Shell Research Center in Modesto. Nevertheless, the Company decided to promote the material for use on cotton pests in the San Joaquin Valley. Shell mounted a massive sales campaign. Radio, television, billboards, bumper stickers, and trade journal ads were employed to move Azodrin out of the warehouses and into the fields. Azodrin was heralded as being unmatched in its ability to kill every major insect likely to damage cotton." The Modesto seminar was given by Robert van den Bosch, one of the nation's outstanding insect ecologists and an expert on ecologically sound control measures. He has said, "our own experiments indicate considerable odds against significant economic gains resulting from the use of Azodrin."

Shell further has been promoting the use of Azodrin on a fixed schedule, whether pests are present or not. But fixed schedule spraying unnecessarily damages non-target organisms, destabilizes the agricultural ecosystem, and creates pest problems that otherwise would not arise. Aside from enhancing these effects, such programs of course promote the development of resistant strains of pests and the destruction of natural enemies. This guarantees the "need" for heavier and heavier doses of Azodrin. As one Azodrin advertisement put it, "even if an overpowering migration (*sic*) develops, the flexibility of Azodrin lets you regain control fast. Just increase the dosage according to label recommendations." The pesticide manufacturer is clearly the only beneficiary of such practices.

Van den Bosch has written that in California a conservative estimate

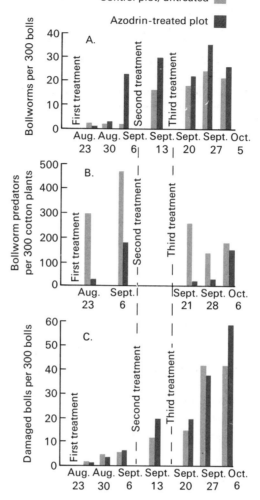

FIGURE 7-6

Results of experiment using Azodrin to "control"
bollworms. A. Number of bollworms in untreated
control plot compared with number found in plot
treated with Azodrin. B. Number of bollworm
predators in control plot and plot treated with
Azodrin. C. Number of damaged cotton bolls in
control plot and plot treated with Azodrin. These
results indicate that Azodrin is more effective against
bollworm predators than against bollworms, so that
the pesticide treatment *increases* the damage to the
crop. (After Shea, "Cotton and Chemicals," *Scientist
and Citizen,* 1968, based on data from R. van den
Bosch et al., *Pest and Disease Control Program for
Cotton,* Univ. Calif. Agricultural Experiment
Station, 1968.)

would be that twice as much insecticide is used as is actually needed. Since the insecticide market in California probably amounts to some $70–80 million a year, one can understand the reluctance of the petrochemical industry to see a sensible use-pattern emerge which would reduce this market by at least 50 percent.

But it would be unfair to blame the petrochemical industry alone for the misuse of pesticides. The United States Department of Agriculture has also contributed heavily to environmental deterioration. That agency has had a long history of promoting pesticides, often displaying a high degree of ecological incompetence in the process. An outstanding example can be found in the history of the fire ant program, in which the USDA, against the advice of most biologists, attempted to "exterminate" this insect over a large portion of the United States by spraying a huge area with chlorinated hydrocarbons. The ensuing disaster is examined in some detail in Appendix 4.

The fire ant program and similar disasters might lead one to conclude that all pest control programs initiated by the USDA are ecologically incompetent. That this is not true is shown by the ecologically sophisticated programs that have been initiated by various individuals within the Department. Perhaps the most brilliant was that against the screwworm, a fly whose larvae (maggots) can be an extremely serious pest on cattle. Annual losses in livestock have been estimated to be as high as $40 million a year. Under the leadership of entomologist E. F. Knipling, the USDA embarked on a massive program of sterilizing male screwworm flies by irradiation and releasing them in infested areas. The female screwworm only mates once. By flooding infested areas with sterile males, the screwworm was essentially eradicated from the southeastern United States. The effectiveness of this biological control program makes an interesting contrast with the futile and destructive fire ant fiasco of the 1950s and early 1960s.

However, when it comes to the fire ant, the USDA apparently is incapable of learning. Armed with a new chlorinated hydrocarbon insecticide, mirex, the Department announced plans in 1970 to spray bait pellets over some 11 million acres in the South. Over the previous 8 years, mirex had already been used over large areas on an "experimental basis" against the fire ant. It was at first touted as the "perfect pesticide" for this program, because virtually all the bait found its way into the ants' nests with very little left to poison non-target organisms, and it appeared to be generally less toxic than other chlorinated hydrocarbons such as dieldrin or heptachlor. But as time and research went on, it was discovered that mirex was not so harmless after all. Like other chlorinated hydrocarbons, it is very persistent and tends to be concentrated in food chains. In laboratory tests, it has been found to be highly toxic to shrimp, crabs, and crayfish, as well as insects other than the fire ant. It is also somewhat toxic to at least some birds and mammals and is carcinogenic in mice. Because of overtreatment (repeated applications after most of the ant nests had been poisoned), enough mirex escaped into the environment to cause problems.

When the USDA announced the new program, the Environmental Defense Fund, together with several other conservation groups, filed suit against it. In April, 1971, their motion for a preliminary injunction against the fire ant program was denied, and the program was immediately initiated. However, the action did serve to delay action. Moreover, perhaps partly bceause of the suit and partly because some of the states failed to produce their share of funds for it, the original program was considerably curtailed.

The fire ant program still must be justified in court. Meanwhile, a number of other government agencies have become interested. The Fish and Wildlife Division of the Department of the Interior long opposed the first fire ant program, and more recently, the Interior Department has put mirex on its list of restricted pesticides. The Department of Health, Education and Welfare disapproved of mirex because of its carcinogenic properties. The Council on Environmental Quality also disapproved of the use of mirex, and the Environmental Protection Agency has put it under scientific review, a step that could lead to its exclusion from interstate commerce. (Similar review is pending against DDT, dieldrin and an herbicide.)

The list of nontarget animals affected by pesticides is now of encyclopedic proportions. The amazing diversity of organisms involved, besides many beneficial insects, includes robins, amphipods, whitefish, earthworms, oldsquaw ducks, warblers, rabbits, quail, lake trout, mosquito fish, foxes, opposums, mice, ospreys, muskrats, pheasants, turkeys, gulls, fiddler crabs, salmon, snakes, and big-game mammals. Poisoning of these or any other organisms, of course, always affects the ecosystems in which they function.

### ALTERNATIVES TO PRESENT PATTERNS OF INSECT CONTROL

It is commonly claimed that only current patterns of chemical control stand between us and starvation or death from insect-borne disease. Nothing could be further from the truth; the alternatives are not death or the continued dosing of ourselves and our environment with chlorinated hydrocarbons. First of all there is a wide variety of highly effective insecticides that are not persistent, and that are thus much less dangerous ecologically (although some may cause considerable environmental disruption and may have much higher immediate toxicity for human beings at application sites). These include the organophosphates, carbamates, and botanical compounds, such as pyrethrum and rotenone. Some of these may be more expensive now than the chlorinated hydrocarbons, but if the chlorinated hydrocarbons are banned it seems likely that the petrochemical industry will find ways to reduce the costs of producing the other compounds.

The most desirable alternative of all is to shift as completely as possible to ecological pest management—that is, to what is often called "integrated control." Integrated control has as its goal the maintenance of potential pest populations below the level at which they cause serious health hazards or economic damage. It does not attempt to exterminate pests—a goal that, incidentally, has never been accomplished by chemical control programs. Integrated control involves using one or more techniques appropriate to the particular pest situation. Mosquitos may be controlled by draining swamps in which some of the larvae live, stocking lakes with mosquito-eating fishes, applying a coat of oil, or perhaps applying small amounts of nonpersistent insecticides to any standing water that will not support fishes and cannot be drained. Similarly, a crop could be protected by practices such as planting it in mixed cultures with other crops, destroying pest reservoirs adjacent to fields, introducing and encouraging appropriate predators and parasites, breeding more resistant crop strains, luring pests from fields with baits, and using nonpersistent insecticides. Insect development may be disrupted by the use of hormonal insecticides. These and other practices may be combined to achieve both a high level of desirable control and a minimum of damage to the ecosystems of the world. Sometimes, as in the successful screwworm program, no chemical control will be necessary; at other times chemical methods may play a major role.

Integrated control programs have been enormously successful in cases where they have been tried. Outstanding examples are the programs in alfalfa and cotton in California, which are discussed in detail in a book edited by Carl Huffaker, *Biological Control*. Robert van den Bosch and his co-authors write (Chapter 17, p. 393) of the control of pests on cotton in California's Central Valley, "Existing pest control practices are both inefficient and expensive, and because of this they are directly contributing to the economic crisis [among cotton growers]. Accumulating evidence indicates that integrated control is much more efficient and less expensive, and the hard-pressed growers are beginning to realize this."

The transition away from the relatively simple chemical techniques will require planning and training, and will perhaps produce some temporary economic stress. Since we must not delay banning the chlorinated hydrocarbons, more expensive methods may have to be used temporarily. But there is no reason that the transition should lead to serious consequences for human health or nutrition. The step would be necessary even if such consequences *were* foreseen as serious, since continued use of persistent insecticides will result sooner or later in an unprecedented catastrophe for the entire planet. In fact, in many areas positive benefits would be immediate, particularly where the development of DDT-resistant mosquitoes is reducing the effectiveness of mosquito control programs. It is important to remember, above all, that the consequences of any control programs, integrated or not, require intelligent surveillance and periodic re-evaluation. *Any* tinkering with ecosystems may result in unforeseen and deleterious consequences.

## Pollutants, Plankton, and Marine Food Chains

The effects of insecticides and other poisonous substances in water are not confined to aquatic animals. Perhaps the most frightening ecological news of

1968 was contained in a short paper entitled "DDT Reduces Photosynthesis by Marine Phytoplankton," which was published in the journal *Science*. The author, environmental scientist Charles F. Wurster of the State University of New York, reports that DDT reduced photosynthesis in both experimental cultures and natural communities of marine phytoplankton (algae, diatoms, etc.), the tiny green plants that float free in the waters of the oceans. Effects were noted at DDT concentrations of only a few parts per billion (ppb), quantities that are commonly found in waters near land sites treated with DDT. Water at a distance from treatment sites ordinarily has DDT concentrations averaging less than 1 ppb, but biological systems clearly have the power and propensity to amplify these amounts.

The effects of DDT on phytoplankton in nature are difficult to evaluate. Phytoplankton are the primary producers responsible for most of the food we take from the sea. If photosynthesis were significantly reduced in marine phytoplankton, the amount of life in the seas would be reduced; if marine photosynthesis ceased, all sea life would die. But significant qualitative changes in the phytoplankton community seem more probable than large quantitative changes. Phytoplankton populations are differentially susceptible to DDT; even extremely low DDT concentrations might result in shifts of dominance, leading to huge blooms of one or a few species. These shifts would, in turn, produce serious consequences throughout oceanic food webs. One possibility is that phytoplankton less acceptable to large herbivores would dominate, so that larger animals would be affected. This shortening of food chains might leave man only microscopic plants and animals as a source of food from the sea. Another possibility is that phytoplankton communities near the shore could become dominated by smaller species, lengthening food chains and dramatically reducing the size of populations of fishes at the upper trophic levels.

Similarly, the problems besetting our inland waters (discussed below) may be aggravated by the effects of DDT on fresh-water phytoplankton. As Wurster says, "Such effects are insidious and their cause may be obscure, yet they may be ecologically more important than the obvious, direct mortality of larger organisms that is so often reported."

Another pollutant was found in 1970 to reduce photosynthesis in phytoplankton, both marine and freshwater. This was mercury, which in organic forms such as methylmercury proved to be extremely toxic to these tiny plants. Photosynthesis was significantly inhibited at concentrations in water of 0.1 ppb, one-fiftieth the amount now tolerated by U.S. Public Health standards (5 ppb). When concentrations reached 50 ppb, growth essentially stopped completely. Mercury's effects on phytoplankton resemble those of DDT; like the chlorinated hydrocarbons, it also tends to be concentrated in food chains. Thus, its potential impact on oceanic food webs may be serious and of a similar nature to that of DDT. Also, like DDT, enough inorganic mercury has already accumulated on lake and stream beds in North America to provide a serious mercury threat (if converted to the soluble organic form) to fresh water and estuarine life for decades to come, unless a way is found to remove it. San Francisco Bay alone was estimated by the U.S. Geological Survey in 1971 to have some 58 tons of mercury on its bottom, with concentrations ranging from 0.25 to 6.4 parts per *million* parts of bottom sediment.

The long-term ecological effects in the seas of other heavy metals, such as lead, cadmium, and chromium, are not known. But since they are known to be toxic to many forms of life, it would be unreasonable to assume their effects to be negligible.

One ocean pollutant which has received a great deal of publicity, mainly because much of it is the result of spectacular accidents, is oil. In 1970, when Thor Heyerdahl sailed a papyrus raft across the Atlantic Ocean, he reported that, "Clots of oil are polluting the mid-stream current of the Atlantic Ocean from horizon to horizon." The oil has reached the sea in a variety of ways. Among them are the massive accidental spills from tankers which have received so much publicity, as well as many smaller spills. These probably account for less than 0.1 percent of the total oil transported at sea. But that volume is so huge, about 360 billion gallons per year, or 60 percent of all sea-transported goods, that the spills amount to a considerable influx. Still more is spilled as fuel oil from ships not involved in transporting oil, especially in connection with refueling operations. In addition to shipping spills, there are accidents in extraction from sea-floor drilling, of which the Santa Barbara leak is the best known example. Finally, some oil reaches the sea in sewage wastes.

The effects of oil pollution on oceanic ecosystems, beyond the immediate and obvious decimation of populations of fish, shellfish, and sea birds at the site of a spill, are now being discovered, thanks to a relatively small spill which occurred in 1969 near the Wood's Hole Oceanographic Institute in Massachusetts. Effects vary with the type of oil, the distance from shore where it is spilled, and how long it can "weather" (be degraded by microorganisms, dissolve and evaporate) before reaching shore, and what organisms live there. Some components of oil are toxic, others are known carcinogens; weathering can reduce their toxicity, but the carcinogenic components are long-lasting. Oil washed to shore lingers on rocks and sand for months or years, but the marine life may need a decade or more to recover, even after the oil is no longer obvious.

Entire populations of some sea birds, especially the diving birds which are most susceptible, have been drastically reduced in recent years, probably largely due to oil contamination. Besides killing thousands of them directly, oil toxins may also reduce egg viability and affect reproduction in these birds.

Detergents used to clean up oil spills have been found to make the situation worse in many cases. Not only are the detergents themselves toxic to many forms of life, they disperse the oil and spread it into new areas. They may also, by breaking up the oil into droplets, render it more easily absorbable by small marine organisms.

Immediately after the Massachusetts spill, there was a 95 percent mortality of fish, shellfish, worms, and other sea animals. Nine months later, repopulation had still not taken place. Surviving mussels failed to reproduce. Some constituents of the oil were still present and killing bottom-dwelling organisms 8 months later. Surviving shellfish and oysters took in enough oil to be inedible and retained it even months after distant transplanting. According to marine biologist, Max Blumer, there is a possibility that the carcinogenic constituents of oil, which are absorbed unchanged by these and other small organisms, may in time be incorporated into and contaminate entire food chains. Thus there is a chance that at levels too low to alter the flavor and aroma of seafoods, some of these oil components could invade a substantial part of the human diet.

Some effort is being made to develop bacterial strains which can quickly degrade spilled oil; more efficient technical means of collecting it before it reaches shore are also being studied. In view of the amount of oil already polluting the oceans and the increasing potential for further spills represented by the rising volume of oil transportation by sea and the increasing size of tankers, efforts to deal with such accidents should be vigorously pursued. At the same time much can be done in the area of prevention without further research. Oil can and should be removed from sewage; safety regulations both for drilling platforms and tankers can be tightened and enforced; the flushing of tankers can be prohibited, and other ships can be forbidden to waste or discard oil products of any kind.

No one knows how long we can continue to pollute the seas with chlorinated hydrocarbon insecticides, polychlorinated biphenyls, oil, mercury, cadmium, and thousands of other pollutants, without bringing on a worldwide ecological disaster. Subtle changes may already have started a chain reaction in that direction, as shown by declines in many fisheries, especially those in areas of heavy pollution caused by dumping of wastes. The U.S. government is now moving toward regulation of ocean dumping; hopefully, other countries will follow suit.

## Pollutants and Soils

The effects of pollutants on soils are difficult to evaluate. Soils are not just collections of crushed rock; they are extraordinarily complex ecosystems in their own right. The animals of the soil are extremely numerous and varied. In forest communities of North Carolina, an estimated 125 million small invertebrates live in each acre of soil, more than 30,000 per square meter. Some 70 percent of these are mites, a group of arthropods that may eventually prove to be as diverse as the insects. In a study of pasture soils in Denmark, up to 45,000 small oligochaete worms, 10 million nematodes (roundworms), and 48,000 small arthropods (insects and mites) were found in each square meter. Even more abundant are the microflora of the soil. More than a million bacteria of one type may be found in a gram (0.035 ounce) of forest soil, as well as almost 100,000 yeast cells, and about 50,000 bits of fungus mycelium. A gram of fertile agricultural soil has yielded over 2.5 billion bacteria, 400,000 fungi, 50,000 algae, and 30,000 protozoa.

In most natural situations, the plants, animals, and microorganisms of the soil are absolutely essential for its fertility. The roles that some of these organisms play in the ecology of the soil were indicated in the discussion of the nitrogen cycle. Everyone is familiar with the beneficial effects of earthworms, but most people are completely unaware of the myriad other complex (and in many cases still poorly understood) ecological relationships within the soil that make it a suitable substance for the growth of oak trees, chaparral, corn, or any other plants. The soil contains microorganisms that are responsible for the conversion of nitrogen, phosphorus, and sulfur to forms available to the plants. Many trees have been found to depend on an association with fungi. The fungi get carbohydrates and other essential substances from the roots, and the root-fungus complex is able to extract from the soil minerals that could not be extracted by the root alone. Such mycorrhizal associations are just beginning to be understood, but it is clear that in many areas the "visible" plant community would be drastically altered if the mycorrhizal fungi were absent from the soil.

Recognizing as they do that most of the complex physical and chemical processes responsible for soil fertility are dependent upon soil organisms, environmental biologists are appalled by continuing treatment of soils with heavy dosages of deadly and persistent poisons. Consider, for instance, a recent study of persistence of chlorinated hydrocarbons in a sandy loam soil at an experimental station. Table 7-1 summarizes the results, which, because of the conditions of the study, may be close to the upper limits for persistence. Of half of these insecticides more than one-third of the amounts applied remained in the soil 14 or more years after treatment. Under normal

TABLE 7-1
*Persistence of Insecticides in Soils*

| Insecticide | Years since treatment | Percent remaining |
|---|---|---|
| Aldrin | 14 | 40 |
| Chlordane | 14 | 40 |
| Endrin | 14 | 41 |
| Heptachlor | 14 | 16 |
| Dilan | 14 | 23 |
| Isodrin | 14 | 15 |
| Benzene hexachloride | 14 | 10 |
| Toxaphene | 14 | 45 |
| Dieldrin | 15 | 31 |
| DDT | 17 | 39 |

SOURCE: Nash and Woolson, *Science,* vol. 157, pp. 924–927 (1967).

agricultural conditions, chlorinated hydrocarbons seem to persist for 3 to 5 years, whereas organophosphates and carbamates are gone in 1 to 3 months or less.

Considerable evidence already exists that the use of insecticides may reduce soil fertility, especially in woodland soils which are subject to spraying but not artificial cultivation. Populations of earthworms, soil mites, and insects are dramatically changed, and these in turn affect the soil fungi, which are their principal food. Even if bacteria were not affected directly, there is no question that the general effects on the soil ecosystem would carry over to these and other microorganisms. But it would be unwarranted to assume that the bacteria are not directly affected. It is known that a few microorganisms can degrade DDT to DDD under the proper conditions; a few can degrade dieldrin to aldrin and several other breakdown products of unknown toxicity. Our ignorance of the interactions of insecticides, herbicides (see next section), and other environmental poisons with soil microorganisms is immense. Our general lack of attention to the possible long-range effects of these and similar subtle problems in our environment could ultimately prove to be fatal to mankind.

## Herbicides and Ecosystems

In recent years there has been an enormous upsurge in the use of herbicides as a substitute for farm machinery and labor in cultivating crops, for keeping roadsides, railroad rights of way, and powerline cuts free of shrubs, and as military defoliants in Vietnam. The rate of increase in herbicide use has far outstripped that of synthetic insecticides. Two kinds of herbicides are in wide use (Box 7-2). Members of one group (2,4D; 2,4,5-T; picloram, etc.) are similar to plant hormones, and cause metabolic changes in the plant that lead to death or leaf drop. The other group (simazine, monuron, etc.) interferes with a critical process in photosynthesis, causing the plant to die from lack of energy. Although their direct toxicity to animals is low, herbicides have great impact on animal populations through their modification and eradication of plant populations, since all animals depend, at least indirectly, on plants for food. Furthermore, as a result of the coevolutionary interactions discussed earlier, most herbivorous animals are specialized to feed on one kind or just a few kinds of plants.

In the light of these considerations, it is possible to evaluate the statements that American government officials have made concerning the lack of danger to animals or the uncertainty of effects on animals of our defoliation activities in Vietnam (Box 7-3), and the reasons for concern on the part of biologists become very plain. Defoliation of tropical jungles inevitably leads to the local extinction of many populations of insects, birds, arboreal reptiles, and arboreal mammals. But, of course, "animals" in official statements can all too often be translated "elephants, tigers, and other large mammals." In temperate forests there is generally a less distinct canopy fauna, but changes in animal populations in response to large-scale defoliation would certainly be tremendous. Recent evidence suggests that herbicides may produce birth defects in mammals (including humans), and it has been shown that 2,4-D can kill bird embryos or induce defective or sterile young. It has been suggested that widespread use of 2,4-D may be responsible for a decline in populations of European gamebirds.

We know very little about direct effects of herbicides on soil microorganisms. Recent research in Sweden indicates that herbicides destroy bacteria that are symbiotic with legumes, although the bacteria apparently are capable of developing some resistance. Some herbicides, such as 2,4-D, are quickly degraded by bacteria and persist for only a few weeks or months; others (2,4,5-T and presumably picloram) are more persistent. Soil microorganisms (primarily bacteria and fungi) do not photosynthesize; they are consumers, not producers. Therefore, they probably will not be affected by herbicides that block photosynthetic processes, although there could, of course, be other metabolic effects. Herbicides that function as simulated plant hormones are unlikely to disturb the growth processes of the soil flora, since there is no evidence that the plant hormone simulated by these substances functions in bacteria or fungi. These herbicides may of course have other physiological effects, since, as noted above, some are metabolized by soil bacteria.

---

BOX 7-2    HERBICIDES

*Chlorophenoxy Acid Herbicides*

This group includes 2,4-D, 2,4,5-T, picloram, and several others. These compounds are chemically similar to the growth-regulating substance indolacetic acid. This plant hormone (or auxin) controls such diverse things as shoot growth, root growth, apical dominance, and phototropism. Overdoses of these herbicides function by causing uncontrolled growth and metabolism; the plant, in essence, grows itself to death.

Indolacetic acid does not function as a growth substance in animals, and therefore it is not surprising that these herbicides have essentially no direct effect on animals. Differential toxicity to broadleafed plants (as opposed to narrowleafed grasses) is a function of the greater ease with which the compounds are absorbed. Some of these herbicides, such as 2,4-D, are rapidly metabolized in woody plants, which usually localize the damage; they are defoliated, but not killed. Other herbicides, such as picloram, remain active for long periods in trees and ecosystems.

*Symmetrical Triazines and Substituted Ureas*

These include simazine, fenuron, diuron, and monuron. Both of these classes of compounds block a critical step in photosynthesis, known as the Hill reaction. The plant, in essence, starves to death. Since animals do not photosynthesize, they are not directly affected by these compounds, with the exception of possible mutagenic effects of the triazines.

BOX 7-3   ECOCIDE IN INDOCHINA

The practice of genocide has, unhappily, a long history in human affairs. Ecocide, the deliberate destruction of ecosystems, is for practical reasons a rather recent development. Destruction of enemy crops has frequently occurred in warfare, and the near extermination of the bison was a decisive factor in America's conquest of the plains Indians (the slaughter was not a purposeful military strategy, but its effects were known at the time). But, until recently, man has not been able to destroy the entire life support system over substantial portions of the surface of the Earth in a short space of time. However, synthetic herbicides, insecticides, and nuclear weapons have now given humanity a greatly enhanced capability to commit ecocide. If the widespread use of biocides continues, despite growing knowledge of the probable consequences, mankind may destroy much or all of the carrying capacity of this planet for human life. If that occurs, however, any survivors will be able to "excuse" what happened as a result of greed and stupidity—after all, no one really wanted the unhappy side-effects of synthetic biocides. But no such excuse can be made for the practice of ecocide in Indochina by the armed forces of the United States.

As of the end of 1969 more than 5 million acres of Indochina, 12 percent of South Vietnam, have been treated with "defoliants," applied at an average of 13 times the dose recommended by the U.S. Department of Agriculture (USDA) for domestic use. Most of the spraying was done in forests in an unsuccessful attempt to "expose" the enemy and secure the area. At such dosages some of the trees, especially mangroves, may not just be defoliated, they may be killed by a single application. Multiple applications kill other kinds of trees. The American Association for the Advancement of Science Herbicide–Assessment Commission (AAAS-HAC) reported that perhaps half of the trees in the mature hardwood forests north of Saigon were damaged. One of the herbicides widely used in Vietnam is Picloram, which is both potent and (like DDT) persistent. It is so dangerous that the USDA has not licensed it for use in the cultivation of any American crop. It may continue to kill plants in Southeast Asia for decades after the last GI has left.

Through 1969 at least one-half million acres of cropland in South Vietnam have been sprayed with herbicides with the stated purpose of denying food to enemy soldiers. It has been done in an attempt to starve civilian populations sympathetic to the National Liberation Front and to force people to move from the countryside into cities where they are more readily controlled. As our military were well aware, the first to suffer when food becomes scarce in wartime are not soldiers, but children, old people, and pregnant and nursing women. The AAAS-HAC reported that virtually all of the crops destroyed would have supplied food to civilians, especially to the Montagnard tribesmen of the central highlands.

The overall effect of these herbicide programs is to degrade Vietnamese ecosystems. Forests attacked with herbicides have been invaded by bamboo, and some areas may have undergone laterization. The danger of laterization is especially severe in farmland attacked with herbicides. According to the AAAS-HAC, large areas of mangrove forest, which grows along waterways and plays a critical role in the maintenance of economically important fisheries, have also been destroyed. Some 1,400 square kilometers, 20 to 50 percent of all the mangroves in South Vietnam, have been killed and the forests show no signs of regeneration. The long term consequences of these actions are incalculable, since they have also certainly had a profound effect on the fauna of the area (and animals in turn are important to the plants for pollination and seed dispersal) and probably also on the organisms of the soil which are essential to its fertility. They also may have left the Vietnamese people with a legacy of birth defects, as evidence is now accumulating that some of the herbicides are teratogenic. At last, however, due in large part to the AAAS-HAC report, and other pressure from the scientific community, the use of herbicides as a military weapon in Vietnam has been discontinued.

Herbicides have not been our only ecocidal weapon. In 1967–1968 alone, more than 3.5 million 500- to 750-pound bombs were dropped on Vietnam, each creating a crater as large as 45 feet across and 30 feet deep. If these craters were placed in a line they would stretch for some 30,000 miles, a distance greater than the circumference of the Earth. They occupy 100,000 acres. We do not know the exact statistics for bombing since 1968 in Vietnam, or the tonnage dropped in Laos and Cambodia, because the Department of Defense has refused to release the exact statistics. Ecologist E. W. Pfeiffer of the University of Montana, estimating an average B-52 mission to consist of six bombers carrying 108 500-pound bombs each, recently calculated that 325,000 acres, mostly in South Vietnam, are now in craters. This estimate may be conservative, as the ending of the herbiciding program has quite possibly caused an increase in sorties-per-mission above six. Even at the lower figure the tonnage of bombs dropped by the USAF on South Vietnam (an area roughly the size of New England) was by mid-1971 some two and one-half times the total tonnage dropped by all belligerents in World War II—some 20 tons per square mile.

Many of the bomb craters pocking the surface of Indochina are permanently water-filled. From observations of World War II bomb craters in New Guinea and the Solomon Islands, it is reasonable to expect natural recovery of cratered areas to take at least a century. The task of filling the 1967–1968 craters alone would require moving 2.5 *billion* cubic yards of earth.

In many areas of Vietnam peasants are afraid to reoccupy bombed fields because of the danger from unexploded ordnance. This problem will worsen if bombing is substituted for both defoliation and ground combat troops. Another ecocidal device now being used with increased frequency, according to Pfeiffer, is the BLU-82B multipurpose bomb, the so-called "daisy-cutter." This 15,000-pound concussion weapon clears an area the size of a football field to make an "instant landing zone" for helicopters. It is being used increasingly as an anti-personnel weapon, as it can kill all animals within a three-quarter-mile radius (over an area of 780 acres). These devices were being dropped at a rate of two or three per week in mid-1971.

Perhaps the crudest tool the United States is using to destroy the ecology of Indochina is the "Rome plow." These are heavily armored D7E caterpillar bulldozers with a 2.5-ton blade. They can plow a swath through the heaviest forest. Rome plows have been used to clear several hundred yards on each side of all main roads in South Vietnam. In mid-1971 five "land clearing companies" were at work, each with some 30 plows, mowing down Vietnamese forests. By then some 800,000 acres had been cleared, and the clearing was continuing at a rate of about 2,000 acres (three square miles) per day! Pfeiffer suspects the plan is to scrape the Earth clean from Saigon to the Cambodian border.

Ecocide in Indochina has not been limited to combat operations. A clandestine

Herbicides have also been adopted by other organisms than man. A flightless grasshopper has been discovered to secrete 2,5-dichlorophenol, apparently derived from 2,4-D, along with other naturally occurring disagreeable substances derived from plants, in its defensive fluid. This unusual ingredient appears to be very successful in discouraging predatory ants; thus, man attacking weeds inadvertently encourages a herbivore. The subtlety of the side effects of biocides is difficult to overestimate.

We know too little also about the effects of herbicides on aquatic life, but the evidence is mounting that they are substantial. Members of the group including 2,4-D particularly are toxic to fish, although less so than most insecticides, and they have also been found toxic to freshwater crustacea.

The runoff of herbicides, especially those that interfere with photosynthesis, into inland and coastal waters could be more serious than the effects of herbicides on soil fertility. The photosynthetic processes of phytoplankton, as well as the growth of other plants, could be disturbed. Again, it is important to remember that changes in basic producer populations will inevitably affect populations higher up in the food chains.

Even with the small amount of information that exists, it is hard to be complacent about widespread indiscriminate use of herbicides under any circumstances. The spraying of potent biocides over large areas because it is easier and quicker than cultivating or weeding is a practice that ecologists can only deplore. The herbicide story may turn out to be a repetition of the insecticide story, but the case for dependence on chemicals is even weaker

---

BOX 7.3 (*continued*)

raid in April 1969 defoliated 173,000 acres in eastern Cambodia and damaged about a third of the rubber trees then in production. The damage was concentrated in an area with the highest yield per acre in Cambodia. In addition to this serious blow to the rubber crop (which is the underpinning of that nation's economy), damage to the local food production was severe. Pfeiffer recently reported that this operation was carried out prior to the Cambodian invasion to put pressure on the Sihanouk government, and that the raid was flown by Air America, an "airline" run by the U.S. Central Intelligence Agency.

Although ecocide itself is not formally a war crime, it has contributed greatly to the "wanton destruction" and "devastation," which are both war crimes and crimes against humanity under the Charter of the International Military Tribunal at Nuremberg. The use of herbicides (and tear gases) is against the Geneva Protocol of 1925 as interpreted in 1969 by the main political committee of the U.N. General Assembly. The vote was 58 to 3, with 35 abstentions. The only nations to vote "no" with the United States were Australia, which has allied herself with us in Vietnam, and Portugal, which wishes to employ these weapons in her own wars in Africa. A large part of the American scientific community must carry a heavy burden of guilt for its failure to develop effective opposition to what we believe to be criminal acts by the American government. Our community developed the weapons, has the expertise to evaluate their impact, and showed in its lobbying effort which eventually forced the military to stop using herbicides that it can have a positive effect when it bestirs itself.

for weed killers. Like insecticides, they should be used with discretion and only when necessary. More attention should be paid to developing integrated control methods for weeds, and in recalcitrant cases where these methods or mechanical weeding proves infeasible, a return to weeding by human labor should be considered. Adjustment of our economic system so that more labor can be profitably employed in agriculture might possibly help solve social and economic problems ranging from unemployment to overurbanization.

## Nitrogen, Phosphates, and Ecosystems

Much of the nitrogen in natural soils is contained in humus, the organic matter of the soil. Humus is a poorly understood complex of compounds of high molecular weight. Inorganic nitrogen in such soils normally accounts for less than 2 percent of the nitrogen present; often the majority is tied up in the large organic molecules of humus, which are derived from such varied sources as the fibrous remains of woody plant tissues, insect skeletons, and animal manure. These substances, in addition to their chemical value, increase the capacity of the soil to retain water. The presence of humus makes the soil a favorable medium for the complicated chemical reactions and mineral transport needed for the growth of higher plants. Bacteria in the soil decompose humus to form nitrates and other nutrient substances required by plant roots.

Roots require oxygen in order to do the work necessary for the uptake of nitrates and other nutrients, but oxygen is not available if the soil is tightly compacted. Thus another important benefit of humus is to maintain soil porosity and so permit oxygen to penetrate to the roots of plants.

In natural soil systems the nitrogen cycle is "tight." Not much nitrogen is removed from the soil by leaching or surface runoff. It has been shown experimentally that by maintaining the supply of humus the fertility of the soil can be perpetuated. This is not possible when fertilizers containing inorganic nitrogen are employed, unless organic carbon (in such forms as sawdust or straw) is supplied to the soil microorganisms. The undesirable decline of humus which often occurs under inorganic fertilization is due to the failure of the farmer to return crop residues (and thus carbon) to his fields. The decline is not caused by any deficiency in the fertilizers themselves. Indeed, if carbon is supplied in the proper proportion with inorganic nitrogen, the supply of humus can be increased and the quality of the soil improved.

If attempts are made to maintain soil fertility by continued applications of inorganic nitrogen fertilizers alone, the capacity of the soil to retain nitrogen is reduced as its humus content drops. In humus, nitrogen is combined into nonsoluble forms that are not leached from the soil by rainwater. Depletion of humus "loosens" the soil cycles and permits large amounts of nitrate to be flushed into rivers and lakes. The use of inorganic fertilizers in the United States has been multiplied some 12-fold in the past 25 years. One result of this dramatic increase has been a concomitant rise in the content of nitrate in surface water, atmosphere, and rain. Another has been a 50 percent reduction of the original organic nitrogen content of Midwestern soils.

The results of the added nitrogen content of our waters are exemplified in part by the now well-documented fate of Lake Erie. The waters of Lake Erie are so polluted that the U.S. Public Health Service has urged ships on the lake not to use lake water taken within 5 miles of the United States shore. The water is so badly contaminated that neither boiling nor chlorination will purify it; although the organisms in it would be killed, the dangerous chemicals it contains would not be removed or broken down.

The sources of Lake Erie's pollution are many. A report to the Federal Water Pollution Control Agency cites as the main source of pollution the raw sewage dumped into the lake by lakeside municipalities, especially Cleveland, Toledo, and Euclid, Ohio; and Wayne County (Detroit), Michigan. The report cites industry as another major source of pollution, and names the Ford Motor Company, Republic Steel, and Bethlehem Steel as significant pollutors. Finally, the basin of Lake Erie contains an estimated 30,000 square miles of farmland, and another important source of pollution is runoff from these farmlands.

Let us examine the last source first. The waters draining the farmlands of the Middle West are rich in nitrogen as a result of the heavy use of inorganic nitrogen fertilizers. Indeed, they have an estimated nitrogen content equivalent to the sewage of some 20,000,000 people—*about twice the total human population of the Lake Erie basin*. Thus, besides fertilizing their farms with nitrogen, the farmers are also fertilizing Lake Erie; their nitrogen contribution is of the same order of magnitude as that of the municipalities and the industrial pollutors. The nitrogen balance of the lake has been seriously disturbed, and the abundance of inorganic nitrates encourages the growth of certain algae. In recent years these algae have produced monstrous blooms—big masses of algae that grow extremely quickly, cover huge areas, foul beaches, and then die.

The bacterial decay of these masses of algae consumes oxygen, reducing the amount of oxygen available for fishes and other animals. Such blooms and oxygen depletions are characteristic of lakes undergoing *eutrophication,* which may be loosely translated as "overfertilization." Phosphate levels in U.S. surface waters have increased 27-fold in recent years. Phosphates, as well as nitrates, are implicated in this problem. Sources include fertilizer runoff and industrial waste, but 60 percent of the phosphate entering U.S. waters comes from municipal sewage. The primary source of phosphates in sewage is household detergents.

The basic sequence of eutrophication is simple in outline. Inorganic nitrates and phosphates are washed into the lake. These inorganic chemicals are converted into organic forms as huge blooms of algae develop; the subsequent decomposition of the algae depletes water of oxygen and kills off animals that have high oxygen requirements. Much of the nitrate and phosphate remains in the lake, settling to the bottom with the decaying mass of algae. The bottom of Lake Erie now has a layer of muck that varies from 20 to 125 feet in thickness; this layer is immensely rich in phosphorous and nitrogen compounds. These compounds are bound by a "skin" of insoluble iron compounds that covers the mud. Unfortunately, the iron compounds change to a more soluble form in the absence of oxygen. Thus the oxygen depletion itself may cause the release into the lake of more of the nutrients responsible for the lake's troubles, and eutrophication may take place even more rapidly. Barry Commoner believes that if this breaking down of the mud skin should continue and result in the release of large amounts of nitrogen and phosphorus, the lake may face a disaster that would dwarf its present troubles.

Lake Erie is just one outstanding example of a general problem that is well known to most Americans—the gross pollution of our lakes, rivers, and streams. All manner of organic and inorganic wastes end up in our inland waters: raw sewage, manure, paunch manure (the stomach contents of slaughtered animals), detergents, acids, pesticides, garbage; the list goes on and on. All of these substances affect the life in the water, all too often exterminating much of it, and at the very least modifying the ecosystems in profound ways. This pollution problem is worldwide; many of the rivers of the Earth are quickly approaching the "too thin to plow and too thick to drink" stage.

In the United States and some other areas, serious attempts have been made to clean up fresh-water systems. These have met with mixed success. It is impossible to know whether we are gaining, holding our own, or losing at the moment, but the situation is bad, and the outlook for the future in the United States is not encouraging. Even an isolated beauty like Lake Tahoe, a high Sierra lake shared by California and Nevada, is threatened. Barry Commoner has estimated that by 1980 urban sewage alone, if left untreated, would consume all the available oxygen in all 25 major river systems of the nation. The eutrophication problems in the U.S. have now even spread to estuarine and inshore waters where sewage is dumped. Many oyster and clam beds have been damaged or destroyed, and some fisheries have all but disappeared. Oxygen depletion and accompanying changes in water quality have been shown to induce marked destabilizing changes in local marine ecosystems.

Similar problems exist in many other parts of the world. Lake Baikal in the Soviet Union seems slowly to be headed for a fate similar to Lake Erie's, despite the protests of Russian conservationists. Many lakes and rivers in Europe and Asia are beginning to show signs of eutrophication, often within 10 to 20 years after the start of human pollution. The rivers in Italy are so badly polluted that Italian scientists fear that marine life in the Mediterranean is endangered. In most UDCs, rivers are simply open sewers. Eutrophication is not usually a problem there, except in a few areas where some industrial development has taken place. However, the Green Revolution, with its required high levels of fertilization, may change the situation.

Inorganic nitrate and phosphate fertilizers must be considered a technological success because they do succeed in raising the amounts of free nutrients in the soil, but it is precisely this success that has led to eutrophication as those nutrients are leached out of the soil by groundwater. It has been predicted that in 25 to 50 years the ultimate crisis in agriculture will occur in the United States. Either the fertility of the soil will drop precipitously, because inorganic fertilizers will be withheld, throwing the nation into a food crisis, or the amounts of inorganic nitrates and phosphates applied to the land will be so large as to cause an insoluble water pollution problem. One would hope that before this comes to pass the rate of fertilizer use will be moderated and laws will require return of plant residues or other means of supplying the organic carbon necessary to build humus. Even these steps might not avert a water crisis produced by two other technological successes: high-compression automobile engines, which produce an inorganic nitrogen fallout, and modern sewage treatment plants, which produce an effluent rich in inorganic nitrates and phosphates. The significance of these inorganic nutrients has only recently been widely recognized.

In the light of these and many other assaults on the environment, it would behoove us to begin immediately to head off future threats. As is becoming apparent, use of the internal combustion engine will have to be greatly reduced. It is imperative that either our present sewage treatment plants be completely redesigned to eliminate nutrients from the effluent, or that a way be found to reclaim the nutrients for fertilizer. Also needed are new sewage plants for the many communities that still pour raw sewage into our waters. Such a program requires money and effort, some of which might be provided immediately by employing the Army Corps of Engineers and the Bureau of Reclamation for such projects.

The problem of controlling the runoff of nutrients from farms is more difficult, but it is known that nitrates leach from soil because they are anions (negatively charged groups of atoms), and the capacity of the soil to retain anions is low. Mixing a resin with high binding affinity for anions into the soil would increase its capacity to hold nitrates. Certainly, experimental work in this area should be initiated immediately, but "solutions" of this sort must be monitored very carefully. Often they have a tendency to create problems more serious than those they solve.

A more immediately available approach to controlling agricultural runoff might be to halt by law the practice of handling manure from farm animals as a waste product. Roughly 80 percent of American cattle are produced on feedlots, and most of their manure is treated as sewage, which more than doubles the sewage volume of the nation. Even if costs prove to be higher, manure should be returned to the land to help build humus.

Sterile, concentrated sewage (sludge) can also be used to improve soil. Sludge from Chicago is now being employed to restore stripmined land in southern Illinois. Crops are being grown very successfully on the reclaimed land. Recycled sewage has long been used as fertilizer in England, Australia, and other countries with excellent results. The prejudices of American farmers are the major obstacle to the development of similar practices in the United States.

## Pollutants and the Atmosphere

Because of its biological origin and its maintenance by biological systems, the atmosphere is an indicator of the health of all ecosystems—in fact, of the entire ecosphere. The climate in a given area is partly a function of the organisms in that area, primarily the plants. The pattern of airflow near the ground is affected by the presence or absence of forests. The amount of water vapor in the air, the rates at which the ground heats up during the day, and thus the occurrence of updrafts, vary according to the vegetation that is present.

Many air pollutants, including hydrofluoric acid, sulfur dioxide, ozone, and ethylene, injure or kill plants, and these changes in plant life lead to drastic changes in the animal populations dependent upon the plants. Other dangerous air pollutants that can also upset ecological systems are the nitrogen oxides. It is thought that the eutrophication of Lake Mendota in Wisconsin is largely attributable to phosphates, but part of the problem can be traced to the automobiles of nearby Madison; rains deposit heavy amounts of nitrogen from auto exhausts, and the nitrogen ends up in the lake. In New Jersey the rains annually bring to earth an estimated 25 pounds per acre of nitrogen from industrial and automobile sources. Where this lands on soil it amounts to very modest fertilization and is a benefit to the vegetation—a rare example of a positive effect from pollution.

Ecologists are very concerned about changes in the atmosphere that may occur, or may be occurring, as a result of man's interference with the Earth's complex biogeochemical cycles. The possible effects of general atmospheric pollution on the climate will be discussed below. But man's influence on biogeochemical cycles could pose other lethal threats. Picture, for instance, what would happen if one of the biocides that we are adding to our environment should show a special lethality for microorganisms in the soil that live by degrading ammonia to nitrites. The death of these microorganisms could be followed not only by a serious decline in soil fertility, but by a buildup of poisonous ammonia in the atmosphere.

On the average, the amount of oxygen produced by photosynthesis is balanced to within one part in 10,000 by the amount consumed when the plant matter is later metabolized in the food chain or by decomposers. The accumulation of oxygen in the atmosphere took place over hundreds of millions of years, and resulted from the relatively exceptional circumstances in which carbon fixed in photosynthesis was sequestered without being oxidized. This is the origin of graphite in older geological deposits and fossil fuels in younger ones. Because the production and consumption of oxygen in photosynthesis and decay is so nearly in balance on a year-to-year basis, and because of the vast reservoir of atmospheric oxygen that has been built up over geological time, there is no danger that man's destruction of forests and other plant communities will cause an oxygen shortage. In the short term, plants are most needed as the basis of everything we eat, rather than as sources of oxygen.

The most substantial drain on atmospheric oxygen comes from the combustion of the fossil fuels. However, given the present estimates of how much of the carbon sequestered in this form is exploitable, even this effect is negligible. The 1970 M.I.T. Study of Critical Environmental Problems concluded that the combustion of all known exploitable reserves of fossil fuels would reduce the atmospheric concentration of oxygen by only fifteen-hundredths of 1 percent. Clearly, the central issue in the quality of the atmosphere is not changes in the concentrations of the two main constituents, nitrogen and oxygen. Rather, the dangers lie in the addition of poisonous or otherwise significant trace contaminants. The carbon dioxide resulting from combustion of all the fossil fuels, for example, could have a measurable effect on world climate.

## Thermal Pollution and Local Climates

Thermal pollution, as the term is most often applied today, refers to waste heat from the generation of electrical power. The adverse consequences of discharging such heat to rivers, lakes, and estuaries is indeed a matter for serious concern, but it is only one aspect of a more fundamental problem. Specifically, *all* human activities—from metabolism to driving (and stopping) an automobile—result in the dissipation of energy as heat. In the case of a power plant, the heat delivered to the environment ultimately includes not only the waste heat at the site, but all the useful output as well: the electricity itself is transformed to heat in wires, filaments, the bearings in electric motors, and so forth. That all the energy we use—electrical and otherwise— is eventually degraded to heat is a consequence of the Second Law of Thermodynamics (see Box 4-1); no technological gimmickery or scientific breakthrough can be expected to relieve this constraint. Thus the thermal load imposed upon the surroundings where energy is consumed can be moderated only by manipulating the number of consumers or the per capita consumption. Of course, the thermal load at the place where power is generated can be reduced somewhat by devising more efficient power plants.

The consequences of man's introduction of heat into his environment can usefully be classified as local, regional, and global. Local effects (cities, the vicinities of power plants) are already prevalent, although not always well understood. Regional effects (river basins, coastlines) could become important before the turn of the century; their exact form is speculative. Global thermal effects could become significant within 70–100 years if current rates of increase persist. They will be considered in the next section, together with the possibly more imminent climatological consequences of man's input into the atmosphere of $CO_2$, particulate matter, and aircraft contrails.

The climate of cities differs appreciably from that of the surrounding countryside in several respects, due in part to the dissipation of heat from the human activities concentrated there. The annual mean temperature in cities in the U.S. is .9 to 1.4° F higher than that in rural surroundings, cloudiness and precipitation are 5 to 10 percent greater, and fog is 30 to

100 percent more prevalent. In the Los Angeles Basin, the rate of energy dissipation by man is equal to 5.5 percent of the solar energy absorbed over the same area. However, it is difficult to sort the climatic consequences of this perturbation from other man-induced effects which accompany it, most specifically the haze of gaseous and particulate pollutants for which Los Angeles is noted.

Better understood and more unequivocally dangerous thermal effects are those at the installations where electrical power is generated. All such plants in commercial operation today, whether powered by fossil fuels or nuclear fission, employ a steam cycle which at the condenser stage transfers heat to a coolant. The numbers involved dictate the use of water (as opposed to air) as the primary coolant. One to two cubic feet per second are required for every megawatt of installed capacity, and the water is warmed by from 12 to 25° F in carrying out its role. The 2,000 cubic feet per second needed for one of today's larger plants amounts to the entire flow of a moderate sized stream.

The effects of an increase in water temperature on aquatic life are several. The dissolved oxygen content of the water is reduced while the metabolic rate of its animal inhabitants increases. Thus, when the animals need more oxygen, they have less available. Some die forthwith, others become more susceptible to chemical toxins or disease. Bacterial decomposition is accelerated, further diminishing dissolved oxygen content. The ultimate consequences of artificial warming are a reduction in species diversity (with the large species of greatest interest to man usually being the first to go) and a reduction in the ability of the water to absorb organic waste.

Nuclear fission power plants present these problems to a greater degree than do their fossil-fueled counterparts, because, at the present stage of technology, the former are thermally less efficient; that is, they produce more heat per unit of electricity. Modern coal-fired plants operate near 40 percent efficiency, fission plants at about 30 percent. This 10 percent difference in overall efficiency translates to more than 50 percent in the amount of heat discharged at the powerplant. Moreover, about 25 percent of the fossil-fueled plant's discharged heat goes up the stack, further reducing the burden on aquatic systems.

Means exist for transferring *all* of the waste heat to the atmosphere at either variety of plant, but power companies find them expensive. Cooling ponds require the acquisition of 2 acres of land per megawatt of installed capacity, the price varying with location. Evaporative cooling towers increase construction costs some 4 percent and operating costs 10 percent. Closed-cycle cooling towers increase capital costs by perhaps 12 percent and operating costs by an amount not yet established.

In considering regional effects, the distinction between discharging waste heat to bodies of water or into the atmosphere with cooling towers or ponds becomes less important. The principal concern here is that man's energy input will become a significant climatic perturbation over large areas, and this can occur for either pathway taken by the heat. It should also be emphasized that such measures as heating homes and apartments with the warm effluent of power plants or using it for irrigation in cold climates do not completely solve even local thermal pollution problems. The heat is ultimately transported to the atmosphere, where it contributes to the regional heat balance and, in the case of the spaceheating application, to the urban thermal effects mentioned above. However, it helps with the larger problem to the extent that it substitutes for other heating, reducing overall fuel consumption and hence environmental heat load. For these reasons, using waste heat from power plants for residential heating is worth doing where feasible. Finally, as already suggested, all of man's *useful* energy consumption must be added to the waste heat from power plants in the reckoning of regional perturbations.

In posing the thermal pollution question for systems larger than a single stretch of river or coastline, some observers have reassured themselves by comparing man's contribution with solar energy input. Such analyses overlook the fact that climate is the result of numerous powerful forces operating in a rather finely tuned balance; phrased another way, the climate we perceive often represents a small difference of large numbers. Thus the important determinants of regional climate include the variation of solar heating with latitude, the winds and ocean currents driven by these differences, the variation in the heat balance on land and adjacent bodies of water, the role of river systems, lakes, bays, and oceans as thermal buffers, the updrafts over mountain ranges, and so forth. While many of the complexities of the meterorological system are still not understood, a few numbers indicate that man's energy input will soon be a force to be reckoned with on these sorts of scales.

For example, if the trends of the past 20 years persist for another 10 to 15, one-fourth of the annual freshwater runoff of the U.S. could be employed in the cooling of electric power stations (the problem will not be quite this bad, since some plants will be sited on the seacoast). But since much of the runoff occurs in short flood seasons, the relevant number for 1980 is actually one half the *normal* flow. Projecting the same trends for 30 years, to about the year 2000, shows that the equivalent cooling demand will correspond to raising the *entire* annual runoff of the U.S. by 20° F (consumption of electric power in the U.S. is doubling roughly every 10 years). In view of the role of river systems in the determination of regional climates and the economic and aesthetic importance of their aquatic life, these numbers are not comforting.

Finally, heavily populated regions such as the Boston-to-Washington megalopolis seem likely to be in climatological difficulty by the turn of the century, even according to the conservative criterion that compares man's energy input to the sun's. In a review of man-made climatic changes, meterologist Helmut E. Landsberg cites projections that, by the year 2000, "Bos-Wash" will contain 56 million people on 30,000 square kilometers, dissipating energy at a rate equal to 50 percent of solar power at the surface in winter, and 15 percent in summer.

## Global Climate and Human Influences

Global climate cannot be thoroughly understood without a study of atmospheric physics and circulation patterns far too complicated to be presented here (several good texts are listed in the bibliography). Nevertheless, some of the most important phenomena and their vulnerability to interference by man can be illustrated in terms of a simplified energy balance for the Earth-atmosphere system. Most of the sun's energy reaches the top of the Earth's atmosphere in the form of radiation of relatively short wavelengths—namely, visible and near-ultraviolet light. About 35 percent of this incident radiation is returned directly to space, either by reflection from clouds, dust particles in the atmosphere, and the surface of the Earth, or by scattering from the air itself. The total reflectivity of the planet due to all these contributors is called the *albedo*. Clouds reflect an average of 50 to 60 percent of the light that actually strikes them, and the surface of the Earth reflects 5 to 10 percent. The local surface value depends strongly on the angle of the sun and on the terrain: deserts reflect more than farmland and forests, and ice and snow may reflect as much as 90 percent.

Of the incident solar energy not directly reflected, about 30 percent is absorbed by the atmosphere and warms it; 35 percent evaporates water at the surface and is released to the atmosphere when the water vapor later condenses to become rain; and 35 percent is absorbed by and warms the ground. On an annual average over the whole Earth, of course, as much energy must leave as enters. If this were not true, the planet would be steadily warming up. The energy leaves as long-wavelength infrared radiation emanating from the surface and from the atmosphere. The atmosphere's role here is very important in that water vapor, water droplets, and carbon dioxide absorb infrared radiation outbound from the Earth's surface and reradiate about half of it back downward. If this "trapping" of heat did not occur the surface of the Earth would have an average temperature around $-10°$ F instead of about $+60°$ F. This phenomenon of heating, which is due to the differential transparency of the atmosphere to long and short wavelengths, is called the *greenhouse effect*. Glass in a greenhouse lets light in, but absorbs the infrared reradiated by the warmed plants and soil of the greenhouse. The glass reradiates some of the infrared back into the greenhouse, which is one reason that greenhouses normally have higher daytime temperatures than their surroundings (that the glass shelters the interior from the wind is also a factor). Similarly, cloudy nights tend to be warmer than cloudless nights, other things being equal. At night the Earth's surface radiates heat accumulated during the day, and clouds absorb part of the heat and reradiate it toward the surface, thus adding to the greenhouse effect. Clouds thus play an important dual role in the heat balance, contributing to the albedo during the day and to the greenhouse effect night and day.

That is a simplified outline of the major factors affecting the average temperature of the Earth's surface. Energy from the sun is partly reflected and partly absorbed by the surface. In the process of absorption the surface is warmed and reradiates infrared radiation, part of which is trapped by the greenhouse effect. A more mathematical formulation of the simple model and a demonstration of its use in making rough estimates of possible changes in the average temperature are given in Box 7-4. These calculations show that, if the simple assumptions were correct and if present rates of increase in energy use persisted for about a century, the mean global surface temperature would increase by more than a degree Fahrenheit. Somewhat more refined calculations, such as those by meteorologist W. D. Sellers, give surprisingly similar results.

As has already been observed, of course, the average temperature is not the whole story of climate. Many other factors determine how the energy received from the sun actually drives the global weather system. These are

---

BOX 7-4    GLOBAL ENERGY BALANCE AND MAN'S CONTRIBUTION

The most simple-minded calculation represents the Earth as a "blackbody" radiating at the mean surface temperature. One has for the energy balance at the Earth's surface:

$$\underbrace{S\,C + M}_{\text{input}} = \underbrace{S\,C\,A + 4\,C\epsilon\sigma T^4}_{\text{output}}, \quad (1)$$

where S is the solar constant, or incident solar flux arriving perpendicular to the cross sectional area of the Earth, C. M denotes miscellaneous inputs of energy to the Earth's surface—tidal (gravitational) energy from the moon and sun, energy released in chemical and nuclear reactions in the Earth's crust, thermal energy from the Earth's core, and energy released by the activities of man. A is the albedo, or fraction of the incident solar energy directly reflected by the Earth (including atmosphere and clouds). Thus, the first term on the output side of Eq. (1) is just A times the solar input. The last term, corresponding to energy absorbed and reradiated to space in the infrared, is multiplied by the entire surface area of the Earth (4C). The usual blackbody radiation law has been multiplied by the "effective emissivity," $\epsilon$, to correct for the fact that the Earth is not really a blackbody at the surface temperature. In reality, the effective "radiator" is in the upper atmosphere, and the

corresponding temperature is $-24°$ C rather than the $15°$ C mean figure at the surface. For crude calculations over a small temperature range, the complexity of the actual global meterological system is often suppressed in the use of the "fudge factor," $\epsilon$, with the time- and space-averaged surface temperature.

The accepted values of these parameters are as follows: S C $= 1.72 \times 10^{17}$ watts, M $= 2.7 \times 10^{13}$ watts (of which $M_m = 5 \times 10^{12}$ watts is man's contribution at the present time), and A $= 37\%$, so that $\epsilon = .55$ then gives T $= 15°$ C. Most observers compare $M_m$ with the radiative term, $4\,C\,\epsilon\sigma T^4$, finding man's contribution to be smaller by a factor of 21,700. Thus, man's contribution will reach 1 percent of the radiative term—a level at which serious effects are plausible—when it is 217 times larger than today's. This amounts to fewer than 8 doublings. Working out the numbers exactly shows that, at the present worldwide rate of increase of energy production (4 to 5 percent per year), we would reach the 1 percent level in 108 to 135 years. The associated mean temperature increase is readily shown to be $1.3°$ F, which doubles with each succeeding doubling of energy consumption.

not entirely understood, but it is known that differential heating is very important, especially the degree of contrast between the equator and the poles. This means that the probable continued input of most of man's energy dissipation in the temperate latitudes could have effects much greater than if the dissipation were evenly distributed. It also means that raising the overall temperature of the planet a degree or two would not necessarily mean a warmer climate for all the world's population. The main effect might be to speed up circulation patterns and to bring arctic cold farther south and antarctic cold farther north.

Man has the potential of altering global climate significantly even before his thermal impact becomes important, however. For instance, when fossil fuels are burned, carbon dioxide ($CO_2$) is added to the atmosphere, and $CO_2$ contributes to the greenhouse effect described above. Since 1880 the $CO_2$ content of the atmosphere has increased about 12 percent, and until the 1940s there was a concomitant rise in temperature. All of this increase in $CO_2$ may not be accounted for by burning of fossil fuels, since some increase in the amount of radioactive carbon (carbon-14) in the atmosphere has been reported. Much more carbon-14 is present in living and recently dead plant materials than in fossil fuels. Therefore the release of $CO_2$ by burning of fossil fuels would not significantly increase the atmospheric load of carbon-14. Part of the increase in $CO_2$ undoubtedly has come from agricultural burning, and part from the slow oxidation of peat bogs which occurred as the climate warmed. The whole $CO_2$ picture is made immensely complex by interactions between the atmospheric pool of $CO_2$ and plant life (which uses $CO_2$ in photosynthesis) and the oceans (which absorb $CO_2$ at different rates in different areas). Unquestionably, man is influencing the climate when his activities add $CO_2$ to the atmosphere, but the degree and significance of that influence are uncertain.

Since the 1940s there appears to have been a slight decline in the average temperature of the Earth, in spite of a continued increase in the $CO_2$ content of the atmosphere. The consensus among meteorologists seems to be that this is a result of increases in the albedo caused by volcanic ash, dust, other particulate pollution, and also increased cloud cover produced by the contrails of high-flying jet aircraft. This increase in reflectivity may have more than counterbalanced the increased greenhouse effect from the $CO_2$. These effects are at present difficult to pin down unequivocally. The "average temperature of the Earth" is itself an elusive quantity, because of the limited number and distribution of measurement stations, and because large year-to-year fluctuations that vary from one region to another tend to mask trends. One should scarcely take comfort from our ignorance in these matters, although some people do—apparently on the grounds that what we don't know won't hurt us.

One major source of atmospheric dust is agriculture; thus food-growing activities could, in principle, change the weather, upon which the success or failure of crops ultimately depends. Automobiles, aircraft, power plants, trash burning, deforestation (leading to wind-erosion of soil) and many other devices and activities of mankind add to the turbidity of the atmosphere. A veil of pollution now covers the entire planet.

Many experts believe that at this time volcanic activity still dominates man's contribution of particulate matter in influencing climate. A look into history can give us some idea of what might be in store for us if we continue increasing particulate pollution, or if there should be an upsurge in volcanic activity. In 1815, the eruption of Mount Tambora on the island of Sumbawa in Indonesia put an estimated 150 cubic kilometers of ash into the atmosphere. The climatic effects were staggering. In 1816 there was "no summer" in the northern United States, and the English summer was one of record cold. The mean July temperature in England was 13.4° C (56° F), in contrast with a 250-year average of 15.7° C (61° F). In fact, the three coldest decades in England's summary weather statistics were 1781–1790, 1811–1820, and 1881–1890, the decades of the eruptions of Mount Asama in Japan and Mount Skaptar in Iceland (both 1783), Mount Tambora (1815), and Krakatoa (1883). It is sobering to consider what a Tambora-scale eruption today would do to the world food supply.

Increases in the planetary albedo resulting from man's activities are not limited to those caused by particulate pollution. Contrails, the long thin clouds produced by the passage of high flying aircraft, also add to the albedo. Contrails often dissipate rather rapidly, but sometimes they apparently trigger the formation of high cirrus clouds. Meteorologists R. A. Bryson and W. M. Wendland have estimated that contrails are responsible for a 5–10 percent increase in cirrus clouds over North America, the Atlantic Ocean, and Europe. Contrails from SSTs could be an especially important factor, since they would be formed above the level of the atmosphere where rapid mixing occurs and could be extremely persistent. Bryson and Wendland indicate that under certain conditions SSTs might generate almost *total* cover in their regions of operation. On the other hand, meteorologist Louis J. Battan thinks that the formation of persistent SST contrails would be unlikely because of the low humidity of the stratosphere.

Unfortunately, it is impossible to predict exactly what will happen to the overall temperature of the Earth over the next few decades, or what the local effects of changes will be. We are especially ignorant of trigger or threshold effects in climatic systems. An increase in a mean summer temperature from 16° C to 18° C might produce little effect, while a further .5° C rise to 18.5° C might bring on a catastrophe. Moreover, it is not even known whether the amount of radiation produced by the sun is a constant—and that is essential information if changes in the heat budget of the planet are ever to be predicted. As a result, although we can be certain that man is affecting the climate (and probably accelerating change), we cannot yet isolate man's contribution to changes we observe.

It is worthwhile to consider some of the climatic changes that *might* occur. If the arctic region should become warmer, the floating ice pack of the Arctic Ocean would disappear. This could result in northward shifts in the positions of storm tracks and thus severely reduce rainfall on the plains of North

America, Europe, and Asia. These areas would rapidly be converted into deserts. Simultaneously, the more northerly storm paths would bring on another age of glaciation; ice sheets would form on the northern parts of the continents. It is unlikely that the Arctic Ocean would freeze again if its mantle of ice were removed, since incoming solar radiation would no longer be reflected by the ice but would be absorbed by the water. Thus the change would not be quickly reversed.

On the other hand, should the south polar region get colder, the Antarctic ice cap could be destabilized by an increase in its thickness. As the weight of ice grew, the bottom layer would liquefy, and much of the mass of the cap might slump into the Antarctic Ocean. The magnitude of such a disaster, thought possible by geologists J. T. Wilson of Victoria University, New Zealand, and J. T. Hollin of Princeton University, is difficult to imagine. It might produce a global tidal wave that could wipe out a substantial portion of mankind, and the sea level could rise 60–100 feet worldwide. Ice would cover an area of the oceans perhaps as large as Asia. There is enough ice stored in the Antarctic and Greenland ice caps together to cover the entire globe with a layer of ice almost 50 yards thick! (In a disaster such as the one just described, only part of the Antarctic ice mass would move into the water.) Polar ice is now a major reflector of solar radiation. If part of the Antarctic ice cap slumped into the sea and spread out, the area of reflecting ice would be enormously increased. The temperature balance of the planet would be drastically altered, producing an estimated average drop of 10° F, and a glacial age would begin that would last until melting and wave action broke up the ice and an interglacial period began. Evidence has been put forward that the last two ice ages began with catastrophic inundations, and that the current situation closely approximates that immediately preceding the last flooding.

Jet aircraft may change the climate in ways other than those already mentioned. For instance, astrophysicist Walter Orr Roberts of the National Center for Atmospheric Research has pointed out that naturally formed cirrus clouds may deflect jet streams, dramatically altering distant weather, and that it is possible that contrail-triggered cirrus clouds may also alter the course of jet streams. A change in the course of a jet stream is suspected to have been partially responsible for starting the formation of the Sahara desert.

Climate, of course, is an ever-changing thing. The past million years or so have shown a pattern of glacial advances and retreats, changes in sea level, changes in rainfall pattern, and so forth, all having tremendous impact on the men alive at the time. Many areas of our planet show the traces of mankind flooded out, frozen out, or forced to migrate because of drought. All of the speculated climatic changes might be viewed merely as a continuation of age-old processes of change and therefore held to involve risks that have always been present in one form or another. But, unhappily, there is a difference. At just the time that man has populated the planet to the point of stretching his food resources to the maximum, he is almost certainly accelerating climatic changes. When climate changes, so must agriculture, and, as has been observed, man is conservative in his agricultural behavior. Consequently, any *rapid* change of climate in whatever direction is bound to decrease food supply. Should rapidly accelerating air pollution, a new volcanic incident, or melting of the North Polar ice pack destroy the Northern Hemisphere's granaries, enormous famines would be inevitable.

## Ecological Accounting

It should now be apparent why ecologists are unimpressed by the claims that only blessings (and profits) have been brought by the use of synthetic pesticides and fertilizers, including the saving of lives through the use of DDT in malaria control. Ecologists and other environmental scientists wince when industrialists talk about the pollution-carrying capacity of inland waters as "a great natural resource," or when government officials caution against making water-pollution standards too high for fear of "discouraging industry." These scientists are not convinced that the costs of heat pollution are negligible or more than compensated by the benefits of power production. They do not think that the accounting has been done properly.

The true costs of our environmental destruction have never been subjected to proper accounting. The credits are localized and easily demonstrated by the beneficiaries, but the debits are widely dispersed and are borne by the entire population through the disintegration of physical and mental health; and, even more importantly, by the potentially lethal destruction of ecological systems. Despite social, economic, and political barriers to proper ecological accounting, it is urgent and imperative for human society to get the books in order.

### UNRECOGNIZED COSTS OF OVERPOPULATION

An important area in which environmental accounting has been faulty is in not anticipating the intensification of disasters by overpopulation. As population density grows, a larger proportion of people tend to live in hazardous locations. Biologists have long recognized that the size of a population relative to the area supporting it almost always influences the death rate when disaster strikes. As ecologists H. G. Andrewartha and L. C. Birch state in their classic book, *The Distribution and Abundance of Animals* (1954): "It is difficult to imagine an area so uniform that all the places where animals may live provide equal protection from the elements, and it is certain that the proportion of animals living in more favorable places would vary with the density of the population. A smaller number is likely to be better protected than a larger number in the same area." Mankind is no exception.

For instance, since the famous 1906 earthquake, a growing proportion of the population of the San Francisco Bay area has been housed on landfill. Geologist R. H. Jahns, discussing the relative impact of earthquakes on buildings constructed on fill, states, "The oft-used analogy of a block of jello on a vibrating platter is grossly simplified but nonetheless reasonable, and assuredly a structure that in effect is built upon the jello must be designed to accommodate greater dynamic stresses if it it is to survive the shaking as effectively as a comparable structure built upon a platter." When the next big earthquake occurs, a great many people will almost certainly die in the overpopulated San Francisco Bay area, simply because they are living in geologically marginal locations.

In November of 1970, a huge tidal wave driven by a cyclone swept over the Ganges Delta of East Pakistan. There a large, mostly destitute population lived exposed on flat lowland, in spite of the ever-present danger of climatic disaster for which the region is famous. They live in constant jeopardy because in grossly overpopulated East Pakistan the choice of places for them to live is greatly restricted. In November, 1970, 300,000 people died who need not have died if their nation had not been overpopulated. This cataclysm has been described as the greatest documented national disaster in history. In a poor, overcrowded nation evacuation was impossible. In a region already nutritionally marginal, people began to starve to death immediately after the disaster.

## Thermonuclear Warfare

A final kind of assault on ecosystems must be mentioned. Much has been written, especially by military theoretician Herman Kahn, on the effects of thermonuclear warfare, the possibilities of limited thermonuclear warfare, and so on. Since modern societies seem bent on continuing to prepare for such conflicts, we have little sympathy for those of Kahn's critics who feel that it is immoral to try to analyze the possible results. It would be pleasant (but probably incorrect) to assume that if everyone were aware of the terrible magnitude of the devastation that could result from a nuclear war, the world's stockpiles of fission and fusion weapons would soon be dismantled. This does not mean that Kahn's analysis is sound—quite the contrary. One major flaw in his evaluation of the results of thermonuclear war is one that is common to the analyses of many physical scientists. He grossly underrates the possible environmental consequences of these projected wars. In addition to the instantaneous slaughter of humans and demolition of property, the effects of any reasonably large thermonuclear exchange would inevitably constitute an unbelievable ecological and genetic disaster—especially for a world already on the edge of nutritional and environmental catastrophe.

Consider the effects that even a rather limited nuclear exchange among the United States, Russia, China, and various European powers would have on the world food supply. Suddenly, all international trade would come to a halt, and the developed world would be in no position to supply either food or any technological aid to the underdeveloped. No more high-yield seed, no more fertilizers, no more grain shipments, no more tractors, no more pumps and well-drilling equipment, trucks, or other manufactured products or machines would be delivered. Similarly, the UDCs would not be able to send DCs minerals, petroleum, and their food products. The world could be pitched into chaos and massive famine almost immediately, even if most countries were themselves untouched by the nuclear explosions.

But of course no country would be left unscathed. All over the world radiation levels would rise and would prevent cultivation of crops in many areas. Blast effects and huge fires burning in the Northern Hemisphere would send large amounts of debris into the atmosphere, probably dwarfing the volcanic and pollution effects previously discussed. The entire climate of the Earth would soon be altered. In many areas, where the supply of combustible materials was sufficient, huge fire-storms would be generated, some of them covering hundreds of square miles in heavily forested or metropolitan areas. We know something about such storms from experiences during the Second World War. On the night of July 27, 1943, Lancaster and Halifax heavy bombers of the Royal Air Force dropped 2,417 tons of incendiary and high-explosive bombs on the city of Hamburg. Thousands of individual fires coalesced into a fire-storm about 6 square miles in area. Flames reached 15,000 feet into the atmosphere, and smoke and gases rose to 40,000 feet. Winds, created by huge updrafts and blowing in toward the center of the fire, reached a velocity of more than 150 miles per hour. The temperature in the fire exceeded 1,450 degrees Fahrenheit, high enough to melt aluminum and lead. Air in underground shelters was heated to the point where, when they were opened and oxygen was admitted, flammable materials and even corpses burst into flame. These shelters had to be permitted to cool *10 days to two weeks* before rescuers could enter.

Anyone interested in further details of what a *small* fire-storm is like is referred to Martin Caiden's excellent book, *The Night Hamburg Died*. From this account one can imagine the ecological results of the generation of numerous fire-storms and the burning off of a large portion of the Northern Hemisphere. In many areas the removal of all vegetation would not be the only effect; the soil might be partly or completely sterilized as well. There would be no plant communities nearby to effect rapid repopulation, and rains would wash away the topsoil. Picture defoliated California hills during the winter rains, and then imagine the vast loads of silt and radioactive debris being washed from northern continents into offshore waters, the site of most of the ocean's productivity. Consider the fate of aquatic life, which is especially sensitive to the turbidity of the water, and think of the many offshore oil wells that would be destroyed by blast in the vicinity of large cities and left to pour their loads of crude oil into the ocean with no way of shutting them off. Think of the runoff of solvents, fuels, and other chemicals from ruptured storage tanks and pipelines.

The survivors of any large-scale thermonuclear war would face a severely devastated environment. If a full-scale war were waged, most of the survivors would be in the Southern Hemisphere. They would be culturally depauperate, since much of mankind's technology would be irretrievably lost. If the technological structure of society is destroyed, man will find it almost impossible to rebuild it because of resource depletion. Most high-grade ores and rich and accessible fossil fuel deposits have long since been used up. Technology itself is necessary for access to what remains. Only if enough scrap metals and stored fuel remained available would there be a hope of reconstruction, and it would have to begin promptly before these rusted, drained away, or were lost in other ways. From what we know of past large disasters, it seems unlikely that survivors, without a source of outside assistance, would psychologically be able to start rapid reconstruction.

If there were extensive use of weapons in the Northern Hemisphere, or if chemical or biological weapons were used simultaneously, the survivors would probably consist of scattered, isolated groups. Such groups would face genetic problems, since each would contain only a small part of mankind's genetic variability and would be subject to a further loss of variability through inbreeding. Studies of certain Japanese and Italian populations have shown that inbreeding profoundly affects infant mortality. In addition it appears that prenatal damage increases linearly with the degree of inbreeding. In such a situation it is problematical whether culturally and genetically deprived groups of survivors could persist in the face of much harsher environmental conditions than they had faced previously. In short, it would not be necessary to kill every individual with blast, fire, and radiation in order to force *Homo sapiens* into extinction.

# Bibliography

Acree, Fred, Jr., Morton Beroza, and Malcolm C. Borman, 1963. Codistillation of DDT with water. *Agricultural and Food Chemistry,* vol. 11, pp. 278–280. Important paper about the mobility of DDT.

American Chemical Society, 1969. *Cleaning Our Environment: The Chemical Basis for Action.* Washington, D.C. Includes good discussion and an extensive bibliography on eutrophication.

Andrewartha, H. G., and L. C. Birch, 1954. *The Distribution and Abundance of Animals.* University of Chicago Press, Chicago. Discussion of animal ecology; indispensable for the serious student.

Anonymous, 1969. Mission to Vietnam (2 parts). *Scientific Research,* June 9–June 23. What two ecologists found in Vietnam following herbicide treatments.

Anonymous, 1970. The Williamstown study of critical environmental problems. *Bulletin of Atomic Scientists,* Oct. pp. 24–30. A summary of the MIT study. (See below, Study on Critical Environmental Problems.)

Anonymous, 1971. Does killing weeds destroy the soil? *New Scientist,* 25 March, p. 663. On the effects of herbicides on soil bacteria.

Antommari, Phillip, Morton Corn, and Lawrence De Mair, 1965. Airborne particulates in Pittsburgh, association with p,p'-DDT. *Science,* vol. 150, pp. 1476–1477. Early paper showing presence of DDT in the atmosphere of a city.

Battan, Louis J., 1966. *The Unclean Sky: A Meteorologist Looks at Air Pollution.* Doubleday and Co., New York.

Battan, Louis J., *Harvesting the Clouds, Advances in Weather Modification.* Doubleday and Co., New York. See especially Chapter 12, "Changing climates," and Chapter 13, "Plants, animals, people, the law, and the weather."

Berger, Rainer, and W. F. Libby, 1969. Equilibration of atmospheric carbon dioxide with sea water: possible enzymatic control of the rate. *Science,* vol. 164, pp. 1395–1397. Illustrates the complexity of the role played by the ocean in regulating the $CO_2$ content of the atmosphere.

Bitman, Joel, Helene C. Cecil, Susan J. Harris, and George F. Frees, 1969. DDT induces a decrease in eggshell calcium. *Nature,* vol. 224, pp. 44–46. Experiments with Japanese quail.

Black, C. A., 1968. *Soil-Plant Relationships.* 2nd edition. John Wiley & Sons, Inc., New York. Technical and comprehensive.

Brown, W. L., Jr., 1961. Mass insect control programs; four case histories. *Psyche,* vol. 68, pp. 75–111. A distinguished entomologist and population biologist evaluates attempts to control the fire ant, gypsy moth, Mediterranean fruit fly, and screwworm.

Bryson, R. A., 1968. All other factors being constant . . . a reconciliation of several theories of climatic change. *Weatherwise* (April).

Bryson, R. A., and W. M. Wendland, 1968. Climatic effects of atmospheric pollution. Paper presented at the American Association for the Advancement of Science meeting, Dallas.

Butler, Philip A., and Paul T. Spruger, 1963. Pesticides—a new factor in coastal environments. *Trans. Twenty-Eighth North American Wildlife and Natural Resources Conference,* pp. 378–390. Summary with good bibliography of earlier papers.

Calder, Nigel (ed.), 1968. *Unless Peace Comes.* Viking (Compass), New York. Projects effects of future weapons systems.

Carson, Rachel, 1962. *Silent Spring.* Houghton-Mifflin, Boston. This classic, thought to be alarmist by many when it was published, now appears to have understated the pesticide problem.

Clark, John R., 1969. Thermal pollution and aquatic life. *Scientific American,* vol. 220, no. 3 (March). Scientific American Offprint No. 1135, W. H. Freeman and Company, San Francisco.

Cloud, P., and A. Gabor, 1970. The Oxygen Cycle. *Scientific American,* vol. 223, no. 3 (Sept.). Reprinted in *The Biosphere,* 1970, W. H. Freeman and Company, San Francisco. Authoritative discussion of the origin of atmospheric oxygen.

Cloudsley-Thompson, J. L., 1971. Recent expansion of the Sahara. *International Journal of Environmental Studies,* vol. 2, pp. 35–39. On the role of human activities in expanding the Sahara Desert.

Coan, Gene, 1971. Oil pollution. *Sierra Club Bulletin,* March, pp. 13–16. Discussion of the immediate and long-term effects of oil pollution on marine life by a marine biologist. Good bibliography.

Cole, LaMont C., 1966. Complexity of pest control in the environment. In *Scientific Aspects of Pest Control.* Pub. 1402, National Academy of Sciences, National Research Council, Washington, D.C.

Commoner, Barry, 1967. *Science and Survival.* Viking, New York. Technology and survival. See especially the material on the ecological effects of thermonuclear war.

Commoner, Barry, 1970. Soil and fresh water: damaged global fabric. *Environment,* vol. 12, no. 3 (April), pp. 4–11.

Cooper, D. F., and William C. Jolly, 1969. *Ecological Effects of Weather Modification.* University of Michigan, School of Natural Resources. This report, sponsored by the Department of the Interior, is an excellent, balanced summary of possible consequences of purposeful weather modification and contains much material related to the effects of gradual climatic change. Good bibliography.

Cornwell, John, 1971. Is the Mediterranean dying? *New York Times Magazine,* Feb. 21, pp. 24–25+. General article on pollution in the Mediterranean.

Cory, L., P. Fjeld, and W. Serat, 1970. Distribution patterns of DDT residues in the Sierra Nevada mountains. *Pesticides Monitoring Journal,* vol. 3, no. 4 (March), pp. 204–211. On nitrates, fertilizer, and polluted water.

Cottam, Clarence, 1965. The ecologist's role in problems of pesticide pollution. *BioScience,* vol. 15, no. 7, pp. 457–463 (July).

Council on Environmental Quality, 1970. *Ocean Dumping,* Report to the President, Oct. Analyzes present and anticipated trends in ocean dumping of wastes and recommends the formulation of a nation policy for regulation.

Council on Environmental Quality, 1971. *Environmental Quality: Second Annual Report* (Aug.), Washington, D.C. This report concentrates on the costs of environmental protection; what is spent now and what will be needed in the future.

Cox, James L., 1970. DDT residues in marine phytoplankton: increase from 1955 to 1969. *Science,* vol. 170, pp. 71–73 (2 Oct.).

De Bach, Paul (ed.), 1964. *Biological Control of Insect Pests & Weeds.* Reinhold Publishing Corp., New York. Covers one of the ecologically sensible components of integrated control.

Deevey, Edward S., Jr., 1958. Bogs. *Scientific American,* vol. 199, no. 4 (Oct.). Scientific American Offprint. No. 840, W. H. Freeman and Company, San Francisco. Describes bog contribution to $CO_2$ in atmosphere.

Doane, Robert R., 1957. *World Balance Sheet.* Harper and Bros., New York. Source of data on land classification.

Dorst, Jean, 1970. *Before Nature Dies*. Wm. Collin Sons, London. A very interesting popular treatment of many of the topics covered in this chapter.

Edwards, Clive A., 1969. Soil pollutants and soil animals. *Scientific American,* vol. 220, no. 4 (April). Scientific American Offprint No. 1138, W. H. Freeman and Company, San Francisco.

Egler, Frank E., 1964. Pesticides—in our ecosystem. *American Scientist,* vol. 52, pp. 110–136. An outspoken ecologist discusses the problems of getting ecologically sophisticated control of pests.

Ehrlich, P. R., J. P. Holdren, and R. W. Holm, 1971. *Man and the Ecosphere*. W. H. Freeman and Company, San Francisco. Contains a number of important articles from *Scientific American* relating to ecosystem deterioration.

Eisner, T., L. B. Hendry, D. B. Peakall, and J. Meinwald, 1971. 2, 5-Dichlorophenol (from ingested herbicide?) in defensive secretion of grasshopper. *Science,* vol. 172, pp. 277–278. Evidence that grasshoppers ingest herbicide and use it to defend themselves against other insects.

Elton, Charles S., 1958. *The Ecology of Invasions by Animals and Plants*. John Wiley & Sons, Inc., New York. A basic source, written by one of the world's most distinguished ecologists.

Epstein, Samuel S., 1970. NTA. *Environment,* vol. 12, no. 7 (Sept.), pp. 3–11. On NTA, a dangerous substitute proposed for phosphates in detergents.

Fiserova-Bergerova, V., J. L. Radomski, J. E. Davies, and J. H. Davies, 1967. Levels of chlorinated hydrocarbon pesticides in human tissues. *Ind. Med. Surg.,* vol. 36, no. 65.

Fisher, J., N. Simon, and J. Vincent, 1969. *Wildlife in Danger*. Viking Press, New York. A comprehensive summary of the state of endangered species of vertebrate animals and plants. Readable and well illustrated.

Flohn, Hermann, 1969. *Climate and Weather*. McGraw-Hill, New York. A fine summary.

Frink, C., 1967. Nutrient budget; rational analysis of eutrophication in a Connecticut lake. *Environmental Science Technology,* vol. 1, p. 425. Technical investigation of nitrogen and phosphorus concentrations in bottom sediments.

Frost, Justin, 1969. Earth, air, water. *Environment,* vol. 11, no. 9, pp. 14–33. Discusses the major role of the atmosphere in distributing chlorinated hydrocarbons.

Galston, Arthur W., 1971. Some implications of the widespread use of herbicides. *BioScience,* vol. 21, no. 17, pp. 891–892 (Sept. 1). See also Johnson reference below.

Gilmour, C. M., and O. N. Allen (eds.), 1965. *Microbiology and Soil Fertility*. Oregon State Univ. Press, Corvallis.

Glass, Bentley, 1962. The biology of nuclear war. *American Biology Teacher,* vol. XXIV, pp. 407–425 (Oct.). On the probable results of nuclear war.

Graham, Frank Jr., 1966. *Disaster by Default: Politics and Water Pollution*. M. Evans & Co., New York.

Graham, Frank Jr., 1970. *Since Silent Spring*. Fawcett-Crest, Greenwich, Conn. Details of pesticide controversies.

Hammond, Allen L., 1971. Phosphate replacements: problems with the washday miracle. *Science,* vol. 172, pp. 361–363 (23 April).

Harper, John L., 1956. Ecological aspects of weed control. *Outlook on Agriculture,* vol. 1, pp. 197–205. An early paper predicting the development of resistance to herbicides by weeds.

Harriss, R. C., D. B. White, and R. B. McFarlane, 1970. Mercury compounds reduce photosynthesis by plankton. *Science,* vol. 170, pp. 736–737 (13 Nov.).

Hass, Ernst, 1968. Common opponent sought . . . and found? *Bulletin of Atomic Scientists* (Nov.). Popular description of Wilson's ice-age theory, and description of possible technological preventions.

Heath, Robert G., James W. Sparn, and J. F. Kreitzer. Marked DDE impairment of mallard reproduction in controlled studies. *Nature,* vol. 224, pp. 47–48.

Hendry, Peter, 1970. Who's afraid of advanced technology? *Ceres,* July–Aug., pp. 45–48. On integrated pest control.

Hickey, Joseph J., and Donald W. Anderson, 1968. Chlorinated hydrocarbons and eggshell changes in raptorial and fish-eating birds. *Science,* vol. 162, pp. 271–273. Correlation of eggshell change with presence of chlorinated hydrocarbon residue.

Hills, Lawrence, 1969. Farming with free fertility for profit. *Journal of the Soil Association* (Oct.). How treated sewage can be successfully used as fertilizer.

Holden, A. V., 1964. The possible effects on fish of chemicals used in agriculture. *Journal of the Institute of Sewage Purification,* pp. 361–368. Analyzes effects of insecticides and herbicides.

Holdren, J. P., and P. R. Ehrlich (eds.), 1971. *Global Ecology, Readings toward a Rational Strategy for Man.* Harcourt, Bracè & Jovanovich, New York. Numerous papers in this collection elaborate on points discussed in this chapter. Holdren's "Global Thermal Pollution" contains a more detailed discussion of the points summarized here in Box 7-3.

Holdren, J. P., and P. Herrera, 1972. *Energy.* Sierra Club Books, New York. Contains good discussion of local, regional, and global thermal pollution.

Hollin, John T., 1965. Wilson's theory of ice ages. *Nature,* vol. 208. no. 5005 (Oct. 2). Describes partial check of Wilson's ice age theory.

Huffaker, Carl B., 1971. Biological control and a remodeled pest control technology. *Technology Review,* vol. 73, no. 8, June 1971, pp. 30–37. An excellent summary paper.

Huffaker, Carl B., 1971. *Biological Control.* Plenum Publishing Corp., New York. A comprehensive, up to date "bible" on ecologically sane pest control practices. Must be read by everyone interested in alternatives to today's disastrous pesticide practices.

Huffaker, Carl B., The ecology of pesticide interference with insect populations (upsets and resurgences in insect populations). A fine discussion of how pesticides upset the "balance of nature." (In press.)

Hunt, Eldridge G., 1966. Biological magnification of pesticides. *Symposium on Scientific Aspects of Pest Control,* Nat. Acad. Sci—Nat. Res. Council, pp. 252–261. Information on buildup of pesticides in food chains.

Inman, R. B., R. B. Ingersoll, and E. A. Levy, 1971. Soil: a natural sink for carbon monoxide. *Science,* vol. 172, pp. 1229–1231 (18 June). On the ability of soil microorganisms to remove CO from the atmosphere.

Institute of Ecology, 1971. *Report of the Workshop on Global Ecological Problems.* John Kedlak, Workshop Coordinator, University of Michigan School of Natural Resources, Ann Arbor, Michigan 48104. Good recent study of many important environmental problems.

Jahns, R. H., 1968. Geologic jeopardy. *Texas Quarterly,* vol. 11, no. 2, pp. 69–83. Deals with geological hazards whose impact may be intensified by overpopulation. (Reprinted in Holdren and Ehrlich, see above).

Johnson, Julius E., 1971. The public health implications of widespread use of the phenoxy herbicides and picloram. *BioScience,* vol. 21, no. 17, pp. 899–905 (Sept. 1). Considers that 2,4-D and 2,4,5-T present little or no public health hazard (see Galston reference above).

Johnston, Harold, 1971. Reduction of stratospheric ozone by nitrogen oxide catalysts from supersonic transport exhaust. *Science,* vol. 173, pp. 517–522 (6 Aug). Another potential threat of SSTs which has been ignored by technological optimists.

Kahn, H., and A. J. Weiner, 1967. *The Year 2000.* Macmillan, New York. An outstanding example of futurism which discounts problems of population, resources, and environment. The words ecology and environment do not appear in the index, which may explain in part why Kahn can view the possibility of thermonuclear war with relative equanimity.

Kassas, M., 1970. Desertification versus potential for recovery in circum-Saharan territories. In *Arid Lands in Transition,* American Association for the Advancement of Science, Washington, D.C. Short discussion of the role of man in enlarging the Sahara and an extensive bibliography of the scientific literature on the subject.

Kearney, P. C., R. G. Marsh, and A. R. Isensee, 1969. Persistence of pesticide residues in soils. *In* Miller and Berg (eds.), *Chemical Fallout,* pp. 54–67. This is the source of our estimates of persistence under normal agricultural conditions.

Kilgore, W. W., and R. L. Dountt, 1967. *Pest Control, Biological, Physical, and Selected Chemical Methods.* Academic Press, New York.

Kormondy, Edward J., 1969. *Concepts of Ecology.* Prentice-Hall, Englewood Cliffs, N.J.

Landsberg, Helmut E., 1970. Man-made climatic changes. *Science,* vol. 170, pp. 1265–1274. How human activities alter climate locally and the potential for global changes. Comprehensive bibliography.

Lichtenstein, E. P., K. R. Schultz, T. W. Fuhrmann, and T. T. Liang, 1969. Biological interaction between plasticizers and insecticides. *Journal of Economic Entomology,* vol. 62, pp. 761–765. Demonstrates toxicity of PCBs to insects and shows that these compounds may increase the toxicity of dieldrin and DDT.

Loftas, Tony, 1971. The unseen dangers of oil. *New Scientist,* 4 Feb., p. 228. Concise account of the effects of oil pollution on marine ecology.

MacDonald, G. J. F., 1968. How to wreck the environment. *In* N. Calder (ed.) *Unless Peace Comes.* Viking Press, New York, pp. 181–205. Describes purposeful weather modification for military purposes.

Marsh, George P., 1874. *The Earth as Modified by Human Action.* Charles Scribner's Sons, New York.

Marx, Wesley, 1967. *The Frail Ocean.* Coward-McCann, Inc., New York.

Matsumura, F., and G. M. Boush, 1967. Dieldrin: degradation by soil microorganisms. *Science,* vol. 156, pp. 959–961. Shows that a few microorganisms can break down dieldrin in the soil.

Matsumura, F., and G. M. Boush, 1968. Breakdown of dieldrin in soil by a microorganism. *Nature,* vol. 219, pp. 965–967. Identifies some of the products of dieldrin breakdown.

McCaull, Julian, 1969. The black tide. *Environment,* vol. 11, no. 9 (Nov.), pp. 2–16. Good general discussion of the effects of oil spills on marine and shore life and how they might be dealt with. Includes references.

Miller, Albert, 1966. *Meteorology.* Charles E. Merill, Columbus, Ohio. Lucid introductory text with especially good treatment of energy balance.

Miller, M. W., and G. G. Berg (eds.), 1969. *Chemical Fallout: Current Research on Persistent Pesticides.* Charles C Thomas, Springfield. An excellent volume containing a number of important papers.

Mitchell, H. H., 1961. *Ecological Problems and Postwar Recuperation: A Preliminary Survey from the Civil Defense Viewpoint.* U.S. Air Force Project and Research Memorandum. A pioneering document, somewhat over-optimistic and now out of date.

Mitchell, J. M., 1968. A preliminary evaluation of atmospheric pollution as a cause of the global temperature fluctuation of the past century. Paper presented at the American Association for the Advancement of Science meeting, Dallas.

Moll, K. D., J. H. Cline, and Paul D. Marr, 1960. *Postattack Farm Problems. Part 1: The Influence of Major Inputs on Farm Production.* Prepared for office of Civil Defense Mobilization under the auspices of Stanford Research Institute (SRI), Menlo Park, Calif. Limited circulation (200 copies). One of the few attempts to investigate systematically the consequences of a nuclear attack. Others by SRI include studies of the effects of a nuclear attack on railroad transport and the petroleum industry.

Moore, N. W., (ed.), 1966. Pesticides in the environment and their effects on wildlife. *Journal of Applied Ecology.* Supplement to vol. 3 (June). This supplement contains many other interesting papers on pesticide ecology.

Mulla, M. S., and Lewis W. Isaak, 1961. Field studies on the toxicity of insecticides of the mosquito fish, *Gambusia affinis. Journal of Economic Entomology,* vol. 54, pp. 1237–1242. Reports high toxicity to mosquito-eating fishes of pesticides used in mosquito abatement programs.

Nash, R. G., and E. H. Woolson, 1967. Persistence of chlorinated hydrocarbon insecticides in soils. *Science,* vol. 157, pp. 924–927. Gives long-term limits on persistence through studies in which pesticides were mixed uniformly into loam in experimental plots.

Neale, Joseph H., 1969. Washing water. *Science and Technology,* June, pp. 52–57. On treatment for water pollution.

Olson, T. A., and F. J. Burgess (eds.), 1967. *Pollution and Marine Ecology.* Interscience Publishers, New York.

Peakall, D. B., 1967. Pesticide-induced enzyme breakdown of steroids in birds. *Nature,* vol. 216, pp. 505–506. Indicates that DDT and dieldrin can change hormone metabolism and upset breeding.

Peakall, D. B., 1970. Pesticides and the reproduction of birds. *Scientific American,* April, pp. 73–74. Up-to-date account of the way chlorinated hydrocarbons affect breeding behavior and egg viability in birds.

Porter, Richard D., and Stanley N. Wiemeyer, 1969. Dieldrin and DDT: effects on sparrow hawk eggshells and reproduction. *Science,* vol. 165, pp. 199–200. Controlled feeding experiments.

Powell, N. A., C. S. Sayce, and D. F. Tufts, 1970. Hyperplasia in an estuarine bryozoan attributable to coal tar derivatives. *Journal of the Fisheries Research Board of Canada,* vol. 27, pp. 2095–2096. Study of abnormal growth in a small marine animal induced by oil pollution.

Ratcliffe, D. A., 1967. Decrease in eggshell weight in certain birds of prey. *Nature,* vol. 215, pp. 208–210. Demonstrates rapid synchronous decline of eggshell thickness at time chlorinated hydrocarbon pesticides introduced. This was key evidence in establishing role of these substances in decline of bird populations.

Ratcliffe, D. A., 1970. Changes attributable to pesticides in egg breakage frequency and eggshell thickness in some British birds. *Journal of Applied Ecology,* vol. 7, pp. 67–115. Expands and updates his 1967 paper, giving more information on the temporal and geographic correlations between eggshell strength and chlorinated hydrocarbon use. Extensive bibliography.

Revelle, R., and H. E. Suess, 1967. Carbon dioxide between atmosphere and ocean and the question of an increase at atmospheric $CO_2$ during the past decades. *Tellus,* vol. 9, no. 1, pp. 18–27 (Feb.).

Risebrough, R. W., R. J. Huggett, J. J. Griffin, and E. D. Goldberg, 1968. Pesticides: transatlantic movements in the northeast trades. *Science,* vol. 159, pp. 1233–1236. Important paper on aerial transport of chlorinated hydrocarbons.

Roe, Frank G., 1951. *The North American Buffalo.* Univ. of Toronto Press, Toronto.

Rosato, P., and D. E. Ferguson, 1968. The toxicity of Endrin-resistant mosquito fish to eleven species of vertebrates. *BioScience,* vol. 18, pp. 783–784.

Rudd, Robert L., 1964. *Pesticides and the Living Landscape.* Univ. of Wisconsin Press, Madison. The prime source on ecological effects of pesticides.

Rudd, Robert L., 1971. Pesticides. *In* W. W. Murdoch (ed.), *Environment: Resources, Pollution and Society.* Sinauer Associates, Stamford, Conn. A fine summary article.

Sanders, Herman O., 1970. Toxicities of some herbicides to six species of freshwater crustaceans. *Water Pollution Control Federation Journal,* vol. 42, part 1, Aug. pp. 1544–1550.

Sellers, W. D., 1969. A global climatic model based on the energy balance of the Earth-atmosphere system. *Journal of Applied Meteorology,* vol. 8, pp. 392–400.

Seshachar, B. R., 1971. Problems of environment in India. In *Proceedings of Joint Colloquium on International Environmental Science,* Report 63–562. U.S. Government Printing Office, Washington, D.C. Documents man's influence in expansion of Rajasthan (Thar) Desert.

Shapley, Deborah, 1971. Mirex and the fire ant. Decline in fortunes of "perfect" pesticide. *Science,* vol. 172, pp. 358–360 (23 April).

Shea, Kevin P., 1968. Cotton and chemicals. *Scientist and Citizen* (Nov.). Gives details of the Azodrin situation.

Shepard, P., and D. McKinley (eds.), 1969. *The Subversive Science*. Houghton Mifflin, Boston. Selected readings in ecology. Excellent.

Singer, S. F., 1970. Human energy production as a process in the biosphere. *Scientific American*, vol. 223, no. 3, pp. 174–190.

Singer, S. F. (ed.), 1970. *Global Effects of Environmental Pollution*. Springer-Verlag, New York, Inc., New York. A symposium on pollution, especially that affecting the atmosphere, the oceans, and soils.

Simon, N., and P. Géroudet, 1970. *Last Survivors: Natural History of 48 Animals in Danger of Extinction*. World Publishing Co., New York. A handsome volume on some vanishing passengers of Spaceship Earth. Highly recommended.

Sladen, W. T. L., C. M. Menzee, and W. L. Rechel, 1966. DDT residues in Adelie penguins and a Craberta seal from Antarctica: ecological implications. *Nature,* vol. 210, pp. 670–673.

Smith, Robt. L., 1966. *Ecology and Field Biology*. Harper & Row, New York. An excellent beginning text.

Stanford Biology Study Group, 1970. The destruction of Indochina. Reprinted in Holdren and Ehrlich (see above). On ecocide.

Stonier, Tom, 1963. *Nuclear Disaster*. Meridian, Cleveland. Describes ecological effects of thermonuclear war.

Study of Critical Environmental Problems (SCEP), 1970. *Man's Impact on the Global Environment*. MIT Press, Cambridge. An excellent assessment of some of the most important environmental problems.

Thomas, William L., Jr. (ed.), 1956. *Man's Role in Changing the Face of the Earth*. An international symposium edited with the collaboration of Carl O. Sauer, Marston Bates, and Lewis Mumford. Univ. of Chicago Press, Chicago.

Tinker, Jon, 1971. One flower in ten faces extinction. *New Scientist,* 13 May, pp. 408–413. More on the loss of stocks for potential food plants and other valuable plants.

Tinker, Jon, 1971. The PCB story: seagulls aren't funny any more. *New Scientist,* 1 April, pp. 16–18. On how PCBs affect sea birds and how one manufacturer is treating the matter responsibly.

Tinker, Jon, 1971. 1969 Seabird wreck: PCBs probably guilty. *New Scientist,* 8 April, p. 69. Report on PCBs and their lethal effect on seabirds under stress.

Ulfstrand, S., A. Södergren, and J. Raböl, 1971. Effect of PCB on nocturnal activity in caged robins, *Erithacus rubecula L. Nature,* vol. 231, pp. 467–468 (June 18).

Van den Bosch, Robert, 1969. The significance of DDT residues in estuarine fauna. *In* Miller and Berg (eds.), *Chemical Fallout*, pp. 205–220. Information on the ability of oysters to concentrate DDT.

Van den Bosch, Robert, 1971. Biological control of insects. *Annual Review of Ecology and Systematics* (in press).

Viets, Frank G., Jr., 1971. Water quality in relation to farm use of fertilizers. *BioScience,* vol. 21, no. 10, pp. 460–467 (May 15).

Wasserman, Larry Paul, 1969. Sweetwater pollution. *Science and Technology,* June, pp. 20–27. Ecological aspects of water pollution.

Watt, K. E. F., 1968. *Ecology and Resource Management*. McGraw-Hill, New York.

Weisberg, Barry (ed.), 1970. *Ecocide in Indochina*. Canfield Press, San Francisco.

Westing, Arthur H., 1971. Ecological effects of military defoliation on the forests of South Vietnam. *BioScience,* vol. 21, no. 17, pp. 893–898 (Sept. 1). A basic source.

Wexler, Harry, 1952. Volcanoes and world climate. *Scientific American,* vol. 186, no. 4 (April). Scientific American Offprint No. 843, W. F. Freeman and Company, San Francisco.

Whiteside, Thomas, 1970. *Defoliation*. Ballantine Books, New York. On the dangers of herbicides, especially as used in Indochina.

Whitten, Jamie L., 1966. *That We May Live*. D. Van Nostrand Co., Inc., Toronto. A clever piece of pro-pesticide propaganda by a U.S. Congressman. It attempts to give the impression that its conclusions are endorsed by scientists, although at least four of the most distinguished scientists interviewed in the course of its preparation disagree totally with its conclusions. Read this if you want to know your enemy. Whitten does not confine his activities to promoting pesticides. U.S. Representative Richard Bolling has written, "Study the unpardonable problem of malnutrition and even starvation in this country and you'll encounter Representative Jamie Whitten of Mississippi, Chairman of the Appropriations Subcommittee on Agriculture and lord of certain operations of the Agriculture Department." (*Playboy,* Nov. 1969, p. 255).

Wilson, A. T., 1964. Origin of ice ages: an ice shelf theory for Pleistocene glaciation. *Nature,* vol. 201, no. 4915 (Jan. 11). The basic source of the Antarctic ice-cap-slump theory of glacial periods.

Woodwell, George M., 1967. Toxic substances and ecological cycles. *Scientific American,* vol. 216, no. 3 (March). Scientific American Offprint No. 1066, W. H. Freeman and Company, San Francisco. Excellent summary. Reprinted in Ehrlich et al. (see above).

Woodwell, George M., 1970. Effects of pollution on the structure and physiology of ecosystems. *Science,* vol. 168, pp. 429–433.

Wurster, Charles F., Jr., 1968. DDT reduces photosynthesis by marine phytoplankton. *Science,* vol. 158, pp. 1474–1475. This may turn out to be one of the most important scientific papers of all time.

Wurster, C. F., and D. B. Wingate, 1968. DDT residues and declining reproduction in the Bermuda petrel. *Science,* vol. 159, pp. 979–981. Shows the effects of DDT on a bird of the open ocean. See also the exchange of letters between the authors of this paper and Lewis A. McLean of Velsicol, Inc., a company which manufactures pesticides (*Science,* vol. 161, p. 387).

Wurster, Charles F., Jr., 1971. Persistent insecticides and their regulation by the federal government. Testimony before the Senate Committee on Agriculture and Forestry, March 25. U.S. Government Printing Office, Washington, D.C.

Wurster, D. H., C. F. Wurster, and W. N. Strickland, 1965. Bird mortality following DDT spray for Dutch Elm disease. *Ecology,* vol. 46, pp. 488–489. Good bibliography of earlier related papers.

# CHAPTER 8

# Optimum Population and Human Biology

*"Maximum welfare, not maximum population, is our human objective."*

—Arnold Toynbee
"Man and Hunger," 1963

The pattern of human population growth and some of its consequences which have been described lead to the conclusion that the size of the population must be controlled. It is to be hoped that all people would agree that the only humane way to control the size of the human population is by limiting the number of births; that an increase in the number of deaths (or reduction in the life expectancy) should be avoided at all costs. But the idea of controlling the size of a population implies the existence of some standard of optimum size. Ways of determining when a population is "too large" and when it is "too small" must be established; that is, the terms "overpopulation" and "underpopulation" need to be defined.

At one extreme, human population sizes are limited by the physical capacity of the Earth itself, and at the other by the smallest group that can reproduce itself. But other factors should enter into considerations of optimum population size, including an individual's relationships with his fellow men and his psychological relationship to his environment—factors that we recognize in such concepts as "the quality of life" and "the pursuit of happiness." Because these factors involve subjective psychosocial and cultural ideals, they cannot be dealt with as directly as biological and physical constraints on population size, where we are able to apply data on resource depletion, photosynthetic efficiency, human nutrition, and thermodynamic limits. Nevertheless, it is clear that questions about the *quality* of human life are inextricably bound to those about the *quantities* of human beings on Earth. And in discussing these questions together, it is important to have some understanding of man's evolutionary background.

## People versus Earth

The idea of consciously controlling the size of the human population is really a new one. Until very recently population limitation has been considered neither possible nor proper, or limits have been set so high that the problem of limitation would, in effect, be postponed into the indefinite future. The tendency to avoid this issue still exists, even in the face of abundant evidence that very large numbers could never be supported. Discussions about fertility control are still far more likely to center on changing *rates of growth;* absolute size is often considered irrelevant to anything. Nevertheless, the *absolute size* of the human race is now so large that it is perhaps the single most important factor we have to consider in discussing man's future, and its present unprecedented rate of growth adds to the urgency of the problem.

Rapid growth rates hinder economic development, particularly in UDCs. Therefore, the population problem is perceived by economists and politicians as a problem of growth rates or maldistribution. That the human population is now putting stress upon the carrying capacity of the Earth itself must be recognized by all responsible people, not just by ecologists. In the next few decades our efforts to support a growing population are bound to result in much more stress, even if we immediately bend most of our efforts toward alleviating the deleterious effects of overpopulation. It is unmistakably clear that the time has come for humanity to take a careful look at its environment, its resources, its ideals, and its numbers, and to try to make some serious judgments about optimum population size, both for individual countries and for the world as a whole. Needless to say, these judgments cannot be made in a purely economic framework as has been done in most of the extensive literature on the subject of optimum population theory.

## Optima and Environment

In order to be meaningful, statements about overpopulation and under-population must be based on consideration of many environmental factors, in addition to numbers of people per unit of land area. One commonly hears that South America is underpopulated because it has relatively few people per square mile in comparison with, say, Asia. It sounds logical at first to use population density as the basis for discussions of optimum population. It becomes evident on further reflection, however, that in most circumstances density alone is one of the *least* important considerations.

Much more critical than density alone will be density in relation to available resources. The Sahara Desert, for instance, might be "over-populated" at a much lower density than the tropical island of Tahiti. More people are able to live well on the resources of the island than they could on the resources of an isolated piece of desert of the same size. Of course, the discovery of valuable resources like oil or water under the desert might alter the situation. The oil could be exchanged for food and other necessities, and in time, the desert might develop into a local population center of very high density. This is essentially what happens in cities, which exchange manufactured goods, technological know-how, and various services for food, commodities, and other needed materials. If, instead of oil, water were discovered and could be made available locally, the surrounding desert might be made to bloom; and intensive agriculture might also permit the establishment of a higher population density than prevails in Tahiti. This, in fact, happens around oases.

However, we cannot be optimistic about the prospects for intensive agriculture in the tropics, where the soils will not, with present technology, support intensive agriculture and high densities of people. Possibly some of these areas, through the development of a "tree culture," with shade-loving vegetables beneath the trees, could successfully support more people than they do now. But the suggestion that all land areas can be made to support population densities as great as those of such European countries as the Netherlands is misleading for two reasons. First, Europe is blessed with very favorable soils and climate, which are not equalled in the tropics, where most poor countries are located. Second, Europe is by no means self-sufficient in food. Even Denmark, an exporter of dairy products, eggs, and meat, must import huge quantities of oilseed cakes and grain to support the livestock. Denmark imports more protein per person than any other country —240 pounds per year. This is three times the average annual protein consumption of each Dane!

The failure to recognize the lack of self-sufficiency of European nations is most frequently seen in statements about the Netherlands. Since the Netherlands has some 18 times the population density of the United States, it is held up as an example of how far the U.S. has to go before it can be considered overcrowded. This notion, which has been christened "the Netherlands Fallacy," ignores the dependence by that country upon large amounts of food and other resources from all over the world to maintain its industries and standard of living. Put another way, the Dutch are supported to a large extent by land outside their borders. That land should somehow be taken into account in estimating the "population density" of this nation. The Netherlands is the second largest per capita importer of protein in the world. It imports 63 percent of its cereals (including 100 percent of its corn and rice), all of its cotton, 77 percent of its wool, all of its iron ore, antimony, bauxite, chromium, copper, gold, lead, magnesite, manganese, mercury, molybdenum, nickel, silver, tin, tungsten, vanadium, zinc, phosphate rock (for fertilizer), potash (fertilizer), asbestos, and diamonds. In 1968 the Netherlands consumed the energy equivalent of over 51 million metric tons of coal, but produced the equivalent of only slightly over 28 million metric tons.

The Netherlands is an extreme case of the general situation of Western Europe. Measured against food needs and production, Europe is already overpopulated. The continent is also a consumer of nonrenewable resources that are largely imported from other areas, and it also has serious population-related pollution problems.

Relative to resources, then, optimum population is not a simple figure to establish. The size and location of the land area and its possibilities for exchange with other areas must be considered. In addition, the question of how long the population is to be maintained is important. An area must be considered overpopulated if it can be supported only by the rapid consumption of nonrenewable resources. It must also be considered overpopulated if the activities of the population are leading to a steady deterioration of the environment. That a potential exists for alleviating environmental impact by means of social or technical changes, even without reducing population size, does not mean that the area is not overpopulated under present conditions. In dealing with the concept of optimum population, we must consider the relationship of human numbers to the carrying capacity of the environment, viewed over both the short and the long term. Taking into account present population sizes, densities, and the other factors involved in carrying capacity, we arrive at the inescapable conclusion that, in the context of man's present patterns of behavior and level of technology, *the planet Earth, as a whole, is overpopulated.*

Biochemist H. R. Hulett of the Stanford University Medical Center, in considering the possible size of an optimum population, has made some interesting calculations that bear on the question of the degree of overpopulation. He assumed that the average United States citizen would not consider the resources available to him to be excessive. He then divided estimates of the world production of those resources by the American per capita consumption. On this basis, Hulett concludes: ". . . it appears that (about) a billion people is the maximum population supportable by the present agricultural and industrial system of the world at U.S. levels of affluence." Hulett's estimate means that, even ignoring depletion of nonrenewable resources and environmental deterioration, the population of the Earth is already almost 3 billion people above a reasonable optimum.

This does not mean that in certain ways some areas of the Earth may not still be underpopulated. For instance, if more people lived in Australia now, that country might be able to afford a better surface transport system and extend paved roads across the continent. Australians would also be in a better position to develop and utilize their mineral and energy resources. But, unhappily, even though a larger population could well live there, the "frontier philosophy" is even more rampant in Australia than in the United States in terms of environmental deterioration and agricultural overexploitation. Thus Australia may be considered overpopulated already in relation to its long-term ability to feed its people, even though the continent is too thinly populated in terms of highway construction and economic development.

Regardless of such examples of present "underpopulation," it is clear that in dealing with population problems we must focus on the Earth as a whole, because it has become a single, closed-loop feedback system as far as human activities are concerned. Air pollution is a global problem, resource depletion is a global problem, food shortage is a global problem, chlorinated hydrocarbons are a global problem, and thus an excessive population in one area of the world creates problems for all other areas.

## Population Growth and Environmental Deterioration

One of the most misunderstood matters that enters into discussions of optimum population is the nature of the relationship between the size of the human population and the effect of that population on the ecology of our planet. In an agricultural or technological society (as distinguished from a hunting-gathering society), each human individual, in the course of obtaining the requisites of existence, has a net negative impact on his environment. His need for food causes some of the simplification (and resulting destabilization) of ecological systems associated with the practice of agriculture. His needs for water, metals, and fibers lead to the conversion of resources into waste; and the procedures of extraction, processing, and waste disposal themselves have simplifying—and therefore adverse—effects on ecosystems. Of course, it may be judged that an individual's beneficial contribution to his culture outweighs his adverse contribution to the stability of the ecosystem. Unfortunately, society's level of culture will be of little consequence if the collective ecological impact exceeds the point of no recovery.

It is axiomatic that the total impact of a society on the ecosystem can be expressed by the relation

$$I = P \cdot F,$$

where $I$ is the total impact, $P$ is the population size, and $F$ is the impact per capita. Obviously, an increase in $I$ can come about if $P$ alone increases, if $F$ alone increases, if both increase simultaneously, or if one increases faster than the other declines. The particularly rapid increase in total impact over the past several decades has occurred because both $P$ and $F$ have, in fact, been increasing simultaneously. The rapidity with which the product of two increasing quantities grows is simply a matter of arithmetic, but this point has apparently not been understood by some writers who have disparaged the role of population growth in producing man's present predicament. Some numerical examples illustrating this situation are given in Box 8-1.

BOX 8-1   THE ARITHMETIC OF INCREASING IMPACT

To examine quantitatively the relative importance of the two components of total impact, when both are increasing simultaneously, let $I$, $P$, and $F$ be the initial values of total impact, population size, and per capita impact, and let $\Delta I$, $\Delta P$, and $\Delta F$ be the observed increases in these quantities during some time period. We assume for the purposes of this purely arithmetic exercise that per capita consumption is independent of population size. The initial total impact is

$$I = P \cdot F, \tag{1}$$

and the subsequent total impact is

$$I + \Delta I = (P + \Delta P) \cdot (F + \Delta F). \tag{2}$$

The relative increase is obtained by dividing equation (2) by equation (1):

$$\frac{I + \Delta I}{I} = \left(\frac{P + \Delta P}{P}\right) \cdot \left(\frac{F + \Delta F}{F}\right), \tag{3}$$

or

$$1 + \frac{\Delta I}{I} = \left(1 + \frac{\Delta P}{P}\right)\left(1 + \frac{\Delta F}{F}\right), \tag{4}$$

where $\Delta I/I$, $\Delta P/P$, and $\Delta F/F$ are the fractional increases in $I$, $P$, and $F$, and

percentage increase = fractional increase $\times$ 100.

Obviously, the fractional increases in $P$ and $F$ do not add up to the fractional increase in $I$, even though many writers have proceeded as if they do. Thus, one can read statements equivalent to "Total impact increased 300 percent but population, which increased only 100 percent, accounted for only one third of the increase." The implication is that the growth of per capita impact must have accounted for the other two-thirds. In reality, the multiplicative effect of popu-

Of course, many variables affect population size and per capita impact on the environment, and population and per capita impact affect each other. These interactions involve more than just arithmetic; they involve biology, technology and economics. Consider the per capita impact alone, which we have called $F$. This quantity is obviously related to per capita consumption— food, water, energy, fibers, metals—but it also depends on the technology used to make the consumption possible. For example, the per capita impact associated with a given level of metals consumption is smaller if recycling is employed in place of the prevalent "once-through" conversion of resources into waste. Similarly, the per capita impact associated with a certain level of electricity consumption is smaller if power plant effluents are controlled than if they are not. Thus, improvements in technology can sometimes hold the per capita impact, $F$, constant or even decrease it, despite increases in per capita consumption.

Some people have argued, on the basis of such examples, that *all* of our

lation and per capita impact increasing simultaneously has produced (in this example) a 300 percent increase in $I$ even though *both* $P$ and $F$ increased only 100 percent:

$$\left(1 + \frac{\Delta P}{P}\right)\left(1 + \frac{\Delta F}{F}\right) = (1 + 1)(1 + 1) = 4 = 1 + \frac{\Delta I}{I},$$

$$\frac{\Delta I}{I} = 3.$$

To take an example from the experience of the U.S., assume that a good measure of environmental impact is energy production (actually a very reasonable assumption). Total energy production increased 140 percent between 1940 and 1969, while population was increasing by 53 percent. We have

$$\frac{\Delta I}{I} = 1.40, \quad \frac{\Delta P}{P} = .53$$

and, from Equation (4),

$$\frac{\Delta F}{F} = .57.$$

The per capita increase in energy production was only 57 percent, yet, combined with an almost identical increase in population, this led to a 2.4 fold increase in *total* energy production:

$$\left(1 + \frac{\Delta P}{P}\right)\left(1 + \frac{\Delta I}{I}\right) = 1.53 \times 1.57 = 2.40 = \frac{I + \Delta I}{I}.$$

The temptation to say population "caused" only 38 percent of the observed increase must be resisted (.53/1.40 = .38); by the same token, the growth in per capita production "caused" only 40 percent of the increase (57/1.40 = .40), and one is left with no "cause" for the remaining 22 percent. In reality, because of the multiplicative effect, the two growing factors contributed about equally to the much faster growth of the product.

environmental impact can be traced to misuse of existing technologies and failure to develop environmentally benign ones. They imply that neither population size nor per capita consumption is important if only the proper technologies are used. The fallacy in this argument is that *no* technology can completely eliminate the impact of a given amount of consumption. For example, recycling is never perfect; there is always some loss of material, which becomes waste and which requires further depletion to replace. Moreover, recycling anything requires energy, although usually less than the once-through method, and energy is *not* recyclable. It can be used only once, and in use it generates waste heat. These facts are sad but unavoidable consequences of the Second Law of Thermodynamics. Pollution control and all other means of minimizing per capita environmental impact are also imperfect: zero release of any contaminant is an unattainable ideal, and attempts to approach it consume great quantities of energy. In a different vein, the ecological disruption caused by agriculture is central to the enterprise, not a peripheral side effect. We may conclude that improving technology to reduce the impact of consumption is worthwhile, but not the entire answer. Under any set of technological conditions, there will be some impact associated with each unit of consumption, and therefore some level of population size and per capita consumption at which the total impact becomes unsustainable.

Analysis of the role of population in environmental deterioration is made particularly difficult by the *causal* interactions that entangle population growth and per capita impact, and those that eventually relate population growth back to total impact. In mathematical terms, the equation connecting *I, P,* and *F* is "nonlinear" and should be written

$$I = P(I,F) \cdot F(P)$$

This is only a compact way of saying that, although *I* equals *P* times *F, F* also depends on *P,* and *P* depends on *I* and *F*. As we indicated, it is a tangled relationship! Although almost none of these interactions has been studied thoroughly, it is easy to give some illustrative examples.

First, consider some ways in which total and per capita impact can cause changes in population growth. Suppose an increase in *F* occurs in the form of an increase in per capita consumption of energy. If the extra energy per person is used to provide medical services, the death rate may drop and increase the rate of population growth, but if the extra energy powers TV sets that keep people up late at night, the birth rate may drop and decrease the rate of population growth. If the total impact, *I,* becomes great enough, the resulting environmental disaster—whether it be loss of fisheries productivity, crop failure, epidemic, or chronic poisoning—will certainly increase the death rate and perhaps reduce the population size more or less instantaneously.

Conversely, population size and growth rate have important effects on per capita impact. A possibility well known to economists occurs when rapid population growth inhibits the growth of per capita income. This means that per capita consumption grows more slowly than it would in the absence of such rapid population growth, so per capita impact grows more slowly, too. In this case the interaction between population and per capita impact has a moderating effect on the growth of the product: increasing the growth rate of one factor (*P*) tends to decrease the growth rate of the other (*F*). This effect is probably important in UDCs but much less so elsewhere.

Effects of the opposite sort, in which increases in population size operate to increase per capita impact on the environment, occur in both DCs and UDCs. These interactions serve to *accelerate* the growth in total impact, compared to what the growth would be if population and per capita impact were independent. They partly explain the very rapid rate of environmental deterioration that has been observed in the DCs, where the disproportionate amount of consumption—and, hence, impact—makes the effects especially visible.

Perhaps the best understood of the effects that link population size and per capita impact is the *law of diminishing returns*. This refers to a situation in which, in the jargon of the economist, the additional output resulting from each additional unit of input is becoming less and less. Here "output" refers to a desired good such as food or metal, and "input" refers to what we must supply—say, fertilizer, or energy or raw ore—to obtain the output. Suppose that per capita consumption of outputs is to be held constant while population increases. If the law of diminishing returns prevails, the per capita consumption of inputs needed to provide the fixed per capita level of outputs will increase. Since environmental impact is generated by the inputs as well as by the outputs, the per capita impact will also increase.

To see how the law of diminishing returns operates in a specific example, consider the problem of providing nonrenewable resources such as minerals and fossil fuels to a growing population, even at fixed levels of per capita consumption. More people means more demand, and thus more rapid depletion of resources. As the richest supplies of these resources and those nearest to centers of use are consumed, it becomes necessary to use lower-grade ores, drill deeper, and extend supply networks. All these activities increase the *per capita* use of energy and hence the *per capita* impact on the environment. In the case of partly renewable resources such as water (which is effectively nonrenewable when groundwater supplies are mined at rates far exceeding natural recharge), per capita costs and environmental impact escalate enormously when the human population demands more than is locally available. Here the loss of free-flowing rivers and other economic, aesthetic, and ecological costs of massive water-movement projects represent increased per capita diseconomies directly stimulated by population growth. These effects would, of course, also eventually overtake a stationary population that demands more than the environment can supply on a perpetual basis; growth simply speeds the process and allows less time to deal with the problems created.

The law of diminishing returns is also operative in increasing food production to meet the needs of growing populations. Typically, attempts are made both to overproduce on land already farmed and to extend agriculture to marginal land. The former requires disproportionate energy use in obtaining and distributing water, fertilizer, and pesticides. Farming marginal land also increases per capita energy use, since the amount of energy invested per unit yield increases as less desirable land is cultivated. Both activities "consume" the fertility built into the natural soil structure. Similarly, as the richest fisheries stocks are depleted, the yield per unit effort drops, and more and more energy per capita is required to maintain the supply. Once a stock is depleted it may not recover—it may be nonrenewable.

In theory, diminishing returns may be counterbalanced by improved technology and by economies of scale. The latter term refers to savings in labor or materials, or both, which may result simply from carrying on an enterprise such as farming or manufacturing on a large scale. In practice, economies of scale hold sway up to a point and then give way to diminishing returns. Improved technology can postpone the onset of diminishing returns but cannot avert it. In the U.S. and in most other DCs, technological innovation and economies of scale are still holding their own in certain service and manufacturing enterprises; but in the critical matter of supplying the raw materials of existence—food, water, fibers, metals—the technologies required to cope with growing populations have been using more inputs per capita, not less.

Population size influences per capita impact in ways other than diminishing returns. One is *increasing complexity,* for the intricacy and unwieldiness of such activities as transportation, communication, and government expand disproportionately as population grows. For example, consider the oversimplified but instructive situation in which each person in the population has links with every other person—roads, telephone lines, and so forth. These links involve energy and materials in their construction and use. Since the number of links increases much more rapidly than the number of people, so does the per capita consumption associated with the links. If $N$ is the number of people, then the number of links is $N(N-1)/2,$ and the number of links per capita is $(N-1)/2.$

Population growth may cause even more rapid increases in per capita impact on the environment through the mechanism we call the *threshold effect.* Below a certain level of pollution, trees will survive in smog. But when a small increment in population produces a small increment in smog, living trees become dead trees. Perhaps 500 people can live around a lake and dump their raw sewage into the lake, and the natural systems of the lake will be able to break down the sewage and keep the lake from undergoing rapid ecological change. But 505 people may overload the system and result in a "polluted" or euthropic lake.

Other phenomena capable of causing near-discontinuities are synergisms. For instance, as cities expand into farmland, air pollution increasingly becomes a mixture of agricultural chemicals with effluents from power plants and automobiles. Sulfur dioxide from the city paralyzes the cleaning mechanisms of the lungs, thus increasing the residence time there of potential carcinogens in the agricultural chemicals. The joint effect may be synergistic; it may be much more than the sum of the individual effects. Investigation of such synergistic effects is one of the most neglected areas of environmental evaluation.

Not only is there a connection between population size and per capita damage to the environment, but the cost of maintaining environmental quality at a given level escalates disproportionately as population size increases. This effect occurs in part because costs increase very rapidly as one tries to reduce contaminants per unit volume of effluent to lower and lower levels (diminishing returns again!). Consider municipal sewage, for example. The cost of removing 80 to 90 percent of the biochemical and chemical oxygen demand (standard indices of pollutants in water), 90 percent of the suspended solids, and 60 percent of the resistant organic material by means of secondary treatment is about 8 cents per 1,000 gallons in a large plant. But if the volume of sewage is such that its nutrient content creates a serious eutrophication problem (as is the case in the U.S. today), or if supply considerations dictate the reuse of sewage water for industry, agriculture, or groundwater recharge, advanced treatment is necessary. The cost ranges from 2 to 4 times as much as for secondary treatment (17 cents per 1,000 gallons for carbon absorption, 34 cents per 1,000 gallons for disinfection to yield a potable supply). This example of diminishing returns in pollution control has its counterpart for gases, automobile exhausts, and so forth.

Consider a situation in which the limited capacity of the environment to absorb abuse requires that we hold human impact in some sector constant as population doubles. This means that *per capita effectiveness* of pollution control in this sector must double (that is, effluent per person must be halved). In a typical situation, this would yield doubled per capita costs, or quadrupled total costs (and probably energy consumption) in this sector for a doubling of population.

Again, the possible existence of "economies of scale" does not invalidate these arguments. Such savings, if available at all, would apply in the case of our sewage example to a change in the amount of effluent to be handled at an installation of a given type. For most technologies, the U.S. is already more than populous enough to achieve such economies and is doing so. They are accounted for in our example by citing figures for the largest treatment plants of each type. Population growth, on the other hand, forces us into quantitative *and* qualitative changes in how we handle each unit volume of effluent; what fraction and what kinds of material we remove. Here economies of scale do not apply at all, and diminishing returns are the rule.

The relations among population and total and per capita impact on the environment are far from being thoroughly understood, but the examples just given should be sufficient to demonstrate that the role of population cannot be lightly dismissed. Many authors who have disparaged the importance of population size and growth rates as contributors to environmental deterioration have apparently misunderstood the multiplier effect of population (Box 8-1), have underestimated the role of diminishing returns, threshold effects, and synergisms, and have ignored the relation between complexity and stability in ecosystems altogether.

Two additional errors should be mentioned. One is the tendency to confuse changes in the *composition* of consumption with absolute increases, and thus to overestimate the role of consumption relative to that of population in generating today's environmental predicament. Consider, for example, the 1971 article by economist Ansley Coale, in which he pointedly notes that since 1940 "population has increased by 50 percent but per capita use of electricity has been multiplied several times." Actually, in this case as in many others, very rapid increases in consumption reflect a shift among alternatives within a larger and much more slowly growing category. Thus, the 760 percent increase in electricity production since 1940 occurred in large part because the electrical *component* of the energy budget was (and still is) increasing much faster than the total energy budget itself. Energy used to produce electricity accounted for 12 percent of the U.S. energy consumption in 1940 versus 23 percent in 1969. These figures take into account the average efficiency of energy conversion from fuel to electricity. Because the efficiency rose considerably between 1940 and 1969, electricity's 8.6-fold increase in kilowatt hours was achieved with a much smaller increase in fuel burned. The total energy production, a more important figure than its electrical component in terms of demands on resources and the environment, increased much less dramatically—by a factor of 2.4 from 1940 to 1969. As noted in Box 8-1, population and per capita production of energy increased by almost identical amounts in this time period and so, in the purely arithmetic analysis, were equally "responsible" for the total increase. Similar considerations reveal the imprudence of citing, say, aluminum consumption to show that population growth is an "unimportant" factor in resource use. Aluminum consumption has increased more than 15-fold since 1940, but much of this growth has been due to the substitution of aluminum for steel in many applications. Thus, a fairer measure is the combined consumption of aluminum and steel, which has risen by a factor of only 2.2 since 1940. Here, in the purely arithmetic analysis, population growth is "responsible" for more than half of the increase.

Sadly, we must here reiterate what we and many other ecologists have pointed out numerous times before: serious environmental deterioration was caused by preindustrial man, and is still being caused by preindustrial groups (as, for example, in the continued southward spread of the Sahara and in contributions of dust to atmospheric pollution made by subsistence farmers). Scattered over the Earth are the remains of past ecocatastrophes, from Angkor Wat to the Tigris and Euphrates Valleys to deforested Europe. One ecological popularizer, in his zeal to "prove" that all environmental problems are caused by faulty technology and are unrelated to population growth, recently wrote:

"As long as human beings held their place in the terrestrial ecosystem— consuming food produced by the soil and oxygen released by plants, returning organic wastes to the soil and carbon dioxide to the plants—they could do no serious ecological harm."

As anyone who has seen the cumulative effects of primitive "slash-and-burn" agriculture in overpopulated areas of the tropics could have informed that writer, Barry Commoner, nothing could be further from the truth.


## Evolution and Human Reproduction

The urge toward maximizing the number of children successfully reared has been fixed in us by billions of years of evolution, during which our ancestors were fighting a continual battle to keep the birth rate ahead of the death rate. That they were successful is attested to by our very existence, for if the death rate had overtaken the birth rate for any substantial period of time, the evolutionary line that led to modern man would have become extinct. Even among our apelike ancestors a few million years ago it was still relatively difficult for a mother to rear her offspring successfully. Most of her children died before they reached reproductive age. The death rate was near the birth rate. Then another factor, cultural evolution, was added to biological evolution. The two kinds of evolution, operating together, resulted in a trend toward larger brains.

Human brain size was eventually limited by the ability of women to carry and deliver large-headed infants without themselves being immobilized. Consequently, more and more brain growth was concentrated in the period after birth. Although this resulted in a longer period of postnatal helplessness for the infants, presumably this was less of an adaptive disadvantage than further pelvic expansion of the mothers would have been.

The long period of helplessness of the human infant had many effects, most of which center on the mother's problem of caring for and protecting the infant. Presumably, a selective premium was placed on keeping the father with the family group, and an essential step in that direction was the elimination of the short, well-defined breeding season characteristic of most mammals. Year-round sexuality and the development of strong mother-offspring and father-mother bonds (pair-bonds), which led to the evolution of family groups, may be traced at least in part to increased brain size. These are, of course, the essential ingredients of what mankind has developed into the vast, varied, complex, and pervasive social phenomenon that is sometimes referred to in our society simply as "sex." This social phenomenon affects the way we raise our children, our family structure and ideals, our sexual mores, and the roles and relative status of the two sexes and their relationships both within and outside the family, to mention only some of the more obvious manifestations. Sex in this sense is not simply an act leading to the production of offspring, but it is also a cultural phenomenon penetrating into all aspects of our lives, including our self-esteem and our choice of friends, cars, and leaders. It is tightly interwoven with our mythologies and history, and it influences our views of nearly everything.

Many plants and animals reproduce without any sort of sexual process. Biologically, sexual reproduction evolved not only as a mechanism of reproduction, but also as a mechanism that provided variability. In many organisms the basic sexual function is to provide the genetic variability that permits natural selection, and sexual processes occur at different stages in the life cycle than do reproductive processes. Most of the vertebrates have two differentiated sexes and generate variability in the process of producing reproductive cells. In these animals, and in man, sex (in the restricted biological sense) and reproduction are closely associated. Just as "biological sex" evolved not only to promote reproduction but to provide variability, "cultural sex" evolved not only to promote reproduction, but primarily as a cultural device to protect the social structure of the family. An essential function of copulation in human beings is to strengthen and maintain the pair-bond; cultural sex reinforces and protects this function in society. Understanding these points makes it easier to evaluate many arguments raised against birth control on the basis of emotional ideas about the "natural" function of sex. Furthermore, a grasp of the cultural importance of sex brings home the difficulty of changing the reproductive habits of a society, since attempts to do so may be perceived by the society as an assault on the very basis of its culture.

## The Natural Environment of Man

In addition to the evolutionary origins of man's attitudes toward reproduction, we must consider what kind of environment man is best adapted to. What size groups does he feel most comfortable in? How important is solitude for the well-being of the human psyche? Is the color green an important component of the environment of *Homo sapiens?* Such questions have been the subject of extensive speculation, but they are exceedingly difficult to answer. In theory, for instance, natural selection could change certain human characteristics dramatically in 6 to 8 generations—in only about 200 years (although this would involve a very large portion of the population not reproducing in each generation). But other characteristics may be so ingrained in the human genetic-developmental system that they would be impossible to change without much longer periods of genetic readjustment, or the changes might even be so traumatic as to lead to extinction. To give an analogy, one may, by selection, experimentally create a strain of fruit flies that is resistant to DDT in 6 to 8 generations, presumably as a result of some minor changes in enzyme systems or behavior. It seems unlikely, however, that any number of generations of selection would produce a fruit fly able to fly with one wing; in fact, an attempt to produce such a change by artificial selection would probably lead to extinction of the experimental population.

Some biologists feel that mankind's evolutionary history has been such that the present environments to which he is subjecting himself are essentially asking him to "fly with one wing." This general viewpoint has been expressed by three biologists at the University of Wisconsin, H. H. Iltis, P. Andrews, and O. L. Loucks. They feel that mankind's genetic endowment has been shaped by evolution to require "natural" surroundings for optimum mental health. They write:

> Unique as we may think we are, we are nevertheless as likely to be genetically programmed to a natural habitat of clean air and a varied green landscape as any other mammal. To be relaxed and feel healthy usually means simply allowing our bodies to react in the way for which one hundred millions of years of evolution has equipped us. Physically and genetically, we appear best adapted to a tropical savanna, but as a cultural animal we utilize learned adaptations to cities and towns. For thousands of years we have tried in our houses to imitate not only the climate, but the setting of our evolutionary past: warm, humid air, green plants, and even animal companions. Today, if we can afford it, we may even build a greenhouse or swimming pool next to our living room, buy a place in the country, or at least take our children vacationing on the seashore. The specific physiological reactions to natural

beauty and diversity, to the shapes and colors of nature (especially to green), to the motions and sounds of other animals, such as birds, we as yet do not comprehend. But it is evident that nature in our daily life should be thought of as a part of the biological need. It cannot be neglected in the discussions of resource policy for man.

There is little consensus among cultures or even within our own culture on what sort of an environment best provides an optimal "quality of life." In addition, there is virtually no experimental evidence on how varying such factors as the density of the population, or levels of noise, or the amount of green in the environment may alter human behavior. We do know from the systematic observations of anthropologist Edward T. Hall that peoples of different cultures have different perceptions of "personal space." It is not clear, however, how much such differences are attributable to the perception of crowding as opposed to the actual tolerance of crowding. For instance, do the residents of Tokyo feel uncrowded at densities that might make residents of Los Angeles feel intolerably crowded, or are the Japanese merely better able to tolerate the crowding, even though their perceptions of it may be essentially the same?

Some psychological studies suggest that individuals who commit violent crimes may have a lower than normal tolerance for crowding. Psychiatrist A. F. Kinzel of the Columbia-Presbyterian Medical Center in New York has found that prisoners convicted of crimes of violence were four times likelier to interpret the close approach of another person as "threatening" than were prisoners convicted of offenses involving property. Evidently there are great differences in amounts of tolerance for crowding among individuals as well as among different cultures.

We have almost no information on the levels of crowding at which people feel most happy and comfortable and can perform various tasks with the greatest efficiency. We do not know whether high density during one part of the daily routine (at work, for example) coupled with low density at another (at home) would have the same effects as medium density throughout the day. We do not know exactly what role high density plays in the incidence of stress diseases and mental health. We do not know whether density alone can be a contributing cause to riots. People have many opinions about such questions, but we have little solid information on which to base conclusions.

Recently, some experimental work on the effects of crowding on human beings has been done by psychologist Jonathan Freedman and his associates in collaboration with one of us. In short-term experiments, no differences were found between crowded and uncrowded groups in performance of a series of tasks. When games were played that permitted competitive or cooperative strategies to be adopted, or when other measures of social interaction were used, the results were more interesting. In all-male groups the crowded situation produced significantly higher levels of competitiveness. In all-female groups the result was reversed; the women in crowded circumstances were more cooperative, while those in less crowded conditions were more competitive. In mixed groups (both sexes present) there was no detectable effect of crowding.

These results must be interpreted with much caution. They suggest that all-male juries should be avoided, as well as groups of men making world-shaking decisions in crowded rooms. The results do not reveal much about the more general effects of crowding in human populations, except to reinforce the notion that human beings will adapt readily to what *a priori* might seem to be difficult conditions—at least as far as task performance is concerned. Statistical studies of cities of varying density have tended to indicate that crowding *per se* is not an important contributor to high crime rates (in fact, the rate of migration into cities seems to be the factor most highly correlated with those rates).

Much of the discussion of effects of crowding on human beings has been based on extrapolation from the results of John Calhoun's classic studies of crowded rats. The assumption is sometimes made that the kinds of social and physical pathologies he observed in crowded rats will sooner or later turn up in populations of people if they get too crowded. Perhaps they would, but it is clear that many other limiting factors will come into play before the human population grows to the point where density itself sets a limit. After all, people living in the most crowded cities, such as Manhattan and Tokyo, do not show social pathologies to a degree sufficient to halt population growth. But if only one-fourth of the land surface of the Earth were populated to the density of Tokyo, the world population would be about 600 billion people. Clearly something besides density itself—famine, plague, war—will stop the growth of the human population long before that point is reached.

Due to the lack of data, we must resort to speculation in further discussion of the psychological and social effects of human crowding. In dealing with a high population density, the Japanese seem to have developed a variety of cultural devices to alleviate the stress. It has been suggested that their very formal and elaborate etiquette may be one mechanism for self-protection against the inevitable frictions of constant human encounter. The Japanese have been relatively crowded for a long time. Around 1870 Japan had some 210 people per square mile. Indeed, because Hokkaido is relatively infertile and inhospitable, the density in many areas is and was much higher than the average for the country. Thus, a century ago, Japan had four times the population density of the United States today. In contrast to the Japanese and the Europeans, who also have had high population densities for several generations, people from currently or recently low-density countries (such as the United States or Australia) are likely to have the reputation of being informal and easy-going, or even bumptious and rude. The Japanese are famous for their interest in aesthetic values and respect for nature, which they demonstrate in their lovely gardens. They also successfully create an illusion of space where there is very little in their homes and buildings, a talent that possibly contributes much to domestic serenity.

People in general remain unaware of the influence that population size and density have upon their ways of life and their perceptions of the world. After all, these factors usually do not change drastically in times on the order of a generation or less. When they do change rapidly, as they are doing in some Latin American countries, the result seems more likely to produce disruption than gradual social change. Around 1910 the United States had about half the number of people that it has today. Society then differed from today's in ways that cannot be entirely explained by the processes of industrialization and urbanization, or by such historical events as two world wars and a depression. Such qualities as friendliness and neighborliness, once common in this country and generally esteemed, now seem to exist primarily in rural areas, small towns, and occasional enclaves in big cities. In myriad ways our lives have become more regulated, regimented, and formalistic, a trend that is at least partly due to population growth. If we add another 100 million people in the next thirty-odd years, this trend will certainly continue and will probably even accelerate.

Cultural and social factors, as well as physical limitations, must be a part of a discussion of optimum populations. A standard of living involves more than per capita income, purchasing power, and possessions. "The best things in life are free," an old song tells us, but they may no longer be available to people in overcrowded populations. Population size and density have a strong influence on social arrangements, and it is certainly appropriate to consider what sort of society we would prefer in trying to reach decisions about population size. Do we like a large degree of personal freedom and free and easy manners? Or do we prefer more formality and a high degree of organization?

Certain values conflict with numbers, even though numbers may also be considered a value by many people, such as economists, politicians (who see more votes), and parents of large families. Those who promote numbers of people as a value in itself may fail to consider the cheapness such abundance often brings. One might well ask whether traditional ideals of cherishing human life have not been eroded by our growing population in the last generation or two. There is some sign of this, especially in the way the nation today barely reacts to such tragedies as devastating floods, hurricanes, and airline crashes—a striking contrast to the prolonged sympathy and relief operations evoked by disasters of lesser magnitude before World War II. The 1970 Pakistani cyclone disaster, which cost half a million lives, was one of the worst in recorded history. Yet it was not one of the ten top news stories of 1970, according to Associated Press editors. The growing impersonality of life in our large cities, in which citizens' cries for help are often ignored by bystanders, further supports this view.

The conflict between values and numbers may arise in a choice between having many deprived children or having only a few who can be raised with the best care, education, and opportunity for successful adulthood. The decision is equally valid whether it is made by a family or a society. It is surely no accident that so many of the most successful individuals are first or only children; nor that children of large families (particularly with more than four children), whatever their economic status, generally do relatively poorly in school and show lower I.Q. test scores than their peers from small families. Studies with very young children conducted at Harvard University by three psychologists, Burton L. White, Jerome Bruner, and E. Robert La Crosse, have lent substance to these findings. They have found that children establish their own level of "competence"—ability to cope with their culture—well before school age. This level of competence is strongly correlated with the amount and kind of attention each child receives from his mother during his earliest years. The significance of this in relation to family size is obviously great.

How much do people really love children? Demographer Lincoln Day of the Harvard School of Public Health suggests that the truth is that Americans, at least, love their *own* children, not their neighbors'. Most adults, in fact, do not ordinarily have much contact with other people's children, and relatively few seek it, unless their occupations bring them into contact with children. Perhaps more opportunities for contact between generations would go a long way toward compensating for large families, when and if a small family norm can be established. The simplest way to provide intergenerational contact is to encourage the development of neighborhoods composed of families of all ages—from newlyweds to senior citizens—and provide communal areas where they can associate. Highly structured child-adult relationships have been developed in such social organizations as hippie communes and Israeli kibbutzim, where all adults in the community come into regular contact with children.

Although human beings are capable of adapting themselves to a wide variety of environments, it is plain that we do much better in some sets of circumstances than others. *Whether we measure adaptive success by how many individuals can survive in a given area or by how many can live healthy, productive, reasonably happy, and comfortable lives is a vitally important point.*

## Determining an Optimum

The approach to establishing optimum population sizes relative to resources is straightforward in principle. We must first determine what material standard of living for people is desired and then determine how many people can be maintained indefinitely at that standard. The minimum size will be determined by the societal complexity necessary for divisions of labor, construction of public works, and so forth. The maximum size will be set by the need to avoid the various unhappy consequences of overpopulation already discussed. It should be noted that the goal expressed in the slogan "the greatest good for the greatest number" is an impossible double maximization. The greater the total number of people, the fewer there will be who can "live like kings" at any given time.

But material standards, as we have seen, are only part of the story. Approaches to optimizing the quality of life should recognize the need for diversity. Population size must be set so that a continuum of density is possible, from crowded cities to utter solitude. People should be able to establish themselves at whatever density makes them feel most comfortable. Public policies might prevent great density changes within specified areas, or encourage desired shifts in density between areas. Such a utopian system would require an overall global density considerably below the maximum "base subsistence density." Not only could the rewards for the human psyche be enormous, but some scope would be left for human social and cultural development, including genuine opportunities to create "free societies," without the need to pour all our efforts into solving the elemental problems of survival.

With the passage of time, both technological change and cultural evolution will inevitably change optima. Therefore, all governments, including eventually a world governmental body, must be ready to encourage appropriate population trends just as they now intervene in attempts to produce desired economic trends. In other words, the size of the human population must be brought under rational control, but not with the idea of establishing some sort of permanent optimum. The ideal of an optimum population size must be a dynamic one, in which population size changes in response to human needs. The number of children that couples may have will not simply be the number of children they desire, but will take into account the children's future well-being, as well as social and physical environmental factors. Arriving at ideals of optimum population sizes, however, will involve more than simply avoiding unwanted births. By virtually every standard the world is already overpopulated, and there is considerable evidence that, even if every unwanted birth were avoided, the global population would still grow. In order to achieve population control, extraordinary changes in human attitudes—attitudes produced by eons of biological and cultural evolution—will have to occur. These changes will inevitably trouble men's minds; death control goes with the grain, but birth control goes against it. Changing people's views of birth control and family size to coincide with the goal of a better future for all mankind is one of the greatest challenges humanity has ever faced.

# Bibliography

Allen, Durward L., 1969. Too many strangers. *National Parks Magazine,* (August).

Althus, William D., 1966. Birth order and its sequelae. *Science,* vol. 151, pp. 44–49. Evidence that first-born children are more likely than others to achieve eminence or educational attainment.

Anonymous, 1969. Children: the intelligent infant. *Time,* March 28, p. 56.

Anonymous, 1970. East Pakistan: the politics of catastrophe. *Time,* Dec. 7, pp. 28–29.

Cassel, John, 1971. Health consequences of population density and crowding. *In* Revelle (see below).

Coale, Ansley J., 1970. Man and his environment. *Science,* vol. 170, pp. 132–136, (Oct.).

Dubos, René, 1965. *Man Adapting.* Yale Univ. Press, New Haven. Deals with all aspects of the individual's adaptation to his environment.

Dubos, René, 1970. Will man adapt to megalopolis? *The Ecologist,* vol. 1, no. 4, pp. 12–15.

Ehrlich, P. R., and J. Freedman, 1971. Population, crowding, and human behavior. *New Scientist,* 1 April, pp. 10–14. On crowding studies.

Ehrlich, P. R., and J. P. Holdren, 1971. Impact of population growth. *Science,* vol. 171, pp. 1212–1217. This is the source of the discussion on the impact of population growth on the environment.

Ehrlich, P. R., and J. P. Holdren, 1972. One-dimensional ecology. *Bulletin of the Atomic Scientists,* vol. 28, May. Presents a detailed documented refutation of Barry Commoner's contention that population growth and affluence do not play significant roles in causing environmental deterioration.

Enke, Stephen, 1970. Zero U.S. population growth—when, how, and why. *Tempo,* General Electric Co., Santa Barbara, January. Includes discussion of the economic impact of population growth in the U.S.

Goldsmith, Edward, 1970. The stable society—can we achieve it? *The Ecologist,* vol. 1, no. 6, pp. 8–11. An interesting essay on achieving an optimum population, primarily oriented toward the United Kingdom. A stable society to Goldsmith includes social and ecological stability as well as numerical stability.

Hall, E. T., 1966. *The Hidden Dimension.* Doubleday, Garden City, N.Y. Basic source on personal space.

Hulett, H. R., 1970. Optimum world population. *BioScience,* vol. 20, no. 3, (March).

Iltis, H. H., O. L. Loucks, and P. Andrews, 1970. Criteria for an optimum human environment. *Bulletin of the Atomic Scientists,* vol. 26, January, pp. 2–6.

Lee, Terence, 1971. The effect of the built environment on human behavior. *International Journal of Environmental Studies,* vol. 1, pp. 307–314. On urban behavior and the planned urban environment.

Marshall, A. J. (ed.), 1966. *The Great Extermination.* Heinemann, London. Describes human destruction of Australia's environment.

Morris, Desmond, 1967. *The Naked Ape.* McGraw-Hill, New York. In spite of some errors of fact and interpretation, this is an excellent book for putting man in perspective.

Odum, Eugene P., 1971. The optimum population for Georgia. *The Ecologist,* vol. 1, no. 9, pp. 14–15. An analysis of how optimum population might be determined, using the state of Georgia as a model.

Pines, Maya, 1969. Why some 3-year-olds get A's—and some get C's. *N.Y. Times Magazine,* July 6. On the Harvard studies of children.

Revelle, Roger (Chairman), 1971. *Rapid Population Growth; Consequences and Policy Implications.* Report of a National Academy of Sciences Study Committee. Johns Hopkins Press. A cautious report that enormously underestimates both the role of population growth in inducing environmental deterioration and the environment's role as a limitation on population growth. Contains a number of interesting papers on social and economic aspects of population growth.

Russell, W. M. S., 1971. Population and inflation. *The Ecologist,* vol. 1, no. 8, pp. 4–8. On economics and population growth.

Sommer, Robert, 1969. *Personal Space.* Prentice-Hall, Inc. Englewood Cliffs, New Jersey.

Spengler, Joseph J., 1968. Optimum population theory, in *International Encyclopedia of the Social Sciences,* vol. 12, pp. 358–362. MacMillan Co., New York. A concise introduction.

Taylor, L. R. (ed.), 1970. *The Optimum Population for Britain.* Academic Press, New York. Proceedings of a symposium on optimum population including political, economic, agricultural, demographic, social, environmental, and resource considerations.

U.S. Commission on Population Growth and the American Future, 1971. Population growth and America's future, Washington, D.C. Reprinted in *Family Planning Perspectives,* vol. 3, no. 2 (April), pp. 45–52. The Population Commission's interim report.

Viel, Benjamin, 1969. The social consequences of population growth. *PRB Selection* no. 30 (Oct.). Population Reference Bureau, Washington, D.C.

Wray, Joel, 1971. Population pressures on families: family size and child spacing. *In* Revelle (see above). A comprehensive treatment of the relationship of family size to the family's health, nutrition, welfare, and I.Q., in both DCs and UDCs.

# CHAPTER 9

# Birth Control

*"Unlike plagues of the dark ages or contemporary diseases we do not yet understand, the modern plague of overpopulation is soluble by means we have discovered and with resources we possess. What is lacking is not sufficient knowledge of the solution but universal consciousness of the gravity of the problem and education of the billions who are its victims."*

——Martin Luther King (1929–1968)
(Speech delivered on receiving the Margaret Sanger Award in Human Rights, 1966.)

An essential feature of any humane program to regulate the size of the human population, and to achieve the goal of a world optimum, is the control of births. This chapter summarizes present techniques by which birth control may be accomplished and describes some others that are under development. For a review of reproductive anatomy and physiology, see Appendix 6.

## History

Many birth-control practices are at least as old as recorded history. The Old Testament contains obvious references to the practice of withdrawal, or *coitus interruptus* (removal of the penis from the woman's vagina before ejaculation). The ancient Egyptians used crude barriers to the cervix made from leaves or cloth, and even blocked the cervical canal with cotton fibers. The ancient Greeks practiced population control through their social system as well as through contraception; they discouraged heterosexual marriage and encouraged homosexual relationships, especially for men. The idea may be distasteful to most of us, but it undoubtedly worked. The condom, or penis sheath dates back at least to the Middle Ages, when it was made of linen, fish skins, or sheeps' intestines. The latter version is still in use today, although it has largely been superseded by the cheaper, more popular, rubber one. Douching, the practice of flushing out the vagina with water or a solution immediately after intercourse, has had a similarly long history in Europe. The widespread practice of withdrawal and a trend toward late marriage are believed to be responsible for the reduction of European birth rates that followed the Industrial Revolution. The simplest, the most effective, and perhaps the oldest method of birth control is abstention; but this method seems to have been favored mainly by older men, particularly unmarried members of the clergy.

Besides the fairly effective methods of birth control mentioned above, a host of others have been tried at various times in various societies, including the use of plants and herbs, chemicals, drugs, saliva and dung from animals, vegetable oils, and even the performance of such rituals as holding one's breath and stepping over graves.

Attempts to limit family size by one means or another appear to be a universal phenomenon. Abortion has a very long history and is believed to be the single most common form of birth control in the world today, despite its illegal status in most countries. Infanticide, which is viewed with horror by prosperous people in industrialized societies, was a rather common practice among the ancient Greeks; the Chinese used it for centuries, especially in times of famine. Only a century or so ago, it was widely practiced in Europe in an institutionalized, although not entirely socially approved, system sometimes called "baby farming" (Box 9-1).

Infanticide today rarely takes the form of outright murder. Usually it consists of deliberate neglect or exposure to the elements. Among the Eskimos and other primitive peoples who live in harsh environments where food is scarce, infanticide is a fairly common practice, since greater importance must be placed on the survival of the group than on the survival of an additional child. It exists even in our own society, especially among the overburdened poor, although intent might be hard to prove. Certainly "masked infanticide" is extremely common among the poor and hungry in underdeveloped countries, where women often neglect ill children, refuse to take them to medical facilities, and show resentment toward anyone who attempts treatment. According to Dr. Sumner Kalman of the Stanford University Medical Center, the average poor mother in Colombia—where 80 percent of a large family's income may be needed to provide food alone—goes through a progression of attempts to limit the number of her children. She starts with ineffective native forms of contraception and moves on to quack abortion, infanticide, frigidity, and all too often to suicide.

The modern family-planning movement began in the United States and England as an outgrowth of the women's rights campaign. In the beginning it was intended primarily to relieve women of the burdens of too many children, which not uncommonly included a threat to the mothers' very lives. In the early years of this endeavor, men (including members of the medical profession), generally opposed the idea or were indifferent to it. Later, when the economic advantages and the benefits to conjugal and family life became evident, men began to support family planning, and the medical profession developed more modern and effective methods of birth control. Nevertheless, more often than not, the wife still holds the primary responsibility for birth control in the family. This is reflected by the fact that the majority of modern birth-control methods, particularly those used by married couples, are designed to be employed by the woman.

## Conventional Methods

Among the so-called conventional methods and devices for birth control are the condom, the diaphragm, and the cervical cap; various creams, jellies, and

---

BOX 9-1   INSTITUTIONALIZED INFANTICIDE IN EIGHTEENTH CENTURY

The following quotation is from George Burrington's pamphlet "An answer to Dr. William Brakenridge's letter concerning the number of inhabitants, within the London bills of mortality," London, J. Scott (1757):

Where the Number of lusty Batchelors is large, many are the merry-begotten Babes: On these Occasions, if the Father is an honest Fellow and a true Church of England-Man, the new-born Infant is baptized by an indigent Priest, and the Father provides for the Child: But the Dissenters, Papists, Jews, and other Sects send their Bastards to the Foundling Hospital; if they are not admitted, there are Men and Women, that for a certain Sum of Money will take them, and the Fathers never hear what becomes of their Children afterwards . . . in and about London a prodigious Number of Infants are cruelly murdered unchristened, by those Infernals, called Nurses; these detestable Monsters throw a Spoonful of Gin, Spirits of Wine, or Hungary-Water down a Child's Throat, which instantly strangles the Babe; when the Searchers come to inspect the Body, and enquire what Distemper caused the Death, it is answered, Convulsions, this occasions the Article of Convulsions in the Bills of Mortality so much to exceed all others. The price of destroying and interring a Child is but Two Guineas; and these are the Causes that near a Third die under the Age of Two Years, and not unlikely under two Months.

I have been informed by a Man now living, that the Officers of one Parish in Westminster, received Money for more than Five Hundred Bastards, and reared but One out of the whole Number. How surprizing and shocking must this dismal Relation appear, to all that are not hardened in Sin? Will it not strike every one, but the Causers and Perpetrators with Dread and Horror? Let it be considered what a heinous and detestable Crime Child-murder is, in the Sight of the Almighty, and how much it ought to be abhorred and prevented by all good People.

foams; the douche; and the rhythm system. All of these are intended to prevent the meeting of sperm and ovum. More recent additions to the arsenal include the contraceptive pill and the intrauterine device (IUD). Some of these methods and devices are more effective than others, and each has advantages and disadvantages that may make it more or less suitable for a particular couple at a particular stage of life. Beyond these contraceptives, for a couple whose family is complete, there is sterilization. For the male especially, this is a simple, harmless procedure that removes the possibility of fathering a child, and has no other effect. In addition to the conventional methods of birth control, certain "folk methods" exist in our culture, which are used mainly by ingenious teenagers. These include douches with soft drinks, and condoms devised from plastic wrapping materials. Despite the ingenuity they reflect, they cannot be recommended, especially the douche. Their effectiveness is unknown, although that of the plastic condom may be quite high.

New methods of birth control are now being developed and tested in laboratories, some of which may be available to the public within the next few years.

### THE CONDOM

Many men have learned about the condom in the armed forces, where it is presented to them as a means of avoiding venereal disease. It is also one of the most popular and most effective means of birth control. Usually made of rubber, the condom is a very thin sheath that fits tightly over the penis during intercourse and retains the semen after ejaculation. Its advantages lie in its simplicity of use and its availability. The failure rate is low, especially if the man has been instructed in its proper use. Care is especially required to insure against spillage of semen at the time of withdrawal. Defective condoms are seldom encountered and can be guarded against by inspection before use. Unlike other devices, condoms require no fitting or prescription by a doctor; but many men complain that they interfere with the enjoyment of intercourse by reducing sensation, and by causing an interruption of foreplay in order to apply them.

### THE DIAPHRAGM

This device, essentially a rubber cup with a rubberclad rim of flexible spring steel, is designed to fit over the cervix, where it acts as a barrier to sperm. It is inserted into the vagina before intercourse, and is left in place for several hours afterward. Before insertion it is coated on the edges and underside with a spermicidal jelly or cream to prevent any sperm from getting through underneath. A well-fitted, properly used diaphragm is a highly effective contraceptive, but it is relatively complicated to use compared to the

condom and some other methods. To ensure a proper fit, it must be prescribed by a doctor, who also instructs the woman about its placement and
use. When in position, it cannot be felt, and its use does not in any way
interfere with either partner's enjoyment of sexual relations.

### THE CERVICAL CAP

Like the diaphragm, the cervical cap bars entrance of sperm into the
uterus. It is made of plastic or metal, fits tightly over the cervix, and may be
left in place for long periods of time. It need be removed only for menstruation. If properly fitted, the cap is extremely effective. Its main disadvantage
lies in the difficulty of placing it correctly.

### SPERMICIDAL AGENTS

A variety of spermicidal jellies and creams are available that can be deposited in the upper vagina with special applicators. Although these agents
are less effective than the devices discussed above, they have the advantage
of being easier to use than mechanical contrivances, and they require neither
fitting nor prescription by a doctor.

Foam tablets, aerosols, and suppositories are similar to the jellies and
creams, and operate on the same principles. The foam varieties may be
more effective than the others, perhaps because they are more thoroughly
dispersed in the vagina.

### RHYTHM

Also referred to as "periodic abstention," rhythm is the only method of
birth control now sanctioned by the Roman Catholic Church. The basic idea
is to abstain from sexual relations during the several days each month when
a woman might be capable of conceiving. The difficulty is that this period is
often hard to determine, particularly in women with irregular menstrual
cycles. To avoid conception, the couple must abstain from coitus for at least
two days before and one-half day after ovulation. Unfortunately the occurrence of ovulation can be determined only after the event, and not too
accurately even then. When ovulation has taken place, the woman's temperature rises about half a degree and drops again when her menstrual period
begins. The time of ovulation must be predicted on the basis of carefully
kept records of her previous menstrual and temperature cycles. To allow an
adequate safety margin, several additional days should be included both before and after the estimated fertile period. Thus, the period of abstention
amounts to a considerable fraction of the month, to the inevitable detriment
of the conjugal relationship, especially since the fertile period may be a time

when the woman is relatively more receptive to sexual relations. What is worse, the rhythm method is one of the least effective of birth-control methods. Approximately one woman in six has a cycle so irregular that the system will not work at all for her. But the Church claims this is the only "natural" form of birth control, since it requires no mechanical devices or chemical solutions—a claim that neglects the necessary preoccupation with calendars, clocks, thermometers, pencils, and graphs.

## THE PILL

The modern steroid oral contraceptive, generally known as "the pill," is the most effective means of birth control generally available today, other than sterilization and abortion. When taken without fail according to instructions, it is virtually 100 percent effective.

The pill is composed of the female hormone estrogen and of progestin, a synthetic substance that is chemically similar to the natural progesterone produced by a woman's ovaries. This combination is believed to act by suppressing ovulation. The pill is taken daily for 20 or 21 days of the 28-day cycle, beginning on the fifth day after the onset of the menstrual period. The steroids may be administered sequentially or in a combined form. In the sequential system, the estrogen is administered alone during the early part of the cycle, with the progestin added only during the latter part. The pills have the effect of regularizing the menstrual cycle to exactly 28 days, even in women who have never had regular cycles before. Moreover, menstrual flow is noticeably reduced, or even occasionally suppressed altogether. Most women consider these effects advantageous.

As is inevitable with any drug, particularly a hormonal drug, there may be undesirable side-effects. Most of these, however, wear off within a few months or can be dealt with by adjusting the dosage or changing brands. Many of them resemble the symptoms of pregnancy, which in a sense is hormonally simulated in the woman's body by the progestin. The most common side-effects are tenderness and swelling of the breasts, weight gain and retention of fluid, nausea, headaches, depression, nervousness and irritability, changes in complexion, and bleeding. About one in four or five women taking the pill experiences one or more of these symptoms.

There are some indications that taking the pill for a long time may extend the period of a woman's sexual activity; in other words, a middle-aged woman who is using the pill may be as sexually active as a woman five years younger who is not on the pill. Some women may even find that they have increased libido. This reaction may simply be the result of not having to worry about pregnancy at the time of coitus, or it may have a hormonal basis.

The advantages of an oral contraceptive are obvious, even apart from the advantage offered by its effectiveness. Its use is far removed in time from the act of intercourse, and there are no mechanical devices or chemicals except the pill to deal with. On the other hand, the woman must remember to take it each day, which requires a fairly high degree of motivation. The chances of pregnancy increase with each forgotten pill.

In the course of up to seven years of testing on large numbers of women prior to its release to the public in 1962 in the United States and its use by millions since then, the pill has produced no serious medical problems for the overwhelming majority of women, although the results of using it over an entire reproductive span of 30 years or so are still unknown. Over the short term it is less dangerous than undergoing a pregnancy. Physicians generally do not prescribe the pill for women who have histories of liver disease, cancer, or thromboembolic diseases. Some kinds of liver disease are known to be aggravated by the hormones produced during pregnancy; the pill seems likely to have the same effect.

Whether the pill plays a role in inducing cancer is still unclear. Early results from a study sponsored by Planned Parenthood of New York were inconclusive. They showed that certain "precancerous" changes in the cervix were more common in women using oral contraceptives than in a control group using diaphragms. This difference remained even after various sociological differences between the two groups of women were accounted for. Nevertheless, the possibility remains that a diaphragm may constitute a positive protection against the "precancerous" condition. This condition, although it is known to precede the development of cancer of the cervix, does not always do so. Whether it would lead to cancer in women who use the pill remains unknown. In any case, the precancerous condition is easily and completely curable. Further studies are now under way in an effort to learn whether use of the pill can lead to cancer.

Another possible hazard, thromboembolism, also presents a complicated picture. Research published in England in 1968 revealed that women over the age of 35 who were using the pill had a significantly higher chance (8 per 200,000) of dying of thrombophlebitis (inflammation of veins together with blood clots) or pulmonary embolism (blood clots in the blood vessels of the lungs) than women of the same age who were not using the pill (1 in 200,000). The risk is less than one-half as high in either case for women under 35. In both age groups the risk of death from thromboembolic disease while using the pill is considerably less than that of death resulting from pregnancy: Demographer Charles Westoff has calculated that the risk of death from complications of pregnancy and childbirth to a population of women who switched from the pill to other, less effective forms of birth control, would be about three and a half times as high as the risk of death from thromboembolism incurred from using the pill. The estrogen component of the pill appears to be reponsible for development of these thromboembolic disorders. Newer versions contain lower doses of estrogen; these are being used exclusively in Britain now. Research in England indicates that this reduces the incidence of thrombosis by a quarter and deaths by half.

The Food and Drug Administration of the United States is currently sponsoring extensive research to find out more about this relationship. Meanwhile, it has required that the labels of the pills warn of possible hazard to women with a history of venous disorders, and has strongly recommended that doctors prescribe only low-estrogen pills.

Much more time will have to pass and much more data will have to be gathered before definite statements can be made about the risks of cancer and thromboembolism involved in the use of oral contraceptives. We are in somewhat the same position as we were when DDT first came into use. The risks must be weighed against the benefits, and the long-term risks are still unknown. From what we know now, it appears that for most women the benefits outweigh the risks; the latter can be minimized through close supervision by an alert physician. Obviously, continued monitoring of the long-term effects of the pill (or any future hormonal contraceptives) is essential.

### THE IUD

The intrauterine device, or IUD as it is generally known, is a plastic or metal object that is placed inside the uterus and left there for as long as contraception is desired. It comes in a variety of shapes, each having its own advantages and disadvantages relative to the others. The most commonly used include the loop, the ring, the spiral, and the bow (Fig. 9-1), although new styles are continually being developed.

That the presence of a foreign body in the uterus would act to prevent pregnancy has been known for a long time, and such devices have been used in animal husbandry. Only the more recently developed forms, made of plastic or flexible steel, have been considered reliable and safe enough to be used widely for humans. Exactly how these devices work is uncertain, but one possibility is that they prevent or disrupt the implantation of the embryo after conception, or they may interfere with fertilization by stimulating the ovum to travel very rapidly through the fallopian tubes. Recent research indicates that in human beings IUDs prevent implantation by changing the condition of the endometrium (lining of the uterus). The degree of this change, also reflected by the pregnancy rate, is proportional to the surface area of the device which can come in contact with the endometrium. Experiments with shield-shaped IUDs at Johns Hopkins Hospital showed that a closed shield gave best results with regard to pregnancy rates, expulsion rates, and other problems, when compared to open shield devices and older styles. The action appears to be the result both of mechanical action and low-level chemical interaction of the plastic material with the endometrial surface.

The advantages of an IUD for the user are several; the primary one is that once in place it can be forgotten. There are no pills to remember, no contraceptive materials to deal with. This is a great advantage for an individual whose lack of motivation, educational background, or financial resources would make other forms of birth control unreliable or beyond her means.

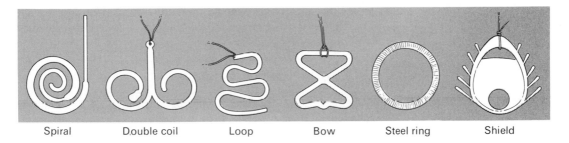

| Spiral | Double coil | Loop | Bow | Steel ring | Shield |

FIGURE 9-1

Various forms of IUDs.

The device costs only a few cents. It must be inserted and subsequently checked by a physician, or a paramedical person.

About 10 percent of women spontaneously expel the device, sometimes without knowing that they have. This tendency varies greatly with age and also with the number of children previously borne. Young women with no children are most likely to expel it; women over 35 with several children are least likely. Expulsion is most likely to occur during the first year of use, and the rate sharply declines thereafter.

For the woman who can successfully retain the IUD, it is a highly effective contraceptive, though the pill is more so when properly used. The pregnancy rate varies somewhat with size and type of IUD, and is higher among young women (as it is under any conditions.) The risk of pregnancy drops considerably after the first year of use and continues to drop for succeeding years.

Many women have to remove the IUD because of such side-effects as bleeding and pain. Some bleeding and discomfort are usual for a short time after insertion; but when these symptoms continue or are excessive, it is best to remove the IUD. Such problems usually disappear immediately after the device is taken out. Less frequently, the IUDs may be associated with pelvic inflammation, though there is some question whether the device is primarily responsible or only aggravates a pre-existing condition. There is no evidence that IUDs lead to the development of cancer. In very rare cases perforation of the uterus occurs. This happens most often with the bow-shaped device, and there is some evidence that it happens during insertion.

The IUD in its present stage of development is probably most suitable for women over 30 who have completed their families; they are least likely to have a birth control failure, to have problems with side-effects, or to expel the IUD.

The various methods of birth control are compared in Table 9-1. The effectiveness of techniques is calculated on the basis of 100 woman-years—that is, the number of women per hundred who will become pregnant in a one-year period while using a given method. Among 100 women using no contraception, 80 can expect to be pregnant by the end of one year. The failure rates are based on actual results, no distinction being made whether the method failed or the individuals were careless in using it. The lower rates are generally achieved by highly motivated individuals under close medical supervision.

TABLE 9-1
*Failure Rates of Contraceptive Methods*

| Method | Pregnancy rates for 100 woman-years of use | |
|---|---|---|
| | High | Low |
| No contraceptive | 80 | 80 |
| Aerosol foam | — | 29 |
| Foam tablets | 43 | 12 |
| Suppositories | 42 | 4 |
| Jelly or cream | 38 | 4 |
| Douche | 41 | 21 |
| Diaphragm and jelly | 35 | 4 |
| Sponge and foam powder | 35 | 28 |
| Condom | 28 | 7 |
| Coitus interruptus | 38 | 10 |
| Rhythm | 38 | 0 |
| Lactation | 26 | 24 |
| Steroid contraception (the "pill") | 2.7 | 0 |
| Abortion | 0 | 0 |
| Intrauterine contraception (averages) Lippes loop (large) | | |
| 0–12 months | 2.4 | |
| 12–24 months | 1.4 | |

SOURCE: After Berelson et al., *Family Planning and Population Programs,* University of Chicago Press, 1966.

## Sterilization

For couples whose families are complete and who wish to rid themselves of concern about contraceptives, sterilization is often the best solution. This procedure can be performed on either partner, but it is much simpler for the male. A vasectomy takes only fifteen or twenty minutes in a doctor's office. The procedure consists of cutting and tying off the vas deferens, thus making it impossible for sperm to be included in the ejaculate (although the absence of the sperm may be detected only by microscopic examination).

The female's operation, called a salpingectomy or tubal ligation, is more complicated, involving an internal surgical operation with the usual attendant risks. The abdomen must be opened under anesthesia and a section of the fallopian tubes cut and removed so that the ova cannot pass through. This operation is best done right after the birth of a baby, when the tubes are in a relatively accessible position. A new method, involving an approach through the vagina, is now being used by some doctors, and may prove to be superior and safer.

Contrary to the beliefs of many people, sterilization does not in any sense end one's sex life. Vasectomy is *not* castration. The hormonal system is left intact, and sperm are still manufactured by the body; they are simply prevented from leaving it. Sexual performance, including orgasm and ejaculation, is normally unchanged. In the few cases in which psychological problems develop, they usually are found to have grown out of previously existing disturbances. In many cases, psychological improvement is reported as worry over unwanted children ends.

The same is true for the female; her hormones still circulate, ova are still brought to maturity and released, the menstrual cycle goes on. All that is changed is that her ova never reach the uterus, nor can sperm travel up the fallopian tubes. Adverse psychological reactions to this operation on the part of the woman are extremely rare.

Many individuals hesitate to take so final a step as sterilization. Although in actual practice only a very small percentage of sterilized people ever ask to have the operation reversed, many want some assurance beforehand that it can be done. For men, successful reversal of the operation can now be achieved in 50 to 80 percent of cases. New methods of sterilization, notably one in which plastic plugs are inserted into the vas deferens, show promise of being virtually 100 percent reversible. The woman's operation can be reversed in 25 to 66 percent of the cases, but women are even less likely than men to request restoration of fertility.

For men who still have lingering doubts about taking the final step of sterilization, it is now possible to preserve a sample of sperm in a frozen sperm bank for up to 10 years. In the future this period can probably be extended. Thus, if a second wife years later wishes children, they can be provided by artificial insemination. Another possibility is that live sperm can be removed from the father's testes and used for insemination.

Sterilization is perfectly legal in the United States, although it is restricted in Utah to cases of "medical necessity." Nevertheless, in many places it is still difficult for an individual to find a doctor who is willing to perform these operations. Why the medical profession has until recently been so demonstrably reluctant is obscure. The obstacles that were raised to sterilization in one major city, San Francisco, are illustrated in the following passage in a letter from Mary Morain of the Association for Voluntary Sterilization in 1969:

> As Board member of the Association . . . I get weekly calls from people asking where they can find a doctor who will give them permanent birth control. The women are faced with a community-wide quota system by which medical committees in hospitals will not give a doctor permission to

'tie their tubes' unless of a certain age with a certain number of children. In San Francisco the *most liberal* standard is this: one must have had five children if one is under thirty, four children if thirty to thirty-four, three children if thirty-five and over. . . . The men have often been sent from pillar to post trying to find a doctor who will do a vasectomy for them.

She went on to mention the substantial "number of cases where couples want no children and for good reason." For these people it was virtually impossible to find help. There was more:

As it is we are forcing parenthood on the unwilling. This is even more striking in the County hospitals, many of which will not sterilize a woman no matter how many children she has had, and of most importance, no matter how much she begs for it.

Apparently many doctors have been reluctant to perform sterilizations because of a fear of lawsuits. The Attorney General's Office of the state of California in 1948 interpreted the performance of vasectomy as "possible mayhem" (originally defined as the rendering of a male unfit for service to his king), regardless of whether the customary release was signed by the patient. This resulted in the withdrawal by insurance companies of insurance coverage for doctors who performed vasectomies. The fact remains that no lawsuit over sterilization has ever been won in a case where a release had been signed. It is possible to protect doctors by law against suits over sterilization, although Virginia, Georgia, and North Carolina are the only states that have made such positive protection available. California law has since been clarified, insurance is now obtainable, and vasectomies are widely available and are often covered by the state's medical insurance plan.

In July 1969 the California District Court of Appeals ruled that "nontherapeutic surgical sterilization was legal in this state where competent consent has been given." The decision was rendered in the case of a couple who desired no more children than they had, but the husband had been denied a vasectomy by a hospital. Similar lawsuits in other states have followed.

Since 1969 hospital restrictions against sterilizations have been loosened to a considerable degree in many states, and many more doctors have begun accepting sterilization requests. National publicity about vasectomies has resulted in a spectacular increase in the number of men obtaining them. A medical survey revealed that 750,000 men in the United States received vasectomies in 1970, approximately a seven-fold increase in only a few years. The expectation for 1971 is even higher. The rate for female sterilization is about one-third as high.

Although many hospitals and many doctors still refuse to cooperate, voluntary sterilization is far more obtainable than in the recent past. Population organizations such as Planned Parenthood, the Association for Voluntary Sterilization, and Zero Population Growth frequently refer individuals seeking these procedures to doctors and clinics where they can be helped. By 1971 there were 38 vasectomy clinics operating in the United States.

# Abortion

In much of the world, induced abortion is illegal. Where it is legal, it is often permitted only under rather strictly defined conditions. Nevertheless, abortion is believed to be the commonest form of birth control in all parts of the world, even in many countries where modern contraceptives are readily available.

Abortion is the arrest of a pregnancy. The medically approved method of inducing abortion in the early stages is through a simple operation known as dilation and curettage (scraping) of the uterus, which removes and destroys the fetus. This is preferably done no later than the 12th week of pregnancy. After the 16th week the procedure is considerably more complicated. A newer, evidently safer method for the early months involving the use of a vacuum device in place of curettage was invented in China and further developed in the USSR. This device is being generally used in many eastern European countries, China, the Soviet Union, England, and has been introduced in the United States and Japan.

When performed under appropriate medical circumstances by a qualified physician, abortion is safer than a full-term pregnancy, but if it is delayed beyond the 12th week, the risks of complications or death rise considerably. Similarly, the risks increase when the abortion is illegal, the amount of increase depending upon the circumstances. These may range from self-inducement with a knitting needle or—almost equally dangerous—unsterile help from untrained or semitrained people to reasonably safe treatment by a physician in a hotel room or a clandestine clinic. In the United States, as in many parts of the world, bungled illegal abortions have been the greatest single cause of maternal deaths, accounting for between 400 and 1,000 deaths per year.

Abortion is practiced in some form in all societies today, and there are records of it throughout history. Disapproval of the practice originated with the Judeo-Christian ethic, yet abortion was not made illegal until the nineteenth century, when it was outlawed on the grounds that it was dangerous to the mother, which it was in those days before sterile medical techniques. Today, even in the countries with the most liberal abortion laws, a woman must go through the legal procedure of applying for and receiving official sanction before she can have an abortion. This is the situation in China, Japan, several countries in eastern Europe, and a few states in the U.S. where abortion is essentially available on request. Rumania and Bulgaria, alarmed at very low birth rates, which were due at least in part to the ease of obtaining an abortion, have recently tightened their regulations. Hungary's abortion rate in 1969 was higher than its birth rate, which suggests that it must be the primary method of fertility control in that country. The U.S.S.R., after several post-revolution population policy changes, now has liberal abortion policies, but does not advertise the fact. Until 1968, the U.S.S.R. did not permit the use of the pill. Now the pill is being used on an experimental basis only, but eventually it will probably be available to all women who want it.

Scandinavian countries and, since 1968, England, have fairly liberal abortion policies, allowing it under a wide range of medical, psychological, and social conditions. However, it is by no means simply granted on request.

By the middle of 1971, most of the United States, virtually all of Latin America, most Asian countries, and southern and western Europe still had very restrictive abortion laws. It was allowed, if at all, only when the mother's life was threatened. However, this situation may change rapidly in the next few years. India legalized abortion in 1971, and some other countries may follow suit, either to ease their population pressures or to put an end to the tragic deaths from botched illegal abortions.

Illegal abortions can probably be obtained in every country in the world. They are most prevalent where laws are most restrictive. In Italy, where contraceptives have been strictly prohibited, the abortion rate is estimated to be nearly equal to the birth rate. Many of these are self-inflicted or accomplished with the aid of an untrained but sympathetic friend. When a woman with hemorrhage is brought to a hospital, she is automatically given tetanus and penicillin shots. She will never admit having had an abortion; under Italian law she has committed a crime and could be sent to prison. Death is estimated to result from about 4 percent of Italian abortions. Some years ago, in a confidential survey of 4,000 married women of all classes, all admitted to having had abortions, most of them not once but many times. The pill is now available on prescription for "medical reasons," and a family planning clinic has opened in Rome. It is to be hoped that this new availability of birth control will have an effect on the appalling rate of medically unsupervised abortions.

In France, contraceptives can be purchased, but their advertisement and the dissemination of information about them are prohibited. Those women pregnant with an unwanted child who cannot afford to visit a Swiss clinic abort themselves in secret, concealing their action even from their husbands. If things go wrong, they often wait too long before seeking medical help for fear of being found out. The result is that France has an even higher rate of death and permanent injury than would exist if help were sought promptly. A movement is now underway to loosen restrictions on birth control and also to legalize abortion. Over 300 prominent French women in April 1971 published a statement that they had had illegal abortions. Early attempts to initiate liberal legislation in France have met with a good deal of opposition from the Catholic Church and some elements of the medical profession. Unfortunately, when nearly 400 West German women attempted a similar public confession, the authorities prepared to take action. In either country women who have had abortions are liable to prison terms of several years.

Illegal abortion is rampant in Latin America. Contraceptives, though legally available, are actually obtainable only by the rich in most places. The poor and ignorant, who make up the bulk of the population in most Latin American countries, are generally unaware of the existence of birth control other than by ancient folk methods, and could not afford modern methods even if they knew of them. There are exceptions to this where governments and volunteer organizations such as Planned Parenthood have established free birth control clinics. Although these help, they as yet reach only a small fraction of the population. In areas where hunger and malnutrition are widespread, a failure of primitive birth control methods leaves women with no alternative but to practice equally crude forms of abortion.

Bungled abortions have been estimated to account for more than 40 percent of hospital admissions in Santiago, Chile. In that country, an estimated one-third of all pregnancies end in abortion. For South America as a whole, some authorities believe that one-fourth of all pregnancies end in abortion. Other estimates are that abortions outnumber pregnancies brought to term.

In the U.S., ten states had moderated their abortion laws by the end of 1969. These new laws permit abortion in cases where bearing the child presents a grave risk to the mental or physical health of the mother, where the pregnancy is a result of incest or rape, and where (except in California) there is a substantial likelihood that the child will be physically or mentally defective. To obtain an abortion, a woman usually had to submit her case to a hospital reviewing board of physicians, a time-consuming and expensive process. Although the laws were relaxed to reduce the problem of illegal abortions, hospital boards in general interpreted the changes in the law so conservatively that they had little effect. The number of illegal abortions per year in the U.S. during the 1960s has been variously estimated at between 200,000 and 2 million, with one million being the most often quoted figure. This amounts to more than one abortion for every four births. At that time, there were estimated to be 120,000 illegal abortions per year in California; in the first year after passage of the "liberalized" law there were just over 2,000 legal ones. The figures were similar for the other states.

During 1970 seven more states and the District of Columbia liberalized their abortion laws. Three states, Hawaii, Alaska, and New York, now essentially have abortion on request, although Hawaii and Alaska have residency requirements. Washington State, interestingly, accomplished its abortion on request (up to the 16th week) not by legislation, but by a referendum. Meanwhile, several states which had partially liberalized their laws, such as California and Kansas, began to interpret their laws much more liberally, and the legal abortion rate rose considerably. In California there were over 135,000 legal abortions in 1971, a rate slightly higher than the estimated previous rate of illegal abortions.

The suddenly liberalized law in New York at first created some special problems. Because there was no residency requirement, more than half of the women seeking abortions were out-of-state residents. But after the first few weeks, New York's hospitals and clinics proved able to cope with the demand. The law allows abortions up to 24 weeks, but the trend has been for an increasing majority to be done in the first 12, when it can be done on an outpatient basis using the vacuum technique. One of the greatest problems was the development of profit-making abortion referral agencies.

Some of their high fees inflated the costs of abortion, which ranged from $100 to $1,000, depending on various factors. These agencies were banned in 1971.

The controversy about abortion in New York was certainly not ended by passage of the law. Anti-abortion groups have lobbied to have the law tightened up (similar attempts have been made in California), while pro-abortion groups want it further liberalized. The latter groups maintain that the poor in particular still meet too many obstacles to abortion in the form of red tape and high costs. However, the availability of Medicaid and other insurance plans to cover costs seems to compensate. During the first six months, nearly half of the abortions were obtained by low-income women.

In the first year there were 200,000 legal abortions in New York, most of them in New York City. It is evident that the number of illegal abortions must have been comparatively very low, if there were any at all. The New York maternal death rates, which include those from abortion, dropped by more than one-half. The number of illegitimate births also declined, as did the birth rate overall for the state. There were only 15 deaths, some of which were from illegal abortions, and all of which occurred in the first eight months after the law was passed. The death rate is expected to remain very low.

The greatest obstacles to freely available, medically safe abortion in most countries are the Roman Catholic Church and other religious groups that consider abortion immoral. The crux of the Catholic argument is that the embryo is, from the moment of conception, a complete individual with a soul. In the Catholic view, induced abortion amounts to murder. Some Catholics also oppose abortion on the grounds that it will encourage promiscuity—exactly the same reason given in Japan for banning the pill and the IUD. There is no evidence to support either point of view on promiscuity, but even if there were an increase it would be a small price to pay for a chance to ameliorate the mass misery of unwanted pregnancies.

Many Protestant theologians hold that the time when a child acquires a soul is unknown and perhaps unimportant. They see no difficulty in establishing it at the time of "quickening," when movements of the fetus first become discernible to the mother; or at the time, around 28 weeks, when the infant, if prematurely born, could survive outside its mother's body. To them, the evil of abortion is far outweighed by the evil of bringing into the world an unwanted child under less than ideal circumstances.

To a biologist the question of when life begins for a human child is almost meaningless, since life is continuous and has been since it first began on Earth several billion years ago. The precursors of the egg and sperm cells that create the next generation have been present in the parents from the time they were embryos themselves. To most biologists, an embryo or a fetus is no more a complete human being than a blueprint is a complete building. The fetus, given the opportunity to develop properly before birth, and given the essential early socializing experiences and sufficient nourishing food during the crucial early years after birth, will ultimately develop into a human being. Where any of these is lacking, the resultant individual will be deficient in some respect. From this point of view, a fetus is only a *potential* human being, with no particular rights. Historically the law has dated most rights and privileges from the moment of birth, and legal scholars generally agree that a fetus is not a "person" within the meaning of the United States Constitution until it is born and living independent of its mother.

From the standpoint of a terminated fetus, it makes no difference whether the mother had an induced or a spontaneous abortion. On the other hand, it subsequently makes a great deal of difference to the child if an abortion is denied and the mother, contrary to her wishes, is forced to devote her body and life to the production and care of the child. In Sweden, studies were made to determine what eventually happened to children born to mothers whose requests for abortions had been turned down. When compared to a matched group of children from similar backgrounds who had been wanted, more than twice as many of these unwanted youngsters grew up in undesirable circumstances (illegitimate, in broken homes, or in institutions), more than twice as many had records of delinquency, or were deemed unfit for military service, almost twice as many had needed psychiatric care, and nearly five times as many had been on public assistance during their teens.

There seems little doubt that the forced bearing of unwanted children has undesirable consequences not only for the children themselves and their families, but for society as well, apart from the problems of over-population. The latter factor, however, adds further urgency to the need for alleviating the other situations. An abortion is clearly preferable to adding an additional child to an overburdened family or an overburdened society, where the chances that it will realize its full potentialities are slight. The argument that a decision is being made for an unborn person who "has no say" is often raised by those opposing abortion. But unthinking actions of the very same people help to commit future unheard generations to misery and early death on an overcrowded planet. One can also challenge the notion that older men, be they medical doctors, legislators, or celibate clergymen, have the right to make decisions whose consequences are borne largely by young women and their families.

There are those who claim that free access to abortion will lead to genocide. It is hard to see how this could happen if the decision is left to the mother. A mother who takes the moral view that abortion is equivalent to murder is free to bear her child. If she cannot care for it, placement for adoption is still possible.

Few people would claim that abortion is preferable to contraception, not only because of moral questions, but also because the risk of death or injury to the mother is usually greater. But large and rapidly growing numbers of people feel that abortion is vastly preferable to the births of unwanted children, especially in an overpopulated world. Until a far more effective form of contraception than we now have is developed, abortion will remain a common method of birth control when contraceptives fail.

Attitudes on abortion have changed before, and they can reasonably be expected to change again in the future. Indeed, polls taken in the United States indicate that the attitudes of Americans changed significantly between 1962 and 1969 (Table 9-2). These polls, conducted at the request of University of California demographer Judith Blake, revealed that within a period of

TABLE 9-2

*Change in Disapproval of Abortion (all white respondents)*

| Reason for abortion | Percentage of disapproval | | | |
|---|---|---|---|---|
| | *1962* | *1965* | *1968* | *1969* |
| Mother's health endangered | 16 | 15 | 10 | 13 |
| Child may be deformed | 29 | 31 | 25 | 25 |
| Can't afford child | 74 | 74 | 72 | 68 |
| No more children wanted | — | — | 85 | 79 |

SOURCE: Judith Blake, Abortion & Public Opinion, *Science* 171: pp. 540–549.

seven years, disapproval of abortion for various reasons declined by from 3 to 8 percentage points. Those who disapproved of abortion to save the mother's life or because the child was likely to be deformed were a very small minority, but from 70 to 80 percent still disapproved of abortion for such social reasons as not wanting or being unable to afford another child. Disapproval tended to be lowest among those with more education and higher incomes, non-Catholics, residents of the Northeast and the West, and younger people. It also was lower among men in most groups than among women. Disapproval seems to be highest among the least-educated, low-income groups. Among non-Catholics, disapproval also seems to be relatively high among fundamentalist, conservative elements of Protestantism. Catholics in general are more disapproving than non-Catholics, but the difference is not great and is diminishing over time. Catholic disapproval is correlated with age, sex, and education, in ways similar to non-Catholics.

Polls taken early in 1970 asked a somewhat different question: Should an abortion be available to any woman who requests one? In apparent contradiction to the earlier opinions, more than half of those interviewed said yes. Although they did not approve of abortion except for the more serious reasons, such as danger to the mother, rape, incest, or the possibility of a deformed child, the majority apparently felt that mothers should be free to make their own decisions.

Continuing this trend, a poll conducted in 1971 for the U.S. Commission on Population Growth and the American Future found that 50 percent of the adults interviewed felt that the decision to have an abortion should be made by the woman and her doctor, 41 percent would permit abortions under certain circumstances, and only 6 percent opposed abortion under all circumstances.

The same poll revealed widespread awareness and concern about the population problem.

In a democratic country such as the United States, there is good reason to question the legality of denying women the right of access to abortion. The American Civil Liberties Union (ACLU) raised this question late in 1968, taking the stand that present laws infringe women's civil liberties, and later that they are unconstitutional because they are based on Roman Catholic dogma. The ACLU maintains that judgments on the morality of abortion "belong solely in the province of individual conscience and religion." At about the same time, the American Public Health Association's governing council and the Planned Parenthood Federation both made public announcements in favor of completely unrestricted access to abortion.

The female half of the world's population has already cast its silent vote. Every year perhaps one million women in the United States, and an estimated 30 to 40 million more elsewhere, make their desires abundantly clear by seeking and obtaining abortions, more often than not in the face of their societies' disapproval and of very real dangers and difficulties.

## Possibilities for the Future

Many possible ways of interfering with the reproductive process have yet to be explored; some of the most promising of these are under investigation in laboratories or are being tested clinically in humans. Within the next decade or two a variety of new methods of birth control should become available for general use. Some of the methods currently being developed show considerable promise as practical approaches for population control in underdeveloped countries, where only the simplest and cheapest methods are likely to result in a substantial lowering of birth rates. Most of the new contraceptives are designed for women, and some are extensions of the research that produced the pill.

### PROGESTINS

Among the developments most likely to prove useful soon are various forms of low, continuous dosages of the steroid progestin. Unlike the higher dosage of progestin combined with estrogen in the present pill, the low dosages do not suppress ovulation. Exactly how the progestin does act is still uncertain, but it appears to be potentially as effective a contraceptive as the pill. It is known to alter the consistency of the mucus of the cervical canal, a change that may prevent the penetration of the uterus by the sperm; it affects the lining of the uterus in a way that may prevent implantation; and it also may cause the ovum to travel too rapidly down the fallopian tubes. It may also inhibit gonadotropic hormones. It is possible that all of these factors may operate to prevent conception.

The use of progestin alone has the advantage of avoiding some of the more dangerous aspects of the pill, such as the increased risks of thrombo-embolism and liver diseases that seem to be associated with the estrogen component. But some side-effects do appear. Some women have complained of headaches and dizziness. A more serious drawback seems to be a tendency toward irregular bleeding and amenorrhea (absence of menstruation).

Very large study programs involving thousands of women around the world have now been carried out with two forms of low dose progestins: a "mini-pill," taken daily with no "time off" to keep track of; and intra-muscular injections at three-month or six-month intervals. The mini-pill has been tested clinically in the U.S., England, and other countries, but several more years of testing will be required before it can be released to the general public. But the mini-pill program has been set back somewhat by the discovery that some progestins caused mammary nodules in beagles which were being used for long-term testing. Since beagles are much more highly prone to develop mammary tumors than are humans, it is not clear how serious this is. Presumably the answer awaits further testing on beagles and a variety of other experimental animals. Meanwhile, the clinical tests have been halted.

The three-month injections of progestins are now in use in over 50 countries around the world, including the U.S., in clinical studies. In 1971 tests were scheduled for the six-month injections. This method of birth control appears to be particularly useful as a post-partum contraceptive to provide spacing between children, as it does not interfere with lactation. Several UDCs, particularly Egypt, are interested in the method on this basis. The International Planned Parenthood Federation is also using the injections in clinics around the world.

Both the mini-pill and injections produce the side-effects of irregular bleeding and amenorrhea, which is disturbing to some women, although the bleeding usually disappears after a few months. This problem can be controlled by administering very small doses of estrogen for a few days each month.

Another way of administering progestin is the "time capsule," which can be implanted under the skin by a hypodermic needle. The material of which the capsule is made—a silicone rubber known as Silastic—releases the steroid at a constant rate over a long period of time, potentially as long as 25 or 30 years. Its effect is completely reversible by removal. The time capsule is now being clinically tested and should be generally available within a few years if it proves successful.

Another version of the continuous low dosage progestin is the vaginal ring. This device fits over the cervix like a diaphragm, but rather than blocking the entrance it slowly releases progestin into the surrounding tissues. It needs replacement only once a month.

Progestin administered in low dosages in any of the ways discussed above shares with the progestin-estrogen pill the advantages of high effectiveness and convenience of use, and has the additional advantages of being far less complicated to use (especially the implanted capsule) and avoiding the hazards of estrogen. It is quite likely that all these forms will be considerably less expensive, at least by the time they can be used in large quantities. If long-term testing does not turn up some new and unanticipated difficulty, progestin holds considerable promise as an agent for effective population control.

### THE MORNING-AFTER PILL

"Morning-after" birth control consists in taking a substantial oral dose of estrogens within a few days after coitus. Pregnancy is prevented, but the woman usually feels quite sick for a day or two. It is therefore not suitable for regular use, at least in this form. This method is still being clinically tested, but is available in some medical centers in the U.S.

### PROSTAGLANDINS

One of the newest and most fascinating developments in the drug business has been the discovery of prostaglandins, a group of hormone-like substances related to fatty acids and normally found in many mammalian tissues. About 14 different prostaglandins have been discovered so far. Their natural function appears to be the local regulation of hormones in cells and organs, although much remains to be learned about them. Various prostaglandins have been found to be useful in treating such diverse ailments as peptic ulcers, thrombosis, hypertension, asthma, and nasal congestion. In addition, they are useful in a variety of areas related to reproduction, as in treatment of male sterility, dismenorrhea (painful menstruation), and for induction of labor, apparently at any stage of pregnancy. They also show interesting promise as a form of birth control. In the very early stages (two weeks) of pregnancy, intravenous injections of prostaglandins seem to cause regression of the corpus luteum, which in turn prevents maintenance of the pregnancy. Its action is therefore actually aborifacient. This new method is still in the early stages of development, but experimental work with women is being carried on in Sweden, the U.S., Chile, and Uganda. In Sweden, intravenous infusions are given at the time of a missed period to induce menses. Some experimentation is also being done with oral and vaginal applications. If either of these methods proves successful, prostaglandins may become a safe, self-administered form of birth control, whose use would probably not be required more than a few times a year.

Some temporary side-effects have been reported in some cases with prostaglandins, usually consisting of nausea, diarrhea, or headaches. It is hoped that further development can reduce or eliminate their incidence. Of course it is far too early to know what if any long-term effects will attend the use of prostaglandins, and many years of research lie ahead before they will be generally available. Nevertheless, they are one of the most promising new developments.

## OTHER CHEMICAL METHODS

A variety of chemicals are in the process of being tested on laboratory animals, in the hope of finding some that will not have the drawbacks of the steroid compounds. But since many seem to act by influencing some part of the natural hormone system, it is not too surprising that similar side-effects have occurred in association with some of them. Nevertheless, these possibilities, which have only begun to be investigated, deserve careful examination.

At least one folk-method of contraception is being looked into. A South American weed, *Stevia rebaudiana,* has traditionally been used by the Indians in Paraguay as a contraceptive. Each day the women drink a cup of water in which the powdered weed has been boiled. Experiments with rats have indicated a reduction in fertility of from 57 to 79 percent compared with a control group, with low fertility lasting up to two months after withdrawal of the drug. Undoubtedly many such folk-methods are known in various human cultures. Some of them may be quite effective and might prove adaptable to the urgent need for population control, particularly in underdeveloped countries.

Some other new ideas being tested in laboratories are more sophisticated versions of contraceptives already in use. These include long-lasting spermicidal creams, removable blocks for the Fallopian tubes, a version of the vaginal ring that releases a spermicide, and IUDs that release hormones or other substances such as copper. There are also experiments on immunizing a woman against her husband's sperm and others on enzymes or chemicals that decapacitate sperm. While many of these ideas may prove impractical for one reason or another, others may ultimately be developed into useful additions to the contraceptive arsenal.

## METHODS FOR MEN

Attempts to find steroid or other chemical forms of contraceptives for men have so far been remarkably unsuccessful. Usually these are aimed at reducing or interfering with spermatogenesis. Several of them have proven to be incompatible with the consumption of alcoholic drinks, a serious drawback in most societies. When progestins were administered to volunteers, spermatogenesis was suppressed, but so was the production of the male sex hormone testosterone.

A nonsteroid chemical derived from the manufacture of dynamite is now being tested in rats. So far no untoward side-effects have shown up, and the chemical seems to have no effect on sexual behavior or desire, nor to interfere with spermatogenesis. But somehow the sperm are rendered incapable of fertilizing the ova.

Two removable mechanical devices, now only in the experimental stage, hold promise as means of reversible sterilization. One, invented by an Indian physician, consists of a clip that can be attached to the vas deferens. The other is a plastic or silicone plug that can be inserted in the vas deferens. Not only could these new devices be used as temporary contraceptives, but they also would satisfy the objections to sterilization from those who fear taking an irreversible step. Unfortunately, sometimes the vas remains permanently closed if the clip is removed after a long period of time. The plugs sometimes have the opposite drawback. The vas may expand so that sperm can pass through, or the plug may eventually deteriorate. The technique shows promise, however, and the plugs are now being tested in human volunteers by the Association for Voluntary Sterilization.

Research is also proceeding along some lines parallel with that for contraceptives for women. Immunizing men against their own sperm would theoretically be a way to halt production. However, this possibility will require many years to develop, if it is even feasible. Another idea is to give men a hormone implant which would suppress sperm production over a period of time.

It appears that the present emphasis on contraceptives for the female will continue for some time in the future, since research on male methods is so far behind in development.

## Research and Development

In the light of the current world population situation, it is clear that research on means of birth control has been neglected for too long. Although some promising projects and possibilities for birth control have come out of recent research, it is obvious that we are still several years away from having the means at hand to help make significant rapid reductions in the birth rates among uneducated and poorly motivated populations. Progress in research is further being hampered in the U.S. and some other DCs by the stringent regulations imposed on human research by such agencies as the Food and Drug Administration. In the U.S., a *minimum* of 8 to 10 years of testing is required before a new contraceptive agent can be released for human use, although limited, short-term clinical testing on humans can begin soon after early tests in animals have been completed. The restrictions on clinical trials in the U.S. and many other DCs (who follow FDA guidelines rather closely) are the reason that so many new contraceptive agents are being clinically tested in UDCs such as Mexico, Chile, and Uganda. Since contraceptive chemicals, unlike most other drugs, are intended for continuous or regular use over long periods of time, perhaps decades, by large numbers of people, the need for exhaustive testing is genuine. But there is no question that it requires a great deal of time and vast quantities of money. As DC laboratories are the best equipped and funded for such research, some changes in the regulations will be needed if they are to make a substantial contribution to population control efforts in the next decade or two.

Chemist Carl Djerassi of Stanford University and Syntex Corporation, who is actively involved in contraceptive research, has offered some proposals to help stimulate such development. Until recently, the costs of developing new contraceptives have been borne almost entirely by the pharmaceutical companies which ultimately market them. But increasingly stringent testing requirements that prolong the development phase and escalate costs are threatening to discourage these companies from embarking on such programs. As an example of the time and funds needed, Djerassi has outlined a project for the development of a male antifertility agent, which would require from 12 to 20 years and between $6 and $18 million to complete. The U.S. government has only begun to allocate funds for contraceptive research, and the amounts so far are only a fraction of what drug companies were spending during the late 1960s. An amount approximately equivalent to the government's is being spent on contraceptive research by various private foundations.

On the assumption that the drug industry, which already has the facilities and personnel, will continue to conduct the bulk of the contraceptive development programs, Djerassi makes the following proposals to stimulate research and accelerate the appearance of new birth control agents:

1. That the FDA establish a period of "conditional approval" for a new agent following a briefer period of clinical testing than is now allowed. During this period of conditional approval, while the agent is marketed, careful follow-up studies of users can be conducted. This would allow for earlier discovery of any low-level side-effects (such as thromboembolism with the pill) which would only show up in a large drug-using population. The shortened clinical studies would still be ample for finding grosser problems.

2. That there be an appeal procedure established for agents that are turned down by the FDA. Such a procedure does not now exist and often results in discontinuance of some potentially valuable projects.

3. That patent protection be extended for new contraceptive agents. With long-term testing periods, patents today often expire soon after a drug reaches the market, which prevents the drug company from recovering the money it invested in developing the product.

4. That the government participate in some of the development costs of contraceptive agents. Besides the conditional approval arrangement, government grants could subsidize some phases of the research, to be repaid by royalties if and when the product was marketed.

Djerassi warns that, unless some incentives such as these are soon established to encourage research and development in the birth control field, new contraceptive agents will be delayed in their appearance on the market even beyond the middle 1980s. In view of the world's need for cheap, simple, and effective means of birth control, the U.S. and other DCs must bend every effort to encourage their development.

# Bibliography

Anonymous, 1968. Emboli and "the pill"—FDA study seeks answers. *Medical World News,* Dec. 6.

Anonymous, 1968. IUDs challenge status of the pill. *Medical World News,* Sept. 20.

Anonymous, 1968. Sterilization fears seem unfounded. *New Scientist,* May 16.

Anonymous, 1970. Prostaglandins. *Medical World News,* Aug. 28:

Anonymous, 1971, Voluntary sterilization. *Consumer Reports,* June, pp. 384–386.

Association for Voluntary Sterilization, 14 W. 40th St., New York, N.Y. Source of much information on sterilization.

Berelson, Bernard, et al., 1966. Family Planning and Population Programs. Univ. of Chicago Press, Chicago. Contains some information on the various birth control methods and their application in different countries.

Blake, Judith, 1971. Abortion and public opinion: the 1960–1970 decade, *Science,* vol. 171, pp. 540–549 (12 Feb.). Documents change in American attitudes toward abortion.

Calderone, Mary S., 1970. *Manual of Family Planning and Contraceptive Practice.* Williams & Wilkins Co., Baltimore. This book includes material on the U.S. family planning movement and the medical, health, social, and educational aspects of birth control. Much more useful than just as a guide.

Djerassi, Carl, 1969. Prognosis for the development of new birth-control agents. *Science,* vol. 166, pp. 468–473 (24 Oct.).

Djerassi, Carl, 1970. Birth control after 1984. *Science,* vol. 169, pp. 941–951 (4 Sept.). Discussion of current state of contraceptive development and suggestions of how the U.S. government might facilitate such development.

Editorial, 1968. Voluntary male sterilization. *Journal of the American Medical Association,* vol. 204, no. 9.

Gilmore, C. P., 1969. Something better than the pill. *New York Times Magazine,* July 20.

Goodhart, C. B., 1965. Criminal abortion in the USA. *Eugenics Review,* vol. 57, no. 2, p. 98.

Goodhart, C. B., 1966. How many illegal abortions? *New Society,* 10 Nov.

Guttmacher, Alan F., 1966. *The Complete Book of Birth Control.* Ballantine Books, New York. Revised. Clear description of all presently used methods of birth control.

Hardin, Garrett, 1966. *Biology: Its Principles and Implications.* W. H. Freeman and Company, San Francisco. Contains a good account of human reproductive physiology.

Hardin, Garrett, 1966. The history and future of birth control. *Perspectives in Biology and Medicine,* vol. 10, no. 1 (Autumn). Contains some interesting historical data.

Hardin, Garrett, 1968. Abortion—compulsory pregnancy? *Journal of Marriage and Family,* vol. XXX, no. 2. Discussion of abortion from a biologist's point of view.

Hardin, Garrett, 1970. *Birth Control.* Pegasus, New York. Excellent up-to-date discussion.

Huldt, Lars, 1968. Outcome of pregnancy when legal abortion is readily available. *Current Medical Digest,* vol. XXXV, no. 5 (May), pp. 586–594.

International Planned Parenthood, 1967. *Victor Fund Report,* no. 6, Summer. Some data on abortions.

Kalman, Sumner M., 1967. Modern Methods of Contraception. *Bulletin of the Santa Clara County* (California) *Medical Society,* March.

Kalman, Sumner M., 1969. Effects of oral contraceptives. *Annual Review of Pharmacology,* vol. 9, pp. 363–378. A good discussion of the hazards associated with the pill.

Lader, Lawrence, 1966. *Abortion.* Beacon Press, Boston.

Lader, Lawrence, 1969. Non-hospital abortions. *Look,* Jan. 21.

Loraine, J. A., 1970. *Sex and the Population Crisis,* Wm. Heinemann Medical Books, Ltd., Surrey, England. A book on contraception in the context of the population explosion.

Lowe, David, 1966. *Abortion and the Law.* Pocket Books, New York.

Moody, Howard, 1968. Protest. *Glamour,* April. A Protestant view of abortion.

Peel, John, and Malcolm Potts, 1969. *Textbook of Contraceptive Practice.* Cambridge Univ. Press. Fairly technical.

Pilpel, Harriet, 1969. The right of abortion. *Atlantic,* June, The ethical and legal problems of abortion.

Pincus, G., 1966. Control of conception by hormonal steroids. *Science,* vol. 153, pp. 493–500. Based on early studies with the pill.

Planas, G. M., and Joseph Kuc, 1968. Contraceptive properties of *Stevia rebaudiana. Science,* vol. 162, p. 1007. Exploring a folk method of birth control.

Population Council, New York. *Studies in Family Planning.* A monthly series. Many contain evaluations of birth control methods.

Ransil, Bernard J., 1969. *Abortion.* Paulist Press Deus Books, New York. Serious discussion of the moral aspects of abortion, written by a Catholic M.D.

Schwartz, Herman, 1967. The parent or the fetus? *Humanist,* July–August. A discussion of legal and ethical aspects of abortion.

Schwartz, Richard A., 1968. Psychiatry and the abortion laws: an overview. *Comprehensive Psychiatry,* vol. 9, no. 2 (March), pp. 99–117.

Segal, Sheldon, 1969. Contraceptive technology: current and prospective methods. *Reports on Population/Family Planning,* Population Council, October.

Soichct, Samuel, 1969. Depo-provera (Medroxyprogerone acetate) as a female contraceptive agent, *International Journal of Fertility,* vol. 14, pp. 33–38 (Jan.–Mar.). On an injectable progestin.

Szasz, T. S., 1966. The ethics of abortion. *Humanist,* Sept.–Oct.

Tietze, Christopher, and Sarah Lewit, 1969. Abortion. *Scientific American,* vol. 220, no. 1 (Jan.). Good general discussion, including some public opinion survey results.

Westoff, L. A., and C. F. Westoff, 1971. *From Now to Zero: Fertility, Contraception and Abortion in America.* Little, Brown & Co., Boston. A comprehensive account of family planning attitudes and practices in the U.S.

Wood, H. Curtis, Jr., 1967. *Sex Without Babies.* Whitmore Publishing Co., Philadelphia. A complete review of voluntary sterilization.

World Health Organization, 1966. Basic and clinical aspects of intrauterine devices. *Technical Report,* no. 332.

World Health Organization, 1966. Clinical aspects of oral gestogens. *Technical Report,* no. 326. Slightly out-of-date analysis of the pill.

World Health Organization, 1967. Biology of fertility control by periodic abstinence. *Technical Report,* no. 360. A study of the rhythm method.

Zañartu, J., 1968. A new approach to fertility control: long-acting injectable progestogens. *Advances in Fertility Control,* vol. 3, no. 3 (Sept.).

Zanetti, L., 1966. The shame of Italy. *Atlas,* Aug. On the abortion problem in Italy.

# CHAPTER 10

# Family Planning and Population Control

*"A common stratagem of those who wish to escape
the swirling currents of change is to stand
on high moral ground."*

—John Gardner
*Self-Renewal: The Individual and
the Innovative Society,* 1964

What is being done in the world today to limit human population size? This chapter considers possible ways in which today's efforts could be converted to genuine population control. Considerable emphasis is placed on family planning programs, since these are now the only programs in existence that claim to have as a goal the regulation of human numbers. However, *family planning and population control are not synonymous.*

## Family Planning in the DCs

At the time of the Industrial Revolution in England an early advocate of limiting the size of families through contraception was labor leader Francis Place. Realizing that a limited labor pool would be likelier to win high wages and better working conditions from employers than would a plentiful supply of workers, Place set forth his views in writings that reached large numbers of people. His original treatise, *Illustrations and Proofs of the Principle of*

*Population,* was published in 1822. It was followed by a series of handbills that urged birth control in the interest of better economic and physical health and also described various contraceptive methods. Additional books on birth control appeared both in England and the United States during the 1830s and continued to circulate until the 1870s, when legal attempts were made to suppress them in both countries. The attempt failed in England, but in the United States the "Comstock Law" was passed by Congress in 1873. It forbade the dissemination by mail of birth control information, classing it with "obscene literature." Many states also passed laws against birth control literature, known as "little Comstock laws," and in 1890, importation of such literature was outlawed.

America's heroine in the family planning movement was Margaret Sanger, a nurse. She has described the incident that triggered her commitment to what became a lifelong cause. In 1912, she and a doctor were called to attend a mother of three who had performed an abortion on herself and had very nearly died. After some weeks of care the woman recovered, but the doctor warned her that another abortion would kill her. The woman understood, and asked the doctor how she could prevent another baby. The doctor's reply was: "You can't have your cake and eat it too, young woman. There's only one way. Tell Jake to sleep on the roof." Three months later the woman was dead of another self-induced abortion.

Within a very few months Margaret Sanger was publishing articles on contraception. Her objective was to free women from the bondage of unlimited childbearing through birth control and her efforts thus became a part of the women's emancipation movement. Although she was prosecuted for her writings, the charges were dropped. In 1916 she opened the first birth control clinic in Brooklyn. This time Mrs. Sanger was arrested and spent time in jail. As a result of her case, however, court decisions subsequently permitted physicians to prescribe birth control in New York for health reasons. These were the first of many such decisions and changes in the laws of various states that ultimately permitted the sale and advertisement of contraceptive materials and the dissemination of information about birth control. The last such court decision was made in 1965, when the Supreme Court ruled that the Connecticut statute forbidding the use of contraceptives was an unconstitutional invasion of privacy. The following year the Massachusetts legislature repealed the last of the state Comstock Laws.

Margaret Sanger and others who joined her rapidly growing birth control movement (then known as the Birth Control League) led the fight for these legal changes and for support from medical, educational, health, and religious organizations. In time, clinics were established throughout the United States, and their activities were expanded to include premarital and preparenthood counseling, assistance for sterile couples, and reproductive research. These additional services are still a part of most family planning programs, even in underdeveloped countries. In 1942 these expanded interests were reflected when the organization changed its name to the Planned Parenthood Federation.

Counterparts to Margaret Sanger existed in many other countries: Dr. Aletta Jacobs in Holland, Dr. Marie Stopes in England, and later, Mrs. Elise Ottesen-Jensen of Sweden, and Lady Dhanvanthis Rama Rau of India. These women, like Mrs. Sanger, were motivated by concern for the health and welfare of mothers and children, and their campaigns emphasized these considerations.

Concurrently, intellectual organizations concerned primarily with population size, known as Malthusian Leagues, were also promoting birth control. These, of course, were intellectual descendants of Robert Malthus, who first put forth warnings about the dangers of overpopulation (see Box 10-1). They were active in several European countries, but after World War I, when European birth rates had dropped substantially, their Malthusian concerns seemed to lose relevance and the movement died out.

The birth control movement in the United States was at first opposed by the medical profession. As the health and welfare benefits of family planning became apparent, the medical profession moved to a position of neutrality, and in 1937 the American Medical Association (AMA) finally called for instruction on contraception in medical schools and medical supervision in family planning clinics. In 1964 the AMA recognized matters of reproduction, "including the need for population control," as subjects for responsible medical concern.

Religious opposition to the birth control movement was initially even stronger than medical opposition. The Roman Catholic Church still opposes "artificial" methods of birth control, but Planned Parenthood clinics cooperate in teaching the rhythm method to Catholics who request it. Acceptance of birth control has come gradually from the various Protestant and Jewish groups after their initial opposition; complete sanction was given by the Anglican (Episcopal) Communion in England and the United States in 1958, by the Central Conference of American Rabbis (Reform) in 1960, and by the National Council of Churches in 1961.

Birth rates in America and Europe had already begun to decline, as a result of the demographic transition, long before the establishment of the first birth control clinics. Nevertheless, the Planned Parenthood movement, particularly in the United States, probably deserves some credit for today's relatively low birth rates. It has also played a great role in increasing the availability of contraceptives and birth control information. This has been accomplished not so much through the clinics, which never reached more than a small fraction of the population, but through the removal of restrictive laws, the development of medical and religious support, and the creation of a social climate in which birth control information can circulate freely.

In 1965 some 85 percent of married women in America had used some method of birth control; 26 percent had used the steroid pill. This represents virtual saturation, since most of the remainder were subfertile, pregnant, or planning to use contraceptives only when their families were complete. Catholic women in the sample showed a level of usage of "artificial" contra-

BOX 10-1    THOMAS ROBERT MALTHUS 1766–1834

The name Malthus and the terms Malthusian and neo-Malthusian are so completely identified with concern about population pressure that a note about the man seems appropriate. Malthus enjoyed what was certainly one of the happiest personal situations ever devised by man; he was an eighteenth century English country gentleman of independent means. His youth and early manhood were in the last years of the Enlightenment, the Age of Reason, a time when learned and wise men saw themselves on the threshold of a world of concord among men and nations in which want and oppression would not exist. Man's imminent entry into this paradise was to be achieved through his discovery of the immutable Laws of Nature which were thought to be such that they could be understood by the human faculty of Reason. All discord, want, and cruelty were held to result from an ignorance of these Laws, which led man to their disobedience. It was an age of very great hope when Nature and Reason were enshrined.

Robert's father, Daniel, the very embodiment of these values, was well connected in the intellectual and philosophical circles of the time, being a close associate of David Hume and a correspondent, friend, and finally, an executor of Jean Jacques Rousseau.

In 1784, after a preparation through home tutoring, Robert entered Cambridge, where in 1788 he graduated with first-class honors in mathematics. With graduation he took Holy Orders in the Church of England but remained at Cambridge where he achieved his M.A. in 1791 and became a Fellow of his College in 1793. In 1796 he became curate of the church at Albury, where his father resided, and settled down to country life.

These were the years of the French Revolution, years which Dickens called "the best of times, the worst of times." Neither the Revolution's war, internal and external, nor even its Terror yet dampened the ambience of optimism which characterized the world of thought. In 1793 William Godwin published his *Enquiry Concerning Political Justice* and the next year saw the appearance of the Marquis de Condorcet's *Essay on the Progress of the Human Spirit,* both of which sought to demonstrate that man's progress from darkness, superstition, and cruelty into the light of Concord through Reason was almost complete. Daniel Malthus, like most of the thoughtful men of the time, was much taken by these writings, but Robert could not share his enthusiasm. Cambridge had not, as he put it, given him "that command over his understanding which would enable him to believe what he wished without evidence." The concern that haunted Robert was population growth. How could a perfect society be achieved, let alone maintained, if population was constantly pressing against resources? Finally, Robert reduced his misgivings to writing so he could present them systematically to his father. Daniel was so impressed with the arguments that he encouraged his son to publish them, which he did anonymously in 1798, under the title, *An Essay on the Principle of Population as it Affects the Future Improvement of Society With Remarks on the Speculations of Mr. Godwin M. Condorcet and Other Writers.* His speculations centered on the proposition that man's "power of population is indefinitely greater than the power in the earth to produce subsistence . . ." which he propounded with strict immutability and mathematical regularity characteristic of the Natural Laws of the Age of Reason as "population, when unchecked, increases in a geometrical ratio. Subsistence increases only in an arithmetical ratio . . ." The first *Essay* challenged the visions of an age and the reactions were immediate and predictably hostile, though many listened. The controversy led to the publication in 1803 of an enlarged, less speculative, more documented, but equally dampening second essay. This one was signed and bore the title, *An Essay on the Principle of Population or a View of its Past and Present Effects on Human Happiness with an Inquiry into our Prospects Respecting the Future Removal or Mitigation of the Evils it Occasions.* Malthus added to and modified the *Essay* in subsequent editions, but it stood substantially unchanged.

In 1804 he accepted a post at the East India Company's college at Haileybury which prepared young men for the rule of India, where he remained until his death. His marriage, in the same year, ultimately produced three children.

The ironies in Malthus' life are obvious. He was one of eight children. He occupied a position of comfort in an intellectual atmosphere of optimism, but was compelled by the rigor of his intellect to argue that nature condemned the bulk of humankind to live in the margin between barely enough and too little. Finally, his message as a teacher fell on the ears of future colonial bureaucrats who would guide or preside over the destinies of India.

Since the conversations between Robert Malthus and his father almost two centuries ago, two sets of factors have entered the scene which were beyond their ken. The first set have combined to put elements into the population-subsistence relationship which Malthus could not have foreseen. On one hand, the introduction of massive death control procedures—immunization, purification of drinking water, the control of disease-carrying organisms, improved sanitation, etc.—have removed many of the checks which Malthus assumed as "natural." On the other hand, developments in agriculture—high-yield plant strains, the powering of equipment with fossil fuels, the use of new techniques of fertilization and pest control—have massively increased food production.

The second set of factors has become widely significant only in the last quarter century and evident to most laymen only in the last decade. These are the deleterious effects on the biosphere resulting from agriculture and industry. With our planet's population bloated by death control and sustained only poorly through an agriculture based on nonrenewable resources and techniques which buy short-run, high yields at the expense of long-run, permanent damage to the "Earth's power to produce subsistence," we face a prospect inconceivable in the Age of Reason. Malthus looked into a dismal future of "vice and misery" begot of an uncontrolled, and to his mind uncontrollable population growth; we look into one where the dismal is compounded with peril, not because humankind cannot control its population, but because it will not.

(For further reading about Malthus, see particularly John Maynard Keynes, *Essays in Biography;* J. Bonar, *Malthus and His Work,* second edition, 1924; G. F. McCleary, *The Malthusian Population Theory;* and of course, Malthus's First and Second Essays.)

ceptives nearly as high as that of non-Catholic women. Ten years earlier, well over half of the contraceptive users employed condoms or diaphragms, the two most effective methods then available.

Europe presents a surprisingly different and diverse picture. *Coitus interruptus* has been given the major credit for lowering birth rates during the demographic transition, with abortion also playing an important role. In most of Europe, both east and west, *coitus interruptus* seems still to be the most widely used method, followed by rhythm and the condom. Among Western European countries, only in England and Scandinavia do contraceptive devices approach being as well-known and readily available as they are in the United States. Even in those countries the condom is the most commonly used device, and withdrawal is much more widely practiced than it is in America. However, use of the pill is increasing. Planned Parenthood groups exist in France, Belgium, and the Netherlands in a quasi-legal status, hampered by laws restricting the dissemination of information and materials. Birth control is still entirely illegal in Spain, Portugal, and Ireland, although a movement for change has begun. Italy has legalized the pill for "medical purposes" (presumably to combat the high illegal abortion rate), and condoms are available "for disease prevention." In 1971, Italian laws prohibiting the dissemination of birth control information were declared unconstitutional, thus opening the way for much greater access to contraceptives.

The Soviet Union and eastern European countries distribute contraceptives through government maternal health clinics, with the intent of reducing the abortion rate. There is evidence that this policy is succeeding in some countries, as it is for example in Japan. The pill, which has been introduced in the Soviet Union and eastern Europe, will probably accelerate this trend away from dependence on abortion for birth control.

Throughout its history, the emphasis and primary concern of the family planning movement has been the welfare of the family; it has stressed the economic, educational, and health advantages of well-spaced, limited numbers of children. Its policy has been to provide information and materials for birth control in volunteer-staffed clinics for the poor, serving any interested client. Once the movement was established, little effort was made to recruit clients until the 1960s, beyond the routine promotion that accompanied the opening of a new clinic. For the United States this policy was apparently adequate; this nation is overwhelmingly committed to family planning. Within the next few years, family planning services will doubtless be extended to the remaining estimated few million women in low-income groups to whom they have not previously been available, either through private agencies or through local or federal government welfare programs.

## Family Planning in the UDCs

In 1952, Mrs. Sanger, Mrs. Ottesen-Jensen of Sweden, Lady Rama Rau of India, and others in the birth control movement joined to form the International Planned Parenthood Federation, a federation of the already established national groups. By the end of 1968, the IPPF had grown to include organizations in 54 countries, 36 of them UDCs. Many of these organizations, notably those in India and Pakistan, operate with funds provided by their own governments. Others are supported by the international organization, which in turn receives funds from private sources and, more recently, from government grants. These grants have come from the United States, Sweden, Denmark, Norway, the Netherlands, and Britain.

In response to rising alarm during the 1950s over the population explosion in underdeveloped countries, several other organizations in the United States began to be involved in population research and overseas family planning programs. Among these were the Ford Foundation, the Rockefeller Foundation, the Population Council, the Population Reference Bureau, and the Population Crisis Committee. The 1960s brought a great proliferation of family planning programs in UDCs (Table 10-1) assisted or administered by one or another of these organizations, or by government-sponsored ones from other countries, such as Sweden. Some federal agencies in the United States, such as the Agency for International Development (AID), have begun to assist such programs also. So far these are the only programs that have been brought into action against the population problem in UDCs, except in the People's Republic of China and a few other countries where other policies supplement family planning.

Characteristically, family planning programs begin with knowledge, attitude, and practice (known as KAP) surveys, which are designed to ascertain the extent of knowledge about and level of practice of birth control, and what attitudes exist toward the idea in the "target population." In most UDCs, few people know anything about birth control (often, only about 10–20 percent of the adult population), and knowledge is mainly restricted to withdrawal. Only a fraction of those who know about birth control practice it. But among people interviewed in surveys, including those previously ignorant of birth control, interest is high, especially in couples with three or more children. Knowledge, practice, and interest are related to economic and educational levels, just as they are in DCs. All are higher in urban than in rural populations, although often not as much higher as one might expect. There is considerable variation from one country to another, but it is a fairly typical experience that when family planning clinics are opened in areas where a high degree of interest and willingness to learn has been indicated, the clientele turns out to be much smaller than expected. People often say one thing, and then do another, and it is difficult for surveys to correct for this. The problem may be especially serious if the interviewer is perceived as a social superior by the person interviewed, in which case answers may be slanted in an attempt to please the interviewer. Tables 10-2 and 10-3 give figures on family sizes desired in both UDCs and DCs.

Family planning programs in UDCs are usually carried out through clinics that are either independent or work in cooperation with maternal and child health agencies, and in some countries mobile units are used to carry

TABLE 10-1

*Family Planning in UDCs*

| Size of population (in millions) | Have an official family planning policy and program | Have limited governmental involvement or support of family planning | Are doing nothing official in family planning |
|---|---|---|---|
| 400+ | People's Republic of China (1962) India (1952, reorganized 1965) | ——— | ——— |
| 100–400 | Pakistan (1960, reorganized 1965) Indonesia (1968) | ——— | ——— |
| 50–100 | ——— | Nigeria (1969) | Mexico Brazil |
| 25–50 | Turkey (1965) United Arab Republic (1966) Iran (1967) Philippines (1970) Thailand (1970) South Korea (1961) | ——— | Burma Ethiopa |
| 15–25 | Morocco (1965) | Colombia (1967) North Vietnam (1964) | South Africa Congo South Vietnam Afghanistan Sudan |
| 10–15 | Taiwan (1964) Nepal (1966) Ceylon (1965) Malaysia (1966) Kenya (1966) | Venezuela (1965) Chile (1965) | Algeria Tanzania North Korea Peru |
| Less than 10 | Tunisia (1964) Barbados (1967) Dominican Republic (1967) Singapore (1965) Jamaica (1966) Trinidad and Tobago (1967) Ghana (1969) Mauritius (1965) Puerto Rico (1970) | Cuba Nicaragua (1963) Costa Rica (1968) Hong Kong (1956) Panama (1969) Honduras (1965) Dahomey (1969) Gambia (1969) Rhodesia (1968) Senegal (1970) Bolivia (1968) Ecuador (1968) El Salvador (1967) | Cameroon Madagascar Uganda Cambodia Iraq Jordan Laos Lebanon Saudi Arabia Syria Yemen |

SOURCE: *Berelson, Studies in Family Planning no. 39,* (supp.) 1969, and Nortman, *Reports of Population / Family Planning, no. 2,* 1970, The Population Council.

workers and equipment to remote villages. Unlike the traditional planned parenthood organizations in DCs, these programs actively recruit clients, employing specially trained field workers for this purpose and utilizing whatever form of mass communication and promotion seems effective. These may include pamphlets and circulars, advertisements in public transportation, billboards, radio and newspaper announcements, or plays and skits produced by traveling troupes. In India an elephant is taken from village to village, and is used to pass out pamphlets and contraceptives.

The propaganda would be familiar to Americans, though perhaps some of the methods of disseminating it would not. The primary emphasis is on preventing the "unwanted child," and the program makes the greatest effort to reach women who already have at least three children. Such women are usually most receptive to the idea of birth control; furthermore, their proven high fertility makes them statistically likely to have several more children if they do not use contraceptives.

Family planning programs generally offer a variety of birth control methods, including sterilization, although the latter has only been used or promoted on a large scale in India and Pakistan. The most popular method in Asia has been the IUD, although it has proved to be less ideal than it first appeared. Barely 50 percent of the women fitted with IUDs still wear them two years later. Malnutrition may contribute to this high discontinuance rate by increasing the tendency to bleed after insertion. This is just one example of how conditions brought on by overpopulation can hinder population control. Great efforts have been made by the family planning workers to reduce the rate of discontinuance by warning women in advance of probable minor complaints and assuring them that they are not serious enough to warrant removal of the IUD. Many who expel IUDs spontaneously are refitted, and those who cannot tolerate them are offered the pill, sterilization, or some other alternative.

Clinic staffs include doctors (usually gynecologists), nurses, midwives, and occasionally social workers. A few programs also employ anthropologists to advise the staff personnel on the best approach to villagers. Midwives are often used as field workers and/or medical workers within the clinic, although some problems have resulted from employing them. Mid-wives commonly see family planning as a threat to their incomes from child delivery, as well as from illegal abortion, in which some are also profitably involved.

Besides offering contraceptives, the family planning programs in the UDCs, like the older ones in DCs, provide counseling services for marriage, parenthood and child-spacing, and assistance for subfertile and sterile couples. Women's discussion groups are often organized in villages to interest wives in birth control. Advice on nutrition and child care may be included in the discussions partly because these subjects will help attract women to the family planning program, and partly because the dissemination of this information supplements the program's child welfare goals.

Some hope of increased effectiveness in reaching younger women early in their reproductive lives is held out by the idea of introducing family plan-

TABLE 10-2
*Desired Family Size Compared to Birth Rate*

| Area | Date | Size sample | Average number of children desired | Percentage desiring: 4 or more | 5 or more | 1971 birth rate |
|---|---|---|---|---|---|---|
| Austria | 1960 | | 2.0 | 4 | | 16.5 |
| W. Germany | 1960 | | 2.2 | 4 | | 15.0 |
| Czechoslovakia | 1959 | 3,192 | 2.3 | | | 15.5 |
| Hungary | 1958–1960 | 6,732 | 2.4 | 13 | 6 | 15.0 |
| Great Britain | 1960 | | 2.8 | 23 | | 16.6 |
| France | 1960 | | 2.8 | 17 | | 16.7 |
| Japan | 1961 | 2,753 | 2.8 | 22 | 8 | 18.0 |
| Switzerland | 1960 | | 2.9 | 22 | | 16.5 |
| Puerto Rico | 1953 | 888 | 3.0 | 19 | | 24.0 |
| Italy | 1960 | | 3.1 | 18 | | 17.6 |
| Norway | 1960 | | 3.1 | 25 | | 17.6 |
| Netherlands | 1960 | | 3.3 | 39 | | 19.2 |
| U.S.A. | 1960 | 2,414 | 3.3 | 40 | 15 | 18.2 |
| Ceylon | 1963 | 302 | 3.2 | 25 | 12 | 32.0 |
| Jamaica | 1957 | 1,368 | 3.4–4.2 | 48 | 19 | 33.0 |
| Colombia | 1963 | | 3.5 | | | 44.0 |
| Turkey | 1963 | 5,122 | 3.5 | 42 | 25 | 43.0 |
| South Africa (white pop.) | 1957–1958 | 1,022 | 3.6 | 54 | 10 | |
| Taiwan | 1962–1963 | 2,432 | 3.9 | 62 | 22 | 26.0 |
| Thailand | 1964 | 1,207 | 3.8 | 54 | 26 | 42.0 |
| Pakistan | 1960 | 2,086 | 3.9 | 65 | 26 | 50.0 |
| Chile | 1959 | 1,970 | 4.1 | 58 | 26 | 34.0 |
| Canada | 1960 | | 4.2 | 70 | | 17.6 |
| India | 1952–1960 | 5,909 | 3.7–4.7 | 57–63 | 25–34 | 42.0 |
| Indonesia | 1961–1962 | 2,208 | 4.3 | 66 | 36 | 47.0 |
| S. Korea | 1962 | 1,884 | 4.4 | 77 | 44 | 36.0 |
| Ghana | 1963 | 637 | 5.3 | 88 | 56 | 48.0 |
| Philippines | 1963 | 7,807 | 5.0 | 71 | 53 | 46.0 |

SOURCE: Data from *Studies in Family Planning no. 7,* Population Council, 1965. Birth rates from 1971 World Population Sheet, Population Reference Bureau.

ning to them immediately after the birth of their first child in the maternity hospital. Pilot studies of this approach in both DCs and UDCs have brought promising results, although to be effective this program may require special personnel in the hospital who do nothing else. Attempts to have regular hospital doctors and nurses add to their other duties the teaching of family planning to their maternal patients have failed. Doctors and nurses, especially in UDCs, are generally overworked already, and they simply have no time for one more function. In addition, they are often not particularly mo-

TABLE 10-3
*Desired Family Sizes of Women in Seven Latin American Cities*

| Latin American Cities | Average number of children wanted | 1971 birth rate of country |
|---|---|---|
| Bogota, Colombia | 3.6 | 44 |
| Buenos Aires, Argentina | 2.9 | 22 |
| Caracas, Venezuela | 3.5 | 41 |
| Mexico City, Mexico | 4.2 | 42 |
| Panama City, Panama | 3.5 | 41 |
| Rio de Janeiro, Brazil | 2.7 | 38 |
| San Jose, Costa Rica | 3.6 | 45 |

SOURCE: Data from Berelson et al., *Family Planning and Population Programs*. Univ. of Chicago Press, 1966. Birth rates from 1971 Population Data Sheet, Population Reference Bureau.

tivated in favor of family planning. A further handicap to this approach is that in most UDCs childbirth seldom takes place in a hospital outside the larger cities.

With the single exception of India, no UDC had an official family planning program prior to 1960. India's began in 1952, but for the first decade it was not strongly supported. Most of that time was spent with surveys, pilot projects, and experiments with the rhythm method. In 1965 the program was completely reorganized, and a much more vigorous effort is now under way, using considerably stronger measures than are employed in most such programs. These include the establishment of clinics (associated with maternal health facilities where possible), temporary camps, and mobile units, all accompanied by a very active education campaign to promote small families. Vasectomy and the IUD are the most used methods, although female sterilization and traditional contraceptives are available. Men who accept vasectomies, and any individual who persuades a man to have one, are paid small fees. Railway stations are often used as vasectomy clinics in place of hospitals, partly because they attract large numbers of people and partly because Indians traditionally regard hospitals as a place to die. In 1971, horrified by the rising death rates from illegal abortions, India's Parliament legalized abortion. In addition, a program of active research and development of new contraceptive methods, including an investigation of folk methods, is being carried on.

But India has run into some problems with her policies, particularly in rural areas. Aside from the monumental logistic difficulty of taking family planning to every village, a good deal of resistance has been met in some places, which has even led occasionally to riots and the destruction of camps and mobile units. This resistance results in part from the existence of three active medical traditions in India—ayurvedic, unani, and homeopathic—besides Western medicine. So far the family planning program has been implemented only through Western medicine, a circumstance that naturally results in resentment and opposition from the others. Resistance also comes from religious and ethnic minority groups who may perceive family planning as discrimination. This opposition has begun to show itself in a drop in the vasectomy contraceptive acceptance rates because of lack of candidates.

In an effort to expand the effectiveness of the program, India has begun experimenting with "family planning festivals." In one district during the month of July, 1971, over 60,000 vasectomies were performed at one festival. IUDs, condoms, and female sterilizations were also available. Greater than usual incentive payments and gifts were offered both to recipients and to recruiters. The festival also included entertainment and cultural events. There was a great deal of publicity, and entertainers toured the surrounding countryside to attract people to the festival. Cooperation and support were secured from voluntary organizations, local government, professional groups and labor unions, which probably contributed much to the success of the campaign.

Pakistan's program was established in 1960 but, as in India, the active, large-scale phase did not begin until 1965. Hong Kong's official program also began in 1960. Taiwan and South Korea began large-scale operations in 1964. Although both programs had been started earlier, Taiwan's was without government support before then. By 1970, some 25 UDCs had established official antinatalist policies and were supporting family planning programs. Another 17 countries were supporting family planning at least to a limited extent.

The earlier and more vigorous programs have made considerable progress in terms of reaching a large proportion of the reproductive population. Yet, as reflected by current birth and growth rates, they show remarkably little progress toward fulfilling their own short-term goals of birth rate and growth rate reduction (Table 10-4), some of which may have been unrealistically optimistic. Taiwan and South Korea have shown a considerable drop in birth rates since the programs were initiated, but birth rates in both countries had begun to decline before then. How much of the recent decline is due to the family planning program is extremely hard to determine, as the administrators of the programs themselves admit. Although neither country has made much effort to propagandize in behalf of small families until recently, there is some evidence that the activities of the family planning program may have stimulated interest in this direction. This was shown by an increasing acceptance of birth control among women in the younger age groups and those with few children. Taiwan may even achieve its 1973 birth-rate goal, although the growth rate goal seems farther away, probably because the death rate has declined to an almost unbelievably low level of 5 per thousand. South Korea, however, fell short of its growth rate goal for 1971.

Taiwan and South Korea may within a few years give us some measure of the potential effectiveness of family planning for reducing population growth in UDCs, although both started with some advantages over most other

TABLE 10-4

*Family Planning Effects Measured Against Goals*

| Country | Program begun | Birth rate per 1,000 Goal* | Birth rate per 1,000 1971† | Growth rate in percent Goal* | Growth rate in percent 1971† | Population of married couples Target‡ (millions) | Population of married couples Protected by 1970 (percent) |
|---|---|---|---|---|---|---|---|
| India | 1965 | 40 to 25 (in 10 years) | 42 | — | 2.6 | 96 | 12 |
| Pakistan | 1965 | 50 to 40 (by 1970) | 50 | — | 3.3 | 20 | >11 |
| S. Korea | 1961 | — | 36 | 2.9 to 2.0 (1962–71) | 2.5 | 4.5 | 32 |
| Taiwan | 1964 | 36 to 24 (by 1973) | 26 | 3.02 to 1.86 (1965–73) | 2.3 | 1.8 | 36 |
| Ceylon | 1965 | 33 to 25 (in 8–10 years) | 32 | 1.6 (by 1976) | 2.4 | 1.7 | > 8.2 |
| Turkey | 1965 | — | 43 | 3.0 to 2.0 (by 1972) | 2.7 | 5.6 | 3 |
| Singapore | 1965 | 30 to under 20 (in 5 years) | 25 | — | 2.4 | 0.3 | 45 |
| Malaysia | 1966 | — | 37 | 3.0 to 2.2 (by 1987) | 2.8 | 1.6 | 7 |
| Dominican Republic | 1967 | 48 to 40 (by 1972) to 28 (by 1978) | 48 | 3.4 to 2.7 (by 1972) | 3.4 | — | — |
| Morocco | 1965 | 50 to 45 (by 1973) | 50 | — | 3.3 | 2.6 | 1 |
| Trinidad and Tobago | 1967 | 38 to 19 (by 1978) | 30 | — | 1.8 | — | — |

* Data on birth and growth rate goals, which have been set by the national family planning programs, are from Berelson, *Studies in Family Planning*, no. 39 (supp.), 1969.
† Data for 1971 birth and growth rates are from the Population Reference Bureau.
‡ The "target population" is the number of married couples in the reproductive ages (15–44). The "protected population" refers to the percentage of the target population which is sterilized or using some form of contraception, whether provided by a government program or through private services. Data from *Studies in Family Planning*, 1965–1970.

UDCs. Taiwan, and to a lesser degree Korea, were fairly highly urbanized (for Asia), relatively literate, beginning to industrialize, and had governments favorable to the idea of family planning programs. In addition, birth rates in both countries had already begun to decline, indicating a pre-existing desire for birth control among the people. Since 1970, Taiwan has supplemented its program by propagandizing for the two-child family and offering incentives for sterilization and IUD acceptance.

Hong Kong and Singapore are also considered to have successful family planning programs, although neither could by any means be considered a typical UDC. Nor has either come close to controlling its population growth, though both have birth rates well below the average for Asia. Both are islands, are overwhelmingly urban, and have fairly high literacy rates and well-organized medical services. Apparently the need to limit population when it is confined to small islands is as obvious to citizens as to the government, and progress in lowering birth rates may be more easily achieved under these special conditions.

## Attitudes and Birth Rates

Unquestionably the single most important factor in a country's reproductive rate is the motivation of the people toward the regulation of family size. The strength of the desire for a small family is critical. If a couple is determined not to have more than two children, they usually will not, regardless of whether there is a birth control clinic down the street. Conversely, if the motivation is weak, the practice of birth control is likely to be a sometime thing, although the motivation often grows with the number of children in the family.

The overriding importance of motivation is made clear by the example of Europe, where the family planning movement has had relatively little influence, particularly in Catholic countries. The continent as a whole has the lowest birth rates of any comparable area in the world, and most European countries have had low birth rates for at least two generations. The population of Europe is growing at considerably less than 1 percent per year (0.8 percent): only Albania, Rumania, and Iceland have growth rates that exceed 1.2 percent. This remarkable record has been and is being accomplished largely in the absence of modern contraceptives. Both information and devices are completely banned in several countries, and they are seriously restricted in others. Yet the birth rates are just as low in these countries as in neighboring countries where information and devices are generally available and in moderately wide use. *Coitus interruptus* is known and practiced everywhere, especially where birth control is restricted, and is generally backed up by abortion, either legal or illegal, depending on the country. In one way or another, most Europeans manage to avoid having children they do not want.

Studies in various countries with different levels of development and different population densities indicate that people tend to have the number of children they say they want. In general, families in DCs fall slightly short of their goals; in UDCs they usually exceed them. But, even if reproductive goals were always perfectly achieved, each country's growth rate would probably be little changed. Surveys show (Table 10-2) that the average number of children wanted per family varies from 2.0 to 3.3 in European countries; in the U.S. it was about 3.3 during the 1960s. By contrast, the average in most UDCs ranges between 3.5 and 5.5. Given the death rates characteristic of DCs, it would require an average of only 2.25 children per married couple over the long run to result in a steady population size. Obviously, population growth, especially in UDCs, cannot be stopped merely by preventing unwanted births, although that is certainly a desirable first step.

A great many socioeconomic factors affect the reproductive goals of individuals and of a society. Among these are the general education level, the degree of urbanization, the social status of women, the opportunities open to women for employment outside the home, and the costs of raising and educating each child. The higher or greater each of these factors is, the lower fertility generally will be. Other factors, such as the average age at marriage (especially of women), the degree of tolerance for illegitimate births, or the usual length of time of breast-feeding, also can directly affect the fertility rates. Later marriage, lower tolerance for illegitimacy, and extended breast feeding all operate to reduce fertility.

Family planning programs in general have made little effort to influence these factors, as demographer Kingsley Davis has pointed out. Most of them try only to influence people by emphasizing the economic and health advantages of small families to themselves and their children. Government officials, economic advisors, and many demographers tend to believe that the process of economic development will automatically bring about the higher levels of education and urbanization that lead to the desire for fewer children and in turn cause a demographic transition in UDCs. Family planning has therefore been introduced in many countries where extremely high population growth rates were impeding the rate of economic development. This is a move in the right direction, but unfortunately this great faith in the possibilities of industrial development, the demographic transition, and the prevention of unwanted children too often encourage governments in these countries to relax under the illusion that their population problems are being solved. (Conversely, many of these officials are lulled into the equally illusionary belief that family planning alone will automatically bring about a solution to their social and economic problems.)

A demographic transition would at best merely reduce growth rates in UDCs to the level of those of the DCs, and thus it cannot be expected to *solve* any country's population problem. In most UDCs, lack of resources and overpopulation will combine to prevent sufficient development for a demographic transition to occur. From all points of view the demographic transition is no solution.

If vigorous family planning programs had been initiated just after World War II when death control and the ideas of economic development were introduced in UDCs, the population situation might be of much more manageable dimensions today. But it plainly would still be with us. Even if the strongest feasible population control measures were everywhere in force today, the time lag before our runaway population growth could be appreciably slowed, let alone arrested, would still be discouragingly long. For UDCs it would be *at least* two generations before the population ceased to expand—unless catastrophe intervened—because of the age composition of their populations.

## Population Growth in the United States

Some people seem to believe that in order to stop growth rates there should be no reproduction at all. Actually, to reduce the 1970 United States birth rate of 18.2 per 1,000 population (higher than most European countries) to a level where it would ultimately balance the death rate (at about 13 per 1,000) would require less of a reduction than took place between 1957 and 1967. During that decade, the United States birth rate fell from 25.3 to 17.8. Reduction of the birth rate to about 13 per 1,000 would eventually stabilize the population—even though the current death rate is 9.3—because such low birth rates would within a few decades change the age composition of the population. The average age of the population would rise from the present 28 to about 37, and with a greater proportion in the older age classes, the death rate would rise significantly.

Of course the projected rise in the number of women of reproductive age (15–44) during the 1970s means that to achieve such a low birth rate there would have to be a substantial reduction in the fertility rates of that segment of the population. The 1970 fertility rate was 87.7 births per 1,000 women of reproductive age, down from a peak of 122.9 in 1957. The lowest fertility rates ever achieved in the United States were 76 to 79 births per 1,000 women of reproductive age during the Depression years of 1933–1939.

TABLE 10-5
*Percentage of Ever-married United States Women,*
*55 to 59 Years Old in 1960, by Numbers of Live Births*

| Number of children | Percentage all women ever married | Children per 100 women |
|---|---|---|
| 0 | 17.5 | 0 |
| 1 | 16.5 | 16.5 |
| 2 | 19.7 | 39.4 |
| 3 | 14.4 | 43.2 |
| 4 | 10.3 | 41.2 |
| 5 & 6 | 11.0 | 60.5 |
| 7 and over | 10.6 | 94.6 |
| | 100 | 295.4 |

SOURCE: Data from *1960 Census of the United States.*

Looking at it another way, if the average desired size of the American family were shifted downward to 2.2, the growth rate of the United States population would be reduced to zero after about 70 years. If American families were to produce less than an average of 2.2 children each, the growth rate would decline more rapidly and would reach zero sooner.

Economist Stephen Enke has calculated a possible distribution of family sizes that would achieve the desired replacement rate. The data in Table 10-5 show the childbearing performance of women whose families were complete in 1960. Enke assumes that many of these women who were childless or had only one child probably wanted more. With the medical assistance available today, sterile and subfertile couples probably would have more children than was possible a generation ago. Under Enke's scheme, 50 percent of married women would have 2 children, which might be considered the norm or the ideal. Some 10 percent might have only one child and 5 percent remain childless. Above the norm, 30 percent might have three children, and another 5 percent more than three, with an average of five. Obviously, this plan still allows for a few large families, but the vast majority of families would have one, two, or three children. Childlessness and large families both would be much rarer than they were a generation or two ago, as can be seen by comparing the Enke distribution with that of Table 10-5.

How much of today's U.S. population growth is due to unwanted births is a matter for debate among demographers. The National Fertility Study of 1965 indicated that 17 percent of all births between 1960 and 1965 were not wanted by both parents and 22 percent were not wanted by at least one parent. The incidence of unwanted births was found, not unexpectedly, to be highest among the poor, to whom birth control and abortion were least available (see Box 10–2). Nevertheless, more than half of these unwanted births were to white, middle class families. Eliminating such a high proportion of unwanted births, according to demographer Charles Westoff, might reduce the U.S. rate of natural increase by as much as 35 to 45 percent.

However, Judith Blake has shown that the high incidence of unwanted births calculated by Westoff for the U.S. during 1960–1965 was because births during that period were occurring disproportionately to women who already had several children. During those six years, there were unusually small proportions of first and second children born and unusually large proportions of births of higher orders (which are more likely to be unwanted). Hence, the *total* proportion of unwanted births in the U.S. was higher for those years than it is now, or than it was at any time as far back as the early 1940s, even if one assumes no change over time in the percentage unwanted within each birth order taken separately. In addition, changes in fertility control, such as the widespread use of the pill and the IUD since the early 1960s, extension of family planning services to the poor, and the moderation of some state abortion laws, probably have substantially reduced the incidence of unwanted births of all orders since 1965. Early results from the 1970 National Fertility Study indicate that this is indeed the case.

There is no question that providing better contraceptives, legalizing abortion, and ensuring that both are easily available to all members of the population could further reduce the incidence of unwanted pregnancy—a desirable end in itself. But even if a perfect contraceptive were available, the contraceptive-using population probably never will be perfect. People forget, are careless, and take chances. They are also often willing to live with their mistakes when they are babies. Therefore, the complete elimination of unwanted pregnancies is probably not possible, and a significant additional lowering of U.S. birthrates without a change in family size goals seems improbable.

Surveys taken between 1965 and 1971 reveal a growing awareness on the part of the American public of the population problem. In 1965, about half of the people interviewed in a Gallup Poll thought that U.S. population growth might be a serious problem; in 1971, 87 percent thought that it was a problem now or would be by the year 2000. Partly reflecting this new concern, in January 1971 only 23 percent of adults polled thought four or more children constituted the ideal family size, in contrast to 40 percent in 1967. The previous low percentage favoring four or more was 34 in 1936; the highest was 49 percent in 1945. One of the three most commonly given reasons for favoring small families was concern about crowding and overpopulation. The others were the cost of living and uncertainty about the future.

In October 1971, a survey sponsored by the U.S. Commission on Popula-

---

BOX 10-2   POVERTY, RACE, AND BIRTH CONTROL

The entrance of the United States government into the field of birth control through the extension of family planning services to the poor has aroused a controversy quite out of proportion to its potential effect on the national birth rate. The majority of poor people are not Negroes, nor are the majority of Negro families poor—about 30 percent of Negro familes were below the poverty level in 1967. But Americans, both black and white, tend to see the two terms as synonymous. This is one reason for the bitterness of the controversy.

Birth rates are higher among the poor and among nonwhites (Negroes, Orientals, and American Indians) than they are among the nonpoor and among whites, but in recent years they have been rapidly declining. In the United States population as a whole, high birth rates are strongly associated both with economic and educational levels. The poorest and least educated have the highest birth rates, with nonwhite families at this level having about one-third more children than comparable whites. At the same time, the poor and nonwhites have had consistently higher death rates, especially among infants and children, than the rest of the population. Both higher birth and death rates doubtless reflect the generally lower

quality of medical care available to the poor and to nonwhite minorities. Above the poverty level, the birth rate difference between races diminishes, and college-educated nonwhites have fewer children than their white peers. Among nonwhite poor, after a generation away from the farm the reproductive difference also disappears.

Some of the truth behind the saying, "The rich get richer and the poor get children," is revealed in the fact that large families tend to be poor. About 42 percent of American families with more than 5 children are poor, whereas only 10 percent with 1 or 2 children are poor. Furthermore, large familes are far likelier to remain poor, especially if they are headed by a woman.

Although there is conflicting evidence regarding desired family sizes among the poor, several surveys conducted in the 1960s indicate that they wish to have only slightly more children than do middle class couples, and nonwhite couples in most socioeconomic classes want fewer children than comparable whites do. This is especially true among the younger couples in their prime childbearing years.

At the same time, the incidence of unwanted children among the poor and near-poor in the early 1960s was estimated to be

tion Growth and the American Future disclosed a greatly increased level of concern about the population explosion among the American people. Specifically, it was discovered that:

1. Over 90 percent of Americans view U.S. population growth as a problem; 65 percent see it as a *serious* problem.

2. Over 50 percent favored government efforts to slow population growth and promote redistribution.

3. Well over 50 percent favor family limitation even if a family can afford more children.

4. About 56 percent favored adoption after two biological children if more are desired.

5. Only 19 percent felt that four or more children were the ideal number

as high as 40 percent. For nonpoor couples the incidence was about 14 percent. The reasons for this disparity between desires and actual reproductive performance appear to lie less in the lack of knowledge of contraceptives than in the availability of effective ones. The poor who used birth control tended to use less reliable methods than did members of the middle class.

Because poor people cannot usually afford contraceptives, and because no family planning information or services were provided through welfare health services until the late 1960s, most poor people were until then deprived of effective methods of birth control. There is some dispute about whether the number of women in need is only 2 million or as high as 5 million, but the experience of the Planned Parenthood clinics and those hospitals and public heath centers that have offered birth control services suggests that the need and the demand are both great. Whatever the actual number of women in need, this help for the poor is long overdue.

Despite the tendency of black militants to regard the provision of birth control to the poor as a policy of genocide against Negroes, it should be emphasized that the government's present program is basically a welfare program, intended to benefit the poor, and poor children in particular. In this connection it is unfortunate that the government has chosen to label it as a "population control" measure, which it is not; rather, it is a logical extension both of the family-planning movement and of the welfare program.

Fears of discrimination have been aroused in areas where middle class social workers or people operating birth control clinics have put pressure on the poor to accept birth control services. The best way to avoid either the appearance or the actuality of such discrimination is to have these services administered by residents of the same neighborhoods they serve.

Although many middle class Americans favor population control for others, especially the poor, they must realize that it is really their own excessive reproduction that accounts for most of the United States population growth rate. Furthermore, the middle class and the wealthy are responsible for the high rate of consumption and pollution, which are the most obvious symptoms of overpopulation in the United States.

for a family; 45 percent favored two or less. The mean was 2.33.

6. Only 8 percent thought the U.S. population should be larger than its present size.

While birth rates began to rise in 1968 as a consequence of the growing proportion of people in the reproductive ages, fertility rates have continued to decline slowly. In the first half of 1971, at about the same time that polls showed a drop in the desire for large families among Americans, the fertility rate dropped precipitously to below 80 births per 1,000 women of reproductive age for the first time since the 1930s.

The time span for this decline is too short to allow interpretation. Whether this is only a brief dip in fertility or the beginning of an important trend, and exactly what factors are producing it, only time will reveal. John Patterson of the National Center for Health Statistics has theorized that one factor may be postponement of marriage and family, but the importance of this factor is uncertain. If postponement proves to be the major cause, the reduction of fertility will be only temporary. If, on the other hand, this decline in fertility heralds a genuine, lasting change in family size goals, population growth will as a result be slowed. But, because of the age composition of the U.S., unless the average family size drops to one child, it will still require a minimum of 70 years to bring growth to an end.

Reflecting the lowered fertility rates of the 1960s and rising public consciousness of population growth, the Census Bureau in 1970 issued two new projections of U.S. population growth based on the attainment of replacement fertility rates in the 1970s, with slight fluctuations around that point between 1970 and 2000 to compensate for age composition differences. One projection assumes that net immigration will continue at the present rate (400,000 per year), the other assumes no net immigration. In the first projection, Series E, the population would be about 266 million in 2000 and would reach 300 million around 2020, stabilizing at a little over 300 million by 2065. In the other projection, Series X, the population would be only about 250 million in 2000 and would stabilize in 2037 at about 276 million. Earlier projections for the year 2000 assumed higher fertility rates and ranged between 280 million and 320 million.

The growth of the women's liberation movement in the U.S. since 1965 may well have become an important influence on birthrates. Young women are expressing more interest in careers and equal opportunities and pay with men in business and the professions and less interest in "homemaking" than they did in earlier years. The movement has been an important force behind the liberalization of abortion laws. Women are also actively campaigning for the establishment of low cost day care centers for children and tax deductions for the costs of child care and household work. Many of these young women are refreshingly honest about their personal lack of interest in having children, an attitude which would have been virtually unthinkable 15 years ago in the U.S. Should these attitudes become widespread in the female population and should the political goals of women's liberation be achieved, the result might well be significantly lower fertility rates.

In late 1968 a new organization, Zero Population Growth, was founded.

Its goal was to promote an end to U.S. population growth through lowered birthrates as soon as possible, and secondarily, the same for world population. It hopes to achieve this by (1) educating the public to the dangers of uncontrolled population growth and its relation to resource depletion, environmental deterioration and various social problems; and (2) by lobbying and taking other political action to encourage the development of antinatalist policies in government. In 1971, ZPG had over 40,000 members in 400 chapters in the U.S., and sister organizations had been established in Australia and Canada. In the U.S. it has taken an active part in promoting such national legislation as the Congressional Resolution for a stationary population, a national abortion bill, equal rights for women, and a number of environmental bills. It has also been involved in lobbying at the state level and in local campaigns to change policies affecting population growth and environmental quality.

## CHANGES IN AGE COMPOSITION

One argument which has been raised against halting U.S. population growth is that the median age would increase from about 28 to about 37. About one-fifth of the population would be under the age of 15, and about the same number would be over 65 years old. It is assumed that such an old population would present serious social problems. Therefore, halting population growth, at least now, is considered undesirable.

It is true that old people tend to be more conservative than young people, and they seem to have difficulty adjusting to a fast-changing, complex world. In an older population there would be relatively less opportunity for advancement in authority (there would be nearly as many 60 year-olds as 40 year-olds—so the number of potential chiefs would be about the same as the number of Indians). There would also be many more retired people, a group already considered a burden on society.

But even those who raise this argument must realize its fundamental fallacy. In the relatively near future population growth *will* stop. If we are extremely fortunate it will stop gradually through birth limitation, rather than by the premature deaths of billions of people. (In the latter case we will have other, more serious problems to worry us.) Therefore, if we do not initiate population control now, we will simply be postponing the age composition problems, leaving them to be dealt with by our grandchildren or great grandchildren. Our descendants will be forced to wrestle with these problems in a world even more overcrowded, resource-poor, and probably environmentally degraded than today's.

Another flaw in this argument against stopping growth is the assumption that an older population *must* be much less desirable than a younger one. This may be so in a society where overemployment and a labor pool constantly replenished by growing numbers of young people force early retirement of the old, making them dependents on society. But if population growth stopped, the pressure of young people entering the labor pool would decline, and the need for forced retirement would abate.

Old people today are obsolete to a great degree. But this is the fault of our social structure and especially our educational system. The problem with old people is not that there are or will be so many of them, but that they have been so neglected. If overemployment were solved and education were continued throughout life (as suggested in chapter 11), older people would be able to continue making valuable contributions well into their advanced years. Such active older people are also less likely to be conservative and inflexible. The savings from a much reduced population of children to educate could easily finance such a program.

## DISTRIBUTION AND NEW CITIES

Obscuring the population controversy in the United States has been the recent tendency of some demographers and government officials to blame our population-related problems on "maldistribution." The claim is that pollution and urban problems such as crime and unrest are the result of uneven distribution, that troubled cities may be overpopulated while other areas of the country are losing population. The cure most often promulgated to resolve this situation is the creation of "new cities" to absorb the 80 million or so people that are expected to be added to the U.S. population by 2000.

It is of course true that there is a distribution problem in the U.S. Some parts of the country are economically depressed and losing population— often the most talented, productive, and capable elements—while some others are growing so rapidly that they are nearly overwhelmed. Patterns of migration and settlement are such that residential areas are becoming racially and economically segregated to an extreme degree, a trend that can be expected to have many undesirable social consequences. Central cities are being economically strangled and abandoned, while industry and the taxpaying middle class flee to the suburbs. But some social scientists have advanced the notion that, rather than being the cause of our social problems, maldistribution and migration might be symptoms of a deeper, more general malady.

Population maldistribution is a different, although related, problem from that of absolute growth, and it demands a different set of solutions. Nevertheless, if growth is not curtailed, the distribution situation will certainly be exacerbated.

Unfortunately, the proposal to create new cities—which would need to be built at the improbable rate of one the size of Tulsa, Oklahoma, per month until the end of the century if *all* expected population growth were to be absorbed—suffers from a number of serious drawbacks. In order to provide the space alone, the U.S. would have to sacrifice large amounts of land now in agricultural production. Far from lessening pollution, new cities would provide additional foci of environmental deterioration. The total impact of pollution on the national environment would not be alleviated by redistribution; the changes would all be local.

Peter Morrison of the Rand Corporation has pointed out several further disadvantages of new cities. The first difficulty is the enormous cost of building each new city, including the creation of a solid economic base to attract immigrants in competition against older cities. The populations of new cities, unless controlled by explicit resettling policies, would be even more homogenous than today's suburbs, and would tend to be even more mobile. Thus they would be quite unstable and would tend to intensify, rather than relieve, the problems of social segregation.

A better solution to distribution problems would be to revitalize existing cities and form policies that encourage migration in desired directions. People who move to new areas are usually attracted to better job opportunities or higher wages. Most go where they already have friends or relatives, a factor which militates against the successful establishment of new cities. Most migration in the U.S. occurs between urban areas; relatively few move from rural to urban areas. Such policies as local tax situations which encourage or discourage the development of industries and differences between states in welfare benefits have considerable potential influence on migration.

A few states and local governments have become aware of the possibilities of limiting local population growth due to immigration by limiting or discouraging industrial and other development. The state of Delaware has banned the further establishment of heavy industries along its shoreline, and other industries must be approved before they can be established. One of the reasons cited for the ban, apart from the severe pollution such industries would bring, was the influx of population they would attract. The Colorado Environmental Commission has proposed that a population size limit be established for the Denver metropolitan area. The city of Los Angeles, which is presently zoned for a completed population size of 7.5 million, is considering a massive zoning rollback to achieve a completed city size of 2.5 million (slightly *less* than the 1970 population). Oregon and Florida have stopped their former policies of encouraging immigration and are restricting industrial development.

Many other areas are changing or reconsidering their zoning regulations as a means of limiting growth. Since zoning merely restricts the use of land, it does not constitute a taking of property by the public for public use, and therefore the landowner is not entitled to compensation. Thus, socially undesirable development may be stopped, without cost to taxpayers, by means of restrictive zoning. The trend toward restrictive development policies can be expected to accelerate as more local governments become aware of the consequences of excessive growth.

## U.S. Population Policies

Until 1970 the only population policies that the United States had were pronatalist policies implicit in tax and other laws and the regulation of immigration. In 1970 Congress passed the Family Planning Services and

Population Research Act and established the Commission on Population Growth and the American Future. Also passed was a Housing and Urban Development Act which authorized urban redevelopment and the building of new towns.

A resolution was introduced in Congress in 1970 by Senator Joseph Tydings, calling for a national goal of zero population growth, to the effect: "That it is the policy of the United States to develop, encourage, and implement, at the earliest possible time, the necessary policies, attitudes, social standards and actions which will, by voluntary means, be consistent with human rights and individual conscience, stabilize the population of the United States and thereby promote the future well-being of the citizens of this nation and the entire world." This resolution died in committee, but was introduced again in 1971 by Senators Taft and Cranston. Passage of the resolution would establish a governmental position in favor of population limitation.

Senator Robert Packwood and Representative Paul McCloskey introduced in each house of Congress a bill to limit tax exemptions for children to two per family. Senator Packwood has also sponsored a bill to legalize abortion nationwide. Neither piece of legislation has gone very far.

The Family Planning Act, sponsored in the Senate by Senator Tydings and passed in 1970, was intended to make family planning information and services available to all women in the U.S. who cannot afford them, provide grants for training and research, and establish a national center for population and family planning in the Department of Health, Education and Welfare. The Act as finally passed unfortunately authorized lower funding than was originally proposed and prohibited the use of any funds for agencies involved in abortion. Moreover, the Administration budget has called for spending only a fraction of the research allocation and considerably less than all of the service allocations in fiscal 1971 and 1972.

President Nixon's concern about population growth would thus appear to be somewhat less deep than his rhetoric suggests. In early 1971, the President reversed an earlier military hospital policy of providing abortion regardless of local laws, thus imposing his personal moral views on the women members and female dependents of the armed forces.

Other proposed legislation in Congress, which if enacted might directly or indirectly affect American reproduction, includes bills to equalize tax rates between single and married people, tax deductions for adoption fees, equal rights for women, and tax deductions and provision for child care.

In March 1971, the Commission on Population Growth and the American Future issued its interim report; the final report is due in March 1972. The Commission was established by Congress to study the effects of population growth and distribution of the U.S. and analyze ways of adjusting to them; it was also required to weigh the resource and environmental implications of growth and explore ways of establishing a population level consistent with American ethical values and resources. The scope and depth of the Commission's inquiry can perhaps best be revealed by quoting the interim report:

The time has come to ask what level of population growth is good for the United States . . . [T]hese are new times and we have to question old assumptions and make new choices based on what population growth means for the Nation today. Despite the pervasive impact of population growth on every facet of American life, the United States has never developed a deliberate policy on the subject. There is a need today for the Nation to consider population growth explicitly and to formulate policy for the future. . . .

The Commission views population policy not as an end in itself but as a means to facilitate the achievement of other social goals desirable in their own right. Such goals would include improvements in the status of women, in the socioeconomic conditions of disadvantaged minorities, and in the health and opportunities of children born because they were wanted, as well as the easing of pressures on our resources and physical environment, health and educational facilities, and the problems of our cities.

The content of a population policy would not be immutable, but would need to be adjusted over time in the light of emerging developments, increased knowledge, and changing attitudes of both policy-makers and the general public. Thus, the Commission sees national population policy as an evolving rather than a static instrumentality. . . .

We do not take future population trends as inevitable. We believe that there are short-run population trends already in process that simply must be accommodated, but that the longer-run future hangs in the balance. And it is not simply population growth itself that is the issue, but rather the quality of life that can be influenced so fundamentally by population. We have the challenge, and indeed the responsibility, to prepare for the future of coming generations of Americans.

The Commission's final report should be a very significant document. We hope that the President, the Congress, and the American public will give it the attention and respect it deserves.

## Population Control

Population control is the conscious regulation of population size by society. Given the threat to our environment and the menace this represents to our already faltering ability to provide food enough for today's population, it is clear that the human population cannot afford *any* further growth, and will soon have to decline. Whatever lands may remain available that seem capable of supporting larger populations than they do now are more than counterbalanced by the vast areas that are grossly overpopulated. In an overpopulated world, no country can have the right to indulge itself in a high growth rate. Since the human population of the world is truly a single interdependent community, such behavior by any country could reasonably be regarded as irresponsible and a threat to all the rest.

No nation has yet adopted as a goal the reduction of its population growth rate to zero, let alone a reduction in absolute population size. In fact, governments in some UDCs—especially in Africa, where the death rate is still well above the average DC level—are hotly pursuing a high birth rate in the belief that their countries need more people in order to develop! (The role of population growth relative to economic development is discussed in Chapter 12). These countries, needless to say, generally do not even have official family planning programs (Box 10-3). As an example of this thinking, in November 1969, Luis Echeverria Alvarez, presidential nominee (now president) in Mexico, announced his opposition to officially sponsored birth control programs, saying, "I don't know whether the birth control pill is effective . . . What I do know is that we have to populate our country and that we have to have faith in our youth and our children."

Before any really effective population control can be established, the political leaders, economists, national planners, and others who determine such policies must be convinced of its necessity. Most of the measures beyond traditional family planning that might be effective have never been tried because they are considered strong and restrictive and they run counter to traditional attitudes. In many countries these measures may not even be considered until massive famines, political unrest, or ecological disasters make their initiation imperative. In such emergencies, whatever measures are economically and technologically expedient will be the likeliest to be imposed, regardless of their political or social acceptability.

We should long ago have begun exploring, developing, and discussing all possible means of population control. But we did not, and time has nearly run out. Measures that may seem totally unacceptable today to the majority of people at large or to their national leaders may be seen as very much the lesser of evils only a few years from now. It must be remembered that even family planning, easily justified on humanitarian grounds alone, and economically feasible for even the poorest of countries, was widely considered totally unacceptable as a government policy only 15 years ago.

Bernard Berelson of the Population Council has analyzed and rated several proposed population control measures according to these criteria: technological, political, administrative, and economic feasibility; ethical acceptability, and presumed effectiveness. Most of the proposals that might be expected to be effective were rated relatively unacceptable on one basis or another. Abortion, for example, was considered low in political and ethical acceptability, uncertain in administrative feasibility, but technically and economically feasible. Compulsory fertility control was rated low on all counts except economic capability. But even such mild measures as incentive programs and tax policies favoring small families were rated moderately low or low in political and economic feasibility, and uncertain in their effectiveness. Berelson's analysis is useful, although his conclusions may have been influenced by his long commitment to family planning.

All of the attitudes on which his evaluations are based are certainly susceptible to change. Indeed, they are changing, as evidenced by the acceptance of legalized abortion by the Indian Parliament. Promising methods that are not now technologically possible should be developed, so that they might be available if and when the need for them arose. Generous assistance

BOX 10-3 POPULATION POLICIES AROUND THE WORLD

## Africa

In general, among past and present colonial countries in Africa, family planning on a private basis has long been available in English colonies, but not in colonies of Catholic countries such as France, Belgium, Spain, Italy, and Portugal. Several former English colonies now have national family planning policies, although they may be promoted only for welfare reasons. (See Table 10-1 for details of UDCs with family planning programs.) A few former French colonies have begun to relax their prohibitions to allow the sale of contraceptives in drugstores and to support some family planning activities. The Portugese colonies remain pronatalist and strongly opposed to birth control. Many of the North African countries have initiated family planning programs, while some others remain pronatalist.

In South Africa and Rhodesia the dominant European populations have traditionally practiced birth control. These countries are now trying to extend family planning services to their African populations. South Africa's family planning is offered only unofficially through private agencies. At the same time, however, South Africa is tending to encourage larger families in its white population.

The belief that more people are needed for development is common among African nations south of the Sahara. Concern about migration is often greater than concern about the high birth rates.

Many African countries still have death rates that are higher than 20 per thousand, and some are even more than 30. A number of demographers and family planning officials believe that interest in population control will remain low until the death rates have been substantially reduced. Ways must somehow be found to change this point of view so that birth rates may be lowered *along with* death rates.

## Asia

Asia presents a widely varied picture in regard to population policies. At one extreme, India and Pakistan are pursuing strong family planning policies accompanied by some social measures, while several of the smaller countries have still shown no interest in population policies. The People's Republic of China has established strong population policies, largely as a part of other social programs. The effectiveness of these is not really known, although the birth rate in China is lower than in many other Asian countries. For political reasons, during the 1950s China did not actively encourage birth control, but the enforced segregation of the sexes in communes must have had an effect on the birth rate. Since the early 1960s, except for a brief period during the "cultural revolution," when young people in the Red Guard associated freely and often married young, a strict policy of late marriage (minimum age 25 for women and 28 to 30 for men) has been in force. The two-child family is strongly promoted, with a space of 3 to 5 years between births. Voluntary sterilization for men who have had two or three children is also encouraged. Birth control methods are apparently widely available; so is legal abortion, utilizing the vacuum device. As is typical of communist countries, women are fully employed outside the home, given limited maternity benefits, and provided with child care. These policies and services apparently are quite well established in the cities and in recent years have spread to villages and communes.

Japan, the only fully industrialized country in Asia, reduced her birth rate rapidly to DC levels after World War II largely by legalizing abortion. A policy of encouraging the use of birth control methods has since reduced the abortion rate without changing the birth rate. The social policy, which was

BOX 10–3 (*continued*)

promoted through massive educational and communications programs, very strongly discouraged having a family with more than two children. Recently, alarmed by a growing labor shortage, the Japanese government has been campaigning for more births.

### North America

Neither Canada nor the United States has an official government population policy, except in respect to immigration. However, there has been a trend toward establishing such a policy. A presidential Commission on Population Growth and the American Future will present its findings and recommendations in 1972 in the areas of demographic development, resource utilization, and the probable effects of population growth on governmental activities. It is hoped that the Commission's recommendations can provide a basis for a strong population policy in the future.

In 1970 Congress passed the Family Planning Services and Population Research Act, which is intended to extend family planning counselling and services to all who need them, particularly the poor, and to sponsor research in the area of reproduction. There has also been a trend toward liberalizing abortion restrictions in the various states. Since 1967, foreign aid agencies have been permitted to include family planning assistance in their programs. Funding for overseas family planning assistance has been steadily increasing since then.

### Latin America

Latin America as a region, despite having the highest population growth rates in the world, has been among the most reluctant to accept a need for population control. This is probably in part due to the influence of the Roman Catholic Church, but there is also a widespread belief, at least in South America, that the continent still contains vast untapped resources of land and minerals, that the answer to all problems is development, and that more people are needed for development. Furthermore, Latin American politicians tend to view proposals originating in the U.S. regarding birth control with understandable suspicion. Some seem to believe we are trying to impose a new and subtle form of imperialism. In some countries this reaction has even had the effect of inhibiting the teaching of demography and family planning in universities. Economists and many politicians have come to accept family planning agencies only on health and welfare grounds and as a means of reducing the horrendous illegal abortion rate. In a few cases they are beginning to realize that the galloping population growth rate is swallowing all the economic progress each year, leaving a per capita rate of progress of zero or less. Most Latin American countries have at least some government support for family planning; but some of the poorest, most overpopulated, and fastest-growing countries, such as Haiti, have none.

### Europe and U.S.S.R.

Western European countries generally have no official population policies, although birth control is almost universally practiced. Sweden is an exception in that there is an official policy for sex education in schools including birth control, a moderately liberal abortion policy, family planning services as part of the national health organization, and a program to assist other family planning programs abroad. England also provides abortions through its National Health Service, and some discussion of developing an antinatalist policy has begun in Parliament. England also provides some family planning assistance to UDCs, mostly former colonies.

Most Catholic countries ban birth control in some degree, but late marriages, high rates of illegal abortions, and the use of withdrawal and the rhythm method help keep birth rates down. There is now a trend to liberalize the laws against contraception and abortion in many of these countries.

Eastern European countries and the Soviet Union provide family planning and abortion through their health services, although Communist ideology officially calls for pronatalist policies. Discouragement of early marriage, an emphasis on training, education, and the full outside employment of women also undoubtedly contribute to the low birth rates.

### Oceania

Australia and New Zealand have historically regarded themselves as underpopulated. Consequently their policies have been pronatalist and proimmigration. There is evidence that these policies are currently being re-evaluated as the public becomes aware of the world population problem. A Zero Population Growth movement was founded in Australia in 1971. As former English colonies, both countries have long had family planning groups and access to contraceptives. Their birth rates are well within the usual DC range, although their growth rates are inflated by high immigration rates.

### United Nations

For many years, the United Nations has limited its participation in population policies to the gathering of demographic data. This has, however, played a role in developing awareness of the need for population policies, especially among UDCs, whose governments often have had no other information about their population growth. Now the U.N. is beginning to take an active role in coordinating assistance for and directly participating in family planning programs of various member nations, while continuing the demographical studies. A special body, the U.N. Fund for Population Activities (UNFPA), advises governments on policies and programs, coordinates private donors and contributions from DC governments and sometimes directly provides supplies, equipment, and personnel through other U.N. agencies.

In 1969 the U.N. Declaration on Social Progress and Development stated that "parents have the exclusive right to determine freely and responsibly the number and spacing of their children." The statement affirmed the U.N.'s increasing involvement in making family planning available to all peoples everywhere and contained an implied criticism of any government policy which might deny family planning to parents who want it. The statement has also been interpreted as a stand against compulsory governmental policies to control births. It is a stand against compulsion; however, the right to choose whether or not to have children is specifically limited in that the right extends only to "responsible" choices. Thus, without violating the Declaration, governments may properly control irresponsible choices.

from developed countries could remove many economic and lack-of-personnel objections for UDCs. Effectiveness can really only be evaluated after a method has been tried. Moral acceptability is very likely to change as conditions change in most societies. The struggle for economic development in the UDCs is producing considerable social upheaval, which will particularly affect such basic elements of society as family structure. Radical changes in family structure and relationships are inevitable, whether population control is instituted or not. Inaction, attended by a deterioration in living conditions, will bring changes everywhere that no one could consider beneficial. Thus, it is beside the point to object to population control measures simply on the grounds that they might change the social structure or family relationships.

Rather than resisting social change, modern communications methods and educational techniques can be used to help develop constructive attitudes and accelerate desirable trends. Trained and sympathetic personnel—for example, social scientists familiar with local cultures and the techniques of introducing change—can work effectively on these problems. Setting up communications centers, training behavioral and other scientists, and supporting technicians and social workers abroad could be major contributions of the DCs to population control efforts.

The moral objections to population control often seem to exist primarily in the minds of political or religious leaders. With regard to abortion, for example, women around the world are plainly unimpressed by the moral objections. The precise number of abortions performed each year is not known, since the majority are illegal, but a U.N. Conference on Abortion in 1965 estimated that there were about 30 million abortions per year (as opposed to about 120 million births). More recent estimates are higher. Moreover, attitudes toward abortion can change considerably in a very short period of time, as witness the change in American attitudes over the last decade.

## Measures for Population Control

Among proposed general approaches to population control are family planning, the use of socioeconomic pressures, and compulsory fertility control. Maximum freedom of choice is provided by traditional family planning, which allows each couple to plan the number and spacing of their children. But family planning alone should not be regarded as "population control," because it includes no consideration of optimum population size for the society, nor does it influence parental goals. Although population growth may be substantially slowed by family planning where individual motivation favors low birth rates and planning is for relatively few children, family planning in other areas may equally well result in average family sizes too large to produce the desired level of population growth, stability, or decline.

The use of abortion and voluntary sterilization to supplement other forms of birth control can quite properly be included as part of family planning.

These methods can be made available at costs everyone can afford. Objections have been raised to the idea of including abortion in family planning programs on the grounds that UDCs lack the trained personnel and medical facilities to carry it out. Even England, after liberalizing her abortion laws, had some difficulty along this line. But the answer to this problem lies in the use of the vacuum device (Chapter 9); it eliminates the need for hospital recuperation and can be operated by a trained midwife or other paramedical person. It has been successfully used on an outpatient basis in eastern Europe, U.S.S.R., China, Japan, England, and more recently in New York City and California.

An extension of family planning that would include legal abortion and sterilization wherever acceptable, might be a first step toward population control. Although many DCs may have very nearly achieved saturation with this completely voluntary approach, there is still a good deal of room for action in the UDCs. Family planning programs can provide the means of contraception, and through their activities and educational campaigns can spread awareness of the idea of birth control among the people. These programs should be expanded and supported throughout the world as rapidly and as fully as possible, *but other programs should be instituted immediately as well*. Given the family size aspirations of people everywhere, additional measures beyond family planning will unquestionably be required in order to halt the population explosion.

## SOCIOECONOMIC MEASURES

Population control through the use of socioeconomic pressures to encourage or discourage reproduction is the approach advocated by, among others, demographer Kingsley Davis, who originated many of the following suggestions. The objective of this approach would be to influence the attitudes and motivations of individual couples. An important part of such an approach would be a large-scale educational program to persuade people of the advantages of small families, to themselves and to society. Information on birth control, of course, should accompany such educational efforts. Programs of this kind should be offered in schools and should also be communicated to adults through a variety of appropriate media, both directly and indirectly. Such an educational campaign is one of the first measures that could be adopted in all countries, UDC or DC, and used at least until its efficacy could be evaluated in terms of other efforts and objectives.

As United States taxpayers know, the federal government uses economic pressure in its present income tax laws to encourage marriage and child-bearing, a pronatalist posture that is no longer appropriate. Tax laws should be adjusted to favor (instead of penalize) single people, working wives, and small families. Perhaps they should even penalize large families that have incomes above certain levels. One suggestion, which has obvious psychological advantages, would be to offer more realistic income tax deductions for the first two children (say $2,000 each) and no deduction for additional children. Tax measures in the United States and other countries might also include marriage fees, taxes on luxury baby goods and toys, and removal of family allowances, where they exist.

Measures like these would clearly be applicable only in countries that have reached a stage of development where a substantial portion of the population is affluent enough to pay taxes, and where tax collection is reasonably honest and effective. Tax policies of this sort have the advantage of shifting the burden of supplying government services more onto the shoulders of those large families who produce the need for them; at least this can be done for large *affluent* families. Tax measures can be designed in various ways to reinforce the idea that population growth is no longer desirable.

Another suggestion related to taxation is that the amount of free education available to a family might be limited to a total of 24 years, enough to put two children through high school. This proposal, however, along with one that would limit maternal benefits, has the potential disadvantage of heavily penalizing children (and in the long run society as well). The same criticism may be made of some other tax plans, unless they can be carefully adjusted to avoid denying at least minimum care for poor families, regardless of the number of children they may have.

A somewhat different approach might be to provide incentives for late marriage and childlessness. Possibilities include paying a bonus to a first-time bride who is over 25 (or to her parents, in countries where bride prices and arranged marriages are customary); a bonus could also be given to couples after five childless years or to men who accept vasectomies after their wives have a given number of children. Lotteries open only to childless adults have also been proposed. Sociologist Larry D. Barnett has calculated the cost of annual fees, based on a percentage of annual income that could be paid to couples who have no more than two children until the wife reaches the age of 45. For example, the cost (based on 5 percent of the annual income up to an income ceiling of $20,000 and calculated on the expected United States population for 1975), would be some $9 billion for that year. Barnett concludes that the savings in pollution and other costs would justify the expenditure.

Adoption can be encouraged through subsidies and simplified procedures, particularly as a measure to satisfy couples who have a definite desire for a son or daughter. Further research on sex determination should be pursued for a similar reason. Many families have additional children in an attempt to have a son, if they have only daughters, or to have a daughter if they have only sons. A special kind of social security pension or bond could be provided for aging adults who have few or no children who might support them in their old age.

There are many possibilities in the sphere of family structure, sexual mores, and the status of women that can be explored, as demographers Kingsley Davis and Judith Blake, and sociologist Alice Taylor Day have suggested. With some exceptions, women have traditionally been allowed to fulfill only the roles of wife and mother. Anything that can be done to diminish the emphasis upon these roles and provide women with equal opportunities in education, employment and other areas is likely to reduce the birth rate. Any measures that postpone marriage and then delay the first child's birth would also help to encourage a reduction in birth rates. The later that marriage and the first child occur, the more time the woman will have to develop other interests. Outside interests, besides employment, can be cultivated, and social life could be planned around these outside interests or the couple's work, rather than exclusively within the neighborhood and family. Adequate care for pre-school children should be provided at low cost, and moreover, it could provide an important new source of employment. Provision of child care seems more likely to encourage employment outside the home with concomitant low reproduction than to encourage reproduction. The deplorable lack of good doctors and medical services in many parts of the United States, for example, could be overcome by actively recruiting and training more women as doctors and other needed specialists. In the Soviet Union more than half of the doctors are female. Women represent a large, relatively untapped pool of intellectual and technical talent; tapping that pool effectively could help reduce population growth and also provide many other direct benefits to any society.

Social pressures on both men and women to marry and have children must be removed. As Stewart Udall has observed in his book, *1976: Agenda for Tomorrow:* "All lives are not enhanced by marital union; parenthood is not necessarily a fulfillment for every married couple." If society were convinced of the need for low birth rates, no doubt the stigma that has customarily been assigned to bachelors, spinsters, and childless couples would soon disappear. But alternative life-styles should be open to single people, and perhaps the institution of an informal, easily dissolved "marriage" for the childless is one possibility. Indeed, the fact that many DC societies already seem to be evolving in this direction suggests that fully developed societies may produce such arrangements naturally. In UDCs, they might be encouraged deliberately, as the status of women approaches parity with that of men.

Although free and easy association of the sexes might be tolerated, illegitimate childbearing could be strongly discouraged. One way to carry out this disapproval would be to insist that all illegitimate babies be put up for adoption. If the mother really wished to keep her baby, she could be obliged to go through adoption proceedings, which might remain more difficult for single people than for couples. Abortion for illegitimate pregnancies might also be required, either as an alternative to placement for adoption or as the only choice, depending on the society.

Somewhat more repressive measures have also been proposed. Whether their effectiveness would counterbalance their social disadvantages is questionable, but at least they should be discussed. These proposals include limiting paid maternal leave (common in many countries) to two children, or reducing it with each child after the first; assigning public housing without regard for family size; and removing dependency allowances from student grants or military pay. The idea behind these is the observation that people in the past have voluntarily controlled their reproduction most stringently during periods of great social and economic stress and insecurity, such as the Depression of the 1930s.

Studies by Judith Blake and by economist Alan Sweezy of the California Institute of Technology, however, have cast serious doubt on the belief that economic considerations are paramount in determining fertility trends. If this view is correct, then severely repressive economic measures might prove to be both ineffective and unnecessary as a vehicle for population control. Clearly, much more needs to be learned about the determinants of fertility trends.


### INVOLUNTARY FERTILITY CONTROL

The third approach to population control is that of involuntary fertility control. Several coercive proposals deserve serious consideration, mainly because we may ultimately have to resort to them unless current trends in birth rates are rapidly reversed by other means. Some involuntary measures may prove to be less repressive or discriminatory, in fact, than some of the socioeconomic measures that have been proposed.

One idea that has been seriously proposed in India is to vasectomize all fathers of three or more children. This was defeated not only on moral grounds but on practical ones as well: there simply were not enough medical personnel available even to start on the eligible candidates, let alone deal with the new recruits added each day! Massive assistance from the developed world in the form of medical and paramedical personnel, and/or a training program for local people, might put such a policy within the realm of possibility, although it still would not be very popular. But probably India's government will have to resort to some such coercive method sooner or later, unless famine, war, or disease takes the problem out of its hands. There is little time left for educational programs and social change, and the population is probably too poor for economic measures (especially penalties) to be effective.

A program of sterilizing women after their second or third child, despite the greater difficulty of the female operation, might be easier than trying to sterilize the fathers. At least this would be the case in countries where the majority of babies are born in maternity hospitals and clinics, and where the medical corps is adequate. The problem of finding and identifying eligibles for sterilization would be simplified in this way.

The development of a sterilizing capsule that can be implanted under the skin and removed when pregnancy is desired opens another possibility for coercive control. The capsule could be implanted at puberty and might be removable, with official permission, for a limited number of births. Various approaches to administering this system have been offered, including one by economist Kenneth Boulding of the University of Colorado. His proposal is to issue to each woman at marriage a marketable license that would en-title her to a given number of children. Under such a system the number could be two if the society desired to reduce the population size slowly. To maintain a steady size, perhaps one out of four couples might be allowed to have a third child if they purchased special tickets from the government or from other women, who, having purchased them, decided not to have a child or found they had a greater need for the money. Another idea is that permission to have a third child might be granted to a limited number of couples by lottery. This system would allow governments to regulate more or less exactly the number of births over a given period of time.

Of course a government might require only implantation of the capsule, leaving its removal to the individual's discretion but requiring reimplantation after childbirth. Since having a child would require positive action (removal of the capsule), many more births would be prevented than in the reverse situation. Certainly unwanted births and the problem of abortion would both be entirely avoided. The disadvantages, besides any moral objections, include the questionable desirability of having the entire female population on a continuous steroid dosage with the contingent health risks, and the logistics of implanting capsules in 50 percent of the population between the ages of 15 and 50.

Adding a sterilant to drinking water or staple foods is a suggestion that, initially at least, seems to horrify people more than most proposals for involuntary fertility control. Indeed this would pose some very difficult political, legal, and social questions, to say nothing of the technical problems. No such sterilant exists today. To be acceptable, such a substance would have to meet some rather stiff requirements. It would have to be uniformly effective, despite widely varying doses received by individuals, and despite varying degrees of fertility and sensitivity among individuals. It would have to be free of dangerous or unpleasant side-effects, and have no effect on members of the opposite sex, children, old people, pets, or livestock.

Botanist Richard W. Schrieber of the University of New Hampshire has proposed that a sterilizing virus could be developed, with an antidote available by injection. This would avoid the problem of finding an appropriate staple food or adjusting doses in water supplies, but it might present some other difficulties. Not the least difficulty might be the appearance of a mutant virus immune to the antidote.

Physiologist Melvin Ketchel, of the Tufts University School of Medicine, has suggested that a sterilant could be developed that would have a very specific action—for example, the prevention of implantation of the fertilized ovum. He proposed that it be used to reduce fertility levels by adjustable amounts, anywhere from 5 percent to 75 percent, rather than to sterilize the whole population completely. In this way, fertility could be adjusted from time to time to meet a society's changing needs, and there would be no need to provide an antidote. Family planning would still be needed for those couples who were highly motivated to have a small family. Subfertile and functionally sterile couples who strongly desire children could be medically assisted, as they are now, or encouraged to adopt.

This plan has the advantage of avoiding those socioeconomic programs that might tend to discriminate against particular groups in a society or that might penalize children. It would also involve no direct action against individuals, such as sterilization operations or implanted capsules. In extremely poor and overpopulated countries, such a program would undoubtedly be far more effective and far easier to administer than any of the others, at least until development and educational levels reached a point where people could be affected by small-family propaganda and be influenced by social or economic pressures. The administration of this sort of program would probably also be easier to safeguard against corruption and abuse in favor of some segments of society, although this is likely to be a problem with any form of population control, just as it is with any government program having far-reaching social consequences.

Compulsory control of family size is an unpalatable idea to many, but the alternatives may be much more horrifying. As those alternatives become clearer to an increasing number of people in the 1970s, we may well find them *demanding* such control. A far better choice, in our view, is to begin *now* with milder methods of influencing family size preferences, while ensuring that the means of birth control, including abortion and sterilization, are accessible to every human being on Earth within the shortest possible time. If effective action is taken promptly, perhaps the need for involuntary or repressive measures can be averted.


## Population Control and Attitudes

No form of population control, even the most coercive or repressive, will succeed for long unless individuals understand the need for it and accept the idea that humanity must limit its numbers. Therefore, the ultimate key to population control lies in changing human attitudes concerning reproductive behavior and goals in all societies. Achieving this throughout the world would be a gigantic task even if it became the world's first-priority goal, as many believe it should be.

But human survival seems certain to require population control programs, at least in some places, even before the necessary changes in attitudes can be brought about in the population. In fact, the establishment of such programs might in itself help to convince people of the seriousness of the population problem.

Most of the population control measures discussed here have never been tried; we know only that their *potential* effectiveness may be great. The socioeconomic proposals are based on knowledge of the sort of social conditions that have been associated in the past with low birth rates. We need to know more about all peoples' attitudes toward human reproduction; we need to know how these attitudes are affected by various living conditions, including some that seem virtually intolerable to us. Even more, we need to know what influences and conditions will lead to changes in these attitudes in favor of smaller families. How can we convince a poor Pakistani villager or a middle-class American that the number of children his wife bears is of crucial importance, not just to himself and his family, but also to his society? How can we make everyone care?

# Bibliography

Adams, E. Sherman, 1969. Unwanted births and poverty in the United States. *The Conference Board Record,* vol. VI, no. 4, pp. 10–17.

Anonymous, 1968. A limit to "wanted" babies? *Medical World News,* Dec. 6.

Anonymous, 1969. Family planning campaign—the Louisiana story. *U.S. News and World Report,* July 28, pp. 55–57. Account of family planning program for the poor.

Anonymous, 1971, P. L. 91–572, milestone U.S. family planning legislation, signed into law. *Family Planning Perspectives,* vol. 3, no. 1, (Jan.), pp. 2–3. Details of the 1970 Family Planning Act.

Anonymous, 1971. Too many Americans? A population expert's view. *U.S. News and World Report,* Feb. 15, pp. 62–64. An interesting discussion of U.S. population trends by a Census Bureau demographer, but with a rather naive view of the environmental aspects.

Anonymous, 1971. U.N. awakens to the problems of a crowded world. *Financial Times* (London), 9 March.

Ayala, F. J., and C. T. Falk, 1971. Sex of children and family size. *Journal of Heredity,* vol. 62, no. 1, pp. 57–59. Study indicating that desire for children of a particular sex may have little influence on family size in the U.S.

Barnett, Larry D., 1969. Population policy: payments for fertility limitation in the U.S. *Social Biology,* vol. 16, no. 4 (Dec.). An analysis of the economics of such a program.

Barnett, Larry D., 1971. Zero Population Growth, Inc. *BioScience,* vol. 21, no. 14, pp. 759–766 (July 15). A sociological study of the membership of ZPG.

Behrman, S. J., L. Corsa, Jr., and R. Freedman (eds.), 1969. *Fertility and Family Planning; A World View.* Univ. of Michigan Press, Ann Arbor. A basic source on family planning.

Berelson, Bernard, et al., 1966. *Family Planning and Population Programs.* Univ. of Chicago Press, Chicago. Basic information on family planning programs.

Berelson, Bernard, 1969. Beyond family planning. *Science,* vol. 163, pp. 533–543. An evaluation of proposed means of population control and an affirmation of the value of family planning programs.

Berelson, Bernard, 1970. The present state of family planning programs. *Studies in Family Planning,* no. 57. The Population Council (Sept.) Useful summary.

Best, Winfield, and Louis Dupré, 1967. Birth control. *Encyclopedia Britannica.* Interesting account of the history of the planned parenthood movement.

Blake, Judith, 1968. Are babies consumer durables? *Population Studies,* vol. 22, no. 1, pp. 5–25 (March). An examination of economic factors motivating family planning.

Blake, Judith, 1969. Population policy for Americans: is the government being misled? *Science,* vol. 164, pp. 522–29. Raises some important questions relative to proposed family planning policies for the poor.

Blake, Judith, 1971. Reproductive motivation and population policy. *BioScience,* vol. 21, no. 5, pp. 215–220 (March 1). An analysis of what sorts of policies might lower U.S. birth rate.

Bumpass, L., and C. F. Westoff, 1970. The "perfect contraceptive" population, *Science,* vol. 169, pp. 1177–1182 (18 Sept.). Discussion of incidence of unwanted births in the U.S.

Campbell, Arthur A., 1966. White-nonwhite differences in family planning in the United States. *Health, Education & Welfare Indicators* (Feb.). U.S. Dept. of Health, Education and Welfare.

Chasteen, Edgar R., 1971. *The Case for Compulsory Birth Control.* Prentice-Hall, Inc., Englewood Cliffs, New Jersey.

Commission on Population Growth and the American Future, 1971. An Interim Report. U.S. Government Printing Office. Also reprinted in *Family Planning Perspectives,* vol. 3, no. 2, pp. 45–52 (April).

Darity, W. A., C. B. Turner, and H. J. Thiebaux, 1971. Race consciousness and fears of black genocide as barriers to family planning. *Perspectives from the Black Community, PRB Selection* no. 37 (June), Population Reference Bureau. An analysis of genocide fears and attitudes toward birth control in the black population of the U.S.

Davis, Kingsley, 1965. Some demographic aspects of poverty in the United States. *In* Margaret S. Gordon (ed.), *Poverty in America.* Chandler Publishing Co., San Francisco.

Davis, Kingsley, 1967. Population policy: will current programs succeed? *Science,* vol. 158, pp. 730–739. One of the most important papers on socio-economic means of population control; excellent.

Day, Alice Taylor, 1968. Population control and personal freedom: are they compatible? *The Humanist,* Nov.–Dec. Contains some excellent ideas in the socio-economic realm of population control measures.

Easterlin, Richard A., 1968. *Population, Labor Force, and Long Swings in Economic Growth.* Columbia Univ. Press, New York. A detailed and scholarly treatment attempting to demonstrate that American fertility patterns are primarily determined by economic factors. Sweezy (see below) does not agree.

Enke, Stephen, 1970. Zero U.S. population growth—when, how, and why. *Tempo,* General Electric Co., Santa Barbara, Jan.

Frederiksen, Harald, 1969. Feedback in economic and demographic transition. *Science,* vol. 166, pp. 837–847. An overly optimistic discussion of the possible benefits of death control in motivating people to have smaller families in UDCs.

Freedman, R., and J. Y. Takeshita, 1969. *Family Planning in Taiwan, an Experiment in Social Change.* Princeton Univ. Press, Princeton, N.J. A detailed analysis of a national family planning program.

Guttmacher, A. F., 1966. *The Complete Book of Birth Control.* Ballantine Books, New York. Contains some history of the family planning movement.

Harkavy, O., F. S. Jaffe, and S. M. Wishnik, 1969. Family planning and public policy: who is misleading whom? *Science,* vol. 165, pp. 367–373. A reply to Judith Blake's article by the family planning establishment.

Hauser, Philip M., 1967. Family planning and population programs. *Demography,* vol. 4, no. 1. Critical review of Berelson's book on family planning, raising some pertinent questions on the approach of family planning as a solution to the population problem.

Heisel, Donald F., 1971. The emergence of population policies in sub-Saharan Africa. *Concerned Demography,* vol. 2, no. 4, pp. 30–35 (March).

Hill, Adelaide C., and Frederick S. Jaffe, 1966. Negro fertility and family size preferences: implications for programming of health and social services. *In* Talcott Parsons and Kenneth B. Clark (eds.), *The Negro American.* Houghton Mifflin Co., Boston.

Johnson, Stanley, 1970. *Life Without Birth.* Little, Brown & Co., Boston. A personal and vivid exploration of the population explosion and family planning programs around the world, particularly UDCs.

Kangas, Lerni W., 1970. Integrated incentives for fertility control. *Science,* vol. 169, pp. 1278–1283 (25 Sept.). Suggestions for improving family planning programs in UDCs.

Ketchel, Melvin M., 1968. Fertility control agents as a possible solution to the world population problem. *Perspectives in Biology and Medicine,* vol. 11, no. 4 (Summer). Discussion of fertility-reducing agents which could be administered impartially to all members of a society.

Lelyveld, Joseph, 1969. Birth curb drive slowing in India. *New York Times,* April 20. Discusses decline in India's sterilizing program.

McElroy, William D., 1969. Biomedical aspects of population control. *BioScience,* vol. 19, no. 1, pp. 19–23 (Jan.). More on the population control controversy; another strong vote for more effective action.

Morrison, Peter, 1970. *Urban Growth, New Cities, and "The Population Problem."* Rand Corporation P-4515-1, Dec. An analysis of population distribution and migration patterns in the U.S. and the new cities approach to dealing with them.

Newman, Lucille F., 1968. *Family Planning: An Anthropological Approach.* Paper presented at the International Congress of Anthropological and Ethnological Sciences, Tokyo, Sept. 6. Raises some pertinent points relative to attitudes and reproductive behavior.

Nortman, Dorothy, 1970. Population and family planning programs: a factbook. *Reports on Population/Family Planning,* no. 2, Population Council, New York. Useful summary.

O'Brien, Fr. John A., 1968. *Family Planning in an Exploding Population.* Hawthorne Books, Inc., New York. A progressive Catholic point of view.

Okorafor, Apia E., 1970. Dialog: Africa's population problems. *Africa Report,* June, pp. 22–23.

Packwood, Bob, 1970. Incentives for the two-child family. *Trial Magazine,* Aug.–Sept., pp. 3–16. Some proposals for population control legislation and details of Sen. Packwood's income tax bill.

Peck, Ellen, 1971. *The Baby Trap.* Bernard Geis Associates, New York. An attack on the traditional pronatalist image of motherhood and an exploration of alternative life-styles.

Population Council, New York. *Studies in Family Planning.* A monthly series. An excellent account of family planning programs around the world.

Population Reference Bureau, *Population Bulletin* and other publications often cover population policies around the world, as well as monitoring the demographic situation. Washington, D.C.

Population Reference Bureau, 1971. Population activities of the United States government. *Population Bulletin,* vol. 27, no. 4 (Aug.).

Potter, R. G., R. Freedman, and Lien-Ping Chow, 1968. Taiwan's family planning program. *Science,* vol. 160, pp. 848–853.

Pradervand, Pierre, 1970. International aspects of population control. *Concerned Demography,* vol. 2, no. 2, pp. 1–16 (Dec.). A discussion of some of the political problems associated with population issues, especially in Latin America.

Revelle, Roger, 1971. *Rapid Population Growth: Consequences and Policy Implications.* Report of a Study Committee, National Academy of Sciences. Johns Hopkins Press, Baltimore.

Smith, Mary, 1968. Birth Control and the Negro Woman. *Ebony,* March.

Sanders, Thomas G., 1971. The politics of population in Brazil. *Fieldstaff Reports, East Coast South America Series,* vol. XV, no. 1. American Universities Field Staff, Hanover, N.H. These Reports contain much of interest in the population field.

Snow, Edgar, 1971. Report from China—III: Population care and control. *The New Republic,* vol. 164, no. 18, pp. 20–23 (May 1).

Stycos, J. Mayone, 1971. Opinion, ideology, and population problems—some sources of domestic and foreign opposition to birth control. *In* Revelle (see above).

Stycos, J. Mayone, 1971. Family planning: reform and revolution. *Family Planning Perspectives,* vol. 3, no. 1, pp. 49–50 (Jan.). On the relevance of family planning to development and politics in UDCs, especially in Latin America.

Sweezy, Alan, 1971. The economic explanation of fertility changes in the U.S. *Pop. Studies,* vol. XXV, no. 2, pp. 255–267 (July). Presents evidence that assumptions that American fertility trends are primarily determined by economic factors are false.

Victor-Bostrum Fund Committee and the Population Crisis Committee, 1730 K St., Washington, D.C. 20006. Population and family planning in the People's Republic of China. (Spring) A collection of articles on China's population policies. Includes a reprint of Edgar Snow's article cited above.

Weiner, Myron, 1971. Political Demography: an inquiry into the political consequences of population change. *In* Revelle (see above).

Westoff, L. A., and C. F. Westoff, 1971. *From Now to Zero: Fertility, Contraception and Abortion in America,* Little, Brown & Co., Boston. Excellent, comprehensive account of demographic structure and population policies in the U.S., although estimates of incidence of unwanted births are out of date. Includes an interesting discussion of fertility in the black population and the impact of population policies on it.

Willie, Charles V., 1971. A position paper. *Perspectives from the Black Community. PRB Selection* no. 37, Population Reference Bureau, June. Discussion of the black community's views on family planning programs and the issue of genocide.

Willing, Martha Kent, 1971. *Beyond Conception: Our Children's Children.* Gambit, Inc., Boston. A woman biologist's view of the population explosion and the future.

# CHAPTER 11

# Social, Political, and Economic Change

*"The ecological constraints on population and technological growth will inevitably lead to social and economic systems different from the ones in which we live today.*
*In order to survive, mankind will have to develop what might be called a steady state.*
*The steady state formula is so different from the philosophy of endless quantitative growth, which has so far governed Western civilization, that it may cause widespread public alarm."*

—René Dubos
*Science,* 14 November, 1969

A change in the attitudes of individuals is the key to population control and to many other measures necessary for the amelioration of the population-environment crisis. Such change is possible. For example, former President of the United States Dwight D. Eisenhower said in 1968: "Once, as president, I thought and said that birth control was not the business of our Federal Government. The facts changed my mind . . . I have come to believe that the population explosion is the world's most critical problem." Changes in our social, political, and economic institutions are also essential. Our problems cannot be solved by destroying our existing institutions, however; we do not have the time or the wisdom to dismantle them and put them back together again in better ways. But these institutions must be successfully altered—and soon—or they and we will not survive. Whether significant changes in attitudes and institutions can occur fast enough to affect mankind's destiny is an open question.

No one is more acutely aware than we are of the difficulties and hazards of trying to criticize and comment constructively on such broad areas of social relevance as religion, education, economics, legal and political systems, and the psychology of individuals and societies. We believe, however, that in order for people to translate into effective and constructive political action what is now known about the roots of the crisis, new, far-reaching and positive programs must be undertaken *immediately*.

Therefore, in this chapter and the next we depart from the realm of relatively hard data in the physical, biological, and social sciences and embark on an exploration of the many other areas of human endeavor which are critically important to a solution of our problems. In doing so we are making the assumption, based upon the facts that President Eisenhower found so compelling, that many reforms are essential. The dangers of making the opposite assumption are beautifully set forth in the following quotation from biologist Garrett Hardin's article, "The Tragedy of the Commons" (*Science,* 1968):

> It is one of the peculiarities of the warfare between reform and the status quo that it is thoughtlessly governed by a double standard. Whenever a reform measure is proposed it is often defeated when its opponents triumphantly discover a flaw in it. As Kingsley Davis has pointed out, worshippers of the status quo sometimes imply that no reform is possible without unanimous agreement, an implication contrary to historical fact. As nearly as I can make out, automatic rejection of proposed reforms is based on one of two unconscious assumptions: (i) that the status quo is perfect; or (ii) that the choice we face is between reform and no action; if the proposed reform is imperfect, we presumably should take no action at all, while we wait for a perfect proposal.
>
> But we can never do nothing. That which we have done for thousands of years is also action. It also produces evils. Once we are aware that the status quo is action, we can then compare its discoverable advantages and disadvantages with the predicted advantages and disadvantages of the proposed reform, discounting as best we can for our lack of experience. On the basis of such a comparison, we can make a rational decision which will not involve the unworkable assumption that only perfect systems are tolerable.

## Religion

Within the theological community, at least in the Western world, there has recently been a heartening revolution in thought and action on human problems in which the quality of life in urban areas, environmental deterioration, and the population explosion have become predominant concerns. Protestant, Catholic, and Jewish clergymen have come more and more to the forefront of public activities in the struggle for human rights, often at great personal sacrifice and risk. For example, Father John A. O'Brien, a distinguished Professor of Theology at Notre Dame University in Indiana, has edited an excellent book, *Family Planning in an Exploding Population,* and he has also been a leader in criticizing Pope Paul VI's 1968 encyclical, *Humanae Vitae,* which condemns the use of contraceptives. Commenting on this encyclical in an article in the January 1969 *Reader's Digest,* Father O'Brien wrote, "Since the decision is bound to be reversed by his (Pope Paul's) successor, it would be far more honorable, proper and just for the Pope to rescind it himself." Ivan Illich, who voluntarily renounced his priesthood after a controversy over birth control in Puerto Rico, wrote that the encyclical "lacks courage, is in bad taste, and takes the initiative away from Rome in the attempt to lead modern man in Christian humanism." Thousands of other Catholics, from Cardinals to common men, have spoken out against the encyclical, which has caused immense anguish among Catholics, millions of whom have followed their consciences and used contraceptives, usually after a period of intense soul-searching.

Bishop C. Kilmer Myers, of the Episcopal Diocese of California, has established an Ad Hoc Metropolitan Planning Group which is deeply concerned with the problems of population and environment. The Social Ministry of the Lutheran Church in America has a highly enlightened policy on population. Methodist groups have been in the forefront of abortion law reform. The numbers of socially concerned clergymen are increasing, and there is every reason to believe that their involvement in population-related problems will continue to grow.

Religious leaders may help to overcome cultural taboos related to population control through an emphasis on the quality of human life rather than on its quantity. Protestant, Catholic, and Jewish theologians have been active in promoting sex education in our schools, and at least Protestant and Jewish theologians and lay people can actively promote the enactment of more liberal abortion laws. Except for the Roman Catholic Church, all major Western religious groups have by now officially sanctioned "artificial" contraception, and even though the Catholic hierarchy has not changed its official policy, enlightened Catholic clerics no longer condemn the use of these methods.

In general, then, there is reason to hope that organized religion could become a powerful force in working toward population control, especially as the suffering caused by overpopulation becomes more widely recognized. The influence of the present Pope's position seems likely to decline as the older members of the hierarchy retire or die and are replaced by administrators more in touch with humanity and modern times. Elderly Catholic economist Colin Clark could still, in 1969, claim on a television program that India would, in a decade, be the most powerful country in the world because of her growing population! He could also write (*Los Angeles Times,* Nov. 9, 1969) that "Population growth, however strange and unwelcome some of its consequences may appear at the time, must be regarded, I think, as one of the instruments of Divine Providence, which we should welcome, not oppose." Such support of outdated dogma among conservative Catholics, especially in governments, still helps to block effective attacks on the population problem both by Catholic countries and by the United Nations. But the new look in Catholic attitudes is typified by those of Catholic biologist John H. Thomas who in 1968 wrote to San Francisco's Archbishop Joseph T. McGucken: "The Church must affirm that the birth rate must soon be brought in line with the death rate—i.e., a growth rate of zero. This is the responsibility of all people regardless of race or religion. The Church must recognize and state that all means of birth control are licit . . . [it] must put its concern for people, their welfare, and their happiness above its concern for doctrine, dogma, and canon law . . . It is time that the Church stop being like a reluctant little child, always needing to be dragged into the present."

The possible role of non-Western religious institutions in the population crisis is more problematical than that of Western religions. For example, within the Islamic religion there is no organized, deep involvement in social problems, although Islamic scholars have recently tried to find religious justification for birth control practices in countries hard-pressed by exploding populations. There are at least 500 million Moslems in the world (roughly half the number of Christians), more than 95 percent of whom live in Africa and Asia, with high concentrations in such problem areas as Indonesia and the Indian subcontinent. Pakistan, with its aggressive family planning program, has made it clear that Moslem countries can take a rational view of their population problems and can make a vigorous attempt to solve them without religious conflict. In the foreseeable future, however, it seems unlikely that Islam will become a positive force for population control.

Much the same can be said of Buddhism, which—if we include as Buddhists those who also subscribe to Shintoism, Taoism, and Confucianism—has perhaps 700 million adherents, almost all in Asia. Since in Asia the barriers to population control and the potential for supporting it both seem to be much more connected with local conditions than with religion, it seems unlikely that changes in the religion will have any substantial effect on population policy.

Similarly, it is hard to picture Hinduism, as an entity, becoming a force in population control. More than 99 percent of the 450 million or so Hindus live in Asia, mostly in India. Like Buddhism, it is a rather heterogeneous, relatively "unorganized" religion. There is still considerable "religious" opposition to population control among Hindus, perhaps based more on medical beliefs and local superstitions than on religious conviction.

For those in the Western world who are interested in population control, one of the best courses of action seems to lie in working with the already established religious groups and using modern methods of shaping attitudes. In the non-Western world, the relative fragmentation of religious groups, their lack of organization and their psycho-social traditions would seem to limit their immediate effectiveness on population control policies.

In the United States, the unorthodox but constructive and quasi-religious attitudes expressed by members of the so-called "New Left" and the Whole Earth "hippie" movements may well help save our environment. The hippies especially have borrowed many religious ideas from the non-Christian East, including Zen Buddhism, the rewards of close personal relationships, spiritual values, a reverence for life and an abhorrence of violence in any form. Members of both these groups of young people share a disdain for material things, a fascination for nature, and an interest in what might be called an ecological way of life. These attidudes on the part of members of the New Left are the antithesis of those of the old left of socialism and communism, which resemble Judeo-Christian attitudes regarding the exploitation of nature. Many older people in our society are horrified at these new attitudes, which go against some cherished religious, political, and economic beliefs, and they are appalled by the actions of some individuals in these groups. Others see in them the vanguard of a new social revolution that could lead to a very different, far better future society. It would be a good idea for those of us who are neither hip nor members of the New Left to pay attention to some of their ideas, whether or not we approve of their dress and general behavior. Those questioners of the status quo may not have the answers, but at the very least they are asking some important questions.

Historian Lynn White, Jr., of the University of California has suggested that the basic cause of Western man's destructive attitude toward nature lies in what he calls Judeo-Christian traditions. He points out, for instance, that before the Christian era men believed trees, springs, hills, streams, and other objects of nature had guardian spirits. These spirits had to be approached and placated before one could safely invade their territories. As White says, "By destroying pagan animism, Christianity made it possible to exploit nature in a mood of indifference to the feelings of natural objects." Christianity fostered the basic ideas of "progress" and of time as something linear, nonseparating, and absolute, flowing from the future into the past. Such ideas were foreign to the Greeks and Romans, who had a cyclical concept of time and did not envision the world as having a beginning. Although a modern physicist's concept of time might be somewhat closer to that of the Greeks than to that of the Christians, the Christian view is nevertheless the prevalent one, in which God designed and started the whole business for our benefit. The world is our oyster, made for man to dominate and exploit. Western science and technology can clearly be seen to have their historical roots in natural theology and the Christian dogma of man's rightful mastery over nature. The European ancestors of Americans had held and developed these attitudes long before the opportunity to exploit the Western Hemisphere arrived. The "frontier" or "cowboy" economy which has characterized the United States seems to be a natural extension of the Christian world view. Therefore, White claims, it may be in vain that so many look to science and technology to solve our present ecological crisis. In his view, "Both our present science and our present technology are so tinctured with orthodox Christian arrogance toward nature that no solution for our ecologic crises can be expected from them alone. Since the roots of our trouble are so largely religious, the remedy must also be essentially religious, whether we call it that or not."

A number of anthropologists and others have taken issue with White's thesis, pointing out that environmental abuse is by no means unique to Western culture, and that animism had disappeared, at least in Western Europe, before Christianity was introduced. As examples they cite evidence of ancient and prehistoric environmental destruction, such as the man-induced extinction of Pleistocene mammals and the destruction of the fertility of the Near East by early agricultural activity, as well as the behavior of contemporary non-Western cultures.

Geographer Yi-Fu Tuan of the University of Minnesota has observed that there is often a large gap between attitudes toward the environment expressed in a religion or philosophy and the actual practices of the people who profess the attitudes. While Chinese religions, for example, stressed the view that man was a part of nature (rather than lord of it) and should live in harmony with it, the Chinese did not always live by this belief. Concern for the environment, especially preserving forests and protecting soils, were expressed throughout Chinese history, but Yi-Fu Tuan suggests that this may often have been in response to destruction that had already taken place. The fact that China was a complex civilization complete with a bureaucracy and a large population doubtless militated against fulfillment of its religious ideals. By the twentieth century, China's once plentiful forests had been nearly destroyed to build cities and clear land for agriculture. All that remained in most areas were small patches preserved around temples. Ironically, the present government, which explicitly rejects the traditional religions, has attempted to restore the forests on a large scale.

Lewis W. Moncrief of North Carolina State University, who may perhaps be described as an environmental anthropologist, feels that the religious tradition of the West is only one of several factors that have contributed to the environmental crisis. Along with some other anthropologists, he has suggested that an urge to improve one's status in society is probably a universal human characteristic, and that expressing this urge through material acquisitiveness and resource consumption is, if not universal, at least common to a great variety of cultures. Perhaps what is unique about Western culture in this regard is the degree of our success.

Moncrief postulates several factors which he feels were equally as influential in determining European and North American behavior toward the environment as the Judeo-Christian ethic. The first of these are the development of democracy and the industrial revolution which, combined, provided control over resources (if only a family farm) for a far greater proportion of the population, and simultaneously provided the means to exploit those resources more efficiently. The existence of a vast frontier fostered the belief in North America that resources were infinite; many of our wasteful habits derive from that. Moncrief thinks it is no accident that the first conservation movement appeared just as the frontier was closing; Americans suddenly and for the first time began to realize that their resources were indeed finite. Urbanization and growing population have multiplied the environmental effects of these various trends in the twentieth century, and we are now confronted with a crisis. Our past institutions never dealt with environmental problems; they were always someone else's responsibility.

The environmental situation is not simply a product of our religious tradition, although that may have played an important part. It probably comes more directly from basic human nature, in Western culture combined with extraordinary social, political, technical and physical opportunities. How we deal with the crisis will depend on much more than a change in philosophical outlook, but such a change will undoubtedly have to accompany whatever measures are taken. After all, human nature is certainly capable of being modified and directed by the appropriate social environment.

## Science and Technology

For many people, science and technology are in effect taking on the aspect of a new religion. How often one hears statements beginning, "any society that can send a man to the moon can . . ." and ending with some problem, usually immensely more complex and difficult than space travel, that science and technology are expected to solve. The population-food imbalance is a common candidate; others are various types of pollution or ecological problems. Two things are generally wrong with these statements. First, science and technology have not yet reached the point relative to those problems that they had relative to the man-on-the-moon project by 1955. The general outlines of a solution are not clear to all competent scientists in the pertinent disciplines. Second, and equally important, there is no sign of a societal commitment to promote a crash program to solve these non-space problems.

The public, indeed, has developed a touching but misplaced faith in the ability of science and technology to pull humankind's chestnuts out of the fire. There is not the slightest question that with clever and cautious use of our scientific and technological resources, a great deal of good could be accomplished. But can we find the required amount of cleverness and caution? In spite of enormous scientific advances during the past thirty years, it is perfectly clear that the *absolute amount* of human misery has increased (because of the enormous growth in the numbers of poverty-stricken human beings), while the chances of civilization persisting have decreased. There has been an abundance of science and technology, but they have been unbalanced and out of control.

Medicine has attacked the death rate with vigor but largely ignored the birth rate, in the process threatening mankind with unprecedented catastrophe. Physics has given us nuclear and thermonuclear weapons, a legacy so weighty on the minus side of the balance that it is difficult to think of any serious pluses with which to balance it. (It is conceivable that the great impatience of many physicists to introduce the use of fission power stemmed from guilt over their participation in building the first A-bombs. Many of the most prominent promoters of nuclear power were involved in the Manhattan project. It is a double tragedy that in an effort to exculpate themselves they may deal humankind yet another blow.) Biology has provided biological warfare weapons and has seen many millions of dollars poured into molecular genetics, a field offering no immediate improvement in human welfare, but with great future potential for curing or preventing inborn defects, curing cancer, etc. Meanwhile, support for environmental studies has been relatively insignificant, in spite of repeated warnings over a quarter of a century by ecologists that man was threatening to destroy the life-support systems of the planet. The behavioral sciences have also languished, despite their potential value in helping to solve human problems.

Most of the great "advances" in technology from DDT and x-rays to automobiles and jet aircraft have caused serious problems for humanity. Some of these problems would have been difficult to anticipate, but most were foreseen, were warned against, and could have been avoided or ameliorated with sensible societal planning. The question now is, how can such planning be done in the future so as to minimize future unfortunate consequences of technological advances?

It is clear from the records of organizations such as the AMA and AEC and from recent statements by technological optimists and scientific politicians that scientists (like other groups in our population) cannot be relied upon to police themselves. Some way must be found to foster greater participation of other segments of society in the major decision-making processes affecting science and technology. This is essential, of course, to the survival of society, but it is also important as protection for scientists themselves. Burdens of guilt such as those borne by the physicists involved in developing atomic weapons must be avoided wherever possible, or at least more broadly shared.

We are not in a position here to propose a detailed structure for controlling science and technology, but some general directions can be suggested. Governmental agencies such as the National Science Foundation and National Institute of Health regularly employ *ad hoc* committees and panels of scientists to evaluate research programs and individual research projects. Universities also on occasion use such groups of scientists to evaluate programs or departments. *Ad hoc* panels of non-scientists might be integrated into these systems, drawing perhaps on citizens with non-scientific expertise serving their "sabbaticals" (see *Education* below). Such panels could both advise agencies directly and also report to a paragovernmental central body (perhaps elected) empowered to intervene whenever it was felt that the public interest was endangered. This power would extend to research under *any* auspices: government, military, university, or industry. The central body could also be charged with continually informing both government and the public of pertinent trends in science and technology.

Increased awareness and scrutiny of science and technology will not, in themselves, suffice. Although laymen can become very knowledgeable about science and technology, as the performance of several congressmen involved in appropriations for science and technical projects has demonstrated, it is often very difficult or impossible for individual laymen (or even scientists) to foresee the consequences of certain trends. A second element is thus required in the control system: an apparatus, possibly in the form of research institutes, concerned solely with such assessment and reporting to the central body described above. Perhaps a set percentage of all funds used in governmental, university, and industrial research should be assessed for the support of these organizations, which should be kept strictly independent of each of those interests.

Some of the work which might be done by such institutes would be an extension of the sort of programs now being run by systems ecologist K. E. F. Watt's group at the University of California at Davis, and by systems analysts Jay W. Forrester and Dennis L. Meadows of the Massachusetts Institute of Technology. Watt, for instance, has forecast the dismal consequences of continuing various prevailing strategies of resource management and social policies. The MIT group has shown, most convincingly, that many of the results of various proposed courses of action are "counterintuitive." Their studies indicated, for example, that a program of reducing demands on resources (by finding substitutes, recycling, etc.), without controlling other influences on the world system such as pollution and population growth, could produce worse results than a future in which resources were exhausted. To quote Forrester's description of the results of his computer simulation model in which resource consumption is substantially curbed, "population and capital investment are allowed to rise until a pollution crisis is created. Pollution then acts directly to reduce birth rate, increase death rate, and to depress food production. Population, which, according to this sample model, peaks at the year 2030, has fallen to one-sixth of the peak population within an interval of 20 years—a world-wide catastrophe of a magnitude never before experienced." Forrester's and Meadow's analysis projects the collective results of various trends in this way, in each case controlling or altering different interacting factors. Their study indicates that different forms of disaster lie ahead unless *all* the factors are controlled: population growth, pollution, resource consumption, and the rate of capital investment (industrialization).

In addition to broad-scope evaluations such as those just described, some research institutes must be involved in much more detailed questions. For example, is medical research being done with adequate attention to the needs of all segments of the population and to birth control as well as death control? Are the benefits and risks of the breeder reactor being studied in proper depth? What are the possible dangerous consequences of further investigating the properties of a given virus or biocidal compound?

Of course, even the most sophisticated assessment apparatus will not avoid all mistakes, but if it is backed by a growing feeling of social responsibility among scientists, we should be able to improve our record greatly. The remainder of the solution of learning to live with science and technology is to leave plenty of margin for error. For safety, we must learn to live somewhat below our means—not to stress ourselves and the Earth's ecosystems to the absolute limit.

## The Conservation Movement

The fascination and profound emotions—essentially religious feelings—aroused in many of us by wilderness areas, wildlife, and beautiful natural scenery are not easily explained to others who do not share them. Disparate beliefs and attitudes are obvious every time those interested in conservation find themselves defending aesthetic values against those who are equally dedicated to "progress." For many years now, people in the conservation movement have fought individually and in groups to halt the extinction of rare animal species and the destruction of the last vestiges of the primitive areas of the Earth. Some of the campaigns conducted by such organizations as the Sierra Club, the Audubon Society, and the Nature Conservancy in the U.S., and similar organizations in other countries, have been successful. It is becoming clear, however, that in the long run the conservation movement as a whole has been fighting a losing battle.

Perhaps the most obvious reason the battle is being lost is that conservation is a one-way street. Essentially each organism or place conserved remains in perpetual jeopardy. Each gain is temporary, but each loss is permanent. Species cannot be resurrected; places cannot be restored to their primitive state. Consequently, even if the conservationists were evenly matched against the destroyers, the battle would probably remain a losing one. But, of course, the battle has been far from even. Powerful economic interests and government agencies, pushed by population pressures, have promoted the development of every possible inch of the United States by building dams in desert canyons, driving roads through the remaining wilderness areas, cutting the last of the primeval forests, drilling for oil on the northern slope of Alaska, and so on. It is a tribute to the conservationists, past and present, that any of our primitive areas remain unspoiled. Political and financial power tend to be arrayed against conservation, and, as people increase and resources dwindle, the situation seems bound to deteriorate further. In many parts of the world the situation is worse than in the United States; in a few it is better.

There are encouraging signs that a new thrust is appearing in the conservation movement. Growing numbers of people are beginning to realize that conservation is a global problem, that in the long run it is not enough to preserve a few isolated treasures such as a grove of redwood trees. If global pollution causes a climatic change, the grove cannot long survive. Many conservationists now realize that if the growth of the human population is not stopped and the deterioration of the planetary environment is not arrested, *nothing* of value will be conserved. They are now also beginning to recognize that *Homo sapiens* itself is an endangered species.

This new understanding and the growing general public awareness of the problems of the environment have given rise to a number of new organizations. Some of these, such as Friends of the Earth (FOE), are more militant offshoots of older conservation groups. Others, including Environmental Action (which grew from the organization that sponsored the first Earth Day) and Ecology Action, are entirely new. Zero Population Growth (ZPG) is primarily concerned with the population problem, but is also interested in the environmental consequences of it. ZPG, a branch of the Sierra Club, and FOE have foregone the tax advantages of an apolitical posture and actively campaign and lobby for their goals, frequently combining their efforts on issues of common concern. These organizations generally differ from many of the older conservation groups in being more oriented to man as an endangered species than to preserving wilderness and wildlife only for their aesthetic and recreational values. Sister organizations of FOE, as well as ZPG, have been established in other countries.

It seems likely that conservation groups will continue to become more militant and more united—at least in their global concerns. While the important local battles must continue to be fought, more general programs of public education and political action should become predominant. It is no longer necessary to plead for conservation on aesthetic or compassionate grounds only. The preservation of the diversity of life and the integrity of the ecological systems of the Earth are absolutely essential for the survival of humanity.

## Education

In the United States and around the world there clearly has been an almost total failure to prepare people to understand and make decisions relating to the population-environment crisis. The universities, which should be leading the way in education, have been too conservative and compartmentalized. Unfortunately, most human problems do not fall neatly into such academic categories as sociology, history, economics, demography, psychology, or biology, and the solutions to these problems require the simultaneous application of the best ideas from many academic disciplines. Our failure to provide a multidisciplinary education explains the optimism of many physical scientists, economists, technologists, and others relative to the environmental crisis. Their kind of optimism is exemplified by a statement made by physicist Gerald Feinberg, who wrote in 1968, "Most of our immediate problems will be solved in a relatively short time by the march of technology and the worldwide spread of those aspects of Western culture that are responsible for our high living standards."

There are many examples of such naive optimism mixed with cultural chauvinism. The illusion that the Green Revolution will save mankind from starvation illustrates a faith in science and technology characteristic of the "well-informed" layman. This faith is all too often shared by academicians who have little insight into biology and into what is involved in agriculture and agricultural development in poor countries. Ignorance of the environmental consequences of population expansion leads many social scientists to underrate the significance of population growth in the DCs and the immediacy of the environmental threat. Such narrowness of outlook is not the exclusive domain of any particular group of scientists. An oceanographer, ridiculing some of the ecological problems associated with agriculture, has told an audience at the University of California at Berkeley that, with modern fertilizing techniques, soil only serves to prop plants up. A very prominent biochemist, writing in *Science* magazine, has attacked those attempting to have DDT banned, and has minimized the health effects of air pollution. A plant physiologist noted for calling attention to various environmental problems has told audience after audience that the population problem in the UDCs will be solved by a demographic transition, and appears incapable of accepting the relationship of population growth to environmental deterioration. An economist who is prominent in the family-planning establishment announced in a symposium at the December 1970 meetings of the American Association for the Advancement of Science that the U.S. birth rate was at an all-time low, although it had by then been rising for about two years.

Many of the solutions put forth by technological optimists are based on ignorance of ecology, demography, anthropology, and other non-technological fields. Those who see a panacea in nuclear agro-industrial complexes are simultaneously required to ignore, among other things, economics, the scale of the problem, the state of reactor technology, the potential ecological damage, and an entire spectrum of political and social problems. Those few scientists who still propose migration (to Australia or to other planets) as a solution to the population problem, or who would accommodate our surplus people in concrete cities floated on the sea, simply need remedial work in arithmetic.

With highly trained and presumably knowledgeable people so uninformed about what is going on, it is hardly surprising that the average citizen has so much difficulty evaluating the situation. Not only do most of our citizens lack even a skeleton of the necessary technical background, but our educational system has seriously straightjacketed the economic thinking of most of our citizens to the point where they are mesmerized by the axiomatic "good" of growth. The thrall in which growth for its own sake holds our "educated" citizens was beautifully exemplified by a statement made on December 2, 1969, by John A. Carver, Jr., a member of the Federal Power Commission. He claimed that Americans would be in "a race for their lives" in order to meet electrical power "needs" up to the year 2000. He foresaw a need for four times the 1970 power generation facilities by 1990, "the equivalent of 670 Hoover Dams," and called for a compromise with environmental quality in order to meet that need. Naturally, his solution is to be found in nuclear power plants. Carver, like many technologists, is evidently incapable of considering the obvious alternative to supplying more power—namely, *regulating demand*. Promoters of increased power consumption also seem unaware that Europeans do not appear to be "racing for their lives," even though European per capita electric power consumption is considerably less than half that of North America.

One would think that these educational problems could be relatively easily solved at the university level, and indeed they might be. Unfortunately, universities are quite determined to perpetuate their antiquated structures. Nevertheless, the possibility of loosening the rigid departmental organization does exist, even though the rate of movement is still very slow. Stanford University, with the help of the Ford Foundation, has developed an interdisciplinary undergraduate curriculum in Human Biology, with the express purpose of avoiding the trap of disciplinary myopia and of preparing students to attack pressing human problems. Some other colleges and universities are also instituting interdisciplinary programs of various sorts, while courses dealing with the problems of the survival of civilization are proliferating and spreading to lower educational levels. Such reforms, however, must continue to accelerate rapidly if the educational system is to contribute in any significant degree to the increase of mankind's chances. Without a growing cadre of well-educated laymen, the kinds of citizen-participation programs suggested in this chapter will not constitute much of an improvement over the present system.

Perhaps the greatest hope for action in our universities and colleges lies with the students. The current group is much more socially aware than were the students of a decade ago, and most of them are determined to change our society for the better. Many are actively working for political and social change. If the behavior of some of them has been reprehensible, few have approached the level of irresponsibility manifested by some of their elders, including certain political leaders and other public figures. Consider, for example, a statement made in 1969 by the late Senator Richard Russell of Georgia: "If we have to start over again with another Adam and Eve, I want them to be Americans, and I want them on this continent and not in Europe." Moreover, of course, young activists have yet to create an abomination remotely on a par with segregation, America's regressive tax system, or the Vietnam War. In our opinion and that of many colleagues, the majority of the most exciting and progressive changes in higher education during the 1960s had their roots in student activism. We hope that these young people may produce equally salutary changes in society as a whole.

To a large extent college students today have a more realistic view of the world than their parents because they do not see it through the rose-colored glasses which were constructed for older generations by society and the educational system. Those who matured just before World War II were young during a time when personal financial insecurity was an overriding consideration for much of the population. Today's students grew up in an era when, for most, financial security could be taken for granted. They grew up in a time of unprecedented change. Moreover, they have had the world brought into their homes through the medium of television, and they have been forced into a global outlook by global threats to personal safety. These students are change-oriented, concerned about other people, and they think about subtle problems that involve all of mankind. That they show such concern should not be viewed as anything but a hopeful sign.

Although the educational system below the college level is in some ways less resistant to change, it is similarly inadequate in preparing people for the realities of the world crisis. In some of the better school systems, however, there are signs that this may be changing—sometimes due to the initiative of the students themselves. Even elementary and junior high school students in some areas have demonstrated their concern for environmental deterioration through various activities. Many teachers have encouraged interest in population and environment, with or without administrative support. Since Earth Day, 1970, in particular, there has been a widespread effort to introduce environmental concern into schools at virtually every level. A program to encourage environmental education has been established at the federal level in the Department of Health, Education and Welfare. A program for population education has also been established, but has been less rapidly implemented.

A lack of adequate sex education is still a serious problem in the U.S. and many other countries. We face both a population problem and a venereal disease epidemic in the United States, and yet powerful groups in this country are determined to keep the "facts of life" from our young people. No subject is more likely to bring out a mob of angry parents than the thought of introducing the most innocuous sex education curriculum into a school, even if the program is endorsed by educators, psychiatrists, and clerics of all faiths. Some of these parents in our sex-saturated society even claim that a straightforward description of sexual intercourse, of the sort that should be perfectly acceptable reading for any child, is part of a communist plot to destroy our youth! This is a vicious cycle, with a minority of ignorant and disturbed parents fighting to guarantee that their children grow up equally ignorant and disturbed.

There are, of course, formidable barriers to reasonable sex education in schools, churches, and in the home. One is a lack of training for potential teachers who need a thorough understanding of the subject. The second is the nearly ubiquitous feeling that sex education must be tied up with a series of moral judgments. In the face of massive ignorance and our current crisis, however, it is difficult to construct an argument against three basic aspects of sex education in the schools. First, children must be thoroughly informed about the anatomy of sex organs and the physiology of sex and reproduction. Second, they must be taught the difference between "sex" and reproduction and about the methods of contraception. Third, they should be informed of the dangers of venereal disease.

These straightforward factual matters are easy. Introducing the student to the role sex plays in society, the attitudes toward it in different religious and social groups, attitudes toward contraception, illegitimacy, marriage, divorce, virginity, and sex-as-just-plain-good-fun must be handled with great care and by specially trained teachers. But the cycle of the blind leading the blind, that of embarrassed and uninformed parents "educating" their children, must be broken somehow. One way in which school systems have successfully introduced sex education programs is to give parents a preview of the material. The parents are invited to evaluate the program; in fact, one purpose is to educate *them*. Such preparations of the adult population would seem essential to avoid perpetuating ignorance. A sex education program has been initiated in West Germany for grandparents, who often care for children while parents work. Perhaps sex education should be compulsory for all American adults with preschool children.

Our educational system is failing to produce not only those competent to teach sex education, but also the ecologists, agricultural and other technicians, social scientists, paramedical personnel, and similar specialists needed to help solve the pressing problems of the world, especially in the UDCs. Indeed, at the moment there is a "brain drain" problem. Trained personnel from the UDCs, especially medical doctors, are attracted to the United States and other DCs. Ironically, this often happens because, despite their usually great needs for trained people, UDCs may have no jobs for them. Even more serious is the fact that many individuals from the UDCs who are educated in the DCs do not wish to return to their homelands. Although some DCs, notably the Soviet Union, virtually force a return, most do not. One relatively humane solution to this problem would be for the DCs to establish and help staff more training centers within the UDCs. This should have the additional benefits of training local people to work on problems of local significance, and of familiarizing visiting faculty members from the DCs with those problems.

Finally, while a great deal can be done to improve our educational system within the general framework now recognized, more fundamental changes will probably be required if large technological societies are to discover ways to govern themselves satisfactorily while avoiding the social and environmental problems which now threaten to destroy them. Ivan Illich has suggested the abolition of formal education and the making of educational materials and institutions available to all on a cafeteria basis. To those struggling in the present system, the idea has considerable appeal, but even Illich recognizes the enormous drawbacks inherent in such an unstructured approach.

We would suggest another strategy, one which expands on ideas already current in education. First of all, we feel that a major effort should be made to extend education throughout the life span, rather than attempting to cram all education into the first 15–25 years of life. It is becoming widely recognized that maturity and experience are often a benefit in learning. Students who have "dropped out," worked, and then returned to school generally do so with much renewed vigor and increased performance. Experience in the "real world" can avoid much wasted effort in the educational world. A program of encouraging interruption of education, perhaps for a one- or two-year period during or directly after high school and another two-year period after receiving an undergraduate degree might be a good start. For example, a student interested in becoming a physician might spend two years after high school doing clerical work in a hospital or doctor's office or serving as an orderly. When his or her undergraduate education was completed, he could spend two additional years working with a doctor as a paramedical person. Similarly, individuals going into business, government, science, bricklaying, plumbing, or what-have-you should have a chance to try out their chosen professions and trades at the bottom before completing their educations.

The benefits of the program would be many, including better understanding of the problems faced by associates (a doctor who has been an orderly should have more insight into the problems facing orderlies), and fewer cases of people committing themselves to careers too early, with too little knowledge of what the commitment involves, and discovering the error too late to make another choice. If a student, on completing high school were unsure of what his future should be, he could try out several possibilities.

What of those who have no desire to go beyond high school or vocational school? Should their education end at that point? We feel that a technological society, if it is to be a democracy, cannot afford a large proportion of poorly educated citizens. Everyone must be drawn into the problems of societal decision-making. We would suggest that *all* people be required to take a sabbatical leave every seventh year, at the expense of society as a whole (the manpower "problems" created by this program will be dealt with in the economic section below). Each person will be required to spend the year bettering society and himself in a way *approved of by his immediate colleagues*. A physician might petition his or her county medical society for permission to go to a center and learn new surgical techniques or study anthropology. A garbage collector might petition co-workers to permit him to take a year's course in sanitary engineering at a university. A secretary might apply to the government for a grant to spend her sabbatical serving on an *ad hoc* citizens' committee to evaluate the direction of research in high energy physics. Her businessman husband might apply for one of the open "sabbatical" chairs which could be established on the city council (as well as in all other legislative bodies). A flight instructor might persuade the local pilot's association to appoint him to one of the exchange positions in the local Federal Aviation Administration office, with his FAA counterpart being required to take over the instructor's job for a year (if he were qualified). *All* bureaucrats should be required to take some of their sabbaticals as nongovernmental workers in the areas they administer; all professors to take theirs outside of the groves of academe, or at least outside their own field. The roles now played by a typical academic sabbatical could be covered by additional leaves, if desirable.

The details of such a program would be complicated, but its benefits we believe would far outweigh its costs. A growing rigidity of roles in our society must be broken, and virtually everyone must be brought into its decision-making processes. Indeed, the discontent expressed today by many groups is based on the fact that they feel cut off from participation in important decisions that affect their lives.

Some moves in this general direction have been made in the People's Republic of China, where city people and academics have been forced to join rural communes and participate in completely different work from what their previous experience had been. It would be interesting to know what success the Chinese have had. We would certainly not advocate forcing people to change their occupations against their wishes, any more than we would advocate adopting the Chinese communist system of government. But the basic idea behind this policy seems valuable, and an adaptation of it that fit our political system might well be worth exploring.

As an example of how citizen participation in political decision-making can work, a group of scientists led by ecologist C. S. Holling at the University of British Columbia have involved local businessmen, politicians, and private citizens in a computer simulation of a prospective development project, as an experiment in the results of citizen decision-making. Everyone contributed to the assumptions of the model, and all were satisfied with the model created. Then various people were allowed to try out their pet development plans on the model. When a politician found that his plan led to environmental disaster, he had to acknowledge his error. He could not blame the model because he had been involved in building what he believed to be a realistic one.

We believe that it is possible, at least in theory, to get away from a we-they system of running the country and give everyone a chance to participate. Grave problems would unquestionably accompany the attempt, but since we are both morally committed to some form of democracy and intellectually convinced that the present system is both undemocratic and lethally ineffectual, we see no choice but to try a change.

## The Legal System

Perhaps the greatest potential for reversing environmental deterioration in the United States and for bringing our population under control lies in the effective utilization of our legal system. A law may be defined as a "rule of conduct for a community prescribed by a governing authority and enforced by sanction." The sanction enforcing a law may be either a reward or a punishment. For instance, to control agricultural production the government might pay a subsidy for not raising crops (a reward) or jail a farmer who raises crops (a punishment). Where a government wishes to induce an affirmative action, a promised reward is often more effective than the threat of punishment. In the United States, constitutional questions involving due process, equal protection, and so forth are more likely to arise where punishment, rather than reward, is involved. Bonuses for not having children would certainly raise fewer constitutional questions than jail for over-reproducers.

Law is also sometimes defined as codified custom. In a sense, legislators, policemen, and judges are merely social instruments for enforcing customary behavior. Historically they have also helped to create custom by defining acceptable conduct. This has been especially true of legislators and is becoming increasingly true of judges. The new problems of local and global overpopulation and pollution clearly require new rules of conduct and new customs: in short, new laws. Just as the ancient laws relating to trespass had to be modified by the courts and by the legislatures to handle the new circumstances created by automobiles and airplanes, new devices are now being developed for dealing with pollution and population pressure. The laws of our free enterprise system are failing to meet the needs of everyone everywhere as long as they *permit unrestricted reproduction and pollution.* We are today witnessing increases in violence and disorder in the United States partly because the legal system has not changed fast enough in response to changing needs. Such symptoms may be just a small taste of what is to come if our legal system does not more effectively assist in solving the population-environment crisis.

### POLLUTION: NUISANCE

Fortunately there are many legal precedents that permit society to attack polluters legally. Under Common Law (the law generally applicable in Britain and her ex-colonies) and under Civil Law (the law generally applicable throughout the rest of the Western world), the concept of nuisance has for centuries permitted some of the coercive powers of government to be brought to bear on those who create excessive smoke, noise, odor, filth, and the like. In some jurisdictions access to sunlight and even an attractive view are among aesthetic values protected by public administrators. Public administrators, however, have not been notable for their diligence in complaining about local businesses. Nuisances have been successfully stopped by individual citizens who have gone to court and obtained injunctions to stop them. Private citizens may receive money damages for the injury caused them by the nuisance.

Existing nuisance laws present a number of difficulties. First, the nuisance doctrine generally serves only to protect rights associated with real property. As things now stand, a private nuisance can be stopped only by a person occupying adjacent or nearby property. Even in the most enlightened jurisdictions, little if anything can be done to protect people in the vicinity who do not own or occupy property.

Second, the nuisance doctrine requires that a complainant show a causal relationship between the condition he is complaining about—for example, smoke or noise—and a direct injury to himself. Generally he has to show that this condition is *the* cause of the injury. Obviously, if each of several polluters contributes a little to the overall problem, the nuisance doctrine is not much help. On the other hand, there is growing authority for the proposition that if a suit is filed against all the persons who are contributing to the nuisance, it is up to them to show to what extent each has contributed. Thus there have been successful cases involving river pollution in which *all* contributors to upstream pollution have been sued.

Third, the nuisance doctrine is applied only if in the eyes of the court the polluter is causing more harm than he is doing good. Unfortunately it has been held by many courts that a so-called lawful business (paint manufacturing, for example) cannot constitute a nuisance. Today there is an increasing public tendency to recognize the dangers from pollution, and, in balancing these against economic considerations, to require businesses to do whatever a court or an administrative agency may think is economically reasonable. The fact that the economic interests of the polluters are taken into consideration by our governmental authorities often leads to spurious arguments based on the notion that restrictions would foster unfair competition: "We can't compete with the Jones Company if we can't spray our crops with DDT." The answer to this argument of course is: "We will stop the Jones Company too." Often the best way of avoiding unfair competition arguments is to pass legislation that affects an entire industry. For example, if a law were passed prohibiting the manufacture of *all* persistent insecticides (for instance, all those with a half-life of more than one week under average field conditions), the chemical companies would very quickly lower prices on those that met the requirements and would develop new ones which also break down rapidly.

The serious defects in the existing nuisance laws might make it appear that they will not really assist in controlling pollution, but this is not so. With some relatively minor adjustments, these laws could be made very effective. These are among the changes that must be made: (1) expand the nuisance doctrine to include people who are hurt by the pollution but who do not necessarily occupy nearby property; (2) permit individuals to bring actions not only on their own behalf, but also on behalf of all other individuals in similar circumstances who are being damaged by pollution; (3) permit recovery of punitive damages (damages in excess of the dollar value of the injury suffered) in cases where the polluter could have avoided some or all of the pollution; (4) organize public-spirited scientists so that they might become a more readily available source of testimony. The real value of the nuisance laws is that they provide an existing framework within which to elaborate newer and more restrictive rules of conduct without also requiring the development of previously unrecognized rights and duties.

POLLUTION: TRESPASS

Another ancient legal doctrine, that of trespass, can also assist in stopping pollution. According to law, if you hit another man with your fist or with your automobile, or if you hike over another man's land, you have committed a trespass. Trespass is both a crime (a public offense) and a tort (an individual, private injury).

For many years there have been metaphysical arguments concerning what constitutes a trespass—for example, whether it is necessary to be able to see whatever hits you or falls on your land. It has been said that rays of light cannot constitute a trespass, and in the past not even smoke could constitute a trespass. However, the old idea that it was necessary to be able to see, feel, and even weigh the offensive object is going out of style. The decision in one California case permitted recovery of substantial damages for lung injuries sustained by a motorist who drove through invisible chemical fumes emitted by a nearby factory.

One serious defect in applying the trespass laws to the control of pollution is that the most an individual can recover are his own damages, which are generally limited to the monetary value of the individual's private injuries. In one case, however, the Oregon Supreme Court permitted a private individual to collect punitive damages in addition to his actual personal damages. The court reasoned that some private wrongs are so evil that the wrongdoer should be punished as well as be forced to pay for the actual injury he has caused the complainant. Punitive damages have long been recognized in our legal systems. If industries guilty of pollution are assessed for punitive damages, private individuals will have some incentive to initiate law suits against them. In the past two years, this possibility has induced some industries to curtail their pollution. It has also induced some insurance companies to withdraw insurance against such suits, and a few states are contemplating the prohibition of insurance for pollution liability.

Like nuisance laws, the trespass laws could be made much more effective merely by permitting an individual to sue for the value of the injuries sustained by *all* individuals similarly situated. Such suits are called class actions, and the individual represents not only himself, but also all others similarly situated or in the same class as himself. There exists ample authority for class actions in other circumstances. For example, a stockholder has long been able to bring a class action on behalf of all stockholders against a corporation or its officers or directors. Today, there is evidence that trespass laws will increasingly be used in what are essentially class actions against polluters. The suits against the Union Oil Company by the State of California and by individuals in connection with the famous 1969 oil leak in the Santa Barbara Channel are class actions.

The 1971 National Environmental Policy Act, if passed, will affirm the right of individuals to take to court others who violate their right to protection and preservation of the environment. The 1970 Clean Air Act provides the same right with regard to abuse of that act's air quality standards if the federal or local governments fail to enforce them.


POLLUTION: LEGISLATION AND ADMINISTRATIVE AGENCIES

In addition to putting pressure on polluters through the courts, there is the vast and fertile field of legislation and administrative law. State and federal legislatures could easily stop pollution if they wished to do so. The courts would find no constitutional objections to any reasonable legislative limitations on the activities of polluting industries—for example, requirements that effluents be purified, reduced, or eliminated. The courts could even sustain statutes that would put certain corporations out of business.

There are two difficult problems in getting effective legislative action. First there is the notion that if a higher governmental authority (for example, the United States Congress) enacts a law regulating a certain kind of activity, it has pre-empted the field and a lesser governmental authority (for example, a state) cannot enact legislation dealing with the same subject. This has led the tobacco and automobile industries to push for federal regulation in order to avoid the enactment of more restrictive state laws. This does create a problem for industry, and there is no easy answer. A national economy does require national standards; it would be extremely difficult for the automobile manufacturers to satisfy 51 different statutory schemes to regulate automobile pollution. Yet some local problems are so severe that they require more drastic solutions than need be applied to the country at large.

The second difficulty with legislative action is that legislators are often not cognizant of new problems, and some are notoriously at the beck and call of established pressure groups, such as the automobile manufacturers and the oil industry. Furthermore, in those situations where the legislature has taken action, the action has generally consisted of setting up regulatory agencies like the Food and Drug Administration, the Federal Trade Commission, or the Federal Communication Commission. Such agencies in time have tended to become dominated by the industries they are intended to regulate; ultimately the foxes wind up minding the chickens. Nevertheless, as public pressure has grown, we have already seen and can expect more results from legislation and from regulatory agencies than we have seen in the past.

An action program to control pollution would require changing the law through the courts, the legislatures, and the administrative agencies. Laws should be enacted to tax polluters, the tax being based on the amount of pollutants released. At the same time, tax deductions could be granted for the costs of developing and installing pollution-control devices. If such relatively nonpunitive steps do not produce the desired results, then statutes forbidding the release of pollutants and permitting the prosecution of violators as felons should be enacted. Laws are needed now to prohibit the use of certain substances (for example, tetraethyl lead in gasoline and such persistent insecticides as the chlorinated hydrocarbons). In some cases, as discussed in the section on economic change, laws should be passed that would spread the burden of responsibility for reducing and eliminating pollution.

The initiation of such a program will require the efforts of many individual citizens. Letters must be written to legislators, to industries, and to news media. Boycotts must be organized. Lawsuits must be instituted against polluters. Individuals with special expertise, particularly scientists and lawyers, must spend the time and effort required to cooperate in bringing lawsuits.

A beginning in scientist-lawyer cooperation has been made by the Environmental Defense Fund (EDF). This group, composed of scientists, lawyers, and other citizens, has been going into the courts and appearing before government regulatory agencies in an effort to protect the environment. They succeeded, for instance, in using the courts to stop DDT spraying in Suffolk County, Long Island, and as a result of the publicity accompanying the EDF suit, the state of Michigan rigidly restricted the use of DDT. In an adversary-style hearing before the Wisconsin Department of Resources, completed in early 1969, EDF was able to demolish the flimsy case of those attempting to defend continued use of DDT. Faced with the certainty of cross-examination, many of the scientists who usually defend the petro-chemical industry were noticeably absent from the witness chair (although not from the public press). As a result of the hearings, DDT can no longer be used in Wisconsin. EDF then carried the battle against DDT to the federal level. Originally a shoestring operation, EDF is everywhere gaining the admiration and support of scientists and others aware of the threats to our survival. It should serve as a model for similar groups.

Another group that has organized to work against both environmental deterioration and overpopulation is composed of students in law schools around the U.S. These students had in 1969 already initiated local actions against development plans and were planning an attack on anti-abortion laws both through legislation and the courts.

The legal machinery and the legal notions necessary to control pollution do exist. Slight changes in the legal notions and diligent application of the legal machinery are all that is necessary to induce a great reduction in pollution in the United States.

POPULATION: THE POWER OF GOVERNMENT

The impact of laws and policies on population size and growth has, until very recently, largely been ignored by the legal profession. The first comprehensive treatment of population law was that of attorney Johnson C. Montgomery (see bibliography), whose ideas are the basis of the following discussion.

To date, there has been no serious attempt in western countries to use laws to control excessive population growth, although there exists ample authority under which population growth can be regulated. For example, under the United States Constitution, effective population control programs could be enacted under the clauses that empower Congress to appropriate funds to provide for the general welfare and to regulate commerce, or under the last clause of the Fourteenth Amendment. Such laws could constitutionally be very broad. Indeed, it has been concluded that compulsory population control laws, even including those requiring compulsory abortion, could be sustained under our existing Constitution if the population crisis became sufficiently compelling to endanger the society. A few consider the situation already serious enough to justify some forms of compulsion.

Unfortunately, our legal system is seriously out of date relative to population policy. Our laws and customs, as embodied in our religious, social, and legal institutions, still reflect the desires of a nation seeking to fill a frontier. We still have laws that restrict access to contraceptives, restrict voluntary abortion and sterilization, and that give tax benefits to large families. These laws, sensible enough at earlier stages of history when society's survival depended on encouraging population maintenance and growth, have become foolish and dangerous in the light of changed circumstances. We no longer need more people. Laws encouraging the production of more people must be changed.

The most compelling arguments that justify governmental regulation of reproduction are based upon the rapid population growth relative to the finite planet and limited resources which are available to us. To provide a quality life for all, there must be fewer people. But there are other sound reasons why the law should regulate reproduction.

It is accepted that the law has as its proper function the protection of each person and each group of people. A legal restriction on the right to have more than a given number of children could easily be based on the needs of the first children. Some studies have indicated that the larger the family, the less likely the children are to realize their potential levels of achievement. Certainly there is no question that children of a small family can be better cared for and better educated than children of a large family, income and other things being equal. The law could properly say to a mother that, in order to protect the children she already has, she can have no more.

A legal restriction on the right to have children could be based on a right not to be disadvantaged by excessive numbers of children produced by others. Different rates of reproduction among groups can give rise to serious social problems. For example, differential rates of reproduction between ethnic, racial, religious, or economic groups might result in increased competition for resources and political power and thereby undermine social order. If some individuals contribute to general social deterioration by overproducing children, and if the need is compelling, they can be required by law to exercise reproductive responsibility—just as they can be required to exercise responsibility in their resource consumption patterns—*providing they are not denied equal protection.*

POPULATION: INDIVIDUAL RIGHTS

Individual rights must be balanced against the power of the government to control human reproduction. Some people—respected legislators, judges, and lawyers included—have viewed the right to have children as a fundamental and inalienable right. Yet neither the Declaration of Independence nor the Constitution mentions a "right" to reproduce. The U.N. Charter describes no such "right." Indeed, the only document that mentions such a "right" is a resolution of the United Nations which affirms the "right *responsibly* to choose" the number and spacing of children (our emphasis). In the United States, individuals have a constitutional right to privacy and it has been held that the right to privacy includes the right to choose whether or not to have children, at least to the extent that a woman has a right to choose not to have children. But the right is not unlimited. Where the society has a "compelling, subordinating interest" in regulating population size, the right of the individual may be curtailed. If society's survival depended on having more children, we could require women to bear children, just as we can constitutionally require our men to serve in the armed forces. Similarly, given the present crisis caused by overpopulation, we can reasonably enact laws necessary to control excessive reproduction.

It is often argued that the right to have children is so personal that the government should not regulate it. In an ideal society, no doubt the State should leave family size and composition solely to the desires of the parents. In today's world, however, the number of children in a family is a matter of profound public concern. The law regulates other highly personal matters. For example, no man may lawfully have more than one wife. Why should the law not be able to prevent a person from having more than two children?

The legal argument has been made that the First Amendment provision for separation of Church and State prevents the United States government from regulating family size. The notion is that family size is God's affair and no business of the State. But the same argument was made against the taxation of church property, prohibition of polygamy, compulsory education of and medical treatment for children, and many similar measures that have been enacted. From a legal standpoint, the First Amendment argument against family size regulation is devoid of merit.

There are two valid constitutional limitations on the kinds of population control policies that could be enacted. First, any enactments must satisfy the requirements of due process of law; they must be reasonably designed to meet real problems, and they must not be arbitrary. Second, any enactments must ensure that equal protection under the law is afforded to every person; they must not be permitted to discriminate against any particular group or person. This should be as true of laws giving economic encouragement to small families as it would be of laws directly regulating the number of children a person may have. This does not mean that the impact of the laws must be the same on everyone. A law limiting each couple to two children obviously would have a greater impact on persons who desire large families than it would on persons who do not. Thus, while the due process and equal protection limitations preclude the passage of capricious or discriminatory laws, neither guarantees anyone the right to have more than his fair share of children, if such a right is shown to conflict with other rights and freedoms.

It is often argued that a fetus or an embryo is a person who has a "right to life" and therefore abortion as a population control measure must be rejected. Supporters of this argument point out that certain rights of a fetus have been legally recognized. For example, some states permit a fetus to recover money damages for personal injuries sustained prior to birth. Under some circumstances the common law has permitted a fetus, if subsequently live born, to inherit property. The intentional killing of a fetus (through injury to the mother) has been declared by statute to constitute murder, although under the statute the fetus is not defined as a human being. Although the fetus after quickening has been protected in some states, most of those states do require that the infant be born and living before the rights vested prior to birth will be actually recognized and enforced. Most jurisdictions afford no protection to property rights or personal rights of the unquickened fetus, and no jurisdiction has protected the rights of embryos. Furthermore, analysis of the situations in which "rights" of the fetus have been recognized disclose that it is generally not the fetus' rights, but rather the rights of its parents or others that are being protected. For example, when a fetus receives money damages for prenatal injuries, it is in reality the parents' and the society's economic interests which are being protected.

Those who argue that a fetus has a right to life usually proceed from the assumption that life begins at or soon after conception. As stated elsewhere, the question, "When does life begin?" is a misleading question. Life does not begin; it began. The real question, from a legal as well as from a religious, moral, and ethical point of view, is as follows: in what forms, at what stages, and for what purposes do we protect human life? Obviously an overweight person regards his fat cells differently from his brain cells. A wandering sperm cell is not the same thing as a fertilized egg; nor is a fetus a child. Yet a fat cell, a sperm cell, a fetus, a child, an adult, and even a group of people are all human life.

The common law and the drafters of our Constitution did not consider a fetus a human being. Feticide was not murder in common law because the fetus was not considered to be a human being, and for purposes of the Constitution a fetus is probably not a "person" within the meaning of the Fourteenth Amendment. Thus, under our Constitution, abortion is apparently not unlawful although infanticide obviously is. This is a very important distinction, particularly since most rights, privileges, and duties in our society are dated from birth and not from some prior point in time. Capacity to contract, to vote, to be drafted, to obtain social security rights, drivers' licenses, and the like, are all dated from birth, which is a very convenient, relatively definite point in time from which to date most rights. Certainly birth is more easily ascertainable than the moment of conception, implantation, or quickening. Such an easily ascertainable point in time is a sensible point from which to date Constitutional rights, which should not depend upon vague imprecisions.

The fact that a fetus is probably not a "person" with Constitutional rights does not, however, mean that the society has no interest in the fetus. The society does have an interest in ensuring that an appropriate number of healthy children are born. To protect the health of the fetus, as well as the health of the mother, some laws regulating abortion may still be necessary.

For example, laws might require that abortions be performed only by doctors or other medically trained personnel. But such regulations should not be confused with the recognition of rights of the fetus as a fetus—rights which do not presently exist.

Although some courts have recently recognized "rights to life" in the developed fetus, the trend of decisions is presently toward more liberal voluntary abortion laws. This is a healthy trend that reduces the possibility that compulsory abortions will ultimately become necessary.

### POPULATION: A PROGRAM FOR LEGAL REFORM

In the United States many laws to discourage population growth would presently be reasonable, constitutional, and desirable. Here are a few possibilities:

1. A federal statute prohibiting any restrictions on safe, voluntary contraception, sterilization, and abortion, and the dissemination of information about them could be enacted.

2. State and federal governments could subsidize voluntary contraception, sterilization, and abortion. Laws could require that birth control clinics be opened at public expense in all suitable locations. They could also require that group and individual health insurance policies cover the costs of abortion and sterilization.

3. Tax laws could be revised, and new laws could be passed that would provide incentives for late marriage, small families, and alternative roles for women, as discussed in Chapter 10. The tax disadvantage of single, childless persons could be eliminated.

4. State and federal laws could make sex education, including instruction about contraception, mandatory in all schools, and the government could sponsor public education programs designed to encourage people to want fewer children.

5. Federal support and encouragement for the development of more effective birth control drugs and devices could be greatly increased.

If such relatively uncoercive laws should fail to bring the birth rate under control, laws could then be written that would make bearing a third child illegal and that would require an abortion to terminate all such pregnancies. Failure to obtain the abortion could be made a felony, as could aiding and abetting over-reproducers. Stiff fines and other penalties could be established, carefully adjusted so that the innocent child would not be penalized for his parents' illegal activities. At the moment there might be little public support for such laws, but if the social and environmental situations are permitted to deteriorate much further, popular support might develop rapidly. Already there has been considerable talk in some quarters of forcibly suppressing reproduction among welfare recipients (perhaps by requiring the use of contraceptives or even by involuntary sterilization). This may sadly foreshadow what our society might do if it wakes up too late. We hope that population growth can be controlled in the United States without resorting to such discriminatory and socially disruptive measures. That is, in fact, a purpose of this book: to stimulate population control by the *least* coercive means before it is too late.

## Business, Industry, and Advertising

Although legal and legislative action are essential to the solution of pollution problems in the U.S., it is to be hoped that American industries will not wait to be coerced into responsible behavior. In fact, a few industries have already taken the initiative for cleaning up their effluents, and some of these have found it possible to make a profit from pollution by-products. Such unexpected bonuses will not be possible in all cases, of course. Tax incentives and pollution clean-up subsidies from the government may be necessary where costs are high (see section on Economic and Political Change).

Meanwhile, many industrial organizations are exploring technological methods for dealing with various kinds of pollution; indeed, new companies are appearing whose entire business is pollution abatement or waste disposal of one sort or another. On the preventive side of the coin, environmental consulting firms have begun to appear. Their business is to advise communities and businesses in planning development with the least possible damage to the environment and the most benefit to the human inhabitants. These trends and others, such as research on recyclable or biodegradable containers, should certainly be encouraged.

A reorientation of businessmen's and consumers' values is in order. Resources of all kinds are limited, but Americans behave as though they were not. The neglected virtues of economy and thrift must be restored to the pedestals that they once occupied in this country. American consumers have been conditioned by advertising to buy gaudy or gimmicky packages, to accept "planned obsolescence," and to want specialized gadgets (such as electric can-openers) that do only one job efficiently. The wastefulness of this system can best be appreciated by a visit to the city dump.

Nowhere is wastefulness more conspicuously enshrined than in the electric power companies. They seem endlessly to be building new facilities and pressing for more power dams and faster development of atomic power. At the same time they spend millions on advertising to promote greater consumption of energy through electric appliances. The huge electricity consumption of Americans, which has doubled in the past ten years, is now creating stress in many areas where power companies cannot meet needs when demand is high. The obvious course out of the problems created by our power glut is *to find ways to lower the demand*. The price of energy (electrical and other) in this country, relative to its real costs in the generation of pollution and other hazards and the depletion of resources, is too low. Moreover, the practice of lower costs per unit of electricity as consumption increases penalizes the poor (who use the least amount), as well as encouraging higher consumption. The Consolidated Edison Company of New York, which has been plagued with blackouts, brownouts, and power station breakdowns, in 1971 announced a change of policy whereby they would, at least temporarily, no longer promote greater consumption of power and that prices would be raised. Charles L. Luce, president of Con Ed, has also proposed that higher rates be applied to "high use" commercial customers to discourage consumption. We can only hope that this policy will be adopted and that other power companies will follow Con Ed's example. The increased revenues could be required by law to be used for reducing pollution from power generation and for upgrading the disgracefully inadequate research programs of the utilities.

Advertising plays a leading role in perpetuating the American system of consumerism. Using the same methods, the advertising industry could play a leading role in reversing the trend, although this presumably would require the cooperation of their clients. Along this line, it is interesting that in the late 1960s many advertisements began to appear featuring various companies' efforts at pollution abatement. This concern over the corporate image with respect to pollution is no doubt a necessary first step. While we hope that the public will encourage pollution-conscious businesses, we also hope that the businesses themselves will do more about pollution abatement (or better, prevention) than merely advertise it.

Environmental activists have been increasingly irritated by self-serving ads showing how clean Company XX's factory in Middleville is (when it is that clean because state or federal laws now or soon will require it). They call these ads "ecopornography." Much more acceptable are ads which offer useful information to consumers on how they can cooperate with business in environmentally beneficial projects, such as recycling aluminum cans. While we certainly would not condone heavy promotion of new versions of products whose environmental contribution is negligible or questionable, such as certain gasoline additives or NTA in detergents, we would welcome ads which feature genuine improvements, such as unleaded gasolines. Admittedly, the line dividing such cases is not always easily drawn.

The advertising industry can do much more than it has so far to encourage its clients to promote products with stress on such qualities as durability, economy, and versatility. For example, automobile advertising should emphasize economy of purchase and operation, especially low gasoline consumption, durability, compactness, comfort (but not roominess), engine efficiency, safety, and low pollution emissions. Advertising that stresses large size and power should be discontinued. The public has to a considerable degree been educated to want large, overpowered vehicles (for that matter, to want personal vehicles at all) and frequent style changes. Presumably it could quickly be educated to want small, efficient, low-powered vehicles that last a long time, particularly if the connections with smog, traffic congestion, and parking space were made clear.

With such a change, the big three American automobile manufacturers could discontinue their larger, more expensive and powerful models immediately. Indeed, one might well ask why they have not already done so. If the automobile industry does not seize the initiative in developing alternatives to the internal combustion engine and the overpowerful, obsolescent automobile, it may one day discover that it is out of business entirely. Sacrificing the largest models now and diverting talent and money into producing genuinely new vehicle designs, rather than trivial model changes, might mean the preservation of the industry. It would be too bad if resources were used instead to continue promoting the same old qualities and to resist the regulations and restrictions that will inevitably be imposed.

To return to advertising, beyond cooperating with clients in antipollution promotions, the advertising companies could by agreement refuse to design ads promoting wasteful or polluting products; for example, ads featuring powerful engines in automobiles, food in throwaway cans and bottles, or goods wrapped in unnecessary layers of packaging.

Advertising agencies can also make a contribution to the population situation by refusing to produce ads featuring large families. There are many other ways to promote heavy-duty washing machines—dormitories, laundromats, boarding schools, and orphanages use them, for instance. In a situation where a family has three children, it could be referred to as a "large family." Women could be featured more often in roles other than homemaker and mother. The convenience of many goods can be stressed more as a value for working women than for the overburdened mother, as they usually are now. The critical problem, of course, is to find a way to swing both advertisers and agencies in the right direction. While public utilities, for example, could and should be prohibited from promoting greater use of power through advertising, such legal controls over all advertising would undoubtedly prove too cumbersome.

A court decision in August 1971 held that under the "fairness doctrine," radio and television stations that carry advertising for big, high-horsepower cars also must broadcast information about the environmental threat such cars represent. The suit had been brought by the Environmental Defense Fund, after the Federal Communications Commission had ruled against such a policy. The FCC, nevertheless, has been studying the question of how far the doctrine should be extended. If it can be widely used, this possibility may itself discourage manufacturers and advertisers from promoting socially and environmentally undesirable products.

The 1970s will be crucial years for everyone. The business community in the U.S. and around the world is faced with a particularly difficult choice. It can continue to pursue the economic goals of the past decades until either an environmental disaster overtakes us or until governments and the public compel a change; or it can actively initiate new approaches to production and industry, with a view to protecting the environment, preserving limited resources, and truly benefiting humanity.

## Medicine

There are signs that the medical profession in the United States is becoming aware of the seriousness of the population problem and the role that medicine has played in creating it, as well as the role that the profession must play if the problem is to be solved. More and more physicians seem to be aware that medical intervention in lowering death rates must be balanced by intervention in lowering birth rates. Courageous doctors in many areas have openly defied antique abortion laws and risked grave financial loss for performing vasectomies. In many UDCs, especially in India, the medical profession is even farther ahead in recognizing the desperate need for population control. Interest in the problems of environmental medicine is on the rise also, and medical doctors have been at the forefront in sounding warnings (often ignored) about the hazards of air pollution, water pollution, and other environmental threats to public health.

On the debit side, the medical profession as a whole has been tardy in backing even such elementary programs as the repeal of laws limiting the distribution of contraceptive information and the establishment of family planning clinics. Furthermore, medical training has militated against abortion except under extremely limited circumstances, and the record of the profession (in contrast to that of some courageous individual physicians) in the area of abortion reform has been atrocious. For some time after a so-called "liberal" abortion law was passed in California, a substantial portion of the abortions in that state continued to be performed by a single group of doctors. The medical profession should take the lead in abolishing not only the abortion laws but all of the pseudolegal hospital rituals attendant to performing abortions. The history of the medical profession's attitude toward voluntary sterilization is similarly reactionary and "moralistic." Beyond establishing that a patient fully understands the consequences of sterilization and will not be physically harmed by the operation, the doctor should have no right to make the ultimate decision as to whether or not an adult should be voluntarily sterilized.

Whether the medical profession in the United States will become a strong force for population control remains to be seen. It has a great potential for helping to solve the population problem, both at home and through technical aid to other countries. It could, for instance, assist in setting up field centers in UDCs, where paramedical personnel could be trained to instruct people in the use of contraceptives and to perform vasectomies and abortions. The American Medical Association (AMA) is an extremely powerful organization and an enormous potential force for good. But, as in many other areas of social reform, such as in providing decent health care to all Americans, the AMA has conspicuously dragged its feet on the population controversy.

It should have been at the very forefront of a crusade for population control measures, particularly those that pertain to medical practice, such as the repeal of abortion laws, increasing the availability of sterilization, and encouraging the dissemination of birth control information. The AMA has now gone on record as supporting these policies, but only after pressure was applied from outside by the public and from within by the younger members. It appears that many physicians, especially younger ones, will no longer permit the AMA to stand firmly against social progress. Perhaps they will be able either to reform it or reduce it to impotence.

## Transportation and Communications

We cannot discuss in detail the changes which might occur in the systems that move people and information around this country and around the world. But there has been considerable discussion in the United States about the possibilities as a long-range trend for a general conversion from automobiles to mass transportation, an idea that has much appeal. It would, among other things, conserve energy resources and help to mitigate the problems of air pollution. Similarly, the crisis in air transportation and suggested cures received wide publicity late in the 1960s. It seems unlikely that transportation systems in the U.S. and other DCs will change significantly for the better until the public becomes sufficiently fed up with smog, noise, delays, and danger that it is willing to forego further growth in both population and gross national product. Automobiles may be made more smog-free, but until the public rebels against them, their numbers will probably increase rapidly enough to keep the overall smog level dangerously high, while more land disappears under freeways. Airport noise may get worse for a while, not better, as more and larger aircraft are used. If and when a transition can be made to a nongrowing population and economy, both the need for business travel and the pressure to build more vehicles and more goods should be reduced; perhaps then these transportation problems could be solved. Hopefully, the kinds of transport problems that now plague the DCs (the U.S. in particular) can be totally avoided in most UDCs.

Unlike the transportation system, the communications system seems to have great potential for instituting positive change. Television and radio seem to have universal appeal, and with relatively little expenditure could have virtually universal coverage. If human problems are to be solved on a worldwide basis, some means of intercommunication among the peoples of the world must be employed. One possibility would be for the DCs to supply UDCs with large numbers of small, transistorized TV sets for communal viewing in villages. These could provide the information channels for reaching the largely rural populations of the "other world." These channels could provide both a route for supplying technical aid and a means of reinforcing the idea that they are members of a global community.

The potentialities of electronic communications, according to Isaac

Asimov, are equivalent to a fourth revolution on a par with the developments of speech, writing, and printing. Considering the enormous influence of radio and television in Western countries, their future impact in largely illiterate societies can hardly fail to be even greater. But this revolution will not realize its full potential until electronic communications are as widespread and commonplace as the printed word now is.

The first small commercial communications satellite station was launched in 1965, with one channel for television and 240 relays for voice transmissions. A much more sophisticated system, Intelsat IV, was scheduled for launching in 1971. By sometime in 1972, some 40 countries around the world will be linked by the Intelsat system. Already a number of countries that previously had had virtually no contact are communicating with each other by satellite. An interesting example is Chile and Argentina; the Andes until now were too great a barrier. As few as three satellites can cover the entire planet. Intelsat can and does transmit data, transoceanic telephone and teletype messages, television broadcasts, and facsimiles of letters, newspapers, or photographs. Plans exist for "distributional" satellites to relay messages within countries, as a supplement to the international Intelsats. After that, the hope is to develop a system of broadcasting directly to each home. This is not expected to become a reality before the 1980s, and even then many think it will be limited to the sort of service described above; programs beamed to schools, community centers, and villages, especially in UDCs.

The potential for creating a true "global village" through such a communications network should not be ignored. Even apart from the opportunity to bring diverse peoples together for exchange of ideas and information, there is a great opportunity for a general lowering of hostilities. Familiarity breeds friendship far more often than contempt.

There remains, of course, the substantial danger that a worldwide communications network will not be used for the benefit of humanity. If, like the television system in the U.S., it is employed to promote the ideas and interests of a controlling minority, the world would be better off without it. The problems of supplying channels for information are thus easily solved in comparison with the problems of determining what information should flow along those channels and in what format. Much programming ought to be informational, even if presented as entertainment. People in the DCs must be made aware of their resource situations, their polluting activities, and the need for population control at home. People in the UDCs must be made aware of the need for population control and the ways it may be achieved. They also need help in solving many other problems such as increasing agricultural production and improving public health. Programming should be carefully designed by social scientists and communications experts thoroughly familiar with the needs and attitudes of the audiences in each country or locality. This will be especially important in the UDCs, and especially difficult there because of the lack of trained people and the radical change in attitudes that is required. Control of the communications media should obviously be public, with maximum safeguard against abuses.

The difficulty of educating the people in the DCs to the problems of population and environment is not as serious, assuming time and space can be obtained in the media. Material can be more straightforward, since in many DCs there is already rather widespread awareness of at least some environmental problems. In the United States a great step forward could be taken by simply requiring that both radio and television assign some of their commercial time to short "spots" calling attention to the problems of population, resources, and environment. This could be justified under the equal-time doctrine that put the anti-smoking message sponsored by the American Heart Association and the American Cancer Society on TV, and that in 1971 was invoked for messages pointing out the environmental hazards of big cars. The FCC might be empowered to require that networks donate time for ads to awaken people to the population-resource-environment crisis. Long documentary "specials," whether prepared by the networks or by educational channels, are relatively ineffective in initiating awareness of a problem, although they are useful in providing detailed information. But, for the most part, they reach only those who are already aware that a particular problem exists. The majority of people want to be entertained; they do not want to hear bad news.

In the longer term, more ambitious exploitation of the potential of communications systems may help to relieve pressure on energy supplies and other resources. Specifically, it is far less costly in terms of energy to move information than to move people and things. Computer terminals coupled to television sets (for graphic display and face-to-face conversations) and to telephone lines (for data transmission) could eliminate the need for commuting to and from work in many kinds of jobs. Newspapers, which today are responsible for the consumption of great quantities of woodpulp, could be displayed a page at a time, under the control of the reader, on the computer-television hookup. Scientific and business meetings, each of which now entails hundreds of thousands of passenger miles of fuel-gobbling jet travel, could be managed on closed circuit television for a tiny fraction of the impact on resources. Of course, there are problems to be surmounted before such schemes can be implemented, not the least of which is the protection of privacy and confidential communications. Such difficulties can, in principle, be solved, and it seems clear that the communication/information processing area is one field in which technological innovation can make important contributions to alleviating the resource-environment crunch.

## Economic and Political Change

In relation to the population-resources-environment crisis, economics and politics can usually be viewed as two sides of the same coin. A very large number of political decisions are made on an economic basis, especially those relating to environmental problems. John Maynard Keynes wrote in *The*

*General Theory of Employment, Interest, and Money* (1936): "The ideas of economists and political philosophers, both when they are right and when they are wrong, are more powerful than is commonly understood. Indeed the world is ruled by little else." Although the major political division of our time—that between capitalist and communist worlds—is thought to be based on differences in economic ideology, the actual differences are relatively few. In fact, a major cause of humanity's current plight lies not in the economic differences between the two superpowers, but in the economic attitudes that they have in common.

### GROSS NATIONAL PRODUCT AND ECONOMIC GROWTHMANSHIP

Economists are not unanimous in their view of economic growth. Paul A. Samuelson wrote in *Economics, An Introductory Analysis* (1967): "The ghost of Carlyle should be relieved to know that economics, after all, has not been a dismal science. It has been the cheerful, but impatient, science of growth." On the other hand, E. J. Mishan states in *The Costs of Economic Growth* (1967): "The skilled economist, immersed for the greater part of the day in pages of formulae and statistics, does occasionally glance at the world about him and, if perceptive, does occasionally feel a twinge of doubt about the relevance of his contribution. . . . For a moment, perhaps, he will dare wonder whether it is really worth it. Like the rest of us, however, the economist must keep moving, and since such misgivings about the overall value of economic growth cannot be formalized or numerically expressed, they are not permitted seriously to modify his practical recommendations." The majority of economic theorists hold Samuelson's view and still tend to be growth-oriented, as do most politicians and businessmen in both DCs and UDCs. However, change is coming slowly but surely. In the eighth edition of his text (1970), Samuelson modified his statement to: ". . . It has been the impatient science of growth."

In much of the world—indeed, in all countries with any aspirations toward "modernization," "progress," or "development"—a general economic index of advancement is growth of the gross national product (GNP). The GNP is the sum of personal and government expenditure on goods and services, plus expenditure on investment. It can be a very useful economic indicator. More important than what the GNP is, however, is what it *is not*. It is not a measure of the degree of freedom of the people of a nation. It is not a measure of the health of a population. It is not a measure of the state of depletion of natural resources. It is not a measure of the stability of the environmental systems upon which life depends. It is not a measure of security from the threat of war. It is not, in sum, a comprehensive measure of the *quality* of life, although, unhappily, it is often misused as such a measure.

When the standards of living of two nations are compared, it is customary to examine their *per capita* GNPs. Per capita GNP is an especially unfortunate statistic. First of all, it is the ratio of two statistics that are at best crude estimates, especially in the UDCs, where neither GNP nor population size is known with any accuracy. More important, comparisons of per capita GNP overestimate many kinds of differences. For instance, a comparison of per capita GNPs would lead to the conclusion that the average American lives almost ten times as well as the average Portuguese, and some sixty times as well as the average Burmese. This, of course, is meaningless, since virtually all services and many goods are much cheaper in the UDCs. Americans pay perhaps five or ten times as much for farm labor, domestic help, haircuts, carpentry, plumbing, and so forth as do people in the UDCs, and the services we get are often of inferior quality. And yet these services, because of the accounting system, contribute between five and ten times as much to our GNP as the same services do to the GNPs of, say, Burma or India. Furthermore, figures on the increase of per capita GNP in UDCs do not take into account such things as rise in literacy rate, and thus may underrate the amount of progress a country has made toward modernization.

Nor does the GNP measure many negative aspects of the standard of living. Although the average Burmese unquestionably lives much less well than the average American, the average American may cause a hundred times as much ecological destruction to the planet as a whole.

A serious criticism that can be leveled at the majority of economists is one that applies equally to most people and societies: they accept a doctrine of economic determinism. The myths of cornucopian economics as opposed to the realities of geology and biology have already been discussed, but the problem is much more pervasive than that. Economic growth has become *the* standard for progress, *the* benefit for which almost any social cost is to be paid.

This problem in economic thought can be fully appreciated by a perusal of Samuelson's excellent *Economics,* one of the best and most influential textbooks ever written. The book is, of course, oriented toward economic growth. Problems of the growing scarcity of nonrenewable resources are presented only briefly as a problem of underdeveloped countries. The physical constraints placed on economic growth by the conversion to heat of all the energy we consume are not discussed in the text, nor are the other basic environmental constraints discussed in our earlier chapters. Implicit in the treatment of economic development is the idea that it is possible for 5 to 7 billion people to achieve a standard of living similar to that of the average American of the 1960s. Uninformed technological optimism is explicit or implicit throughout the book.

Nevertheless, Samuelson's book reveals more understanding of population and environment than the writings of many other economists. He does realize that growth of GNP must be "qualified by data on leisure, population size, relative distribution, quality, and noneconomic factors." In the 1970 edition, Samuelson added two new chapters dealing with economic inequality: the quality of life, race, cities, and pollution. Furthermore, in a 1969 *Newsweek* column, Samuelson wrote, ". . . most of us are poorer than we realize. Hidden costs are accruing all the time; and because we tend to ignore them, we overstate our incomes . . . Thomas Hobbes said that in the state of nature the life of man was nasty, brutish and short. In the state of modern civilization it has become nasty, brutish and long."

The discussion of the problems of American society and of UDCs in Samuelson's text is a model of realism when contrasted with the ideas of such economic conservatives as Milton Friedman of the University of Chicago, who in 1970 wrote an article for the *New York Times Magazine* (Sept. 13) entitled "The Social Responsibility of Business is to Increase its Profits." Most economists subscribe to the "bigger and more is better" philosophy. The growing mixed economy is something to analyze, improve, and by all means to keep growing. In an article that appeared in the *New York Review of Books,* economist Wassily Leontief of Harvard remarked that ". . . If the 'external costs' of growth clearly seem to pose dangers to the quality of life, there is as yet no discernible tendency among economists or economic managers to divert their attention from this single-minded pursuit of economic growth." That economists have clung to this idea is not surprising. After all, natural scientists often cling to outmoded ideas that have produced far less palpable benefits than have the mixed economies of the Western World. The question of whether a different economic system might have produced a more equitable *distribution* of benefits is not one that Western economists like to dwell on. Furthermore, ideas of perpetual growth are congruent with the conventional wisdom of most of the businessmen of the world; indeed, of most of the world's population. The people of the UDCs naturally wish to emulate the economic growth of the West and they long for "development" with all of its shiny accoutrements. Why should they be expected to know that it is physically and ecologically impossible for them to catch up with us when many of our most erudite citizens are still unaware of that fact?

Perhaps most serious is the common idea that not only is growth of the GNP highly desirable, but that population increase, at least in DCs, *promotes* such growth. However, some economists have made a point of attacking the idea that population growth is necessary to keep the GNP growing in DCs. Certainly in the DCs there is no perfect correlation between population growth and growth of GNP. For instance, J. J. Spengler of Duke University has written, "It is high time . . . that business cease looking upon the stork as a bird of good omen." He points out that a substantial portion of the GNP consists of services, and that these may continue to expand with a stationary population. As we in the United States become more willing to acknowledge the maldistribution of our wealth, we will become increasingly aware of ways to expand our services by extending them to a greater portion of our population.

Whether or not population growth helps to raise the GNP, it is clear that the GNP cannot grow forever. Why should it? As John Kenneth Galbraith points out in *The New Industrial State,* it would be entirely logical to set limits on the amount of product a nation needs, and then to strive to reduce the amount of work required to produce such a product (and, one might add, to see that the product is much more equitably distributed than it is today). But, of course, such a program would be a threat to some of the most dearly held beliefs of our society. It would attack the Protestant work ethic, which insists that one must be kept busy on the job for 40 hours a week. It is even better to work several more hours moonlighting, so that the money can be earned to buy all those wonderful automobiles, detergents, appliances, and assorted gimcracks which *must* be bought if the economy is to continue to grow. But this tradition is outmoded; the only hope for civilization in the future is to work for *quality* in the context of a nongrowing economy, or at least an economy in which growth is carefully restricted to certain activities.

A number of interesting suggestions about GNP have been made by economist Edwin G. Dolan in his fine little book, *TANSTAAFL: The Economic Strategy for Environmental Crisis*. TANSTAAFL (which stands for There Ain't No Such Thing As A Free Lunch) contains the most lucid brief consideration of population-environment economics we have come across, and we recommend it highly even though we differ with the authors on some points. Dolan, along with some other economists, would rename the GNP the Gross National Cost (GNC). More importantly, he would distinguish between Type I GNC and Type II GNC. Type I GNC would measure that fraction of GNC produced with renewable resources and recycling of wastes. Type II GNC would be that depending on the depletion of nonrenewable resources and the production of indestructible wastes. The problems of doing the discrimination would be difficult (consider, for instance, calculating in the energy component involved in the production of Type I GNC), but the basic aim is sound. As Dolan says, "Politicians and economists would then design their policies to maximize Type I and minimize Type II. In the eyes of world opinion a high Type I component would be a source of national pride, while high production of the Type II variety would be a source of shame."

Economist Kenneth E. Boulding has begun to develop an exciting set of economic concepts dealing with the population-resource-environment crisis, by recognizing the existence of biological and physical limitations to growth. In "The Economics of the Coming Spaceship Earth," he described the need to shift from our present "cowboy economy," in which both production and consumption are regarded with great favor, and which is "associated with reckless, exploitative, romantic and violent behavior," to a "spaceman economy." In the spaceman economy there are no unlimited reservoirs, either for extraction or pollution, and consumption must be minimized. In a classical understatement, Boulding describes the idea that production and consumption are bad things as "very strange to economists." But even economists can change, and perhaps this section on economics can end on an optimistic note. Economists of the next generation may be weaned away from their concentration on perpetual growth and high production-consumption, and learn, in Boulding's words, to measure economic success in terms of the "nature, extent, quality and complexity of the total capital stock, including in this the state of the human bodies and minds included in the system."

POPULATION, OVERPRODUCTION, AND EMPLOYMENT

Population growth in any nation absorbs capital and resources that could be used to increase the average standard of living (as discussed in Chapter 8). It is, in fact, almost certain that economic growth in the DCs is, or soon will be, hindered by population growth, just as it is clearly hindered in the UDCs now. In the United States, for instance, there is no need for additional people in the labor force. Indeed, today we suffer simultaneously from overproduction and both actual and disguised unemployment.

The best example of overproduction is perhaps seen in the automobile industry. The introduction of annual automobile model changes by General Motors in 1923 quickly pushed most competitors out of business, reducing the number of American automobile manufacturers from 88 in 1921 to 10 in 1935. Only four remain today. This has permitted a few companies in an essentially non-competitive situation to manipulate both demand and quality in a way that has resulted in a continual high output of overpriced, overstyled, under-engineered, low durability (compared to what is possible) automobiles. This overproduction is responsible for a substantial portion of the problems of environmental deterioration and resource depletion faced by our society. Immediate relief from a major portion of our air pollution problems, for instance, would result from the replacement of our present automobiles with small, low-horsepower, long-lasting cars designed for recycling. We might start by removing tariffs and import restrictions on automobiles that met our exhaust emission standards, so that small foreign cars would be even more attractive to American buyers. Exhaust emissions and the components of air pollution produced by the wear of tires on asphalt and from the asbestos of brake linings would be reduced. Recycling old automobiles or building longer lasting ones would reduce resource pressure and the pollution associated with automobile production, as well as that from obtaining the materials used in automobile production. These would include such operations as iron and coal mining and the transporting and smelting of the ores. The rewards of such a program would not be limited to pollution abatement and the reduction of resource depletion, especially of petroleum. Since small cars need less room on the highway and in parking lots, transportation would, through that change alone, become pleasanter, safer, and more efficient.

But, of course, there would be several unhappy consequences of a general program of automobile control. A very substantial portion—perhaps 10–20 percent—of the American population derives its living, directly or indirectly, from the automobile; its construction, fueling, servicing, selling, and the provision of roads and other facilities for it. Thus, a large fraction of our population would face problems similar to those faced by individuals whose jobs were dependent on continuation of the SST program. And economic difficulties for such a large group would have a serious impact on the American economy as a whole.

Unless there were careful planning to ameliorate the consequences, a sudden attempt to shift from big, short-lived automobiles to small, long-lived automobiles, let alone to some completely different system of transportation, might lead to a national calamity. The economy, however, is demonstrably capable of accommodating itself to very far-reaching changes. Even without extensive planning, the United States economy during the period from 1946 to 1948 converted almost 50 percent of its productive capacity from war-related products to peacetime products. The flexibility of our economic institutions is often grossly underestimated. Clearly, an apparatus should be established immediately to do the planning and lay the groundwork for dealing with the automobile problem without destroying the national economy, as well as for other actions necessary for making the transition to a stable, ecologically sound economy. The task is enormous. In the short term, alternative activities must be found for various industries. The productive capacity of the automobile manufacturers, for example, might be diverted to meeting other pressing national and international needs. Many Americans need new housing, and many localities need mass transit systems; many UDCs need modern systems of food storage and transport. Detroit is surely capable of making valuable contributions in these areas.

In the long run, however, we must find a way to reduce our overall productive capacity, recycle everything possible, and limit our use of energy. We must outgrow the idea that a high level of production is *per se* good. A relatively small fraction of the American work force is quite capable of producing all of the things necessary to provide a reasonably "good life" for all Americans, even 207 million of us.

The problems of reducing overproduction are greatly exacerbated by unemployment. The 4–6 percent unemployment figures commonly quoted do not indicate the true seriousness of the problem. First of all, this overt unemployment is very unevenly distributed in the population. Racial minorities, young workers, and, above all, young minority workers suffer disproportionately. The pressure of unemployment at the younger end of the labor pool is probably a major reason that we have been so rigid about retirement around the age of 65. Many talented people are removed from the labor force even though they may still be capable of 10 years or more of productive work and do not wish to be "put out to pasture." The enforced separation of older people from their economic life (not included in unemployment figures) is clearly a contributing factor to the problems of the aged discussed in Chapter 10.

Added to these components of the employment problem is disguised unemployment: people doing jobs that are either unnecessary or detrimental to society or both. Anyone familiar with government, big business, universities, the military, or any large bureaucracy, knows how many people are essentially "feather-bedding" or just "pushing paper." When those people are combined with the workers who are engaged in such fundamentally anti-social activities as building freeways, overproducing cars and appliances, manufacturing DDT, napalm, and jet fighters, or being slum landlords, the number of people who are in some sense unemployed is a substantial portion of the work force.

Of course, the whole problem would be made infinitely worse if we attempted simply to discontinue those jobs which are unnecessary or dangerous to society. Many of those jobs are probably necessary in the short run. For instance, until and unless rational solutions are found to the problem of international conflict, it will doubtless be necessary to continue to manufacture some jet fighters. But now is the time to start planning and maneuvering to phase out both disguised unemployment and antisocial products without damaging society and without creating enormous levels of overt unemployment. Shifting productive capacity to socially useful goals is a major component of the medium-term solution. The long-term solution, as hinted by Galbraith, lies in drastic reduction of the amount of work done by each worker, in order to create more jobs. Shortening the work week (to 20 hours or less) or decreasing the number of weeks per year worked (companies could have different spring-summer and fall-winter shifts) would accomplish this. The result would be more leisure, which hopefully will be better enjoyed by a more educated population. It would also provide the time for people both to obtain that education and to put it to good use participating in the running of society. There should be little but positive consequences from such a reduction in working time. Pay would perhaps be reduced, but so would many expenses, if material goods were built to endure and there was no longer social pressure to consume for the sake of consuming. The pace of life would undoubtedly slow down, with attendant psychological and physical benefits. If a stable economic system could be achieved, life would indeed be different from what it is today.

### PERSONAL FREEDOM AND THE QUALITY OF LIFE

"We have had no environmental index, no census statistic to measure whether the country is more or less habitable from year to year. A tranquility index or a cleanliness index might have told us something about the condition of man, but a fast-growing country preoccupied with making and acquiring material things has had no time for the amenities that are the very heart and substance of daily life." Stewart Udall was Secretary of the Interior when he wrote those words. His bold challenge to Americans, expressed in *1976: Agenda for Tomorrow,* has not yet been accepted. Is there any way to break into the present system and persuade our society to weigh economic goals carefully against other possible goals of human existence? Can we proceed with Mr. Udall's urgent agenda? The obstacles are great, since economics and politics are so intertwined, and the various elements of the power structure in the U.S. all want and promote "growth." If there is any chance of getting a reversal of this attitude, it lies in convincing those in power as well as the electorate that their own personal lives and freedom are at stake. More men with dedication and perception must be elected to public office, and ways must be found to convince the present leaders of the nation that population growth and accelerating resource utilization, coupled with environmental decay, are injuring their children and progressively limiting their possible futures. Two points may be made:

1. While the American economy has been growing, freedom has been shrinking. Greater and greater controls must be applied to everyday living, and restrictions will inevitably grow more severe as population increases. The use of automobiles, boats, and private airplanes will become even more circumscribed. The keeping of pets, especially those that are noisy or consume substantial amounts of protein, will be forbidden. Increasingly, access to recreational areas will be strictly rationed. Bureaucracy will continue to grow as the government tries to solve more and more pressing problems with less and less success. Each citizen, assuming that at least an illusion of "democracy" will persist, will have an ever-decreasing say in the affairs of state. For instance, consider what has happened to the average citizen's "say" in the past 150 years. In 1810 each of 52 Senators represented, on the average, about 140,000 citizens. Today each of 100 Senators represents about 2,100,000 Americans—15 times as many! A parallel dilution of representation has occurred in the House of Representatives.

2. While the American GNP has been growing, the quality of life in the United States has been deteriorating. The GNP roughly doubled in the decade 1960–1969. Can anyone claim that the average individual's life has greatly improved in the same period? Here is a short list of the negative changes that have occurred in the quality of his existence: The air that he breathes has become more foul, and the quality of the water he uses has probably declined. His chances of being robbed or murdered have increased, as have his chances of losing his life in a highway accident or his home or business in a civil disorder. His chances of dying of emphysema, bronchitis, and various kinds of cancer have increased. He must travel further to reach solitude, either on increasingly crowded highways, increasingly shoddy trains, or increasingly delay-prone airlines. His children have a more difficult time being accepted into a first-class college than they did in 1960. If he has sons they are more likely to be killed in a war, or to flee the country to avoid being drafted. Can a list of *improvements* twice this long easily be constructed?

We suspect that these arguments will not have the desired effect, even if a great many influential people get the message. To a large extent the political-economic system has a life of its own; it possesses emergent qualities beyond those of the individuals who constitute it. There is no conscious conspiracy on the part of individual military men, businessmen, and government officials to destroy the United States and the world, but the total effect of their actions and those of their counterparts in other governments nonetheless is moving us toward that end. People in groups, be they mobs, university committees, armies, or industrial boards, simply do not behave the way single individuals behave. But basically we must try, by changing the behavior of many individuals, to produce the desired changes in the corporate behavior of the economic and political establishment.

### ECONOMICS AND THE POLITICS OF THE ENVIRONMENT

One way in which changes in our economic system might be accomplished would be to develop a new economics of the environment. There is a pressing need to re-examine the way cost-benefit calculations are done in our society. Such calculations are usually made over too short a time span. For example, consider the history of a contemporary housing development. A developer carves up a Southern California hillside, builds houses on it, and sells them, reaping the benefits in a very short time. Then society starts to pay the costs. The houses have been built in an area where the native plant community is known as *chaparral*. Chaparral, known to plant ecologists as a "fire climax," would not exist as a stable vegetation type unless the area burned over every once in a while. When it does the homes are destroyed, and the buyers and the public start paying hidden costs in the form of increased insurance rates and emergency relief. Of course, there are hidden costs even in the absence of such a catastrophe. The housing development puts a further load on the water supply and probably will be a contributing political factor in the ultimate flooding of distant farmland to make a reservoir. Perhaps wind patterns cause smog to be especially thick in the area of the development, and as it begins to affect the inhabitants they and society pay additional costs in hospital bills and high life insurance premiums. And, of course, by helping to attract more people into the area, the development helps to increase the general smog burden. Then there are the problems of additional roads, schools, sewage treatment plants, and other community requirements created by the new subdivision. While the builder may have put the roads in the subdivision, increased taxes must pay for increased upkeep on roads in the subdivision area, and eventually for new roads demanded by increasing congestion. Among the saddest phenomena of our time are the attempts by politicians and chambers of commerce to attract industry and developers to their areas to "broaden the tax base." The usual result, when the dust has settled, is that the people who previously lived in the area have a degraded environment and *higher* taxes.

In short, the benefits are easily calculated and quickly reaped by a select few; the costs, on the other hand, are diffuse, spread over time, and difficult to calculate. For example, how would one assess the cost of weather modification by pollution, which might result in the death of millions from starvation? What is the value of an ecological system destroyed by chlorinated hydrocarbons or of one death from emphysema?

The disparity between the few elements accounted for in present methods of cost-benefit analysis and the real costs borne by society is even more obvious when the problem of industrial pollution is considered. Here the benefit is usually the absence of a cost. Garbage is spewed into the environment, rather than being retained and reclaimed. The industry avoids real or imagined financial loss by this process. The term "imagined loss" is used because some industries have found that reclaiming pollutants has more than paid for the cost of retaining them. More often than not, however, the industry benefits, and the public pays the short- and long-term costs. Air pollutants damage crops, ruin paint, soil clothes, dissolve nylon stockings, etch glass, rot windshield wiper blades, and so on. Pollutants must be removed, often at considerable expense, from water supplies. People with emphysema, lung cancer, liver cancer, and hepatitis must be given expensive hospitalization. Insurance costs go up. In these, and in myriad more subtle ways, *everyone* pays. These costs are what accountants euphemistically call "external diseconomies," because they are external to the accounting system of the polluter. A persuasive case can be made that these diseconomies far outweigh the benefits of growth. Such a case has been made recently in some detail by economist Ezra Mishan in his book, *The Costs of Economic Growth.*

One way to attack external diseconomies would be to require industry to internalize them. They could be forced to absorb the costs by laws prohibiting the release of any pollutants. Profits would have to be added on after *all* costs were paid. Clearly, the only solution is for society to insist on pollution abatement at the source. It would be cheaper in every way to curtail it there, rather than attempt to ameliorate the complex problems pollutants cause once they are released into the environment.

Society, having permitted the pollution situation to develop, should now shoulder some of the burden of its correction. As a theoretical example, Steel Company X, located on the shores of Lake Michigan, is pouring filth into the lake at a horrendous rate. A study shows that it would cost $2.00 per share of common stock to build the necessary apparatus for retaining and processing the waste. Should the company be forced to stop polluting and pay the price? Certainly they must be forced to stop, but it seems fair that society should pay some of the cost. When Company X located on the lake, everyone knew that it would spew pollutants into the lake, but no one objected. The local people wanted to encourage industry. Now, finally, society has changed its mind; the pollution must stop. But should Company X be forced into bankruptcy by pollution regulations, penalizing stockholders and putting its employees out of work? Should the local politicians who lured the company into locating there and the citizens who encouraged them not pay a cent? Clearly society should order the pollution stopped *and pick up at least part of the bill.* It would be a bargain in the long run. Society is already paying a much higher cost for the pollution. The legal tools for forcing compliance with pollution-abatement decisions are essentially at hand.

A similar situation occurred in real life in 1971. Congress refused to vote funds for the continuance of the SST project, in part because of environmental considerations. The decision cost thousands of workers their jobs. Society must find mechanisms to compensate such people, retrain, and if necessary, relocate them. Such dislocations are certain to occur more often and on a larger scale as polluting, energy wasting, and socially dangerous industries and projects are phased out. Fortunately, time should be available to smooth the transitions in most situations.

The profound changes necessary to save the environment and ourselves will not be made easily, however. Powerful opposition can be expected from economic interests. Such opposition has already been mounted by the petrochemical industry, whose behavior may foreshadow that of other industries. This industry has applied constant political pressure (through friends in Congress and such agencies as the USDA) and has resorted to outright lies about the safety of pesticides in order to avoid regulation, particularly since the publication in 1962 of Rachel Carson's book, *Silent Spring,* which was addressed to the public at large. The industry has attempted to discredit responsible scientists who have nothing to sell, but who oppose current patterns of pesticide usage because they have learned through careful and patient study that DDT and related pesticides are not mere killers of insects, but threaten the capacity of the Earth to support human life. Desperately worried biologists have attempted, through public education and by going to court, to keep more of these poisons from entering the environment, and concerned conservationists have done what they can. But until 1969 the petrochemical industry was successful in forestalling any effective regulation of its activities.

The industry's tactics were typified by an editorial that appeared in the journal *Farm Chemicals* (January 1968), which not only labeled every biologist critical of current pesticide practice as a member of a "cult" and a "professional agitator," but also claimed that "scientists themselves literally ostracized Rachel Carson, and they will come to grips with this eroding force within their own ranks. Of course, it is not unusual that the character of the scientific community is changing. It may be a sign of the times. The age of opportunism!" This editorial appeared four years after Rachel Carson's death, yet the ghost of this remarkably sensitive and extremely capable marine biologist apparently still haunted those whose products she had found were dangerously polluting the environment.

Unquestionably, some chemists and entomologists attempted to discredit Rachel Carson. Most of those who did, however, were either employed by the petrochemical industry or were too narrowly trained (as most entomologists are) to appreciate the dangers in the use of such powerful chemicals. Scientists in other disciplines disagreed with her too, but for the wrong reasons: some argued that she was speaking outside of her field of expertise; others charged her with emotionalism. Hundreds of biologists, however, admired her tremendously for her breadth of view and for awakening the general public to the hazards posed by the use of dangerous chemicals in attempts to increase the production of food.

It is true that there were a few factual errors in *Silent Spring,* but in many ways Rachel Carson *underestimated* the hazards of DDT and certain other chlorinated hydrocarbons. Nevertheless, she succeeded in awakening the public—and did so in a way that a more "technical" and highly documented book like Robert L. Rudd's *Pesticides and the Living Landscape* could not do. Rudd, a zoologist, came to many of the same conclusions that were presented in *Silent Spring,* but because his book was not addressed to the general public it did not engender the level of attack that was directed toward *Silent Spring.* In our opinion, no biologist has made a greater contribution to mankind in this century than Rachel Carson.

The petrochemical industry is now on the defensive because scientists and other citizens have discovered that there are still some legal remedies against environmental degradation and health hazards, and, through the Environmental Defense Fund, they are using these remedies. It seems unlikely that the reaction of the industry is based on the DDT or chlorinated hydrocarbon issue alone. A more likely reason is apprehension about the precedents which will be set if any or all these chemicals are banned or restricted in use. The industry would prefer to account primarily to the friendly and compliant USDA, not to groups of scientists who are concerned with the ecological effects and long-term dangers to human well-being caused by their activities. Even the USDA finally seems to have seen the handwriting on the wall, however, as in late 1969 it began to discuss, along with the Department of Health, Education and Welfare and the Department of the Interior, the phasing out of all "nonessential" uses of DDT.

When the Environmental Protection Agency (EPA) was created in 1970, it assumed responsibility for the regulation of pesticides. It did proceed to ban the use of DDT for households and certain crops (for which DDT was seldom used anyway). EDF litigation produced a court order early in 1971 for EPA to issue notices of cancellation of registration and review DDT for suspension. Cancellation takes effect after 30 days, provided that the manufacturers do not appeal. The process of appeal can go on for years. Suspension, on the other hand, takes effect at once, even as appeal proceeds. As of summer 1971, the notices of cancellation for DDT, as well as aldrin, dieldrin, mirex, and the herbicide 2,4,5T were of course being appealed. But EPA had declined to suspend DDT or the other pesticides, so EDF went back to court. It is not yet clear whether this will lead to the necessary, almost total discontinuance of persistent pesticides throughout the world, although some countries are ahead of the U.S. in this respect. DDT has been at least partially or temporarily banned in Canada, Sweden, Norway, Hungary, Cyprus, and Japan, and pesticide regulation is being seriously considered in many other countries. Of course, even if DDT is completely discontinued, it may already be too late. Still, this glacially slow process is in the right direction.

Defensive reactions similar to those of the pesticide manufacturers can be expected from other industries whose activities contribute heavily to pollution. Representatives of the inorganic nitrogen fertilizer industry have given extensive testimony before Congress, which confirmed the belief of biologists that the industry simply cannot (or does not want to) grasp the dimensions of the problems that result from the failure to maintain an adequate supply of humus in the soil.

It is most difficult to protect the environment when economists, industries, and governmental agencies team up to wreak havoc, as in the case of the supersonic transport. The SST was "justified" in the United States largely on the grounds that it was needed economically to protect the balance of payments. President Nixon, in endorsing the SST program in 1969, stated, "I want the United States to continue to lead the world in air transport." The economic penalties which would be incurred from sonic boom damage were probably not included in the administration's consideration of whether to proceed with the project, nor were the psychological and emotional damages that people would suffer, nor the possible effects on the world's climate (which themselves may cause heavy economic damage) of the operation of these high altitude jets. Fortunately, a combination of factors, including intensive lobbying by conservation organizations and testimony by several distinguished economists that the SST was an economic boondoggle, convinced Congress that the SST's disadvantages outweighed its very questionable advantages.

If our government is serious about leading the world in air transport, it could, having denied funds for American SSTs, ban the operation of foreign SSTs over U.S. territory or their landing at U.S. airports, forbid American travel agents to book passengers on foreign airlines which fly SSTs, and try to persuade other governments to abandon their SST projects. With the billions saved from the SST project, real effort could be put into improving air safety, alleviating airport congestion, and improving transportation to, from, and within airports.

The problem of preventing environmental deterioration caused in part by governmental agencies will almost certainly have to be attacked by changes in government structure. President Nixon, to his credit, has made some progress along this line. Early in 1970, the Council on Environmental Quality was established in the President's Executive Office. Soon afterward, the CEQ issued a report which superficially listed our environmental problems, but offered no serious programs for dealing with them other than to recommend a national land use policy. Other government agencies have been required to submit reports on the environmental impact of new projects to the CEQ for review, but many have not been bothering. Moreover, these reports are not being released to the public until after the project has been approved, thus hampering public monitoring of the CEQ's performance. This is specifically against the provisions of the National Environmental Policy Act of 1969. Hopefully, the Act will soon be properly administered by the Executive Branch.

In July 1970, the President proposed the creation of two new agencies which would absorb some of the activities of older ones. Pollution monitoring and control for air and water, solid waste management, regulation of pesticides and radiation have all been centralized into the independent Environmental Protection Agency (EPA). This new agency, under the administration of William D. Ruckleshaus, is also responsible for ecological research and the development of environmental policy. The other new agency is the National Ocean and Atmospheric Administration, which was created within the Department of Commerce to unify research and other matters pertaining to the ocean and atmosphere.

Whether this reorganization of government regulating agencies will result in more effective federal action in dealing with the environment remains to be seen. But some important roadblocks to action have been removed simply by transferring the power to license or ban pesticides away from the Department of Agriculture and transferring the regulation of nuclear power and radioactive wastes away from the Atomic Energy Commission. Given appropriate funds and support from Congress, the President, and the public, the Environmental Protection Agency has the potential to evolve into a powerful friend of our environment.

Nevertheless, in an age when the most significant problems of humanity lie in the areas of ecology and the behavioral sciences, it is extraordinary that the President of the United States has not appointed a single behavioral scientist or biologist, let alone ecologist, as his advisor, as a member of the CEQ, or as head of either of the two new agencies. His science advisors have been a physicist and an electrical engineer. Ruckleshaus was an Assistant Attorney General before joining EPA. Is it any wonder that, at least from outward appearances, the President still does not seem to grasp the true magnitude of the environmental crisis?

President Nixon in early 1971 announced a plan to reorganize the Cabinet and thus the entire structure of the Administration (Fig. 11-1). Needless to say, such an overhaul is long overdue, and many of the proposed changes are potentially very beneficial. Environmental and resource affairs are nicely centralized in the Department of Natural Resources, except for the monitoring and regulating agencies, CEQ and EPA, which will remain independent. However, many of the activities that might affect population growth are scattered throughout the four new departments. Some centralized agency or department should be developed that would be responsible for establishing and maintaining quality standards for the lives of all Americans. It should, by recommending policy changes or legislation, monitor and regulate the size of our population so that such standards can be met.

We hope that the Department of Natural Resources, if and when it is formed, will be a major center of policy planning relative to the environment, and will carry out a program of public education in that general area.

As President Nixon seems to have recognized, our governmental structure is no longer suitable for the task before it. The fragmentation of responsibility among government agencies makes even less sense than the university depart-

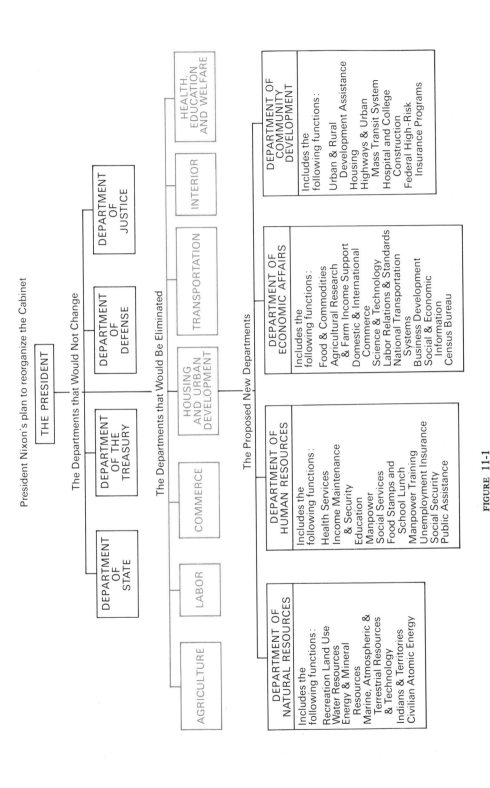

**FIGURE 11-1**

**President Nixon's plan to reorganize the Cabinet.**

mental structure mentioned earlier. The lack of overall control of environmental matters and the impossibility of dealing with problems in any coordinated way are illustrated by the fact that the area of urban affairs now comes under the jurisdiction of the Department of Housing and Urban Development, the Department of Health, Education and Welfare, and the Departments of Labor, Commerce, Interior, Justice, and Transportation, to name just the main ones. It is clear that the Executive branch gravely needs reorganizing. Substantial changes in the Legislative branch are also called for, especially reorganization of the committee system.

Perhaps one of the most fundamental changes needed is that an upper age limit—of perhaps 65 years—be established for appointed and elected federal officials. Older people who have experience and wisdom and are still fit, could be asked to serve in formal advisory bodies in the government, or informally as consultants. But the actual work of running the country in our complex world is simply too great a strain for most older men, especially in an era when instant worldwide communications are capable of putting extraordinary loads of responsibility on individuals. A second reason for age limits is the principle that in a dangerous and rapidly changing world those responsible for making decisions should have a reasonable expectation of having to live with the consequences of those decisions.

Some cogent suggestions on reforming the Legislative Branch may be found in the books listed in the bibliography of this chapter. The Center for the Study of Democratic Institutions has had, under the direction of R. G. Tugwell, an ongoing project designed to produce a modern constitution for the United States. This project deserves much more publicity, and the constitution, now in its 33rd draft, deserves wide circulation and study.

One of the features of the Tugwell Constitution is a Planning Branch of the government, with the mission of doing long-range planning. As should be apparent from the preceding discussion, without planning we have little chance of saving ourselves. Human societies have shown little aptitude for planning so far, but it is a skill that we must soon develop. A private organization, California Tomorrow, has produced a document which can serve as a preliminary model for the kind of planning that might be done. *The California Tomorrow Plan: A First Sketch* presents a skeletal plan for the future of the state of California. It describes "California Zero," the California of today, and two alternative futures: California I and California II. California I is a "current trends continue" projection. California II is a projection in which various alternative courses of action are followed. The plan considers 22 major problem areas (Fig. 11-2) and looks at both the causes of the problems and policies to ameliorate them. California I is compared with California II, and suggestions for phasing into the California II projection are given. The details of the plan need not concern us here (the document can be purchased; see bibliography), but the subjects of concern in the plan are roughly those of this book. What is encouraging is that a private organization could put together a comprehensive vision of the future of one of the largest political entities in the world. Intelligent, broad-spectrum planning can be done.

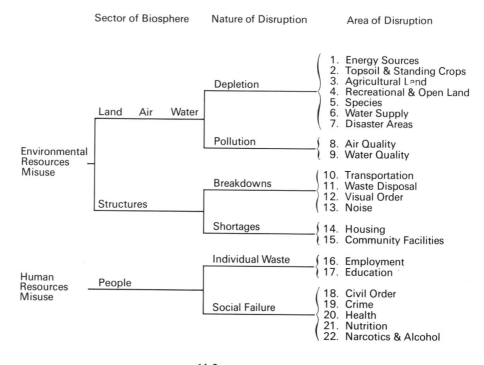

FIGURE 11-2

(from California Tomorrow Plan)

The next question is, how can we in "U.S.A. Zero" start toward "U.S.A. II"? It may well be necessary for a new political party to be formed, one founded on the principles of population control, environmental quality, a stabilized economy, and dedication to careful long-range planning. Such a party would be national and international in its orientation, rather than basing its power on parochial issues as our current parties do. In 1854 the Republican party was created *de novo,* founded on the platform of opposition to the extension of slavery. It seems probable that in the 1970s the environmental issue will become even more prominent than the slavery issue was in the 1850s, and the creation of a powerful new party might be possible. It could, indeed, grow out of such political organizations as Zero Population Growth and Friends of the Earth.

Obviously, such changes as those briefly proposed above will threaten not only numerous politicians of both major parties, but many economic institutions and practices. They are likely to be opposed by vast segments of the Industrial State; by much of the oil and petrochemical industry, the steel industry, the automobile industry, the nuclear power industry, the heavy construction industry, and by many subdividers, the Army Corps of Engineers, the USDA, the AEC, the Chamber of Commerce, to name only a few. Even a cursory knowledge of the pervasive nature and degree of control of these interests leads to the conclusion that the necessary changes in attitudes and behavior are extremely unlikely among the individuals and organizations where it would be most helpful. But the name of the game is *human survival,* and each one of us is dealt in, whether we like it or not. These individuals and organizations have an unprecedented opportunity to help everyone win. Will they accept the challenge?

# Bibliography

Ayres, Edward, 1970. *What's Good for GM*. Aurora, Nashville. An indictment of the degree to which the U.S.A. is run for the automobile. Full of little gems like "In 1969, as a result of auto and highway clout, the federal government spent $50 on highways for every dollar it spent on mass transit."

Bolling, Richard, 1965. *House Out of Order*. E. P. Dutton, New York. Critique of the House of Representatives by a congressman.

Boulding, Kenneth E., 1966. The economics of the coming spaceship earth. *In* H. Jarrett (ed.), *Environmental Quality in a Growing Economy*. Johns Hopkins Press, Baltimore. A superb article about making the transition from a "cowboy" to a "spaceman" economy.

Cipolla, Carlo M., 1965. *The Economic History of World Population*. Penguin Books, Baltimore.

Cirino, Robert, 1971. *Don't Blame the People*. Diversity Press, Box 45764, Los Angeles. A systematic description of the way the news media filter and distort the information that reaches the American public.

Clark, Colin, 1967. *Population Growth and Land Use*. Macmillan, London. The author of this book once claimed on a television show that India would be the richest country in the world in ten years or so *because* of population growth! Read his book, paying careful attention to his treatment of environmental problems.

Clark, Joseph S., 1964. *Congress: The Sapless Branch*. Harper and Row, New York. Senator Clark criticizes our moribund legislature.

Coombs, P. H., A. Pearse, J. Hutchinson, L. T. Khoi, T. P. Llaurado, R. Colin, and P. Freire, 1971. Seven articles on education in UDCs in *Ceres,* vol. 4, no. 3, pp. 23–51 (May–June).

Coale, Ansley, 1970. Man and his environment. *Science,* vol. 170, pp. 132–136 (9 Oct.) A simplistic and undocumented view of the relationship between population, resources, and environment.

Dales, J. H., 1968. *Pollution, Property, and Prices*. Univ. of Toronto Press, Toronto. An economist's suggestions for cleaning up our environment.

Dolan, Edwin G., 1969. *TANSTAAFL: The Economic Strategy for Environment Crisis*. Holt, Rinehart and Winston, Inc., New York. Brief and highly recommended.

Ehrlich, P. R., and R. L. Harriman, 1971. *How To Be a Survivor: A Plan To Save Spaceship Earth*. Ballantine Books, New York. Covers many of the problems discussed in this chapter. Contains the text of the Tugwell Constitution.

Enke, Stephen, 1966. The economic aspects of slowing population growth. *The Economic Journal,* vol. LXXVI, no. 301 (March), pp. 44–56.

Enke, Stephen, and Richard G. Zind, 1969. Effects of fewer births on average income. *Journal of Biological Sciences,* vol. 1, pp. 41–55.

Fagley, Richard M., 1960. *The Population Explosion and Christian Responsibility*. Oxford Univ. Press, New York. A Protestant perspective on the population explosion, and a good source of information on religious attitudes toward population control.

Forrester, Jay W., 1971. Counterintuitive behavior of social systems. *Technology Review,* Jan., pp. 52–68. Forecasts future states of the world based on computer simulations. A fascinating and important study.

Friedman, Milton, 1970. The social responsibility of business is to increase its profits. *New York Times Magazine,* Sept. 13. Argues that as long as businessmen operate within the law, it is an unfair tax on stockholders to devote resources to anything but maximizing profits, neglecting the role businessmen play in determining the passage and administration of those laws.

Galbraith, John K., 1967. *The New Industrial State*. Signet, New York. A most interesting, logical, and controversial thesis about the nature of the military-industrial-university-government complex.

Gardner, John, 1964. *Self-Renewal: The Individual and the Innovative Society*. Harper & Row, New York. A personal approach to change within the individual and within society.

Graham, Frank, Jr., 1970. *Since Silent Spring*. Fawcett-Crest. Greenwich, Conn. Details of the pesticide controversies.

Hamilton, William F., II, and Dan K. Nance, 1969. Systems analysis of urban transportation. *Scientific American,* vol. 221, no. 1 (July). Problems of urban transport and some possible solutions.

Hardin, Garrett, 1968. The tragedy of the commons. *Science,* vol. 162, pp. 1243–1248.

Hardin, Garrett (ed.), 1969. *Population, Evolution, and Birth Control* (2nd ed.). W. H. Freeman and Company, San Francisco. A fine collection of readings edited by one of the best writers among biologists.

Harvard Law Review Association, 1971. Note. Legal analysis and population control: the problem of coercion. *Harvard Law Review,* vol. 84, no. 8, pp. 1856–1911 (June).

Hayes, Denis, 1971. Can we bust the highway trust? *Saturday Review,* June 5, pp. 48–53.

Heilbroner, R. L., 1959. *The Future as History*. Harper and Row, New York. This brief classic on modern society, American optimism, revolutions, progress, etc., is highly recommended.

Heller, Alfred (ed.), 1971. *The California Tomorrow Plan*. California Tomorrow, San Francisco.

Heller, Walter (ed.), 1968. *Perspectives on Economic Growth.* Random House, New York. A compendium of the conventional wisdom of economic growth.

Hilu, Virginia (ed.), 1967. *Sex Education and the Schools.* Harper and Row, New York.

Illich, Ivan, 1970. *Celebration of Awareness.* Doubleday and Co., Garden City, New York. Brilliant book by one of today's most imaginative thinkers.

Illich, Ivan, 1971. *Deschooling Society.* Harper and Row, New York. A call for radical reform of education.

Istock, Conrad E., 1971. Modern environmental deterioration as a natural process. *International Journal of Environmental Studies,* vol. 1, pp. 151–155. A concise and important article which should be read by all economists.

Jarrett, Henry (ed.), 1966. *Environmental Quality in a Growing Economy.* Johns Hopkins Press, Baltimore. An interesting collection—see especially the article by Boulding, "The Economics of the Coming Spaceship Earth."

Kelso, Louis O., and Mortimer J. Adler, 1958. *The Capitalist Manifesto.* Random House, New York. The original exposition of Kelso's theory of universal capitalism, a proposal for capitalist rather than socialist redistribution of wealth.

Kelso, Louis O., and Patricia Hetter, 1967. *Two-Factor Theory: The Economics of Reality.* Vintage Books, New York. A revolutionary book by a capitalist. The authors point out that *less than one percent of United States households are capitalist,* and set out proposals to change all that.

Kozol, Jonathan, 1967. *Death at an Early Age.* Houghton Mifflin, Boston. A devastating examination of one of our educational system's major failures.

Landau, N. J., and P. G. Rheingold, 1971. *The Environmental Law Handbook.* Ballantine Books, New York. How to fight pollution in the courts.

Lear, John (ed.), 1968. Science, technology, and the law. *Saturday Review* (Aug. 3). This is one of a series of five essays, all of which are pertinent to the question of the law and our population and environmental problems.

Leonard, George B., 1968. *Education and Ecstasy.* Delacorte Press, New York. A most thoughtful and original book on education. Highly recommended.

Lundberg, Ferdinand, 1968. *The Rich and the Super-rich.* Bantam Books, New York. An eye-opening book for those bedazzled by "people's capitalism" and the high-school civics class versions of how our government functions.

Marx, Leo, 1970. American institutions and ecological ideals. *Science,* vol. 170, pp. 945–952. A thoughtful discussion of the profound changes in our institutions that really "cleaning up the environment" will require.

Means, Richard L., 1970. *The Ethical Imperative: the Crisis in American Values.* Anchor Books, Garden City, New York. Excellent.

Meek, Ronald L. (ed.), 1971. *Marx and Engels on the Population Bomb.* Ramparts Press, Berkeley. Reprints the attacks of Marx and Engels on

Malthus; contains a most interesting introductory essay by New Left theorist Steve Weissman.

Mintz, M., and J. S. Cohen, 1971. *America, Inc.: Who Owns and Operates the United States.* Dial Press, New York. A very important book dealing with the evils of concentrated economic power and the possible ways of diffusing it. See especially the material on big oil companies.

Mishan, Ezra J., 1967. *The Costs of Economic Growth.* Frederick A. Praeger, New York. An excellent discussion.

Mishan, E. J., 1970. *Technology and Growth: The Price We Pay.* Praeger, New York. A more popular version of *The Costs of Economic Growth.*

Moncrief, Lewis W., 1970. The cultural basis for our environmental crisis. *Science,* vol. 170, pp. 508–512 (30 Oct.).

Montgomery, Johnson C., 1971. Population explosion and United States law. *Hastings Law Journal,* vol. 22, no. 3, pp. 629–659 (Feb.) First definitive treatment of this subject.

O'Brien, Fr. John A. (ed.), 1968. *Family Planning in an Exploding Population.* Hawthorne Books, Inc., New York. Statements by scholars inside and outside of the Catholic Church, edited by an outstanding Catholic theologian who has strongly disagreed with the Church's stand on birth control.

Pearson, Drew, and Jack Anderson, 1968. *The Case Against Congress.* Simon and Schuster, New York.

Pilpel, Harriet, 1965. Sex vs. the law. *Harper's Magazine,* January.

Pilpel, Harriet, 1969. The right of abortion. *Atlantic Monthly,* June. The ethical and legal aspects of abortion.

Pirages, Dennis (ed.), 1971. *Seeing Beyond: Personal, Social and Political Alternatives.* Addison-Wesley Publishing Co., Reading, Massachusetts. A fine collection of readings bringing together a wide variety of articles dealing with contemporary human problems.

Platt, John, 1969. What we must do. *Science,* vol. 166, pp. 1115–1121. A classification of the urgency of our multiplicity of crises and suggestions on how we might meet them.

Ross, D., and H. Wohlman, 1970. Congress and pollution: the gentleman's agreement. *Washington Monthly,* vol. 2, no. 7, pp. 13–20 (Oct.). Behind the scenes in Washington.

Samuelson, Paul A., 1970. *Economics,* 8th ed. McGraw-Hill, New York. One of the great texts of all time.

Skinner, B. F., 1971. *Beyond Freedom and Dignity.* Knopf, New York. Skinner finally says it in terms understandable even to those who have not followed his work—individuals can neither be "blamed" for their failures nor credited with their accomplishments. The book caused an uproar even before publication. Must reading, if you are concerned with societal survival, even if you disagree.

Spengler, Joseph J., 1960. Population and world economic development. *Science,* vol. 131, pp. 1497–1502.

Stone, Tabor R., 1971. *Beyond the Automobile: Reshaping the Transportation Environment.* Prentice-Hall, Inc., Englewood Cliffs, New Jersey. An interesting book that explores some new directions for transportation in the U.S.

Tuan, Yi-Fu, 1970. Our treatment of the environment in ideal and actuality. *American Scientist,* vol. 58, pp. 244–249 (May–June).

Udall, Stewart L., 1968. *1976, Agenda for Tomorrow.* Harcourt, Brace & World, Inc., New York. See especially Chapter 8, "The renewal of politics." Many cogent points made on population, environment, and the quality of life.

Wagar, J. Alan, 1970. Growth versus the quality of life. *Science,* vol. 168, pp. 1179–1184. A critique of the cult of growth with an interesting "simplified calculus for the good life."

White, Lynn, Jr., 1967. The historical roots of our ecological crisis. *Science,* vol. 155, pp. 1203–1207. A classic paper.

# CHAPTER 12

# The International Scene

*"Let us in all our lands . . . including this land . . .
face forthrightly the multiplying problems of our
multiplying populations and seek the answers
to this most profound challenge to the future
of all the world. Let us act on the fact that
five dollars invested in population control
is worth one hundred dollars invested
in economic growth."*

—President Lyndon B. Johnson
Speech to United Nations
June 25, 1965

*"A planet cannot, any more than a country, survive half
slave, half free, half engulfed in misery, half careening
along toward the supposed joys of almost unlimited
consumption. Neither our ecology nor our morality
could survive such contrasts. And we have perhaps
ten years to begin to correct the imbalance and
to do so in time."*

—Lester Pearson, 1969

Assuming that the United States makes a start on solving its own serious domestic problems, what might we and other developed nations do to help improve conditions for people in the underdeveloped world? To date we have generally done more to worsen their situation than to improve it. The U.S. has, since World War II, expanded our economic horizons to the far corners of the Earth, investing many billions of dollars to develop a trade network designed in our own self-interest. Like other powerful nations, we have used economic, political, and military means to maintain this network. Our comparatively small foreign aid programs are far more economic and political in orientation than humanitarian; our resources have been devoted to providing additional material goods for ourselves and to an expensive and dangerous arms race, rather than to the improvement of the lot of our fellow men. It is time that our past performance be re-evaluated and a new set of national objectives be established in relation to the rest of the world.

The problem the U.S. faces in helping the rest of mankind is greatly complicated by Western attitudes toward the underdeveloped countries. Western countries, both capitalist and communist, seem convinced that they know what is best for the nations of the "third world." An unspoken assumption of all "aid" seems to be that the best hope of survival for the UDCs lies in emulating the path followed by the DCs; that by applying the ideas of Marx, Malthus, or perhaps Henry Ford, the UDCs can pull themselves out of the mire of poverty. This is called "development" or "modernization." The *hubris* of this view is lost on most citizens of the DCs, but it is obvious to many inhabitants of the third world. The peoples of Indochina developed, among others, the culture that produced Angkor Wat. The Chinese had a venerable civilization when the British still lived in caves and painted themselves blue. The civilization of India is nearly as old. Asians and the proud peoples of Latin America and Africa do not appreciate being considered somehow "backward" and in need of charity.

The time has come for both the DCs and the UDCs to recognize that each has something to offer the other. Human dignity and inventiveness are certainly not the sole possession of any human group. It is possible, for instance, that UDC governments seriously interested in helping their citizens might do better to look to China and Cuba for basic ideas than to Washington or Moscow. Indeed, it is quite likely that both the Americans and the Soviets themselves could learn from both China and Cuba. Americans might learn a lot about delivering food and medical care to people from Cubans. The Russians might learn how to relieve the strangling grip of bureaucracy from the Chinese, and Americans might learn from them how to rediscover a sense of national purpose. Both the U.S. and U.S.S.R. might learn something about population control from the Chinese.

That is not to say that both Cuba and China cannot in turn learn from the U.S. and U.S.S.R. Both Cuba and China are badly in need of the kinds of technical expertise that the DCs have developed in so many areas, but they are certainly in the best position to judge their own needs. Fundamentally, *all* countries must re-evaluate a long series of assumptions about such things as population growth and size, environmental deterioration, economics, progress, equity of material distribution, and the quality of life. Perhaps the biggest step of all toward survival would be the recognition that what is required is not a process of DCs teaching UDCs, communists teaching capitalists (or vice-versa), or scientists teaching peasants, but a process of mutual learning.

## Development, Exploitation, and Aid

When one reads the literature on DC-UDC relationships—especially that dealing with economics—it is difficult to believe that the writers are all describing the same situation. Consider the question of whether or not DCs "exploit" UDCs (or, as it often is stated, do the DCs practice "neo-colonialism" or "economic imperialism?"). On one side, economist Ansley Coale states, in connection with the extraction of raw materials from the UDCs, "The most effective forms of assistance that the developed countries (including the United States) give to the less developed countries are the purchases they make from the less developed countries in international trade." On the other hand, socialist economist Pierre Jalée writes that UDCs "are not poor because of a curse of nature, that they are not lacking in natural wealth, least of all in raw materials for heavy industry. They are poor only because, as we shall see, this natural wealth has been, and still is being, plundered by imperialism for the needs of its own industrialization, at the expense of those countries from which it flows away in its raw state."

Which of these views is correct? Our answer would be neither, although Jalée's is closer. It is quite true that great damage would be done to UDC economies if DCs decreased their purchases of commodities. UDC economies are set up to supply commodities to DCs, and are not in a position to use those commodities themselves. But one must question why UDCs are in such a position; that is, what historical events channeled their economic development into such narrow pathways? One must also ask who determines the prices paid for the commodities? And, perhaps most important, one must ask who (that is, what group) within the UDCs benefits from the trade in commodities? Is it the mass of the people or is it a small ruling elite? If it is the latter, are the DC commodity "consumers" in any way involved in keeping those elites in power? No special economic expertise is needed to find a partial answer to those questions.

The shortcomings of the Coale position do not, however, validate Jalée's. There is no reason to believe that present-day UDCs would have "developed" their natural "wealth" by now if it were not for the rapacious interference (or at least influence) of the DCs. The cultural conditions for an industrial revolution were hardly universal; after all, the Chinese did not undergo such a revolution even though they were civilized long before western Europe. It is also questionable whether the wisest course for most UDCs now would be to turn away from their roles as commodity-suppliers, even if that were economically possible.

Given the world ecology-resource situation, a much more intelligent strategy might well be to strive toward obtaining a much higher return on their commodities, especially their irreplaceable mineral wealth. A start in this direction was made in 1971 when the oil-rich countries of the Middle East successfully bargained as a group for higher prices for their oil. At the same time, agricultural production could be shifted more toward supplying the food needs of indigenous populations, rather than luxuries for DCs. This, of course, would require revision of DC-UDC relations, since it is effective demand (interest plus cash) from the DCs which maintains the present pattern. No strategy adopted by the UDCs will be successful without essential changes in DC attitudes. Until the DCs decide to make an all-out effort to help the UDCs, it seems certain that the gap between the rich and the poor nations will inevitably continue to widen.

In general, the flow of aid from DCs to UDCs has thus far been much too small. The United Nations, for instance, declared that 1960–1970 was to be the "Development Decade." Each DC was urged to contribute 1 percent of its GNP to the UDCs during that period. But even that pathetic goal was not achieved. In the calendar year 1967, for instance, United States foreign aid grants (nonmilitary) totalled 1.8 billion dollars, out of a GNP of 790 billion. That is less than *one-fourth* of the level advocated by the U.N. In addition, the aid that has been given has too often been wasted or has even done direct harm, although some direct benefits have also accrued. We have supplemented our economic aid with military aid, with very limited demonstrable advantage to ourselves or to the average citizens of the recipient countries. A certain amount of economic aid has gone into prestige items— for example, airlines and steel plants, in countries that lack food and housing for their people. But the desire for such "monuments" is understandable in a world dominated by Western economic values. On the positive side, DCs have also accomplished a great deal in agricultural programs generally aimed at helping UDCs increase their own food production.

### LATIN AMERICA AND THE UNITED STATES

Relations between DCs and UDCs are exemplified by U.S. behavior toward Latin America. When Sol Linowitz resigned in 1969 as U.S. Ambassador to the Organization of American States, he warned of the possibility of "a series of Vietnams" in Latin America. The same year Governor Nelson Rockefeller, on a fact-finding tour south of the border for President Nixon, was greeted with a violence that underlined the Linowitz warning. Rockefeller was, of course, an especially ironic choice since his family's Standard Oil empire is so much a symbol of U.S. economic imperialism. But one does not have to look far for more fundamental reasons for his reception. Population growth in Latin America is proceeding at an average rate of 2.9 percent per year; during the first eight years of the Alliance for Progress, economic growth averaged only about 1.5 percent per year, a full percentage point below the Alliance target. Latin Americans are, for the most part, living in appalling poverty. Diets are inadequate, infant and child mortality sky-high, and decent houses often nonexistent. If 10,000 houses *per day* were built in Latin America between 1969 and 1979, something on the order of 100 million of our southern neighbors (more than one-fifth of the expected population) would still be inadequately housed at the end of that time.

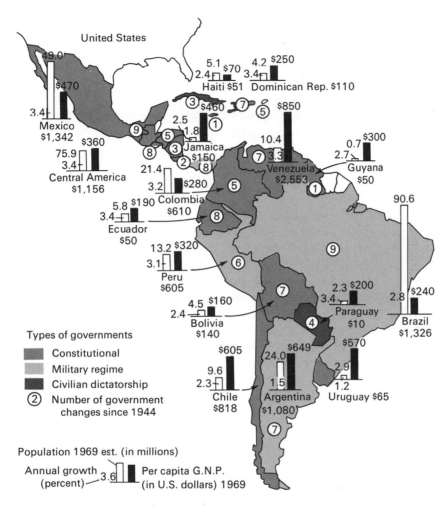

FIGURE 12-1

Latin American summary: population, per capita gross national product, form of government, number of government changes since 1944, amounts of American investment. (Various sources.)

Latin America's political instability is legendary (Fig. 12-1). Between 1961 and 1969, political changes were made by military force in Argentina, Bolivia, Brazil, Dominican Republic, Ecuador, Guatemala, Honduras, Panama, and Peru. Although land reform is beginning to take place in some countries, most recently in Peru, progress toward a more equitable distribution of what income there is has been slow. Some 10 percent of the people still own 90 percent of the land. Resentment toward the United States is widespread. Although the days when American corporations directly controlled small countries are over, there is a huge reservoir of ill-will remaining from the days when the U.S. openly took what it wanted of the mineral and agricultural wealth of the continent. United States economic exploitation of

Latin America is still far from over. While some U.S. companies are now so well behaved that they can serve as examples of benevolence and have made enormous contributions to their host nations, they still drain vast amounts of badly needed capital from those nations.

In 1969, Latin American governments, meeting at Viña del Mar, Chile, drew up a memorandum presenting their program for improving U.S.–Latin American economic relations. They requested the United States to lower its tariff barriers against Latin American goods and asked for a preferential market for their manufactured products. Basically, they sought redress for the economic imbalance in which Latin America still gives to the United States more than it receives in return. American aid to Latin America amounted to $11 billion in the first eight years of the Alliance. But profits extracted by U.S. corporations operating in Latin America, interest on American loans, and arrangements in which aid funds must be spent for goods on the expensive U.S. markets (and shipped on U.S. ships) have more than compensated for the aid.

The announced result of Governor Rockefeller's 1969 trip meant disappointingly little change in U.S. policies toward Latin America. More equitable economic relations are to be fostered through tariff changes and other means, and the policy of economic "punishment" for governments that nationalize such local industries as copper without compensating to their satisfaction the American companies that developed them is to be abandoned. Whether these changes will be far-reaching enough to counteract to some degree Latin American resentment of economic exploitation remains to be seen; that they can reverse the present exploitative situation is too much to expect. Rockefeller also recommended that the U.S. continue to support all governments that happen to be in power (whether we approve of them or not) and that we sell arms and military equipment to them when requested, a policy which can only contribute to the volatility of the Latin American political situation.

There is little question that American economic interests will be the source of continuing potential trouble with Latin America. Our corporations have an investment of more than $10 billion in the area, much of it concerned with the extraction of nonrenewable resources that are in critically short supply. Major examples are a $2 billion investment in Venezuelan oil, and a $500 million investment in Chilean copper (now nationalized by the Chilean government). As the long-term significance of continued U.S. exploitation of these and other resources becomes clear to Latin Americans, the resulting resentment may be catastrophic for American interests and for the regimes that permit the exploitation.

DEVELOPMENT AND THE ENVIRONMENT

An unhappy aspect of some development programs has been their ecological incompetence, a direct consequence of the environmental nearsightedness which has so long afflicted the politicians and technologists of the DCs. Western technology exported to the UDCs has certainly been a mixed blessing, whether or not that technology has been part of a formal aid program. The consequences of the export of death control technology to the demographic situation have been examined earlier, as have such problems as are created by the disastrous export of our pesticide technology to places like the Cañete Valley of Peru. The list, however, runs far beyond this: the misuse of pesticides in Malaysia, the encouragement of schistosomal parasites in Africa, soil deterioration and erosion in many areas, and so forth. In almost every case, great problems could have been avoided or ameliorated if an ecologically sound approach had been taken.

What is perhaps the classic example of misplaced aid in development has been supplied by the Soviet Union. This is the construction of the Aswan High Dam, which may well prove to be the ultimate disaster for Egypt. As is characteristic of much foreign aid, the ecological consequences and social alternatives were not considered in advance. Irrigation from the dam project will not increase food production enough to feed the number of people that were added to the Egyptian population during the dam's construction period. This is not a criticism of the dam itself, except insofar as it has absorbed resources that might better have been put into population control or agricultural development. Further, it seems certain the conversion of some 500 miles of Nile floodplain from a one-crop system of irrigation to a four-crop rotation system will have deleterious effects on the health of that population. Perennial irrigation creates conditions that are ideal for the spread of certain snails, which are the intermediate hosts of the blood flukes that cause the serious parasitic disease *bilharzia*. Parasitologists expect the Aswan Dam to be the ultimate cause for an explosive outbreak of this disease. In addition, the change in the flow of the Nile has had deleterious effects on fisheries in the eastern Mediterranean. It will also have a negative impact on the fertility of the soil of the Nile Delta, since nutrients were previously deposited annually by the Nile flood, which the Aswan Dam will restrain. This problem will be exacerbated by growing several crops a year. Attempts to solve it will undoubtedly include an accelerating use of inorganic fertilizers, with attendant ecological complications.

On the plus side, new fisheries may become established in the Mediterranean and in Lake Nasser (forming behind the dam), it is conceivable that new drugs will help control bilharzia, and technology may be able to maintain yields on the newly irrigated land. But even if most of the problems created by the dam can be solved, two important principles will not be changed. The first is that *all* major development projects are bound to have ecological consequences, which should be carefully evaluated at the time of *planning,* not dealt with haphazardly after the deed is done. The second is that an effort equal to the Aswan Dam project channeled into population control would have benefited Egypt far beyond the rewards of a totally problem-free dam, especially since in the long run the reservoir behind the dam will silt up and become useless.

Bringing land under cultivation through irrigation has long been recognized as no permanent solution to population-food imbalances. Charles Galton Darwin pointed out that the Sukkur Barrage on the Indus River diverting water to irrigate 6 million acres of India, did not result in adequate diets for people who were previously hungry. As he put it, "After a few years the effect was only to have a large number of people on the verge of starvation instead of a small number." Population can easily increase enough to overstrain any resource, which is precisely what is happening in Egypt today. In 1971 the birth rate in the United Arab Republic was estimated to be 44, the death rate 15, and the growth rate 2.8 percent (doubling time 25 years). In this context the Aswan Dam project, which required more than a decade to construct and added an equivalent of 2 million acres (one-third of the previously cultivated land) to the arable pool, is a small project indeed. The UAR will have to complete the equivalent of four more Aswan Dam projects in the next 24 years just to maintain its present inadequate level of nutrition. Worst of all, the propaganda associated with the Aswan Dam lulled many Egyptians and others into a false sense of security, so that little was done either to control the population of the UAR or to improve her stagnant agriculture. When the dam was completed, its inadequacy to solve Egypt's food and development problems became evident. Recently, the government has been supporting Egypt's family planning program with more enthusiasm than before.

## THE SOFT STATE

We must mention here what Gunnar Myrdal describes as the problem of the "soft state." Viewed from the Western cultural context, many UDCs are not political units equivalent to most DCs. They face grave problems of equity and organization, and these problems present formidable barriers in the path of the Green Revolution and other steps toward development. Two of the most critical difficulties are the general lack of progress toward land reform and the prevalence of graft.

Myrdal has suggested that the problems of "soft states" are in part an unfortunate legacy of anarchic attitudes which arose during colonial times. The patterns of civil disobedience, non-cooperation, and overt rebellion, which developed during the struggles for independence, persist and are now operating to the detriment of new indigenous governments. This is not very surprising, especially in countries where an elite trained by a colonial power has, on gaining independence, simply continued the operation of the governmental apparatus as they inherited it—and adopted many of the attitudes of the previous colonial rulers as well.

These patterns flourish along with the "corruption" which has historically characterized many UDC governments and which is almost invariably a corollary of an illiterate, ill-informed, or misled populace. Graft has long been a way of life in most UDCs, and is recognized as such by the citizens of those countries themselves. For example, in 1968 Indian Minister for Foreign Affairs and Labor, S. Rajaratnoam, described government by graft as "kleptocracy." He said:

> It is amazing how otherwise excellent studies on development problems in Asia and Africa avoid any serious reference to the fact of corruption. It is not that the writers do not know of its existence but its relevance to the question of political stability and rapid economic development appears not to have been fully appreciated. It may also be that a serious probing of the subject has been avoided lest it should offend the sensibilities of Asians.

Most UDCs are traditional societies in which "connections," large-scale graft and petty bribery (with little loyalty to community or nation) have thrived as an acceptable form of transaction in both business and government. Such a system can be described as "corrupt" or "irrational" only in a context of Western values. Although DCs are not wholly free from graft, the populace in those nations generally recognizes graft as an evil, and it is seldom as open and pervasive as it is in many UDCs. Circumstances compel us to accept this culture-bound Western value judgment. Western medicine and public health procedures have been a key factor in promoting overpopulation; Western economic goals are accepted by UDC governments, educational systems and large segments of UDC populations. As far as we can see, Western-style organizational solutions are, at this time, the only kind available which offer substantial hope of ameliorating the crises that now face us. Therefore, culture-bound as it appears—and is—our discussion will be within that framework.

Whatever its origins, corruption undoubtedly increased when partial vacuums were created by the withdrawal of colonial administrations. In general, it has tended to increase since independence and has helped to block many needed social changes, including land and tenancy reforms. It often prevents foreign aid from reaching its intended recipients. It greatly weakens local respect for government and for planning, and thus helps to block programs to improve the standard of living. It also makes more difficult the kind of coordinated international action required if programs like the Green Revolution are to achieve maximum success. In short, the "blame" for the dismal state of world efforts to help the needy may lie largely at the doorstep of the DCs, but not entirely so.

## Development: A New Approach

As should be apparent by now, the problems of "development" are a complex of population, food, environmental, social, political, and economic problems. Population growth, for instance, is in itself a major barrier to economic development. Goran Ohlin wrote in *Population Control and Economic Development:* "The simple and incontestable case against rapid population growth in poor countries is that it absorbs very large amounts of resources which may otherwise be used both for increased consumption and above all, for development. . . . The stress and strain caused by rapid demographic growth in the developing world is actually so tangible that there are few, and least of all planners and economists of the countries, who doubt that per capita incomes would be increased faster if fertility and growth rates were lower. . . ."

Although economic problems are important in development there are many reasons why most UDCs cannot and should not be industrialized along DC lines. The most impressive constraints are probably the environmental ones. As one biologist put it, "Just think of what would happen to the atmosphere if 700 million Chinese started driving big automobiles!" But even below these limits it seems highly unlikely that the problems posed by the depletion of nonrenewable resources would permit more than a very limited industrial development of most UDCs, unless, of course, there were some sort of massive de-industrialization of most DCs. The most pressing problem for the UDCs is one of ecologically sensible agricultural development, with supporting facilities for distribution, storage, and marketing—that is, for "semi-development." But as already noted, agricultural development is necessarily connected with general economic improvement; road building, fertilizer production, farm machinery availability, increased demand, etc., are all involved.

If industrialization is not going to occur in the UDCs, how then are they to semi-develop? The answer lies in the DC-UDC relationship. Without a drastic change in DC attitudes and aid patterns, the UDCs are not going to develop in any sense; rather, most are likely to collapse into chaos.

The value of population control in aid programs to UDCs has been studied intensively. Economist Stephen Enke has done much of the analysis, and his conclusions may be summarized in three points: (1) channeling economic resources into population control rather than increases in production "could be 100 or so times more effective in raising *per capita* incomes in many UDCs"; (2) an effective birth control program might cost only 30 cents per capita per year, about 3 percent of current development programs; (3) the use of bonuses to promote population control is "obvious in countries where the 'worth' of permanently preventing a birth is roughly twice the income per head." Enke's results are strongly supported by recent computer simulation work by systems analyst Douglas Daetz, who examined the effects of various kinds of aid in a labor-limited, nonmechanized agricultural society. His results brought into sharp question the desirability of aid programs not coupled with population control programs. They might provide temporary increases in the standard of living, but these are soon eaten up by population expansion. In many circumstances, population growth and aid inputs may interact to cause the standard of living to decline below the pre-aid level.

The necessity for population control to permit even semi-development of UDCs is thus plain from practical experience (per capita income gains being small in the face of record population growth) and from economic analysis and computer simulation. The obstacles to UDC development go far beyond this, however. The underdeveloped world today has an entirely different, unfavorable demographic situation that differs markedly from that of the DCs during their industrialization (for an example, see Box 12-1). In addition, the UDCs face competition from the DCs if they attempt to compete in international markets for manufactured goods. Most of today's DCs did not have vastly more advanced nations to compete with when they were developing. This is one factor that keeps UDCs in the role of commodity producers, concentrating on the production of agricultural goods and minerals. Furthermore, the UDCs generally lack the cultural traditions which led to industrialization in the DCs. As economist Neil Jacoby of the University of California wrote, "development requires a people to choose a new set of philosophical values." The UDCs do, however, have the advantage (or potential advantage) of the accessibility of the technological expertise of the DCs.

---

### BOX 12-1    THE MANPOWER EXPLOSION IN THE UDCS

One of the unhappy consequences of the rapid increase in UDC population growth rates in the 1950s and 1960s is that the children born during that period are now entering the labor pool in large numbers. In India, for instance, 170 million youngsters born between 1955 and 1965 will turn 15 during the decade of the 1970s. About 90 million of those young people will enter the labor force. Other additions to that force will include almost 2 million students now in tertiary education. During the same decade it is estimated that only some 27 million workers will die or retire, so the net gain in the 15-and-over labor pool will be some 65 million people. If current levels of employment are to be maintained, this means that at the beginning of the decade *India must create about 100,000 new jobs per week, and by the end of the decade some 140,000 new jobs will be required every week.*

These statistics are particularly staggering when it is realized that unemployment and underemployment are already creating enormous problems throughout India's economy, and that competition for jobs has already been described as "cut-throat." Furthermore, no successes in birth control, regardless of how spectacular they are, can affect these statistics, since the people involved have already been born. The situation in India is more or less characteristic of that in other UDCs. The manpower explosion will require dramatic efforts to provide jobs in both the urban and rural sectors of UDC economies. Much can be accomplished by concentrating on labor-intensive agricultural practices and introducing "social security" programs which will permit old or otherwise marginal workers to withdraw from the labor pool without tragic results. Development in general can similarly produce more jobs if it is carefully planned so that unnecessary mechanization is sharply limited. But if the labor problem is not solved, unemployment and associated disruption may themselves present serious barriers to development. The problems created by forcing peasants off the land and the support this gives to militant groups, such as the Naxalite movement in India, may be a harbinger of worse to come.

There is still considerable debate among economists on technical points of policies relating to development. Tariff and trade policies are especially in dispute, with UDCs arguing strongly for measures to raise prices of their commodities and to obtain trade preferences. These measures have generally been opposed by the DCs, and the United Nations Conferences on Trade and Development (UNCTAD) have generally seen battle lines drawn on a DC-UDC basis. The UDCs claim that there is a built-in bias in world trade and finance in favor of the DCs, and they see in UNCTAD an opportunity to eliminate or even reverse that bias. Also disputed are the roles of colonial history and traditions, the present political decision-making apparatus, land reform, and a wide array of governmental economic policies. Unfortunately, the usual narrow focus on economics characterizes these discussions. For instance, economists often point out that the coffee trade has "enriched" Brazil, ignoring the ecological effects of what Georg Borgstrom describes as the "almost predatory exploitations by the coffee planters." Brazil's dependence on this commodity has not only ruined much of her soil, but is also a major reason why she cannot adequately feed her population today.

The economic and political aspects of UDC development and DC-UDC relationships are extremely complex. But whatever the "answers" are to the disputed policy points, it has become abundantly clear that no solution to the general problem can be found until, in effect, the rules of the game are changed. In our opinion, major changes must occur in the areas of foreign aid, development, and international politics.

## FOREIGN AID

The DCs must recognize that their fates are inextricably bound up with those of the UDCs. They must further recognize that their patterns of resource utilization cannot continue, and that dramatic measures must be taken to effect some level of redistribution of the wealth of the world. Two scientists, Lord C. P. Snow of Great Britain and Andrei D. Sakharov of the U.S.S.R., have made rather similar proposals along these lines. Sakharov, "father of the Russian hydrogen bomb" and one of the youngest men ever elected to the Soviet Academy of Sciences, expressed his views in an extraordinary document entitled, "Progress, Coexistence, and Intellectual Freedom," which was not published in the U.S.S.R. Among his many proposals is that after the U.S.A. and the U.S.S.R. have "overcome their alienation" they should collaborate in a massive attempt to save the UDCs. This attempt would be financed by a contribution to the effort on the part of the DCs of some 20 percent of their national income over a 15-year period. Lord Snow, an eminent physicist and novelist, supports the suggestion of Academician Sakharov. He recommended that the rich nations devote 20 percent of their GNP for 10–15 years to the task of population control and development of the poor countries. By the scale of the effort, and by its no-strings-attached nature (a substantial portion might be channeled through international agencies under control of UDCs themselves), the people of the "other world" might be convinced that the developed countries *do* care. Though there is much suffering today in the UDCs and more is unavoidable, a substantial lowering of DC-UDC tensions could occur if the UDCs felt that help was really on the way. And, of course, the joint DC effort could help to bring about that community of feeling that psychologists regard as so essential to the abolition of war.

SEMI-DEVELOPMENT

A large-scale effort on the part of the DCs will not suffice, however, unless there are basic changes in the value systems related to development. If industrialization of the entire world is neither possible nor desirable, new standards of value will have to be established which will permit *all* peoples to have access to the basic human needs of adequate food, shelter, clothing, education and medical care, regardless of the economic value of their productivity.

The first question asked of any aid project should be: will it benefit the *people* or only the government or some special interest group in the beneficiary country? If the project benefits only the latter groups, it should be rejected unless it can be proved that it will ultimately benefit the general population in some real and measurable way. Thus a steel mill might be a poor project for a UDC, even though it might provide employment and contribute to the economy. A fertilizer plant, on the other hand, would also provide employment and benefit the economy. Beyond that, it would produce fertilizers for agricultural development, contributing to the country's ability to raise its food production and feed its population. An example of a small-scale program aimed at solving one particular problem with a minimum of outside intervention and social disruption is described in Box 12-2.

As examples of semi-development, Kenya and Tanzania might be semi-developed primarily as combination agrarian-recreation areas. They, and some other African nations, can supply the world with a priceless asset: a window on the past when vast herds of animals roamed the face of the Earth. They could also provide one of the many living stockpiles of organic diversity, stockpiles which may prove of immense value as humankind attempts to replenish the deteriorated ecosystems of the planet. These and similar areas could serve as rest-and-rehabilitation centers for people from the more frantic industrialized parts of the planet.

They would also serve as guarantors of cultural diversity, as areas specifically reserved to permit peoples to maintain their traditional ways of life. One of the grim dangers facing *Homo sapiens* is the continued homogenizing of cultures, the erosion of mankind's spectacular array of cultural differences. Urbanization, mass communications, and the explosive spread of Western technology and Judeo-Christian attitudes have already irretrievably reduced this diversity. But who is to say that one world view is "better" than another, that a British scientist's way of structuring the world is superior to that of a Hopi Indian, that a militant Christianity is superior to a gentle Oriental religion, that the Australian aboriginal view of kinship is inferior to that of a jet-set sophisticate?

Preserving this diversity will require nothing less than a restructuring of our ideals and values. A demand must be created for what Aborigines, Eskimos, Kenyans, and Hondurans can supply, something that might be called "cultural resources." These priceless resources are in short supply, they are dwindling rapidly, and they are nonrenewable. A way must be found to permit these people access to more of the fruits of industrial societies without attempting to industrialize the entire world. At the moment the trinkets of in-

---

BOX 12-2 A PROGRAM TO COMBAT MALNUTRITION

One of the most serious problems in many UDCs is widespread malnutrition, particularly protein malnutrition. This is usually most severe in young children, whose protein needs are greater than those of adults in proportion to body weights, but who are, through their parents' poverty, ignorance, or custom, often given quite restricted diets. This is in many ways a different problem from that of insufficient total food, and requires different solutions.

In Haiti, where fatal malnutrition among children was very common, a program that has attempted to meet this problem, especially to help malnourished children, was initiated in 1959 by the Haitian Department of Public Health in collaboration with the Department of Biochemistry and Nutrition at Virginia Polytechnic Institute, with financial support from Research Corporation, a foundation.

Realizing that lack of transportation and economic conditions made the distribution of a food supplement from elsewhere to isolated villages impractical, and that an unfamiliar food, even if accepted, would probably be too complicated an addition for village cooking methods, the project researchers started by looking for suitable supplements among indigenous food plants. Ultimately, they came up with a happy combination of a cereal (corn, rice, or millet) and any of three varieties of beans. Although separately these were low-quality protein foods, each compensated for the other's amino acid deficiencies, resulting in a mixture containing protein of excellent quality, and a superior source of vitamins as well.

Since Haitian mothers ordinarily feed their children a gruel of cereal, in order to improve the children's diets it was necessary only to convince the mothers to add a handful of beans with every two handfuls of cereal when making the gruel. Beans were already a part of the regular diet; they simply were not customarily fed to very young children.

To introduce the use of the new food mixture to the population, "Mothercraft Centers" were established in villages. Each center was run by a girl with a high-school education and six weeks of special training in child care, including nutrition and sanitation. The thirty most malnourished children in the village were invited to join the center with their mothers. The children were expected to spend six days and the

dustrial civilization have the strongest appeal to the naive, both within and outside of industrial society. If we continue to train our own people to think of the power lawn mower and automatic ice maker as the finest achievements of mankind, it seems unlikely that the "rising expectations" of the UDCs will rise above them either. But if we can learn to recognize and attempt to correct our own gruesome errors, then perhaps the UDCs will see their way clear to establishing new goals: development within resource limitations and with careful attention to the *quality* of life.

In short, the DCs must not only give unprecedented aid to the UDCs, they must help the UDCs to avoid the mistakes made by the DCs. Something like this message must come across: "By making the fundamental error of basing our standard of progress on expansion of the GNP, we have created

mother one day a week at the center. The girl who ran the center was expected to feed the children exclusively from local market produce and to do it at the same cost per child as the villagers spent. While she and the mothers prepared the food for the children, the center supervisor explained the nutritional and economical reasons for her particular food choices. Thus the mothers learned not only how to obtain better food but also more food for their money.

Within about three weeks, the children's symptoms of malnutrition were disappearing. Originally listless and apathetic, the children became alert, lively, and disobedient. The mothers, unaccustomed to such behavior, thought "that these alert and frisky children were either sick or under a curse of some kind." By the time the first group "graduated" after four months at the center, the mothers had begun to regard the changed behavior of their children as normal. Then the next group was invited to the center.

The program proved to be very successful beyond reducing the incidence of fatal malnutrition among young children. The diets of all the villagers were considerably improved through the mothers' new knowledge of nutrition and economical food-buying.

The Haitian food-supplement program has been a model for the development of similar ones in several countries: Algeria, Brazil, Colombia, Costa Rica, Equador, Guatemala, Nigeria, Peru, Uganda, and Venezuela. Programs of this sort, utilizing indigenous foods that are known to be acceptable, and introducing the new ideas in a sympathetic way, may prove to be among the most effective that have been proposed for alleviating malnutrition. The approach is simple, not horrendously expensive, and it causes a minimum of disruption in the society that the program was designed to help.

The method of introducing the new ideas can also serve as a model for the introduction of many other changes for the society, such as birth control and improved agricultural practices. Indeed, the success of the food-supplement program itself, in greatly reducing child mortality from malnutrition, will soon lead to a need for both in these villages.

a vast industrial complex and great mental, moral, and aesthetic poverty. Our cities are disaster areas, our air often unbreathable, our people increasingly regimented, and our spirit increasingly domitable. We require far too large a slice of the world's resources to maintain our way of life. We, in short, are not developed, we are *overdeveloped*. We now realize that our current patterns of consumption and exploitation cannot and should not be sustained. While we are correcting our mistakes and de-developing, we want to help you to semi-develop—not in our image but in whatever way is most appropriate for your culture."

What semi-development might mean in practice would, of course, differ from area to area. Certainly, ecologically sound agricultural development, rather than industrialization, should receive priority virtually everywhere. In general the DCs would, where needed, supply medical services, educational facilities and teachers, and especially technical assistance, in population control. Roadways, electrification, and communications adequate to the demands of an agrarian society would be an almost universal need as would help in developing improved local systems of agriculture. In all of these endeavors, the most efficient means of meeting the needs should be the first consideration: how to make the limited resources do the most good. Roads can be built without the sort of heavy machine equipment used in DCs. In fact, the simpler techniques of several decades ago would probably be more efficient in poor countries and would provide employment for unskilled labor. The same is true of electrification and communications; a single power supply or telephone for each village, with its use being shared communally, makes more sense than attempting to provide electricity to each home, which is impossible anyway. Transportation should not be designed along DC lines. Buses, whether imported or locally manufactured, make far more sense than cars, where only a fraction of the population can afford the latter. A suitable vehicle should be provided for UDC farmers, low-powered, economical, and sturdy. Several owners of small farms might own one communally, or the government might provide the transport of agricultural produce to market on a pickup and delivery basis.

Farm machinery need not be highly mechanized to be efficient; Japan and Taiwan have developed very efficient agricultural systems without mechanization. Economist Bruce F. Johnston of Stanford University's Food Research Institute has written that "simple, inexpensive farm equipment that is well suited to local manufacture in small- and medium-scale rural workshops" would be far more beneficial to the economies of UDCs and more practical than the use of heavy machinery. Not the least benefit of such a system would be its dependence upon abundant farm labor.

Education is an obvious area for aid, but setting up systems that mimic those of the DCs should be avoided. Education must be tailored to the needs of the local culture, not designed to destroy it. One of the great tragedies of Latin America is the university system which has evolved there. This system produces many attorneys, philosophers, poets, and "pure" scientists, but not the agriculturalists, ecologists, and public-health experts which the area so desperately needs. Education for Eskimos or Bushmen should be designed to produce first-class Eskimos or Bushmen, not caricatures of Americans or Russians, although the option to acquire technical or academic educations should remain open to those who may desire them. These special educations could be available to children of affluent classes at their own expense and to the poor through scholarship programs.

Education is particularly an area where innovations in methods are sorely needed. In the past two decades, due mainly to the population explosion, the literacy rate in many UDCs has dropped, not risen. Mass education in traditional Western style of so many children is simply beyond the means of most poor countries. It has been suggested that basic education of the masses be deferred to adulthood (or possibly adolescence), when it can be accomplished far more economically in terms of both time and money; an adult can acquire in a year the equivalent of an entire grade-school education. If effort were now concentrated on adults, including mothers, these adults could then begin to teach their children. Some educational resources might profitably be devoted to producing and distributing locally designed versions of the sorts of toys and games that prepare children in Western societies to learn in school. Satellite television programming can substitute economically for much of the educational apparatus, especially if an entire school or village shares a single receiver. Such a system has great potential for eradicating illiteracy and generally informing vast segments of any population with a common language, while requiring a minimum of trained people. A single teacher could, for instance, teach a course in basic arithmetic to a whole country's population in a few weeks.

Above all, the standard for aid and development should not be to make a nation or area "self-sufficient" in terms of today's economic standards. Just as some areas within Western countries today are maintained at economic expense because they supply other values, so in the future some parts of the world will have to be maintained at economic expense because they supply other values: natural beauty, biological or cultural diversity, survival and happiness for fellow human beings and, in the long run, survival for us all. Similarly, while some states in the U.S. are largely agricultural, others are heavily industrialized. There is no reason why UDC countries could not be developed differentially, some might have considerable industry and others be limited almost entirely to agricultural development. Such disparate economic entities could perhaps be loosely federated in economic associations similar to the Common Market.

### DE-DEVELOPMENT

As indicated above, the success of a planet-wide program of semi-development of UDCs will depend in large part on the degree to which present-day overdeveloped countries are able to de-develop. As long as the United States, most European countries, the Soviet Union, Australia and Japan have cowboy economies, it is unlikely that UDCs will change their development goals. It has become increasingly apparent that the key to saving the world (if such a key exists) lies in the behavior of those countries which might accurately be described as overdeveloped countries (ODCs). If the ODCs can successfully move toward spaceman economies, systematically eliminate the wasteful, frivolous, and ecologically harmful aspects of their behavior, shift the economic emphasis to Type I GNC, and divert their excess productivity and technological expertise into helping the poor people of the world, rather than exploiting them, then perhaps the citizens of the Third World will accept semi-development as their most desirable goal. On the other hand, if the ODCs continue to loot the world of its high-grade resources, use their technology to produce doomsday weapons and senseless gadgets for super-consumers, and permit the gap between the rich and the poor to continue to widen, it can be predicted that the people of the UDCs will continue to strive toward overdevelopment themselves.

As we see it, de-development of the ODCs should be the top priority goal. Only when that course is firmly established will there be any real hope for all of humanity to generate a worldwide spirit of cooperation rather than competition and to consider the problems of the "development" of our spaceship in the holistic perspective which is so essential to our survival.

The whole idea of de-development has met with considerable misunderstanding and resistance, and will undoubtedly meet with much more. Some people have mistakenly assumed that the idea of de-development is basically anti-technological. The extreme emotionalism which accompanies this resistance is exemplified by the reaction of AEC scientist Alvin M. Weinberg, who wrote in *BioScience* (April 1, 1971) that the de-development message was "we should destroy technology since technology got us into this dilemma, and this will set things right."

As should be obvious to any but the most defensive technologist, nothing could be farther from the truth. Technology must be brought under control and turned to the service of humanity. It is essential to de-development, but as de-development proceeds, we must be more discriminating in the use of technology and much more cautious about its potentially disastrous side-effects. Technologists must learn the physical and biological limitations of their disciplines and be prepared to put social limitations on its use. But to turn away from technology itself would be to condemn to death many hundreds of millions of people now living on our overcrowded planet. We need to make the fullest use of our technological expertise to maximize agricultural production, while minimizing the destructive effects of agriculture on the ecosystems of the planet. We must develop new technologies for recycling, for control of pollutants, for efficient transport systems, and for population control. We must improve our efficiency in power generation from fossil fuels to give us time to develop safe methods for the generation of nuclear and thermonuclear power. Technologists will be needed at all stages to help with the change from a cowboy to a spaceman economy; technology will play a key role in the processes of both semi-development and de-development.

We can expect hysterical opposition to de-development from many technologists who are used to having their schemes for "progress" accepted without question by a dazzled public. SSTs, ABMs, manned space ships, thermonuclear weapons, geodesic domes over cities, nuclear power, giant automobiles, plastic wrappings, genetic engineering, disposable packages and containers, synthetic pesticides, and the like are supposed to be accepted as self-evidently desirable. However, many technologists correctly perceive that, if the ODCs are to be de-developed and civilization is to persist, those halcyon days of unquestioning public acceptance must disappear forever.

## International Politics

The third area of rule-changing is political. Because of their own backgrounds and capabilities the two most powerful DCs, the U.S. and the U.S.S.R., have approached aid differently: the U.S. with a vast store of capital to draw on, has seen the problems of the UDCs primarily in terms of a shortage of capital. Shortage of capital is, of course, a major problem. The Soviets, on the other hand, because of their relatively recent history of revolution, and the recent success of revolutions in two UDCs, China and Cuba, tend to emphasize the export not of capital but of political change, of revolution. The need for dramatic political change is obvious in many countries. Haiti (with a per capita GNP of $70) had no chance while it was being ground under the heel of a dictator like François Duvalier, and its present prospects seem no better. A reasonable life cannot be available to the majority of the inhabitants of Angola and Mozambique while the Portuguese control their countries. It is not just a coincidence that these two colonies have among the lowest per capita GNPs on the African continent, $40 and $55, respectively. Moreover, in nominal "democracies," land reform unquestionably is badly needed to give the people incentive to improve their agricultural practices. Revolution might be one way to achieve land reform.

Both the capitalist and revolutionary points of view on aid have a certain validity, but both are also sadly deficient. If progress is to be made, both superpowers will have to change their ways. The United States must stop supporting assorted dictators around the world simply because they are "anti-communist." We must face the fact that in many countries the majority of the people might be better off under a regime that we perceive as "communist" than under their present regimes. In Latin America in particular, the need for social justice as a first step toward economic development has been widely recognized. If badly needed reforms do not take place peacefully, they will sooner or later take place by revolution. It is imperative that U.S. officials in the UDCs realize that their contacts within these countries are all too often totally unrepresentative of the people as a whole.

There is, of course, no doubt that corporate interests, sensitive to the resource poverty of the United States and motivated by the desire for profits, play a substantial role in shaping American foreign policy. The interlocking directorates of our government and various industrial giants are well known. Executives move freely from big business into administrative positions in the government, while high level bureaucrats and military men are welcomed into executive positions with corporations doing government business. The significance of the activities of the Central Intelligence Agency in Latin America, our open military intervention in Southeast Asia, Cuba, and the Dominican Republic, and such devices as the Hickenlooper Amendment (which discourages expropriation by foreign governments of American property within their territories) is not lost on people in the UDCs.

It seems unlikely that there is much to be gained in attempting immediately to break the power of international corporations that, among other things, are busily engaged in the exploitation of UDC resources. A primary reason is that it probably would be impossible in the absence of dramatic changes in DC attitudes. As long as economic standards reign supreme, economic power will tend to become concentrated; only more fundamental changes will suffice. And these changes must be made with great care. International corporations supply planning coordination, capital, and expertise in their operations in UDCs, and considerable economic hardship could result from the sudden dissolution of the giants. But they could be quickly stopped from draining capital away from the UDCs.

It is evident that the UDCs can undertake, and would profit from, control over their own resources and destinies. The contrary view is often held as doctrine by the DCs—but recall the dire and erroneous warnings that the Egyptians would be unable to run the Suez Canal when they took it over from the British. Some way must be found to make the people wielding the vast economic power of the West's steel, oil, banking, and other empires realize that their own survival depends on a graceful abdication of much of that power. Such a move would be unprecedented, but so are the dangers humanity faces.

On the other side of the coin, Russia should face the facts of life, too. Blaming all the problems of the world on capitalist imperialism simply is not supported by the evidence. For instance, India has, in many ways, gotten deeper into trouble since she gained her political freedom from England. Revolution is, at best, a partial answer; India today is in great need of thoughtful, technically competent help, especially in achieving population control. No kind of revolution can remove the biological and physical constraints upon development, although it might well remove some of the economic barriers. Furthermore, the Soviet Union's intervention in other countries in defense of what she perceives as her vital interests has been fully as blatant and brutal as that of the "capitalist imperialists," as the Czech invasion of 1968 so clearly demonstrated. It is ironic that the U.S.S.R., in the Mediterranean and elsewhere, now seems to be emulating the "gunboat diplomacy" pioneered in the last century by western European powers and the United States.

In attempting to save the world, the U.S. and the U.S.S.R. must not merely lead the way by making resources available. Rather than try to bury each other, they must bury their compulsion toward destructive competition to an extent that will permit them to move toward cooperative planning. A simple GNP transfer from DCs to UDCs is probably neither possible nor desirable; the United Nations estimates that the UDCs could not usefully absorb more than $20 billion per year in aid. Much more than "aid" in the familiar sense will be necessary if the world is to be restructured, and much thought must go into ways of increasing the "absorptive power" of the UDCs. It is hardly credible that they are unable to utilize more than $10 per capita in assistance annually (as the UN figure indicates), unless one assumes that only the type of economic aid which has become more or less traditional since 1950 could be given. Clearly, material goods alone worth more than $10 could benefit the average UDC citizen a great deal. We must find ways to revolutionize the DC-UDC aid situation, possibly by a reorganization of the economic structure of the world. At the same time care must be taken so that aid does not become counterproductive. Food shipments from the United States hindered the modernization of Indian agriculture in the mid-1960s, and the Aswan Dam lulled Egypt into a false sense of security for a decade. Finding ways to supply aid to UDCs without doing harm to their social and economic structure is a major challenge for the future.

An important problem is that of the allocation of resources. How much should go into improving worldwide systems for food distribution and subsidizing redistribution? How many more agricultural research teams must be trained and established in experiment stations in the UDCs? How many paramedical personnel are to be trained to teach birth control techniques, where are they to be trained, and how are they to operate? How are communications systems to be set up in the UDCs? Who will run them? Where are the anthropologists, economists, and sociologists to be educated who will help plan the aid programs so they are minimally disruptive and maximally acceptable? What is to be done with the dictators who do not want the lives of their people improved? How can an equitable distribution of aid be achieved within countries controlled by ruling elites? Which countries should receive outright gifts of food? The questions are exceedingly complex and nearly infinite in number. The kind of planning and decision-making which the Paddocks proposed in their book, *Famine—1975!* will have to be adopted by worldwide policy planning groups (Box 12-3).

It seems likely that, at least at first, a great deal of the financial resources of DCs that are allocated to help the UDCs will involve large expenditures within the DCs themselves—a factor which might make the entire program more palatable to DC citizens. The DCs must plan and initiate their own de-development to take the pressure off UDC resources and preserve the Earth's environment. At the same time, ships, wheat, bulldozers, fertilizer, condoms, and many other items will have to be procured and moved to UDCs. Vast education and training programs will have to be established, and scarce talent organized into planning and teaching teams. Many people will be employed in new research programs on everything from efficient inte-

BOX 12-3   TRIAGE

William and Paul Paddock in their 1967 book *Famine—1975!* considered the difficult question of how the United States might allocate its limited food aid as the world food situation worsens in the 1970s. They suggested a policy based on the concept of "triage" borrowed from military medicine. Briefly the idea is this: when casualties crowd a dressing station to the point where all cannot be cared for by the limited medical staff, some decisions must be made on who will be treated. All incoming casualties are placed in one of three classes. In the first class are those who will die regardless of treatment, in the second are those who will survive regardless of treatment, and the third contains those who can be saved only if they are given prompt treatment. When medical aid is severely limited, it is concentrated only on the third group; the others are left untreated.

The Paddocks suggested that we devise a similar system for classifying nations. Some will undergo the transition to self-sufficiency without enormous aid from us. They will be ones with abundant money for foreign purchases, or with efficient governments, strong population control programs, and strong agricultural development programs. Although our aid might help them, they could get along without it. The Paddocks suggested that Libya is probably such a country because it has the resources, in the form of oil, that will allow it to purchase food as its population expands.

Some nations, on the other hand, may become self-sufficient if we can give them some food to tide them over. The Paddocks thought that Pakistan, at least West Pakistan, might be such a country. Considering the recent behavior of West Pakistan toward East Pakistan, and the disastrous turmoil which has overtaken that nation, one wonders if they were not too optimistic.

Finally there is the last tragic category: those countries so far behind in the population-food game that there is no hope our food aid could see them through to self-sufficiency. The Paddocks said that India was probably in this category.

The development of the Green Revolution may have set back the predicted time schedule of the Paddocks' prognosis for perhaps a decade and may have changed the status of several countries (India, for example) in regard to their ability to cope with the food problem. But it does not invalidate their general analysis or the importance of their contribution to the debate on how to deal with a food crisis. The Paddocks' prescription, of course, is not necessarily an ideal one. One obvious drawback is the notion that existing political boundaries should be used to separate people who can be helped from those beyond saving. Actually, the prospects of large groups *within* a country may differ tremendously, owing to geographical, climatological, and political circumstances.

The crucial lesson which the world should learn from the Paddocks' proposal is the need to evaluate rationally any program to help people; to ask how whatever aid is available can be used to the greatest humanitarian effect. That agricultural experts such as the Paddocks were so despairing of the food production situation that they felt the necessity of proposing triage should jolt the world into some realization of the predicament. The United States cannot by itself feed the world, and the UDCs cannot avoid massive famines indefinitely, no matter how successful programs to expand food production may be. If the Green Revolution is successful, then we have perhaps bought a little time before we will again be faced by a need for triage or some similar, hard-headed approach, which would be preferable to thoughtless dispersal of limited food reserves without regard for their long-range effects.

grated control of insects and the psychology of food acceptance to worldwide policy planning to maintain the quality of our environment and prevent
international conflict. The challenge of carrying out such an idealistic program is immense. The reward could be survival, and hopefully, a much
better world for future generations.

## War

In *The Naked Ape* (1967), Desmond Morris observed that ". . . the
best solution for ensuring world peace is the widespread promotion of contraception and abortion . . . moralizing factions that oppose it must face
the fact that they are engaged in dangerous war mongering." As this indicates, and as was discussed in Chapter 3, population-related problems seem
to be increasing the probability of triggering a thermonuclear Armageddon.
Avoiding such a denouement for *Homo sapiens* is the most pressing political-
economic problem of our time.

### POPULATION, RESOURCES, AND WAR

In 1969 the world saw in a microcosm what may be in store. Two grossly
overpopulated Central American countries, El Salvador and Honduras, went
to war. El Salvador had an estimated population of 3.3 million, a population density of 413 people per square mile, and a doubling time of 21 years.
Honduras had a population of 2.5 million, a density of only 57 per square
mile, and the same doubling time as El Salvador. More significant statistics
have been provided by the Latin American Demographic Center; they show
that in El Salvador the population density per square mile of *arable* land was
782 persons, while in Honduras it was only 155 persons. Almost 300,000
Salvadorans had moved into Honduras in search of land and jobs because
of the population pressure and resulting unemployment at home. Friction
developed among the immigrants and the Honduran natives, El Salvador
accused Honduras of maltreating the Salvadorans, and the problem es-
calated into a brief but nasty war. The conflict was ended by the intervention
of the Organization of American States (OAS). In a precedent-shattering
move the OAS recognized demographic factors in its formula for settling the
dispute. An international body acknowledged that population pressure was a
root cause of a war.

Systematic analyses of the role of population pressures in generating wars,
carried out by political scientist Robert C. North and his colleagues at
Stanford University, have begun to support earlier conclusions based on anec-
dotal evidence. Pilot statistical studies of war involvement of major European
powers in modern times have revealed very high correlations among rates of
population growth, rising GNP, expanding military budgets, and involvement
in wars, although technical considerations make drawing conclusions about

causes and effects hazardous. In more detailed multivariate analyses, Professor North has found a complex causal chain involving population growth in relation to static or slowly growing resources, technological development, a tendency to invest energy beyond previous boundaries of society, and increases in the presumed "needs" and demands of a populace. In North's own words, "Differential rates (from society to society) of population growth, technological growth, and access to resources gave rise to differential demands, differential capabilities, and differential expansions of interests and influence, to competitions, conflicts, arms races, crises, and wars."

In ancient times such tendencies were buffered to a degree by oceans, mountain ranges, deserts, vast distances, and slow means of travel. Rome could raze Carthage, but not China or the cities of South and Central American Indians. Today, however, with vast increases of population and unprecedented developments in technology, transportation, and communications, the people of the world are cheek by jowl, and there is little geographical buffering left. North points out that states in nonaggressive phases, like modern Sweden, tend to share certain characteristics: "A relatively small and stable population, a relatively high and steadily developing technology, and good access to resources (either domestic or acquired through favorable trade)."

Finite resources in a world of expanding populations and increasing per capita demands create a situation ripe for international violence. The perceived need to control resources has been a major factor in U.S. military and paramilitary involvements around the globe since World War II. The overt manifestation of aggressive American resource policies in Southeast Asia may, with luck, bring about a careful reconsideration of the resource demands created by our present cowboy economy.

The resource element in the United States intervention in Southeast Asia has been stated explicitly by many American political leaders. Richard Nixon said in 1953, when he was Vice President: "If Indo-China falls, Thailand is put in an almost impossible position. The same is true of Malaya with its rubber and tin." President Eisenhower wrote in 1963: "The loss of all Vietnam together with Laos in the west and Cambodia on the southwest . . . would have spelled the loss of valuable deposits of tin and prodigious supplies of rubber and rice." In an interview with *U.S. News & World Report* (April 16, 1954), Mr. Eisenhower also mentioned tungsten as being an important resource found in Indo-China. The same issue of this magazine was headlined "Why U.S. Risks War in Indo-China." The subhead of the article was: "One of the world's richest areas is open to the winner in Indo-China. That's behind the growing U.S. concern. Communists are fighting for the wealth of the Indies. Tin, rubber, rice, key strategic raw materials are what the war is really about. U.S. sees it as a place to hold—at any cost." A listing in the article of the components of "The Big Prize: Southeast Asia" includes tin, rice, rubber, oil, minerals (tungsten, iron, zinc, manganese, coal, and antimony), and foodstuffs. Nothing was changed by our active entry into the war during the 1960s, despite a great deal of propaganda to the effect that we were saving the people from communist control. President Johnson in 1966 bluntly told the soldiers at Camp Stanley in Korea: "They want what we've got and we're not going to give it to them."

Greatly increased oil exploration in Southeast Asia and the mapping out of oil leases in the waters off South Vietnam in 1970 have added to the resource component of the United States involvement. The U.S. is clearly willing to fight under some circumstances to protect its resource base and to deny resources to its enemies. It is also willing to intervene in the internal affairs of UDCs to ensure that governments friendly to American investors and sympathetic with our resource needs remain in power. Economist Percy W. Bidwell, writing for the Council on Foreign Relations, stated what he thought should be the goals of our policy: "Our purpose should be to encourage the expansion of low-cost production and to make sure that neither nationalistic policies nor Communist influences deny American industries access on reasonable terms to the basic materials necessary to the continued growth of the American economy."

Such thinking clearly is still a major factor in making American foreign policy, and it will continue to be if the business community has its way. An article in the August 1, 1971, issue of *Forbes* magazine complains about the growing U.S. dependence on foreign sources of raw materials: "Unfortunately, all this is happening at a time when the Vietnam war and the world balance of power make it almost impossible for the U.S. to defend its overseas supply sources. When we practiced gunboat diplomacy, we really didn't need it. Now, when we need it, we can't use it."

If the developed countries insist on continued expansion of their cowboy economies, accelerating competition over the dwindling resources of the planet can be expected. Moreover, if nations do not establish rational control of the oceans, shrinking fishery yields may also precipitate serious conflicts. Since, even if nations should move in the right direction, resource competition is likely to increase for some time, it is crucial that legal devices be quickly developed for the resolution of international conflicts.

### INTERNATIONAL CONFLICT IN THE NUCLEAR AGE

Indeed, it is in the area of international conflict above all else that the old rules must be changed. Most national leaders still view war as an extension of politics, as Clausewitz did in the early nineteenth century. They have not yet learned that thermonuclear war itself is a far more deadly enemy than any other nation; they still talk of winning, when in reality only losing is possible. It it to be expected that older people will have more trouble in adjusting to change than the young, and changes in the world military situation over the past 25 years have been so unprecedented as to constitute a serious test of even the adaptability of the most flexible young people. It is lamentable that at the time of its most extreme crisis the world is still largely ruled not just by old men, but by an unfortunate selection of old men.

In the United States, the leadership consists mainly of those people who are most likely to have the ethnocentrism of their society embedded in their characters. Our images of leadership and our political and elective processes seem to require this. Our leaders are unlikely to be familiar with the values and attitudes of other cultures. They are equally unlikely to know anything about the psychology of aggression. They are most likely to have deep emotional investments in patriotic ideals and the glorification of the American way of life, and to have contempt for other cultures. Few have any insight into the psychological tricks which we have built into our world view in order to conceal reality. They do not understand why we talk of military "hardware" instead of weapons, why we say we can "take out" an enemy city instead of "destroy it, killing every man, woman, and child," why we talk of "casualties" in Vietnam instead of "dead and maimed." They do not understand how our preconceptions about the Russians, the Chinese, the Cubans, and other unfamiliar peoples badly distort our perceptions of their behavior. *Moreover, American leaders do not understand that the leaders of the other countries have equally distorted perceptions of our actions and motives.* They have no way of understanding. If the men now leading most nations really had been sensitive to such things as cultural relativity, it is unlikely that they ever would have become political leaders.

In spite of these handicaps, there has been an increasing attempt on the part of the American establishment to gain some degree of understanding of the motives of the Russians, and even to open communications with them. The existence of a White House–Kremlin "hotline" testifies to progress in the area of communications. it is, of course, a device to help prevent misinterpretation of Soviet actions by Americans and vice versa. Americans seem to have learned something since the 1950s, when rigidity and paranoia set the tone of our relations with the U.S.S.R. Similarly, Russian leadership has been more reality-oriented since the demise in 1953 of Joseph Stalin. But the change has not been great, and a lack of basic understanding still seems to exist on both sides of the Iron Curtain.

The conclusion seems inevitable that if nations continue to collect nuclear arms and biological weapons, sooner or later World War III will occur. And it *will* be the war that ends all wars, at least all world wars, for a very long time, if not forever. Unfortunately, a great deal of our governmental policy with regard to national defense is founded on the idea of a "balance of terror," the creation of a group of scientists specializing in what has become known as the "theory of nuclear deterrence." What the politicians apparently do not know (or refuse to believe) is that this theory is based on assumptions which have been demonstrated to be untenable, analyses which are inapplicable, and nonexistent or irrelevant data (see Green's *Deadly Logic* for details). A similar foundation has been developed in parallel by the Soviet Union for their military policy.

Why would presumably intelligent men be taken in by transparent theorizing? Simply because the "analysis" can be conveniently arranged to produce desired results. Naturally the answers are engineered to fit precisely the expectations of the appropriate government officials. Leaders of nations believe that their nations must be *strong* if they are to survive. Nuclear weapons fit right into a pattern which has, for all of man's history, dictated arming against an enemy in order to avoid attack. In the past, if a strong society was attacked, it won. But nations have not been able to adjust to the new set of rules. With thermonuclear weapons, regardless of which side is stronger and which attacks, both sides will lose.

Four elements make recognition of the new rules and action based on them difficult. First, there are always scientists who tell the politicians that nuclear or CBW wars can be won. If the other side is utterly destroyed and 20 million of us survive the conflict, is that not victory? Remember Senator Russell and his "American Adam and Eve."

A second element is the notion that the weapons will not be used; that the balance of terror will be a stable one. This notion has been examined in detail by behavioral scientists, and few of them seem anxious to bet on it.

Most Americans seem to feel that the chances of thermonuclear war are remote. Many, for instance, seem to believe that the limited test ban treaty has greatly reduced the chances of thermonuclear war. Their confidence stands in sharp contrast to the apprehension of those most concerned with the arms race. In 1964, for instance, a survey of experts at Rand Corporation (a military-industrial "think tank") revealed the following estimates of the subjective probability of thermonuclear war: 10 percent in 10 years, 25 percent in 25 years. Those less enamored of the idea of a nuclear holocaust than the Rand-Hudson Institute type of cold warriors do not seem to consider World War III any less likely to occur.

On the contrary, they realize that the deployment of multiple independently targeted reentry vehicles (MIRVs) and anti-ballistic missiles (ABMs) promises to *destabilize* the balance of terror. A missile equipped with a MIRV can strike at a series of targets. The payload is a vehicle known as a "bus," which drops off a series of warheads aimed independently at different targets. An ABM is a system for destroying incoming enemy missiles. The combination greatly increases the advantages of making a first (pre-emptive) strike. Each missile with a MIRV is a single target in its silo, but a "salvo" once launched. A pre-emptive strike against the enemy's missiles might, with the multiplicative advantage of MIRVs, saturate the enemy ABM capability and destroy much of the opponent's strike capability. The aggressor can launch a pre-emptive strike and then hope to use his ABMs to shoot down most or all of the enemy's weakened second strike. He can thus hope to escape with little or no damage (the ecological and radiation dangers to the entire planet rarely are considered major factors in military-governmental war scenarios).

The basic assumption of deterrence theory that leaders will behave rationally is not only weak, but has been contradicted by history. Scientists may make guesses about the "probability" of a thermonuclear war, but they are really no better than the guesses of an informed layman. (A good introduction to this problem is to read the three books by Herman Kahn listed in the bibliography of this chapter, followed by Green's *Deadly Logic,* Frank's *Sanity and Survival,* and York's *Race to Oblivion,* Plate's *Understanding Doomsday,* and finally Robert F. Kennedy's *Thirteen Days.* These will provide the reader with some background for his own predictions.)

The third element of difficulty in changing the rules is uncertainty about the best way to achieve disarmament and security in a world where security has usually in the past been provided by brute force, either overtly exercised or used as a threat. Unfortunately, the effort going into the study of this aspect of the problem has been infinitesimal compared with that going into military research, although almost no area demands greater immediate attention. The basic need is evident: once again it is a change in human attitudes so that the "in group" against which aggression is forbidden expands to include *all* of humanity.

If this could be accomplished, security might be provided by an armed international organization, a global analogue of a police force. Many people have recognized this as a goal, but the way to reach it remains obscure. The first step might involve partial surrender of sovereignty to an international organization. It seems probable that as long as most people fail to comprehend the magnitude of the threat, that step will be impossible. At the very least we must learn to weigh the risks inherent in attempting controlled disarmament against those run by continuing the arms race. An attempt at disarmament could lead to a war, or the destruction or domination of the United States through Chinese or Soviet "cheating." But, if we were successful at disarming and if we achieved an international police force, the reward would be a very much safer world in which resources would be freed for raising the standard of living for all humankind. Few problems deserve more intensive study. The dynamics of disarmament appear to be even more complex than those of arms races. In spite of this, in 1970 the Arms Control and Disarmament Agency (ACDA), the only U.S. agency charged with planning in this area, had a budget of only a few million dollars (contrasted with $80 billion for "defense"). Moreover the ACDA is heavily influenced by the State Department, a stronghold of cold war bureaucracy.

The fourth element of difficulty involves economics and the military. Although this will be discussed in terms of the United States, there is every reason to believe that an analogous situation exists in the Soviet Union. Civilians should realize that peace and freedom from tension are not viewed as an ideal situation by many members of the military-industrial-government complex. By and large, professional military officers, expecially field grade and higher, hope for an end to the cold war about as fervently as farmers hope for drought. When there is an atmosphere of national security, military budgets are usually small, military power minimal, and military promotions slow. The founders of the United States recognized that the military services were unlikely to work against their own interests, and carefully established ultimate civilian control over the Army and Navy. It worked rather well for a long time. But times have changed. Wars are no longer fought with simple, understandable things like axes, swords, and cannon. Now we need "weapons systems" with complex and often arcane components, such as acquisition radar, VTOL fighters, doppler navigators, MIRVs, heat-seeking missiles, and nuclear submarines. These cannot be produced rapidly, on demand, by a few government contractors. Long-term planning is required, involving not only the military services, but also a large number of different industrial organizations which supply various components. These organizations, not unnaturally, often hire retired military men to help them in their negotiations with the government, where decisions on armament appropriations are made. The necessary intimacy of the military and industry in areas of weapons development and procurement has thus given rise to the term "military-industrial complex." The term military-industrial-government complex sometimes seems more accurate. In his heavily documented book, *Pentagon Capitalism,* industrial engineer Seymour Melman of Columbia University shows that even this description is inadequate for the Frankenstein's monster we have created.

This complex seems to have an aversion to peace, but it is not composed of a group of evil, conspiring men determined to napalm babies and keep the world on the edge of thermonuclear disaster. Rather, it is composed of men who, because of their personal histories and associations, are convinced that our only hope of survival lies in confronting the Soviet Union with overwhelming strength. On the other side, of course, their Russian counterparts see Soviet preparedness as the only thing preventing an attack by the capitalists who want to destroy their way of life. The Soviets tend to forget that we did not attempt to destroy them when we enjoyed a nuclear monopoly. Americans, on the other hand, tend not to appreciate the valid roots of Soviet anti-Western paranoia. Members of both complexes are generally not long on introspection; that by keeping the cold war going they are adding to their own prestige and power is not viewed by them as a major factor in their behavior. In individual instances, however, it must be difficult even for members of the complex to avoid admitting the truth to themselves.

With the military budget now in the vicinity of $80 billion annually, one does not have to look far to find a quick $20 billion a year or so that could be used by the United States to try to save itself and the rest of the world. Melman has shown how more than $50 billion could be trimmed from the 1970 military budget without compromising our security (see appendix to Plate, *Understanding Doomsday*). Naturally, if large cuts were made in military budgets, substantial economic dislocations and unemployment would occur, unless very careful planning preceded the cuts. It is probably politically unrealistic to expect the funds necessary for the solution of our population-environment problems to be diverted in great amounts from military or space programs. Higher taxes will be necessary, at least at the start, to reach the level of effort discussed earlier.

The problem of breaking the power of the military-industrial-government complex (and its analogues in other nations) and the related problem of finding a way to world peace are, as we have seen, among several general problems which mankind must solve if civilization is to survive. Two French scientists, Marcel Fetizon and Michel Magat, have stated, "We must either eliminate science or eliminate war. We cannot have both." One might go even farther. Man's science and technology are incompatible with his present attitudes. Either the attitudes must change or science and technology will disappear, and one way or another most of *Homo sapiens* will go with them.

### CONVENTIONAL ARMS

One of the unhappy facts of today's military situation is that while attention is focused on the nuclear arms race, a spectacular conventional arms race is going on relatively unheralded. The DCs in general and the U.S. and U.S.S.R. in particular are culpable in supplying vast amounts of arms to other nations. India and Pakistan, for instance, fought a bloody war in 1964 with arms supplied by the U.S. to both sides. Needless to say, our military aid hardly helped these two UDCs toward development (although, in all probability, if the arms hadn't been obtained from us, the Russians, British, or French would have been happy to supply them). George Thayer has written a detailed study of the conventional arms trade, *The War Business*. His treatment is clearly not anti-American (or pro-communist), and yet he feels constrained to state (p. 376):

> Still, today's arms trade is essentially an American problem. No nation talks more loudly about peace, yet no nation distributes as many weapons of war. No nation has spoken so passionately in favor of nuclear controls, yet no nation has been so silent on the subject of conventional arms controls. Nor has any nation been as vocal in its desire to eradicate hunger, poverty, and disease, yet no nation has so obstructed the fight against these ills through its insistence that poor countries waste their money on expensive and useless arms.

The effects of this conventional arms race can be deduced from Figure 12-2. As you can see, although military expenditures have peaked in the DCs, they are still skyrocketing in the UDCs, the countries least able to afford them. If the DCs really believe their rhetoric about helping the UDCs, the flow of arms from DCs to UDCs should be cut off. The Pentagon maintains that since Thayer's book was written, they have stopped vigorously promoting arms sales. This is a helpful step, but likely to result only in the U.S. losing its share of the market, unless we are joined in this policy by the other DCs.

## International Controls

It has been apparent for some time that the nations of this planet cannot long survive without a system of controls for dealing with the world eco-

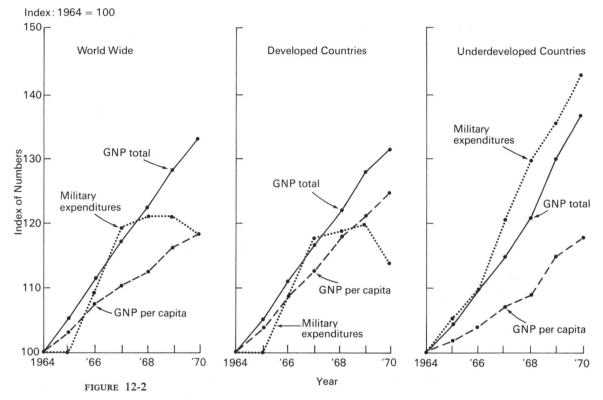

Index: 1964 = 100

FIGURE 12-2

Trends in military expenditures in relation to GNP (corrected for inflation). Ordinates are index numbers where 1964 = 100. Note that in UDCs military expenditures continue to outstrip per capita GNP, even though the average income per capita in those countries is only about $200 per year. (From U.S. Arms Control and Disarmament Agency, World Military Expenditures 1970.)

nomic system, the world ecosphere, and world population growth. Such a system must above all be capable of resolving national differences. This, for instance, is the basic conclusion of international lawyer Richard Falk's analysis of the present situation, as exemplified by his projections of alternate futures (Box 12-4).

In our opinion, one of the first and perhaps most easily accomplished areas where international controls could and should be established is over what may be called the "world commons." All of *Homo sapiens* must extract needed materials from the atmosphere and waters of the Earth, and the hydrologic and biogeochemical cycles bind these together into an indivisible entity. Although nations vary in their mineral endowment, it would clearly be wise to consider all supplies of non-renewable resources as a commons also.

Idealistically, we might put in a plea here for a surrendering of national sovereignty to a world government, but it is apparent that any movement in that direction will be extremely slow at best. There does seem to be, how-

BOX 12-4 THE FALK PROJECTIONS

In his superb book, *This Endangered Planet,* international lawyer Richard A. Falk of Princeton University gives two fundamental scenarios of the course of politics in a world threatened by ecological catastrophe. In the first scenario, he envisions that the 1970s will see *The Politics of Despair.* People will come to realize that governments cannot deal with the problems of society. The gap between rich and poor nations will continue to widen, ecocatastrophes will become more frequent, the arms race and technological circuses will continue, while governments continue to pursue growth of GNP. The world system will face crisis after crisis, but no organized attempts will be made to attack underlying causes. Governmental repression will become more commonplace, and "people will increasingly doubt whether life is worth living."

The decade of the 1980s will feature *The Politics of Desperation.* Governments will realize their helplessness in the face of human problems, but the elites who run them will turn more and more to repression to maintain their privileges. The suffering people of the world will become increasingly hostile toward the fortunate few living in islands of affluence. UDCs may start to develop nuclear or biological warfare capability in an attempt to force resource redistribution on the DCs. Realignments of power among DCs and token concessions to the UDCs will not halt their drive, and DCs may "recolonize" some in order to enforce "peace" and maintain the world trade system which favors them. The U.S. finds itself powerless to intercede.

*The Politics of Catastrophe* will take over in the 1990s. In that decade an immense disaster, ecological or thermonuclear, will overtake mankind. The reorganization (if any) of the post-catastrophe world will de-pend on the exact form of the disaster and who survives. The reorganization would most likely be world-oriented rather than nation-state oriented. If, by chance, the outmoded world-order system is not irremediably damaged in the 1990s, then it certainly will be in the 21st century, which Falk labels the *Era of Annihilation.*

Falk's second scenario is more optimistic. It envisions a rapid recognition that the world-system based on sovereign states cannot possibly deal with the problems of the endangered planet. In this scenario, the 1970s would be *The Decade of Awareness,* in which people in general face squarely the nature of the emergency which engulfs us. The 1980s would be *The Decade of Mobilization,* in which awareness would be converted into action taking mankind away from the primacy of the sovereign state. A new world political movement, based on transnational thinking, would overwhelm the conservative forces dedicated to maintenance of the status quo.

The 1990s would be *The Decade of Transformation,* in which mankind moves in the direction of stability in both population and economic systems. "A new political man will emerge from such a climate of opinion and change. The planet will be governed as a system that needs to guard against relapse and reversion, and regards the diversities within itself as a source of vitality and vigor." That decade will lead to the 21st century as *The Era of World Harmony*—based on ecological humanism and men living in harmony with nature.

Obviously, we find Falk's first scenario more probable. His second seems wildly optimistic, especially in light of the growth potential built into the age structure of the human population. But it is a noble target at which to aim!

ever, some chance that humanity might be able to move much more rapidly than it has in the past toward international agreements on the control of the world commons. Treaties have been worked out to control the uses of outer space and Antarctica, and there is now growing interest in a treaty to control the use of the oceans. A draft of such a treaty has been prepared by Elisabeth Mann Borgese of the Center for the Study of Democratic Institutions. It is based on previous ocean treaty drafts and the Treaty on Outer Space. The proposed Ocean Treaty would do more than set rules for the behavior of nations; it would establish an *Ocean Regime,* an institution charged with the development of a code of conduct for nations, non-governmental entities, and individuals who use the sea. The Regime would also modify that code in response to changing ecological, economic, or technological developments. It would provide for the development, administration, conservation, and distribution of the resources in the seas and in the sea-bed on a cooperative, international basis, limiting all use to peaceful purposes. This would include the regulation of fisheries and sea-farming, exploitation of sea-bed resources, the control of pollution, the supervision of exploration and research, and the settling of disputes among nations or groups regarding ocean use. The Ocean Regime and the proposed route to its establishment are discussed in Mrs. Borgese's article, which is listed in the bibliography.

Should an Ocean Regime be established, it could serve as a model for a future Atmosphere Regime to regulate the use of airspace and to control atmospheric pollution. Perhaps these two might eventually be developed into a Planetary Regime. Experience gained in dealing internationally with the oceans and the atmosphere could, in theory, be combined with that gained within national governments dealing with problems of population and environment. The Planetary Regime might thus incorporate the United Nations into a sort of International Agency for Population, Resources, and Environment.

As an extension of the Ocean and Atmosphere Regimes, the comprehensive Planetary Regime could control the development, administration, conservation and distribution of *all* natural resources, renewable, or nonrenewable, at least so far as any international implications exist. Thus, the Regime could have the power to control pollution not only in the atmosphere and the oceans, but also in such fresh-water bodies as rivers and lakes that cross international boundaries. Any river that discharged pollutants into oceans might also be subject to control by the Regime.

The Regime would also be the logical central agency for regulating all international trade, particularly assistance from DCs to UDCs, and including all food on the international market, as well as all that comes from the oceans.

The Regime could have the responsibility for determining the optimum population for the world and for each region and for arbitrating various countries' shares in their regional limits. Population control might be the responsibility of each government, but the Regime should have power to enforce the agreed limits. As in the Ocean Regime, all regulations for population sizes, resource development and pollution control should be subject to revision and modification in accordance with changing conditions.

The Planetary Regime might have the advantage over earlier proposed world government schemes in not being primarily political in its emphasis. Since most of the areas it would control are not now being regulated or controlled by nations or anyone else, its establishment would involve far less surrendering of national power. Nevertheless, it might function powerfully to suppress international conflict simply because such an interrelated resource-environment structure would not permit such an outdated luxury.

# Bibliography

American Museum of Natural History, 1969. The unforeseen international ecologic boomerang (supplement to the Feb. 1969 issue of *Natural History*). The misuse of western technology in UDCs.

Arms Control and Disarmament Agency (U.S.), 1970. *World Military Expenditures, 1970* USACDA Publication 58, Government Printing Office, Washington, D.C. Basic source on the size and impact of military expenditures.

Aron, Raymond, 1957. *On War*. W. W. Norton & Co., Inc. New York. A European view of the influence on international relations of nuclear armaments and planetary politics.

Barnet, Richard J., and Richard D. Falk (eds.), 1965. *Security in Disarmament*. Princeton Univ. Press, Princeton, N.J. A collection of essays dealing with such subjects as systems of inspection, violations of arms control agreements, and supernational versus international models for disarmament.

Bolton, Roger E. (ed.), 1966. *Defense and Disarmament*. Prentice-Hall, Inc., Englewood Cliffs, N.J. A series of essays on the economics of disarmament.

Boulding, Kenneth E., 1962. *Conflict and Defense*. Harper and Row, New York. A pioneering attempt to create a general theory of conflict.

Borgese, Elisabeth Mann, 1968. The Ocean Regime. *Center Occasional Papers,* vol. 1, no. 5. Center for the Study of Democratic Institutions, Santa Barbara. A model statute and program which, if enacted, could go a long way toward solving the problem of the "ocean commons" and perhaps serve as a trial for a similar governing of the "world commons."

Buchan, Alistair (ed.), 1966. *A World of Nuclear Powers?* Prentice-Hall, Inc., Englewood Cliffs, N.J.

Calder, Nigel (ed.), 1968. *Unless Peace Comes.* Viking Press, New York. A description of future weapons systems.

Chedd, Graham, 1969. Famine or sanity? *New Scientist,* Oct. 23.

Coale, Ansley J., and Edgar M. Hoover, 1958. *Population Growth and Economic Development in Low-Income Countries.* Princeton Univ. Press, Princeton, N.J.

Culbertson, John M., 1971. *Economic Development; An Ecological Approach.* Alfred A. Knopf, New York. Outlines a theory of economic development which, to quote the author, "indicates that the pessimistic warnings that present day civilization may come to an early end merit serious consideration. It also explains why the optimistic theories of economic development are believed, although they are false—or because they are false."

Daetz, Douglas, 1968. *Energy Utilization and Aid Effectiveness in Nonmechanized Agriculture: A Computer Simulation of a Socioeconomic System.* Ph.D. Dissert., Univ. of California.

Doane, Robert R., 1957. *World Balance Sheet.* Harper and Brothers, New York.

Ehrlich, P. R., and R. L. Harriman, 1971. *How to be a Survivor: A Plan to Save Spaceship Earth.* Ballantine, New York. A concise description of a strategy that might get mankind through the crisis now developing.

Enke, Stephen, 1966. The economic aspects of slowing population growth. *The Economic Journal,* vol. LXXVI, no. 301 (March), pp. 44–56.

Enke, Stephen, 1969. Birth control for economic development. *Science,* vol. 164. pp. 798–802.

Falk, Richard, 1971. *This Endangered Planet.* Random House, New York. A most interesting view of the global crisis.

Food and Agriculture Organization of the United Nations. *Production Yearbook.* FAO-UN, Rome.

Forrester, Jay W., 1971. *World Dynamics.* Wright-Allen Press, Inc. Cambridge, Mass. The first results of the MIT simulation studies of the human future.

Frank, Jerome D., 1967. *Sanity and Survival.* Vintage Books, New York. The psychology of war and peace.

Frederiksen, Harald, 1969. Feedbacks in economic and demographic transition. *Science,* vol. 166, pp. 837–847. An overly optimistic discussion of the possible benefits of death control in motivating people to have smaller families in UDCs.

Green, Philip, 1968. *Deadly Logic.* Schocken Books, New York. An analysis of deterrence theory—a critically important work.

Greene, Felix, 1971. *The Enemy: What Every American Should Know About Imperialism.* Vintage Books, New York. A classical Marxist analysis of the role of the West in the world of today and yesterday. Read this to know what intelligent critics of the capitalist system say, based on a world-view entirely different from that of the average American. Note his acceptance of the labor theory of value.

Halperin, Morton H., 1966. *Limited War in the Nuclear Age.* John Wiley & Sons, Inc., New York.

Heilbroner, R. L., 1959. *The Future as History.* Harper and Row, New York. A classic, recommended.

Henkin, Harmon, 1969. Side effects. *Environment,* vol. 11, no. 1 (Jan.–Feb.). More on unexpected ecological results from development projects.

Hersh, Seymour M., 1969. *Chemical and Biological Warfare.* Doubleday (Anchor Book), Garden City, New York.

Hertzog, Arthur, 1965. *The War-Peace Establishment.* Harper and Row, New York. An introduction to the views of those researchers concerned with our military-foreign policy stance.

Illich, Ivan, 1969. Outwitting the "developed" countries. *New York Review of Books,* Nov. 6.

Illich, Ivan, 1970. *Celebration of Awareness.* Doubleday and Co., Garden City, New York. Brilliant book by one of today's most imaginative thinkers. See especially Chapter 10, "Sexual Power and Political Potency," in which Illich discusses the population situation in Latin America.

Jacoby, Neil H., 1969. The progress of peoples. *Center Occasional Papers,* vol. 2, no. 4. Center for the Study of Democratic Institutions, Santa Barbara. A most interesting discussion of the problems of development.

Jalée, Pierre, 1968. *The Pillage of the Third World.* Modern Reader, New York.

Jarrett, Henry (ed.), 1966. *Environmental Quality in a Growing Economy.* Johns Hopkins Press, Baltimore. An interesting collection—see especially the article by Boulding, "The Economics of the Coming Spaceship Earth."

Kahn, Herman, 1960. *On Thermonuclear War.* Princeton Univ. Press. Princeton, N.J. This book brought much unfair personal criticism of Kahn. It is the subject of devastating professional analysis by Green in *Deadly Logic.*

Kahn, Herman, 1962. *Thinking about the Unthinkable.* Horizon, New York. An able reply to the personal attacks made on Kahn after *On Thermonuclear War* was published.

Kahn, Herman, 1965. *On Escalation.* Penguin Books, Baltimore. The most recent work by the best known of the deterrence theorists.

King, Kendall W., 1969. The world food crisis—a partial answer. *Research Development* (Sept.). Describes a successful program for dealing with malnutrition among children in UDCs.

Lockwood, Lee, 1967. *Castro's Cuba, Cuba's Fidel.* Vintage Books, New York. Contains an interview in which Castro describes his approach to Cuban semi-development.

Meadows, D. L., 1972. *The Limits to Growth; A Global Challenge.* Universe Books, Washington, D.C. An important new study.

Melman, Seymour, 1662. *Disarmament, Its Politics and Economics.* American Academy of Arts and Sciences, Boston, Mass.

Melman, Seymour, 1970. *Pentagon Capitalism; The Political Economy of War.* McGraw-Hill, New York. See especially Chapter 7 for a summary of myths about the military establishment. Melman sees it as independent of real U.S. needs, defense or economic.

Myrdal, Gunnar, 1968. *Asian Drama.* Pantheon, New York. A three-volume monument on politics, economics, planning, and population in Asia. Comprehensive, and rather depressing.

Myrdal, Gunnar, 1970. *The Challenge of World Poverty: A World Anti-Poverty Program in Outline*. Pantheon, New York. Based on *Asian Drama,* this is much shorter but goes beyond it. A "must" for all those interested in the problems of development.

Paddock, William, and Paul Paddock, 1967. *Famine, 1975!* Little, Brown & Co., Boston.

Pearson, Lester B., 1969. *Partners in Development*. Praeger Publishers, New York. Report to the World Bank by the Commission on International Development.

Peccei, Aurelo, 1969. *The Chasm Ahead*. Macmillan, London. A distinguished Italian industrialist and member of the "Club of Rome" examines mankind's predicament and reaches conclusions startlingly close to those of many ecologists.

Pincus, John A. (ed.), 1968. *Reshaping the World Economy*. Prentice-Hall, Englewood Cliffs, N.J. Especially useful source on world trade problems.

Platt, John, 1969. What we must do. *Science,* vol. 166, pp. 1115–1121. A classification of our multiplicity of crises and suggestions on how we might meet them.

Rathjens, George W., 1969. *The Future of the Strategic Arms Race: Options for the 1970's*. Carnegie Endowment for International Peace.

Sakharov, Andrei D., 1968. *Progress, Coexistence and Intellectual Freedom*. W. W. Norton and Co., New York. Heroic statement by the brilliant physicist called "Father of the Russian H-Bomb."

Sanders, Sol., 1969. *A Sense of Asia*. Charles Scribner's Sons, New York.

Schelling, Thomas C., 1968. *The Strategy of Conflict*. Oxford Univ. Press, Oxford. Well worth reading. Schelling is one of the brightest of the deterrence theorists.

Spengler, Joseph J., 1960. Population and world development. *Science,* vol. 131, pp. 1497–1502.

Sprout, H., and M. Sprout, 1971. *Toward a Politics of the Planet Earth*. Van Nostrand-Reinhold Co., New York.

Thayer, George, 1969. *The War Business: The International Trade in Armaments*. Avon Books, New York. A detailed description of the conventional arms trade.

United Nations. *Statistical Yearbook*. Statistical Office of the U.N., New York. A gold mine of information on population, manufacturing, agriculture, trade, consumption, etc. Produced annually.

York, Herbert, 1970. *Race to Oblivion: A Participant's View of the Arms Race*. Simon and Schuster, New York. Merciless examination of the military-industrial complex and its "ideas." From an impeccable source.

# CHAPTER 13

# Conclusions

*"The only trouble with our time is that
the future is not what it used to be."*

—Paul Valéry
(1891–1945)

*"The future is a cruel hoax . . .
I am terribly saddened by the fact that
the most humane thing for me to do
is to have no children at all."*

—Valedictorian Stephanie Mills, 1969
Mills College

## Summary

To recapitulate, we would summarize the present world situation as follows:

1. Considering present technology and patterns of behavior our planet is grossly overpopulated now.

2. The large absolute number of people and the rate of population growth are major hindrances to solving human problems.

3. The limits of human capability to produce food by conventional means have very nearly been reached. Problems of supply and distribution already have resulted in roughly half of humanity being undernourished or malnourished. Some 10–20 million people are starving to death annually.

4. Attempts to increase food production further will tend to accelerate the deterioration of our environment, which in turn will eventually *reduce* the capacity of the Earth to produce food. It is not clear whether environmental decay has now gone so far as to be essentially irreversible; it is possible that the capacity of the planet to support human life has been permanently impaired. Such technological "successes," as automobiles, pesticides, and inorganic nitrogen fertilizers are major contributors to environmental deterioration.

5. There is reason to believe that population growth increases the probability of a lethal worldwide plague and of a thermonuclear war. Either could provide a catastrophic "death rate solution" to the population problem; each is potentially capable of destroying civilization and even of driving *Homo sapiens* to extinction.

6. There is no technological panacea for the complex of problems comprising the population-food-environment crisis, although technology, properly applied in such areas as pollution abatement, communications, and fertility control can provide massive assistance. The basic solutions involve dramatic and rapid changes in human *attitudes,* especially those relating to reproductive behavior, economic growth, technology, the environment, and conflict resolution.

## Recommendations: A Positive Program

Although our conclusions must seem rather pessimistic, we wish to emphasize our belief that the problems can be solved. Whether they *will* be solved is another question. A general course of action that we feel will have some chance of ameliorating the results of the current crisis is outlined below. Many of the suggestions will seem "unrealistic," and indeed that is how we view them. But the system has been allowed to run downhill for so long that only idealistic and very far-reaching programs offer any hope of salvation.

1. Population control is absolutely essential if the problems now facing mankind are to be solved. *It is not, however, a panacea.* If population growth were halted immediately, virtually all other human problems— poverty, racial tensions, urban blight, environmental decay, warfare— would remain. The situation is best summarized in the statement, "whatever your cause, it's a lost cause without population control."

2. Political pressure must be applied immediately to induce the United States government to assume its responsibility to halt the growth of the American population. Once growth is halted, the government should undertake to regulate the birth rate so that the population is reduced to an optimum size and maintained there. It is essential that a grassroots political movement be generated to convince our legislators and the executive branch of the government that they must act rapidly.

The program should be based on what politicians understand best—votes. Presidents, Congressmen, Senators, and other elected officials who do not deal effectively with the crisis must be defeated at the polls and more intelligent and responsible candidates elected.

3. A massive campaign must be launched to restore a quality environment in North America and to *de-develop the United States.* De-development means bringing our economic system (especially patterns of consumption) into line with the realities of ecology and the world resource situation. Resources and energy must be diverted from frivolous and wasteful uses in overdeveloped countries to filling the genuine needs of the underdeveloped. This campaign would be largely political, especially with regard to our overexploitation of world resources, but the campaign should be strongly supplemented by legal and boycott action against polluters and others whose activities damage the environment. The need for de-development presents our economists with a major challenge. They must design a low-consumption economy of stability, and an economy in which there is a much more equitable distribution of wealth than in the present one. Redistribution of wealth both within and among nations is absolutely essential. Marxists claim that capitalism is intrinsically expansionist and wasteful, and that it automatically produces a monied ruling class. Can our economists prove them wrong?

4. Once the United States has clearly started on the path of cleaning up its own mess it can then turn its attention to the problems of the de-development of the other DCs, population control, and ecologically feasible semi-development of the UDCs. It must use every peaceful means at its disposal to bring the Soviet Union and other DCs into the effort, in line with the general proposals of Lord Snow and Academician Sakharov. Such action can be combined with attempts to achieve a general detente with the Soviets and the Chinese. Citizens, through the ballot, letter writing, and continued peaceful protest, must make clear to American leaders that they wish to move toward disarmament in spite of its possible risks. They must demand detailed appraisal of the risks of continuing the "balance of terror" versus the risk that the other side might "cheat" in a controlled disarmament situation. Americans should inform themselves of what is known about the causes and the psychology of conflict and about deterrence theory, and attempt to elect officials who are similarly informed. They must, above all, learn to behave in ways that will convince the poor of the Third World that the days of exploitation will end and that genuine aid is on its way.

5. It is unfortunate that at the time of the greatest crisis the United States and the world have ever faced, many Americans, especially the young, have given up hope that the government can be modernized and changed in direction through the functioning of the elective process. Their despair may have some foundation, but a partial attempt to

institute a "new politics" very nearly succeeded in 1968. In addition many members of Congress and other government leaders, both Democrats and Republicans, are very much aware of the problems outlined in this book and are determined to do something about them. Others are joining their ranks as the dangers before us daily become more apparent. These people need public support in order to be effective. The world cannot, in its present critical state, be saved by merely tearing down old institutions, even if rational plans existed for constructing better ones from the ruins. We simply do not have the time. Either we will succeed by bending old institutions or we will succumb to disaster. Considering the potential rewards and consequences we see no choice but to make an effort to modernize the system. It may be necessary to organize a new political party with an ecological outlook and national and international orientation to provide an alternative to the present parties with their local and parochial interests. The environmental issue may well provide the basis for this.

6. Perhaps the major necessary ingredient that has been missing from a solution to the problems of both the United States and the rest of the world is a goal, a vision of the kind of Spaceship Earth that ought to be and the kind of crew that should man her. Society has always had its visionaries who talked of love, beauty, peace, and plenty. But somehow the "practical" men have always been there to praise the smog as a sign of progress, to preach "just" wars, and to restrict love while giving hate free rein. It must be one of the greatest ironies of the history of the human species that the only salvation for the practical men now lies in what they think of as the dreams of idealists. The question now is: can the "realists" be persuaded to face reality in time?

# About this Book

It has been our aim to produce a reasonably comprehensive and reliable sourcebook for the study of questions related to population, resources and environment—a book that can serve the needs of teachers and students as well as the needs of general readers who may not be enrolled in any formal courses.

We have tried to make clear, by providing adequate detail and documentation, our reasons for sharing with many well-informed and concerned citizens of the world a gloomy prognosis for mankind. We have also tried to include many constructive proposals and suggestions that offer possible means of brightening that prognosis.

The wide diversity of sources we have drawn upon is indicated in the annotated bibliographies at the ends of the chapters, and in the general bibliography at the end of the book. We have listed only a small selection of references from technical journals, but these should provide the interested student with adequate guidance for a further exploration of this literature. We have not hesitated to include, in addition, bits of information from such sources as newspapers and the scientist's "grapevine," if such information seemed sufficiently important and timely, even though this might entail some risk of possible small losses in scientific accuracy.

Because, as indicated in the acknowledgments, the various drafts of our manuscript were thoroughly reviewed by a large number of critics who are competent in the various areas covered, we believe that the factual basis of the book is sound throughout. We do not believe that such minor errors as may be revealed in any of our figures, estimates, or interpretations will change the thrust of our major conclusions. In many areas, of course, it is impossible to determine exactly what has happened, or to know what the significance of certain trends may be. Data are often unreliable or unavailable, and our understanding of the complexities of ecological systems and human behavior is still fragmentary. But in dealing with the population-resource-environment crisis, it is important to recognize that people are going to have to learn to make decisions in the face of such uncertainty. Possible benefits will have to be weighed against possible risks, and a great deal of thought given to possible future events which may seem unlikely *but which will be catastrophic if they do occur*. It would be a major step forward for mankind if all people could know the general state of the world and could be informed as to just what chances are being taken with their lives and the lives of future generations.

From the almost limitless number of subjects which might have been included in this book, choices of those that were to be treated in detail had to be made. We have tried to emphasize those which seemed to us to be of the most general importance, and we make no apology either for our selection of subjects or for the personal style and approach we have used throughout. We have not attempted to give equal weight to both sides of all controversial issues; where we think one side is correct we have so indicated. We also make no claim to having tried to detail all exceptions to general rules. We hope that this book will provide concerned readers with enough background to enable them to make informed political decisions about environmental issues and to combat what C. P. Snow has referred to as the "excessive unsimplicity" which, in his words, "crops up whenever anyone makes a proposal which opens up a prospect, however distant, of new action. It involves a skill which all conservative functionaries are masters of, as they ingeniously protect the status quo: it is called the 'technique of the intricate defensive.' "

Finally, we hope that all of our readers will understand that the primary purpose of this book is to inform and convince them about the elements and the dimensions of the environmental crisis, rather than merely to frighten or discourage them. Nothing in this book is intended to cause feelings of guilt, resentment, or defensiveness in anyone who happens to be a parent or a child of a large family. It is not our purpose to offend anyone; in fact, to do so would only help to defeat our own goals. The future is our concern, and clearly, any measures that may help to brighten the prospects for mankind will require the understanding, the goodwill, and the enthusiastic support of all.

# Acknowledgments

Most of the people who helped us with the first edition have been involved in the hectic process of revision. Things are moving so fast that while one part of the manuscript is being revised another is going out of date—and our problems of information overload at times seem insurmountable.

Special thanks must go to first edition veterans Lester R. Brown, Dana Dalrymple, and Nathan Keyfitz, all of whom supplied critically important inputs in their areas of expertise. John Montgomery not only provided most of the information for the legal section but also took the time to read the entire manuscript and has given us many useful ideas. John Holdren (now of the Lawrence Radiation Laboratory of the University of California) has continued his collaboration with us, and his thoughts and prose are sprinkled liberally throughout the book. Without his help our task would have been enormously more difficult.

Critical readings of the revised manuscript by D. L. Bilderback, Department of History, Fresno State College; N. S. Demerath, American Council on Education; Edwin G. Dolan, Department of Economics, Dartmouth College; Gail Firstenbach, Washington, D.C.; Charles E. Hunt, Department of Geography and Environmental Engineering, Johns Hopkins University; Roderic B. Park, Department of Botany, University of California, Berkeley; Dennis Pirages, Department of Political Science, University of Georgia (on leave with the Population Biology Group, Department of Biological Sciences, Stanford); and S. Fred Singer, Advanced Study Program, The Brookings Institution, have been extremely helpful, and many of these reviewers' comments have been directly incorporated. Paul Grobstein and Peter M. Ray, Department of Biological Sciences, Stanford, Judith Blake, Department of

Sociology, University of California, Berkeley, and Charles F. Wurster, Marine Sciences Research Center, State University of New York, have reviewed portions of the manuscript and have made most helpful suggestions. Doctors Bilderback and Pirages have been closely involved with us in research projects on the sociopolitical aspects of the population-environment crisis and have had a major influence on our thinking.

The staff of the Falconer Biology Library has continued to show great patience and resourcefulness in helping us in our attempt to keep track of a flood of literature. Typing chores for this edition have been handled expertly by Frances Duignan, Patricia Mersman, and Susan Thomas. Dorothy Decker's successor, Jane Lawson Bavelas, has coordinated operations with great finesse and we are deeply in her debt.

Finally we would like to express our appreciation to William Kaufmann and his wife Virginia. This book grew out of a long friendship with Bill and Ginne, and the first edition was published while Bill was associated with W. H. Freeman and Company. Bill has since retired from Freeman and so the strict company rule of no "in-house" acknowledgments no longer applies. Bill's contributions to the book have been immense, far beyond those normally expected of an editor. They have ranged from correcting our faulty prose and unearthing pertinent epigrams to sitting up late at night in our living room working on the index. Without Bill and Ginne's encouragement this book would never have been written.

# World Demography

*Figures are from the 1971 Data Sheet of the Population Reference Bureau,*
*except for those on literacy and life expectancy,*
*which are from the 1968 Data Sheet.*

The data include, for each country and continent, current population sizes, birth rates, death rates, growth rates, and doubling times. In addition, infant mortality figures, percent of population under 15 years of age, population projection for 1985, and per capita gross national product are also included. These data are compiled from various sources, the United Nations being the principal one. The population figures given are mostly extrapolations from the most recent census data (censuses are not taken annually). Estimates for many countries undoubtedly contain a large margin of error. In many cases census data are extremely unreliable, in others undetected changes in birth or death rates since the latest census may introduce considerable error into extrapolations. And, of course, in some instances the figures may represent faulty extrapolations from incorrect census data.

Nonetheless, these are the best estimates available, and because errors in different countries are probably in different directions (and thus cancel each other out) a 1960 U.N. analysis concluded that the world total is probably accurate within plus or minus 50 million. Whether the U.N. analysts were correct is open to question. Needless to say, most of the figures should be considered to represent rough magnitudes. A difference of a point or two in birth rates between two countries may have no significance whatever. The most accurate census data come from the DCs; those of many UDCs are extremely suspect. The per capita gross national product figures should be used with special caution; as ratios of estimates they are especially liable to error. The major features of the current world demographic picture are clear in these data, but in using them their limitations should always be kept in mind.

| Region or Country | Population Estimates Mid-1971 (millions)† | Annual Births per 1,000 Population‡ | Annual Deaths per 1,000 Population‡ | Annual Rate of Population Growth (percent)° | Number of Years to Double Population □ | Annual Infant Mortality (Deaths under one year per 1,000 Live Births) ‡ | Population under 15 Years (percent)▶ | Population Projections to 1985 (millions)† | Life Expectancy at Birth (years)‡ | Population Illiterate 15 Years and Over (percent)‡ | Per Capita Gross National Product (US $)§ |
|---|---|---|---|---|---|---|---|---|---|---|---|
| World | 3,706¹ | 34 | 14 | 2.0 | 35 | — | 37 | 4,933 | 53 | 39 | — |
| AFRICA | 354² | 47 | 20 | 2.7 | 26 | — | 44 | 530 | 43 | 82 | — |
| *Northern Africa* | 89 | 47 | 16 | 3.1 | 23 | — | 45 | 140 | — | — | — |
| Algeria | 14.5 | 50 | 17 | 3.3 | 21 | 86 | 47 | 23.9 | — | 75–85 | 220 |
| Libya | 1.9 | 46 | 16 | 3.1 | 23 | — | 44 | 3.1 | — | 80–87 | 1,020 |
| Morocco | 16.3 | 50 | 15 | 3.3 | 21 | 149 | 46 | 26.2 | 50–55 | 80–90 | 190 |
| Sudan | 16.3 | 49 | 18 | 3.2 | 22 | — | 47 | 26.0 | — | 80–88 | 100 |
| Tunisia | 5.3 | 45 | 14 | 3.1 | 23 | 74 | 44 | 8.3 | — | 75–85 | 220 |
| UAR | 34.9 | 44 | 15 | 2.8 | 25 | 118 | 43 | 52.3 | 50–55 | 75–80 | 170 |
| *Western Africa* | 104 | 49 | 23 | 2.6 | 27 | — | 44 | 155 | — | — | — |
| Dahomey | 2.8 | 51 | 26 | 2.6 | 27 | 110 | 46 | 4.1 | 30–35 | 90–95 | 80 |
| Gambia | 0.4 | 42 | 23 | 1.9 | 37 | — | 38 | 0.5 | — | 90–95 | 100 |
| Ghana | 9.3⁴ | 48 | 18 | 3.0 | 24 | 156 | 45 | 14.9 | 40–45 | 70–75 | 170 |
| Guinea | 4.0 | 47 | 25 | 2.3 | 31 | 216 | 44 | 5.7 | 25–35 | 80–90 | 90 |
| Ivory Coast | 4.4 | 46 | 23 | 2.4 | 29 | 138 | 43 | 6.4 | 30–35 | 85–92 | 260 |
| Liberia | 1.2 | 41 | 23 | 1.9 | 37 | 188 | 37 | 1.6 | — | 90–95 | 210 |
| Mali | 5.2 | 50 | 25 | 2.4 | 29 | 120 | 46 | 7.6 | 30–35 | 85–95 | 90 |
| Mauritania | 1.2 | 45 | 23 | 2.2 | 32 | 187 | — | 1.7 | 40–45 | 90–97 | 180 |
| Niger | 4.0 | 52 | 23 | 2.9 | 24 | 200 | 46 | 6.2 | 35–40 | 95–99 | 70 |
| Nigeria | 56.5 | 50 | 25 | 2.6 | 27 | — | 43 | 84.7 | — | 80–88 | 70 |
| Senegal | 4.0 | 46 | 22 | 2.4 | 29 | — | 42 | 5.8 | 35–45 | 90–95 | 170 |
| Sierra Leone | 2.7 | 45 | 22 | 2.3 | 31 | 136 | — | 3.9 | — | 80–90 | 150 |
| Togo | 1.9 | 51 | 24 | 2.6 | 27 | 127 | 48 | 2.8 | 30–40 | 80–90 | 100 |
| Upper Volta | 5.5 | 49 | 28 | 2.1 | 33 | 182 | 42 | 7.7 | 30–35 | 85–92 | 50 |
| *Eastern Africa* | 100 | 47 | 21 | 2.6 | 27 | — | 44 | 149 | — | — | — |
| Burundi | 3.7 | 48 | 25 | 2.3 | 31 | 150 | 47 | 5.3 | 35–40 | 85–92 | 50 |
| Ethiopia | 25.6 | 46 | 25 | 2.1 | 33 | — | — | 35.7 | — | 90–95 | 70 |
| Kenya | 11.2 | 50 | 20 | 3.1 | 23 | — | 46 | 17.9 | 40–45 | 70–75 | 130 |
| Malagasy Republic | 7.1 | 46 | 22 | 2.7 | 26 | 102 | 46 | 10.8 | — | — | 100 |
| Malawi | 4.6 | 49 | 25 | 2.5 | 28 | 148 | 45 | 6.8 | — | 85–93 | 50 |
| Mauritius | 0.9 | 27 | 8 | 1.9 | 37 | 72 | 41 | 1.2 | 58–65 | 35–40 | 230 |
| Mozambique* | 7.9 | 43 | 23 | 2.1 | 33 | — | — | 11.1 | — | 90–95 | 200 |
| Reunion* | 0.5 | 37 | 9 | 3.1 | 23 | — | — | 0.7 | — | — | 610 |
| Rwanda | 3.7 | 52 | 23 | 2.9 | 24 | 137 | — | 5.7 | — | 85–90 | 70 |
| Somalia | 2.9 | 46 | 24 | 2.4 | 29 | — | — | 4.2 | — | 90–95 | 60 |
| Southern Rhodesia | 5.2 | 48 | 14 | 3.4 | 21 | 122 | 47 | 8.6 | 50–55 | 70–75 | 220 |
| Tanzania (United Republic of) | 13.6 | 47 | 22 | 2.6 | 27 | 162 | 42 | 20.3 | 35–45 | 80–90 | 80 |
| Uganda | 8.8⁴ | 43 | 18 | 2.6 | 27 | 160 | 41 | 13.1 | — | 65–75 | 110 |
| Zambia | 4.4 | 50 | 20 | 3.0 | 24 | 259 | 45 | 7.0 | 40–45 | 55–60 | 220 |

| Region or Country | Population Estimates Mid-1971 (millions)† | Annual Births per 1,000 Population‡ | Annual Deaths per 1,000 Population‡ | Annual Rate of Population Growth (percent)° | Number of Years to Double Population □ | Annual Infant Mortality (Deaths under one year per 1,000 Live Births)‡ | Population under 15 Years (percent)▲ | Population Projections to 1985 (millions)† | Life Expectancy at Birth (years)‡ | Population Illiterate 15 Years and Over (percent)‡ | Per Capita Gross National Product (US $)§ |
|---|---|---|---|---|---|---|---|---|---|---|---|
| *Middle Africa* | 37 | 46 | 23 | 2.2 | 32 | — | 42 | 52 | — | — | — |
| Angola* | 5.8 | 50 | 30 | 2.1 | 33 | — | 42 | 8.1 | 40–50 | 90–97 | 190 |
| Cameroon (West) | 5.9 | 43 | 21 | 2.2 | 32 | 137 | 39 | 8.4 | 35–40 | 80–90 | 140 |
| Central African Republic | 1.6 | 48 | 26 | 2.2 | 32 | 190 | 42 | 2.2 | 35–40 | 70–79 | 120 |
| Chad | 3.8 | 48 | 23 | 2.4 | 29 | 160 | 46 | 5.5 | 30–35 | 75–82 | 60 |
| Congo (Dem. Republic) | 17.8 | 44 | 21 | 2.3 | 31 | 104 | 42 | 25.8 | 35–45 | 80–85 | 90 |
| Congo (Republic of) | 1.0 | 44 | 23 | 2.3 | 31 | 180 | — | 1.4 | 35–40 | 50–55 | 230 |
| Equatorial Guinea | 0.3 | 35 | 22 | 1.4 | 50 | — | — | 0.4 | — | — | 260 |
| Gabon | 0.5 | 35 | 26 | 0.9 | 78 | 229 | 36 | 0.6 | 25–45 | 85–90 | 310 |
| *Southern Africa* | 23 | 41 | 17 | 2.4 | 29 | — | 40 | 34 | — | — | — |
| Botswana | 0.6 | 44 | 23 | 2.2 | 32 | — | 43 | 0.9 | — | 70–80 | 100 |
| Lesotho | 1.1 | 40 | 23 | 1.8 | 39 | 181 | 43 | 1.4 | 40–50 | — | 80 |
| South Africa | 20.6 | 40 | 16 | 2.4 | 29 | — | 40 | 29.7 | 50–60 | 65–70 | }650 |
| Namibia (Southwest Africa)* | 0.6 | 44 | 25 | 2.0 | 35 | — | 40 | 0.9 | — | 60–70 | |
| Swaziland | 0.4 | 52 | 22 | 3.0 | 24 | — | — | 0.7 | — | — | 200 |
| **ASIA** | 2,104² | 38 | 15 | 2.3 | 31 | — | 40 | 2,874 | 50 | 54 | — |
| *Southwest Asia* | 79 | 44 | 15 | 2.9 | 24 | — | 43 | 121 | — | — | — |
| Cyprus | 0.6 | 23 | 8 | 0.9 | 78 | 27 | 35 | 0.7 | 70 | 20–25 | 830 |
| Iraq | 10.0 | 49 | 15 | 3.4 | 21 | — | 45 | 16.7 | — | 75–85 | 260 |
| Israel | 3.0 | 26 | 7 | 2.4 | 29 | 23 | 33 | 4.0 | 72 | 10–15 | 1,360 |
| Jordan | 2.4 | 48 | 16 | 3.3 | 21 | — | 46 | 3.9 | — | 60–70 | 260 |
| Kuwait | 0.8 | 43 | 7 | 8.2 | 9 | 36 | 38 | 2.4 | — | 50–55 | 3,540 |
| Lebanon | 2.9 | — | — | 3.0 | 24 | — | — | 4.3 | — | 40–50 | 560 |
| Muscat and Oman | 0.7 | 42 | 11 | 3.1 | 23 | — | — | 1.1 | — | — | 250 |
| Saudi Arabia | 8.0 | 50 | 23 | 2.8 | 25 | — | — | 12.2 | — | 85–95 | 360 |
| Southern Yemen | 1.3 | — | — | 2.8 | 25 | — | — | 2.0 | — | — | 120 |
| Syria | 6.4 | 47 | 15 | 3.3 | 21 | — | 46 | 10.5 | — | 65–70 | 210 |
| Turkey | 36.5 | 43 | 16 | 2.7 | 26 | 155 | 44 | 52.8 | 50–60 | 60–65 | 310 |
| Yemen (Arab Republic) | 5.9 | 50 | 23 | 2.8 | 25 | — | — | 9.1 | — | 90–95 | 70 |
| *Middle South Asia* | 783 | 44 | 16 | 2.7 | 26 | — | 43 | 1,137 | — | — | — |
| Afghanistan | 17.4 | 50 | 26 | 2.5 | 28 | — | — | 25.0 | — | 85–95 | 80 |
| Bhutan | 0.9 | — | — | 2.2 | 32 | — | — | 1.2 | — | — | 60 |
| Ceylon | 12.9 | 32 | 8 | 2.4 | 29 | 48 | 41 | 17.7 | 62 | 25–30 | 180 |
| India | 569.5⁴ | 42 | 17 | 2.6 | 27 | 139 | 41 | 807.6 | 45 | 70–75 | 100 |
| Iran | 29.2 | 48 | 18 | 3.0 | 24 | — | 46 | 45.0 | — | 75–85 | 310 |
| Nepal | 11.5 | 45 | 23 | 2.2 | 32 | — | 40 | 15.8 | — | 85–95 | 80 |
| Pakistan | 141.6 | 50 | 18 | 3.3 | 21 | 142 | 45 | 224.2 | 45 | 75–85 | 100 |

| Region or Country | Population Estimates Mid-1971 (millions)† | Annual Births per 1,000 Population‡ | Annual Deaths per 1,000 Population‡ | Annual Rate of Population Growth (percent)° | Number of Years to Double Population □ | Annual Infant Mortality (Deaths under one year per 1,000 Live Births)‡ | Population under 15 Years (percent)▶ | Population Projections to 1985 (millions)† | Life Expectancy at Birth (years)‡ | Population Illiterate 15 Years and Over (percent)‡ | Per Capita Gross National Product (US $)§ |
|---|---|---|---|---|---|---|---|---|---|---|---|
| *Southeast Asia* | 295 | 43 | 15 | 2.8 | 25 | — | 44 | 434 | — | — | — |
| Burma | 28.4 | 40 | 17 | 2.3 | 31 | — | 40 | 39.2 | 40 | 30–40 | 70 |
| Cambodia | 7.3 | 45 | 16 | 3.0 | 24 | 127 | 44 | 11.3 | 44 | 60–70 | 120 |
| Indonesia | 124.9 | 47 | 19 | 2.9 | 24 | 125 | 42 | 183.8 | 42 | 55–60 | 100 |
| Laos | 3.1 | 42 | 17 | 2.5 | 28 | — | — | 4.4 | — | 70–80 | 100 |
| Malaysia | 11.1 | 37 | 8 | 2.8 | 25 | — | 44 | 16.4 | 44 | 70–80 | 330 |
| Philippines | 39.4 | 46 | 12 | 3.4 | 21 | 72 | 47 | 64.0 | 47 | 25–30 | 180 |
| Singapore | 2.2 | 25 | 5 | 2.4 | 29 | — | 43 | 3.0 | — | 40–50 | 700 |
| Thailand | 37.4 | 42 | 10 | 3.3 | 21 | — | 43 | 57.7 | 65–70 | 30–35 | 150 |
| Vietnam (Dem. Republic of) | 21.6 | — | — | 2.1 | 33 | — | — | 28.2 | — | — | 90 |
| Vietnam (Republic of) | 18.3 | — | — | 2.1 | 33 | — | — | 23.9 | — | — | 130 |
| *East Asia* | 946 | 30 | 13 | 1.8 | 39 | — | 36 | 1,182 | — | — | — |
| China (Mainland) | 772.9 | 33 | 15 | 1.8 | 39 | — | — | 964.6 | — | 40–50 | 90 |
| China (Taiwan) | 14.3 | 26 | 5 | 2.3 | 31 | 19 | 44 | 19.4 | 65–70 | 35–45 | 270 |
| Hong Kong* | 4.3 | 21 | 5 | 2.5 | 28 | 21 | 40 | 6.0 | 65–70 | 25–30 | 710 |
| Japan | 104.7 | 18 | 7 | 1.1 | 63 | 15 | 25 | 121.3 | 71 | 0–2 | 1,190 |
| Korea (Dem. People's Rep. of) | 14.3 | 39 | 11 | 2.8 | 25 | — | — | 20.7 | — | — | 250 |
| Korea (Republic of) | 32.9 | 36 | 11 | 2.5 | 28 | — | 42 | 45.9 | 55–60 | — | 180 |
| Mongolia | 1.3 | 42 | 10 | 3.1 | 23 | — | 44 | 2.0 | 30 | 5 | 430 |
| Ryukyu Islands* | 1.0 | 22 | 5 | 1.7 | 41 | 11 | 39 | 1.3 | | | 580 |
| NORTHERN AMERICA | 229[2] | 18 | 9 | 1.2 | 58 | — | 30 | 280 | 71 | 2 | — |
| Canada | 21.8 | 17.6 | 7.3 | 1.7 | 41 | 20.8 | 33 | 27.3 | 72 | 0–3 | 2,460 |
| United States[3] | 207.1 | 18.2 | 9.3 | 1.1 | 63 | 19.8 | 30 | 241.7 | 71 | 0–3 | 3,980 |
| LATIN AMERICA | 291[2] | 38 | 9 | 2.9 | 24 | — | 42 | 435 | 60 | 34 | — |
| *Middle America* | 70 | 43 | 9 | 3.4 | 21 | — | 46 | 112 | — | — | — |
| Costa Rica | 1.9 | 45 | 8 | 3.8 | 19 | 60 | 48 | 3.2 | 62–65 | 10–20 | 450 |
| El Salvador | 3.6 | 47 | 13 | 3.4 | 21 | 63 | 45 | 5.9 | 57–61 | 45–50 | 280 |
| Guatemala | 5.3 | 42 | 13 | 2.9 | 24 | 94 | 46 | 7.9 | 50–60 | 60–70 | 320 |
| Honduras | 2.8 | 49 | 16 | 3.4 | 21 | — | 51 | 4.6 | — | 50–60 | 260 |
| Mexico | 52.5[4] | 42 | 9 | 3.4 | 21 | 66 | 46 | 84.4 | 58–64 | 30–35 | 530 |
| Nicaragua | 2.1 | 46 | 16 | 3.0 | 24 | — | 48 | 3.3 | — | 45–50 | 370 |
| Panama | 1.5 | 41 | 8 | 3.3 | 21 | 41 | 43 | 2.5 | — | 20–30 | 580 |

| Region or Country | Population Estimates Mid-1971 (millions)† | Annual Births per 1,000 Population‡ | Annual Deaths per 1,000 Population‡ | Annual Rate of Population Growth (percent)° | Number of Years to Double Population □ | Annual Infant Mortality (Deaths under one year per 1,000 Live Births)‡ | Population under 15 Years (percent)▶ | Population Projections to 1985 (millions)† | Life Expectancy at Birth (years)‡ | Population Illiterate 15 Years and Over (percent)‡ | Per Capita Gross National Product (US $)§ |
|---|---|---|---|---|---|---|---|---|---|---|---|
| *Caribbean* | 26 | 34 | 10 | 2.2 | 32 | — | 40 | 36 | — | — | — |
| Barbados | 0.3 | 21 | 8 | 0.8 | 88 | 42 | 38 | 0.3 | 63–68 | 0–10 | 440 |
| Cuba | 8.6 | 27 | 8 | 1.9 | 37 | 40 | 37 | 11.0 | — | 15–25 | 310 |
| Dominican Republic | 4.4⁴ | 48 | 15 | 3.4 | 21 | 64 | 47 | 7.3 | 57–60 | 40 | 290 |
| Guadeloupe* | 0.4 | 32 | 8 | 2.4 | 29 | 35 | 42 | 0.5 | — | — | 510 |
| Haiti | 5.4 | 44 | 20 | 2.5 | 28 | — | 42 | 7.9 | 35–45 | 80–90 | 70 |
| Jamaica | 2.0 | 33 | 8 | 2.1 | 33 | 39 | 41 | 2.6 | 63–68 | 15–20 | 460 |
| Martinique* | 0.4 | 30 | 8 | 1.9 | 37 | 34 | 42 | 0.5 | — | — | 610 |
| Puerto Rico* | 2.9 | 24 | 6 | 1.4 | 50 | 29 | 39 | 3.4 | 68–73 | 15–20 | 1,340 |
| Trinidad & Tobago | 1.1 | 30 | 7 | 1.8 | 39 | 37 | 43 | 1.3 | 63–68 | 15–25 | 870 |
| *Tropical South America* | 155 | 39 | 9 | 3.0 | 24 | — | 43 | 236 | — | — | — |
| Bolivia | 4.8 | 44 | 19 | 2.4 | 29 | — | 44 | 6.8 | — | 55–65 | 150 |
| Brazil | 95.7 | 38 | 10 | 2.8 | 25 | 170 | 43 | 142.6 | — | 30–35 | 250 |
| Colombia | 22.1 | 44 | 11 | 3.4 | 21 | 78 | 47 | 35.6 | — | 30–40 | 310 |
| Ecuador | 6.3 | 45 | 11 | 3.4 | 21 | 86 | 48 | 10.1 | — | 30–35 | 220 |
| Guyana | 0.8 | 37 | 8 | 2.9 | 24 | 40 | 46 | 1.1 | 60–65 | 15–25 | 340 |
| Peru | 14.0 | 43 | 11 | 3.1 | 23 | 62 | 45 | 21.6 | 55–60 | 35–40 | 380 |
| Surinam* | 0.4 | 41 | 7 | 3.2 | 22 | 30 | 46 | 0.6 | — | — | 430 |
| Venezuela | 11.1 | 41 | 8 | 3.4 | 21 | 46 | 46 | 17.4 | 65–70 | 30–35 | 950 |
| *Temperate South America* | 40 | 26 | 9 | 1.8 | 39 | — | 33 | 51 | — | — | — |
| Argentina | 24.7 | 22 | 9 | 1.5 | 47 | 58 | 29 | 29.6 | 63–70 | 5–8 | 820 |
| Chile | 10.0⁴ | 34 | 11 | 2.3 | 31 | 92 | 40 | 13.6 | — | 13–16 | 480 |
| Paraguay | 2.5 | 45 | 11 | 3.4 | 21 | 52 | 45 | 4.1 | — | 20–25 | 230 |
| Uruguay | 2.9 | 21 | 9 | 1.2 | 58 | 50 | 28 | 3.4 | 65–70 | 8–10 | 520 |
| **EUROPE** | 466² | 18 | 10 | 0.8 | 88 | — | 25 | 515 | 70 | 5 | — |
| *Northern Europe* | 81 | 16 | 11 | 0.6 | 117 | — | 24 | 90 | — | — | — |
| Denmark | 5.0 | 14.6 | 9.8 | 0.5 | 140 | 14.8 | 24 | 5.5 | 72 | 0–1 | 2,070 |
| Finland | 4.7 | 14.5 | 9.8 | 0.4 | 175 | 13.9 | 27 | 5.0 | 69 | 0–1 | 1,720 |
| Iceland | 0.2 | 20.7 | 7.2 | 1.2 | 58 | 11.7 | 34 | 0.3 | 73 | 0–1 | 1,680 |
| Ireland | 3.0 | 21.5 | 11.5 | 0.7 | 100 | 20.6 | 31 | 3.5 | 70 | 0–1 | 980 |
| Norway | 3.9 | 17.6 | 9.9 | 0.9 | 78 | 13.7 | 25 | 4.5 | 73 | 0–1 | 2,000 |
| Sweden | 8.1 | 13.5 | 10.4 | 0.5 | 140 | 13.0 | 21 | 8.8 | 74 | 0–1 | 2,620 |
| United Kingdom | 56.3 | 16.6 | 11.9 | 0.5 | 140 | 18.6 | 23 | 61.8 | 71 | 0–1 | 1,790 |
| *Western Europe* | 150 | 16 | 11 | 0.6 | 117 | — | 24 | 163 | — | — | — |
| Austria | 7.5 | 16.5 | 13.4 | 0.4 | 175 | 25.4 | 24 | 8.0 | 70 | 0–1 | 1,320 |
| Belgium | 9.7 | 14.6 | 12.4 | 0.4 | 175 | 21.8 | 24 | 10.4 | 71 | 0–3 | 1,810 |
| France | 51.5 | 16.7 | 11.3 | 0.7 | 100 | 16.4 | 25 | 57.6 | 71 | 0–3 | 2,130 |
| Germany (Federal Republic of) | 58.9 | 15.0 | 12.0 | 0.4 | 175 | 23.3 | 23 | 62.3 | 71 | 0–1 | 1,970 |
| Luxembourg | 0.4 | 13.5 | 12.6 | 1.0 | 70 | 16.7 | 22 | 0.4 | 68 | 0–3 | 2,170 |
| Netherlands | 13.1 | 19.2 | 8.4 | 1.1 | 63 | 13.2 | 28 | 15.3 | 74 | 0–1 | 1,620 |
| Switzerland | 6.4 | 16.5 | 9.3 | 1.1 | 63 | 15.4 | 23 | 7.4 | 71 | 0–1 | 2,490 |

| Region or Country | Population Estimates Mid-1971 (millions) † | Annual Births per 1,000 Population‡ | Annual Deaths per 1,000 Population‡ | Annual Rate of Population Growth (percent)° | Number of Years to Double Population ☐ | Annual Infant Mortality (Deaths under one year per 1,000 Live Births) ‡ | Population under 15 Years (percent)▸ | Population Projections to 1985 (millions)† | Life Expectancy at Birth (years)‡ | Population Illiterate 15 Years and Over (percent)‡ | Per Capita Gross National Product (US $)§ |
|---|---|---|---|---|---|---|---|---|---|---|---|
| *Eastern Europe* | 105 | 17 | 10 | 0.8 | 88 | — | 25 | 116 | — | — | — |
| Bulgaria | 8.6 | 17.0 | 9.5 | 0.7 | 100 | 30.5 | 24 | 9.4 | 70 | 10–15 | 770 |
| Czechoslovakia | 14.8 | 15.5 | 11.2 | 0.5 | 140 | 22.9 | 25 | 16.2 | 71 | 0–5 | 1,240 |
| Germany (Dem. Republic) | 16.2 | 14.0 | 14.3 | 0.1 | 700 | 20.1 | 22 | 16.9 | 71 | 0–1 | 1,430 |
| Hungary | 10.3 | 15.0 | 11.3 | 0.4 | 175 | 35.7 | 23 | 11.0 | 70 | 0–5 | 980 |
| Poland | 33.3 | 16.3 | 8.1 | 0.9 | 78 | 34.3 | 30 | 38.2 | 68 | 0–5 | 880 |
| Romania | 20.6 | 23.3 | 10.1 | 1.3 | 54 | 54.9 | 26 | 23.3 | 68 | 5–15 | 780 |
| *Southern Europe* | 130 | 19 | 9 | 0.9 | 78 | — | 27 | 146 | — | — | — |
| Albania | 2.2 | 35.6 | 8.0 | 2.7 | 26 | 86.8 | — | 3.3 | 65 | 20–30 | 400 |
| Greece | 9.0 | 17.4 | 8.2 | 0.8 | 88 | 31.9 | 25 | 9.7 | 69 | 15–20 | 740 |
| Italy | 54.1 | 17.6 | 10.1 | 0.8 | 88 | 30.3 | 24 | 60.0 | 70 | 5–10 | 1,230 |
| Malta | 0.3 | 15.8 | 9.4 | −0.8 | — | 24.3 | 32 | 0.3 | 69 | 35–45 | 640 |
| Portugal | 9.6 | 19.8 | 10.6 | 0.7 | 100 | 56.8 | 29 | 10.7 | 64 | 35–40 | 460 |
| Spain | 33.6 | 20.2 | 9.2 | 1.0 | 70 | 29.8 | 27 | 38.1 | 70 | 10–20 | 730 |
| Yugoslavia | 20.8 | 18.8 | 9.2 | 1.0 | 70 | 56.3 | 30 | 23.8 | 65 | 15–25 | 510 |
| *USSR* | 245 | 17.0 | 8.1 | 1.0 | 70 | 25.7 | 28 | 286.9 | 70 | 12 | 1,110 |
| OCEANIA | 20[2] | 25 | 10 | 2.0 | 35 | — | 32 | 27 | 71 | 0–2 | — |
| Australia | 12.8 | 20.0 | 9.1 | 1.9 | 37 | 17.7 | 29 | 17.0 | 71 | 0–1 | 2,070 |
| Fiji | 0.5 | 29 | 5 | 2.7 | 26 | 22 | 45 | 0.8 | — | — | 330 |
| New Zealand | 2.9 | 22.5 | 8.7 | 1.7 | 41 | 16.9 | 33 | 3.8 | 71 | 0–1 | 2,000 |

## World and Regional Population (millions)

| | World | Asia | Europe | USSR | Africa | North America | Latin America | Oceania |
|---|---|---|---|---|---|---|---|---|
| Mid-1971 | 3706 | 2104 | 466 | 245 | 354 | 229 | 291 | 20 |
| UN Medium Estimate, 2000 | 6494 | 3777 | 568 | 330 | 818 | 333 | 652 | 35 |

† Estimates from United Nations. *"Total Population Estimates for World, Regions and Countries, Each Year, 1950–1985,"* Population Division Working Paper No. 34, October 1970.

‡ Latest available year. Except for Northern American rates, estimates are essentially those available as of January 1971 in UN *Population and Vital Statistics Report.* Series A, Vol. XXIII, No. 1, with adjustments as deemed necessary in view of deficiency of registration in some countries.

▸ Latest available year. Derived from UN *World Population Prospects, 1965–85, As Assessed in 1968,* Population Division Working Paper No. 30, December 1969 and UN *Demographic Yearbook, 1967.*

§ 1968 data supplied by the International Bank for Reconstruction and Development.

° Annual rate of population growth (composed of the rate of natural increase modified by the net rate of in- or out-migration) is derived from the latest available published estimates by the United Nations, except where substantiated changes have occurred in birth rates, death rates or migration streams.

☐ Assuming no change in growth rate.

* Nonsovereign country.

[1] Total reflects UN adjustments for discrepancies in international migration data.

[2] Regional population totals take into account small areas not listed on the *Data Sheet.*

[3] US figures are based on Series D projections of the 1970 census and vital statistics data available as of April 1971.

[4] In these countries, the UN estimates show a variation of more than 3 percent from recent census figures. Because of uncertainty as to the completeness or accuracy of census data, the UN estimates are used.

NOTE: The completeness and accuracy of data in many developing countries are subject to deficiencies of varying degree. In some cases, the data shown are estimates prepared by the United Nations.

# Population Estimates, 1960–2000

*United Nations Population Studies, no. 41, and the*
*less comprehensive "World Population Prospects, 1965–2000*
*as assessed in 1968, U.N. Document ESP/P/WP.37*

Projections of population growth, even more than estimates of population sizes and growth rates, are subject to a substantial margin of error. Besides the problem of scanty or inadequate data to start with, predicting the future reproductive behavior of any society, even one whose population structure may be known in detail, is notoriously difficult. In the past demographers have erred fairly consistently on the low side.

All of these projections, except the "constant fertility, no migration" projection, assume some degree of success for family planning programs and economic development in UDCs. The constant fertility projection assumes a continuation of present fertility rates.

The following tables correspond to Figure 3-12, the regions of the world for which United Nations demographic projections have been made.

*1963 Population Estimates According to the U.N. "Low" Variant, 1960–2000, for Major Areas and Regions of the World*

*(Population in thousands)*

| Major areas and regions | 1960 | 1965 | 1970 | 1975 | 1980 | 1985 | 1990 | 1995 | 2000 |
|---|---|---|---|---|---|---|---|---|---|
| WORLD TOTAL | 2,998,180 | 3,265,555 | 3,544,781 | 3,840,439 | 4,147,337 | 4,462,720 | 4,782,859 | 5,109,362 | 5,448,533 |
| More developed regions[a] | 976,414 | 1,028,862 | 1,069,745 | 1,110,340 | 1,153,323 | 1,195,026 | 1,234,313 | 1,266,219 | 1,293,175 |
| Less developed regions[b] | 2,021,766 | 2,236,693 | 2,475,036 | 2,730,099 | 2,994,014 | 3,267,694 | 3,549,546 | 3,843,143 | 4,155,358 |
| A. *East Asia* | 794,144 | 839,970 | 883,366 | 926,689 | 966,092 | 1,002,895 | 1,039,118 | 1,079,058 | 1,118,122 |
| 1. Mainland region | 654,181 | 689,000 | 722,000 | 754,000 | 782,000 | 808,000 | 834,000 | 864,000 | 893,000 |
| 2. Japan | 93,210 | 97,159 | 100,328 | 104,081 | 107,762 | 110,750 | 112,950 | 114,378 | 115,326 |
| 3. Other East Asia | 46,753 | 53,811 | 61,038 | 68,608 | 76,330 | 84,145 | 92,168 | 100,680 | 109,796 |
| B. *South Asia* | 865,247 | 975,777 | 1,101,743 | 1,237,117 | 1,378,496 | 1,526,188 | 1,675,465 | 1,825,655 | 1,984,435 |
| 4. Middle South Asia | 587,277 | 659,977 | 743,752 | 832,611 | 922,138 | 1,012,824 | 1,101,103 | 1,188,439 | 1,283,065 |
| 5. South-East Asia | 218,866 | 248,792 | 281,465 | 317,082 | 356,997 | 401,363 | 449,372 | 499,081 | 549,594 |
| 6. South-West Asia | 59,104 | 67,008 | 76,526 | 87,424 | 99,361 | 112,001 | 124,990 | 138,135 | 151,776 |
| C. *Europe* | 424,657 | 439,340 | 449,988 | 458,742 | 467,081 | 475,079 | 481,578 | 486,999 | 490,777 |
| 7. Western Europe | 134,536 | 139,160 | 142,570 | 145,452 | 148,151 | 150,648 | 153,132 | 155,101 | 156,920 |
| 8. Southern Europe | 117,488 | 121,543 | 124,503 | 126,838 | 128,958 | 131,203 | 132,707 | 134,115 | 134,753 |
| 9. Eastern Europe | 96,852 | 101,193 | 104,439 | 107,446 | 110,651 | 113,653 | 116,219 | 118,263 | 119,700 |
| 10. Northern Europe | 75,781 | 77,444 | 78,476 | 79,006 | 79,321 | 79,575 | 79,520 | 79,520 | 79,404 |
| D. 11. USSR | 214,400 | 230,627 | 243,486 | 255,768 | 268,865 | 282,387 | 296,533 | 307,306 | 316,464 |
| E. *Africa* | 272,924 | 305,859 | 343,633 | 386,653 | 434,486 | 486,730 | 545,614 | 611,088 | 684,132 |
| 12. Western Africa | 85,973 | 98,269 | 112,093 | 127,711 | 145,401 | 165,336 | 189,339 | 217,461 | 250,284 |
| 13. Eastern Africa | 75,032 | 81,884 | 89,773 | 98,847 | 109,155 | 120,572 | 133,531 | 148,217 | 164,976 |
| 14. Middle Africa | 28,345 | 30,471 | 32,969 | 35,816 | 39,080 | 42,755 | 46,990 | 51,835 | 57,395 |
| 15. Northern Africa | 65,955 | 75,282 | 86,119 | 98,418 | 111,400 | 124,770 | 138,452 | 152,152 | 165,899 |
| 16. Southern Africa | 17,619 | 19,953 | 22,679 | 25,861 | 29,450 | 33,297 | 37,302 | 41,423 | 45,578 |
| F. 17. *Northern America* | 198,664 | 212,028 | 222,156 | 234,102 | 248,250 | 261,592 | 274,207 | 284,736 | 294,337 |
| G. *Latin America* | 212,431 | 244,828 | 281,805 | 321,313 | 362,278 | 404,483 | 446,466 | 488,133 | 532,388 |
| 18. Tropical South America | 112,479 | 131,334 | 153,168 | 176,533 | 200,745 | 225,453 | 249,924 | 274,147 | 299,977 |
| 19. Middle America (mainland) | 46,811 | 54,844 | 64,304 | 74,908 | 86,443 | 98,525 | 110,699 | 122,976 | 136,241 |
| 20. Temperate South America | 32,796 | 35,914 | 38,906 | 41,633 | 44,067 | 46,724 | 49,463 | 52,080 | 54,586 |
| 21. Caribbean | 20,345 | 22,736 | 25,427 | 28,239 | 31,023 | 33,781 | 36,380 | 38,930 | 41,584 |
| H. *Oceania* | 15,713 | 17,126 | 18,604 | 20,055 | 21,789 | 23,366 | 24,878 | 26,387 | 27,878 |
| 22. Australia and New Zealand | 12,687 | 13,794 | 14,881 | 16,014 | 17,298 | 18,494 | 19,582 | 20,720 | 21,685 |
| 23. Melanesia | 2,166 | 2,332 | 2,523 | 2,741 | 2,991 | 3,272 | 3,596 | 3,967 | 4,393 |
| 24. Polynesia and Micronesia | 860 | 1,000 | 1,200 | 1,300 | 1,500 | 1,600 | 1,700 | 1,700 | 1,800 |

[a] Including Europe, the USSR, Northern America, Japan, Temperate South America, Australia and New Zealand.
[b] Including East Asia less Japan, South Asia, Africa, Latin America less Temperate South America and Oceania less Australia and New Zealand.

*1968 Total Population Estimates and Annual Rates of Growth According to U.N. "Low" Variant, 1965–2000, Less Developed Regions Only*

| Regions | (Population in thousands) | | | | | Annual Rates of Growth (percent) | | | | |
|---|---|---|---|---|---|---|---|---|---|---|
| | 1965 | 1970 | 1980 | 1990 | 2000 | 1965–70 | 1970–75 | 1980–85 | 1990–95 | 1995–2000 |
| Less developed regions[a] | 2,251,510 | 2,522,681 | 3,136,625 | 3,819,836 | 4,523,382 | 2.3 | 2.2 | 2.0 | 1.8 | 1.6 |
| *A. East Asia* | | | | | | | | | | |
| 1. Mainland region | 700,076 | 752,802 | 855,508 | 945,776 | 1,034,638 | 1.5 | 1.4 | 1.0 | 0.9 | 0.9 |
| 3. Other East Asia | 53,851 | 61,046 | 76,468 | 92,659 | 107,712 | 2.5 | 2.3 | 2.0 | 1.6 | 1.4 |
| *B. South Asia* | 981,046 | 1,121,456 | 1,438,771 | 1,785,862 | 2,119,009 | 2.7 | 2.6 | 2.3 | 1.8 | 1.6 |
| 4. Middle South Asia | 664,868 | 758,481 | 967,173 | 1,191,467 | 1,403,391 | 2.6 | 2.5 | 2.2 | 1.7 | 1.6 |
| 5. South East Asia | 249,349 | 286,062 | 369,499 | 461,531 | 550,240 | 2.7 | 2.6 | 2.4 | 1.9 | 1.7 |
| 6. South West Asia | 66,829 | 76,914 | 102,100 | 132,864 | 165,378 | 2.8 | 2.8 | 2.7 | 2.3 | 2.1 |
| *E. Africa* | 303,150 | 343,596 | 448,006 | 582,872 | 734,159 | 2.5 | 2.6 | 2.7 | 2.4 | 2.2 |
| 12. Western Africa | 89,546 | 100,928 | 130,536 | 168,751 | 210,587 | 2.4 | 2.5 | 2.6 | 2.3 | 2.1 |
| 13. Eastern Africa | 86,448 | 97,637 | 126,633 | 165,633 | 211,152 | 2.4 | 2.6 | 2.7 | 2.5 | 2.3 |
| 14. Middle Africa | 32,318 | 35,766 | 44,757 | 57,033 | 71,306 | 2.0 | 2.2 | 2.4 | 2.3 | 2.2 |
| 15. Northern Africa | 74,520 | 86,470 | 116,964 | 154,130 | 194,285 | 3.0 | 3.1 | 2.8 | 2.4 | 2.2 |
| 16. Southern Africa | 20,318 | 22,795 | 29,117 | 37,325 | 46,829 | 2.3 | 2.4 | 2.5 | 2.3 | 2.2 |
| *G. Latin America* | | | | | | | | | | |
| 18. Tropical South America | 129,854 | 150,035 | 198,648 | 257,832 | 325,152 | 2.9 | 2.8 | 2.7 | 2.4 | 2.2 |
| 19. Middle America (Mainland) | 56,961 | 67,136 | 92,831 | 127,219 | 167,641 | 3.3 | 3.2 | 3.2 | 2.9 | 2.6 |
| 20. Caribbean | 23,068 | 25,762 | 31,713 | 38,814 | 47,677 | 2.2 | 2.1 | 2.0 | 2.1 | 2.0 |
| *H. Oceania* | | | | | | | | | | |
| 23. Melanesia | 2,452 | 2,765 | 3,533 | 4,579 | 5,786 | 2.4 | 2.5 | 2.6 | 2.5 | 2.2 |
| 24. Polynesia and Micronesia | 1,053 | 1,213 | 1,632 | 2,179 | 2,733 | 2.8 | 3.1 | 3.0 | 2.4 | 2.1 |

[a] The totals for the Less Developed Regions have been slightly adjusted to take into account the discrepancies between international immigration and emigration assumptions.

[457]

1963 Population Estimates According to the U.N. "Medium" Variant, 1960–2000, for Major Areas and Regions of the World

(Population in thousands)

| Major areas and regions | 1960 | 1965 | 1970 | 1975 | 1980 | 1985 | 1990 | 1995 | 2000 |
|---|---|---|---|---|---|---|---|---|---|
| WORLD TOTAL | 2,998,180 | 3,280,522 | 3,591,773 | 3,944,137 | 4,330,037 | 4,746,409 | 5,187,929 | 5,647,923 | 6,129,734 |
| More developed regions[a] | 976,414 | 1,031,759 | 1,082,150 | 1,135,587 | 1,193,854 | 1,256,179 | 1,318,433 | 1,379,812 | 1,441,402 |
| Less developed regions[b] | 2,021,766 | 2,248,763 | 2,509,623 | 2,808,550 | 3,136,183 | 3,490,230 | 3,869,496 | 4,268,111 | 4,688,332 |
| A. East Asia | 794,144 | 851,520 | 910,524 | 975,935 | 1,041,097 | 1,104,903 | 1,167,882 | 1,228,006 | 1,287,270 |
| 1. Mainland region | 654,181 | 700,000 | 748,000 | 799,000 | 850,000 | 900,000 | 950,000 | 998,000 | 1,045,000 |
| 2. Japan | 93,210 | 97,523 | 101,465 | 106,174 | 111,064 | 115,169 | 118,280 | 120,561 | 122,400 |
| 3. Other East Asia | 46,753 | 53,997 | 61,059 | 70,761 | 80,033 | 89,734 | 99,602 | 109,445 | 119,870 |
| B. South Asia | 865,247 | 976,341 | 1,106,905 | 1,256,352 | 1,420,258 | 1,596,329 | 1,782,525 | 1,973,889 | 2,170,648 |
| 4. Middle South Asia | 587,277 | 659,977 | 746,892 | 846,932 | 953,709 | 1,064,374 | 1,177,133 | 1,288,246 | 1,398,810 |
| 5. South-East Asia | 218,866 | 249,213 | 283,035 | 320,720 | 364,310 | 414,686 | 471,973 | 535,170 | 603,272 |
| 6. South-West Asia | 59,104 | 67,151 | 76,978 | 88,700 | 102,239 | 117,269 | 133,419 | 150,473 | 168,566 |
| C. Europe | 424,657 | 440,303 | 453,918 | 466,772 | 479,391 | 491,891 | 503,858 | 515,674 | 526,968 |
| 7. Western Europe | 134,536 | 139,456 | 143,766 | 147,876 | 151,845 | 155,724 | 159,769 | 163,635 | 167,699 |
| 8. Southern Europe | 117,488 | 121,831 | 125,671 | 129,205 | 132,569 | 136,342 | 139,238 | 142,539 | 145,360 |
| 9. Eastern Europe | 96,852 | 101,414 | 105,354 | 109,341 | 113,597 | 117,414 | 121,601 | 125,181 | 128,426 |
| 10. Northern Europe | 75,781 | 77,602 | 79,127 | 80,350 | 81,380 | 82,411 | 83,250 | 84,319 | 85,483 |
| D. 11. USSR | 214,400 | 231,000 | 245,700 | 260,800 | 277,800 | 296,804 | 316,090 | 334,845 | 353,085 |
| E. Africa | 272,924 | 306,173 | 345,949 | 393,257 | 448,869 | 513,026 | 586,702 | 671,207 | 767,779 |
| 12. Western Africa | 85,973 | 98,359 | 112,862 | 129,851 | 149,818 | 173,369 | 201,832 | 236,082 | 277,192 |
| 13. Eastern Africa | 75,032 | 81,957 | 90,397 | 100,505 | 112,515 | 126,518 | 142,528 | 161,153 | 183,119 |
| 14. Middle Africa | 28,345 | 30,553 | 33,299 | 36,632 | 40,592 | 45,225 | 50,610 | 56,965 | 64,519 |
| 15. Northern Africa | 65,955 | 75,351 | 86,712 | 100,408 | 116,369 | 133,920 | 152,577 | 172,185 | 192,148 |
| 16. Southern Africa | 17,619 | 19,953 | 22,679 | 25,861 | 29,575 | 33,994 | 39,155 | 44,822 | 50,801 |
| F. 17. Northern America | 198,664 | 213,150 | 226,803 | 242,942 | 261,629 | 283,105 | 305,926 | 329,186 | 354,007 |
| G. Latin America | 212,431 | 244,880 | 283,263 | 327,584 | 378,437 | 435,558 | 497,920 | 565,681 | 638,111 |
| 18. Tropical South America | 112,479 | 131,334 | 153,838 | 179,798 | 209,506 | 242,902 | 279,613 | 319,463 | 361,985 |
| 19. Middle America (mainland) | 46,811 | 54,844 | 64,595 | 76,359 | 90,433 | 106,662 | 124,655 | 144,469 | 165,901 |
| 20. Temperate South America | 32,796 | 35,966 | 39,302 | 42,708 | 46,221 | 49,778 | 53,227 | 56,771 | 60,514 |
| 21. Caribbean | 20,345 | 22,736 | 25,528 | 28,719 | 32,277 | 36,216 | 40,425 | 44,978 | 49,711 |
| H. Oceania | 15,713 | 17,155 | 18,711 | 20,495 | 22,556 | 24,793 | 27,026 | 29,435 | 31,866 |
| 22. Australia and New Zealand | 12,687 | 13,817 | 14,962 | 16,191 | 17,749 | 19,432 | 21,052 | 22,775 | 24,428 |
| 23. Melanesia | 2,166 | 2,338 | 2,549 | 2,804 | 3,107 | 3,461 | 3,874 | 4,360 | 4,938 |
| 24. Polynesia and Micronesia | 860 | 1,000 | 1,200 | 1,500 | 1,700 | 1,900 | 2,100 | 2,300 | 2,500 |

[a] Including Europe, the USSR, Northern America, Japan, Temperate South America, Australia and New Zealand.
[b] Including East Asia less Japan, South Asia, Africa, Latin America less Temperate South America and Oceania less Australia and New Zealand.

*1968 Population Estimates and Annual Rates of Growth According to U.N. "Medium" Variant, 1965–2000, for Major Areas and Regions of the World*

| Regions | (Population in thousands) | | | | | Annual Rates of Growth (percent) | | | | |
|---|---|---|---|---|---|---|---|---|---|---|
| | 1965 | 1970 | 1980 | 1990 | 2000 | 1965–70 | 1970–75 | 1980–85 | 1990–95 | 1995–2000 |
| World total[a] | 3,289,002 | 3,631,797 | 4,456,688 | 5,438,169 | 6,493,642 | 2.0 | 2.0 | 2.0 | 1.8 | 1.7 |
| More developed regions[a] | 1,037,492 | 1,090,297 | 1,210,051 | 1,336,499 | 1,453,528 | 1.0 | 1.0 | 1.0 | 0.9 | 0.8 |
| Less developed regions[a] | 2,251,510 | 2,541,501 | 3,246,637 | 4,101,670 | 5,040,114 | 2.4 | 2.5 | 2.4 | 2.1 | 2.0 |
| A. East Asia | 851,877 | 929,932 | 1,095,354 | 1,265,343 | 1,424,377 | 1.8 | 1.7 | 1.5 | 1.2 | 1.1 |
| 1. Mainland Region | 700,076 | 765,386 | 901,351 | 1,042,864 | 1,176,176 | 1.8 | 1.7 | 1.5 | 1.3 | 1.1 |
| 2. Japan | 97,950 | 103,499 | 116,347 | 125,330 | 132,760 | 1.1 | 1.2 | 0.8 | 0.6 | 0.6 |
| 3. Other East Asia | 53,851 | 61,046 | 77,656 | 97,148 | 115,442 | 2.5 | 2.4 | 2.4 | 1.8 | 1.6 |
| B. South Asia | 981,046 | 1,125,843 | 1,485,714 | 1,911,819 | 2,353,841 | 2.8 | 2.8 | 2.6 | 2.2 | 2.0 |
| 4. Middle South Asia | 664,868 | 761,809 | 1,001,046 | 1,279,761 | 1,564,963 | 2.7 | 2.8 | 2.5 | 2.1 | 1.9 |
| 5. South East Asia | 249,349 | 286,925 | 380,367 | 491,775 | 607,709 | 2.8 | 2.9 | 2.7 | 2.2 | 2.0 |
| 6. South West Asia | 66,829 | 77,109 | 104,302 | 140,283 | 181,169 | 2.9 | 3.0 | 3.0 | 2.7 | 2.4 |
| C. Europe | 444,642 | 462,120 | 497,061 | 532,636 | 568,358 | 0.8 | 0.7 | 0.7 | 0.7 | 0.6 |
| 7. Western Europe | 143,143 | 148,619 | 158,214 | 168,679 | 179,266 | 0.8 | 0.6 | 0.6 | 0.6 | 0.6 |
| 8. Southern Europe | 122,750 | 128,466 | 140,059 | 151,605 | 162,674 | 0.9 | 0.9 | 0.8 | 0.7 | 0.7 |
| 9. Eastern Europe | 100,060 | 104,082 | 112,392 | 119,607 | 127,277 | 0.8 | 0.8 | 0.7 | 0.7 | 0.6 |
| 10. Northern Europe | 78,689 | 80,953 | 86,396 | 92,740 | 99,141 | 0.6 | 0.6 | 0.7 | 0.7 | 0.7 |
| D. 11. USSR | 230,556 | 242,612 | 270,634 | 302,011 | 329,508 | 1.0 | 1.0 | 1.2 | 0.9 | 0.8 |
| E. Africa | 303,150 | 344,484 | 456,721 | 615,826 | 817,751 | 2.6 | 2.8 | 3.0 | 2.9 | 2.8 |
| 12. Western Africa | 89,546 | 101,272 | 133,406 | 180,059 | 240,158 | 2.5 | 2.7 | 3.0 | 3.0 | 2.8 |
| 13. Eastern Africa | 86,448 | 97,882 | 128,757 | 173,639 | 233,245 | 2.5 | 2.7 | 2.9 | 3.0 | 2.9 |
| 14. Middle Africa | 32,318 | 35,893 | 45,785 | 60,449 | 80,214 | 2.1 | 2.4 | 2.7 | 2.9 | 2.8 |
| 15. Northern Africa | 74,520 | 86,606 | 119,385 | 163,230 | 214,404 | 3.0 | 3.2 | 3.2 | 2.9 | 2.6 |
| 16. Southern Africa | 20,318 | 22,832 | 29,387 | 38,450 | 49,730 | 2.3 | 2.5 | 2.7 | 2.6 | 2.5 |
| F. 17. Northern America | 214,329 | 227,572 | 260,651 | 299,133 | 333,435 | 1.2 | 1.3 | 1.5 | 1.1 | 1.0 |
| G. Latin America | 245,884 | 283,253 | 377,172 | 499,771 | 652,337 | 2.8 | 2.9 | 2.8 | 2.7 | 2.6 |
| 18. Tropical South America | 129,854 | 150,660 | 203,591 | 272,495 | 358,447 | 3.0 | 3.0 | 2.9 | 2.8 | 2.7 |
| 19. Middle America (Mainland) | 56,961 | 67,430 | 94,706 | 132,387 | 180,476 | 3.4 | 3.4 | 3.4 | 3.2 | 3.0 |
| 20. Temperate South America | 36,000 | 39,378 | 46,731 | 54,783 | 63,266 | 1.8 | 1.7 | 1.6 | 1.5 | 1.4 |
| 21. Caribbean | 23,068 | 25,785 | 32,145 | 40,107 | 50,148 | 2.2 | 2.2 | 2.2 | 2.2 | 2.2 |
| H. Oceania | 17,520 | 19,370 | 24,025 | 29,639 | 35,173 | 2.0 | 2.1 | 2.2 | 1.8 | 1.6 |
| 22. Australia and New Zealand | 14,015 | 15,374 | 18,785 | 22,659 | 26,214 | 1.9 | 2.0 | 2.0 | 1.5 | 1.4 |
| 23. Melanesia | 2,452 | 2,767 | 3,583 | 4,743 | 6,107 | 2.4 | 2.6 | 2.8 | 2.6 | 2.4 |
| 24. Polynesia and Micronesia | 1,053 | 1,229 | 1,657 | 2,237 | 2,853 | 3.1 | 3.1 | 3.1 | 2.6 | 2.3 |

[459]

[a] The totals for the world, more developed and less developed regions have been slightly adjusted to take into account the discrepancies between international immigration and emigration assumptions.

*1963 Population Estimates According to the U.N. "High" Variant, 1960–2000, for Major Areas and Regions of the World*

*(Population in thousands)*

| Major areas and regions | 1960 | 1965 | 1970 | 1975 | 1980 | 1985 | 1990 | 1995 | 2000 |
|---|---|---|---|---|---|---|---|---|---|
| WORLD TOTAL | 2,998,180 | 3,305,862 | 3,659,157 | 4,070,083 | 4,550,733 | 5,096,198 | 5,689,910 | 6,325,593 | 6,993,986 |
| More developed regions^a | 976,414 | 1,038,410 | 1,102,074 | 1,170,451 | 1,244,728 | 1,321,537 | 1,402,019 | 1,485,660 | 1,574,079 |
| Less developed regions^b | 2,021,766 | 2,267,452 | 2,557,083 | 2,899,632 | 3,306,005 | 3,774,661 | 4,287,891 | 4,839,933 | 5,419,907 |
| A. *East Asia* | 794,144 | 869,950 | 956,283 | 1,056,589 | 1,170,951 | 1,289,018 | 1,405,321 | 1,515,953 | 1,623,170 |
| 1. Mainland region | 654,181 | 718,000 | 791,000 | 875,000 | 971,000 | 1,070,000 | 1,167,000 | 1,258,000 | 1,345,000 |
| 2. Japan | 93,210 | 97,865 | 102,972 | 109,536 | 116,554 | 122,819 | 128,216 | 133,311 | 138,731 |
| 3. Other East Asia | 46,753 | 54,085 | 62,311 | 72,053 | 83,397 | 96,199 | 110,105 | 124,642 | 139,439 |
| B. *South Asia* | 865,247 | 976,550 | 1,107,569 | 1,262,512 | 1,447,692 | 1,665,607 | 1,909,998 | 2,174,390 | 2,443,531 |
| 4. Middle South Asia | 587,277 | 659,977 | 746,892 | 850,684 | 974,841 | 1,120,290 | 1,280,930 | 1,450,581 | 1,614,152 |
| 5. South-East Asia | 218,866 | 249,422 | 283,699 | 322,951 | 369,613 | 425,211 | 489,796 | 563,154 | 645,358 |
| 6. South-West Asia | 59,104 | 67,151 | 76,978 | 88,877 | 103,238 | 120,106 | 139,272 | 160,655 | 184,021 |
| C. *Europe* | 424,657 | 441,268 | 457,850 | 474,801 | 491,701 | 508,703 | 526,139 | 544,349 | 563,159 |
| 7. Western Europe | 134,536 | 139,752 | 144,962 | 150,299 | 155,539 | 160,800 | 166,407 | 172,168 | 178,478 |
| 8. Southern Europe | 117,488 | 122,119 | 126,839 | 131,573 | 136,180 | 141,481 | 145,770 | 150,962 | 155,968 |
| 9. Eastern Europe | 96,852 | 101,636 | 106,270 | 111,236 | 116,542 | 121,175 | 126,983 | 132,100 | 137,151 |
| 10. Northern Europe | 75,781 | 77,761 | 79,779 | 81,693 | 83,440 | 85,247 | 86,979 | 89,119 | 91,562 |
| D. 11. USSR | 214,400 | 233,853 | 253,827 | 274,157 | 296,032 | 319,891 | 346,010 | 373,775 | 402,772 |
| E. *Africa* | 272,924 | 306,563 | 348,468 | 399,989 | 462,886 | 538,972 | 629,061 | 736,266 | 864,282 |
| 12. Western Africa | 85,973 | 98,535 | 114,007 | 132,973 | 156,165 | 184,631 | 219,799 | 263,572 | 317,915 |
| 13. Eastern Africa | 75,032 | 82,120 | 91,342 | 102,955 | 117,330 | 134,780 | 155,244 | 179,841 | 209,946 |
| 14. Middle Africa | 28,345 | 30,559 | 33,548 | 37,361 | 42,104 | 47,971 | 54,917 | 63,402 | 73,792 |
| 15. Northern Africa | 65,955 | 75,351 | 86,712 | 100,408 | 116,884 | 136,236 | 157,732 | 180,749 | 204,982 |
| 16. Southern Africa | 17,619 | 19,998 | 22,859 | 26,292 | 30,403 | 35,354 | 41,369 | 48,702 | 57,647 |
| F. 17. *Northern America* | 198,664 | 215,513 | 232,746 | 252,113 | 274,818 | 298,182 | 323,083 | 348,542 | 376,141 |
| G. *Latin America* | 212,431 | 244,935 | 283,436 | 328,902 | 383,243 | 449,815 | 521,603 | 600,624 | 686,084 |
| 18. Tropical South America | 112,479 | 131,334 | 153,842 | 180,327 | 211,871 | 251,892 | 294,611 | 343,866 | 386,113 |
| 19. Middle America (mainland) | 46,811 | 54,845 | 64,597 | 76,595 | 91,522 | 109,223 | 128,856 | 149,725 | 171,574 |
| 20. Temperate South America | 32,796 | 36,020 | 39,469 | 43,184 | 47,236 | 51,704 | 56,479 | 61,542 | 67,077 |
| 21. Caribbean | 20,345 | 22,736 | 25,528 | 28,796 | 32,614 | 36,996 | 41,657 | 46,491 | 51,320 |
| H. *Oceania* | 15,713 | 17,230 | 18,978 | 21,020 | 23,410 | 26,010 | 28,695 | 31,694 | 34,847 |
| 22. Australia and New Zealand | 12,697 | 13,891 | 15,210 | 16,660 | 18,387 | 20,238 | 22,092 | 24,141 | 26,199 |
| 23. Melanesia | 2,166 | 2,339 | 2,568 | 2,860 | 3,223 | 3,672 | 4,203 | 4,853 | 5,648 |
| 24. Polynesia and Micronesia | 860 | 1,000 | 1,200 | 1,500 | 1,800 | 2,100 | 2,400 | 2,700 | 3,000 |

^a Including Europe, the USSR, Northern America, Japan, Temperate South America, Australia and New Zealand.
^b Including East Asia less Japan, South Asia, Africa, Latin America less Temperate South America and Oceania less Australia and New Zealand.

*1968 Population Estimates and Annual Rates of Growth According to U.N. "High" Variant, 1965–2000, Less Developed Regions Only*

| | (Population in thousands) | | | | | Annual Rates of Growth (percent) | | | | |
|---|---|---|---|---|---|---|---|---|---|---|
| | 1965 | 1970 | 1980 | 1990 | 2000 | 1965–70 | 1970–75 | 1980–85 | 1990–95 | 1995–2000 |
| Less Developed Regions[a] | 2,251,510 | 2,563,561 | 3,378,768 | 4,424,950 | 5,650,426 | 2.6 | 2.7 | 2.7 | 2.5 | 2.4 |
| A. *East Asia* | | | | | | | | | | |
| 1. Mainland Region | 700,076 | 785,095 | 983,009 | 1,183,317 | 1,369,757 | 2.3 | 2.3 | 2.0 | 1.5 | 1.4 |
| 3. Other East Asia | 53,851 | 61,046 | 78,845 | 102,115 | 123,424 | 2.5 | 2.5 | 2.7 | 2.1 | 1.7 |
| B. *South Asia* | 981,046 | 1,126,115 | 1,518,153 | 2,032,456 | 2,617,382 | 2.8 | 2.9 | 3.0 | 2.7 | 2.4 |
| 4. Middle South Asia | 664,868 | 761,993 | 1,024,890 | 1,363,525 | 1,742,573 | 2.7 | 2.9 | 2.9 | 2.6 | 2.3 |
| 5. South East Asia | 249,349 | 286,925 | 387,315 | 522,096 | 677,570 | 2.8 | 3.0 | 3.0 | 2.7 | 2.5 |
| 6. South West Asia | 66,829 | 77,197 | 105,947 | 146,835 | 197,239 | 2.9 | 3.1 | 3.3 | 3.1 | 2.8 |
| E. *Africa* | 303,150 | 345,818 | 466,366 | 648,854 | 905,702 | 2.6 | 2.9 | 3.3 | 3.4 | 3.3 |
| 12. Western Africa | 89,546 | 101,705 | 136,590 | 190,624 | 269,314 | 2.5 | 2.8 | 3.3 | 3.5 | 3.4 |
| 13. Eastern Africa | 86,448 | 98,203 | 131,361 | 182,218 | 256,970 | 2.5 | 2.8 | 3.2 | 3.4 | 3.5 |
| 14. Middle Africa | 32,318 | 36,013 | 46,754 | 63,457 | 88,626 | 2.2 | 2.5 | 3.0 | 3.3 | 3.4 |
| 15. Northern Africa | 74,520 | 87,027 | 121,883 | 172,708 | 236,900 | 3.1 | 3.3 | 3.5 | 3.3 | 3.0 |
| 16. Southern Africa | 20,318 | 22,871 | 29,778 | 39,847 | 53,892 | 2.4 | 2.6 | 2.8 | 3.0 | 3.0 |
| G. *Latin America* | | | | | | | | | | |
| 18. Tropical South America | 129,854 | 151,266 | 208,241 | 288,203 | 394,822 | 3.1 | 3.2 | 3.3 | 3.2 | 3.1 |
| 19. Middle America (Mainland) | 56,961 | 67,498 | 96,505 | 138,609 | 196,659 | 3.4 | 3.5 | 3.7 | 3.5 | 3.5 |
| 20. Caribbean | 23,068 | 25,851 | 32,754 | 41,915 | 53,842 | 2.3 | 2.3 | 2.5 | 2.5 | 2.5 |
| H. *Oceania* | | | | | | | | | | |
| 23. Melanesia | 2,452 | 2,771 | 3,645 | 4,963 | 6,625 | 2.4 | 2.6 | 3.0 | 3.0 | 2.8 |
| 24. Polynesia and Micronesia | 1,053 | 1,230 | 1,737 | 2,472 | 3,337 | 3.1 | 3.4 | 3.6 | 3.1 | 2.9 |

[a] The totals for the Less Developed Regions have been slightly adjusted to take into account the discrepancies between international immigration and emigration assumptions.

1963 Population Estimates According to U.N. "Constant Fertility, No Migration," 1960–2000, in Major Areas and Regions of the World

(Population in thousands)

| Major areas and regions | 1960 | 1965 | 1970 | 1975 | 1980 | 1985 | 1990 | 1995 | 2000 |
|---|---|---|---|---|---|---|---|---|---|
| WORLD TOTAL | 2,998,180 | 3,297,482 | 3,640,970 | 4,042,761 | 4,519,146 | 5,088,112 | 5,763,577 | 6,564,584 | 7,522,218 |
| More developed regions[a] | 976,414 | 1,037,209 | 1,100,340 | 1,168,202 | 1,241,660 | 1,319,857 | 1,401,980 | 1,488,187 | 1,580,049 |
| Less developed regions[b] | 2,021,766 | 2,260,273 | 2,540,630 | 2,874,559 | 3,277,486 | 3,768,255 | 4,361,597 | 5,076,397 | 5,942,169 |
| A. East Asia | 794,144 | 863,258 | 942,256 | 1,034,364 | 1,142,609 | 1,272,236 | 1,424,527 | 1,601,016 | 1,810,678 |
| 1. Mainland region | 654,181 | 711,000 | 776,000 | 852,000 | 942,000 | 1,051,000 | 1,180,000 | 1,330,000 | 1,509,000 |
| 2. Japan | 93,210 | 98,011 | 103,341 | 108,861 | 114,055 | 118,457 | 121,948 | 124,809 | 127,160 |
| 3. Other East Asia | 46,753 | 54,247 | 62,915 | 73,503 | 86,554 | 102,779 | 122,579 | 146,207 | 174,518 |
| B. South Asia | 865,247 | 975,940 | 1,105,563 | 1,259,456 | 1,446,153 | 1,674,235 | 1,952,050 | 2,290,246 | 2,701,865 |
| 4. Middle South Asia | 587,277 | 660,148 | 746,062 | 848,430 | 972,506 | 1,123,880 | 1,308,534 | 1,534,394 | 1,811,220 |
| 5. South-East Asia | 218,866 | 248,641 | 282,523 | 322,149 | 370,409 | 430,006 | 502,966 | 590,983 | 696,620 |
| 6. South-West Asia | 59,104 | 67,151 | 76,978 | 88,877 | 103,238 | 120,349 | 140,550 | 164,869 | 194,025 |
| C. Europe | 424,657 | 442,416 | 460,136 | 478,209 | 496,448 | 514,820 | 533,108 | 551,655 | 570,785 |
| 7. Western Europe | 134,536 | 139,157 | 143,583 | 148,036 | 152,284 | 156,621 | 161,183 | 166,123 | 171,520 |
| 8. Southern Europe | 117,488 | 123,273 | 129,224 | 135,221 | 141,304 | 147,498 | 153,492 | 159,291 | 164,962 |
| 9. Eastern Europe | 96,852 | 101,654 | 106,234 | 111,105 | 116,313 | 121,475 | 126,498 | 131,411 | 136,213 |
| 10. Northern Europe | 75,781 | 78,332 | 81,095 | 83,847 | 86,547 | 89,226 | 91,935 | 94,830 | 98,090 |
| D. 11. USSR | 214,400 | 233,411 | 252,498 | 272,415 | 294,594 | 318,896 | 345,084 | 372,800 | 402,077 |
| E. Africa | 272,924 | 306,563 | 347,791 | 397,830 | 458,251 | 531,213 | 619,748 | 728,013 | 860,462 |
| 12. Western Africa | 85,973 | 98,535 | 114,007 | 132,973 | 156,165 | 184,631 | 219,799 | 263,572 | 317,915 |
| 13. Eastern Africa | 75,032 | 82,120 | 90,910 | 101,579 | 114,355 | 129,384 | 146,976 | 167,803 | 192,725 |
| 14. Middle Africa | 28,345 | 30,559 | 33,303 | 36,578 | 40,444 | 45,001 | 50,389 | 56,832 | 64,427 |
| 15. Northern Africa | 65,955 | 75,351 | 86,712 | 100,408 | 116,884 | 136,843 | 161,215 | 191,104 | 227,748 |
| 16. Southern Africa | 17,619 | 19,998 | 22,859 | 26,292 | 30,403 | 35,354 | 41,369 | 48,702 | 57,647 |
| F. 17. Northern America | 198,664 | 213,840 | 230,409 | 249,840 | 272,238 | 297,348 | 324,955 | 354,914 | 388,264 |
| G. Latin America | 212,431 | 245,080 | 283,899 | 330,488 | 386,856 | 455,131 | 537,450 | 636,447 | 755,579 |
| 18. Tropical South America | 112,479 | 131,334 | 153,838 | 180,933 | 213,792 | 253,728 | 302,118 | 360,626 | 431,302 |
| 19. Middle America (mainland) | 46,811 | 54,926 | 64,775 | 76,878 | 91,921 | 110,535 | 133,312 | 161,037 | 194,816 |
| 20. Temperate South America | 32,796 | 35,896 | 39,287 | 43,018 | 47,123 | 51,647 | 56,587 | 61,966 | 67,786 |
| 21. Caribbean | 20,345 | 22,924 | 25,999 | 29,659 | 34,020 | 39,221 | 45,433 | 52,818 | 61,675 |
| H. Oceania | 15,713 | 16,974 | 18,418 | 20,159 | 21,997 | 24,233 | 26,655 | 29,493 | 32,508 |
| 22. Australia and New Zealand | 12,687 | 13,635 | 14,669 | 15,859 | 17,202 | 18,689 | 20,298 | 22,043 | 23,977 |
| 23. Melanesia | 2,166 | 2,339 | 2,549 | 2,800 | 3,095 | 3,444 | 3,857 | 4,350 | 4,931 |
| 24. Polynesia and Micronesia | 860 | 1,000 | 1,200 | 1,500 | 1,700 | 2,100 | 2,500 | 3,100 | 3,600 |

[a] Including Europe, the USSR, Northern America, Japan, Temperate South America, Australia and New Zealand.
[b] Including East Asia less Japan, South Asia, Africa, Latin America less Temperate South America and Oceania less Australia and New Zealand.

1968 Total Population Estimates and Annual Rates of Growth According to U.N. "Constant Fertility, No Migration" Variant, 1965–2000, Less Developed Regions Only

| | Population (in thousands) | | | | | Annual Rate of Growth (percent) | | | | |
|---|---|---|---|---|---|---|---|---|---|---|
| | 1965 | 1970 | 1980 | 1990 | 2000 | 1965–70 | 1970–75 | 1980–85 | 1990–95 | 1995–2000 |
| Less Developed Regions[a] | 2,251,510 | 2,559,001 | 3,381,131 | 4,583,220 | 6,368,737 | 2.6 | 2.7 | 3.0 | 3.2 | 3.4 |
| **A. East Asia** | | | | | | | | | | |
| 1. Mainland Region | 700,076 | 780,941 | 991,228 | 1,275,390 | 1,673,559 | 2.2 | 2.3 | 2.5 | 2.7 | 2.8 |
| 3. Other East Asia | 53,851 | 61,573 | 82,445 | 113,879 | 156,700 | 2.7 | 2.8 | 3.2 | 3.2 | 3.2 |
| **B. South Asia** | 981,046 | 1,126,074 | 1,515,875 | 2,100,924 | 2,988,562 | 2.8 | 2.9 | 3.2 | 3.5 | 3.6 |
| 4. Middle South Asia | 664,868 | 761,904 | 1,023,084 | 1,414,629 | 2,012,112 | 2.7 | 2.9 | 3.2 | 3.5 | 3.6 |
| 5. South East Asia | 249,349 | 287,050 | 387,272 | 537,323 | 762,368 | 2.8 | 2.9 | 3.2 | 3.5 | 3.5 |
| 6. South West Asia | 66,829 | 77,121 | 105,509 | 148,972 | 214,081 | 2.9 | 3.0 | 3.4 | 3.6 | 3.7 |
| **E. Africa** | 303,150 | 344,496 | 456,620 | 622,901 | 872,798 | 2.6 | 2.7 | 3.0 | 3.3 | 3.4 |
| 12. Western Africa | 89,546 | 101,272 | 133,360 | 180,901 | 252,231 | 2.5 | 2.7 | 3.0 | 3.3 | 3.4 |
| 13. Eastern Africa | 86,448 | 97,882 | 128,711 | 174,009 | 241,750 | 2.5 | 2.7 | 2.9 | 3.2 | 3.4 |
| 14. Middle Africa | 32,318 | 35,958 | 45,603 | 59,449 | 79,683 | 2.1 | 2.3 | 2.6 | 2.9 | 3.0 |
| 15. Northern Africa | 74,520 | 86,606 | 119,719 | 170,143 | 247,424 | 3.0 | 3.2 | 3.4 | 3.7 | 3.8 |
| 16. Southern Africa | 20,318 | 22,779 | 29,227 | 38,399 | 51,710 | 2.3 | 2.4 | 2.7 | 2.9 | 3.0 |
| **G. Latin America** | | | | | | | | | | |
| 18. Tropical South America | 129,854 | 151,523 | 209,966 | 295,754 | 420,972 | 3.1 | 3.2 | 3.4 | 3.5 | 3.6 |
| 19. Middle America (Mainland) | 56,961 | 67,485 | 96,413 | 140,425 | 206,814 | 3.4 | 3.5 | 3.7 | 3.8 | 3.9 |
| 20. Caribbean | 23,068 | 26,041 | 33,725 | 44,540 | 60,115 | 2.4 | 2.5 | 2.7 | 2.9 | 3.1 |
| **H. Oceania** | | | | | | | | | | |
| 23. Melanesia | 2,452 | 2,767 | 3,612 | 4,886 | 6,798 | 2.4 | 2.6 | 2.9 | 3.2 | 3.4 |
| 24. Polynesia and Micronesia | 1,053 | 1,229 | 1,733 | 2,478 | 3,544 | 3.1 | 3.3 | 3.6 | 3.6 | 3.6 |

[a] The totals for the Less Developed Regions have been slightly adjusted to take into account the discrepancies between international immigration and emigration assumptions.

# The Essential Nutrients

## Carbohydrates and Fats

Energy for the life processes and for activity is obtained through "burning" food in the process known as metabolism. Usually this energy is provided by carbohydrates and fats, although if they are undersupplied, proteins may be utilized to make up the deficit. This potential energy from food is measured in "calories." One calorie is the amount of energy (in the form of heat) required to raise the temperature of one kilogram of water one degree centigrade.

Carbohydrates are sugars and starches. They are both made of the same elements, carbon, hydrogen, and oxygen. In digestion, starch (which is a structurally more complicated kind of molecule) is broken down to simple sugars. These may then be metabolized at once or stored for future needs.

Sugars are found most commonly in fruits, and to a lesser extent in vegetables, milk, and milk products. Refined sugars, which are used in cooking, baking, and preserving, come from sugar cane or sugar beets. Starches are found in grains and vegetables, especially such root vegetables as potatoes and yams.

Fats are present in both plant and animal foods, as well as eggs and dairy products. Besides being a source of energy, whether used directly or stored as a reserve, fats are important structural constituents of cell membranes. They provide the sheaths that surround nerves, help to support internal organs, and assist in the utilization of fat-soluble vitamins.

When insufficient supplies of carbohydrates and fats are eaten, the stored reserves are consumed, and weight is lost. There is usually an accompanying curtailment of physical activity. If the weight loss continues until the reserves are gone, the individual starves. Calorie starvation is very hard to separate from other deficiencies. Even if enough protein is provided in the diet to meet protein needs, it will be metabolized for its caloric value, and protein deficiencies will result. Vitamins and minerals are also likely to be undersupplied when intake of carbohydrates and fats is insufficient.

A diet deficient in fats is likely to produce nervous irritability and possibly deficiencies in the fat-soluble vitamins.


## Proteins

Proteins are the structural materials of life, including human life. They also serve in many other roles, as enzymes (biological catalysts), and as oxygen transport compounds (hemoglobin). Most of the parts of the body, muscles, bones, skin, even hair and blood are made up largely of proteins. While there are millions of different proteins, all of them are built from about 20 amino acids. The differences are in the arrangements and proportions of the amino acids. These subunits, in turn, are composed primarily of carbon, nitrogen, oxygen, and hydrogen. The complicated protein molecules we eat are broken down in digestion into their constituent amino acids, which are then reassembled in our bodies to meet our protein needs. Nine of these amino acids (eight for adults) are essential in our diets; the others can be synthesized from simple precursors.

Proteins are essential for growth and development, for tissue maintenance and repair, and for healing and recovery from disease. They also play a part in regulating the metabolism of sugar. To support growth, infants and children need higher proportions of protein relative to their body weight than adults. So, for similar reasons, do pregnant and lactating (nursing) women.

Proteins are found in virtually all foods, but in enormously differing quantities and qualities. "Complete protein" foods, those which contain all of the nine essential amino acids, are found primarily in animal foods: meat, fish, poultry, eggs, and dairy products. Nuts and soybeans also provide complete proteins, but of lower quality. This means that while all essential amino acids are present, they do not occur in ideal proportions for meeting nutritional needs. Protein of the highest quality (except for mother's milk) is found in eggs, and that of cow's milk is of the next best quality.

Substantial amounts of incomplete proteins are found in cereal grains and pulses, such as lentils, peas, and beans. By combining these with other foods (for example, cereal combined with milk), a meal of very high quality protein can be achieved. Additional amino acids can be obtained from other fruits and vegetables, thus supplementing the diet further.

A diet deficient in protein results in a lack of energy, stamina, and resistance to disease. In children the result is retarded growth and development. If the deficiency is severe and continues over a long period of time, the child may never fully recover. The severe form of protein starvation in children is called "kwashiorkor." This form of malnutrition is discussed in greater detail in chapter 4.

## Vitamins

Vitamins are essential nutrients needed in minute amounts compared with carbohydrates, fats, and proteins. They fill a variety of needs in the regulation of life processes. The lack of any of the 13 or more essential vitamins leads to problems of cellular metabolism, which may lead to a serious deficiency disease and ultimately death.

Vitamins fall into two general classes: the fat-soluble (vitamins A, D, E, and K) and the water-soluble (B-complex and C) ones. The fat-soluble vitamins can be absorbed only in the presence of bile salts, which are brought into the digestive system by fat in the diet.

Many vitamins are depleted or destroyed by exposure to light, air, heat, or alkaline conditions. They are therefore often lost from food through improper storage or cooking methods.

Vitamin A exists in vegetables and fruits in a precursor form known as carotene, which is converted in the liver to vitamin A. It is found as vitamin A most abundantly in animal liver, eggs, and dairy foods. It is needed for normal vision, healthy skin, gums, and soft tissues, and resistance to respiratory illnesses. Vitamin A is a precursor of retinene, which together with a protein makes up visual purple, the photosensitive substance of the retina.

A lack of vitamin A first shows up in "night blindness," skin problems, and susceptibility to colds. When it is more extreme, the visual and skin problems intensify, and blindness may ultimately result (xerophthalmia).

The B vitamin complex consists of at least eight separate essential vitamins. They were originally thought to be only one when first discovered. Although they perform different functions, they seem to act somewhat synergistically, and they occur in many of the same foods, the richest sources being liver, whole grains, yeast, and unpolished rice. Deficiencies often occur that involve several of them simultaneously. The lack of one also may interfere with the action of the others. These vitamins are necessary for efficient metabolism.

Thiamin (vitamin $B_1$), besides having an important role in carbohydrate metabolism, is necessary in regulating growth, maintaining the health and functions of the circulatory, digestive, and nervous systems. Its absence leads to the disease known as beriberi, whose symptoms are lack of energy, nervous and emotional disorders, and digestive and circulatory disturbances.

Riboflavin (vitamin $B_2$) is also involved in carbohydrate metabolism, functioning as a coenzyme. Deficiency leads to problems with eyes, central nervous system, and skin (ariboflavinosis). This deficiency frequently appears together with vitamin A deficiency. Riboflavin is found in the usual B vitamin foods, plus milk and eggs.

Pyridoxin (vitamin $B_6$) also functions as a coenzyme involved in protein and fat metabolism. It is needed for healthy skin, nerves, and muscles.

Vitamin $B_{12}$ is, unlike the other B vitamins, not found in vegetable sources. It is obtained mainly from milk and liver. It is used mainly for treatment of pernicious anemia, and probably normally prevents its occurrence.

Niacin (nicotinic acid) participates in a wide variety of metabolic processes as part of the $NAD \rightleftharpoons NADP$ electron transfer system. It is essential for normal function of the nervous system, soft tissues, skin, and the liver. The symptoms of deficiency include mental disorders, skin problems, swollen gums and tongue. The severe deficiency disease, pellagra, is characterized by the "three D's"—diarrhea, dermatosis, dementia.

Choline is essential for normal functioning of several glands, the liver and kidneys, and for fat metabolism.

Pantothenic acid functions as a component of coenzyme A, involved in carbohydrate, fat, and protein metabolism. It is needed for growth, for the health of the skin, the digestive tract, and the adrenal gland.

Folic acid is involved in the regulation of red blood cells and the function of the liver and glands. Deficiency may lead to liver and digestive disturbances.

Biotin is essential to cellular metabolism, functioning, among other places, in the Krebs cycle. Deficiency produces an anemia, skin and heart disorders, sleeplessness, and muscular pain.

Other B vitamins are para-aminobenzoic acid (PABA) and inositol. PABA is an intermediate in folic acid synthesis, and inositol is involved in the metabolism of fats.

Vitamin C (ascorbic acid) is essential for healthy skin, gums, and blood vessels. It is also built into cell walls and is necessary for their continuing strength. Vitamin C also is an important factor in resistance to stress and infection. This vitamin is widely found in fruits and leafy green vegetables, the richest sources being the citrus fruits. It is relatively unstable, being destroyed by heat, and cannot be stored in the body for any length of time.

Symptoms of vitamin C deficiency include bleeding gums, a tendency for small blood vessels to break and hemorrhage, and low resistance to infection. Extreme deficiency is the familiar disease of sailors and explorers, scurvy.

Vitamin D is sometimes known as the "sunshine" vitamin. The precursor ergosterol, which we obtain from green plants, is changed to vitamin D in the skin when it is exposed to sunlight. Today in developed countries milk is enriched with vitamin D through irradiation. The only satisfactory source of converted vitamin D, if sunshine and irradiated milk are unavailable, is fish liver oils. It is quite likely that the thick blanket of smog hanging over American cities interferes with the manufacture of vitamin D in urban populations, which has implications for adults who do not drink milk.

Vitamin D is intimately involved in the absorption and utilization of calcium and phosphorus, and consequently in the growth and maintenance of the bone structure. Rickets is a disease of children who lack vitamin D and/or calcium and phosphorous. In these children the growth and development of the bones is disturbed and retarded. The corresponding disease in adults is osteomalacia. This occurs when calcium is being drawn from the bones to meet daily needs, and is not sufficiently replaced in the diet.

Vitamin E seems to be involved in reproductive functions; lack of it may lead to repeated miscarriage. It is obtained from vegetable oils, particularly wheat germ oil.

Vitamin K is essential to normal blood-clotting activity. This vitamin is ordinarily manufactured by intestinal bacteria, and is also found in green leaves, fat, and egg yolks. The intestinal supply may be cut off temporarily following an antibiotic regime, especially if it is orally administered.

## Minerals

Some 17 essential nutrients are minerals. Many of them are required in very minute amounts.

Bones and teeth are composed primarily of calcium and phosphorous. Calcium also plays a part in the regulation of nerves and muscles, and is necessary for healthy skin and for blood-clotting. The best source of calcium is milk, followed by yellow cheeses. It can also be obtained from the bones of fish and other animals and from green vegetables, shellfish, and lime, which is sometimes used in the preparation of food. Hard water used for drinking or in cooking also contributes calcium.

Phosphorous is closely involved with calcium in bone-building and nerve and muscle regulation. It is also important in sugar metabolism and the utilization of vitamins, and is critically involved in transfers of energy in living systems. Phosphorous is found in dairy foods, poultry, eggs, and meat. Deficiency is relatively uncommon.

Iron is an essential component of hemoglobin, the protein in red blood cells which carries oxygen to the cells of the body. Iron-deficiency anemia is the commonest kind of anemia. Its symptoms include lack of energy and stamina. It is more common among women, whose iron needs are higher due to blood loss in menstruation and the demands of pregnancy. Anemic women are susceptible to stillbirth and miscarriage, and are likely to produce anemic children. Iron is found most abundantly in liver, other organ meats, eggs, molasses, oysters, and apricots. Smaller amounts are found in meat and green vegetables.

Sulphur is necessary for the building of some proteins in the body and must be ingested in amino acids. It is found in many high protein foods, both plant and animal.

Sodium chloride—ordinary table salt—is essential to life, although toxic in too large doses. It occurs naturally in sea foods, meat, and a few fruits and vegetables. It is also found in processed foods such as cheese and bread. Vegetarians may have difficulty getting enough salt; otherwise deficiency is unlikely except where there is danger of heat prostration.

Potassium is a widely available mineral found in meat and many dried fruits and vegetables. It is needed most during periods of rapid growth.

Iodine is an essential component of thyroid hormones which regulate growth, development, and metabolic activities. It is found in foods grown in iodine-rich soil and in iodized salt. Its lack results in goiter, characterized by a swelling of the thyroid gland in the neck. In extreme forms of this disease, cretinism or deaf-mutism may be produced in children.

Zinc is a component of insulin and therefore involved in utilization of carbohydrates and protein. It is found in pulses (peas and beans), organ meats, and green vegetables.

Magnesium is necessary for the utilization of both calcium and vitamin C. It is found in a wide variety of foods.

Manganese is necessary for lactation and some other glandular functions. It is obtained from a variety of nuts and vegetables.

Some other trace elements that are necessary for health are: chromium, cobalt, copper, molybdenum, and selenium.

It is quite possible that other essential nutrients exist that have not yet been isolated. The importance of trace elements cannot be overemphasized. Because they are often required in such minute amounts, and perhaps because there seems to be considerable individual variation in requirements, there is some tendency to overlook them. Yet without them human life would cease.

# The Fire Ant Program:
# An Ecological Case Study

The fire ant is a nasty, but not-too-serious pest in the southeastern United States. Its nests form mounds that interfere with the working of fields. Its stings may cause severe illness or death in sensitive people, but it is a considerably smaller menace in this regard than are bees and wasps. The ant is best described as a major nuisance. After limited and inadequate research on the biology of the fire ant, the USDA in 1957 came up with the astonishing idea of carrying out a massive aerial spray campaign, covering several states, against the ant. Along with other biologists, including those most familiar with the fire ant, I protested the planned program, pointing out, among other things, that the fire ant would be one of the *last* things seriously affected by a broadcast spray program. A quote from a letter I wrote concerning the problem to Ezra Taft Benson, then Secretary of Agriculture, follows:

> To any trained biologist a scorched earth policy involving the treatment of 20 million acres with a highly potent poison such as dieldrin should be considered as a last ditch stand, one resorted to only after all of the possible alternatives have been investigated. In addition such a dangerous program should not even be considered unless the pest involved is an extremely serious threat to *life* and property.
>
> Is the Department of Agriculture aware that there are other consequences of such a program aside from the immediate death of vast numbers of animals? Are they aware that even poisoning the soil in a carefully planned strip system is bound to upset the ecological balance in the area? We are all too ignorant of the possible sequelae of such a program. Has it been pointed out that an adaptable and widespread organism such as the Fire Ant is one of the least likely of the insects in the treated area to be exterminated? It is also

highly likely that, considering its large population size, the Fire Ant will have the reserve of genetic variability to permit the survival of resistant strains.

I would strongly recommend that the program be suspended: 1) until the biology of the ant can be thoroughly investigated with a view toward biological control, baiting, or some other control method superior to broadcast poisoning, and 2) until trained ecologists can do the field studies necessary to give a reasonable evaluation of the chances of success, and the concomitant damage to the human population, wildlife, and the biotic community in general of *any* contemplated control program.

I hope that the United States will learn from the disastrous Canadian Spruce Budworm program and hesitate before carrying out a program whose consequences may be a biological calamity.

This reply came from C. F. Curl, then Acting Director of the USDA Plant Pest Control Division. Note the emphasis on "eradication" in this excerpt:

Surveys do indicate that the imported fire ant infests approximately 20,000,000 acres in our southern states. This does not mean, however, that the eradication program is embarked on a "scorched earth policy." The infestation is not continuous and the insecticide is applied only to areas where it is known to exist. The small outlying areas are being treated first to prevent further spread and of the large generally infested areas only a portion is treated in any one year.

The method of eradication, namely, the application of granular form of two pounds of either dieldrin or heptachlor per acre is based on an analysis of research information compiled from State and Federal sources. Use experience on other control programs such as the white-fringed beetle and Japanese beetle was also taken into consideration before the final decisions were made. All the data indicated that a program could be developed which would be safe and would present a minimum of hazard to the ecological balance in the areas to be treated.

To date approximately 130,000 acres have been treated. This includes a block of 12,000 acres at El Dorado, Arkansas, treated nearly a year ago. Reports indicate the program is successful in eradicating the ants. No active mounds have been found in the El Dorado area and the results look equally good in other locations treated to date. Observers vitally interested in the impact of this program to other forms of life have not reported serious disturbances in the area as a whole.

Close liaison has been established with the Fish and Wildlife Service to continue their observations and to keep us informed currently as to the effect this program may have on fish and wildlife in the area. Experience to date indicates that a successful program can be carried out with a minimum hazard to the beneficial forms of life present.

We believe that the points mentioned in your letter were given ample consideration before the initiation of the fire ant eradication program. We recognize of course that in any program where insecticides are used, certain precautions are necessary. Our experience has shown that insecticides can be applied successfully using very definite guidelines which can be established to minimize the hazard to fish and wildlife and to preclude any hazard to domestic animals and human health. Such guidelines are being followed in the operation of all control and eradication programs in which the U.S. Department of Agriculture participates.

In order to permit you to judge for yourself who was right, here are parts of an article on the results of the program by Dr. William L. Brown, Jr., of the Department of Entomology of Cornell University. Dr. Brown, an outstanding biologist and a world authority on ants, wrote:

> With astonishing swiftness, and over the mounting protests of conservation and other groups alarmed at the prospect of another airborne 'spray' program, the first insecticides were laid down in November, 1957. The rate of application was two pounds of dieldrin or heptachlor per acre . . . Dieldrin and heptachlor are extremely toxic substances—about 4–15 times as toxic to wildlife as is DDT. Many wildlife experts and conservationists as well as entomologists both basic and economic, felt a sense of forboding at the start of a program that would deposit poisons with 8–30 times the killing power of the common forest dosage of DDT (one pound per acre in gypsy moth control).
>
> . . .The misgivings of the wildlife people seem to have been justified, since the kill of wildlife in sample treated areas appears to have been high in most of those that have been adequately checked. The USDA disputes many of the claims of damage, but their own statements often tend to be vague and general.
>
> . . .Although the USDA claims that the evidence is inconclusive in some cases, there does exist contrary information indicating that stock losses from ant poisons may sometimes be significant.
>
> . . .A serious blow was dealt the program in late 1958, when treatments were only one year old; Senator Sparkman and Congressman Boykin of Alabama asked that the fire ant campaign be suspended until the benefits and dangers could be evaluated properly. Then, in the beginning of 1960, the Food and Drug Administration of the Department of Health, Education, and Welfare lowered the tolerance for heptachlor residues on harvested crops to zero, following the discovery that heptachlor was transformed by weathering into a persistent and highly toxic derivative, heptachlor epoxide, residues of which turn up in milk and meat when fed to stock. Some state entomologists now definitely advise farmers against the use of heptachlor on pastures or forage.
>
> . . .The original plan set forth in 1957 called for eradication of the ant on the North American continent, by rolling back the infestation from its borders, applying eradication measures to more control foci in the main infestation, and instituting an effective program of treatment of especially dangerous sources of spread, such as nurseries. Nearly four years and perhaps 15 million dollars after the plan was announced, the fire ant is still turning up in new counties, and is being rediscovered in counties thought to have been freed of the pest in Arkansas, Louisiana, Florida, and North Carolina.

Recently a bait has been found which gives effective fire-ant control on a rate of insecticide application of less than one tenth ounce per acre. It is claimed that the insecticide, Mirex (a chlorinated hydrocarbon) is virtually harmless to vertebrates and bees. Even if it is not, this program shows what improvement is possible if one pays some attention to the ecology of a situation, rather than launching vast broadcast spray programs. Note that baiting was suggested to the USDA before 1960.

This rather lengthy discussion should give you some insight into two of the government agencies which should be most active in preserving the quality of our environment. The USDA, against the advice of the most competent people in the field, launched a fruitless eradication campaign which could only have positive results for the stockholders of pesticide companies, and the FDA discovered that another of its tolerance levels was set too high.

# Some Important Pesticides

*(Adapted from Bulletin of Entomological Society of America, 1969, vol. 15, pp. 85–135.)*

The left-hand column below gives the commonest name for the insecticide, other names by which it is known, and the chemical designation. Sometimes on labels the chemical designation may be simplified. For instance, aldrin will sometimes be listed simply as "hexachlorohexahydro-*endo, exo*-dimethanonaphthalene. The second column gives the general use of the chemical, coded as follows.

Acar. = Acaracide (used against mites)
Ins. = Insecticide (used against insects)
Syn. = Synergist (makes insecticide more potent)
MP = Moth Proofer
C. Fum. = Commodity or space fumigant
S. Fum. = Soil fumigant
Sys. = Systemic insecticide (taken up by plant)
Nem. = Nematocide (kills roundworms)

The right-hand column indicates mammalian toxicity judged by experiments on rats (no symbol), rabbits (Rb), white mice (M) or dogs (D). They are mostly given as $LD_{50}$, that is the dose level which killed 50% of the experimental animals. The doses used in studying acute toxicity are in parts per million of live animal weight. AO = acute oral toxicity; AD = acute dermal (skin application) toxicity. Chronic oral toxicity (CO) is the highest level (parts per million in diet) at which no effect is seen in 90 days or more.

Fumigant toxicities: VA = acute vapor toxicity, the highest level in ppm thought not to be dangerous to man with 60 minutes exposure; VC = chronic vapor toxicity, same for 8 hours per day, five days per week.

For example, chlordane killed 50 percent of rats tested in different experiments at oral doses of 283–590 milligrams per kilogram (mg/kg) of body weight. When chlordane was applied to the skin, 50 percent of the rats died at doses of 580 mg/kg in at least one experiment, but in another a dose of 1600 mg/kg did not produce 50 percent deaths. In rabbits more than 50 percent were killed with a skin dose of 780 mg/kg. In mouse experiments diets with greater than 25 or less than 150 ppm did not produce symptoms in 90 days or more.

As a general rule there will be a reasonable correlation between other mammals and man in the toxicity of these compounds. Thus TEPP with an AO of 0.5–2 in rats in exceedingly toxic to man. An amount equal to about one-millionth of your body weight will kill you. DDT, on the other hand, is much safer as far as acute exposure is concerned.

Note that the chlorinated hydrocarbons appear in several groups: Chlorinated Aryl Hydrocarbons, DDT relatives, and Fumigants (paradichlorobenzene).

| Common and Technical Names | Use | Mammalian Toxicity |
|---|---|---|
| **ACTIVATORS OR SYNERGISTS FOR INSECTICIDES** | | |
| Piperonyl butoxide (Butacide[R]) | Ins. | AO>7500, M3800 |
| α–[2–(2–butoxyethoxy)-ethoxy]–4,5– methylenedioxy–2–propyltoluene | Syn. | D>7500 Rb>7500 AD Rb>1880 CO 1000, D700 |
| **BOTANICALS** | | |
| Rotene powder and resins (derris) (cubé) | Ins. | AO 60–1500, M350 AD Rb>1000–3000 CO 25, D>400 |
| 1,2,12,12α,tetrahydro–2–iso–propenyl–8,9– dimethoxy–[1]benzopyrano–[3,4–b]furo[2,3–b][1] benzopyran–6 (6aH)one | | |
| Pyrethrins (cinerin) | Ins. | AO 200–2600 |
| Pyrethrum (principally from plant species chrysanthemum cinariaefolium) | | AD>1800 CO 1000 |
| Allethrin (synthetic pyrethrins) | Ins. | AO 680–1000 |
| 2–allyl–4–hydroxy–3–methyl–2–cyclopenten– 1–one ester of 2,2–dimethyl–3–(2–methylpro– penyl)–cyclopropanecarboxylic acid | | M480, Rb4290 AD>11200 CO 5000, D 4000 |
| Nicotine (sulfate) | Ins. | AO 50–91, M24 |
| Black Leaf 40[R] | | AD 140, Rb50 |
| ℓ–1–methyl–2–(3–pyridyl)–pyrrolidine | | |
| **CHLORINATED ARYL HYDROCARBONS** (containing 6 or more chlorines) | | |
| Benzene hexachloride (BHC) | Ins. | AO 600–1250 |
| 1,2,3,4,5,6–hexachloro-cyclohexane, mixed isomers and a specified percentage of gamma | | CO 10 (Toxicity depends on ratio of isomers) |

| Common and Technical Names | Use | Mammalian Toxicity |
|---|---|---|
| CHLORINATED ARYL HYDROCARBONS (*continued*) | | |
| Lindane (gamma BHC)<br>1,2,3,4,5,6–hexachlorocyclo-hexane, 99%<br>  or more gamma isomer | Ins. | AO 76–200, M86<br>  Rb60–200, D40<br>AD 500–1200<br>  Rb300–4000<br>CO 50, 25<br>  D>15 |
| Chlordane<br>1,2,4,5,6,7,8,8–octachloro–3α,4,7,7α–<br>  tetrahydro–4,7–methanoindane | Ins. | AO 283–590<br>AD 580->1600<br>  Rb<780<br>CO>25–<150 |
| Heptachlor<br>1,4,5,6,7,8,8–heptachloro–3α,4,7,7α–tetra-<br>  hydro–4,7–methanoindene | Ins. | A040–188, M68<br>AD 119–320<br>  Rb2000<br>CO 0.5->5<br>  D4–5 |
| Aldrin<br>Not less than 95% of 1,2,3,4,10,10–hexa-<br>  chloro–1,4,4α,5,8,8α–hexahydro–1,4–endo-<br>  exo,5,8–dimethano-naphthalene | Ins. | AO39–60, M44<br>  D65–90, Rb50–80<br>AD 80->200<br>  Rb<150<br>CO 0.5, 25, D1 |
| Dieldrin<br>Not less than 85% of 1,2,3,4,10,10–hexa-<br>  chloro–6,7–epoxy–1,4,4α,5,6,7,8α–octa-<br>  hydro–1,4–endo–exo–5,8–dimethano-<br>  naphthalene | Ins. | A040–100<br>  D65–95, M38<br>  Rb45–50<br>AD 52–117, Rb250–<br>  360<br>CO 0.5, Dcal |
| Endrin<br>1,2,3,4,10,10–hexachloro–6,7–expoxy–<br>  1,4,4α,5,6,7,8,8α–octahydro–1,4–endo–endo–<br>  5,8–dimethano-naphthalene | Ins. | AO 3–45, Rb7–10<br>AD 12–19, Rb60–<br>  120<br>CO >1–<25 |
| Endosulfan (Thiodan[R])<br>6,7,8,9,10,10–hexachloro–1,5,5α,6,9,9α–<br>  hexahydro–6,9–methano–2,4,3–benzodioxa-<br>  thiepin 3–oxide | Acar.<br>Ins. | AO 30–110<br>AD 74–130, Rb360<br>CO 30, D30 |
| Toxaphene<br>Chlorinated camphene containing 67–69%<br>  chlorine | Ins. | AO 40–283, M112<br>  D15, Rb<780<br>AD 600–1613<br>  Rb780–4000<br>CO 10, 25<br>  Dca400 |
| Mirex<br>Dodecachlorooctahydro–1,3,4–methano–<br>  1H–cyclobuta[cd]pentalene | Ins. | AO 235–702<br>AD Rb800 |
| DDT RELATIVES<br>(Diphenyl Aliphatics) | | |
| DDT (dichloro diphenyl trichloro-ethane)<br>1,1,1–trichloro–2,2–bis-(p–chlorophenyl)<br>  ethane | Ins.<br>MP | AO 87–500<br>  M150–400<br>  Rb250–400<br>AD 1931–3263<br>  Rb2820<br>CO 5, 1, D400 |

| Common and Technical Names | Use | Mammalian Toxicity |
|---|---|---|
| **DDT RELATIVES** (*continued*) | | |
| DDD (TDE) <br> Dichlorodiphenyl dichloro-ethane <br> 1,1–dichloro–2,2–bis–(p–chlorophenyl) ethane | Ins. | AO 400–3400 <br> M2500 <br> AD Rb 4000–>5000 <br> CO ca100–900 |
| Kelthane[R] (dicofol) <br> 4,4′–dichloro–α–(tri-chloromethyl)– benzhydrol | Acar. | AO 575–1331 <br> D>4000 <br> Rb1810 <br> AD 1000–1230 <br> Rb2100 <br> CO 20–100, D300 <br> D100 |
| Methoxychlor <br> 1,1,1–trichloro–2,2–bis–(p–methoxyphenyl) ethane | Ins. | AO 5000–7000 <br> M1850, Rb>6000 <br> AD >2820–>6000 <br> CO 100, >200 <br> D>4000 |
| **FUMIGANTS** | | |
| Methyl bromide <br> Bromomethane | C. fum. <br> S. fum. | VA 200 <br> VC 20 |
| Cyanide (prussic acid) (HCN) <br> Hydrocyanic acid | C. fum. <br> S. fum. | AO Rb4 <br> CO >300 <br> VA 40 <br> VC 10 |
| Paradichlorobenzene (PDB) <br> p–dichlorobenzene | C. fum. <br> MP | AO 500–5000 <br> M2950 <br> AD Rb>2000 <br> VA 500 <br> VC 75 |
| Naphthalene | C. fum. <br> MP | VC 10 |
| Carbon disulfide | C. fum. | VA 200 <br> VC 20 |
| Vapam[R] <br> Sodium methyldithio-carbamate | Nem. <br> S. fum. | AO 820, M285 <br> AD Rb800 |
| **ALIPHATIC DERIVATIVES OF PHOSPHORUS COMPOUNDS** | | |
| Tepp (TEPP) <br> Tetraethyl pyrophosphate | Ins. | AO 0.5–2, M1–7 <br> AD 2–20, Rb5 |
| Dipterex[R] (trichlorfon) <br> Dimethyl (2,2,2–trichloro–1–hydroxyethyl) phosphonate | Ins. | AO 450–699 <br> M300–500 <br> AD>2800, Rb5000 <br> CO<100–125 |
| DIBROM[R] (naled) <br> 1,2–dibromo–2,2–dichloroethyl dimethyl phosphate | Acar. <br> Ins. | AO 430 <br> AD Rb1100 <br> CO D7.5 <br> mg/kg |
| Vapona[R] (dichlorvos) <br> 2,2–dichlorovinyl dimethyl phosphate | C. fum. <br> Ins. | AO 25–170 <br> AD 59–900, Rb107 <br> CO <50 |

| Common and Technical Names | Use | Mammalian Toxicity |
|---|---|---|
| **ALIPHATIC DERIVATIVES OF PHOSPHORUS COMPOUNDS (*continued*)** | | |
| Phosdrin[R] (mevinphos) | Ins. | AO 3–7, M8–200 |
| Methyl 3–hydroxy–alpha–crotonate, dimethyl phosphate | Sys. | AD 3–90, Rb13–55 CO 0.8, D1 |
| Azodrin[R] | Ins. | AO 21 |
| 3–hydroxy–N–methyl–cis–crotonamide dimethyl phosphate | Sys. Acar. | AD Rb354 CO 1.5 |
| Systox (demeton) | Acar. | AO 2–12 |
| Mixture of 0,0–diethyl S–(and 0)–2–[(ethylthio)ethyl] phosphorothioates | Ins. Sys. | AD 8–200, Rb24 CO 1, D1, D2 |
| Malathion | Ins. | AO 885–2800 |
| Diethyl mercaptosuccinate, S–ester with 0,0–dimethyl phosphorodithioate | | M720–4060 AD >4000->4444 Rb4100 CO 100–1000, D100 |
| **ARYL (PHENYL) DERIVATIVES OF PHOSPHORUS COMPOUNDS** | | |
| Methyl parathion | Ins. | AO 9–42, M32 |
| 0,0–dimethyl 0–p–nitrophenyl phosphorothioate | | AD 63–72, Rb1270 |
| parathion | Acar. | AO 3–30, M6–25 |
| 0,0–diethyl 0–p–nitrophenyl phosphorothioate | Ins. | Rb10, D3 AD 4–200 Rb40–870 CO 1, 50, D1 |
| **HETEROCYCLIC DERIVATIVES OF PHOSPHORUS COMPOUNDS** | | |
| Diazinon | Acar. | AO 66–600 |
| 0,0–diethyl 0–(2–isopropyl–4–methyl–6–pyrimidyl) phosphorothioate | Ins. | M80–135 Rb130–143 AD 379–1200 Rb 4000 CO 1, D 0.75 |
| **SULFONATES** | | |
| Mitin FF[R] | MP | AO 750–1380 |
| Sodium 5–chloro–2–(4–chloro–2–(3–(3,4–dichlorophenyl)–ureido)phenoxy)benzenesulfonate | | |
| **CARBAMATES** | | |
| Baygon[R] | Ins. | AO 95–175 |
| 0–isopropyoxyphenyl methylcarbamate | | AD >1000 CO 800 |
| SEVIN[R] | Ins. | AO 307–986 |
| Carbaryl | | D>759, Rb710 |
| 1–naphthyl methylcarbamate | | AD >500->4000 Rb>2000 CO 200, D200–400 |

# Reproductive Anatomy and Physiology

According to those who have been involved in the Planned Parenthood movement, the two greatest obstacles to successful birth control are ignorance and prudery. In fact, the two often go together. Women who have been raised to fear and dislike sex will often resist learning the facts of reproduction and be very reluctant to discuss any aspect of the subject, including birth control, with their doctors or anyone else. Women without such psychological problems, who are ignorant of their own anatomy and the significance of the menstrual cycle, are still very likely to have failures in their birth control programs, simply because they do not understand how they work or why. Here is one more argument for good sex education programs in schools, churches, and in the home. A sound understanding of the reproductive process is essential to the effective use of at least the conventional methods of birth control. There is even enough uncertainty among educated persons about human reproductive biology and contraception to make a brief review appropriate here.

Conception occurs when a spermatozoan (sperm cell) from a man meets and fertilizes an ovum (egg cell) within a woman's body. The various forms of contraception are designed to prevent that occurrence in a number of different ways, either by erecting a physical or chemical barrier between sperm and egg or through adjustment of the hormone system.

Spermatozoa are manufactured continuously by the millions daily in a man's testes. This goes on from the age of puberty, around fourteen, until very old age. Each spermatozoan contains the genetic information which the man passes on to the child in the event conception takes place. But unless it meets and fertilizes an egg cell, it dies within a few days. These microscopic, active cells which resemble minute tadpoles, are emitted in the hundreds of millions each time a man ejaculates. The testes are also the source of production of the male hormone, testosterone, which is released to the blood stream and is responsible for sexual activity and for the development of a man's secondary sexual characteristics such as a deep voice, a beard, and typically male body structure.

When the spermatozoa are mature, they are moved upward through one of a pair of tubes called a vas deferens to the seminal vesicle (Fig. A-1). This acts as a reservoir for storage until the man ejaculates. Each vas deferens opens into the urethra, a tube which extends the length of the penis. During intercourse when the man experiences his climax, or orgasm, a series of muscular contractions force the sperm cells in a fluid matrix known as semen through the urethra, injecting it into the vagina. The semen is a mixture produced in several glands including the prostate. It provides the spermatozoa with protection after they are deposited in the vagina, which is a relatively hostile environment.

The woman's reproductive cells (ova) are present in immature form in her ovaries from birth (Fig. A-2). From puberty (around 13) until she reaches menopause, somewhere around the age of 45 or 50, one egg cell or *ovum* (or occasionally two or more, which may result in multiple births, usually twins or triplets) is brought to maturity approximately every 28 days. A single ovum is so small it would be visible to the naked eye only as a tiny speck, yet it is many thousands of times larger than a spermatozoan. Besides the mother's genetic contribution to the potential child, the egg cell contains nourishment to support the early development of the embryo, should the ovum be fertilized.

Besides being the source of ova, the ovaries also secrete the female hormones, which, along with certain pituitary hormones, regulate the woman's menstrual cycle and the successful completion of a pregnancy. Estrogen, which is also responsible for the secondary sexual characteristics of a woman, such as the developed breasts and the pelvic bone structure adapted for the bearing of children, initiates the maturation of the ovum and the preparation of the uterus for pregnancy. In one of the two ovaries each month, an ovum, which is surrounded by a group of cells called a follicle, ripens and is released (ovulation). It enters the adjacent flared end of a trumpet-shaped structure known as a fallopian tube and travels slowly down it toward the uterus (womb). If fertilization does not take place during the one or two days of this journey, the ovum begins to deteriorate and eventually dissolves.

After the ovum is discharged from the follicle, the latter develops into a structure called a corpus luteum, which begins to secrete the other female hormones, including progesterone. Progesterone further stimulates the buildup of a lining of cells and extra blood vessels in the uterus, in preparation to receive a developing embryo for implantation. If conception (fertilization) does not occur, the corpus luteum degenerates and ceases to produce progesterone. In the absence of fertilization, about 14 days after ovulation the lining of the uterus is sloughed away through the vagina over a period of 5 or 6 days in the process of menstruation (Fig. A-2). Then the cycle begins again.

Spermatozoa which have been deposited in the vagina during coitus still have a long way to go relative to their size and vulnerability before fertiliza-

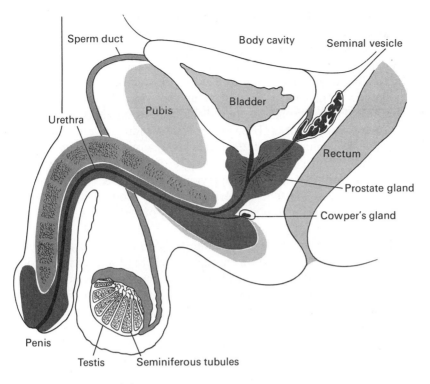

FIGURE A-1

FIGURE A-2

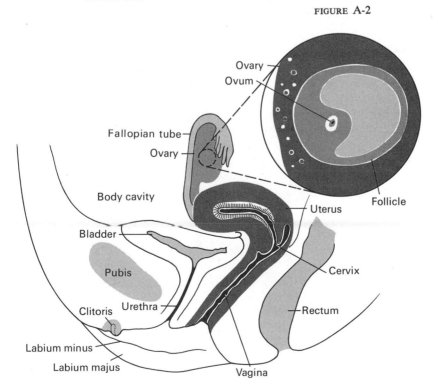

tion can take place. The mucus lining of the vagina is acid, and the sperm cells cannot live long in such an environment. They must find their way into and through the thick mucus filling the cervical canal of the uterus. They are equipped with an enzyme capable of dissolving the mucus, but apparently it requires large numbers of them to dissolve enough to allow them to reach the uterus. Many, of course, are lost along the way. The uterus provides a favorable, alkaline environment, but the spermatozoa must still find their way into the fallopian tubes. If an ovum is descending one of the fallopian tubes as the remaining several thousand spermatozoa swim up it, one of them may succeed in penetrating the capsule of the egg cell. Once one has penetrated, the fertilized ovum is impervious to all of the others. The ovum continues to descend the tube, undergoing cell division as it goes. When it reaches the uterus and is implanted in the wall of the uterus, it is a rapidly developing embryo.

Within several weeks, the growing embryo is about an inch long and has established its placenta, the organ through which food and oxygen from the mother and wastes and carbon dioxide from the fetus, as it is now called, are exchanged. Nine months from conception, the infant is born. With powerful contractions from the uterus, the child is forced through the cervix and vagina, which expand to accommodate it.

Throughout the pregnancy, the corpus luteum continues to secrete progesterone, which protects the implantation of the early fetus and suppresses ovulation and menstruation. During lactation (the period when the mother is producing milk) menstruation is also usually suppressed, although ovulation may or may not occur.

# General Bibliography

For more detailed references, see bibliographies at the end of each chapter.

American Chemical Society, 1969. *Cleaning our Environment: The Chemical Basis for Action*. American Chemical Society, Washington, D.C. On pollution control for air, water, solid wastes, and pesticides.

Appleman, Philip, 1965. *The Silent Explosion*. Beacon, Boston. An excellent general treatment, strong on attitudes toward control of population.

Bates, Marston, 1960. *The Forest and the Sea, A Look at the Economy of Nature and the Ecology of Man*. Random House, New York.

Behrman, S. J., L. Corsa, Jr., and R. Freedman (eds.), 1969. *Fertility and Family Planning; A World View*. Univ. of Michigan Press, Ann Arbor. A basic source on family planning.

Blake, P., 1964. *God's Own Junkyard, the Planned Deterioration of America's Landscape*. Holt, Rinehart & Winston, New York.

Borgstrom, Georg, 1967. *The Hungry Planet*. Collier, New York. Excellent.

Borgstrom, Georg, 1969. *Too Many, A Story of Earth's Biological Limitations*. Macmillan, New York. A fine, impassioned treatment of the population-food crisis.

Bronson, W., 1968. *How to Kill a Golden State*. California Tomorrow, San Francisco.

Brown, Harrison, 1954. *The Challenge of Man's Future*. Viking, New York. A fine early work on population and resources.

Brown, Harrison, J. Bonner, and J. Weir, 1957. *The Next Hundred Years*. Viking, New York. A classic dealing with population and environmental problems.

Brown, Harrison (ed.), 1967. *The Next Ninety Years*. California Institute of Technology, Pasadena. Updates *The Next Hundred Years*.

Brown, Lester R., 1970. *Seeds of Change: The Green Revolution and Development in the 1970s*. Frederick A. Praeger, New York. A current analysis of the Green Revolution and its impact on the various aspects of development strategy by an author eminently qualified to discuss the topic.

Carson, Rachel, 1962. *Silent Spring.* Houghton-Mifflin, Boston. Probably the most important book by a scientist in the last 25 years.

Cloud, Preston E., Jr. (ed.), 1969. *Resources and Man.* W. H. Freeman and Company, San Francisco.

Comfort, Alex, 1966. *The Nature of Human Nature.* Discus Books (Avon), New York.

Commission on Population Growth and the American Future, 1971. An Interim Report. U.S. Government Printing Office. Also reprinted in *Family Planning Perspectives,* vol. 3, no. 2, pp. 45–52 (April).

Dasmann, Raymond F., 1963. *The Last Horizon.* Macmillan, New York. A distinguished conservationist looks at the plight of man and wilderness.

Day, L. H., and A. T. Day, 1965. *Too Many Americans.* Delta, New York. Important work on overpopulation in the United States.

Esposito, John C., 1970. *Vanishing Air.* Grossman Publishers, New York. Ralph Nader's Study Group's report on air pollution.

Ehrlich, Paul R., 1971. *The Population Bomb,* 2nd ed. Ballantine, New York.

Ehrlich, Paul R., and R. L. Harriman, 1971. *How to Be a Survivor: A Plan to Save Spaceship Earth.* Ballantine Books, New York.

Ehrlich, Paul R., J. P. Holdren, and R. W. Holm (eds.), 1971. *Man and the Ecosphere.* W. H. Freeman and Company, San Francisco. Important papers from *Scientific American* with critical commentaries.

*Environment* (formerly *Scientist and Citizen*). An official publication of the Scientists' Institute for Public Information, this journal is published monthly by the Committee for Environmental Information, 438 N. Skinker Blvd., St. Louis, Mo. 63130. The best source of sound, relatively nontechnical information on environmental problems. Depressingly weak coverage of the relationship of population growth to environmental deterioration.

Enke, Stephen, 1970. Zero population growth, when, how, and why. *Tempo,* General Electric Co., Santa Barbara (Jan.). A discussion of population momentum, and economic aspects of stopping population growth.

Fagley, R. M., 1960. *The Population Explosion and Christian Responsibility.* Oxford Univ. Press, Oxford. A Protestant perspective on population control.

Falk, Richard, 1971. *This Endangered Planet.* Random House, New York. A most interesting overview of the global crisis.

Food and Agriculture Organization of the United Nations, *Production Yearbook.* FAO-UN. Rome. A basic source for agricultural data. Issued annually.

Food and Agriculture Organization of the United Nations. *The State of Food and Agriculture.* An annual volume of information.

Frejka, Tomas, 1968. Reflections on the demographic conditions needed to establish a U.S. stationary population growth. *Population Studies,* vol. XXII, pp. 379–397 (Nov.).

Gofman, J. W., and A. R. Tamplin, 1971. *Poisoned Power.* Rodale Press, Emmaus, Pa. Livermore scientists present their case on radiation and the hazards of nuclear power.

Hardin, Garrett, 1970. *Birth Control.* Pegasus, New York. Excellent, up-to-date discussion.

Hardin, Garrett (ed.), 1969. Population, Evolution, and Birth Control. W. H. Freeman and Company, San Francisco. A superb collection of readings, including numerous gems by the editor.

Harrison, Gordon, 1971. *Earthkeeping.* Houghton-Mifflin, Boston. A fine recent overview.

Heer, David M. (ed.), 1968. *Readings on Population.* Prentice-Hall, Englewood Cliffs, N.J. A good collection of demographic papers, most of which will be understandable to the layman.

Heer, David M., 1968. *Society and Population.* Prentice-Hall, Englewood Cliffs, N.J.

Holdren, J. P., and P. R. Ehrlich (eds.), 1971. *Global Ecology.* Harcourt Brace Jovanovich, New York. Significant papers on several subjects.

Holdren, J. P., and P. Herrera, 1972. *Energy.* Sierra Club Books, New York. Thorough, readable and well-documented treatment of the energy situation: technology, economics, environmental impact, and a history of utility-environmentalist confrontations.

Hopcraft, Arthur, 1968. *Born to Hunger.* Houghton-Mifflin, Boston. An excellent and personalized account of hunger in the world.

Huffaker, Carl B., 1971. *Biological Control.* Plenum Publishing Corp., New York. A comprehensive, up to date "bible" on ecologically sane pest control practices. Must be read by everyone interested in alternatives to today's disastrous pesticide practices.

Illich, Ivan, 1970. *Celebration of Awareness.* Doubleday and Co., Garden City, New York. Brilliant book by one of today's most imaginative thinkers. See especially Chapter 10, "Sexual Power and Political Potency," in which Illich discusses the population situation in Latin America.

Istock, Conrad E., 1971. Modern environment deterioration as a natural process. *International Journal of Environmental Studies,* vol. 1, pp. 151–155. A concise and important article which should be read by all economists.

Jarrett, Henry (ed.), 1969. *Environmental Quality in a Growing Economy.* Johns Hopkins Press, Baltimore. An interesting collection. See especially Boulding's "The Economics of the Coming Spaceship Earth."

Keyfitz, N., and W. Flieger, 1971. *Population: Facts and Methods of Demography.* W. H. Freeman and Company, San Francisco. Gives life tables and other calculations for most countries where birth and death statistics exist, and explains methods used in these calculations. Age distributions, sex ratios, and population increase are among its themes. Highly recommended.

Landau, N. J., and P. G. Rheingold, 1971. *The Environmental Law Handbook.* Ballantine Books, New York. How to fight pollution in the courts.

McHarg, Ian, 1969. *Design With Nature.* Natural History Press, Garden City, New York. Excellent discussion of how our urban environment *could* be planned.

Marine, Gene, 1969. *America the Raped.* Discus Books, New York. An angry book on the destruction of the U.S.

Marsh, George P., 1874. *The Earth as Modified by Human Action.* Charles Scribner's Sons, New York. An early classic showing that environmental concerns are nothing new.

Marx, Wesley, 1967. *The Frail Ocean.* Coward-McCann, Inc., New York.

Meadows, D. L., et al., 1972. *The Limits to Growth: a Global Challenge.* Universe Books, N.Y.

Mishan, E, J., 1970. *Technology and Growth: the Price We Pay.* Praeger, New York. A more popular version of *The Costs of Economic Growth.*

Montgomery, Johnson C., 1971. Population explosion and United States law. *Hastings Law Journal,* vol. 22, no. 3, pp. 629–659 (Feb.). First definitive treatment of this subject.

Morris, Desmond, 1967. *The Naked Ape.* McGraw-Hill, New York. In spite of some errors of fact and interpretation this is an excellent book for putting man in perspective. Highly recommended.

Murdoch, William W. (ed.), 1971. *Environment: Resources, Pollution and Society.* Sinauer Associates, Stamford, Connecticut. A topnotch collection.

Myrdal, Gunnar, 1970. *Challenge of World Poverty: A World Anti-Poverty Program in Outline.* Pantheon, New York.

National Advisory Commission on Civil Disorders, 1968. *Report of the National Advisory Commission on Civil Disorders.* Bantam Books, New York.

Odum, Howard T., 1971. *Environment, Power and Society.* John Wiley & Sons, Inc., New York.

Osborn, Fairfield, 1948. *Our Plundered Planet.* Little, Brown & Co., Boston. An early warning which, unhappily, was ignored. See the comments on DDT, pp. 61–62.

Paddock, W., and P. Paddock, 1967. *Famine—1975! America's Decision: Who Will Survive?* Little, Brown & Co., Boston. Everyone should read this controversial work.

Park, Charles F., Jr., 1968. *Affluence in Jeopardy.* Freeman, Cooper & Co., San Francisco. An important discussion of mineral resource problems in a world with an exploding population.

Petersen, Wm., 1965. *The Politics of Population.* Doubleday (Anchor Book), New York. A collection of essays on how population relates to social psychology.

Pirages, Dennis (ed.), 1971. *Seeing Beyond: Personal, Social and Political Alternatives.* Addison-Wesley Publishing Co., Reading, Massachusetts. A fine collection of readings bringing together a wide variety of articles dealing with contemporary human problems.

Population Council. *Studies in Family Planning.* A monthly series. Evaluations of birth control methods, and discussions of family planning programs.

Population Reference Bureau, Inc., 1775 Massachusetts Ave. N.W., Washington, D.C. 20036. Publishes the *Population Bulletin, PRB Selections,* and the *World Population Data Sheet.* Everyone interested in population problems should subscribe to all three.

President's Science Advisory Committee, 1965. *Restoring the Quality of our Environment.* Report of the Environmental Pollution Panel, Washington, D.C. An important source on environmental deterioration and what might be done about it. The recommendations of this report have been largely ignored.

President's Science Advisory Committee, 1967. *World Food Problem* (3 vols.). Washington, D.C. A comprehensive treatise invaluable for reference.

Rattray-Taylor, Gordon. *The Biological Time Bomb*. World Publishing Co., New York. A very competent popular treatment of the revolution in the biological sciences. Highly recommended.

Reinow, R., and L. T. Reinow, 1967. *Moment in the Sun*. Dial, New York. A superb popular work on the deterioration of the American environment.

Rudd, R. L., 1964. *Pesticides and the Living Landscape*. Univ. of Wisconsin Press, Madison.

Sax, K., 1955. *Standing Room Only*. Beacon, Boston. Another excellent "early warning."

Shepard, Paul, and Daniel McKinley (eds.), 1969. *The Subversive Science*. Houghton-Mifflin Co., Boston. A classic collection.

Singer, S. F. (ed.), 1970. *Global Effects of Environmental Pollution*. Springer-Verlag, New York, Inc., New York. A symposium on pollution, especially that affecting the atmosphere, the oceans, and soils.

Sprout, H., and M. Sprout, 1971. *Toward a Politics of the Planet Earth*. Van Nostrand Reinhold Co., New York.

Study of Critical Environmental Problems (SCEP), 1970. *Man's Impact on the Global Environment*. MIT Press, Cambridge. An excellent assessment of some of the most important environmental problems.

Udall, Stewart, 1963. *The Quiet Crisis*. Holt, Rinehart & Winston, New York. The history and future of the fight to save the American environment.

Udall, Stewart, 1968. *1976, Agenda for Tomorrow*. Harcourt, Brace, and World, Inc., New York. A fine book outlining a positive action program for Americans.

United Nations, 1966–1967. *World Population Conference, 1965* (vol. 1, Summary Report; vol. 2, Fertility, Family Planning, Mortality; vol. 3, Projections, Measurement of Population Trends; vol. 4, Migration, Urbanization, Economic Development). U.N., New York. The papers by Soviet scientists A. Y. Boyarsky and B. Y. Smvlevich (vol. 2) are especially noteworthy. Their attacks on "Malthusianism" show interesting parallels with those of old-time Catholic dogmatists such as Colin Clark.

United Nations. *United Nations Statistical Yearbook*, U.N., New York. The most important summary source of statistical information, published annually.

United Nations. *Demographic Year Book*. U.N., New York. Published annually.

U.S. Department of Commerce, 1970. *Statistical Abstract of the United States* (41st edition). U.S. Government Printing Office, Washington D.C. A gold mine of varied information.

U.S. Department of Health, Education, and Welfare. *Vital Statistics Report*. Health Services and Mental Health Adm., Washington, D.C. Current data on U.S. population, published monthly.

Vogt, William, 1948. *Road to Survival*. Sloane, New York. *Time* magazine thought this book was alarmist, but time has shown Vogt to have been right.

Vogt, William, 1960. *People, Challenge to Survival.* Hillman-McFadden, New York. Another fine book to which people should have paid attention.

Watt, K. E. F., 1968. *Ecology and Resource Management.* McGraw-Hill, New York. Excellent book for anyone interested in the technical aspects of ecology.

Westoff, L. A., and C. F. Westoff, 1971. *From Now to Zero: Fertility, Contraception and Abortion in America.* Little, Brown & Co., Boston. A comprehensive account of family planning attitudes and practices in the U.S.

Whyte, William H., 1968. *The Last Landscape.* Doubleday, Garden City, New York. An important book on refurbishing our urban disaster areas.

Wrigley, E. A., 1969. *Population and History.* McGraw-Hill, New York.

# Index

In this index 48f means separate references on pp. 48 and 49; 48ff means separate references on pp. 48, 49, and 50; 48–50 means a continuous discussion. *Passim,* meaning "here and there," is used for a cluster of references in close but not consecutive sequence (for example, 13, 14, 16, 17, 20 would be written as 13–20 *passim.*)

# CONVERSION CHARTS

## LENGTH

ENGLISH
    Mile = 1,760 yards = 5,280 feet = 63,360 inches

METRIC
    Kilometer (km) = 100 decameters = 1,000 meters
    Meter (m) = 10 decimeters = 100 centimeters (cm) = 1,000 millimeters (mm)

ENGLISH TO METRIC
    Mile = 1.609 kilometers = 1,609 meters
    Yard = .914 meters = 91.4 centimeters
    Foot = 30.48 centimeters
    Inch = 2.54 centimeters

METRIC TO ENGLISH
    Kilometer = .62 miles = 1,091 yards = 3,273 feet
    Meter = 39.37 inches
    Centimeter = .39 inches
    Millimeter = .04 inches

## AREA

ENGLISH
    Square mile = 640 acres
    Acre = 4,840 square yards = 43,560 square feet

METRIC
    Square kilometer ($km^2$) = 100 hectares (ha) = 1,000,000 square meters ($m^2$)
    Hectare = 10,000 square meters
    Square meter = 10,000 square centimeters ($cm^2$)

ENGLISH TO METRIC
    Square mile = 2.59 square kilometers = 259 hectares
    Acre = .405 hectares = 4,047 square meters
    Square yard = .836 square meters

METRIC TO U.S.
    Square kilometer = .3861 square miles
    Hectare = 2.47 acres = 11,955 square yards
    Square meter = 1.196 square yards

## VOLUME AND CAPACITY

U.S. LIQUID MEASURES
    Gallon = 4 quarts = 8 pints = 231 cubic inches
    Cubic foot = 7.48 gallons

METRIC
    Cubic kilometer ($km^3$) = 1 billion cubic meters
    Cubic meter = 1,000 cubic decimeters
    Cubic decimeter = 1 liter

U.S. LIQUID TO METRIC
    Gallon = 3.785 liters
    Quart = .946 liters

METRIC TO U.S. LIQUID
    Cubic kilometer = $2.64 \times 10^{11}$ gallons
    Liter = 1.057 quarts

## WEIGHT

ENGLISH (Avoirdupois)
    Ton (short) = 2,000 pounds

METRIC
    Metric ton = 1,000 kilograms = 1,000,000 grams

ENGLISH TO METRIC
    Ton (short) = .907 metric tons = 907 kilograms

METRIC TO ENGLISH
    Metric ton = 1.1 short tons = 2,205 pounds